THE PRESIDENT MAKERS

*The Culture of Politics and Leadership
in an Age of Enlightenment
1896-1919*

MATTHEW JOSEPHSON

With a new Introduction by Robert Engler

A CAPRICORN BOOK

•

G. P. PUTNAM'S SONS

NEW YORK

Library of Congress Cataloging in Publication Data

Josephson, Matthew, 1899-
   The president makers.
   Reprint of the 1964 ed. published by Ungar, New York, in
series: American classics.
   Bibliography: p.
   Includes index.
   1. United States—Politics and government—1865–1933.
2. Statesmen—United States. I. Title.
[E743.J65 1979]   973.91   78-26912
ISBN 0-399-50387-0

CONTENTS

INTRODUCTION

Robert Engler

MATTHEW Josephson's life and writings were of a piece. They reflected a lively curiosity combined with conviction tinged with irony about art, literature, business and politics. As a social historian he was sensitive to the interplay between ideas and institutions, between individuals and their social milieu. His lucid narratives conveyed the spirit of dadaism and surrealism with feeling and accuracy. The transformations within modern capitalism and the mores of the jazz age received equally vivid treatment.

Josephson had a special eagerness to know the frontiers in each field of his interest and to ascertain who was crossing them. The "who" was vitally important to him, for while convinced of the necessity to understand social forces, he never lost sight of the creators, disciples and camp followers of each critical movement. He was to gain great distinction as a portraitist defining the quality and exposing the conflicts of those at the cutting edge of experimentation.

Josephson was always a voracious reader; he combed libraries for the journals and diaries of a wide range of creative figures of nineteenth-century Europe and the United States. He also thoroughly enjoyed the company of contemporary artists and writers who were to appear later in his accounts of the twenties and the thirties. Josephson, in turn, was a character in the chronicles of such fellow critics as Malcolm Cowley. Increasingly, he focused upon the politicians and tycoons who commanded the headlines of the day and shaped the immediate directions of an America which although he found troubling, he nevertheless viewed as home. He had a keen eye for detail and could not resist a revealing story about the passions and pretensions of men and women determined to make history. His sophisticated appraisals of maneuvers "at the top" were built upon careful research into the social currents his central figures may have been riding or bucking. Biographies of individual robber barons were developed with full appreciation of the emergence of the corporate order, while the careers of visible political figures and behind-the-scenes brain trusters were sketched within the framework of the political system.

Matthew Josephson was one of the relatively rare biographers and historians who did not dwell inside the university. Indeed he was often critical of academics who, he felt, under the pretense of objectivity ground out neither good history nor biography—nor literature. In an essay in 1940 he voiced impatience with "the conventional historians, with their antiquated Spencerian individualism and their Chamber of Commerce mentalities," who did not provide either stimulation or counsel. His wariness was sometimes reciprocated, especially by those uncomfortable with his skepticism about the glories of the American way and with his lack of formal credentials. And Josephson's highly readable prose, which marshaled substantial documentation without losing the narrative or the reader, was a feat suspect to those who believed scholarship and intelligibility were incompatible. Although he was reviewed and cited by scholars frequently, Josephson's writing may have missed some of the ongoing collegial interchange which the best of that world can offer. But he was spared the mindless taxonomy which infests the academy. Rather than assign people and movements to familiar bins, he preferred, along with many of his creative subjects, to move on to new and uncharted intellectual adventures. His prodigious output of some twenty books and numerous contributions to little magazines and university reviews as well as to *The New Yorker, The New Republic* and *The Saturday Evening Post* demonstrated that he was first and always a professional who cared about the craft of writing from which he earned the bulk of his living. At the time of his death in March 1978, he was actively engaged in research.

Josephson was born in 1899. He recalled his boyhood in the "backwater" that was Brooklyn when illumination was mostly by gas and the world "seemed stable and peaceful and still appearing very much as it did in the time of President Grant." The tempo of life was at the pace of an old rented carriage horse which traveled "about six miles an hour" to take his family on Sunday outings. Yet the period was a dramatic watershed in American history and along with many of his literary generation he was to speculate later about the dissolution of old forms. But at the time there was little immediate pressure for coming to personal terms with discontinuities. His parents lived comfortably and familiarity with business and public affairs (his father was a small banker and local political bigwig) came easily.

The world of letters became his calling while he was still in high school, and the trolley car enabled him to cross the East River to settings where such concerns were natural. At Columbia University he gravitated toward writers and their world. Greenwich Village became his home briefly before joining the overseas migration in 1921 for several long stays. In Paris he and his bride, Hannah Sneffen, a future collaborator and independent writer, became friends with many painters and poets, European and expatriate. But "expatriate" conveyed only a partial truth, he was to explain. "We were really removing ourselves for a while from our business civilization, and from our middle class families that counted fondly on our making our careers in an advertising office or a bank." He and his compatriots hoped to broaden themselves through exposure to the rich texture of older heritages and the creative workshop that was Paris. No great social or political conviction guided their transplanted lives. "Our ruling idea then was to approach the practice of our art from the point of view of serious craftsmen concerned, above all, with mastery of form and technique."

He tried his hand at "an experimental sort of poetry" and was an editor of several avant-garde publications which sought to expound militant modernism in literature and art. But Josephson's encouragement and recognition were to come from his ambitious literary histories and biographies. *Life Among the Surrealists* affectionately recalled the bold and sometimes merry irreverence of the dadaists and the surrealists whom he knew so well. They had wished to smash old forms of expression and thus free the imagination for new possibilities. Josephson appreciated this unbelief but he also recognized that it was not a substitute for belief. He immersed himself completely in the lives and times of Zola, Rousseau, Hugo, and Stendhal and the scholarship and vitality of his biographies helped to renew public interest in their work. Rousseau's role as the eighteenth century's friend of man and father of revolutions excited Josephson. Was an era of enlightenment likely to return again? he wondered. What forces would usher it in and what role could artists and intellectuals play? Zola's career, first as a devoted man of letters whose naturalistic novels appeared nonpartisan, and then as a social activist whose life became "ennobled and transfigured" as he became the conscience for all mankind in the Dreyfus case, made a deep impression on the young writer. Much later the pen and voice of Victor Hugo, another writer who turned public man in defense of democracy in France, was to engage Josephson. His favorite figure remained Stendhal, who wrote without illusions and whose psychologist's eye helped penetrate the private torments and public jungles of modern life.

In *Portrait of the Artist as American* (1930) Josephson lamented the twentieth-century burden of living in an unfeeling, mechanized order. Looking backward, he concluded that the foothold of art in America had always been precarious. Emily Dickinson, James Whistler, Herman Melville, Stephen Crane, Henry James, Henry Adams and others who had made a slender but genuine contribution had to battle an environment of insatiable expansion, gasping for want of a sympathetic audience. A nation mortgaged to the railroads had no time for thought, Adams complained. Walt Whitman ultimately was to find that the material absorption of the new world democracy left it with little or no soul. To Henry James the plainest burgher among the Florentines had a taste for beauty, while his own countrymen were the disinherited of art, possessing the freedom to grow up blighted. "I feel I am an exile here," Melville cried out. All essentially were fugitives rather than rebels, Josephson decided. But the real deprived were the American people. And yet, might it not be the time "to hope, to begin calculating the chances for a kind of moral revolution," one which accepted the advantages offered by the machine but rejected the status of automation for its users?

In the late twenties, Josephson was ready to abandon the precious public of "diminutive magazines" in favor of the more intimidating challenge of reaching a broader segment of America to come to terms with the goliath. "I want to live here and see the battle fought out, see the nature of the change that will take place . . . and find out whether the Machine will ultimately triumph over ideas." He urged his wandering countrymen to do the same.

Josephson found the Depression a stimulant for experimentation and hopefulness. He shared with Edmund Wilson the view that American intellectuals were never busier or happier and joined other writers eager to propose alternate solutions for an economy that appeared to have run its course. In 1932, along with many of his literary associates, he supported the Communist ticket. Later, he was to keep a close and sympathetic eye on the New Deal. During the next forty years Josephson explored the corridors of power in New York and Washington. He completed full-length biographies of Juan Trippe, Thomas Edison (for which he was awarded the Francis Parkman prize), Sidney Hillman, and with his wife, Alfred E. Smith (which received the Van Wyck Brooks prize). There were also numerous sketches of other business and political figures in national journals. *Life Among the Surrealists* and *Infidel in the Temple*, two volumes of memoirs, appeared in 1962 and 1967.

The President Makers was first published in 1940. The last of a trilogy tracing patterns of American development between the Civil War and the First World War, it recounted the national political debates between 1896 and 1919. To Josephson this was relatively an age of enlightenment. A galaxy of public-minded men had sought selected office; behind them were networks of writers and philosophers with conflicting views about public policy. Together they helped produce a political culture that was fascinating and at times noteworthy.

This was contrast to the evidence presented in the first volume of the series, *The Robber Barons* (1934), which described the rise to power of the money kings between 1861 and 1901, whom Charles and Mary Beard had described as "the peerage of a new industrial age." Dedicated to the Beards, his friends and Connecticut neighbors, this book recorded the destruction of a free market and the capture of political institutions that followed in the wake of the empire building of Carnegie, Harriman, Morgan, Rockefeller and other industrial captains. Such men had advised their sons against entering politics: "We buy these people." *The Politicos* (1938), the middle work, examined the professional politicians of the same epoch "who spoke all too much while doing as little as possible" while the nation was being organized for plunder. "One might read a thousand pages of the speeches of a Blaine, a Garfield or a Cleveland, and not find a single new idea," Josephson observed. This study ended with the defeat of the Democratic Populist forces under William Jennings Bryan in the election of 1896. "God's in his Heaven, all's right with the world!" exclaimed Mark Hanna, the millionaire who became a national political boss. The conservative McKinley was in the White House, the political party was in good hands, and business was safe from democratic politics.

The Robber Barons became the most widely known work of the series. It educated a Depression-scarred generation, which wanted to know what had gone wrong, about the preemption of resources and the concentration of power under monopoly capital. But all three volumes received considerable attention. The scourging portrait of political morality in a business civilization was to be tapped by numerous historians. Richard Hofstadter viewed *The Politicos* as a superb study, "the most illuminating book on the politics of the entire period." In his own work he drew upon what he saw as Josephson's penetrating analyses of the new imperialist elites and the progressives. Robert H. Wiebe concurred, calling *The Politicos* and *The President Makers* the best introduction to the political history of that era. Students of the new nationalism and the new freedom found the summary analyses insightful. Historians and political scientists of varying persuasions applied *The President Makers* to their own interpretations of the gaps between the major political parties, whether the populists and progressives were truly radical, and why the latter two groups ultimately failed. There was considerable admiration for Josephson's sensitivity to literary and intellectual factors. And his focus upon biography was respected as a genuine contribution to historiography, for as John Higham has noted, until the thirties few professional historians took such approaches seriously. A graduate student named C. Vann Woodward wrote to Josephson that a reading of an advance copy of *The President Makers* inspired him to write history.

There were also dissenting voices. His approach to political economy, which owed so much to such interpreters as Thorstein Veblen, Lincoln Steffens, Gustavus Myers and Charles Beard, troubled those who detected muckraking or, worse yet, economic determinism. To Josephson the empire builders were aggressive, sometimes lawless men who tended to act without those established moral principles which fixed the conduct of the common people of the community. They had no sentimental ties to either political party over a long period of time. Although Josephson's illustrations and quotations often suggested their limited sensitivity to all areas of life, whether art or childbearing, except for money-making, he also admired their energy. And at times he described these empire builders as agents of progress in furthering the process of economic integration. Some believed Josephson oversimplified when he implied that the advocates of the new nationalism and the new freedom fundamentally agreed more than they disagreed about the relation of capitalism to political democracy and that he played down the independence of the party leaders and their machines.

Allan Nevins, in a debate with Josephson in the fifties, was to call upon his colleagues in history to right the great injustice done to the architects of industrial growth by those espousing "feminine idealism." Instead of apologizing for our material power we should credit it for enabling the United States to mobilize the genius of mass production to win global war and assume global leadership against communism. A few entrepreneurs may have been disreputable, but the term "robber barons" was unscientific; their contribution was constructive and supportive of the nation's moral and spiritual values. Herbert Agar concluded that the robber baron interpretation was based on two major and contradictory fallacies: "first, that there was something a little glamorous about these 'robber barons'; and second, that they were economically determined, that the whole process of which they formed a part was inevitable, and therefore not a proper subject for moral comment." In Henry Steele Commager's view, Josephson saw people responding only to pecuniary interests, leading him to put the worst construction upon the words and actions of political leaders and scholars. Reviewing *The President Makers* for *Time* magazine, Whittaker Chambers wrote, "Matthew Josephson continues to tell Americans that their administrators and respectable citizens are a bunch of crooks." More than a history of the making of presidents, it "is a history of what he calls 'the central task of modern capitalist statesmen to save society from revolutionary breakup.' He tells the story of their efforts and of U.S. social unrest in great detail, makes a brave try at controlling his irritation when the revolutionary breakup does not progress faster." Given the publication of *The President Makers* on the eve of American entry into World War II, some reviewers were uncomfortable with Josephson's discovery that the progressives and reformers of the Roosevelt-Wilson era, "so humane and democratic in all other respects," could be carried away by calls to international adventures and war.

The President Makers remains valuable for those concerned about understanding when American politics offered genuine choices. And to better appreciate Matthew Josephson's excitement and his reservations about the national debates of the opening decades of the twentieth century it is helpful to recall the tenor of the preceding period.

Private acquisition and expansion were national priorities. Law and the frontier ethic encouraged the conquest of nature. Elected officials presided over circumscribed arenas for furthering such development, whether through tariffs, money, land or immigration policies. Presidents promoted the new industrial order while limiting their accountability to the popular will. There was scant deference to what Henry Adams had preferred as a Ciceronian model of the national interest, one defined by statesmen who, trained in the values of earlier professional and religious elites, guided public opinion but were little ruled by it.

There were moral and esthetic forebodings about the violence of "the machine in the garden" and the perverted priorities it generated. The cutting off of man from nature, from his fellows, and ultimately from himself were seen by a few as casualties wrought by the uncritical embrace of technological changes. Josephson sympathized with the plight of Henry Adams. Viewing the dynamo in the Gallery of Machines at the Great Exposition of 1900, its force mysterious, scarcely humming, and yet infinite, Adams found "his historical neck broken by the sudden irruption of forces totally new." In his past studies he had always sought unity, bowing his neck to railways, banks, corporations, trusts, the capitalist system and even to the popular will, as far as he could understand it, "yet the greater the unity and the momentum the worse became the complexity and the friction." Now Adams wondered about the whole mechanical consolidation of force which "ruthlessly stamped out the life of the class into which he was born but created monopolies capable of controlling the new energies that America adored."

Regional discontent was widespread and focused against bankers, supply merchants, grain and cotton dealers and the railroad interests who were exacting tribute from southern and western farmers over the flow of raw materials and finished goods. The crop lien system, as Lawrence Goodwyn and others have documented, became little more than a modified form of slavery for millions of white and black farmers in the south. Cheap land and the public domain were going to large speculators. The political levers for arresting such patterns seemed to be beyond the effective jurisdiction of local and state governments. The agrarian revolt rejected nostalgia as the focal point for building a people's movement. Its counterstrategies included specific land, banking and railroad reforms for checking private power and creating democratic alternatives to finance and industrial capitalism. White tenant farmers and black sharecroppers courageously joined forces to challenge the crippling credit system through cooperative buying and selling. Farmers in this alliance reached out to industrial workers in the Knights of Labor in quest of a coalition.

Industrial workers faced periodic depressions and severe unemployment. Daily living was often grim and the American dream seemed remote for many immigrants and blacks. Their cities were run by machine bosses responsive to the privileged class. The railroads, which had worried Thoreau because of the harsh invasion of bucolic settings, did more than forge a nation from settlements; they spread the nationalizing power of a new industrial elite which could build empires, inflate values and buy state legislatures. This elite could also call upon federal troops to put down strikes.

This grass roots ferment had only a limited positive impact upon the two major parties. As Josephson points out, they competed for office and its advantages, but united in the worth of business development and overseas expansion.

The agrarian populism incorporated by the Democrats under Bryan in 1896 obscured much of the fundamental social criticism. With eyes primarily upon small farmers, it failed to offer a meaningful program for the industrial workers of the northeast. The latter were ethnically divided and unskilled in politics. McKinley's victory, with the northeast supporting the Republican call for progress and development, meant the destruction of a populist vision based on a national alignment of industrial workers and small southern and western farmers. Northern Republican business and southern conservative Democratic forces were to dominate political life until the 1930's. Racial and sectional loyalties were magnified to prevent any new democratic coalition. Poor whites and blacks in the south were disenfranchised. The myth was fostered that populists had always been simply racists and anti-intellectuals, just as a later generation was to hear the fallacious claim that Joseph McCarthy and his anti-communism were creatures of modern populism. Politics had been tamed.

Against this backdrop, the emerging debates at the core of *The President Makers*, polarized around "the new nationalism" and "the new freedom," offered hope for new directions. And readers should have little difficulty relating them to the agitation of the New Deal period and to today's dilemmas about wealth and commonwealth. Theodore

Roosevelt and Herbert Croly argued for a strong centralized government which would harness all the resources of the society, including the concentrated energy of the trusts, guided by a meritocracy of specially trained public servants. Their model was not to be confused with Hamiltonian mercantilism which sought to thwart popular rule in the interest of a social stability favorable to rising Federalist merchants. The planning envisioned would express a collective will, somehow involving mass participation, and thus liberating American democracy from a Jeffersonian mythology which had provided rationalization for selfish accumulation and aggrandizement.

Mobilization for World War I accelerated industrial integration and the subsequent push for industrial self-government. The system required smooth running; it could not afford breakup or breakdown. When it did sputter badly, as during the great Depression, the first response was to centralize guidelines and controls. Some New Deal planners argued that national direction was more likely to bring responsible performance than grass roots participation. Many contemporary economists insist that the giant corporations which dominate the economy are products of technological imperatives; the problem is how to guide them for public purposes. And a handful of corporate leaders now call for some form of national, public planning. They do this not as closet socialists but because of their concern that private management of transnational businesses is hazardous without the helping hand of the state.

But as Josephson shows, the Jeffersonian and Jacksonian ideals underlying the new freedom have not been abandoned. In Woodrow Wilson's time, Louis Brandeis warned against the curse of bigness. Accepting centralization as part of the heady optimism of the democratic promise meant accepting irresponsible power and with it the demise of the regenerative force of individual and community initiatives. Big government did not mean big democracy; it meant the strangulation of popular expression, just as rule by experts removed the rule from popular will and review. If the democratic spirit was to prevail it had to be given leeway in decentralized settings. Appropriate intervention was needed to ensure that the rules of the system were defined and respected. Capitalism must be defended from its own worst follies and transgressors must be deterred.

Antitrust remains a classic element of this position. More vigorous enforcement of the antitrust laws continues to be a solemn pledge of candidates and presidents. It is insisted that rules about money in politics will narrow the possibilities for corruption, just as rules about conspiracy and improper practices will limit the opportunities for administering the economy privately. With such constraints, there is confidence that good men and women on regulatory agencies could make the crucial difference.

Perhaps the most powerful rejoinder to the cult of bigness comes from the increasing vulnerability of the American political economy. As corporations extol their global capacities, the social indifference of such remote control which may mean the abandonment of towns, regions and even nations becomes painfully apparent to affected citizens and communities. Incremental reforms in welfare, civil rights and sexual equality become immediate casualties. Disadvantaged groups are asked to compete for a diminishing economic pie, as if to invite civil war among the very elements of the society who might become the core of a new political movement for justice and accountability.

The experiences of the twenty-five years after 1896 discussed by Matthew Josephson remain most instructive. Populists, progressives, other "splinter" groups and men like Debs and La Follette tried to place on the nation's agenda alternatives for an economic environment supportive of democratic political ideals. But neither the Square Deal, the New Freedom, the New Deal, the New Frontier nor the Great Society appreciably altered the structure of power or the distribution of wealth, however much they ameliorated conditions and kept alive a hope that the next round might produce a more humane environment. Now a new president, James Carter, viewing problems as technical, and himself a moralist, searches for a middle ground on fundamental issues of the political economy. Once more the American people are left without a clear picture of what public policy might be, including alternative programs which challenge the prevailing deference to giant technology under corporate stewardship and a cumulative slide into a one-party state. And as this is written, once more a president finds it easier to talk tough with a foreign power.

As an historical inquiry, *The President Makers* does not tell us the political requirements for contemporary social change. But Matthew Josephson's review of where we have been contributes substantially to an informed political discourse on precedents and possibilities. One can only welcome its reissue.

Robert Engler is author of *The Brotherhood of Oil: Energy Policy and the Public Interest* (Chicago, University of Chicago Press, 1977) and also of *The Politics of Oil: Private Power and Democratic Directions* (New York, Macmillan, 1961; The University of Chicago Press, Phoenix edition, 1967). He is professor of political science at the City University of New York.

BOOK ONE

I. THE GOLDEN YEARS

OF McKINLEY AND HANNA

THE DECISIVE victory of the conservative Republicans over the Democrats and Populists, upon the clear issue of money inflation, seemed to bring at last, in the fall of 1896, release from an intolerable burden of anxiety that had oppressed many good men. While the citizens of the predominantly rural West and South were deeply cast down, those of the typically industrial and commercial regions, the North Central and Northeastern states, were loudly exuberant. They exulted because "anarchy" and "repudiation" were beaten; because "Danton, Robespierre, and Marat" (Bryan, Altgeld, and Tillman) and all the others who, in the phrase of the young Theodore Roosevelt, "made war on the elegancies and decencies of life" were hurled down to defeat.

"God's in his Heaven, all's right with the world!" Mark Hanna had telegraphed to McKinley on the night of November 3, 1896. In his bedroom in Canton, Ohio, Mr. McKinley knelt and prayed for joy. In Union League Clubs sedate old men danced in each other's arms. The golden years had begun; the golden years of those whom the Jacobins of 1896 called Gold-bugs.

"Recent events may well cause those who represent business interests to rejoice on their escape from threatened perils," wrote the outgoing President, Grover Cleveland, with statesmanlike moderation.[1] In truth, the McKinley administration seemed to open an era of sunlit hope and promise for those whom we may

[1] Grover Cleveland, *Letters*, Nov. 16, 1896, p. 461.

call the party of business. It was as consummation and reward after long, arduous struggle. Compliments were showered as often upon Mark Hanna, the national chairman of the Republican party, as upon the successful candidate; for it was Hanna's aggressive generalship in the campaign, and especially the "scare" he threw into the country, that seemed the largest factor in defeating Bryan. Now Hanna, the "triumphant business man in politics," was widely expected to play a very large part in the new government. This gave assurance that the ruling party—though its President had sometimes in the past been a wavering politician—would rule frankly in the name of business interests.

McKinley was aware of the distress among the people. Depression in business and popular distress would be his chief concern, he promised in his first inaugural address. To bring recovery and the "full dinner pail" he would urge two principal measures: the enactment of a higher tariff; the defense of the gold standard.

And what could be better, from the point of view of large business interests? Their owners earnestly believed that if the government could but safeguard their capital by sound financial laws, and increase their profits by favoring tariff acts, a portion of their prosperity would not fail to circulate or seep downward to the masses of laborers and farmers. They asked for aid and encouragement, and where this could not be given they asked only to be "let alone." Such were the concepts of policy embraced by the most eminent capitalists at the end of the last century. Such they are now.

The Republican party, which, we must remember, was founded by men like Lincoln, and as recently as 1890 favored currency inflation, now in 1896 seemed more firmly wedded to big business interests than ever before. Moreover, the McKinley-Hanna partnership seemed to be the strongest political combination known by this party since the Civil War. It was also, in many ways, the final flower of our professional politics as cultivated for a generation past.

William McKinley himself was a finished product of the old professional school. John Hay, who knew him well, sometimes likened him to a medieval Cardinal of Mother Church. With Congressmen, whose ways he knew deeply, he dealt with a fine, Italian hand. He knew and enjoyed the arts of combination and conciliation; he distributed the patronage with a light touch. McKinley was effusively sentimental in his personal relations, and in public sometimes concealed his ignorance under an air of gravity and excessive virtue which could be unwittingly funny. His very pompous speeches, according to Edwin L. Godkin, were utterly devoid of meaning and showed that the Republican party had reached limits of "intellectual poverty and moral weakness" in choosing its standard-bearer.[2]

But under McKinley not only were relations between the White House and Congress harmonious, but the executive departments also were managed by an imposing group of like-minded financiers and Republican elders, who functioned with ease and authority. The Cabinet members and the leading diplomatic appointees had been chosen from among the representatives and friends of large business interests. Several of them had even belonged to the well-known McKinley "syndicate" which, under Mark Hanna's initiative, had rescued McKinley from bankruptcy in '93 and financed his subsequent campaign for the Presidency. John Hay, one of the generous subscribers, an experienced diplomat, a distinguished writer, and a man of fortune by marriage, was named Ambassador to Great Britain, and would soon replace the aged party leader, John Sherman, as Secretary of State. General Russell Alger, the lumber baron and political boss of Michigan, was made Secretary of War; Lyman Gage, president of the First National Bank of Chicago, Secretary of the Treasury; Cornelius Bliss, also a banker, from New York, Secretary of the Interior.

Then, at the President's side there stood always the formidable Hanna, a truly national boss, who had rebuilt the party organization and subdued the great regional bosses under his command. Under Hanna, the relationship of the Republican party with big business was more intimate and effective than ever before. Under

[2] Godkin, *Problems of Democracy*, p. 267.

Hanna, the great corporations expected that "protection against hostile legislation" for whose cost regular taxes had been assessed against them. Under Hanna, the Republican party itself now displayed a gratifying financial responsibility like that of a great commercial corporation.

Thus the road lay open, straight ahead. A business men's government, dreamed of in the days of the spoilsmen Politicos, had come at last.

After the panic of 1893, a strong movement of consolidation, mainly led by J. Pierpont Morgan, New York's leading investment banker, steadily eliminated the quarrelsome "robber barons" in both the railroad and the industrial field. Judging, after November 3, 1896, that all signs were propitious, Morgan boldly extended his operations beyond the railroad world that had been his special province hitherto. In one great industry after another he brought about "community of interests" by throwing together the leading corporations into great, centralized holding companies or trusts. McKinley's inauguration marked the beginning of the greatest movement of consolidation in American business. In 1897 alone, while the government looked on tolerantly, new incorporations were established with a total nominal capital of 3.5 billions of dollars. Within the several years that followed, the nation's dominant trusts in the copper, sugar, tobacco, oil, marine, smelting, and steel industries were formed—the steel trust being the biggest of all holding companies, and the seven together having an aggregate capital of 2.5 billions of dollars.

With the launching of the great trusts and of their new securities (chiefly under the sponsorship of the Morgan and Rockefeller banks), there came a tremendous financial boom. Mr. Morgan was widely recognized as the "hero" of the great boom, which appeared to reach its climax between 1899 and 1901. In the wake of the giant consolidations there followed hundreds of smaller promotions and speculative coups; and soon the newly made nabobs of coal, coke, and barbed wire, along with their relatives, servants, and even their favorite ministers, flung themselves upon the market places in a frenzy of speculation. Into the fashionable centers of metropolitan cities they crowded; to the watering places they bustled, to join in an orgy of conspicuous expenditure, with their fine clothes, their glittering carriages, and their jingling pockets.

The prosperity of 1899, after the quick war with Spain, made it a year of "miracles." John Hay spoke with wonder and apprehension of the "insolent prosperity" of the United States. Men of gentle breeding and social pretension found their exclusive social world invaded by new-rich vulgarity in every form. These were the days of stupendous "international marriages"—when American heiresses purchased foreign titles at stupendous prices—of "$5,000 breakfasts," "$10,000 luncheons," and "$15,000 suppers," social functions which the popular press now qualified only according to the sums of money expended for them. The popular press, typified by Pulitzer's New York *World* and Hearst's New York *Journal,* in terms of pretended moral censure, gave fulsome reports of the Lucullan feasts of the new grandees, reports calculated to arouse lustful envy among the people.

These were the golden years of McKinley and Hanna.

"Almost every morning paper was filled with accounts of the . . . new railroad and industrial combinations. The relations between this process of business consolidation and the existing Republican supremacy was unmistakable." Thus the authorized biographer of Mark Hanna drew the implications of the McKinley-Hanna program.[3] Instead of professing a decent abhorrence of the new financial monsters, as political men usually did in public, Mark Hanna placed the trust boom directly to the credit of his party. "Mr. Hanna did not fear or hesitate to come out frankly in favor of these combinations," Croly relates. Despite the Sherman Anti-Trust Law and the common law, the government stood squarely behind the movement of financial concentration.

At this period Henry Adams, descendant of Presidents and patricians, and (as he described himself) the inveterate "stable companion" of statesmen, resided permanently in Washington,

[3] Herbert Croly, *Marcus Alonzo Hanna*, p. 296.

watching events as one absorbed in the great game of history. His own family fortunes had been linked with two revolutionary periods in American history, and this gave him an added perspective, a strong sense of the past. From his devoted friend John Hay, who was high in the inner circle of the ruling party, he gathered not a little inside stuff about the present. Thus armed, Henry Adams was enabled to make interesting judgments concerning the political-social upheavals of the 1890's. They marked, he concluded, one of those decisive epochs in the nation's history; their outcome was to be not merely "the final surrender of the country to capitalism," but a surrender to capitalism in its higher phase, that of great finance capitalists and investment bankers, centralizing and ruling virtually all industry. Adams' prophecies were written down in letters of the time (1896), as well as in his *Education*, several years later.

With the victory of 1896, Adams judged, the bankers had become "the greatest single power in the country, and infallibly control the drift of events." He himself pretended to an old-fashioned dislike of bankers and capitalistic society. But, as he wrote afterward in *The Education*, "All one's friends, all one's best citizens, reformers, churches, colleges, educated classes, had joined to force submission to capitalism." It had come; and, as a dividend-receiver, Adams resigned himself with cheerful cynicism. For, if such a society were to run at all, it must be run by capital. ". . . Nothing could surpass the nonsensity of trying to run so complex and so concentrated a machine by Southern and Western farmers in grotesque alliance with city day-laborers. . . ." [4]

Then, in passages full of insight, Adams sketches the flowering of America's imperial age. A favorable trend of commercial exchanges was causing the accumulation here of colossal bank deposits and gold, making the United States independent of European capital and herself one of the great creditor nations of the world, driven, in turn, to seek new outlets, new markets, new investment opportunities for her mountains of capital and expanded

[4] Henry Adams, *Letters*, Vol. II, p. 96.

productive energies. These momentous developments determined the politics of "McKinleyism"—for this was the name that Adams and later historians gave to the program to which McKinley himself may have contributed unconsciously only a part.

"McKinleyism," in essence, was "the system of combinations, consolidations, trusts, realized at home, realizable abroad." To the President—or perhaps, rather, to the silent partner, Hanna—this meant "the pooling of interests . . . in a general trust into which every interest should be taken, more or less at its own valuation, and whose mass should, under his management, create efficiency." [5]

At home "McKinleyism" required that the rival party bosses, as well as the competing captains of industry, were to be merged into a grand alliance, a kind of super-trust. Abroad, beyond the water's edge, the chance of combining the growing world force of America with that of nations which held the balance of power on earth, would offer itself ostensibly as the task of imperial diplomacy. This was the task to which the subtle John Hay, as Ambassador to England, and as Secretary of State, set himself for the decade after 1896. "Having looked with such a benevolent eye upon the merger of railroads and . . . industrial combinations, McKinley permitted Hay to see what he could do in the way of bringing the Powers abroad into a grand concert of agreement upon their common world-wide interests." [6]

It was a bold concept, worthy of those crowded hours when the stern, lonely, ill-favored Morgan labored like a titan to cement his vast "community of interests," when the crass, bullet-headed Hanna bestrode the land like a national boss.

McKinley and his partners, thought Henry Adams, in furthering trusts and combinations at home and abroad, "achieved very remarkable results." But, he added reflectively: "How much they cost was another matter."

[5] Adams, *The Education of Henry Adams,* p. 373.
[6] Dennett, *John Hay,* pp. 328, 330.

2

Under McKinley, the political government appeared very strong, in contrast with preceding administrations. Its high councils were filled mainly with rough-handed men of the "practical" type, probably the strongest men of professional politics and business in their generation. To be sure, Edwin L. Godkin, a sort of Gloomy Dean of the period, characterized them as being "mostly ignorant and completely secluded from foreign influences and without knowledge of any other state of society, with great contempt for history and experience. . . ." This political character would have its dangers. Yet accustomed as they were to handling large ventures in a large way, they worked to fulfill Hamilton's old dream of centralized, authoritative rule by "talents and wealth" —with the qualification that deficiency of talent was to be offset by mass of wealth.

The passion for order, for consolidation, pervaded even Congress. Much had been done in recent years toward co-ordinating the old "bear garden" that was the House of Representatives; while, in the Senate, new arrivals found the power of Nelson Aldrich, of Rhode Island, by his control of party caucus and Senate committees, little less than that of a dictator. Within a few minutes of a caucus meeting the program of a whole session of Congress might be dispatched. The Dingley Tariff Act, with its hundreds of complex schedules, was passed in the early weeks of the McKinley administration with almost no discussion worth the name. Opportunities for public hearings on this measure were negligible. Louis D. Brandeis, then a young Boston lawyer, presented himself before Representative Dingley's committee in behalf of a recently formed association favoring low tariff rates. "I desire to speak," he said, "on behalf of those, who, I believe, form a far larger part of the people of this country than any who have found representation here. . . . The consumers. . . ." He was greeted with jeering laughter.[7]

[7] Lief, *Brandeis*, p. 49.

But behind the executive and legislative organs of the government there stood always the supporting party institution, with its army of "workers," the men who managed primary conventions and gathered votes. Here in the party institution, more vital than at any time since Andrew Jackson's reign, there was (on the Republican side), an unheard-of regimentation and discipline under one man: Mark Hanna.

The Ohio coal and iron magnate was one of those key figures of the period who typified, for the caustic Godkin, contempt for learning, ignorance of the ways of other civilized society, indifference to the lessons of history. Certainly he was a new kind of political hero. Though John Hay thought him "a born general in politics," he ruled not among crowds, by eloquence, but from a desk in a private office.

His dictatorial temper, his blunt epithets, his shocking candor about the use of money, made men fear him, as they feared the red-nosed Morgan. Men of gentle feeling, at sight of the paunchy figure, the jowled face, the heavy mouth and piercing eye of the Ohio boss, would be taken aback. He seemed feudal, warlike; a man who would crush out or buy all those who stood in his way. In time, more credit would be given to the "benevolence" which underlay Hanna's feudalism; and to the shrewd wisdom with which he read the forces of his time. A peculiar glory adhered to him for having "made" a President, not by chance, but by long planning; many rich, ambitious Americans suddenly desired to imitate him, and become President Makers in their own right.

Entering politics late in life, Hanna had discovered nothing, invented nothing. He had taken the tools that were at hand, the machinery for gathering "voting cattle," and improved them. The alliance between large corporate business and political parties had long existed; Hanna perfected it, regularizing the tax laid upon business. It was his boast that money entrusted to him suffered little waste; that he and his lieutenants could be counted on to "use every cent of it right."

Washington, as a capital, often strikes one as a façade, ornate of marble, hollow-sounding. There you may see the President, like the polished figure in bronze of a typical politician, shaking people's hands, making conventional speech. Or the legislators on Capitol Hill performing their parts in a well-rehearsed play. The realities of political power are often to be felt elsewhere: in the field, at the grass roots.

Hurrying away to the banks of the Ohio River or of Lake Erie, we may glimpse the President Maker arduously at work, at the battle front itself. There is a state election campaign on, and Mr. Hanna, besides being national chairman of the Republican party, is, in his own right, boss of the Ohio suzerainty, and must oversee its action in person. With a retinue of Congressmen, aides, and "distinguished Ohioans," as well as baggage containing goodly store of cash, the great man journeys upon a tour of his state in a private train, stopping at hotels in small cities, conferring everywhere with county chairmen and district leaders, counting noses, distributing money.

In the papers of William C. Beer, a lawyer who acted as political liaison agent and lobbyist for a great insurance company of New York, there has been preserved for us a most graphic and candid picture of Mark Hanna in action at the front, in the summer of 1899, two years after McKinley's inauguration. Here we see, to our surprise, that there is great concern in inner circles over the results of the election. For Ohio is a "pivotal" state, and renewed success in the national elections will depend greatly upon the outcome here.

The first thing that surprises us is the strain, the difficulty, the apprehension everyone shows. Evidently the "protecting" of business from hostile legislation is a far less simple or easy affair than one would have assumed. McKinley himself, as Beer who has just visited him in Washington reports, is highly anxious about the results of the local Ohio elections.

"He has d—— good reason to be!" explodes Hanna. And he adds: "Please tell Pres. McCall [of the New York Life Insurance

Company] that I have had a very hard fight. . . . It has been hard work and has nearly worn me out." [8]

Then Hanna relates, for the benefit of the insurance company, how he himself has gone through the smaller towns and cities calling together the leaders, and "personally given out the necessary funds, one hundred dollars here, one hundred dollars there, and so on."

That night from Hanna's hotel room in Lima, Ohio, letters giving reports of the current situation and appealing urgently for funds go forth to Mr. J. Pierpont Morgan, to the heads of the Pennsylvania railroad and other railroads.

"I wrote by hand for Hanna," notes Beer in his memorandum, "twenty-two letters to railroad presidents, general managers and superintendents, and to Senator [Thomas C.] Platt and other prominent express officials." These letters urged the "extreme necessity" upon the large employers, "to get out every vote among their employees and shop-men on election day." By all this expenditure, by laborious preparation, by constant vigilance, Hanna hoped they could carry Ohio by a narrow, but safe, plurality.[9]

Why the "extreme necessity"? Why was it necessary that the leader of the victorious party work night and day in order to influence the voice of the electorate in the desired sense? Were not the Boy Orator and the Free Silver agitators defeated for good and all? Was the country not safely surrendered to high capitalism, as Henry Adams surmised? The actual picture in Ohio, then the most boss-ridden and "corrupted" of states, was utterly different from the expected one.

After two years of orthodox Republican leadership, in both peace and war, the old Western Reserve, including the large cities of Cleveland and Toledo, was aflame with opposition. That year, an opponent of Hanna's regular machine was to be elected Mayor of Cleveland; and soon afterward another opponent, Tom L. Johnson, formerly a public-utility magnate himself, and now converted to radical Single Tax doctrines, was to capture Hanna's

[8] Beer, *Hanna*, appendix, p. 306.
[9] *Ibid.*, pp. 307-308.

own city, Cleveland, and reign over it for long years. In nearby Toledo, also, another singular character, Samuel Jones—called "Golden Rule" Jones—had arisen to challenge the regulars in 1897. A prosperous small manufacturer, Jones had made himself loved and celebrated for his profit-sharing enterprises. Entering local politics, he quickly won over his townspeople, preaching to them in language so simple that even the foreign-born workers could understand the most deeply radical of doctrines: those of the Golden Rule, of the Declaration of Independence, of Thomas Jefferson. The newspapers of both parties, combining to slander him, accomplished nothing in a series of elections.

Though Mark Hanna controlled the national party machine, the state and its legislature, local revolt of surprising vigor and dangerous scope threatened him repeatedly. In 1899 Mayor Jones planned to run for the Governorship itself as an independent candidate, using the same picturesque methods that had succeeded so well in smaller contests. The anxiety Hanna showed in the nocturnal interview with Mr. Beer, and his decision to go himself to Toledo by a morning train, to checkmate the enemy, becomes explicable.

I have quietly summoned all our leaders there . . . and am going to follow the same tactics I used to beat Jones in the Convention—to get the delegation—you remember? They sent word a few days ago that if they had five thousand they could buy up all of Jones's lieutenants—his head men. Those fellows understand perfectly well that Jones can't be elected Governor, that there will be no offices, and they are not in this for their health. They convinced me as to the scheme, and I sent them a thousand dollars yesterday, and will give them the rest tomorrow.[10]

Thus bribery—oh, unpleasant word!—as ancient as the arts of assassination, seems clearly to have been used in completing the "educational" program in Ohio. Nor was money spared in hiring carriages to transport the voters of the countryside. "It is quite easy to see where 25,000 votes were changed . . . within the

[10] Beer, *Hanna*, appendix, pp. 307-308.

week before election day," runs Beer's secret memorandum to his employers. Money was well expended, since the added votes brought exactly the narrow margin of victory that year.

Yet it was like holding a dike against the ceaselessly pounding, invading sea. Local revolt would be overcome in Ohio; but it made new breaches and broke through at other points. It was at this very period, when national party organization came into such strong hands, that political unrest assumed a specially local or municipal shape. Now was the heyday of city reformers and Single Taxers who hoped to establish their experiments in taxation or Good Government in a local frame. And everywhere in these localities one could hear expressions similar to those reported in Ohio: "The people are sick of Hanna. . . . They have all they want of Hannaism." [11]

In Illinois, for example, where Governor John P. Altgeld had gone down to defeat in 1896, the Republican machine had installed a more complaisant Governor, approved by Charles T. Yerkes, Chicago's baron of street-cars. Preparations were then made to revive those "eternal monopoly bills" that Altgeld had vetoed; and the legislature at Springfield was known to be ready to pass them. But in Chicago the masses of Mr. Yerkes' "straphangers," forewarned by Altgeld's men, were roused to a fever suggesting renewed mob violence. Delegations of citizens marched on Springfield; and at their approach the Illinois legislators yielded in panic.

Then a few weeks later, when the excitement had abated, the utility ring planned a sudden thrust by which measures favoring the purpose of Yerkes' corporations were to be rushed, this time through the Chicago City Council. But the citizens rose again; some of them came with rope in their hands, showed it to the Aldermen, saying that it was intended for them if the street-car franchise bills were passed. They were not passed.[12]

Thus it was an unending struggle; and the fight must be carried over and over again to many points of the system. The Presi-

---

[11] *Ibid.*, pp. 310-311.
[12] Lloyd, *H. D. Lloyd*, Vol. II, p. 283.

dent Maker was, in reality, a harassed ruler, increasingly apprehensive of an opposition that mounted even among the educated middle class. The very prominence given to Mr. Hanna's methods at the hour of his triumphs aroused fear as to the effect of such methods on public morals and even public safety. The very measures taken by the large business interests (that he represented) to protect themselves by an alliance with corrupt professional politics "served only to inflame the irritation." [13]

What would become—a young New York reformer, John Jay Chapman, asked at this time—of a people who for long years lived, as a community, completely under boss rule? What would their habits be after a generation or so? What views could we expect to find in their hearts? "The masses will have been controlled by bribery and terrorism. . . . Money and place will have been corrupting them. A conviction will spread throughout the community that nothing can be done without a friend in court; that honesty does not pay and probably never has paid in the history of the world."

Yet the business leaders, believing that that system which enabled them to make money was "the only safe government," resisted all change and "clung to abuses as to a life-preserver." Reform, they argued, was expensive and served but "to excite the poor against the rich." To put honest politicians in office was something they feared, lest these might prove unable "to bribe the thieves not to steal from them!" [14]

Contemporary with the Mugwumps, rising in the Eastern cities of Boston and New York, were the Single Taxers and municipal reformers of Ohio, who were roused to intense activity by Hanna's ruthlessness. Here the followers of Tom L. Johnson and Golden Rule Jones strove to apply the Single Tax doctrines of Henry George to the local situation. As latter-day Christians in politics they reacted strongly against the extremes of poverty and squalor and vulgar wealth which their cities displayed. They hoped that the Single Tax, by eliminating ground rent, would transform their

[13] Croly, *op. cit.*, p. 326.
[14] Chapman, *Causes and Consequences*, pp. 28 ff.

towns into happy and beautiful places, with the artisan and mechanic rendered eternally prosperous. They too labored "to free the cities from privilege and partisanship" which retarded progress and battened on poverty. They trusted that they would bring about "the free city of today, which is the hope of democracy; tomorrow . . . the triumph of democracy." [15] They too, like the Eastern Mugwumps, or civil service reformers, centered their attack upon the groundwork of local government on which the whole national party system was based. In time the current of their agitation would merge also with the broader stream of democratic resurgence in the rural West.

3

Had anything truly been settled by the contest of 1896? How real was the victory of "McKinleyism"? No sooner had the battle ended than the victors realized that they had won only a truce, a temporary respite. For the warning that Edwin L. Godkin, the Cassandra of American journalism, had given them in 1894 still held true:

> . . . *The politics of the world are becoming more and more a controversy between rich and poor.* The influential and the rich men are taking the place of the feudal baron and the absolute monarch as objects of popular attack. . . .[16]

And Godkin, though he had not the slightest desire that the rich should give way to their inferiors, was independent enough to reproach the men of business themselves for having brought disaster nearer by their own follies. Had they not for years, by their demand for a protective tariff, made the government a partner in their enterprises and made every Presidential election "an affair of the pocket"? Had not the capitalists themselves spread the notion that the government owed assistance to individuals in carrying on business and making a livelihood?

[15] Brand Whitlock, *Letters*, pp. 84, 97.
[16] E. L. Godkin in *The Forum*, Mar., 1894; italics mine.

Another cultivated member of the conservative upper class, Theodore Roosevelt, was also convinced, like Godkin, that the victory of the Gold-bugs had brought little more than a temporary halt in hostilities. The young author, sportsman, clubman, and amateur of politics had given active help to his party from the stump in 1896. At the height of the panic over Bryan, he had written privately of his surprise at the "savage hatred of the unprosperous for the prosperous" that clearly underlay the whole silver movement. Here was the greatest crisis in our history, he felt, saving only that of the Civil War. "It is a semi-socialistic, agrarian movement, with free silver as a mere incident. . . ." Organized labor and all the other "ugly forces that seethe beneath the social crust," and feed "on class and sectional hatred," had supported Bryan. Though these were "the very people one would wish to help"—there was nothing to be done but to beat them back.[17]

Weeks passed after the election victory, and Theodore Roosevelt would still confide to his friend and fellow-Republican, Henry Cabot Lodge, his fears that Bryanism was still "too real and ugly a danger . . . and our hold on the forces that won the victory for us by no means too well assured."[18]

For what reply had the Gold Standard Republicans given to the insistent demands raised on behalf of the masses of people in great sections of the country? Complaint was made of the scarcity of money and credit; the winning party responded by reaffirming and defending the gold standard. Millions of farmers protested at the high cost of manufactured or consumer goods in relation to the price of grains; the conservative Republicans answered by raising the protective schedules higher than ever before. Labor had pressed for the right to collective bargaining, the eight-hour day, and a living wage, making bitter cry against the Federal courts that outlawed their strikes and imprisoned their leaders. The ruling party had simply proclaimed the sacredness of Court and Constitution. The average small man had shown a most vehement

[17] Cowles, *Letters from Theodore Roosevelt*, pp. 192-194; Sept. 27, 1896.
[18] Lodge, *Correspondence*, Vol. I, p. 240.

dislike for the new railroad and industrial trusts; he had petitioned for control of them by the government. The party in
power answered by doing nothing, abandoning nearly all pending
trust suits. Popular anxiety at the increasing, machinelike subjection of the political government to secret controls had been aired;
many had urged that party nominations and elections be made
more directly responsive to the popular will. Yet they had come
to see the party machine transformed into the terrible Steam
Roller; they had seen money and intimidation used more openly
than ever before.

Truly they might say, as Bryan had said at Chicago: "We have
petitioned, and our petitions have been scorned; we have entreated
and our entreaties have been disregarded; we have begged, and
they have mocked. . . ."

In short, none of the genuine social and "sectional" issues of the
time had been fairly dealt with; and the regime of practical men
seemed bent on forgetting or avoiding them as far as possible.

Beyond the Mississippi, Bryan still spoke from the Chautauqua
platform, as a beloved leader of the West, and vowed that it was
only "the first battle" that was ended. Yet, though the same profoundly democratic and "Jacobin" impulses still ruled the people
of the Valley of Democracy, they turned away, nowadays, from
the simpler nostrums of the Populist and Free Silver parties. Gold
was more plentiful now; and farmers were relatively more prosperous after 1897. In the decade that followed they were to turn
to solutions other than that of currency inflation.

Responding to the proposals of the more intelligent and inven-
tive of the new sectional leaders, such as William S. U'Ren of
Oregon, and Robert M. La Follette of Wisconsin, they began to
consider the procedure of democracy itself and the possibilities of
purifying it. The old equalitarian tendencies showed themselves
again in demands that political government, local and Federal, be
rescued from "invisible," machine control. The hope of more
"direct democracy" was what U'Ren fostered when he succeeded
in introducing the popular referendum, a device borrowed from

the plebiscite of the Swiss. By this means the power of a hated public-utility corporation was suddenly broken in Oregon.

Meanwhile in Wisconsin, La Follette, another champion of the plain people, made persistent, vigorous agitation for the direct primary system of party nominations. Thus he hoped to wrest control of the state's dominant party organization from its old, corrupt masters, so that a just system of taxation, control of the private monopolies, and enlightened social laws might follow.

Banished from public life in 1891, after his rupture with the Republican machine, La Follette knew that it would require a struggle of many years to win over the party for his own independent faction. Sometimes he wondered seriously if the game were worth the candle for himself and his friends.

But there was the good State of Wisconsin ruled by a handful of men, who had destroyed every vestige of democracy in the Commonwealth. They settled in private conference practically all nominations for . . . offices, controlled conventions, dictated legislation, and . . . even sought to lay corrupt hands on the courts of justice.[19]

To revive democracy, to rescue it from corrupt machine control and make it once more the instrument of popular will—these, rather than the economic cure-all of currency inflation, were the objects of the new Western leaders, still obscure in a national sense at the turn of the century.

In a speech of 1897, before students of the University of Chicago, La Follette both challenged the reigning Mark Hannas and, in characteristic fashion, addressed an appeal to youth. "Abolish the caucus," he cried. "Go back to the first principles of democracy; go back to the people." [20]

The Jacksonian temper still lived in the West and especially in its middle border. In spite of defeat, there was no want of determination and faith. Many hands were at work.

But even in the "plutocratic" East, in the bosom of the ruling party itself, there was an ambitious, adventurous faction of

---

[19] La Follette, *Autobiography*, p. 172.
[20] *Ibid.*, p. 197.

younger men who held their own ideas of policy and leadership, and dreamed of supplanting the old chieftains.

4

All things after March 4, 1897, seemed perfectly ordered for a millennial age of business prosperity. Yet why was it that when one looked a little under the surface, or listened to the talk of leading personages in Washington or New York society, one received an impression of abiding gloom, of brooding apprehension for the future?

The seed of opinion, ideas, talents, of history and civilization, often flourished best in small, homogeneous social groups. These favoring conditions were often to be found in compact England or France, and were less discernible in sprawling America. Yet during the '90's there did exist for a time, in Washington, a few such "centers of culture," circles of men and women of charm and wit, ever engaged in the discussion of human affairs, to be met usually at the luxurious mansion of John Hay or at the equally fastidious home of Henry Cabot Lodge, the young Senator from Massachusetts, called "the Scholar in Politics." Here were to be seen not only literary notables and visiting foreign celebrities, but also those native public figures who embodied such talent as the new Hamiltonian dynasty of wealth contained. Here, as the French would say, was *un monde*, a definite little social microcosm, with its members drawn from the wealthy class, or men of influence and office who enjoyed the social graces. Speaker Thomas B. Reed, the cynical, witty elder statesman, was one of the circle, but not Mark Hanna; the corporation lawyer and Cabinet member, Elihu Root, but not Edward Harriman; Theodore Roosevelt and Albert Beveridge, but not Matt Quay.

Here the news of the day was studied, the political reverberations of events throughout the world were avidly discussed; ideas were born and plots laid; and men and women departed to lobby, to cajole Senators or Cabinet Secretaries to take some new "line";

or even to intrigue for somebody's Presidential boom; or bring on a war.

It was these people whom James Bryce saw much of during his visit to the United States, and whom he had in mind when he remarked, in *The American Commonwealth,* upon the prevailing "apathy among the luxurious classes and fastidious minds, who . . . are disgusted by the superficial vulgarities of public life." America's educated and wealthy class, he said, "find no smooth and easy path lying before them. Since the masses do not look to them for guidance, they do not come forward to give it. If they wish for office, they must struggle for it, avoiding the least presuming upon their social position."

Another English observer, Cecil Spring Rice, then Secretary of Legation at Washington, also wrote home similar intimate impressions of Hay, Adams, Lodge, Roosevelt, and other American luminaries. He too said of these cultivated men that in their talk "there was something melancholy." On political questions those who were in politics would make "open profession of partisanship and bitterness, with an open contempt of any of the ordinary considerations of honor or honesty or high feeling." Others who were not in politics, when touching on public questions, spoke with "a sort of bitter despair in their minds which is hard to describe and not pleasant to listen to. . . ." [21]

John Jay Chapman, who also knew well these men of leisure and education, said of them with a flash of insight: "Though they may think they are not affected by commercialism, their attitude of mind is precisely that of a lettered class living under a tyranny." [22]

For they did not conceal their misgivings concerning the supposedly strong but ignorant men who ruled our government. John Hay often and again lamented the "corruption, the self-seeking, the cowardice," that filled our official life ever since the days when he served as Lincoln's private secretary. While, next door, Henry Adams would look out from his library window across LaFayette

---

[21] Gwynn, *Sir Cecil Spring Rice,* Vol. I, pp. 64-65, 102.
[22] Chapman, *op. cit.,* p. 40.

Square toward the White House, and ponder upon "democracy's neglect of the well-born and intelligent." [23] But most of all these men of culture, who thought often of the lessons of history, suffered from a fear of "the mob" which, though expressed constantly in the form of jests, remained nevertheless their deepest obsession.

To the young Theodore Roosevelt, a Governor Altgeld was a "demagogue," a Benedict Arnold. The dispatch of Federal troops to Chicago during the general railway strike of 1894 had saved us from "a repetition of what occurred during the Paris Communes!" [24]

"I know the Populists and the laboring men well and their faults . . ." he had written in a letter of December, 1894. "I like to see a mob handled by the regulars, or by good State-Guards, not overscrupulous about bloodshed." [25] The election of 1896; he felt, had "raised the evil spirit of revolution. . . ." The legend persisted that in his youthful spirits he had thought of issuing armed challenges to the radical adversaries; that he had said they should be suppressed "as the Communes of Paris were suppressed by taking ten or a dozen of their leaders out, by standing ten or a dozen of them against a wall and shooting them dead!" [26]

But while fear of the mob animated the young leaders, they also expressed in private a deep disgust for that "unholy alliance" of corrupt professional politics and big business that stood over them. Quietly they deplored "Dollar Mark" Hanna, and longed for the coming of civil-service reform, which would halt jobbing and thievery in public office. McKinley they rated an "infirm" man, who would be unequal to gigantic labor riots, they feared, or to the danger of a foreign conflict. Of the business men's government that McKinley had established, Henry Cabot Lodge, himself a millionaire by inheritance, spoke with unconcealed scorn, saying that "the business man dealing with a large political question is

[23] Dennett, *Hay*, p. 164.
[24] T. Roosevelt in *The Forum*, Feb., 1895.
[25] *Matthews Papers*, to Brander Matthews.
[26] Willis J. Abbot in the New York *Journal*, Oct. 29, 1896.

really a painful sight." [27] And Roosevelt, amid the tumult of labor uprising, reminded himself also that the banker and merchant too needed "education and sound chastisement." He inveighed against those men who deified "success through financial trickery," who had but "the imagination of a green-grocer," and to whom trade and property were more sacred than honor or national glory. Could the values of justice, humanity, and culture be propagated by such as these? he questioned.[28]

Though placed within the Hamiltonian party, as the epoch of "McKinleyism" opened, the faction of conservative upper-class intellectuals, typified by Lodge and Roosevelt, was already embarked upon a search for new doctrines, for a new ideology of leadership. They had premonitions of the gravity of the real situation and of historic opportunities as well. These "scholars in politics" were convinced that McKinley, Hanna, and their associates were ignorant and without insight into the forces of history; their ideas, like those of the typical "Old Guard" Republicans, dated from the Civil War, and would have to be changed one day. Hence they, the new men, already pressed forward impatiently to shoulder them aside.

In truth, the apparently invincible Old Guard and the businessmen-in-politics, who now headed a movement that seemed so powerful, were nearly all to be scattered and decimated in a surprisingly short time. In how few years illness, age, or electoral misfortune would overtake nearly all of them!—while the less "sound," younger men rushed into their offices as with the effect of a palace revolution.

Nor was the concern with the future pattern of political leadership limited to the conservative intellectuals only in the one party. In August, 1897, at Richmond, Virginia, shortly after McKinley and Hanna took over the reins of government, we find Professor Woodrow Wilson of Princeton University, a Southern Democrat,

[27] Cowles, *op. cit.*, pp. 182-183.
[28] *Matthews Papers*, T. R. to Brander Matthews, Dec., 1894; *Forum*, Feb., 1895.

delivering an address significantly entitled "Leaderless Government," whose line of thought paralleled most remarkably that of Lodge and Roosevelt.

There was much unrest, much "vague radicalism" abroad, he said.

The nation is made—its mode of action is determined; what we now want to know is: what is it going to do with its life, its material resources and its spiritual strength? How is it to gain and keep a common purpose in the midst of complex affairs . . . ? How is the nation to get definite leadership and form steady, effective parties? . . . How shall we settle questions of economic policy? Who is to reconcile our interests . . . ?

Who, in short, would provide "wisdom in action"? Only, he asked as if in deep doubt, "our men of affairs"? [29] Wilson, for his part, would continue to doubt them, and in the pages of his private letters to confide his own long-cherished hopes for a role in public life.

It was at this time, while new tactics of leadership and new ideologies were being sought in the circles I have described, that the very curious American philosopher of history, Brooks Adams, turned up, almost providentially, with his prophetic study of historical trends, *The Law of Civilization and Decay*, published in December, 1895, and widely read and discussed by the literati in the years that followed, then unjustly forgotten. The younger brother of Henry Adams, himself eccentric enough, had shifted suddenly from the practice of law and the pursuit of reform in Massachusetts politics to furnishing historical theories for the younger statesmen, such as Lodge (to whom he was related) and Roosevelt, his friend, whom he strongly influenced.

Brooks Adams resembled the Italian philosopher Vico, as he foreshadowed the German Spengler, in his ingenious use of historical parallels and "cycles of culture." His own cycles—differing from the biological cycles of Henry Adams—were based on the

[29] W. Wilson, *Public Papers*, Vol. I, pp. 338, 339.

shiftings of the great trade routes of the world and the rise and fall of commercial empires. The United States, he held, now dominated the main trade routes of the modern world, running from the Atlantic to the Pacific, as Rome had once dominated Mediterranean commerce. Although here "the conventions of popular government were still preserved," he argued, the country was already falling subject to an aristocracy of money-lenders as absolute as that of Rome. Soon our commercial civilization, with its love of gain and usury, would grow less energetic, less warlike, less "heroic." Ultimately its rulers would be unequal to the mastery of fearfully complex social problems; and, using copious illustrations from past history, Brooks Adams forecast inevitable revolutions and catastrophes to come in a comparatively early future. The very weaknesses and default of the ruling class, as in the French Revolution, would contribute to the debacle.

However doubtful in validity these theories may have appeared to most men at the time, we find that they gained currency with Roosevelt, with Lodge, and evidently with the young Beveridge. We find the terms of Brooks Adams occurring constantly in Roosevelt's early speeches and writings, as in Lodge's. They provide an orientation toward a reviving nationalism, toward the "soldierly virtues," which Roosevelt nowadays admired, and seem to rationalize the increasingly critical spirit (among the new Hamiltonians) toward the crass commercialism of the age. Greed and demagogy, both disturbing and dividing our society, must be struck down, and a virile, fraternal sentiment for the glory of the nation made to rule in their place.

Albert Beveridge, who shone as a stump speaker for the Republicans in 1896, attacked those who fomented sectional and clan conflict—in terms that might have been borrowed from Brooks Adams. "Today the issue is national life," he said. "Are the American people a nation, or are they an aggregation of localities? Is the Stars and Stripes the flag of a vital nation . . . of an invincible people?" [30]

[30] Bowers, *Beveridge*, p. 63.

At the time of the Venezuela crisis, in the winter of 1895-1896, both Lodge and Roosevelt brimmed over with war fever, the latter expressing the most fervent hope that our government would now adopt a more "spirited" foreign policy. Brooks Adams meanwhile wrote to Roosevelt in dark tones that the crisis with England seemed to offer a possible way of escape or regeneration. "The whole world seems to be rotting, rotting. The one hope for us, the one chance to escape from our slavery, even for a year, is war, war which shall bring down the British Empire." [31]

Even after the momentary danger of war with England had passed, Roosevelt and Lodge continued to search for war and preach foreign adventure and annexation. The moral and historical arguments with which each adorned his purpose resembled strongly those of Brooks Adams. Let men cease to hold trade and manufacture sacred and set above them "national honor and glory . . . courage and daring and loyalty and unselfishness," wrote the young Theodore Roosevelt. He prayed that this rich nation might not, by growing timid and slothful, fall an easy prey to those people who embodied "those most valuable of all qualities, the soldierly virtues." [32]

Sometimes Roosevelt hoped for a war on grounds of "humanity and self-interest" combined. At others he admitted that he desired it for the sake of "the benefit done to our people by giving them something to think of which isn't material gain. . . ." [33] He reproached our trade-unionists for thinking too much of material gain; and regarded with ill-concealed dislike the barons of the bag, typified by the former grocer Hanna, who "owned" the administration in 1897 and seemed resolved to direct it only toward the paths of peaceful commerce.

On the whole the conservative intellectuals, typified by Roosevelt and Lodge, when the Golden Years of McKinley and Hanna opened, were discontented and restless. They conceived of no large, constructive, domestic projects to occupy their own ener-

[31] *T. R. Papers*, Brooks Adams to T. R., Feb. 25, 1896.
[32] Speech of Jun. 2, 1897.
[33] *T. R. Papers*, T. R. to Commander W. W. Kimball, Nov. 19, 1897.

gies and appeal to the aspirations of the people. Within their party, their hidden opposition to the reigning leaders resolved itself into a persistent, intriguing agitation for a war, any war that would yield those thrills of generous emotion, those pulse-throbbings that gave to statesmen and to patriots, to warriors and to poets, as Roosevelt said, their grandest opportunities.

The temper and historical circumstances of the late 1890's are an extraordinary parallel to those of America exactly a century before. Then too the Federalists, the party of talents and wealth, held power, though with increasing difficulty. Meanwhile the anti-Federalists, championing that "ever-increasing class which labor under the hardships of life," as Madison said, by their hunger for equality offered a certain threat to the "gentry." The mood of the latter, who still ruled the republic firmly, grew both pessimistic and cynical. Though the Federalist leaders coldly defied popular opinion, they constantly feared a democratic upheaval, and groped for ways to outflank it. One of them, the dour Yankee, Fisher Ames, even went so far as to lament the fortunate geographical position of our country which made the possibility of war with a foreign power so remote that no threat from this direction served to check domestic political strife. Would, he said, that there were some formidable neighbor close at hand, whose threat might for a time at least "inspire stronger fears than demagogues can inspire." [34] For in those days, too, they who attacked the rule of the "gentry" were but demagogues.

[34] Ford, *Rise and Growth of American Politics*, p. 71.

II. THE SCHOLARS IN POLITICS

O N A Friday evening of November, 1894, Theodore Roosevelt, then a mere Civil Service Commissioner, stood before a large gathering of the Harvard Civil Service Reform Club, at Cambridge, making a thumping speech on the need for governmental reform and the still more burning need of educated young men to carry this out.

Decent people, he said, wanted decent politics. But corruption was organized—by office-holding mercenaries—while decency was unorganized. "The only way to break up this organization is by taking away from the political leaders the offices by which they pay themselves." Our political government must be salvaged by a concerted drive for civil service reform. And Harvard men, cried the thick-set, energetic, bespectacled alumnus in ringing tones, must take an increasingly active part in this effort; they must recall that they had "special duties as well as special privileges."

But, he went on to warn them, they must be prepared to change their methods and manners. They must be active in politics not from a theoretical "collegian" point of view, but from a "practical" one. They must proceed not merely as "good men" but as "manly" men. "Away with mere feebleness," he cried, "this is a rough, work-a-day, practical world." Too often had people of the better sort turned with mingled scorn and discouragement from contact with the lower ranks of politics and party life. But what a sad and evil thing it would be if men of culture and social position, men possessed of a moral sense and "devotion to what is right," should show themselves lacking in the energy and manliness necessary to

impose their will. We must make our blows against evil count and
not let those rude, unlettered elements who stand for evil alone
"have all the virile qualities." The new crusaders must be, above
all, virile; they must, he would exclaim, baring his teeth, be ready
even to be "tough."[1]

The speech which Theodore Roosevelt gave when he was thirty-
five was true in type to those he would be giving twenty years
later. Its message, its spirit, was deeply characteristic of the conservative élite which pushed itself vigorously into American public
life at the turn of the century, and which was to play so bold and
brilliant a part in the politics of the new century.

Here, necessarily, there will be much to say of Theodore Roosevelt and his career. Of the new men in politics he becomes easily,
by his many-sided, tireless activities, by the high gifts of his temperament, his infectious example and influence, the central or key
figure. He was unmistakably a man of his time, and the Zeitgeist
was lusty in him. All that happened to him from beginning to
end seems, in afterthought, in the highest degree symptomatic
rather than accidental.

That he was a man of "average" mental attainments, as he himself sometimes admitted, rather than one of unusual intellectual
powers, is all the more helpful to our plan of studying the pattern of political leadership as it took shape in the beginning of
the present century. He sprang, to be sure, from the bosom of
the upper class; but with passing time he would learn to swallow
many of his inherited prejudices and speak for the aspirations of
much larger groups.

He reflected intensely the ideas and interests of his epoch; indeed he echoed, or responded to, the pulsations of popular feeling with remarkable sensitiveness, becoming himself an instrument
of public opinion, a sort of "sounding board" for *vox populi*, as
he said. While responding, he also, as the embodiment of changing popular sentiment, stimulated and provoked even better than

[1] *Harvard Crimson*, Dec., 1894, No. 41, Vol. XXVI; also J. E. Spingarn to
author.

he knew. Decisive measures of law, sweeping reforms from which he himself shrank, were to be enacted by others, thanks to the momentum he had helped to generate.

Most important of all, he introduced a new note, a breath of fresh air into our public life, after thirty years of degraded spoils politics, of uncritical and complacent drifting. His eloquent public utterances sounded more forcefully than any others the new political attitude, at once more critical toward the social canons of the preceding generation and more enlightened and refined in its approach to the massive social questions that had been accumulating under those who had gone before him.

Theodore Roosevelt was to mount to the highest office probably as the first man in forty years who, in that sanctified place, actually questioned or dreamed of questioning the accepted standards of respectability of his predecessors. Perhaps most of all he himself would have liked to be remembered as a moral motive force, one who turned himself and other men of his time to "higher things" than thoughts of "factories and railways," or "piled-up riches," or "roaring, clanging industrialism." [2]

For nearly forty years American public life had been degraded; Presidents and Senators and Governors had been puppets of the great overlords of industry and finance who held real power after the industrial revolution. But with Roosevelt the Political Man, *homo politicus*, was to be revived. The era of Enlightenment that came in with him—both enlightened and repentant in contrast with the age of the "robber barons" and the spoilsmen—was in effect an American counterpart of the Liberal or Social Democratic movements that ruled western Europe also at the end of the nineteenth century. The era was stamped so deeply with the first Roosevelt's virtues and defects (which linger to our own day) that in all justice we are disposed to call it "Rooseveltian."

But—to return to Theodore Roosevelt's speech at Harvard in 1894—his Macedonian appeal to men of his university and social

[2] *T. R. Papers*, T. R. to Frédéric Mistral, Dec. 15, 1904.

class to come and rescue our politics represented in one sense nothing new in itself. It was, indeed, an old Mugwump or Non-Partisan idea. The Mugwump leaders, Carl Schurz, George William Curtis, Godkin, who with the various members of the Adams family initiated the first civil service reform organizations, were the mentors of Roosevelt's youth. Since the days of the Tweed Ring and the Crédit Mobilier affair they had been distressed by the accumulated public scandal and shame, and frightened at the very costs of partisan, spoils politics. Their hope of elevating the tone of our government service resided in introducing honest, educated, and able men into the administrative corps. To this end they attempted to stimulate an enlightened public opinion and summon up an independent bloc of voters controlling the balance of power between the two corrupt parties.

In short, the older reformers strove to force their influence upon the party institution "from above." They called indignation meetings of good citizens, organized state and even "national" conventions, while ministers from the pulpit, university presidents, and the independent press supported them. Not a few wealthy capitalists who had been gouged by the politicos came to their aid.[3]

Yet while scheming to name Presidents and pull wires on a grand scale, they developed at no time any hold upon the masses of voters. The net results of their crusades were ludicrous; one fiasco followed another, and many of the original Mugwump leaders deserted the reform movement. Bitter with disappointment, Henry Adams in 1881 had warned his young colleague and pupil at Harvard, Henry Cabot Lodge, to shun politics; saying,

---

[3] For many years the long-range objectives of the Independent group had been to break down the narrow walls of partisan loyalties, attached to some leader who headed a "Blaine Legion," or aroused by the waving of "the bloody shirt," yet actually grounded in the lust among the lower ranks for the spoils of office. Men like Edwin L. Godkin believed that, if we were to arrive at good government, the unpledged or Independent vote in large states such as New York and Massachusetts must be increased and carefully wielded in the balance of election contests; the bonds of party discipline must be relaxed, and "the expression of open dissent from party programmes" made "respectable." (Godkin, *op. cit.*, pp. 211-212.)

"I have never known a young man to go into politics who was not the worse for it." [4]

But the procedure of Roosevelt and of his friend Lodge, as well, in one sense did represent a departure from that of the older men, those whom the arrogant boss Roscoe Conkling had called the "man-milliners," the "carpet-knights" of reform. Roosevelt in his Harvard speech urged that educated and well-bred men should no longer shrink from the "rough, work-a-day" side of politics; they must establish contact with the plain people; they must be ready to undergo apprenticeship among the lowest ranks of party "workers."

This was precisely what Roosevelt himself had done, upon being graduated from Harvard and returning to New York. He had applied for membership and had been admitted—after overcoming some natural suspicions—to his district Republican club, which met in a room above a corner saloon. He had stubbornly refused the advice—or the solemn warnings—of his family and his family's friends; and his determination to enter politics at the bottom of the ladder had seemed as scandalous to them as if he had decided to devote himself to poetry or the theater. They told him that politics were "low," that local party organizations were not the place for "gentlemen" but were run rather by saloon-keepers and horse-car conductors, who would be brutal and unpleasant to deal with. He answered that if this were true, then the people he had been frequenting did not belong to the governing class, "whereas the horse-car conductors and their like plainly did"; and that he for his part "intended to be one of the governing class." [5]

The young man's unconventional behavior suggests already that clairvoyance that leads to veritable discoveries or innovations. He showed qualities of intense curiosity, the desire to learn for himself of the realities of political life and power; he showed independence of mind in judging that those who passed for "gentlemen" should begin among the rank and file the work of elevat-

[4] Adams, *Letters*, Vol. I, p. 331.
[5] Roosevelt, *An Autobiography*, pp. 55-56.

ing our public life. Thus there began for Roosevelt twenty years of apprenticeship, a long period of training, marked with many painful contretemps, a preparation for his later climb to the political heights which was so erroneously considered "meteoric" or even "accidental."

The decision of a young man of "old Knickerbocker" family and independent means to enter politics—rather than railroading or banking—appeared without rhyme or reason at the time, in view of the low estate to which political life had sunk in the 1880's. Probably the love of literature and history that Roosevelt had absorbed during his Cambridge years was not unrelated to this decision. No doubt he pictured to himself a world filled with William Pitts, Edmund Burkes, and Wellingtons rather than the humbler members of the "Jake Hess Republican Club" of the Twenty-first District of New York, who were his first colleagues.

The impulse to public life, and especially to reform activities such as now gripped the cultivated and wealthy circles in Boston, frequented at this time by Roosevelt, in itself suggested the beginning of a higher stage in our great economic revolution after the Civil War. Leisure-class ideals of literary-political glory, such as the eighteenth-century Americans had known, were spreading again, if slowly. The plundering of the public treasury, winked at during the more frenzied phases of wealth-getting, was now strongly deplored in good company.

Lodge, when Roosevelt met him at Harvard, was divided in his mind between the choice of a career in literature and one in politics. This son of New England patricians, who had a local reputation for industry and talent, had been counseled by Henry Adams to turn his steps toward the "historico-literary line," as a career that could be made to pay well in money, reputation, and other solid values. In their most respectable town of Boston, Adams observed: "No one has done better and won more in any business or pursuit, than has been acquired by men like Prescott, Motley, Frank Parkman, Bancroft and so on in historical writing. . . ." Yet none of these had been men of extraordinary gifts; and now that they were passing, Boston was "running dry of literary authorities." By his ability Lodge might with ease "enthrone himself as a species of literary lion. . . . With it comes social dignity, European reputation, and a foreign mission to close." [6]

Lodge had decided, however, to combine from the beginning both the "historico-literary" and the political career. His wealth, which rumor traced to a great "rum-and-nigger" fortune, and his cultured background disposed him to the effort. His boyhood memories were filled with the eloquence of great men such as Daniel Webster, Charles Sumner, and Emerson, who used to call upon his father and discourse upon the state of the world. Inspired with their example he prepared himself, it is said, to become a master of languages and of letters, a poised speaker at the dinner table or from the public rostrum. One of his friends, John T. Morse, recalls that even from earliest years Lodge "always had himself well in hand." He bore himself with almost too much measure and pride; and his popularity among his Massachusetts neighbors was never "strictly personal." [7]

When he came of age and inherited his fortune, Lodge gave great dinners at his home, and with the aid of a cellar of famous old Madeira maintained a high level of talk. To a Roosevelt, Lodge was the cultured young man of letters, "writing brilliant books in his handsome library in the forenoon and entertaining agreeable company at his hospitable mahogany in the evenings." Roosevelt heard much from his friend, eight years his senior, of the need for "philosophic statesmanship" and for "introducing education, training, character" into our public life. [8]

Often among the company were those other young Mugwumps, such as Moorfield Storey, who had been the secretary and protégé of Sumner, and Brooks Adams, with whose aid Lodge launched the Commonwealth Club, devoted to the "purification of politics." [9]

From 1880 on, Lodge made serious efforts to play a part in local politics; he sought to become a delegate to national Repub-

[6] Adams, *Letters*, Vol. I, p. 228.
[7] *Harvard Graduates' Magazine*, Mar., 1925.
[8] *H. C. Lodge Papers*, Harvard College, Lodge to Goss.
[9] Howe, *Moorfield Storey*, pp. 141-142.

lican conventions. Though Henry Adams scolded him, he continued his efforts, despite some disappointments. Mornings he continued to work at his historical literature: the biographies of his Federalist ancestor, George Cabot, and George Cabot's famous friend, Alexander Hamilton. Afternoons, he repaired to South Boston, seeking out the local professionals of politics, through whom he hoped to secure his election to Congress.

This Boston swell "had always got what he wanted," as his friend Morse relates. But in some manner the partisans of reform, and Lodge, their active local leader, begot for themselves by 1884 a certain ill-repute during their struggle with the dreadful spoilsman General Ben Butler. In fact rumors of Lodge's Jekyll-and-Hyde character, circulating even at this time, had it that Butler's own shady methods had been turned against him; a hired "rowdy element" seemed to have become uppermost in the respectable faction itself. Those rumors Lodge indignantly denied as miserable calumnies, against which he set the record of his past life, his position, his education, his character.[10]

Roosevelt at Harvard has been pictured as both bookish and passionately fond of sports, an indifferent student and yet full of impetuous curiosity for all things. He became a member of fashionable clubs; he was fastidious, even a little showy in dress, with a touch of the exhibitionism that often clings to men who love public life. He had also a serious side that led him to direct a Sunday school class every week.[11]

His social connections with Boston deepened when he met Alice Lee, who became his first wife. She was the daughter of George Cabot Lee, one of Boston's leading bankers, and like his partner, Higginson, a convinced Mugwump. The fervor for civil service reform so strong in Boston at this time now swept up the young Roosevelt.[12]

[10] *H. C. Lodge Papers,* letter of Oct. 22, 1884.
[11] Pringle, *Roosevelt,* pp. 32-33.
[12] Not long before, the fierce political strife of the "Dreadful Decades" in New York, with its Democratic Tweeds and Republican Conklings, had pene-

In childhood Theodore Roosevelt evidently received a firm, Christian upbringing from his father, whom he pictures as just and wise, "the best man I ever knew." One might almost say that he inherited from him a disposition to political reform. It was Lodge, however, who evidently imparted to him the twin ambitions of becoming a great tribune and a great man of letters. Roosevelt thought Lodge, who possessed already a literary reputation, one of the most brilliant and forceful men he had ever met; and his friend was to gain over him an empire which another contemporary at Harvard, Owen Wister, rated as that of an "evil genius." But those who knew Cabot Lodge only as a cold and scheming man were ignorant of the hidden side of him which brought tears to his eyes when he read poetry to a friend.

Roosevelt too was soon deep in the historico-literary line. At the age of twenty-two he set to work on his long chronicle, *The Naval War of 1812.* Thereafter biographies and historical studies, essays on travel and political subjects, flowed from his pen.

In his early twenties he pictured himself, in his letters, as living an intense life of the mind; he described his joy at visiting a literary club, "a kind of Boston 'Century,'" where he met writers like Henry James and Edward Everett Hale. Dreams possessed him of a life more cultured, more filled with large events, in short, *less boresome,* than that of most others in his class. He looked forward to that "far distant salon, wherein we are to gather

trated to the very home of the Roosevelt family. The worthy Theodore Roosevelt, Sr., widely known in New York as a rich merchant and public-spirited citizen, had been "interested in every social reform" movement of the time, working with the Citizens' Committee which fought the Tweed Ring, and with the moderate Republicans who opposed the "Stalwart" machine. Thus President Hayes, in a sudden movement against Senator Roscoe Conkling, in 1877 nominated the elder Roosevelt for Collector of the Port of New York, a tremendous patronage job, overseeing half the customhouse business of the country—a business long in the hands of the machine, and a nest of corruption. But the "courtesy of the Senate" invoked by Conkling for two years blocked confirmation of Roosevelt, Sr., who died suddenly in 1878. Thus the public career he had been ready to embrace at a sacrifice was killed in the bud. Although the incident has not been noticed much, the younger Roosevelt could not have failed to associate the spoilsmen's opposition to his father with sorrow at his early death.

society men who take part in politics, literature and art, and politicians, authors and artists, whose bringing up and personal habits do not disqualify them for society." For the paramount thing was to escape from the desperately dull life that most of his friends appeared to lead. He continues: "The ———s are two fine-looking fellows of excellent family and faultless breeding, with a fine old country-place, four-in-hands, tandems, a yacht, and so on; but, oh, the decorous hopelessness of their lives!" [13]

The ideals of a Lodge and Roosevelt thus corresponded to those of many members of the leisure class in England. Literature, history, the arts, good society, were the ornaments of a good life; to stand for Parliament, to play a leading part in politics, both dispatched a duty and made life fuller still. But in America things were vastly different; and to pass directly from Harvard College to the Senate was no easy matter.

2

Fifteen years of political apprenticeship had passed for Theodore Roosevelt, the "silk stocking dude," before the critical year of 1896. He held minor public offices almost constantly, being elected Assemblyman from his district for three years, 1881 to 1884; running unsuccessfully for Mayor of New York in 1886; and being appointed a United States Civil Service Commissioner under President Harrison in 1889, President of the New York City Police Board in 1895, and finally, Assistant Secretary of the Navy in 1897, following McKinley's election. It was a record of varied experience and service, not lacking in distinction, yet on the whole unsatisfying, and certainly less brilliant than that of William Howard Taft, who also as a young reformer of respectable upper-class connections entered Ohio local politics at the same time and rose to be a Solicitor General and Federal judge while still in his early thirties. Nor did Roosevelt, like another contemporary, that strange young Texan of independent fortune and

[13] Cowles, *op. cit.*, pp. 77-78.

literary tastes, Edward M. House, become one of the "powers behind the throne" in the party organization of a great state. Nor did his record show that admirable consistency and zeal in pursuit of reform that distinguished certain of his acquaintances, such as the Bostonian Moorfield Storey, who despite high abilities was nearly all his life excluded from political office.

Imbued in the beginning with the Mugwump's belief in the primacy of "righteousness" above "partisanship," Roosevelt's early career could be summed up as a series of strategic retreats from such ideals—retreats, however, which brought him ever closer to the conquest of power.

In his *Autobiography*, often very pertinent and revealing, though disingenuous with its glaring omissions, Roosevelt has given a colorful picture of his early days in the lower ranks of his trade. The party, which he formally joined after providing suitable credentials, he describes as having still some of the character of a "private corporation," made up of a network of local district sub-organizations or clubs. The fiction of free and secret balloting in a democracy was dissolved for him soon after he joined the "Jake Hess Club," named after one of Republican boss Platt's city henchmen. Meetings were held once or twice a month in a large, dismal, barnlike room over a saloon, having the usual dingy benches, spittoons, and dais, and also the usual picture of General Grant on the wall. Here the real soldiers of democracy plied their trade. Under the command of Jake Hess and his "heelers," primaries were "managed," nominations were "arranged," and election campaigns were "organized." Here Roosevelt, the thin, blond, bespectacled, overdressed young man, after overcoming the hostility of his rough comrades—much to his credit, and thanks to the human warmth, charm, and high spirits he always had under his "dude's" dress—came at last to feel himself one of the "governing class," one of the nation-wide guild of political workers to whom public affairs were a constant rather than a spasmodic object of interest.

Owing to dissensions within the Republican party in New York the chance of being nominated for Assemblyman came early; and with the aid of prominent residents of his "silk stocking" district, such as Joseph H. Choate and Elihu Root, he was elected to the State Legislature in November, 1881. At Albany other myths concerning "government by discussion" and parliamentary action were dispelled. Laws were enacted not by juristic debate but by the pressure of powerful interests standing behind the local politicians. "There was no real party division. . . ."[14] The notorious Black Horse Cavalry, who alternately accepted bribes and extorted blackmail money in return for passing or obstructing certain legislative acts, drew their members from the Republican as well as the Tammany side. "Probably a third" of the legislators were crooked, Roosevelt estimated, and the rest were more or less helpless.

After a time Roosevelt, as an outsider, began open and vigorous attacks upon one of the most generally hated of the "special interests" who ruled the local parliament from behind the scenes: Mr. Jay Gould himself. He succeeded in carrying through one day a resolution for the investigation of various stock-jobbing scandals touching elevated railway finance, and charging the sinister Gould with the corruption of a New York Supreme Court judge. Nothing came of the affair beyond the investigation and its report; yet the metropolitan newspapers that were not then owned by Jay Gould applauded the youthful Assemblyman as one, at least, who "called men and things by their right name," which took no little courage "in these days of subserviency to the robber-barons of the Street." "There is a splendid career open for a young man of position, character, and independence like Mr. Roosevelt who can denounce the legalized robbery of Gould and his allies without descending to the turgid abuse of the demagogue, and without . . . the cowardly caution of the politician."[15]

Soon the dude was hailed by the spokesmen of reform, especially by Godkin in the *Post* and in the *Nation,* as a shining model to all his fellow society men. A banquet was given in his honor at Delmonico's by eminent Goo-Goos; and it was said that

[14] Roosevelt, *An Autobiography,* p. 64.
[15] The New York *Times,* Apr. 6, 1882; Bishop, *Roosevelt,* Vol. I, p. 12.

his example was sufficient "to shame thousands who complain that politics are so dirty no decent gentleman can engage in them." [16]

At the beginning of his second year in the Albany Legislature he had been honored by being given the minority vote of his party for Speaker. But the following year, when the Republicans regained the majority in both houses of the Legislature, he resolved to be Speaker in more than an honorary sense. Unabashed, he ran about everywhere and canvassed several up-state counties, soliciting support in the autumn of 1883. But now that actual control of the Legislature was located in the post of the Speaker, the Republican managers ended their dissensions and, in caucus, elected a "regular" Speaker over Roosevelt by a very heavy vote. It was a stinging lesson in party discipline. Roosevelt had counted decidedly upon his advancement in New York State politics; and he attributed this crushing reverse, which left him standing alone and without prospects for the future, to his frequent independence, his voting without paying heed to "teamwork" or to the views of his party.

At this period also another deep lesson was administered to the young statesman. An old family friend and prominent lawyer had invited him to lunch, and, in a heart-to-heart chat, attempted to open his artless mind to the realities of politics and business. He both liked young Roosevelt and was sorry for him. The "reform play" in the Legislature, the airing of the Westbrook-Gould scandal, was all very well; Roosevelt had acquitted himself creditably in the Legislature and shown that he could make himself useful in the right kind of law firm or business concern. But he had gone far enough and must not overplay his hand. It was time, his friend advised, "to leave politics and identify [himself] with the right kind of people, the people who would always in the long run control others and obtain the real rewards which were worth having." Did that, Roosevelt asked, mean yielding to "the ring" in politics? The lawyer answered impatiently that talk of "rings" was all poppycock. The real "ring," the inner circle, was made up

[16] Bishop, *op. cit.*, Vol. I, p. 29.

in actuality of "certain big business men, and the politicians, lawyers and judges who were in alliance with and to a certain extent dependent upon them." The successful man, whether in business, law, or politics, had to win his success by the backing of those same forces—or go down to failure.[17]

Here, he recalls in his memoirs, he received his "first glimpse of that combination between business and politics which I was in after years so often to oppose."

Meanwhile his friend Cabot Lodge, whose constant advice and aid counted for so much both in literary and political enterprises, began to make rapid progress in mastering the intricacies of Massachusetts politics, receiving the Republican nomination for Congress and becoming state chairman of his party in 1884. It was not through his personal charm, according to common report, that the wealthy scholar won the electoral support of the Lynn shoemakers and the Charlestown Navy Yard workers.

That year the two friends went together as delegates to the Republican national convention, and shared an experience that was decisive for Lodge and that tried the soul of Roosevelt. Still playing the reformer, Lodge was the active head of the group of New England Mugwumps who fought to oppose the nomination of the immitigable James G. Blaine. The candidate supported by Lodge, Schurz, Moorfield Storey, Charles W. Eliot, Josiah Quincy, and other Massachusetts Independents was the able but colorless Senator George F. Edmunds, Vermont's Favorite Son, who had the advantage of never having been touched either by recent public scandal or factious strife. To their cause Roosevelt was able to bring over a small, Independent minority of the New York delegation as well.

Because the real race lay between President Arthur and Blaine,

[17] Roosevelt, *An Autobiography*, pp. 76, 77, 85.
That Roosevelt did not weakly and unreflectingly accept the counsel of the lawyer speaks for his own originality, force of will, and desire for *innovation*, which make his career so noteworthy. Otherwise we should not be writing of him today.

leaders of the two rival factions in the Republican party, our earnest reformers hoped for a long deadlock out of which their candidate would be chosen as a compromise figure. Thus the two young politicians, Lodge and Roosevelt, filled with excitement at the prospect of "making a President," worked day and night to win over doubtful state delegations.

The struggle was brief. At the proper moment the "stampede" for the immensely popular Blaine, idol of the professionals, overwhelmed them as with the force of an avalanche. *"Blaine! Blaine! James G. Blaine!"* thundered the exultant followers of the Plumed Knight whose plumes were besmirched by scandal.

Of all men in politics at that time none aroused more revulsion in Independent breasts than James G. Blaine. Henry Cabot Lodge has related that during a private conference in May, 1884, he and Roosevelt had agreed to remain "regular" and abide loyally by the majority decision of the party convention.[18] But whatever private pledges Theodore Roosevelt may have given Lodge, he felt himself placed in a terrible quandary. His whole purpose in entering politics as a moral venture had been to contend against such an example of official corruption as Blaine was reputed to be. Meanwhile, all of his closest friends and fellow reformers both in New York and Boston, all the men whose good opinion he had earned, were preparing to "bolt." That is, they were organizing as a group to influence public opinion in favor of the expected reform candidate whom the Democrats would offer that season, Governor Grover Cleveland. By all his lights, Roosevelt too should have "switched" to Cleveland. That Roosevelt was racked by doubts, that he felt his position most critical, is all too clear. He made several contradictory statements: early reports reflected his extreme disillusionment, and indicated that he expected to join the "bolt" against Blaine. But these were promptly denied by him, although in private he wrote to his sister, Mrs. Cowles, of his bitter sense of betrayal, of the betrayal of "all the men of the broadest culture and highest character" in his party.[19]

18 Lodge, *op. cit.*, Vol. I, pp. 13-14.
19 Cowles, *op. cit.*, pp. 54-55.

Meanwhile he took sudden flight to the cattle ranch which he had acquired the year before in Dakota Territory, and remained there silent, alone, wrestling with his soul during several weeks. One alternative that was always left to him, one that the educated man of wealth always held, was that of quitting politics entirely. Certainly he might choose to be silent, abstaining from any active canvassing for Mr. Blaine.

But his "alter ego" of those days, Cabot Lodge, would leave him no rest. Lodge had come to the parting of the ways with his more discriminating Mugwump friends. He was already heavily committed to Massachusetts organization politics, even in a pecuniary sense; and he proposed now to continue along that line. To Carl Schurz (whom he, like so many other intellectuals of the period, admired as one of the nobler types in American politics, and who now pleaded with Lodge to "obey a noble impulse," to "bolt") he defended his decision to remain "regular" as the only feasible course for him. "By staying in the party I can be of some use. By going out, I destroy all the influence and power for good I possess." [20]

It was in these terms that he must have appealed to the sulking Roosevelt, who, during a hurried trip East shortly before July 19, 1884, saw Lodge and was won over by him.

In his well-known biography of Alexander Hamilton, published two years before, Lodge had written some meaningful passages concerning Hamilton's decision to vote for the adoption of the Constitution despite his own dislike for many of its provisions. These sentences tell us much concerning the author's outlook on life:

Had he been an agitator or a sentimentalist of muddy morals and high purposes, a visionary and an idealist, he would have stood up and howled against this constitution. . . . As he was none of these things, but a patriotic man of clear and practical mind, he knew that the *first rule of successful and beneficial statesmanship was not to sulk because one cannot have just what one wants, but to take the best thing obtainable, and sustain it to the uttermost.* [21]

[20] Fuess, *Schurz*, p. 288.   [21] Italics mine.

"Sentimentalist" and "agitator"—such may have been the reproaches with which Lodge tackled his younger friend's *crise de conscience*. Meanwhile the fate of their whole grandiose Hamiltonian design for the future conquest of Congress, Senate, Cabinet, or even the White House turned upon accepting "the best thing obtainable," following the party line and observing party discipline. For, in a close election, even the "bolting" of young minor leaders would have its weight for independent voters—and would be neither forgotten nor forgiven. Roosevelt resisted no more that day. There is a telling phrase which occurs at this period in his intimate correspondence with his sister: "Cabot has felt that I was a brand snatched from the burning. . . ." [22]

How often in those early years the sagacious Cabot was to snatch him from danger and carry him off safely for the Republican party! For Cabot recognized high qualities in the young Roosevelt, fed his boundless ambitions, and sustained him when others doubted. From this moment in 1884—when Roosevelt issued to the New York press his prepared statement that after mature consideration he had decided to vote for Blaine—from this moment dates the period of closest political collaboration between the two friends, and the long ascendancy of Lodge's will and direction over Roosevelt. His words were almost identical with those Lodge had used in writing to Schurz: "Whatever good I have been able to accomplish in public life has been accomplished through the Republican party." He could not, he declared, act at the same time as a "guerilla chief," outside the party, and as a "colonel in the regular army." [23]

The "treason" of the reformer Lodge caused a tempest in Boston. Lifelong friendships were broken at this time. Moorfield Storey never spoke to Lodge for forty years after, though both served together as Overseers at Harvard. Roosevelt, who came to Boston in October to stump for Lodge in the Congressional campaign, was also bitterly condemned by his Boston friends, espe-

[22] Cowles, *op. cit.*, p. 149.
[23] Bishop, *op. cit.*, Vol. I, p. 36.

cially when the exposure of the famous "Mulligan Letters" appeared to blacken Mr. Blaine's public reputation beyond repair. Roosevelt is alleged to have said: "I hope to God he [Blaine] will be defeated." The reasons he and Lodge gave for their conduct appeared to be a mixture of personal ambition and hope of promotion through the elimination of rivals who "bolted." [24]

In New York, censure of Roosevelt was also frequently heard. Edwin L. Godkin appeared all the more disappointed in him, inasmuch as he had formerly praised him, and now delivered some merciless drubbings. "Jack in the Box" and "ranting young humbug [who] made the very term reform redolent of hypocrisy" were some of the epithets reserved for Roosevelt after 1884 in the independent press.[25]

"I have been called a reformer, but I am a Republican," Roosevelt was reported to have said by a Boston newspaper. This interview he repudiated in part.[26]

Censure that stung only hardened the young man's resolve. By October he took to the stump, speaking in behalf of the party if not noticeably of the candidate. He guarded thereafter a bitter dislike for his reformist friends, which they cordially returned, whereas he now found unexpected beauties of character in his professional associates. They at least were "men of action." "They are not always polished, but they are strong, and as a whole I think them pretty good fellows," he wrote somewhat later to one of his

[24] "Diary of Storey" in Howe, *op. cit.*, pp. 154-155.

[25] H. C. Lodge, *op. cit.*, Vol. I, p. 121, citing the New York *World*.

[26] In a somewhat indiscreet speech at Boston in October, 1884, Theodore Roosevelt attributed the nomination of Mr. Blaine ("against the wishes of many of us, against my wishes and votes") to the stupidity of the masses. Blaine was nominated "because those whom Abraham Lincoln in one of those quaint remarks of his called 'the plain people' wished to see him President. He was nominated against the wishes of the most intellectual men, the most virtuous and honorable men, but he was nominated fairly and honorably . . . and I for one am glad to abide by the judgment of the 'plain people.'" (Howe, *op cit.*, pp. 157-158, footnote.) Thus T. R. against his own inclinations appeared to be following a "popular" line for "practical" reasons. Moorfield Storey thought Roosevelt was "unprincipled" ever after. He would never support an unpopular cause because it was right. He would, however, support a cause that seemed "righteous" to him, if it were popular.

literary friends, Brander Matthews. "Oh, you Mugwumps!" he would exclaim resentfully. "The way you arrogate all virtue to yourself is enough to exasperate an humble party man like myself." [27]

Despite the somersaults of our Mugwump renegades, Blaine was defeated; in Boston, Lodge, who stood for Congress, was likewise defeated—although his "regularity" gained him the post of state chairman of his party. The party which could have rewarded Roosevelt was out of power for four years. These years in which he posed as "an humble party man" were not in any sense happy ones. Indeed, they represented a phase of extreme moral and intellectual confusion, during which the "practical" politician was somewhat prematurely and crudely superimposed upon his own better nature. In that same year, 1884, his gloom was deepened by the sudden death of his first wife, Alice Lee Roosevelt. In his autobiography he passes quickly over most of these events.

3

Do not think that Theodore Roosevelt in his mood of disillusionment relapsed wholly into the character of "an humble party man." He was to be no more faithful to orthodox Republicanism than to Mugwump reform. With the purely political man, loyalty to ideas and doctrines is relative rather than absolute. Even the dogmatic or "fanatical" type of political leader is found to pursue often a devious rather than a head-on march toward his objectives.

Roosevelt's apprentice years were compounded of irresolute waverings and contradictory impulses, reflecting well the contradictions within the middle-class republic and its institutions. In those years the amateur of politics—as Grover Cleveland, who observed him both at Albany and Washington, remarked—"was looking to a public career, studying political conditions with a care that I had never known any man to show." [28] The problem of developing a substantial following of voters, building a functional

---

[27] *Matthews Papers*. T. R. to Brander Matthews, Feb. 10, 1890; July 31, 1889.
[28] Josephson, *The Politicos*, p. 442.

strength of his own from the ground up, remained for a long time unsolved.

He preserved within him some pure white flower, sprung perhaps from his decent moral upbringing, his environment and inheritance, that made it less possible for him to enjoy downright dishonesty or skulduggery than it was for that other Harvard swell, Boies Penrose, who, beginning as a reformer in Philadelphia politics, turned wickedly and cheerfully into the henchman of boss Matt Quay. Roosevelt was not obviously a handy man of the party hierarchy at administering bribes or swinging "deals." Thus his sphere of usefulness seemed limited for a long time to "mere scavenging work," as he himself called it, or to ornamenting minor administrative posts, his very appointment representing something of a concession to those who demanded "good men in office."

His work as Civil Service Commissioner at Washington during the six years from 1889 to 1895 was also creditable, especially for vigorous attempts to enforce the new merit and examination system and for hounding criminal characters out of government offices. Yet here too he was to learn bitter lessons concerning the narrow limits of governmental reform. There were collisions with Senators and cabinet members, party bosses who vehemently opposed the elimination of their henchmen from government payrolls. Once more the newspapers spoke well of the vigorous and courageous civil service reformer in Washington. Then he was forgotten. He found that his usefulness was restricted; that he was expected to "cleanse the Augean Stables" only up to a point where he did no hurt to the larger interest of his party in the spoils of office. Mr. Harrison, "the little grey man in the White House," he reported privately, "treated him with a cold and hesitating disapproval." [29]

The label of the reformer clung to him, whether he chose it or not. As Civil Service Commissioner under Harrison and then for several years under Cleveland (who retained him with a worthy gesture), Roosevelt could be seen "battling the spoilsmen" with a

[29] Cowles, *op. cit.*, p. 113.

gusto that was native and a forthrightness that made his advancement in politics more interesting and more difficult at once.

Then when the more Machiavellian Lodge would come forward to caution him, warning him not to precipitate quarrels which would injure his party's election prospects, he would retreat for a time. He would promise to behave with a more "statesmanlike reserve" in the future.[30]

With the November, 1894, elections fresh opportunities for practical experience had come to Roosevelt just when he was growing bored with civil service reform. In his native city of New York, sensational exposures (by the Lexow Committee) of corruption in the police and street-cleaning departments had led to the defeat of the Tammany "rascals" and their replacement by a non-partisan or "Fusion" ticket, allied with the city's regular Republican minority. The Goo-Goos promptly bethought themselves of Theodore Roosevelt, and invited him in December, 1894, to become Street Cleaning Commissioner. It was an office that plainly needed his reforming hand.

With Lodge's advice this offer was refused as touching a position Roosevelt "could not afford to be identified with." [31] But a few weeks later there came the offer of membership in New York's Police Commission; and further—thanks to Lodge—the offer carried with it the promise that young Roosevelt would be named president of the board of four by an understanding with the new Mayor, William L. Strong. That he regarded the appointment as a career opportunity in which he intended to prove himself fit for higher stations is shown by his letter to Lodge written in May, 1895, shortly after he bustled into the damp, gloomy Mulberry Street headquarters: ". . . In a couple of years or less . . . the department will be in good running order. . . . I shall be quite ready . . . to take up a new job."

Opportunities and dangers were large as the youthful Commissioner at the age of thirty-six took over one of the most important

[30] Lodge, *op. cit.*, Vol. I, p. 82.
[31] Cowles, *op. cit.*, p. 149; Lodge, *op. cit.*, Vol. I, p. 142.

and difficult of offices. The police department of New York was very nearly at the heart of the system of political corruption then flourishing. For nearly three years the Rev. Charles H. Parkhurst had been fulminating from the pulpit of his Madison Square Church against the iniquities of Tammany and the organized trade in vice and gambling carried on by a Tammany-ruled police.

Then, in 1894, the probings of the Lexow Committee of the New York State Legislature had brought out facts more complete and more shocking still. The rank and file of the police were shown to be completely demoralized; appointments and promotions in the force were based frankly on cash payments. Throughout the metropolis, huge revenues, an unofficial tax or tithe, were regularly collected from the unlawful sale of liquor, the operation of gambling and brothel houses, and other indulgences. The illicit "licensing" activities by the New York City police were believed to yield more revenue than the legal licensing privileges exercised by the city or state governments themselves. Roosevelt, as an Assemblyman ten years ago, and member of the City Affairs Committee, had already glimpsed something of these conditions and even made a beginning toward exposing them. It was the partial knowledge of these conditions that had made him originally so strong for reform. The fact that the sale of police indulgences, gambling and liquor privileges, was but a minor department in the larger working alliance between the political rings and business interests does not seem to have dawned upon him at the time. What followed, as the eager Roosevelt leaped into the fray, took the pattern of a classical comedy which may be called "The Reform Wave."

The first act was an affair of popular revulsion and the turning out of the rascals by the Good Government men. Before the storm of public opinion Chief Croker, the master of Tammany Hall, retreated to Ireland for a temporary vacation, though muttering darkly as he left that he would soon return at the people's command.

Roosevelt, who now showed his flair for battle, began with a sudden, sharp thrust. He persuaded his fellow commissioners to dismiss the formidable and sinister Inspector Byrnes, one of those permanent officials who, because of long working relations with the criminal class, were considered more powerful than any mere commissioner. This bold move was followed up a few weeks later, on June 23, 1895, by an order to enforce the Sunday closing law for saloons throughout the metropolis. As Roosevelt said afterward: "The saloon was the chief source of the mischief. It was with the saloon that I had to deal, and there was only one way to deal with it. That was to enforce the law." [32]

On that Sunday morning when Roosevelt's bluecoats began closing up the public houses and making hundreds of arrests all over the city, there began the creation of a legend. A group of newspaper reporters who admired Roosevelt—among them Jacob Riis, the humanitarian author of *How the Other Half Lives;* Lincoln Steffens, then a police reporter; and Joseph Bucklin Bishop, afterward Roosevelt's biographer—all championed the commissioner with their pens. In addition, ministers of the pulpit and academic leaders helped to call favorable attention to this unique political figure, about whom a storm of mingled applause and denunciation henceforth raged.

Joseph B. Bishop thought him impulsive to the point of naïveté, with "essentially a boy's mind." Yet he said out loud the things that others knew but would not mention. He seemed to court head-on opposition. To those who warned him that in carrying out an unpopular blue law he should at least enforce it with some "discrimination," he replied bluntly that to do so would be "like believing in truthful mendacity." He would go on "enforcing honestly a law that has hitherto been enforced dishonestly." [33]

The second act is, thus, an exhilarating one. Amid high excitement the cleansing of the Augean Stables from basement to attic proceeded unremittingly. Honest men were in the saddle. The public rubbed its eyes at the unwonted sight of its officers actually enforcing the law. Indeed, it was a hopeful sign that many of the citizens of Gotham, not yet too lost in iniquity, responded warmly

[32] Roosevelt, *An Autobiography,* p. 191.
[33] Bishop, *op. cit.,* Vol. I, pp. 61, 63.

at first to the appeal of the devoted, strenuous official. His unconventional tours of inspection through the wicked city by night (he wore evening clothes covered with a long cloak), his tracking down of delinquent officers, his raids into dens of evil, became the talk of the town during the summer of 1895. "Teddy the Scorcher," a bellicose reformer ready to give blow for blow, in his cowboy costume, wearing pince-nez, and smiling with all his buck teeth, figured in newspaper story and cartoon until he became a colorful national celebrity.

The first enthusiasm over his law-enforcement campaign, as he reported modestly to Cabot Lodge, had made "the Good Government Club and their ilk regard me as a hero." [34] From Europe his faithful mentor, reading of Theodore's exploits in the London *Times* itself, sent warm compliments, happy that his anticipations for his pupil were being borne out. The Senator from Massachusetts—for he had recently attained this high station—now replied:

> I am glad that I have known you long and loved you well and that you are a person of loyal disposition, for you are rushing so rapidly to the front that the day is not distant when you will come into a large kingdom and by that time I shall be a back number and I shall expect you to give me a slice. . . . That Senatorship is getting well into sight, my dear boy.

But Lodge, who had a vision of his younger friend as a growing power in the practical politics of the Empire State, soon began to point out to him that being a hero to the Goo-Goos might prove an embarrassment. Theodore must indicate that his reformatory actions were aimed at the Democratic enemy and furthered a full-fledged, four-square Republicanism. He must even refuse to speak in public save at Republican gatherings.

To this line of advice Theodore shows himself fairly submissive, writing in answer: "This summer, I have, as you know, been careful to identify myself in every way with the Republicans. Hill has attacked me violently as a Republican. . . ." And again, sometime later, he writes, "During the two years I have been

[34] Lodge, *op. cit.*, Vol. I, p. 169, letter of Aug. 27, 1895.

here . . . I have in every way avoided any kind of attack upon the organization Republicans, and all I could legally do that they have asked me, I have done."

To such dutiful reports "Dear Cabot" would respond with praise and even flattery: Theodore was now doing "rightly, wisely and splendidly." He was showing good sense in avoiding any "personal quarrel with the machine." His work would "lead surely to even better things." But Theodore was so constituted that he suffered qualms, and sometimes exclaimed with disgust: "I feel all the time that very uncomfortable sensation of sailing under false colors." [35]

In the third act of the Reform Wave, popular enthusiasm flags, difficulties mount, the forward and uplift movement drags against an increasing resistance.

We must remark that the New York City Fusion administration of 1895-1897, of which Roosevelt was the most important officer after the Mayor, had a most superficial, an ephemeral, program. Goo-Goo reform, ignoring the deeper social evils of the day, changed in no sense those material conditions of poverty and hideously crowded, filthy housing which caused the proletarians to congregate in the saloons that were "poor men's clubs," or to seek excitement in gambling resorts, and submit on election days to the influence of the local heelers who were kindred to them and often befriended them in time of trouble. The characteristic measures of the civil service reformers, especially their more rigorous policing, seemed to strike directly at the few pleasures and liberties open to the masses.

Roosevelt, a typical upper-class product of Mugwump thought, never understood the working class well, and in his earlier phase concealed but little of his instinctive hostility to them. While in the State Legislature, as one of his later biographers, Henry Pringle, has shown, this aristocratic reformer considered no revolutionary changes within the pattern of his proposed improvements. He would support a bill to abolish sweatshop labor in tene-

[35] Lodge, *op. cit.*, Vol. I, pp. 169, 256.

ment houses, "as a measure of health." But when measures raising the wages of city laborers in Buffalo and New York to $2 a day, or fixing twelve hours as the maximum for street-car workers, were brought up, he denounced them as visionary, un-American, and "socialistic." [36] Any other line of action, in the view of reformers of comfortable means in his day, would be tantamount to "playing the demagogue."

At this period of his life Theodore Roosevelt's first-hand knowledge of the oppressed classes, the "other half," was extended somewhat, thanks to his friendship with Jacob Riis and Lincoln Steffens. With these two journalists he would sometimes wander upon slumming expeditions at night through the lower East Side, and would grow horrified at the things to be seen only a few minutes' walk from Gramercy Park or his own "silk stocking" district. He recalled vividly in his memoirs, long afterward, the hot, stinking, summer nights, the piles of refuse, the occasional dead horses lying in the streets, the incredible squalor and filth of the tenement quarters that made New York one of the world's hell-holes. To the influence of the tender-hearted Jacob Riis he attributed his own belated awareness of the cruelly contrasting extremes of showy wealth and wretched poverty to be seen everywhere in American cities. Yet nodding acquaintance with the slum-dwellers in no way changed his real prejudices.

Toward the labor movement, toward the rising trade-union organizations as a growing institution, eager to play its full-grown part within the social organism, he remained hostile. To be sure, these were "the very people one would wish to help," he would say paternally—they must never learn to help themselves! And he could still say, at the time when he was New York's police commissioner in 1896, that the remedy for our social troubles lay not in radical action, in "Popocracy," but in "inculcating higher ideals of citizenship and developing a nobler order of manhood." [37]

Thus Roosevelt's fear of the proletarians and of their rebellious instincts persisted strongly. That "organized labor," of which

[36] Pringle, *Roosevelt*, p. 78.
[37] New York *Journal*, Oct. 29, 1896.

he spoke often with contempt, might in its own behalf seek political instruments and directions of its own—as in turning to Mr. Bryan's party and free silver—was a development that he resented with every fiber of his nature. Addressing a trade-union audience on the East Side one night, he made a pleasing impression, and the union leaders proposed to him that he seek the endorsement of trade-unionists for some public office. Reporting this incident to Cabot, he relates how offended he was at the proposal, and how he thrust it away with scorn. And the working classes instinctively returned his suspicion and dislike, all through his career. With them the Reform Wave was not popular; and Roosevelt never developed a following among them comparable to that of the Tammany leaders who sometimes winked at the law for the sake of a trade-unionist in distress.

Moreover, the delicate, complex adjustments of the political parties, in relation to both large business interests and illicit commerce, were being disturbed by the reformers. The liquor dealers' associations were up in arms, and on them depended much of the vote-gathering in November. Their protests were joined with those of the lower classes, accustomed to taking their beer on Sundays, *en famille*, at the Viennese beer gardens of the Bowery. Soon the friends of the old order, noticing the changing tide, threw up cleverly contrived obstacles in the shape of obsolete blue laws, vexing local ordinances which their politicians ordered enforced and which caused spreading confusion and resentment. After a year in office, Commissioner Roosevelt found himself more and more exposed to blows from unseen hands, to flanking maneuvers.

He now felt himself in serious straits, with his popularity waning. Most embarrassing of all was the passage of the Raines Law by the State Legislature in April, 1896. While innocently pretending to be another liquor-control measure, it provided that hotels equipped to serve meals, and therefore permitted to serve liquor also on Sundays, could henceforth be located only in structures having ten rooms. ". . . The ten rooms required by law were used for prostitution in order to pay the overhead," records Henry Pringle in his often ironical biography of Roosevelt. This statute constituted, in concealed form, "the greatest boon to commercialized vice in the history of New York." [38] Hundreds upon hundreds of the new "hotels" were opened, and soon it was plain that the exertions of the reformers had produced but a greater outburst of general lechery.

The troubles of the Police Department, obliged to conduct raids in all directions, were multiplied rapidly. Its Board of Commissioners, two of whose four members submitted readily to machine orders, ceased to support Roosevelt. A hopeless deadlock ensued, and the bitter wranglings of the Board became known to the public in 1896.

To Roosevelt it was now plain that the leaders of his own Republican organization were combined "half-secretly" with the Tammany forces to undo him, as he hinted in several angry press interviews. Behind his increasing misfortunes, he suspected, was the cunning old hand of Thomas C. Platt, the so-called Easy Boss of New York Republicans, who was known to co-operate with the Tammany machine by a system of division of labor, the Democrats controlling the metropolitan spoils down-state while the Republicans managed the Albany Legislature up-state.

The young Police Commissioner now grew as despondent as he had been sanguine the season before. Hope of rising to grander offices, even of becoming President—such hope now lay always in the back of his mind, as Lincoln Steffens discovered—was dwindling fast. Even the respectable elements seemed weary of the uproar over the blue laws. Thus victory over the saloons seemed to leave him politically "without any opening." He lamented to Lodge: "It leads nowhere." [39] To another confidant he said: "I have offended so many powerful politicians that no political preferment in future will be possible for me. All the liquor interests . . . and all the party bosses will oppose me. . . . I realized this when I began my fight." [40]

But at this crisis "Dear Cabot" showered him with advice.

[38] Pringle, *op. cit.*, pp. 148-149.
[39] Lodge, *op. cit.*, Vol. I, pp. 168, 174-176, 181.
[40] Bishop, *op. cit.*, Vol. I, pp. 68-69.

Though hard pressed, Theodore could still strengthen his position in the party by sagacious conduct in the future. Above all, no outspoken accusations in the press. "Talk as little as possible," concluded Lodge, already aware of Theodore's weakness for publicity.

Theodore, however, replied in words that sounded as if he were girding himself to some desperate stroke, one that might throw his whole career into the balance but would at least save his honor as an independent in politics. Rumors came that the Republican party at its approaching state convention would, at Platt's bidding, pass resolutions which showed retreat on the question of Excise Law enforcement, thus repudiating Roosevelt's labors and mollifying the liquor dealers' association. The Commissioner felt himself betrayed, a martyr of the machine whose interests he had dared to oppose. Even Mayor Strong now seemed cowardly, and as for Platt, his conduct had been such "that a decent man must oppose him." [41]

These days he found himself "living in a welter of political intrigue of the meanest kind. . . ." With his own eyes he had witnessed electoral frauds that horrified him: a local primary election carried for his own party by 600 votes raised up from "vacant lots, from houses where [no one] lives, from houses of ill-fame and the like." And he is forced to remain silent, enduring the rebuffs of Platt's henchmen, "who intend to read me out of the party." [42] And yet none must know of the secret, inward torment devouring the hero of the Goo-Goos, and which now speaks to us from page after page of his correspondence with "Dear Cabot." One might say that, as with Brutus, shame for his city and for himself was borne in upon him during sleepless nights. Perhaps, even, he heard voices calling: "*Speak, strike, redress!* Brutus, thou sleepest! Awake and see thyself. . . ."

Finally he bursts out to Lodge that he proposes to speak out, to attack the machine:

I have so far with no little self-command, refrained from hitting at any of the Republican people; but after the election is over, I am far from certain that I shall keep my hands off them. However, if possible, I shall wait until I see you before taking action.[43]

When Lodge, who was then traveling overseas, received this letter some ten days later, he flew into a perfect panic. Theodore's whole future was at stake. He sat down and cabled from Paris a dispatch of solemn warning:

You may be surprised to get a cable from me today [he wrote at the same time by letter] but one sentence in your letter of the 18th. troubled me and that was where you said that you might attack the Machine after the election. That I would not have you do for all the world. I know how trying it all is . . . but to come out and denounce Platt is simply playing Platt's own game.[44]

And once driven out of the party, where they wanted him, his hope of wresting leadership from the others would be ended.

As in similar crises, Roosevelt bowed once more before his mentor's will. When the cablegram from Paris had arrived, October 29, 1895, his wife Edith joined his friend in dissuading him from following the promptings of his heart, saying: "I do believe that dear Cabot cares more for you than anyone else in the world does." The reply to Cabot went forth: "All right! I won't attack anyone." [45]

Lodge preached regularity and discipline. Roosevelt must even force his attentions upon his fellow Republicans, whether they wanted him or not. "Do not fail to go on the stump—not through the city, where it is needless," Cabot counseled, "but through the State where . . . the masses of Republicans are with you. Make speeches for all the State Senators and Assemblymen that you can properly support, and . . . they must see you and get to know you. I regard this as of the utmost importance."

Finally "Dear Cabot" cheered on his protégé, tempting him with the strong wine of ambition: "I can judge of your standing and reputation better than you. . . . You have a great chance to take

[43] Lodge, *op. cit.*, Vol. I, p. 189, Oct. 18, 1895.   [45] *Ibid.*, Vol. I, p. 196.
[44] *Ibid.*, Vol. I, p. 197, Oct. 30, 1895.

the leadership of powerful and controlling elements of the party which can put you in the Senate. . . . I do not say you are to be President tomorrow. I do not say it will be—I am sure it may and can be." [46]

"During my two years as Police Commissioner," Roosevelt told his English friend, Cecil Spring Rice, "I may say I accomplished a great deal, but gradually things have so shaped themselves that I couldn't do anything more." [47]

He now turned to national affairs, bored with the local politics of cartage contracts and appointments for street-sweepers. Hand in hand with Lodge, his fellow conspirator, he continued to scheme for Senatorships or Presidencies. In the winter of 1896 the two devoted schemers had earnestly opposed the boom for McKinley, supporting instead Speaker Thomas B. Reed of Maine, a man of keen intellect, and breadth and force of character. For twenty years Reed had worn the collar of his party in Congress, though he knew how to laugh privately at himself and his colleagues. Yet in spite of the veteran Speaker's distinguished services, his claims to the nomination, supported by the "better element," were brushed aside by the all-powerful Mark Hanna. The elimination of the brilliant Reed, and his consequent decision to retire from public life, was a heartbreaking disappointment, whose meaning Roosevelt could scarcely miss. He sent the Speaker his condolences, and Reed answered in bitter vein that he was long used to "waiting for others to pass." He remarked: "Hanna's coarse ways are pretty hard to stand, especially when you appreciate that a great office can be retained by purchase as well as obtained by purchase." [48]

Yet Roosevelt, as did Lodge and Reed as well, labored with the habitual discipline of his calling for the success of McKinley that year.

At repeated intervals Theodore Roosevelt felt keenly the fickleness of crowd favor and the rebuffs of dominant party bosses.

[46] *Ibid.*, Vol. I, pp. 179-180.   [48] *T. R. Papers*, Jul. 28, 1896.
[47] *T. R. Papers*, Apr. 28, 1897.

Then the assault upon the heights of public power would appear but a slow, unrewarding progress—already extended over fifteen years by 1896—and he would reflect the gloom which visiting foreigners such as Viscount James Bryce noticed in circles of upperclass intellectuals.

In such moods the influence of the pessimistic philosopher of history, Brooks Adams, weighed upon him and was harder to throw off. Early in 1896 Roosevelt had read and written a review of Adams' *The Law of Civilization and Decay*. This writer's interpretation of the "natural laws of force and energy" determining the rise and fall of "concentrations" of civilization along the great trade routes of the world had a curious vogue. Roosevelt tended to thrust aside Adams' darker prophecies, refusing to believe that the American republic, abandoned to love of gain and usury, ruled by a purely money-lending class, was as inevitably doomed to collapse as the Roman republic. But Brooks Adams continued the debate between them firmly; he persisted in attaching himself to the young politician, in whom he, like Cabot Lodge, discerned high possibilities. The struggle over bimetallism, he argued, showed that the "producing classes," crushed under debt, were to be as subject slaves henceforth. Even the administrative leader or the military captain was but a paid official who must take his orders from the ruling class. Roosevelt's future turned upon his ability to submit to events with good grace, upon whether he fought or made his peace with the "system," the Machine.

Brooks Adams wrote him now:

I have watched your career with deep interest. You may remember a year ago in Washington, *I told you to sell*. You may understand me better now. You are an adventurer and you have but one thing to sell—your sword. You can take your wages like Nelson and Clive, and fight where you are sent, just as every soldier must in a commercial age, or you can lie and rot. Capital will not employ you if you have a conscience, a heart, patriotism, honesty or self-respect.

But the earlier mercenary soldiers had still believed in the country and cause for which they fought. Today one must apparently fight only for "Wall Street," and "Wall Street is a harder master . . . wants men it can buy and own," concluded Adams bitterly—this descendant of Yankee Presidents and capitalists.

I feared for you last year. I knew that courage and honesty would not help you. I hope, however, that you may still pull through and make your peace.

In this world we must all live if we can—what is hardest is to be so made that you cannot sell. If you can sell, do. If you don't, others will. The world will be no better and you much the worse.[49]

A few weeks later Adams, having received, apparently, a despondent letter from his friend, returned to the attack. He alluded to his own failures in fighting for a lost cause, civil service reform in Massachusetts. "What use?" he summed up. "Why not live and be hired by a force which masters you, rather than be crushed in a corner to no purpose?" The men of money would be willing to buy Roosevelt out, at almost his own price, for "Wall Street has desperate need of men like you." Let Roosevelt, who was "instinctively a fighter," hire out his sword as barbarian chieftains did for the Romans. "Why fall? Better to be Caesar in the chair of State, than the broken soldier in the arena."[50]

How much the subversive ideas of Brooks Adams ruled the mind of Roosevelt we cannot know. Certainly the terms in which his scholarly friend defined the dilemma of society, faced with the choice of violent proletarian revolution or social decadence eating at the top of the society, were always present in his writings and speeches. They run through his private thoughts like a thread which shows the figure in the carpet: the "weakening fibre" of latter-day Americans; the prospects of "race suicide," whereby the older Anglo-Saxon stock was to be submerged by the masses of alien immigrants; the preoccupation with the "strenuous life," the revival of "soldierly virtues," and reaction against the merely

[49] *T. R. Papers*, Brooks Adams to T. R., Feb. 25, 1896.
[50] *T. R. Papers*, B. Adams to T. R., Apr. 26, 1896.
Search of the Roosevelt Papers did not yield the letters written in reply to Brooks Adams at this period.

"commercial type of mind" in politics—haunted by these notions, Roosevelt, with Lodge and other intellectuals of the conservative class, searched for an alternative way out of the doom not seldom predicted for their world.

Brooks Adams' influence may perhaps be detected in the apparent heartiness with which Roosevelt at length "hired" his verbal sword to Mark Hanna for the fierce stump campaigns of '96; and in the swashbuckling violence with which he attacked the "anarchists" and "Popocrats," Bryan, Altgeld, and Debs, that season.

Little wonder that the restive masses of New York trusted not their city's Goo-Goos, and turned in large numbers not only to the party of Bryan but to Tammany afterward. For civil service reformers came and went, yet the inequalities existing under the constitutional law of the land, which Bryan challenged, remained unaltered. What did the Mayor Strongs or the Commissioner Roosevelts bring them but needless vexations—as in enforcing more rigorously laws that helped them not to slake their thirst and forget the wretchedness and weariness of summer nights in the slums? In 1897 the people turned once more to their old friends of Tammany Hall, those who had always remained close to them, who, while exploiting, had at least understood their misery, their inarticulate fears and wants.

When the fourth act of the comedy of reform was reached, and the full storm of local reaction broke upon the Good Government men in November, 1897, Theodore Roosevelt—fortunately for him—was already somewhere else, placed in a higher political post at the national capital and watching events as from a safe remove. (While suffering the loss of the city of New York, the Republican organization had worked successfully to win the nation for Republicanism; thus the Police Commissioner had found avenues open to him in Washington again.) "New York, as a whole, was glad to see him go. A small dose of reform, as practical politicians well know, lasts for years." [51]

[51] Pringle, op. cit., p. 151.

The summer before, boss Richard Croker had hurried back from Ireland to take command of the Tammany revival, which he had predicted two years before. The people, he had said, would return to his camp after "an extravagant and hypocritical Republican reform administration." [52] Doubtless he knew also that Republican boss Tom Platt would hold hands with him this year, not for the first time so far as city affairs were concerned. That year the Citizens' Union, or non-partisan, reform candidate for Mayor, Seth Low, ran without grace of Republican fusion; though he made a strong demonstration in winning over 150,000 independent votes, the defection of the regular Republicans insured the sweeping victory of Tammany with nearly 234,000 votes.

Early on that Election Day, November 4, 1897, the huge city crowds gathered in the streets and squares to celebrate the expected outcome. The press reported:

TENDERLOIN MAKES MERRY

GOOD OLD DAYS ARE EXPECTED TO RETURN WITH THE TIGER—IT WILL BE "WIDE OPEN"

From six in the evening the dense crowds made Broadway, from Forty-second to Fourteenth Street, impassable; there was a sound of revelry, a fearful din of tin horns and rattles, of jovial crowds besieging bars and hotel corridors where "wine flowed in rivers." The bands played "Hard Times Come Again No More," and "Hot Time in the Old Town Tonight," and "Hear Dem Bells."

At eight o'clock, when the election returns were definitely known, New York seemed to go mad with joy. "The repression of years found vent in every description of boisterous license." [53] A Tammany leader cried to the crowds before the doors of Tammany Hall: "Do you think we'll sneak out the back way, this year?" "Never!" roared the crowd in answer. Tipsy men and women saluted the downfall of the hated Raines Law. Street-

---

[52] The New York *Times*, Nov. 4, 1897.
[53] The New York *World*, Nov. 4, 1897.

walkers proceeded everywhere, mocking at recent city police regulations.

In a large café at the Haymarket on Sixth Avenue a woman stood on a table tossing off one schooner of beer after another, whirling each one around her head and shouting: *"To hell with reform!"*

Banners were quickly produced bearing the same legend. Soon the cry seemed to be taken up all over the great city; and the thousands who had chafed at the bridle danced, sang, and shouted in refrain all that night: *"To hell with reform!"* [54]

[54] The New York *World*, Nov. 4, 1897.

III. A "SPLENDID LITTLE WAR";

AND THE MAKING OF A PRESIDENT

ONCE more Theodore Roosevelt was back in Washington; this time as Assistant Secretary of the Navy, an important post in the more or less brilliant McKinley administration. It had been no simple matter for Roosevelt's political friends, Cabot Lodge, the Senator for Massachusetts, and Speaker Reed and John Hay to overcome McKinley's misgivings about the Police Commissioner as a young hothead of some sort. Cabot had been forced to stretch the truth a little when he insisted that his protégé thought only to "push on the policies . . . in operation for the last two or three administrations." [1] More embarrassing still had been the preliminary requirement of winning the endorsement of New York's Republican boss, Senator Tom Platt. Roosevelt was virtually ordered to "step up and see him about the place," and must needs come hat in hand before the oily and cunning old man whom he detested, and who accorded assent rather than approval—"because Roosevelt would do less harm to the Organization," Platt thought, if removed from New York to Washington. [2]

Once more escaped from the "scavenging" labor and the dreary squabbles of local politics, Roosevelt could plunge himself into national, history-making affairs, as he had longed to do. Moreover, he was a figure again in those literary-political salons that made social life in the capital so much more amusing and stimulating in

[1] Lodge *op. cit.*, Vol. I, p. 241.
[2] Lodge, *op. cit.*, Vol. I, p. 264.

the '90's than in two or three preceding decades. There were good musicales at the discriminating and yet cosmopolitan homes of those two reigning hostesses, Mrs. Henry Cabot Lodge and Mrs. J. Donald Cameron, wives of wealthy Eastern Senators. There were distinguished men of letters to be met, a Rudyard Kipling observing his American admirers critically, a William Dean Howells; there were foreign diplomats and native financiers. There was good food and animated conversation with it, ranging in subject from the world of ideas and books to the Chinese curios of Henry Adams and the Botticelli purchased by John Hay. But above all there was talk of politics, now the very breath of life to Roosevelt, Lodge, and their circle of friends. At a *bal de début* given by the affluent Charles J. Bonapartes for their daughter, between the cotillions "they talked of civil service . . . even with the ladies." On vacations in the New Hampshire mountains "one nearly walked over a cliff talking politics." [3]

The political talk in influential circles close to the imperial McKinley regime embraced not only national affairs but, more than ever nowadays, international relations, the course of empire and trade, the acquisition and completion of the Isthmian canal, naval bases, expansion on the ocean to the south and the west, all the various moves in the game of world power politics, and America's part in them.

"You have a war on your hands," the outgoing President Cleveland said to McKinley on Inauguration Day. McKinley answered: ". . . If I can only go out of office . . . with the knowledge that I have done what lay in my power to avert this terrible calamity . . . I shall be the happiest man in the world." [4] But while McKinley hesitated, the whispers, the intriguing that foreshadowed an approaching conflict went on in the salons.

Ever since the Cuban insurrection had begun in 1895, agents of the revolutionary junta apparently had thronged Washington and held deep consultations with Republican leaders in the Senate such as Cameron of Pennsylvania, and Lodge. "I am kept here by

[3] John Hay, *Diaries*, Vol. II, p. 236.

[4] Rhodes, *op. cit.*, Vol. 18, p. 41.

Cuba, which I appear to be running . . ." is the curious phrase that occurs in a letter of Henry Adams to his brother Brooks. And again, to an English friend, not entirely in jest: "You had better sell all you have and buy with me in Cuba." [5]

Meanwhile, in high naval circles there was not only talk of a coming war but active preparation for it. Admiral Charles Henry Davis, the father-in-law of Lodge, learning that Theodore Roosevelt sought the office of Secretary of the Navy, wrote him: "There is a tremendous chance in that office," and expressed the earnest hope that the President would appoint him. [6] Roosevelt had been willing enough to take, as the best he could get, the subordinate post of Assistant Secretary in this strategic department.

2

Bored and disillusioned with reform politics, Roosevelt embraced the ideas of militant nationalism and "Americanism"; he dreamed of entering upon some great martial enterprise while thoughts of reform and "good citizenship" waned, not only in his mind, but in those of the other younger prophets in the ruling party. Their ambitions and frustrations, their fear of class-sectional divisions in the country, their "Hamiltonian" and distinctly anti-democratic views and historical concepts, their impatience with the McKinley-Hanna "politics of the cash-register," all disposed Roosevelt and his friends to join in the war-making of 1896-1898.

For more than a decade the orientation toward the cult .of "Americanism" had been apparent in Roosevelt's writings. Married again in 1886 to one whom he had known as a childhood friend, Edith Carow, he lived more happily; he resumed, especially at periods when he was out of office, the prolific writing of biographies and historical studies which had been held out to him and to Lodge as a path to public glory. Roosevelt's early writings contained many crudities, yet they were not wanting in talent and vigor; removed from public life he might have made his mark as

---

[5] Henry Adams, *Letters*, Vol. II, pp. 96, 99.
[6] *T. R. Papers*, C. H. Davis to T. R., Nov. 11, 1896.

a man of letters. But here it is the ideas in the early writings, *simpliste* or naïve though many of them were, that interest us most.

Very marked is the anti-democratic bias in Roosevelt, especially in the period of his career when he was under the influence of Cabot Lodge, the biographer of Alexander Hamilton. Lodge had written almost with nostalgia of the time when America was ruled by men who were "powerful by their talents if not by their numbers." He had written always of Jefferson as the villain in the piece—as that kindred soul, Beveridge, did later in his monumental *Life of John Marshall*. The followers of Jefferson were "worthless, noisy" persons, "given to useless agitation" and showing "anarchical tendencies." But for the earlier, "aristocratic" republic, dominated by Hamilton, Lodge could scarcely conceal his admiration, while condoning his hero's willingness at times to "accomplish a great right by doing a little wrong." Such tendencies, Lodge reflects, half-revealing his own faith, would never be wanting "to the champions of order, the saviours of society, the 'strong men' and the imperialists of this world." [7]

Similar principles are frankly expressed in Roosevelt's second published book, the rather amateurish, hastily written biography of Thomas Benton. Here too he shows a hearty dislike of the champions of thoroughgoing democracy, the "timid, shifty doctrinaire" Jefferson, the unruly Andrew Jackson who had brought on an explosion of "caste antagonism" in 1828. The author condemns all the "vague and senseless clamor" against a "supposititious aristocratic corruption" raised by "the mass of the ignorance of the country," and easily exploited by scheming demagogues to bring about that spoils system that Good Government men now contended against. [8]

But Thomas H. Benton, the long-winded Senator from Missouri, though an ally of Jackson in leading "the party of the multitude," possessed in the author's eyes the virtue of having sounded forth, perhaps earlier and more powerfully than all others, the call

[7] Lodge, *Alexander Hamilton*, p. 228; cf. also pp. 130, 184, 185.
[8] T. Roosevelt, *Thomas Benton*, pp. 72, 137.

to "Manifest Destiny." He aroused the "hardy and restless back-woodsmen," those American Vikings who had conquered wilderness and prairie, to move against their weaker neighbors and seize their territories. Benton embodied an "intense Americanism" that visioned the farthest expansion of the republic toward the Pacific and even to the mysterious Orient. And Roosevelt recalls with emotion those Texans of a "barbaric age," who raised the flag of the Lone Star State and precipitated a war of conquest with Mexico: "They were restless, brave and eager for adventure, excitement and plunder. . . . They had all the marks of a young and hardy race, flushed with the pride of strength and self-confidence." [9]

Thus the historical thinking of our latter-day Hamiltonians turned often with admiration to the earlier American pioneers who had overrun and conquered a whole vast continent. (It was, to be sure, a thinly populated, ill-defended continent.) Theodore Roosevelt, driven by some ill-defined "historic-literary" inspiration, had even gone to seek renewal of those experiences at first hand, when he traveled to the Far West in 1883 and acquired a part ownership in two cattle ranches. Was it a mere outburst of romanticism, whim of the eternal small boy in Roosevelt who, having once been sickly, attempted to brave hardships and live dangerously? Ranch owning was a fashionable speculation of the 1880's with their cattle booms, and brought then not a few titled Europeans to Western prairies in quest of adventure, big game, or quick wealth. Roosevelt's intuitions here led to financial loss, but to intangible gains.

He had escaped at last from the life of the Eastern cities, at once soft, confining, and unnatural. He would recall long afterward in his autobiography: "It was still the Wild West in those days. In that land we led a free and hardy life, with horse and rifle." He himself had been one of those "reckless riders who, unmoved, look in the eyes of life and death. We knew toil and hardship and hunger and thirst; and we saw men die. . . ."

[9] *Ibid.*, p. 178.

There was something of Lord Byron in the extravagantly costumed, slightly exhibitionist gentleman cowboy of 1883 to 1887. But there was also the instinct to leave his study and see things for himself, to renew contact with the land and the people, something which it was said most Americans of the wealthy class had already lost.

Afterward, back in his country house at Long Island, writing of the exploits of Meriwether and Clark, his convictions about the historic destiny of his people became crystallized. The Americans, he wrote, sprang fully into national life, became a distinct nation, *only at the moment when they began their work of conquest.*[10] He understood the deeds of the early border people all the better, and for him to write of them was "a labor of love," because he too had helped to settle the lonely cattle ranges of the Far West.

For a number of years I spent most of my time on the frontier and lived and worked like any other frontiersman. . . . We guarded our herds of branded cattle and shaggy horses, hunted bear, bison, elk and deer, established civil government, and put down evil-doers, white and red, on the banks of the Little Missouri and . . . the Big Horn, exactly as did the pioneers who a hundred years previously had built their log-cabins beside the Kentucky or in the valleys of the Great Smokies. The men who have shared in the fast-vanishing frontier life of the present feel a peculiar sympathy with the already long-vanished frontier life of the past.[11]

Roosevelt, cherishing the American legend of the frontiersman, re-entered those experiences, embraced those memories, that he found most admirable in our history. All these epitomized for him the essence of "Americanism," the "great work" of conquest. Was it not time to return to "Americanism," to resume the "great work" of the early "conquering" Americans in new fields?

Thenceforth Roosevelt propounded "Americanism" in literature as well as in politics, almost with violence. "We must work according to our own ideas."[12]

[10] T. Roosevelt, *The Winning of the West,* Vol. I, p. 40.
[11] *Ibid.,* Preface, Vol. I, p. 16, written May, 1889, at Sagamore Hill.
[12] *Brander Matthews Papers,* letter of Jun. 29, 1894.

Meanwhile Henry Cabot Lodge was himself—though there was nothing of the cowboy in his exquisite composition—the most perfervid exponent of militant "Americanism" in Congress. Determined, ever since parting with his Mugwump friends, to essay the role of the "strong man" in politics, like the great Federalist statesman who was his chosen model, he shrank from nothing that would serve to extend his immediate power. David Graham Phillips, when he came some years later to investigate the Massachusetts political ring, found Lodge in absolute command of the state Republican organization, the ruthless machine boss under the robe of the scholar and man of letters. The old "Blaine gang" in Boston, entrenched in the Federal offices, had been taken over by him. Thenceforth, while still giving lip service to reform, he devoted himself unsleepingly for thirty years to securing offices and sinecures for his "boys." Every county, township and district in the state was carefully supervised by him personally. Does the southern Berkshire district appear doubtful? He dispatches agents capable of "organizing and arousing the district" in preparation for an election. The agent is told to visit the local committees and report accurately the condition of affairs. Sums of money are designated "to properly compensate" the agents in charge.[13] And combined with this organizing effort he makes appeals to the Irish masses of Boston by all sorts of oratorical somersaults and verbal "twists" of the lion's tail, narrow vindictive speeches against England in the best manner of James G. Blaine, so that Henry Adams who had known Lodge all his life, reading his anti-English speeches, rubbed his eyes and likened him to a cheap actor who "talks pure rot to order."[14]

On the other hand, J. T. Morse in his memoir of Lodge relates that the Senator admired the English intensely, envied especially their aptitude for imperial politics, and strove to emulate their aristocracy. It was simply that he had become convinced through negotiations with the English that they were successful

[13] *Lodge Papers* (Library of Congress), H. C. L. to Wellington Smith, Oct. 12, 1892.
[14] Adams, *Letters*, Vol. II, pp. 313, 267.

through being domineering and grasping. The United States, he argued, "must be as insolent and overbearing and ready to show fight as the others."[15] To Roosevelt, also, Lodge explained his pose of aggressiveness in similar terms. In the contests of international politics, he held, we must be more ruthless than the others; we must strike at them and strike hard if we would have them respect us and treat us well.

Through his post in the Senate Foreign Relations Committee, Lodge pressed the government toward a "spirited" foreign policy. In the magazine press he also conducted a shrill agitation for aggressive territorial expansion. "From the Rio Grande to the Arctic Ocean," he wrote, "there should be but one flag and one country. . . ." British dominion in Canada must be ended; like-wise the strong places that Britain had fortified in the West Indies must be seized. With the Isthmian canal completed, Cuba would become necessary to us, and the Hawaiian Islands and Samoa no less. He concluded:

We have a record of conquest, colonization and expansion un-equalled by any people in the Nineteenth Century. We are not to be curbed now by the doctrines of the Manchester School which . . . as an importation are even more absurdly out of place than in their native land.[16]

To Lodge, as to Roosevelt, our people's conquests of Indian nomads and Mexican peasants represented the chief glory of our history. Would not this history repeat itself soon upon a grander stage?

The closing years of the nineteenth century were rendered dramatic by the world-wide race of the great powers to seize and colonize the remaining, undefended territories of Africa, Asia, and even Polynesia. England vibrated with the martial poetry of Rudyard Kipling and the speeches of "Joe" Chamberlain. In the African deserts columns of French free-booters collided danger-

[15] *Harvard Graduates' Magazine*, Mar., 1925.
[16] *Forum*, Mar., 1895.

ously with British forces. Germany, entering the world contest tardily, now roared and clanged with naval and marine construction, rivaling that taking place along the Clyde. Incidents of extreme international tension succeeded each other rapidly in the years after the financial depression of 1893, as accumulated capital and industrial surpluses in the older nations sought new markets and avenues for investment overseas.

In the summer of 1895, a stormy year in British politics, Cabot Lodge visited London and found himself lionized in a most agreeable manner. He spent whole days conferring with leading statesmen, such as Balfour, Curzon, and Joseph Chamberlain. His long letters reporting these meetings to Roosevelt, who followed his course with envious interest, show no signs of the anti-British sentiment assumed upon the American rostrum. Rather he appears infected with the imperial visions of the English politicians who, following Chamberlain's new lead, prepared to abandon their historic Free Trade doctrines and worked to strengthen the British Empire bonds. At this time some basis for an Anglo-American rapprochement may well have been laid.

Joseph Chamberlain too had been a reformer, concerned for twenty years as an enlightened captain of industry with all sorts of benevolent social legislation, "concessions" to labor in the shape of city parks, workers' homes, and municipal improvements. These, Chamberlain argued, were the "ransom" which industry "must pay to society for prosperity." But was it not plain now that the cycle of domestic reform and concession approached its limits? To a Cecil Rhodes, uneasy witness of large riots of the unemployed in London at this period, the paramount problem was to open up new provinces and markets, taking up the surplus population and goods "if only in order to preserve the forty million inhabitants of the United Kingdom from a murderous civil war." The need for new drives toward colonial trade obsessed even the Liberal statesmen; and Chamberlain perorated, on the eve of the Boer War: "Providence intended us to be a great governing power, conquering, yes, conquering, but only in order to civilize."

Cabot Lodge returned from England to witness episodes in

United States politics apparently no less alarming, as symptoms of unrest, than those of Europe. His own purposes were now more fully revealed to himself; his speeches were marked with the unmistakable accents of the British imperialists, those of belligerency justified in the light of an assumed humanitarian, "civilizing" mission.

Early in 1896, while tales of insurrection and the horrors of civil war in the Antilles agitated Americans, and proposals for formal recognition of the rebels occupied the Senate, Lodge had assumed the floor leadership of the faction that pressed for intervention. Our "pecuniary" interests in Cuba, he argued, were great, and our humane interests were likewise not to be denied.

Free Cuba would mean a great market for the United States; it would mean an opportunity for American capital invited there by signal exemptions. . . . But we have a broader political interest in the fate of Cuba. She lies athwart the line which leads to the Nicaragua canal.

. . . But, Mr. President, I am prepared to put our duty on a higher ground than either of these, and that is the broad ground of common humanity.[17]

The gospel of American imperialism was preached at this time even more eloquently by the still younger Republican prophet, Albert Beveridge of Indiana. The issue before the country, this disciple of the old Federalists now proclaimed constantly, was "national life." The conflicts and discontents of sections and classes must be resolved, under the one flag of the Stars and Stripes. On the eve of a war which he passionately courted he spoke in Boston in reverberant phrases: *"We are a conquering race. . . . We must obey our blood and occupy new markets, and if necessary new lands."* For, were not our American factories and American soil already producing more than our people could consume? He added:

Fate has written our policy for us; the trade of the world must and shall be ours. . . . We will cover the ocean with our merchant marines. We will build a navy to the measure of our greatness. Great col-

[17] Millis, *The Martial Spirit*, pp. 46-47.

onies governing themselves, flying our flag and trading with us, will grow about our posts of trade. . . . And American law, American order, American civilization, and the American flag will plant themselves on shores hitherto bloody and benighted, but by those agencies of God henceforth to be made beautiful and bright.[18]

Adding his own high-pitched voice to the growing chorus of the jingoes, Assistant Secretary of the Navy Roosevelt, in a speech on April 2, 1897, exhorted his fellow countrymen to abandon the timid leadership of the rich bankers and industrialists and to turn instead to the example of a Farragut. No nation could hold its place in the world unless it stood ready to "guard its rights with an armed hand." Liberty itself could be preserved only by men "willing to fight for an ideal." Then in an access of lyrical militarism, he cried:

No triumph of peace is quite so great as the supreme triumphs of war. The courage of the soldier, the courage of the statesman who has to meet storms which can only be quelled by soldierly virtues—this stands higher than any qualities called out merely in times of peace.

. . . No national life is worth having if the nation is not willing to stake everything on the supreme arbitrament of war, and to pour out its blood, its treasure, and tears like water rather than submit to the loss of honor and renown. . . .

The purpose was clear; the course was marked. It needed, however, the instruments and the materials for victorious warfare in modern times. Therefore Roosevelt said, in the same speech: *"We ask for a great navy. . . ."*

The sailor, with his rolling gait and flapping trousers, had replaced the bowlegged cowboy as a *beau idéal* in the mind of the adventurous dude in politics.

3

The seafaring and sea-fighting tradition of the Americans was an old and colorful one, with its high point probably the daring

[18] Bowers, *Beveridge*, p. 69 ff.

naval exploits of the war of 1812, which Roosevelt had chronicled. But it was Captain Alfred T. Mahan, a little-known American naval officer, and another of the strong historical thinkers working upon our later politics, who did most to define for the imperialist age the role and meaning of naval power and the program of the great navy. His book, *The Influence of Sea-Power upon History: 1660-1783*, published in 1890, became at once the most important work of military history and theory since Clausewitz in the early part of the nineteenth century, and was read and expounded by the statesmen and military leaders of all the great powers, from Britain to Japan.

Mahan had based his historical analysis on the peculiar effectiveness of British "control of the seas" ever since the seventeenth century, when the Dutch rivals had been crushed. From Britain's maritime dominance and her superior mobility in fighting landlocked enemies (including the French under Napoleon I) Mahan deduced his theory of the supremacy of the naval arm in modern warfare. Nations which would frankly pursue their "self-interest" (interchangeable with "extending foreign commerce"), he concluded, must devote themselves to a program for increasing their sea-power in systematic fashion: first, by strengthening armor and gun capacity, size and quantity of men-of-war; second, by acquiring naval stations, ports, and colonies helpful to the fueling and repair of the war vessels. Thus the acquisition of colonial territories overseas supported naval power, and naval power in turn helped to win greater territorial possessions and commercial expansion. The rightness of such expansion, such forcible pursuit of national self-interest, Mahan in his fatalistic vein (like Clausewitz or Machiavelli earlier) never seemed to question. Indeed, though a good, professing Christian in private life, he was one of the prophets of "total warfare," opposing nearly all those "sentimental" movements which tried to limit the increasing destructiveness and cruelty of modern arms by international agreements.

Mahan's ideas of sea-power were taken up with enthusiasm first abroad, and then found followers at home as well. From 1893 on, Mahan, by articles in the press and in magazines, urged a policy of a large navy and a small army for the United States, for like Britain we were an "island power" fronting on two great oceans. With a great navy we could "round out" our American empire, and dominate the Western Hemisphere, long regarded as the special province of United States commerce. Moreover, once the Isthmian canal were finished, our naval forces would stand athwart the new world-trade routes between Europe and the China Sea; and it must be our endeavor, he argued, to control the approaches to the canal in the Caribbean, as well as the strategic stations at its exit in the Pacific. Ever since 1880, when Lesseps had begun the building of the canal at the Isthmus of Panama, Captain Mahan had thought it imperative for American naval forces to dominate this position.

America had long repelled the notion of foreign entanglements. But "The canal at the Isthmus may bring our interests and those of foreign nations into collision," he surmised, "and in that case, which is for statesmen to forecast, we must without delay begin to build a navy which will at least equal that of England. . . ." Else, who would pay heed to the Monroe Doctrine? Our navy had long been neglected, Mahan pondered with the bitterness of a disappointed career officer. He dreamed for years of an "awakening." [19]

Toward 1893, both Roosevelt and Lodge became acquainted with Mahan, and turned into enthusiastic disciples of his great navy doctrine and his plans for the founding of a Naval College. Through the Senate Foreign Relations Committee and the Navy Department they acted later as his protectors and patrons.

With Mahan's aid, Roosevelt drew up programs of strategy and intensified naval preparation. Roosevelt's big-navy speech at Newport in April, 1897 (already quoted), made after receiving his new appointment, is stamped with Mahan's influence. Dreams of far-off naval conquests now possessed the ambitious young politician. His correspondence with Mahan in the spring of 1897 touched on the matter of secret preparations for strengthening the Pacific fleet and finding the most aggressive officer possible

[19] Puleston, *Mahan*, pp. 60, 131.

for its command. He confided to Mahan his feeling of dissatisfaction with his cautious superior, Secretary of the Navy John D. Long, whose restraining authority he sometimes attempted to override.[20]

President McKinley would have found his worst fears realized concerning Roosevelt's impetuous and headstrong spirit if he had known of Roosevelt's discussions with Mahan concerning provisions for the seizure of Hawaii, the dispatch of added munitions for the Pacific fleet, an attack upon the Philippines, and a possible brush with the Japanese.[21]

More and more, military reasoning replaced legal reasoning in Roosevelt's mind. Mahan in his letters admits that he knows no other reasoning. How should Hawaii be annexed, for instance? How was "the political problem" to be solved? He advised: "Do nothing unrighteous; but . . . *take the islands first and solve afterward.*"[22]

These plans were pushed rapidly after April, 1897, a year before war came. In September, 1897, the Assistant Secretary of the Navy told Lodge of dining with President McKinley and outlining to him the action to be taken in case of war with Spain. "I gave him a paper showing exactly where all our ships are." The disposition of the ships for a Cuban expedition was sketched in outline; and also, looking farther off in the Pacific, special arrangements were made to prevent the Japs from chipping in. To this end, "our Asiatic squadron should blockade, and if possible, take Manila."[23]

4

The Republican party in its platform resolutions of 1896 had promised to use its offices to bring peace and independence to Cuba, charging at the same time that the Spanish government

[20] *T. R. Papers*, T. R. to A. T. Mahan, May 1, May 6, 1897; Mahan to R., May 4, 1897.
[21] *Ibid.*, May 3, 1897, T. R. to Mahan.
[22] *Ibid.*, Mahan to T. R., May 6, 1897. Italics added.
[23] Lodge, *op. cit.*, Vol. I, p. 278, letter of Sept. 21, 1897.

showed itself unable to protect the property and lives of American citizens residing in her colony. But thereafter President McKinley had proceeded with a studied restraint, while constantly applying diplomatic pressure to the Spanish government. The horrors and atrocities of civil war (practiced by both sides), which agitated American opinion deeply, the herding of natives into concentration camps by the Spanish army authorities, the large destruction of property (fifty millions of it estimated as American-owned), would not be tolerated here for long. McKinley pressed the Spanish government to put an end to the Cuban warfare, and to grant some form of autonomy to the Cubans. Yet he accepted Spanish assurances, and showed a courteous patience, knowing like Cleveland that the Spanish would be unable to hold Cuba indefinitely, and that the island could be purchased by us eventually, if need be. Moreover, McKinley had set his heart upon restoring prosperity at home, and appeared remarkably sensitive to the financial shocks registered in our securities markets whenever the threat of war appeared.

"I do not think a war with Spain would be serious enough to cause much strain on the country or much interruption to the revival of prosperity . . ." Theodore Roosevelt had written to Lodge in December, 1896.[24] Here was the clear difference between the war party and the Big Business faction. Meanwhile McKinley drifted, as Walter Millis has pictured him in his detailed study of the Spanish-American war, *The Martial Spirit*. The President resisted the war-mongers, yet never shut the door against their agitation.

The Spanish ambassador, Dupuy de Lome, in a secret letter that became all too famous, characterized the President accurately enough as one who was "weak and a bidder for the admiration of the crowd, besides being a common politician who tries to leave a door open behind himself while keeping on good terms with the jingoes of his party." [25]

[24] Millis, *op. cit.*, p. 63.
[25] *Ibid.*, p. 98.

The exposure of this letter (as a result of theft) in a sensational New York newspaper on February 8, 1898, ended Dupuy de Lome's tenure of office here, and did much to bring war nearer. The mysterious explosion which destroyed the American battleship *Maine,* stationed in Havana harbor, occurred a week later and seemed to make hostilities inevitable.

For three years the drums of war had been sounding both on the political rostrum and in the sensational popular press, typified by Hearst's New York *Journal* and Pulitzer's *World,* both exploring or experimenting with the possible effects of war upon reader circulation. Accounts of beautiful spies, tragic martyrs, and unbelievably daring heroes among the Rebel cohorts had figured constantly in their front pages. With the destruction of the *Maine,* headlines of a size such as had never been seen before strengthened the hands of the war party.

Yet Mark Hanna, the man from the midlands, now in the Senate as the "fit representative" of business men, reflected their prevailing caution when he said, as late as the days following the *Maine* disaster, "I am not in favor of heedlessly precipitating the country into the horrors of war." He was also convinced that Spain would now "back down," yield autonomy to Cuba, or cede the island to us.[26] That the United States, just emerging from depression, and until now in dire need of foreign capital to develop its own immense resources, should suddenly seek to conquer backward territories in the sub-tropics seemed to him and to other hard-headed business men sheer madness.

Meanwhile the business groups interested in sugar and tobacco, and the light-waisted speculators who bought worthless bonds of the future "Cuban Republic" in the hope of their validation by a war, represented actually a small influence. An array of conservative politicians, including Aldrich's powerful clique in the Senate, and Speaker Reed in the House, struggled to bring calm to the country in February and March, and as late as the early days of April. They had the aid of a large, enlightened minority

26 Rhodes, *op. cit.,* Vol. IX, p. 56.

of "anti-imperialists," typified by President Charles W. Eliot of Harvard and other academic and religious leaders.

But emotion rose throughout the country. Late in March a group of Senators headed by Redfield Proctor of Vermont told in the upper chamber a harrowing tale of horrors seen everywhere in Cuban cities, and of mass starvation in the camps of the *reconcentrados*. And Senator Thurston, a member of this delegation, whose wife had died of illness during the visit, cried out in a voice torn with passion, before crowded galleries, that the only people who now opposed a just war for the liberation of Cuba were the heartless financiers of Wall Street.[27]

In Congress, elements opposed to the McKinley administration, including the Western bloc of Republicans, the "radicals" of silver inflation, used the Cuban issue and the President's hesitant policy as a means of attack. In their mood of exasperation and discontent they pressed McKinley to end the interminable negotiations with Spain and to make a declaration of war. A secret caucus of forty or fifty Republican members of Congress sent a committee to him conveying the threat that they would introduce a resolution for war and vote with the Democrats to carry it through.[28] Even the formidable Bryan himself, national leader of the Democratic party, now at a great public dinner demanded that the Cubans be set free and that the United States recognize the Cuban "government."

Thus, fear that important Republican groups were at the point of revolting against party discipline, that the Western silver men might join with the hordes of Bryan in singing of a new "crown of thorns"—the failure to intervene in Cuba—now possessed McKinley and even Mark Hanna himself. General Russell Alger, the Michigan lumber baron who was Secretary of War, and Senator Cushman K. Davis, the strongly anti-labor Senator from Minnesota, both sent warning to McKinley that he must declare war soon. "He is in danger of ruining himself and the Republican

[27] *Congressional Record*, Mar. 23, 1898.
[28] Olcott, *McKinley*, Vol. II, p. 28.

party by standing in the way of the people's wishes. . . . He'll get run over and the party with him." [29]

War was inevitable. The young imperialists in the Government, such as Roosevelt, had been confident of the outcome since February 15, 1898, the day of the *Maine* disaster. "*Our internal political conditions will not permit its postponement,*" ran one significant newspaper editorial comment. For if war were avoided, out of the frustration of the people, embittered by other vexations, there might come not only a political cyclone, but who knew what other political developments or legislation "ruinous to every sober interest in the country . . ."? [30]

Thus the war-makers were confident that for *internal political reasons*, despite the waverings of McKinley and his continued negotiations with Spain, war must come. This war would be "righteous," wrote another of the "literary fellows," John Hay, who now occupied the post of Ambassador to England and was possessed by new, glamorous ideas of imperial policy. "I have not for two years seen any other issue." [31]

The inner circle of conservative Republicans suddenly shifted to a position of leadership in the war movement, in the last days of March, 1898. Important financial figures now swung to the war party, men like John Jacob Astor, William Rockefeller, Thomas Fortune Ryan, and Stuyvesant Fish, making public statements on March 24, 1898, that they favored driving Spain from her last possessions in America. [32]

On March 27, 1898, the President sent to Madrid his ultimatum, which asked virtually the immediate abandonment of Cuba by Spain. From Madrid the zealous American ambassador, General Woodford, sent message after message urging delay. The Queen's government was yielding slowly; he reported then that Spain promised to suspend hostilities, to call a Cuban parliament and accord autonomy. The President (using sleeping powders)

[29] Olcott, *McKinley*, Vol. II, p. 28.
[30] Chicago *Times Herald*, cited by Millis, *op. cit.*, p. 124.
[31] Thayer, *John Hay*, Vol. II, p. 167.
[32] Beer, *Hanna*, pp. 199-200.

waited two weeks; then, as he was about to succeed by peaceful methods, professed himself dissatisfied with the Spanish replies and yielded suddenly to the war party, delivering to Congress on April 11, 1898, his message calling for war.

It proved to be a fortunate move. Six months later, with the successful election of November out of the way, Mark Hanna would be writing to McKinley of his contentment because the Western political ferment had been diverted or had died down. The "splendid little war" (as John Hay called it) had by then apparently closed the sectional divisions of the country, enabling the Republican party to hold in line the "silver states" west of the Missouri.[33] The baffled passions of a long period of depression, always ready to turn against a regime so profoundly conservative as that of the Gold-bug Republicans, had been safely channeled away.

The pulse of the country quickened to the excitement that warfare brings. The foreign devil drew attention from the domestic demons troubling the American family. Western cowboy and Eastern bourgeois, Yankee and Southerner, fought side by side. The "sense of common national feeling and interest, weakened after a generation of economic, sectional and class conflicts, was reawakened . . . in a sense favorable to the Administration."[34] The next Congress, the Fifty-sixth, would see the elimination of the Western bimetallists from Republican ranks, and the presence of a full and "regular" conservative majority. Thus the McKinley administration would proceed, in the afterglow of military triumph, to the enactment of the Gold Standard Act, which the politicians themselves had dreaded, postponing its passage for three years.

5

The Spanish-American war, the "splendid little war" in John Hay's apt words, had curious, unexpected overtones and by-products. One was the sudden thrust of the American naval force into the Far East, where Commodore Dewey with his Pacific squadron

[33] Stephenson, *Aldrich*, p. 448.
[34] Croly, *Hanna*, p. 279.

prevailed so brilliantly at Manila and added a generally unexpected, unknown imperial possession to the United States. The preparations for this move had been secretly ordered well in advance of the war, on February 25, 1898, by the high-handed Assistant Secretary of the Navy, Roosevelt, on a day when his superior Mr. Long had left him in temporary charge as Acting Secretary.[35] A few men only, in the inner circle of the war party, expected this extension of the war for the "liberation" of Cuba to the conquest of the Philippine Islands at the antipodes of the world. Albert Beveridge, a friend of Lodge and Roosevelt, in a speech at Boston on April 27, 1898, several weeks before any actual fighting had begun, gave almost the first public hints of this action.

Cuba must fall into our hands, but that will be only when Spain is conquered. . . . In the Pacific is the true field of our earliest operations. There Spain has an island empire, the Philippine Archipelago. It is poorly defended. . . . In the Pacific the United States has a powerful squadron. The Philippines are logically our first target.[36]

Thus the armed force of the United States hurled her into the the race for imperial colonies in the tumultuous Orient.

An immediate problem now before the American politicians was the effect of such a war against Spain upon our relations with the other great powers. Here, too, swift and significant developments followed. From 1896 dates the beginning of a marked rapprochement with Britain, which was soon afterward to be cemented into a tacit alliance, a kind of "secret axis."

President Cleveland's recent Venezuela message had formed the climax of a long period of some thirty years of ill-feeling and strain between the United States and Britain. But its very explosion, with such unexpected force, had compelled Britain to overhaul her American policy in the light of an approaching fear of Germany and general war in Europe. The English proved conciliatory in recognizing the emphatic assertion of the Monroe Doctrine in its stronger form; the Venezuela boundary dispute was

[35] Mayo, *America of Yesterday*, p. 169.
[36] Bowers, *op. cit.*, pp. 69-70.

tactfully composed in a manner which accepted virtually all of the British boundary claims against Venezuela as just; and the two great nations closed the incident with a glow of good feeling induced by the framing of an arbitration pact now earnestly sought by Cleveland and Olney, which President McKinley eagerly signed in March, 1897. The difficulties of Britain in South Africa, the bellicose gestures of Emperor William II, further stimulated British courting of friendship with the United States. In 1898, while Germany and even France (having sizable investments in Spain) condemned the "bullying" tactics of the United States toward a weaker power, the British by broad hints gave their benedictions. From London, American Ambassador John Hay reported on April 5, 1898, a few days before the outbreak of war, that the commonest opinion left with him was: "I wish you would take Cuba at once. We wouldn't have stood it this long." Hay, of course, conveyed to Washington news of the "friendship and sympathy" shown in England as perhaps selfish in intent, but so "important and desirable in the present state of things. . . ." [37]

In high military circles in America, with some exceptions, fear of Britain seemed to depart. Mahan, in his program for increasing our sea-power, declared that he saw no need in the future to provide for renewed contests between America and Britain, whose interests, while they clashed at some minor points, now "coincided generally throughout the world." [38]

John Hay went even further. In a speech given after the opening of the war, on April 21, 1898, using the refrain "sharing of the white man's burden," he spoke of the thousand ties of origin, language, and kindred pursuits binding America and Great Britain: reasons enough for attaining a "good understanding." Finally he concluded, ". . . There is a sanction like that of religion which

[37] Thayer, *op. cit.*, Vol. II, p. 166.

[38] Where they appeared not to coincide, as at the time of the Venezuela boundary dispute, there were reasons enough for British moderation toward us. The unfortified border of Canada was a pawn for her good behavior. As Theodore Roosevelt remarked in January, 1896, at the time of the dispute, "We will settle the Caribbeans in Canada." (Puleston, *Mahan*, p. 131.)

binds us to a sort of partnership in the beneficent work of the world. Whether we will it or not, we are associated in that work by the very nature of things. . . . We are joint ministers of the same sacred mission of liberty and progress. . . ." The German ambassador at Washington, reading this speech, formed suspicions of a secret Anglo-American alliance.[39]

These omens, if omens they were, were plainer still in the speech of the young Albert Beveridge, who was soon to enter the Senate. Beveridge knew already of the expressions of good-will by leading English statesmen with regard to America's war in the Caribbean against Spain. But he knew also that Britain looked with favor at our penetration of the Pacific.[40]

The new American imperialism, according to Beveridge, plainly foreshadowed a partnership between the two nations. He continued:

If it means Anglo-Saxon solidarity; if it means an English-American understanding upon the basis of a vision of the world's markets so that the results may be just . . . if it means such an English-speaking people's league of God for the permanent peace of this war-worn world, the stars in their courses will fight for us and countless centuries will applaud.[41]

From England in the powerful voice of the Liberal leader, Joseph Chamberlain, there came on May 13, 1898, as if in answer, the surprising speech prophesying a ripening accord between the two long-hostile sister nations: "What is our next duty? It is to establish and maintain bonds of permanent amity with our kinsmen across the Atlantic. . . . The union—the alliance if you please—the understanding between these two great nations is indeed a guarantee of the peace of the world."

[39] Dennett, *op. cit.*, p. 189.

[40] John Hay, after a conference with Lord Salisbury, reported to Washington that American retention of a "permanent foothold in the Philippines" brought no objections. England would be content if America should retain the Philippine Islands, asking only "an option in case of future sale," lest they fall into other, possibly German, hands. (Dennett, *op. cit.*, p. 191.)

[41] Bowers, *op. cit.*, p. 69.

Thus the entrance of the United States into that war which has been called our first war of commercial empire was accompanied by a positive, though tacit, extension of America's foreign connections, a departure from Washington's doctrine of isolation and "no entanglements." Thenceforth a tacit understanding, a shadowy "axis" or community of interests, appeared to be operating between Britain and the United States, and even between the United States and Britain's allies, Japan and France. There would be henceforth much well-informed talk of that vague "Atlantic System of States" which combined to hold the balance of world power against certain inland empires, notably Germany, and sometimes Russia. "McKinleyism," product of trusts and combinations at home, favored such a policy of combination, of an imperial world trust abroad. Many hands now worked to cement the Atlantic System, which was to bring such fateful consequences in the new century.

6

Meanwhile Theodore Roosevelt, who had so often and so vigorously inveighed against the comfortable classes in America for their want of patriotism, resigned from his civilian post and enlisted for active military duty, receiving the commission of Lieutenant-Colonel. With the aid of the more experienced Colonel Leonard Wood, he raised a volunteer cavalry regiment of "Rough Riders."

His motives were mixed and perhaps not even clear to himself, though as usual his intuitions were deep. Friends and family, who had sought to dissuade him, were firmly resisted. Suggestions that he pursued military glory for political purposes irritated him deeply. Secretary of the Navy Long, though he sometimes felt Roosevelt a perfect "bull in a china shop," urged him to remain at the helm of the Navy. Roosevelt refused; and Long a few years later wrote in his diary that, absurd as this action had appeared at the time, it had proved wonderfully right later. "His going into the army led straight to the Presidency." [42]

[42] Mayo, *op. cit.*, p. 162.

Roosevelt lived his dream of charging an enemy upon a horse at the head of a column of cowboys. He reveled in victory and gore—the "primitive" in him content even with the heavy battle casualties in his spirited but ill-trained regiment. Out of the disorder and comic opera that attended the Cuban skirmishes, the "political colonel" returned with a reputation for martial spirit and valor—enough for most men. In the field, by his colorful and pugnacious personality he attracted the attention of the press correspondents unerringly, as was his wont nowadays, and they made much of him. The legend of "Teddy" spread broadly. The charge of the Rough Riders on the little hills outside of Santiago was in effect a charge on the political heights that Roosevelt, in peacetime, had for many years been unable to scale.

The *mystique* of war which the swashbuckling Roosevelt expounded by voice and by example seized upon men of good society like a fever and had strangely varying effects. They entered the war with poor Spain as a high imperial lark. For example, the young multi-millionaire "radical" William Randolph Hearst, not content to fight the war with his "yellow" newspapers, equipped his own naval squadron, consisting of a large private yacht and several tugboats, with which he followed up the action of Sampson's conquering fleet at Santiago, and personally participated by capturing and rescuing several wretched, drowning sailors of the Spanish squadron.

Another of Roosevelt's contemporaries, his Harvard friend and clubmate Winthrop Chanler, also a son of old "Knickerbockers," had adventures still more curious which were a parody of those of the Rough Rider himself. Bored with social life at Newport and New York and Florence, Italy, and with his own pranks and escapades, the whimsical "Winty" Chanler inspired himself now with the martial fever of the hour and resolved to give battle even before the main armies met. He departed from Florida's coast one night in a filibustering tugboat, fitted out at his own expense, and landed somewhere on the uncharted beach of Cuba with the design of meeting and joining the besieged Insurgents. But "Winty" lost his way in the bush, was nearly bitten to death by mosquitoes, and was finally driven to his ship by Spanish guards, carrying with him a minor wound in the arm and feeling weary, starved, sick, and much the worse for wear.

Colonel Roosevelt, on the other hand, soon heard at the battlefield in Cuba, as he wrote to "Dear Cabot," that "The good people in New York . . . at present seem to be crazy over me." And Lodge replied at once: "I hear talk all the time about your being run for Governor or Congressman and at this moment you could have pretty much anything you wanted. . . ." [43]

But a few weeks after his "crowded hour" at Santiago (fully reported in the idolatrous newspapers), Roosevelt came bustling back to the States, landing at Montauk Point, Long Island, with the first returning troop transports. The war was clearly won; American armed forces had wrested possession of Cuba, Puerto Rico, even the distant Philippines from Spain. There was apparently no pressing need for Colonel Roosevelt's personal leadership in the field. Still in uniform, from his regimental tent he began promptly his march on Albany.

While his praises were sung and thousands cheered him as a new idol of the people, the agents of party organizations for the first time courted him. In Cuba he had received a letter from Benjamin B. Odell, lieutenant to boss Platt, informing him in effect that he would in all likelihood be awarded the Republican nomination for Governor—provided that he proceeded with tact. [44] The Republican party prospects had lately been injured by grievous public scandals arising from their corrupt and wasteful administration of the New York canal system; and a new popular hero, wearing the garland of victory in war, was exactly what was needed in this crisis.

The inner circle of the Republican party fixed upon Roosevelt as their candidate, despite many misgivings concerning his character. Chauncey Depew, the venerable president of the New York Central railroad, and one of the wisest old heads among Republican

[43] Lodge, op. cit., Vol. I, p. 334 ff.
[44] Alexander, Four Great New Yorkers, p. 304.

elders, had won them over by his merry arguments. If Governor
Frank Black were nominated, he said, there would be heckling on
the subject of the canal frauds and Depew would be forced to state
in public that the amount stolen "was only a million, and that
would be fatal." But if Colonel Roosevelt were named, he could
climb up on the stump and say with conviction:

> We have nominated for Governor a man who has demonstrated in
> public office and on the battlefield, that he is a fighter for the right,
> and is always victorious. If he is elected, you know and we all know
> from his demonstrated characteristics—courage and ability—that every
> thief will be caught and punished. . . . Then I will follow the Colonel
> leading his Rough Riders up San Juan Hill and ask the band to play
> the "Star Spangled Banner." [45]

The party leaders were convinced. They sent word to Roosevelt
that they were ready to name him the regular Republican candidate for Governor if he would but call on Senator Tom Platt and
give assurances that, once nominated and elected, he would not
oppose or seek to injure the party organization or its chieftain.

In 1898 there was only one unpleasant, perhaps unimportant,
incident that marred the Colonel's triumphal march on Albany. It
is connected with Roosevelt's final parting from his Mugwump,
his reformer, friends.

Though the Citizens' Union ticket had been defeated in the
New York City mayoralty election the previous year, its showing
had been so strong that plans were now laid for expanding the
same movement into a state-wide Independent party. For the
subsidiary offices of the state ticket, Independent candidates were
to be named; but the most logical nominee for Governor would
be the new hero of the day, Colonel Roosevelt. Had he not—save
for certain regrettable lapses—long stumped with them for civil-
service reform? And would not the endorsement of the intelligent
voters (even though he was obviously to have also the "regular" Republican nomination) be in accord with his own innermost
desires?

[45] Depew, *My Memories*, pp. 160-162.

The reformers too opened parleys with Roosevelt; and on September 1, 1898, a very earnest delegation appeared at the Montauk Point camp, among them the young littérateur John Jay Chapman, another amateur of politics, who knew Roosevelt socially and who has left us an intimate account of the proceedings. After a heated discussion of all the aspects of the case, the Colonel decided to accept the Independent nomination.[46] But no sooner had Platt and his stalwarts heard of the Independents' plan than they were thrown into alarm. For they had accepted Roosevelt as a political Lesser Evil, so that his bright shield might cover the regular machine men returning to state office under him, and not to have him encourage their enemies and detractors. A tug of war began. On September 10, 1898, Platt sent his lieutenant, the veteran Congressman Lemuel Quigg, to warn Roosevelt that he must absolutely disavow the "poisonous Mugwumps" and their " 'good government' entanglements." A clear agreement was drawn up providing that Roosevelt was

to acknowledge and respect his [Platt's] position at the head of the Republican organization . . . and you would consult with the Senator fully and freely . . . adopt no line of policy and agree to no important matter of nomination without previous consultation, and that you wanted him to agree to the same thing on his part.[47]

To the written memorandum of this conference Roosevelt at the time subscribed by letter, except for the reservation that he gave no promise to act "otherwise than in accord with my conscience." A week later he had a private interview with boss Platt, and was accepted into the fold. Then immediately after, on September 19, 1898, he wrote to his friend Chapman:

Dear Jack,
    I do not see how I can accept the Independent nomination and keep good faith with the other men on my ticket.

There followed two weeks of explanations and recriminations, in which the Goo-Goos and, particularly, Chapman wrestled for

[46] Howe, *op. cit.*, p. 138.   [47] Roosevelt-Barnes suit, pp. 2362-2363.

Roosevelt's soul. There was anguish on both sides; it was the parting of ways. Without Roosevelt the Independents' party and even the city reform clubs would vanish as going concerns. "I unloaded the philosophy of agitation upon Roosevelt," relates Chapman in his memorandum. "I pictured him as the broken-backed, half-good man . . . the trimmer who wouldn't break with his party, and so, morally speaking, it ended by breaking him." At times, during the long dispute, Roosevelt is said to have broken down and "cried like a baby." [48] Yet he held firm to his decision to renounce the Independent nomination, a decision which he made public in a letter to the newspapers on September 25, 1898. After this struggle with his reformer friends (and his own conscience) was over, Roosevelt always tended to speak of them most bitterly, even accusing them of "treachery." He claimed that he had not been given to understand that they intended to run candidates for the lower offices on his ticket in opposition to the rest of the Republican ticket. Yet this had been the very essence of their plan for building a new party throughout the state.

The significance of this incident, and of the minor public controversy that followed, was that Roosevelt dropped all connections with the reformers, but also gave up all chance of building a distinct and independent organization of his own, and so left himself henceforth entirely in the hands of the professionals.

Once more it was his "evil genius" Cabot Lodge who did most to persuade Roosevelt to abandon the Independents in a final break. They would lead but "to the defeat of the sound money men" and would undermine the results of the war, Cabot argued. John Hay, too, complimented Roosevelt upon his having shown himself in this painful affair both honest and practical, "a reformer by instinct and a wise politician; brave, bold, uncompromising, and yet not a wild ass of the desert." [49]

There was a brief scandal in the clubs, as reports of Roosevelt's faithlessness and his "surrender to Platt" were given by trust-

[48] Howe, op. cit., pp. 140-143.
[49] Lodge, op. cit., Vol. I, pp. 348-349; Roosevelt, An Autobiography, pp. 272-273.

worthy persons. But soon the obscure quarrel was forgotten. Roosevelt, wearing the sombrero of a Rough Rider, toured the state with an escort of cowboy warriors and a collection of flags for his rallies. There was talk of war and its rich fruitage, and not of reforming canal administrations. When embarrassing mention of the canal scandals was made, the bugles would blow and the drums roll. The citizens were exhorted not to help the Spaniards with their votes. "He really believes," remarked Roosevelt's embittered friend Chapman, that "he is the American flag." [50]

For all its brass music, the New York campaign was comparatively calm, as if the New Yorkers cared little for the war. However, the large corporations gave liberal donations to the party chest, Mr. J. P. Morgan coughing up $10,000; and the party workers labored willingly at the canvass. Colonel Roosevelt prevailed over his Democratic opponent by the close margin of 18,000 votes—yet without him the Old Guard might have lost this important election through its own follies.

A strong current of reaction against the war and its aftermath of prolonged, bloody conflict with the Filipinos now ran through the country. The typical Mugwumps, with whom Roosevelt had parted company, Schurz, Godkin, and Moorfield Storey, addressed the country more vigorously than ever as Anti-Imperialists. William Graham Sumner's eloquent protests that our great nation, in the name of patriotism, had "knocked to pieces a poor old bankrupt state" were widely noticed. Soon Bryan embraced the cause of Anti-Imperialism as furnishing the burning issue of the day. Thus Roosevelt's "spread-eagle" campaign in New York was of the greatest moment to the national administration. He brought happy omens that the "splendid little war" had been, after all, effective as a diversion, that the majority of the people would not repudiate a regime which carried the laurels of military victory, however dubious they might be.

At the outset of his term as Governor of New York, Roosevelt exuded confidence and good cheer. He told himself that he was

[50] Howe, *op. cit.*, p. 470.

going "to achieve results, not merely issue manifestoes of virtue." To his intimate friends, such as Winthrop Chanler, he confided that in spite of the Goo-Goos he expected to make "a pretty decent governor." And the charming Winty hastened to reply that no one doubted this, or believed Roosevelt doubted it. Otherwise "the imagination fairly boggles at the panic I should have suffered." Chanler pledged that he would give aid to the new Governor "by shooting Jack Chapman and his co-kickers with a putty blower." [51]

Theodore Roosevelt's term as Governor was neither brilliant nor interesting, like that of Tilden's reform administration a generation earlier, or Charles E. Hughes's or Alfred Smith's afterward. He made, actually, little more than "a pretty decent governor." He reigned by virtue of a compromise agreement with boss Platt, a compromise that was observed with tolerable good faith by both men, but was awkward and satisfied neither one. In those days the powers of the Governor of New York were peculiarly circumscribed, both as an executive and as an initiator of legislation. His office was apparently held "in trust" for the ruling party organization; while, as Elihu Root admitted, the wily Mr. Platt "simply ruled the State; for nigh upon twenty years he ruled." The capital was not at Albany, but at the corner of the sofa in the Fifth Avenue Hotel, where the county leaders met with Platt and said "Amen!" to his rulings. [52]

Platt, with a quietness and efficiency that made him famous under the soubriquet of the Easy Boss, managed a kind of central clearing house for political privilege, receiving fees regularly from the large corporations in his province and delivering services to them faithfully. This system of political-economic relationships, functionally similar to those in the other important states, was so firmly knit, so highly perfected by 1898, that even the popular hero Colonel Roosevelt, under the circumstances by which he tacitly accepted or recognized it, could do little.

[51] *T. R. Papers*, W. Chanler to T. R., Mar. 10, 1899.
[52] Root, *Addresses*, p. 202.

There is no doubt that he strongly desired to dismiss dishonest, corrupt officials from the public service and actually proceeded to do so, but in each case he had to consult, as agreed, the Easy Boss in order to replace them with reputedly more honest men selected from the organization's approved list. He would have liked to formulate some large policy with regard to the taxation and supervision of corporations and public-utility monopolies chartered by the state—a subject growing fashionable at the time, as we shall see—yet here too his hand was stayed.

Before he took office, Roosevelt relates, Platt asked him in a moment of pleasant humor what committee appointments he wished to suggest for the Legislature. Roosevelt had replied that he had no suggestions, and that in any case the Speaker had not yet been chosen. "Oh," responded Platt, "he has not yet been chosen, but of course whoever we choose as Speaker will agree beforehand to make the appointments we wish." [53]

It would be incorrect to say that Colonel Roosevelt as Governor of New York was merely the puppet of the boss. This was not the view entertained of him privately in professional political circles. The chronicle of Roosevelt's political growth is one alternately of compromise or "trimming," and of rebellious, bold-handed assertions of his independence, his integrity of character. Alternately, he accepts the system, makes his bargain with the boss, and then revolts. (We have seen his backward and forward movements while serving as Police Commissioner; and it is still the same.) Meanwhile his contradictory behavior illuminates all the more strongly the political conditions of the time because he is so atypical, so refreshingly different, so much more enterprising, than the common-garden variety of politician in his time.

In this connection we must remark Senator Tom Platt's careful efforts to pin down the young politician, as far as possible, by written agreements limiting his sphere of action. Such care evidently was unnecessary with those who preceded and followed him in office. A McKinley, in Ohio, did not have to be given sermons by

[53] Roosevelt, *An Autobiography*, p. 284.

Mark Hanna calculated to strengthen his respect for substantial moneyed interests in his state, nor weaned away from reputedly "unsound" or "heretical" notions. Roosevelt on the other hand came to the weekly Sunday breakfasts in New York with Senator Platt, those private conferences which were *de rigueur*, with obvious distaste. He apparently feared to be left alone with the oily, crafty old man; sometimes he brought his sister, Mrs. Anna Roosevelt Cowles, with him.

Attractive and jovial as was the picture that Governor Roosevelt made before the public (the mythical Rough Rider in politics, with his mask of furious energy, of "pure act" as Henry Adams described it), there was in him a more troubled, inward self known to only a few intimate friends, such as Cabot Lodge and Brooks Adams. It was that of an upper-class intellectual of uncertain convictions and limited knowledge, now facing the deeper questions of his time, in more responsible office, while endeavoring to push himself toward the further goal of his overweening ambitions.

The paradox of his character, which has so long troubled historians, derived from his being at the same time the playboy in politics, the picturesque Rough Rider who caught the eye of the crowds, all encircled by followers and flatterers, and the troubled intellectual, the "literary fellow" of aristocratic background who glimpsed something of the dangers and needs of his time, who was sensitive to the moods of the people—yet, at heart unsympathetic to them—who felt all these things and yet suffered from his own incapacity to rationalize them. Thus we may explain the recurrent lapses from announced high principles to gross compromise, the striking contradictions between word and deed, disparities far more prominent in a Theodore Roosevelt than in less honest and less sensitive political characters. We may understand the better also why, throughout the career of this "strong man," there seem to be hands guiding, propelling, manipulating him at every turn, the hands of men who were far more certain of their purpose than he.

The synthesis of political principles and maxims which were fittingly to be known as "Rooseveltian" took more definite form in his mind during the interlude at the Governor's mansion in Albany. In serious vein, he wrote now to his British friend, Cecil Spring Rice: "We have tremendous problems in the way of relations of labour to capital to solve." [54]

In his first annual message to the State Legislature, he found it politic to introduce some conciliatory sentences about the need for bettering the conditions of working men. But as soon as a serious strike broke forth in Buffalo, a short time later, he dispatched state militia to preserve order and property on the spot. Again, in a strike of construction workers at the Croton Dam project, he could not restrain himself from intervening with the armed forces at his disposal, who helped to defeat the strike. Labor, when it showed itself as an organized power, always made him react with instinctive violence. Union men knew this and remembered him for it all his life.

But at the same time the Colonel persisted in his critical attitude toward those whom he amusingly named in private conversation "the criminal rich." In 1899 the tremendous post-war "boom" was on; the bull market roared unceasingly in the stocks of companies being currently absorbed by the giant trusts created under Morgan's leadership. The Democratic leader Bryan now made the problem of the trusts, like that of "imperialism," one of his principal issues. He toured Ohio to oppose personally the re-election of Mr. Hanna to the Senate in 1899, holding that the voters must choose there "between plutocracy and democracy." [55] These would also be the terms of the national campaign in 1900, as anyone could see. Governor Roosevelt, who had so often ridiculed Mr. Bryan, now faced the problem of the multiplying and expanding trusts, everywhere laid to his own party's declared policy of tolerance. He told Cabot Lodge in April, 1899, that despite the booming prosperity seen on every hand, he noted a mood of "sullen discontent" and growing anger among the working classes and small tradespeople of his state—disturbing symptoms to the profes-

[54] Gwynn, *The Letters and Friendships of Cecil Spring Rice*, Vol. I, p. 293.
[55] Croly, *op. cit.*, p. 248.

sional student of the public pulse, who would soon adopt the very terms of Mr. Bryan in order to deal with them.

I have been in a great quandary over trusts. I do not know what attitude to take. I do not intend to play the demagogue. On the other hand, I do intend, so far as in me lies, to see that the rich man is held to the same accountability as the poor man; . . . this is not always easy.

For many years Roosevelt and his friends had been wont to raise the slogans of nationalism and patriotism in opposition to sectional and class divisions. But now at Albany, facing a period of peace, he entertained doubts that the catalyzing force of militant patriotism would always be enough. Searching for Live Issues, he groped for new tactics and emblems, those which composed gradually the vague program called "The Square Deal." Brooks Adams, paying a week-end visit to Albany in the summer of 1899, held serious discourse with the Governor of the twin dangers of the materialistic trade-union and eight-hour-day movement among the lower classes, and of the possible "enslavement" of the nation by its trust magnates. Their minds played with the possibility of Roosevelt's "heading some great outburst of the emotional classes which should at least temporarily crush the Economic Man." [56]

Despite the hostages that he had given to conservative Republicanism, he was most eager at the outset of his term to figure as a vigorous reformer. He waited a few months, cast about for an issue, and soon found one in the shape of the Ford Franchise Tax Bill, long entombed in the committee rooms of the Legislature. This measure proposed a more adequate though quite moderate scheme of taxation to be placed upon public-service corporations of the state in ratio to the value of the franchises which they had obtained. Roosevelt's special emergency message late in April, 1899, calling for passage of the Ford Bill out of its turn, created a sudden excitement in financial and party circles, and brought the Republican elders hurrying to Albany to admonish him.

In the serious altercation with Platt which arose over the fran-

[56] *T. R. Papers*, T. R. to Hay, Jun. 17, 1899.

chise tax bill the differences between the ideas of the young and the old leader are well revealed. Platt urged the Governor to do nothing. He reminded the Governor warningly:

When the subject of your nomination was under consideration there was one matter that gave me real anxiety. . . . I had heard from a good many sources that you were a little loose on the relations of capital and labor, on trusts and combinations, and, indeed, on those numerous questions which have recently arisen in politics affecting . . . the right of a man to run his own business in his own way, with due respect of course, to the Ten Commandments and the Penal Code. Or, to get at it even more clearly, I understood . . . that you entertained various altruistic ideas, all very well in their way, but which before they could safely be put into law needed very profound consideration.

Platt concluded with an expression of fear lest "the notions of populism, as laid down in Kansas and Nebraska," would soon be exemplified by the leadership of the Republican party in the State of New York.

In answer, the Governor now set forth *virtually his whole profession of faith, that which he adhered to all his life.* He pointed out that "on the one hand" during the recent strike at Buffalo, he had "unhesitatingly acted . . . to put down mobs, without regard to the fact that the professed leaders of labor furiously denounced me for so doing. . . ." But "on the other hand," neither would he tolerate wrongs committed in the name of property, as by the public-utility corporations. He objected strongly to "the tendency to force everybody into one of two camps, and to throw out entirely men like myself, who are as strongly opposed to Populism in every stage as the greatest representatives of corporate wealth. . . ." On this score Roosevelt desired not to be misunderstood in any sense. He insisted emphatically that

these representatives of enormous corporate wealth have themselves been responsible for a portion of the conditions against which Bryanism is in ignorant revolt. I do not believe that it is wise or safe for us as a party to take refuge in mere negation and to say that there are no evils to be corrected. It seems to me that our attitude should be one of cor-

recting the evils and thereby showing that, whereas the Populists, Socialists, and others really do not correct the evils at all . . . we Republicans hold the just balance and set ourselves as resolutely against improper corporate influence on the one hand as against demagogy and
mob rule on the other. . . . I think it is in the long run the only wise
attitude. . . .[57]

Despite the ill humor of the leader and his henchmen in the
Legislature, Roosevelt therefore persisted in pressing for enactment of the Ford Bill. He threatened to call a special session;
skillfully he used interviews with the press to arouse popular opinion, and implied that a disagreeable internal party struggle might
ensue in the event that his wishes were resisted. Reluctantly the
party machine yielded, although the bill was passed only on condition that certain compromise clauses be inserted which were designed to render its constitutionality doubtful.

From such victories Roosevelt's popularity waxed. Platt would
warn him solemnly, however, that his future was being ruined;
that no large corporations would be willing to contribute to his
campaign expenses; they would neither forget nor forgive, while
the public with its fickle memory would forget him in a brief season or two. There are signs that Roosevelt bore these strictures in
mind. Once having scored a point for himself, he would turn about
and allow a few cards to the adversary who still controlled the
party's purse.

One of Governor Roosevelt's most helpful acquaintances of this
period was Elihu Root, the gray-headed corporation lawyer who
either as a legal representative or a lobbyist for his clients had
been active in behind-the-scenes politics ever since the days of Boss
Tweed in the 1860's. When certain legal technicalities appeared to
disbar Roosevelt from the gubernatorial nomination in 1898, owing to his having declared residence in Washington rather than
New York, the resourceful Root had quickly found an ingenious
way out of the difficulty, winning Roosevelt's everlasting gratitude. A legendary remark suggesting Elihu Root's resourceful-

[57] Roosevelt, *An Autobiography*, pp. 300-301.

ness, and variously attributed to W. C. Whitney, Thomas Fortune Ryan, and J. Pierpont Morgan, was: "I have had many lawyers who have told me what I cannot do; Mr. Root is the only lawyer who tells me how to do what I want to do." [58] It was to the Ulysses of the New York bar (recently appointed Secretary of War by McKinley) that Roosevelt turned repeatedly for advice, especially on the new trust question.

After wrestling for long hours in December, 1899, with his annual message to the State Legislature, regarding measures for supervising monopolistic, semi-public corporations, Roosevelt sent the draft of his message to Root, confessing that he felt himself beyond his depth, and appealing for aid.

Root reads it and tutors him as follows:

. . . You say "some of the wealth has been acquired by means which are inconsistent with the highest rules of morality and which yet under our present laws cannot be interfered with." I think that is a dangerous suggestion. It is not a function of law to enforce the rules of morality. . . . There is altogether too general an impression that it is immoral to acquire wealth, and far too little appreciation of the fact that the vast preponderance of the *grand fortunes which now exist in this country have been amassed, not by injuring any living being, but as an incident to the conferring of great benefits on the community.*

The "trust problem," according to Root, boiled down to seeing that wealth-getting did not infringe upon any individual's legal rights. So long as the rights of individuals were protected by law sufficiently, it was unnecessary to enact any legislation that would confine or injure business.

Roosevelt replied humbly:

I see entirely the danger . . . such as my phrase might carry. I think that for it I shall substitute some of the sentences you write in your letter. There are, however, certain fortunes which do seem to me to be unfortunate in their effects with the country. . . .

---

[58] Jessup, *Elihu Root*, Vol. I, p. 185.

In his message to the New York Legislature, Roosevelt, as he admitted to Root, "cribbed" unblushingly.[59]

The grand fortunes may have been amassed, as Root argued, without injury to any living being; yet Governor Roosevelt now learned from the state banking examiners that there had been scandalous goings-on in the affairs of a certain trust company, purchased lately by a group of eminent financiers including W. C. Whitney and Thomas Fortune Ryan. The Governor's informants wrote him:

They got rid of the old officers, put in creatures of their own, and proceeded to borrow for their own speculative uses, a large portion of the deposits. The collateral they gave was speculative . . . unmarketable in large degree, almost valueless in many cases. . . . They deliberately violated the Banking Laws and the Penal Code.[60]

Through the bank, the directors got control of an insurance company and disposed of the credit and funds of the latter in ways useful to themselves which the reigning Superintendent of Insurance made no effort to oppose. Roosevelt heard that the latter, Lou Payn, former Congressman, lobbyist and henchman of boss Platt, was the trusted intermediary of the ring of big speculators.

. . . Being a frugal man, out of his $7,000 a year salary he [Payn] had saved enough to enable him to borrow nearly half a million dollars from a Trust Company, the directors of which are also the directors of an insurance company under his supervision. As Insurance Superintendent, he last year rendered such disinterested aid to Mr. Whitney, when Mr. Whitney's Metropolitan Railway was in danger of being made to pay a tax to the State, etc., etc., that in a burst of similar disinterestedness Mr. Whitney lends him offhand a hundred thousand. . . .[61]

The worst of it was that the newspapers, notably the *World* (March 12 and 13, 1900) with the help of a disgruntled em-

---

[59] *Root Papers*, E. Root to T. R., Dec. 13, 1899; T. R. to Root, Dec. 15, 1899; Jan. 4, 1900. Cf. also Jessup, *op. cit.*, Vol. I, pp. 208-210. Italics added.

[60] *T. R. Papers*, C. Bacon to T. R., April 19, 1900; also G. R. Sheldon to T. R., Jan. 18, 1900.

[61] Lodge, *op. cit.*, T. R. to Lodge, Jan. 22, 1900, Vol. I, p. 438.

ployee, ventilated these scandals, and Elihu Root was seen to have been the corporation counsel who approved the objectionable transactions. Roosevelt in this case acted with discretion. The *World,* which under Pulitzer often subjected him to its raillery, charged that he shielded certain high political and financial figures, notably Elihu Root. But in any case, he resolved that Lou Payn, Senator Platt's handy man, must give way to a new Superintendent of Insurance.[62]

The ousting of Payn brought fierce outcries from the party's stalwarts. Platt grew bitter; prominent financial leaders made testimonials on behalf of Payn, who for some time defied the Governor's efforts to dismiss him. In the end he departed. But Platt, who was grievously offended by the affair, was partly conciliated in having one of his "boys," whose reputation was not yet sullied, appointed in Payn's place.

A few "altruistic" measures (as Tom Platt cynically called them) were passed during Governor Roosevelt's term, including a tenement-house law, improved civil service regulations, and a new game law. But he had done nothing to prosecute the perpetrators of the canal frauds of 1897-1898; and while he was at odds with the party machine, he was charged by Goo-Goos with having "bowed to Platt on many an appointment." [63]

To his detractors he now answered in terms that were very characteristic of his temperament: "the fool reformers" were as bad as corrupt machine politicians. He ridiculed men who championed their favorite causes only as "a kind of tribute to their own righteousness," and without regard to opportuneness or the need for realistic compromise. To temporize, he held, was often the mark of the highest statesmanship. Or, as he said some years later,

[62] Elihu Root, now Secretary of War, remained silent, though it is evident the affair nettled him. "It is most distressing," he wrote at this time to one of his business associates, "to have the State Government made the tool of a lot of blackmailing scoundrels. I should be glad to know just what part Governor Roosevelt played in it." (*Root Papers,* E. Root to W. S. Johnston, Feb. 19, 1900.)

[63] Pringle, *Roosevelt,* p. 214.

during his libel suit against William Barnes: "I say emphatically that you must have regard for opportunism in the choice of the time and method of making the attack. . . ." [64]

Meanwhile the position of Colonel Roosevelt in the politics of New York State and his party continued to be precarious. Cabot Lodge was now curiously pessimistic when they discussed the "troubled waters" of New York machine politics, in which so many ambitious careers had foundered.

In a certain measure Roosevelt had "hired" his sword, as Brooks Adams had cynically advised him to do, to the masters of political parties; he had made his peace with the machine, which all his instincts and his education taught him to dislike. Yet he felt that his actual prospects were dark; his "career" might soon be ended. He heard of plans afoot to eliminate him from the Governorship, to deny him re-election, which he merited. Boss Platt wanted him out of New York altogether, Roosevelt heard. The big insurance companies, the corporation magnates who represented for him the "criminal rich"—involved in recent scandals, and incensed by the dismissal of Payn—pressed the Senator to rid them of the Rough Rider. "All the high monied interests that make campaign contributions of large size," he confided to Lodge, "and feel that they should have favors in return are extremely anxious to get me out of the State." [65] And beyond Albany the possible advance of the Rough Rider, popular figure though he might be, was limited. The McKinley-Hanna regime with its military conquests and prosperity was to seek vindication before the voters in 1900; and Roosevelt, though inwardly discontented, must remain regular. He could not hope to climb to the Cabinet offices, the realm of national and foreign affairs which truly fascinated him, or the highest office of all, unless he avoided "making mistakes," as an older counselor, H. H. Kohlsaat of Chicago, intimate of McKinley and Hanna, now warned him. He must, in short, take his orders and go where he was told. Especially upon the

[64] Barnes vs. Roosevelt, 366 ff.
[65] *T. R. Papers*, G. H. Lyman to T. R., Dec. 28, 1899.

"trust question" must Roosevelt avoid outspokenness. "I am anxious to have you inherit the McKinley machinery—& following," wrote the Chicago newspaper publisher. "You can get that only by sticking close to the President." He added mysteriously: "A man is often put in a hole by his would-be-friends." [66]

How vastly different was the situation of one of Roosevelt's Western contemporaries, the former Congressman Robert M. La Follette of Wisconsin, also a Republican, who now battled his way to leadership of his state organization. La Follette had been cast out of the temple in 1891 for the high crime of insubordination. Then, after a period of retirement, La Follette had determined to enter the struggle for public office in opposition to the entire Wisconsin machine, a course that Roosevelt, Lodge, and company had so sagely avoided. Wisconsin's party machine was as corrupt and complete as anything in the older regions of the country; yet it was not so deeply entrenched in the rural world; there were fewer crowded city alleys where its roots might flourish rankly as in Boston or New York. Thus La Follette could "go to the people" in a more effectively democratic commonwealth, agitating, educating them tirelessly against the bribe-givers. With the aid of his wife and a few college friends at Madison, he patiently built up his "personal machine." He and Mrs. La Follette by hand addressed thousands of letters, distributed tens of thousands of circulars. Evenings he made long carriage rides, to see his farmers and village shopkeepers face to face. His strength grew steadily from year to year, and his enemies accused him of "working stealthily" by candlelight. This was literally true; because he had no newspapers supporting him, no wealthy patrons, and was forced to knock at the farmers' doors after working hours, and make his appeals man to man, without formality, and by the light of a lantern or a guttering candle.

Thus by 1898 the relentless independent La Follette succeeded in forcing his own political program of administrative, fiscal, and electoral reform upon the state Republican party, though the nom-

[66] *Ibid.*, H. H. Kohlsaat to T. R., Aug. 9, 14, 1899.

inating convention, still partially under the Sawyer-Spooner control, denied him the Governorship. The obstruction of this program thereafter, the failure to enact the party resolutions into law, aroused a wave of popular anger, which made inevitable La Follette's triumphant election in 1900, an event that caused reverberations throughout the country. La Follette had transformed the dominant party in a great Western state "from below," after a decade of grim, incessant warfare. As its undisputed leader he now took over, with his own incorruptible band of followers, the University of Wisconsin "experts," Van Hise, Ely, and Commons, and the agrarian organizers who were sons of the Populists. Henceforth he need "consult" no one, take orders from no one—save the people, who, as La Follette said, "have never failed us. . . ."

But in New York, Governor Roosevelt, courageous and well-intentioned though he might be, felt the ground give way under his feet. For his strength was not built solidly upon a mass following, but derived from a bargain with the old professional organization. Thus he felt himself more or less helpless as many hands combined now to thrust him toward a kind of outer political darkness in 1900.

He should seek re-election as Governor, his admirers urged; then, retiring in 1903, hold himself in readiness for Presidential lightning to strike him. In one year as Governor there was too little time to enact a distinguished legislative program, or to render other signal services; but in his second term there would be opportunity to do this. It was against such a probability, Roosevelt knew, that the machine made ready to remove him. "Hurrahs" greeted the Colonel nowadays when he went forth to speak to the people, but he told himself always that mere "Hurrahs" did not encompass election victories.

After the death of Vice-President Hobart in November, 1899—he had indicated earlier that he wished to retire—there arose a "spontaneous" demand for Governor Roosevelt as running mate to President McKinley in 1900. Several months earlier, Cabot Lodge had written to Theodore that the Vice-Presidency offered interesting possibilities. "I have thought it over a great deal and I am sure I am right," he concluded. Later he wrote that Roosevelt was "tempting Providence by staying in Albany," where he might come a cropper, and firmly advised him to consider the Vice-Presidency if it was offered. Then on December 29, 1899, he reported confidentially that Elihu Root had been offered the nomination and had refused it.[67]

Other admirers and informants now brought word to the Governor that plans were being laid to bar his re-election and thrust him upon the Vice-Presidential "shelf." If he resisted, the whole press would be turned against him; and if he fought for the gubernatorial nomination, unlimited funds would be expended in aid of the Democratic candidate that year.[68]

Gripped by indecision, Roosevelt wavered for many weeks. He knew that the ways of Platt were dark and double; and he had won in 1898 by a slender margin which could be perhaps easily reversed. Moreover, he had managed to offend the trade unions; the American Federation of Labor, he thought, now seethed with anger against him because he had ordered out the militia at the recent Croton strike.[69]

Meanwhile the humorous little conspiracy of Platt and his collaborator, boss Quay of Pennsylvania, proceeded apace, though Mark Hanna openly disapproved of it. An emissary of the Easy Boss came to Albany a few days before the convention opened and advised Roosevelt that his renomination for Governor was improbable, and that public sentiment, especially among the Far Western delegates with whom the war had been popular, would make it hard for him to reject the Vice-Presidential office.[70] Waveringly Roosevelt thrust away the fool's cap of the Vice-President in public, while privately admitting that he saw nothing else to do

[67] *T. R. Papers*, Lodge to T. R., Jul. 12, 1899; Dec. 7, 1899; Dec. 29, 1899.
[68] *Ibid.*, C. P. Bacon to T. R., Apr. 19, 1900; Redfield Proctor to T. R., Apr. 21, 1900; Frederick Holls to T. R., May 3, 1900.
[69] Cowles, *op. cit.*, pp. 232, 240, 244, letters of Feb. 2, 1900; Apr. 30, 1900.
[70] Pringle, *op. cit.*, p. 218.

and was not abandoning the idea of it irrevocably. Lodge, the staunch old friend and mentor, continued to urge his acceptance of the office, though in guarded language, arguing that it would bring Roosevelt close to the Administration: ". . . I did not want you to think that with my views I was encouraging you to get into a position where you would be forced to take the Vice-Presidency." [71]

After some misgivings, the Rough Rider attended the national convention of his party at Philadelphia, wearing his "Acceptance Hat," the old cowboy sombrero of 1898. The only enthusiasm shown at this machinelike ceremony came with the "stampede" to nominate him for the Vice-Presidency. Mark Hanna's opposition to Roosevelt had ceased at the last moment, after telephone communication with President McKinley. "Don't you know that there is only one life between the Presidency and the Vice-Presidency . . . ?" he had exclaimed when another's name had been proposed, one even less offensive to him than the "wild man" of the Republican party.[72]

Although Roosevelt enjoyed the demonstrations made in his honor at the convention, he left it in a mood of deep depression. The Vice-Presidency seemed the tomb of all his hopes. He would pass four years in a futile and farcical role, presiding in routine fashion over the Senate debates which had never interested him, at an age when he might well have shone in more active parts.

His friend Cabot Lodge seemed curiously contented with the outcome. Much might be said of his strange behavior in this affair. Henry Adams, who had known both men for a whole generation, commented privately at the time that Cabot had resolved to "cut the throat" of his friend.[73]

Another intimate friend of both men, Winthrop Chanler, on hearing of the Vice-Presidential nomination, wrote to Roosevelt:

Well, well, well! Long ago, when you first got the nomination for Governor, the astute Cabot told me that he wanted you to be Vice-

President and enumerated all the advantages therein for you and the country. The Wily One has won the day, in spite of your titanic struggles to disappoint him. It is the first time that you have been beat, old man. Let the thought that it took the delegates from every State of the Union to do so, console you. I am glad because your being on the ticket makes a Republican victory almost a certainty. . . ."[74]

Under marching orders, Roosevelt was designated to lead the nationwide stumping for his party, while the President, according to tradition, remained passive. The Vice-Presidential candidate was a "hybrid duckling" whom the Republican party had hatched, and, as Mark Sullivan has said, "the Republican party was Mark Hanna." [75] The humorous conspiracy to dispose of the adventurous amateur in politics and of his uncomfortable "heresies" was heartily enjoyed by boss Platt, Quay, and Boies Penrose, who had a hand in it, as well as by those great financiers who evidently approved of the scheme.

The long-cherished aspirations of the political adventurer and soldier Roosevelt, just as he attained a national popularity, seemed to have ended in farce. The Vice-Presidency was traditionally a "blind alley," a political grave. Yet McKinley and Hanna, heartily disliking the idea of having Roosevelt so near them, had ceased their opposition only at the last hour. In a sense, was not all the busy scheming to "shelve" Roosevelt a tribute to the force he now represented in their little world of practical politics? Unorthodox as were his methods, he had thrust himself into the field. Then by the romantic adventure in the Cuban battlefield he had won crowd popularity, had become for the first time a power as a vote-getter. The crowds in the Western cities had cheered him "like a Presidential candidate" when he attended veterans' gatherings and made a speaking tour in 1899. "Teddy," the emphatic stump speaker, all pent-up passion, with his bared teeth and clenched fists, was now a familiar figure to the millions, a force to be reckoned with. Moreover, it was an evil omen that the Western politi-

[74] T. R. Papers, W. Chanler to T. R., Jul. 10, 1900.
[75] Sullivan, Our Times, Vol. II, p. 380.

cians who disliked the McKinley administration's financial conservatism and the domineering of Mark Hanna, turned to the "unsafe" Roosevelt and joined with Platt and Quay to force him upon the Republican ticket, as a means of expressing their secret discontent. On the floor of the convention at Philadelphia in June, 1900, the little conspiracy had turned into a general ovation for the younger politician.

At any rate, one year and three months later—after the sweeping victory over Bryan—on September 6, 1901, the point of Senator Platt's clever joke was suddenly lost when the assassin Czolgosz discharged his revolver into the body of President McKinley. In high financial circles where solid contentment and confidence had been flourishing, panic raged; and Mr. Morgan himself was heard to swear mighty oaths. Eight days later the gentle William McKinley lay dead, and "that damned cowboy," as Mark Hanna called him, who had come hurrying down from his vacation retreat in the Adirondacks, was being sworn into office as President.

IV. TOWARD NATIONAL
POLITICAL LEADERSHIP

THE MANAGERS of the ruling party had laid their plans with utmost care for 1900 and after. In the campaign for the re-election of McKinley, Mark Hanna, again the national chairman of the Republican party, sought both vindication by the voters and a crushing defeat of the old opposition party, now deeply committed to a partnership with Bryan's Western "radicals." Chairman Hanna, before an Ohio gathering in April, 1900, pointed with pride to the good fortune that had come in foreign war and in home business. His party, he promised, would continue to devote itself mainly to "the material interests" of the country. The opponents urged various reforms or experiments with the money system and the regulation of trusts, and demanded the liberation of the Philippines. In answer, Mark Hanna, often colorful and blunt in speech, coined a slogan from the terminology of poker players, a slogan that was to be a famous synonym for orthodox Republicanism: "I say, 'Stand pat!' "[1]

The silver-tongued Bryan, chosen again as the Democratic standard bearer, inaugurated a nation-wide debate that season upon the issues of "imperialism" and the trusts, which he linked together in a very intelligent manner. Driven by a "greedy commercialism," he argued, our native monopolists, after exploiting the laborer and farmer at will, and crushing out small enterprisers, caused the country to depart from its democratic traditions in subjugating foreign people by force. For the Filipinos, under Agui-

[1] Croly, *Hanna,* pp. 303-304, 417.

naldo, were now engaged in tremendous guerilla war against American armed rule.

But the "boy orator" of Nebraska (no longer a youth) cast a less potent spell over the citizens than in 1896. His favorite financial cure-all, the free coinage of silver, began to seem old-fashioned in an era of roaring prosperity and good prices. Coming to New York during his tour, he had made an open alliance with Tammany Hall, saying: "Great is Tammany! and its prophet is Croker." It was a move that made the reformers and Anti-Imperialists unhappy, though it reflected well the divided character of the Democratic party, an amalgam of the "solid South," the Western agrarians, and the Eastern city machines.

Moreover, the new, glamorous war hero Colonel Roosevelt was a counter-attraction to Bryan during his own nation-wide stumping tour. ". . . The war had had the interesting and powerful psychological effect of diverting the mind of the American from his own woes, his currency troubles, his hard times," Ray Stannard Baker commented at this period. The citizens thought now "of glory and patriotism and expansion. . . ."[2] To these new interests the swashbuckling Roosevelt directed his appeals with a vehemence of speech and gestures that made him a favorite Republican orator. On all other questions Roosevelt spoke in a conservative key, warning his hearers against the insincere demagogism of the adversary, and deploring indiscriminate attacks upon large business interests.

It was Elihu Root, the Secretary of War, however, who sounded the strongest notes on behalf of the Hamiltonian party, which he did in a speech at McKinley's native Canton, Ohio, October 24, 1900. How pleasing this speech was to the greatest patrons of the Republican party is shown by the fact that Mr. J. P. Morgan thought it the finest oration of its kind he had ever heard or read, and obtained a manuscript of it to keep with his collection of the manuscripts of Rousseau and Keats, and the Shakespeare folios.[3]

[2] R. S. Baker, in the *Cosmopolitan Magazine*, May, 1900.
[3] Jessup, *Root*, Vol. II, p. 234.

The material results of "wise and successful government," Root said, were visible on every hand. Never in the history of the world was there a body of people "so well fed, well clothed and well housed." (That very summer, however, a desperate strike of 140,-000 anthracite coal miners in Pennsylvania had been settled only through the urgent intervention of Mark Hanna.) Yes, continued Mr. Root, the country flourished, because "wise government" while not interfering with business and labor "gives to capital that confidence in security for its investment which draws it from the hiding places of distrust." As for Mr. Bryan and his followers, they had "learned nothing and abandoned nothing." They sought now, as in 1896, "to excite animosities and foment discord among the people; to deceive by the false promises of the demagogue; and to profit themselves by creating a warfare of class against class." Mr. Bryan would destroy the trusts? But most of the so-called trusts were great and strong "because they sell cheaper . . . are more efficient. This is not monopoly but competition." Bryan attacked those great industrial enterprises which employed labor and increased the wealth of the country; he had even proposed Federal licensing of large corporations engaged in interstate commerce. "Shades of Thomas Jefferson! What doctrines to be preached in thy name." Here was not "democracy" but domestic "Imperialism" with a vengeance. Absolute control over every business interest in the country would be established at Washington; the effect of politics and favoritism would bring an appalling destruction of values and liberties. Such a proposal was as grotesque as it was absurd.

Bryan had also charged that the existence of a large army, and the growing practice of using it in labor disputes, showed that "it was intended to suppress by force that discontent that ought to be cured by legislation!" But Root in his peroration cried that this was a defamation. "The American soldier is not a danger to liberty and law but their defender. . . . I challenge the just judgment of the people as between him and those men who, for their own selfish purpose, are aspersing and maligning him, while in distant lands he is braving hardship and disease and wounds and death in defence of our country's flag." [4]

The waving of the flag brought cheers that drowned out the cries of the Anti-Imperialists.

The Republican victory of 1900 was more sweeping, more decisive, than in 1896 and brought that which Chairman Hanna had craved: "a clear mandate to govern the country in the interests of business expansion." [5] Greater credit than ever now adhered to the President Maker who, as if with some future design, now for the first time endeavored to speak from the public rostrum and show himself more humorous, more tolerant, more prepossessing than in earlier years.

Years of undisputed rule were easily foreseen for the party of business men; and the large projects which had waited upon the November elections were pushed forward confidently. In New York, on the day of McKinley's second inauguration, the newspapers announced the approaching formation of Mr. Morgan's United States Steel Corporation, the world's first "billion-dollar-trust." At the same time reports were circulated of the combination of two rival transcontinental railroads, the Great Northern and the Northern Pacific, under the leadership of J. P. Morgan and James J. Hill. While in the Senate, Hanna, now a convinced Imperialist, pushed energetically his favorite measure, the Shipping Subsidy Bill, by whose provisions the friendly government would extend direct money subsidies to an expanding merchant marine competing with that of other imperial powers for the world's export trade.

The boom continued, and its foundation, as Hanna said in the summer of 1901, was "confidence—confidence in the future."

Then, on September 6, 1901, the shock of tragedy suddenly shattered all the smoothly working arrangements and plans. Mark Hanna, watching over the deathbed of the President, was seen to break down and weep like a child. Not only was his affection for

[4] Root, *Military and Colonial Policy*, pp. 27-64.
[5] Croly, *Hanna*, p. 341.

McKinley old and strong—though their agreement had become less perfect in the last days—but the patient labor of many years, and big deals planned for the future, seemed undone as the man's life ebbed away.

William McKinley may have been "nothing more than a very supple and highly paid agent of . . . capitalism," as Henry Adams remarked at the time.[6] Yet our government system was cumbersome at best; and McKinley's "suppleness" had made the divided authorities of the government function more effectively in the interests of business expansion than in nearly forty years. This successful functioning was grounded upon a structure of relations and understandings with the national party boss, Hanna, with the veteran leaders of Congress, and with the representatives of great financial and industrial concerns, that was inherently delicate and confidential. To entrust the command of this system to a youthful Theodore Roosevelt seemed grotesque.

It was not that Roosevelt was a Single Taxer or a Socialist in disguise; his background was in fact irreproachably conservative. But this political soldier, this playboy of reform politics, had never worked seriously at any trade; he had never had important business men as his clients nor acquired the respect for money that McKinley instinctively showed. To Hanna he appeared always "impulsive," frivolous, and "unsound"—for who could overlook his remarks upon the "criminal rich" or the "timid," "greedy" commercial interests? His restless ambitions would be urging him always to "do something," to "save" the country, when men like Hanna and Platt knew that there was no danger of a revolution, and all that was needed was to "stand pat." Finally to fix the contrast between the meddlesome young Roosevelt and the veteran, professional politician McKinley, one need but recall the awkward experience of the New York machine, which was a matter of common knowledge in the inner circles of the party. Those letters of agreement defining the sphere of the Governor and the boss, the reservations of Roosevelt regarding affairs affecting his "con-

---

[6] Adams, *Letters*, Vol. II, p. 356.

science"—such things were, of course, wholly unnecessary with a McKinley. Little wonder that a "bear market" raged in Wall Street.

With but a single thought the strong men in the ruling party hastened to encircle the "accidental" President with their counsel and their warnings. At Buffalo, whither Roosevelt had hurried instantly upon news of McKinley's fatal relapse, most of the Cabinet members were assembled. On behalf of the Cabinet, Elihu Root asked him to take the oath of office; and Root has related that Roosevelt whispered a question to him as to whether he should make any statement.

Root told him he thought . . . the country was much disturbed and needed some assurance that would create confidence. He thought Roosevelt should declare his intention to continue unbroken the policy of President McKinley for the peace, prosperity and honor of the country. Roosevelt repeated the words just as Root suggested them to him, and Judge Hazel administered the oath. Root intended that Roosevelt's statement should constitute a binding obligation.[7]

The power of Mark Hanna, Roosevelt recalled in later years, was "such as no other man in our history has had." He was aware of this power, hedging in his own office, as McKinley's unofficial prime minister and national boss called upon him in Buffalo on that same morning. And to Hanna the same assurances given to the Cabinet were repeated. That evening Hanna returned by appointment, and the two men, who had never liked each other, held frank, intimate conversation. Without any beating about the bush, and without unmanly bowings to the new rising sun, Hanna assured Roosevelt that he would do all in his power to make his administration a success—subject to Roosevelt's following the McKinley policies. Hanna made it clear, however, that he was not committing himself to favor Roosevelt's nomination at the next election, but must leave that to the future to decide. Roosevelt thanked him and told him that he understood his position.

[7] Jessup, *op. cit.*, Vol. I, p. 238.

2

Theodore Roosevelt at forty-three aroused the interest of the country as the youngest President in our history, and one of the most attractive and sympathetic figures who had reached that office in recent decades. He assumed his burdens and dignities cheerfully on the whole, despite the tragic circumstances under which they had been gained. His energetic and informal methods of working, the ease with which he received and dismissed hundreds of visitors every day, his lively sallies, his original turns of speech, all occupied the press and the popular mind. "Every day or two," a correspondent reported, "he rattles the dry bones of precedent and causes sedate Senators and heads of departments to look over their spectacles in consternation." [8] From the outside, Roosevelt's many-sided career now appeared dazzling, meteoric; his personal force, irresistible.

In reality, Roosevelt knew that he was, so to speak, a *captive* President. As at Albany, so at Washington a nearly omnipotent boss, with power to make or ruin him, stood close by. Deferentially Roosevelt invited the boss to hold conferences with him at an early date at Washington; and from Cleveland came Hanna's reply, hinting plainly that the President must wait until he arrived to advise him "on many important matters to be considered from a political standpoint. . . ." Meanwhile, Hanna urged, " 'Go slow.' You will be besieged from all sides. . . . *Hear* them all patiently but *reserve* your decision—unless in cases which may require immediate attention. Then if my advice is of importance, Cortelyou [Private Secretary to the President] can reach me over the 'long distance.' "

Roosevelt answered that he would do exactly as advised. He would "go slow." [9]

Indeed from all sides, even by his relatives, he was besieged with the warnings to be cautious, to be "close-mouthed" and con-

[8] Sullivan, *op. cit.*, Vol. II, p. 394.
[9] *T. R. Papers*, Hanna to T. R., Oct. 12, 1901; T. R. to Hanna, Oct. 12, 1901.

servative. In truth, he understood the situation; and the urgency of these warnings seemed scarcely necessary. To his friend and biographer, Joseph B. Bishop, he confided his intention of avoiding disputes, of seeking to work with the managers of his party, rather than spend his term in strife with them as Grover Cleveland had done.

Moreover, he had felt in honor bound to retain McKinley's Cabinet, even his Private Secretary, Cortelyou, at his side. It was a conservative Cabinet at best; and two of its leading members were old friends and patrons, given to treating him with amused tolerance rather than respect. To the right of him sat Secretary of State John Hay; to the left, Secretary of War Elihu Root. The connections of these men ran straight to the highest circles of Wall Street. Possibly Hay was "one wheel of the old machine of Hanna and Pierpont Morgan, and Root the other," as the old gossip, Henry Adams, surmised.[10]

Another thread which led to the House of Morgan was the appointment by Roosevelt of Robert Bacon, one of the bank's partners, as Assistant Secretary of State—Bacon had been an admired classmate at Harvard. The frequent visits of George W. Perkins, whom Roosevelt had met at Albany, and who was generally charged with handling lobbying and political relations for J. P. Morgan and Company, also pointed to the continued political ascendancy of the great banking house. Perkins wrote frequently from Number 23 Wall Street to the young President whom he warmly liked, giving information of large financial projects in a manner that might commend them to Presidential tolerance. In urgent cases Mr. Perkins would sometimes call the White House on the long-distance telephone.

With regard to legislative matters, as in the preparation of his first message to Congress, Roosevelt went directly to Senator Aldrich's "Philosopher's Club" for advice and approval. "I shall want to see you before I write my message," he told the ancient Senator Allison of Iowa, "because there are two or three points

[10] Adams, *Letters*, Vol. II, p. 383; letter of Apr. 6, 1902.

upon which I do not desire to touch, until after consultation with you." [11] Mark Hanna, John Hay, Elihu Root, Aldrich, Allison, O. E. Platt, Robert Bacon, and George W. Perkins—all were consulted in the production of Roosevelt's first, eagerly awaited message to Congress.

Yet, notwithstanding these eminent advisers, Theodore Roosevelt as a young Republican had a contribution of his own to make. He clung tenaciously to those principles he had begun to advocate as Governor. In a confidential letter to his brother-in-law, Douglas Robinson, a New York stock broker who had besought him not to "upset the confidence . . . of the business world," he wrote in very characteristic terms that he intended to propound an attitude of even-handed "righteousness" toward the trusts.

> I intend to be most conservative, but in the interests of the corporations themselves and above all in the interests of the country, I intend to pursue cautiously, but steadily, the course to which I have been publicly committed . . . and which I am certain is the right course.[12]

For two years, as we have noted, the great movement toward concentrating industries into single trusts had been absorbing the attention of the country. Then, in the spring of 1901, came the launching of the colossal steel trust, followed by the fierce financial struggle for control of the Northern Pacific Railroad, which terminated in the pooling of the opposing Morgan and Harriman interests in the Northern Securities Company, a $400,000,000 holding company. McKinley himself had noticed, at the time of the Northern Pacific "corner" and panic, the virulence of the trust issue, and according to his official biographer, Olcott, during his second term "reached a firm determination to deal seriously with the evils inseparable from the rapid multiplication of the so-called trusts." [13] Roosevelt had learned that President McKinley had been turning over in his mind what to do in this matter. One often-advocated method of approach would have been to mod-

---

[11] Stephenson, *Aldrich*, p. 174.
[12] Oct. 14, 1901; Bishop, *op. cit.*, Vol. I, p. 159.
[13] Olcott, *McKinley*, Vol. II, pp. 299-300.

erate the protective tariff, which was "the mother of trusts." Despite his lifelong championing of protection, McKinley's final public speech at Buffalo proposed a series of reciprocity treaties with various countries for the mutual reduction of tariffs.

Roosevelt in preparing his first message had recourse to this identical solution: reciprocity. But when he broached this point to Senator Nelson Aldrich on October 28, 1901, he was advised to drop the whole business. This the President humbly agreed to do, saying: "All I shall do about the [reciprocity] treaties will be to say I call the attention of the Senate to them." Aldrich was also promised "a last looking over" of the message.[14]

To Hanna, intimately connected with the great oil and steel trades, Roosevelt also turned for advice on the trust question. Hanna wrote:

I have been thinking (hard) about that portion of your message regarding "Trusts." It seems to me that there are some suggestions which may furnish ammunition to the enemy in a political contest—the question of "overcapitalization" which seemed to have created a doubt in your own mind strikes me as a delicate one.

The mention of "overcapitalization" Hanna advised him to drop entirely, assuring him also that organized labor was in general not opposed to combinations of capital. "They are not worried about the 'Trust' question. . . . Therefore may I suggest that you do not give it so much prominence in your message." Roosevelt had proposed some form of enforced publicity and investigation of books; but Hanna remarked, "The inquisition feature is most objectionable. . . . Pardon my suggestions—which have come from careful consideration. I see 'dynamite' in it." [15]

Roosevelt thereupon dropped his reflections upon the "overcapitalization" of the trusts.

True to character, Roosevelt in his first message to Congress did sound, at times, a critical note toward the huge monopolies whose apparition now frightened the average citizen. And this

[14] Stephenson, op. cit., p. 180.
[15] T. R. Papers, Hanna to T. R., Nov. 10, 1901.

was the distinguishing feature of a very ambitious, long, involved paper, which touched a hundred different topics. He pointed frankly to the evil concerning which others had been silent. He also retained the statement that "knowledge of the facts—publicity" should be secured as a means of keeping the trusts a force for good and curbing their "occasional" tendencies to evil. When some of the corporations in their "eagerness to reach great industrial achievements" went too far, the government, he suggested, might inform itself and, while not "prohibiting" or "confining," should in some manner "supervise and regulate."

But modern business was delicate and could easily be thrown out of adjustment, he admitted. "Prosperity can never be created by law alone. . . ." It was not true, he argued, that "the rich were growing richer and the poor poorer." The country continued in an amazingly healthy and flourishing condition, thanks to Republican rule, and nothing must be done to disturb this needlessly.

Such is the gist of an essentially middle-road document that brought welcome relief to the anxious watchers in the counting-houses. It was a performance that ran constantly from "one hand" to the "other hand," as the informal political philosopher, Mr. Dooley, soon noted. Yet to dismiss it as purely opportunist would be to miss its nuances and to differentiate a Theodore Roosevelt in no way from his predecessor McKinley. Though still very moderate, the expression of a spirit critical toward the canons of the respectable can already be observed here. There are also, in references to the new imperial policies, accents of an intense nationalism. But here Roosevelt differs from the older leaders of the Hamiltonian party, who ignored the popular demand for the safeguarding of democratic, equalitarian rights under new forms of attack; he differs from them in seeking to give "a democratic meaning and purpose to the Hamiltonian tradition and method." [16]

Theodore Roosevelt, arriving suddenly in the office of President with its enormous powers under the Constitution, found that

[16] Croly, *The Promise of American Life*, pp. 168-169.

he actually held not much real power. Control of the party organization and of parliamentary activities seemed pretty thoroughly vested in Hanna, Aldrich, and a few of their associates. These men with their managerial or pivotal controls, buttressed by vast resources of money, could easily have moved to discredit and crush the unwelcome successor of McKinley, though it would have been a costly business, as in the case of Andrew Johnson. But Roosevelt acted warily, and, at the outset, respected the existing arrangements. He respected the huge, crude strength of Hanna, and the silent, confident force of the more polished Aldrich. How much he deferred to these men and their lieutenants is shown by the disposition of Federal patronage in his first administration—an inescapable sign, since the machinery of their "indirect" rulership rested as always upon the loaves and fishes of office.

To the famous corned-beef-hash breakfasts which Hanna served at the Hotel Arlington in Washington, Roosevelt came frequently for "consultations," just as he had formerly come to Platt's Sunday breakfasts in New York. A stupendous amount of patronage, in the shape of petty appointments, continued to be cleared through Hanna in 1902 and 1903, as is shown by the voluminous private correspondence between the two men. "I see by the papers," runs a characteristic message from Hanna, "that you are thinking of appointing Mr. ——— as ———. Please go slow about this. Will see you tomorrow." [17] Thus the army of Republican "workers," holding post-office, revenue, and lighthouse jobs throughout the country, continued to be provisioned by the national party boss.

In a similar manner Senator Matthew Stanley Quay of Pennsylvania, almost as powerful a boss as Hanna, was freely provided with minor offices. Concerning this old knave, who had been close to the gates of the penitentiary, Roosevelt once remarked, shrugging his shoulders, that it was not his fault if the people of Pennsylvania had elected the man as United States Senator. Also in the Western states, Roosevelt reinforced party orthodoxy against in-

---

[17] *T. R. Papers*, Hanna to T. R., Dec. 5, 1902.

surgence, by furnishing Henry C. Payne, his Postmaster General —rather than Governor La Follette—with Federal patronage in Wisconsin. Payne, who "represented" public-utility and railroad interests, was a "Standpatter."

In quiet fashion, Roosevelt passed out the desired loaves and fishes to these men who dominated what would later be known as our "invisible government." More publicly, however, he would point with pride to his selection of meritorious and distinguished young administrators to office, wherever possible, for in his heart the Mugwump, the civil-service reformer, still lived. Regarding the administration of the new colonies, where war and danger lurked, he decreed publicly that "no appointments . . . will be dictated or controlled by political considerations." [18]

But Theodore Roosevelt was never made to be a yielding, a complaisant character. Though he found his sphere sharply limited, he could not refrain from pressing instinctively, everywhere, to win more power; and this unremitting process was to end by changing the very traditions surrounding the office of the President.

At Albany he had learned how to carry out "horse trades" even with the wily Tom Platt, winning consent to reformist legislation, and credit for ousting crooked office-holders, in return for concessions to the boss's requirements in other directions. So in Washington, in a series of conferences with the wise old men of the party, the younger politician played a shrewd, determined game for the sake of concessions opening the road for his own ambitions.

A very plausible and appealing theory has been worked out by the late Professor Nathaniel W. Stephenson (based on a study of the Aldrich private papers) that Roosevelt at the outset of his term worked out a truce or "gentleman's agreement" with Hanna and Aldrich, which though circumscribing his field of operations gave him a free hand in certain areas. On August 23, 1902, there was a private gathering of the elder Senators, including Mark Hanna, at Oyster Bay, for an all-day conference. Again, on Sep-

[18] Bishop, *op. cit.*, Vol. I, p. 155.

tember 16, 1902, Roosevelt sailed across Long Island Sound to Narragansett, near Newport, where Aldrich's great castle stood, and conferred all day with the gentleman from Rhode Island and his colleagues in the Senate.

The upshot was that the President agreed to leave undisturbed the protective tariff system and the monetary system, those monumental achievements of the Republican party. However, as reports ran, he was "to have his head on all things outside of economics and finance." For instance, Roosevelt might have thought of "Bryanizing" a little. There was now a powerful popular movement for the Eight-Hour Day earnestly pushed by the trade unions and many liberal sympathizers throughout the country. Did Roosevelt agree with Hanna, Aldrich, Cannon, and company to avoid this subject? The idea of the Eight-Hour Day for labor was to spread widely, but without the blessing of the White House, where the counsels of Aldrich, Spooner, Allison, O. H. Platt (of Connecticut), and Mark Hanna were to prevail.[19]

Concerning the whole vague "trust question," which engrossed public opinion, the Republican elders, save for Senator Hanna, showed a certain resignation amounting almost to indifference. Much doubt existed that the government could actually curb the monopolistic corporations under existing laws and court rulings. Moreover, the legal character of the trusts was now being rapidly transformed by clever lawyers into new guises permitted by the New Jersey and Delaware charters. When Roosevelt, soon afterward, opened a government suit against one of the notorious new "holding companies," none of the Aldrich group objected.

Shortly after the second of these conferences, in September, 1902, Roosevelt departed upon a Western tour, and stopping at Logansport, Indiana, made an important "policy" speech touching questions of tariff and finance. Though there was said to be much discontent in the Middle West regarding the tariff and the trusts, he urged the need for continuity in our government revenue laws. To make abrupt changes was dangerous. "What we really need is

---

[19] Stephenson, *op. cit.*, p. 196; p. 243; Appendix, p. 453.

to treat the tariff as a business proposition," he declared, "and not from the standpoint of a political party." The nation could adjust its business to a given tariff schedule. But changes should be managed by experts, working "primarily from the standpoint of the business interests."

The philosophers of the Senate, both Allison and Spooner, at once wrote Roosevelt that his were brave words, "sound and wise . . . will do much to clear the atmosphere." They concluded: "Have done immeasurable good." And he replied (to Allison): "I thought I had substantially the idea that we agreed upon at the time you were in Oyster Bay." [20]

Roosevelt in short was not to disturb the economic legislation which favored industrial capitalism, nor the financial policy, the gold standard, favored by the Eastern bankers. In truth he was never highly interested in these matters, confessing that economic questions were beyond his grasp. But, in compensation, he could pursue freely a "spirited" foreign policy, and he could engage to his heart's content in vigorous but essentially "moral" crusades against the trusts, those "heejeous monsthers," as Mr. Dooley styled them.

3

As at Albany, so at Washington, Roosevelt studied the popular mood carefully and searched for Live Issues, the ideological raw material of the genuine politician. Nor were they far to seek.

For two years an agitated discussion of the coming of the great trusts was whipped up in the popular press; though it did not reach the intensity of the period between 1904 and 1912, discussion of the trust question was the paramount subject of the Rooseveltian Era. In the Middle West the problem of the high cost of living aroused discontent among an important minority that had always been allied with the Republican party. The high cost of living was widely attributed there to the appearance of the monopolies in steel, nails, barbed wire, shoes, wool, tobacco, all

[20] *T. R. Papers*, T. R. to W. Allison, Sept. 27, 1902.

the consumer goods which the farmer must purchase. In the usually safe State of Iowa, the rise of Albert Cummins as a dominant political leader, toward 1901, was a symptom; Cummins, though a Republican, preached tariff reduction as a measure with which to combat the trusts. In Wisconsin, where the radical La Follette now ruled, a strong anti-railroad movement flourished. And in Minnesota the merging of the two competing trunk lines, the Great Northern and Northern Pacific, had led to an attempt at a suit by Governor Van Sant against the parent holding company, the Northern Securities.

Rumblings of protest could be heard by sensitive ears throughout the Mississippi Valley, and especially in the "Granger" states, which so often threatened to quit the orbit of the Republican party. This movement, it was plain to see, Bryan would attempt again to take advantage of. In the winter of 1902, Bryan's followers in Congress, such as Albert S. Burleson of Texas, prepared to open fire upon the new President because of his initial "mildness" toward the big corporations.[21] But though breaches showed themselves here and there in the historic alliance between the Eastern capitalists and the Middle-Western farmers, it is doubtful that Hanna or Aldrich would have moved. They would have continued to "stand pat," while the breach widened.

Roosevelt, however, held different views; and was as confident of the correctness of his judgment as upon the eve of the Spanish-American War. He agreed with Bryan that the trust question was the Live Issue of the day. But in attempting vigorous legal action against the trusts, he alarmed the wise old men of the party far less than if he had struck at the protective tariff.

Not long before this, the railroad bankers, after the violent "Northern Pacific panic" of May, 1901, had composed their quarrel and decided to fling together, by a simple exchange of stock, the assets of three giant trunk lines. This alarmed even men of conservative opinion. A few more such moves on the chessboard of finance capitalism and, as Professor W. Z. Ripley com-

[21] *Bryan Papers,* W. J. Bryan to A. C. Burleson, Mar. 11, 1902.

mented at the time, the industries of the nation might be contained within one great holding company, controlled from one banking office, such as that at the corner of Broad and Wall Street in New York. The Northern Securities Company was widely held to be a menacing "Trojan Horse." James J. Hill, who was to be its titular head, admitted afterward that there had been talk of having him manage all of the railroads west of the Mississippi, covering two-thirds of the area of the United States, by means of one great holding company. Even Mark Hanna thought that Hill and Morgan might have gone too far, and McKinley himself would have acted against them in time.[22]

Shortly after his entrance into office, early in February, he asked his Attorney General, Philander C. Knox, who was formerly the attorney of Andrew Carnegie, for an opinion as to the legality of the new railroad holding company, the Northern Securities, whose creation had caused such an outcry. Knox advised that it was a violation of the Sherman Anti-Trust Act of 1890. Whereupon, in absolute confidence, Roosevelt ordered Mr. Knox to prosecute and bring the case to court.

News of the sudden, secretly prepared government action came to financial circles on February 18, 1902, with the effect of the proverbial bombshell. Mr. J. Pierpont Morgan, receiving the news while at dinner, appeared to lose his appetite, and expressed strong resentment at not having been told of the action in advance. Neither Elihu Root nor John Hay had known anything of it.[23]

Three days after the announcement of the government's suit to dissolve the Northern Securities Company, Mr. Morgan, "chaperoned" by Senators Mark Hanna and Chauncey Depew, arrived at the White House to pay a social call upon the new President. Theodore Roosevelt had met Mr. Morgan before and knew him slightly. But the encounter was dramatic.

The one man taciturn, huge, old, craggy and ugly of counte-

---

[22] Pyle, *James J. Hill*, Vol. II, p. 185; Beer, *op. cit.*, p. 246.

[23] "Root was much upset by it." (Adams, *Letters*, Vol. II, p. 374; Feb. 23, 1902.)

nance, was now almost a legendary figure in newspaper prose and caricature, legendary enough to terrify little children. Actually he was not the wealthiest of financiers, but the aggressive leader, heart and soul of the movement of combination in industry and finance, omnipotent in his control of affiliated banks and trust companies, seemingly invincible in his gigantic promotions. The movement he led, moreover, was held to be a part of progress and "natural evolution," hence inevitable. Creating ever new masses of debts and securities, huge new areas of capital investment, Morgan accelerated a tremendous credit inflation which wrought for a time a "boundless prosperity." He now stood at the very zenith of his strange, lonely career, as one of the sovereigns of the modern world.

The comparatively youthful, ebullient Roosevelt, on the other hand, was a kind of political adventurer to Mr. Morgan. He had never been in trade, though he sprang from the more comfortable or upper middle class. He had been a writer of books, a sportsman, a soldier, a government official. He occupied, in fact, a middle ground, and had said with conviction in his First Annual Message to Congress: "We are neither for the rich man as such nor the poor man as such; we are for the upright man, rich or poor." He had a thoroughly middle-class fear of labor in its militant moods, and had shown that he would not hesitate to use force against it. But on the other hand he shared a growing resentment and fear also of the mighty industrial overlords, including the one before him, who had accumulated a degree of power that seemed to brook all efforts of government to restrain them. He would soon say: "Of all forms of tyranny, the least attractive and the most vulgar is the tyranny of mere wealth, the tyranny of a plutocracy." The accent here upon vulgarity is not of the proletarian rebel, but of the aristocrat who, aware of the diminished power of his class, nevertheless professes to scorn mere "money-grubbers."

Linked with the aristocratic impulse another impulse could be noted, typical of a large *bureaucratic* class, the men in political or military service in Europe as well as America at this time, who stood outside of commercial life, but often felt bitterly that their devotion and exertions were unjustly overlooked. Roosevelt shared their "moral" conviction that ambitions might be nobly satisfied, not merely by the acquisition of wealth but by a patriotic career in arms, in service, or in directing grand imperial plans for the glory of country and people.[24] In short, no two men could have offered greater contrast than the youthful statesman and the old banker who confronted each other.

At this time there were few men who cared to face the gaze of this fierce old man. Railroad presidents and great bankers habitually avoided debate with "Jupiter" Morgan over his commands. Now Morgan evidently measured the politician and pondered over the possible difficulties he presented, for this politician was unlike others, whom he usually despised. Roosevelt, who had faced death in the Bad Lands of the Dakotas and in Cuba, stood on the precarious ground he had chosen. He was not to be dealt with by a direct approach. Morgan's impulse to violence, expressed in a letter he wrote the President from his hotel that night—a letter never delivered—was in some manner checked by his counselors. The first collision between these two men was less than deadly.

It was probably at a later, less public conference, that day (February 21, 1902) or the day after, that Morgan's complaints at not having been informed in time were heard.[25] It was then that Morgan made his famous, blunt proposal: "If we have done anything wrong, send your man [meaning the Attorney General] to my man [naming his lawyer] and they can fix it up." The President, however, held this to be impossible; while the Attorney

---

[24] Cf. C. A. Beard and A. Vagts, *The New Republic*, June 28, 1939, for a discussion of this bureaucratic outlook on life. Mahan in a letter wrote: ". . . The mere *opportunist*, the mere dollars and cents view, the mere appeal to comfort and well being as distinct from righteousness and foresight, in a word, mere selfishness and regard for present ease are being dropped rapidly behind and nobler, if somewhat crude and vainglorious, feelings are taking possession of the people. For after all, if the love of mere glory is selfish, it is not quite as low as the love of mere comfort." (Puleston, *Mahan*, p. 200.)

[25] Pringle, *op. cit.*, p. 256.

General, perhaps simulating the Rooseveltian pugnacity, added that they intended not to "fix it," but to "stop it."

"Are you going to attack my other interests, the Steel Trust and the others?" Morgan asked. To learn of this was the real object of his call.

"Certainly not," replied Roosevelt, "unless we find out that . . . they have done something that we regard as wrong."

After the banker was gone, Roosevelt pointed out to Knox how well "the Wall Street point of view" had been illuminated at this meeting. Mr. Morgan, he reflected, "could not help regarding me as a big rival operator, who either intended to ruin all his interests or else could be induced to come to an agreement to ruin none." [26]

Though it amused the President, there was not a little allegorical truth and keen insight in this notion of Mr. Morgan's. The political man could rise to the force of "a big rival operator," instead of remaining merely a "supple, paid agent" of the capitalist. That the political government might stand "above" the great capitalists, and act as impartial broker between the other great pressure groups, was another question that would wait long for its answer.

Meanwhile the actual outcome of the suit against the Northern Securities Company waited two years, until March, 1904, in the hands of the Supreme Court, which then issued a dissolution order favorable to the government's contention. The disposition of the company's assets, controlled by the court, inflicted no serious punishment upon the monopolists. Jim Hill, who angrily called Theodore Roosevelt "a political adventurer" and a poseur, vowed in 1902 that the purposes of the railway magnates would be met "in another way." Two certificates of stock, printed in different colors, would be issued instead of one, and that, as Hill remarked derisively, "would constitute the main difference." [27]

[26] Bishop, *op. cit.*, Vol. I, pp. 184-185.
[27] Pyle, *J. J. Hill*, Vol. II, p. 187.

The press and public opinion heartily approved of Roosevelt's suit against Northern Securities—though conservative organs denounced the action. Joseph Pulitzer, the owner of the independent, Democratic *World*, though personally hostile to Roosevelt, supported him at this time, on the ground that his actions appeased the masses of people. "The greatest breeder of discontent and socialism," wrote Pulitzer to his editor Frank Cobb, "is the . . . popular belief that the law is one thing for the rich and another for the poor." [28]

It was with the purpose of contending against such dangerous counsels of despair as Pulitzer alluded to, that Roosevelt, in the late summer of 1902, took the stump in a speaking tour of New England and the Middle West. In explaining and defending his action, which had roused up a spirited controversy, he argued that the trust question was essentially a *moral* question, and that he endeavored but to deal with it righteously. It was inevitable, with his half-aristocratic, half-bureaucratic outlook (detached from the economic motives of both the House of Morgan and the American Federation of Labor), that he should seek a synthesis emphasizing "the superiority of the moral to the material."

"Material prosperity without the moral lift toward righteousness," left to its own devices, he said, would bring but unhappiness and degradation to our country.[29]

He prophesied dangers to come from the jealousy of the classes.

Not only do the wicked flourish, when the times are such that most men flourish, but what is worse, the spirit of envy and jealousy and hatred springs up in the breasts of those who, though they may be doing fairly well themselves, yet see others who are no more deserving, doing far better.[30]

Finally, Roosevelt argued, as one who but opposed the "misuse of property," who would prevent "wrongdoing" lest greater wrongdoing follow:

[28] Seitz, *Pulitzer*, p. 320.
[29] Speech at Bangor, Sept. 13, 1902.
[30] Speech at Providence, Aug. 23, 1902.

I am far from being against property when I ask that the question of the trusts be taken up. I am acting in the most conservative sense in property's interest. . . . Because *when you can make it evident that all men, big and small alike, have to obey the law, you are putting the safeguard of law around all men.*[31]

Roosevelt's words were timely; they came at a moment when the bright noon of McKinleyan prosperity sensibly declined; though business activity remained high, the distinctly higher cost of living began now to offset the gains of the four boom years after 1898. Roosevelt's mounting popular strength, however, maintained a unified support for his party among its old followers in the Congressional elections of 1902. His popular strength waxed even greater as a result of the part he played in the great coal miners' strike of that autumn. Here too he came to grips with the most powerful capitalists of the age; and here too his chosen tactics and maxims were vividly illustrated in action.

4

By 1898 the anthracite coal fields of eastern Pennsylvania were completely dominated by the combination of five coal-carrying railroads, either controlled or financed by the Vanderbilt family and Morgan. Centralization and well-maintained prices brought handsome profits to the coal operators and the railways, but the distressed position of the miners reflected the remarkable unevenness of our prosperity. The average earnings of a miner were increased, but the higher costs of the boom years after 1897 brought a sharp decline in "real" wages, leaving him not much better off than in 1880. Thus a union movement, corresponding in force to the monopoly movement at the top, and spurred by desperation, swept the coal fields in 1897.

Under the inspired leadership of the young, self-educated miner John Mitchell, the United Mine Workers organized the anthracite field and conducted the successful strike of 1900, bring-

[31] Speech at Boston, Sept. 6, 1902; italics mine.

ing a 10 per cent increase of wages, which was forced—during a Presidential campaign—by secret pressure of frightened Republican party leaders. In 1902 the miners struck again, this time with the object especially of winning union recognition as well as wage improvement. But the large mine operators, which meant the coal railroads typified by President George F. Baer of the Reading, were adamant; this time they would brook no secret political pressure and were resolved to administer—as Henry Frick used to say—a memorable lesson to the union.

On May 12, 1902, some 140,000 miners ceased work and remained idle throughout the spring and summer. Mark Hanna's National Civic Federation, organized lately to conciliate labor and capital, and numbering distinguished industrialists in its membership, sought in vain to intervene. Appeals were directed to President Roosevelt to press arbitration upon both parties, but no easy solution offered itself to him. An incident of mid-July, when a friend of the miners inveigled out of President Baer, and made public, the famous "divine right" letter—to the effect that "the Christian men to whom God in His infinite wisdom has given the control of the property interests of this country," would alone care for the interests of the laboring men—both hardened the miners and rallied public opinion to their cause.

Ten thousand militia patrolled the Pennsylvania coal field by September, but the mines were shut down, and their owners called for more troops, and Federal troops, as a means of protecting the strikebreakers whom they tried to bring in. Yet the union men behaved with admirable discipline and committed no violence. Meanwhile coal grew scarce and dear, rising from $5 a ton to over $30. September brought the first hints of autumn cool, especially to New England, whose high Republican leaders trembled for the consequences of the strike.

Lodge, in great anxiety, wrote Roosevelt in September that the price of coal was something one could not "argue with." The schoolhouses were closing. "Political disaster" loomed ahead. He ended: "We have powerful friends in business. . . . Can nothing be done—*not in public,* of course, I know that is out of the question, but by pressing the operators?" [32]

The coal barons remained obdurate. But behind the coal barons there stood, as everyone knew, one omnipotent being whose command they would doubtless heed more readily than that of the King in Heaven, whom Mr. Baer professed to worship. When interviewed at the end of August, the great man declared, however, that he knew nothing of the strike; he would not interfere. [33]

Meanwhile, "little flames of violence began to flicker out here and there, where cars carrying coal were seized and looted as they trundled past the dwellings of people who had no fires." [34] Inconspicuous news reports such as that of "prominent citizens of Arcola, Ill., including officials, lawyers, ministers," seizing a coal train and looting the coal, figured in the newspapers. "The coal strike of 1902 revealed how quickly a people's reverence for law becomes exhausted, when the pinch comes." [35]

Though the mood of alarm spread, and heart-rending petitions reached the President from miners and consumers, he remained embarrassed for a time. He had no legal authority to take action, he recognized; he had behaved independently toward the "big monied men," and doubted whether he could ask them for favors or exert secret pressure upon them; lastly, the coal operators were the more obstinate, because they had yielded to their employees owing to political interference in 1900.

Nevertheless he consulted Elihu Root, and turned to Mark Hanna for aid. The latter proceeded directly to New York on September 29, and saw in secret both Mr. Morgan and John Mitchell, President of the United Mine Workers. The terms of a settlement appeared within reach. But Mr. Baer, on behalf of the mine owners, when called upon in Philadelphia, absolutely refused to agree to a settlement save one brought about by starv-

[32] Lodge, *Correspondence,* Vol. I, p. 528.
[33] Corey, *House of Morgan,* p. 213.
[34] Wister, *Roosevelt,* p. 195.
[35] L. J. Ghent, *Mass and Class,* p. 127.

ing out his employees.[36] Finally, at the urgent suggestion of Governor Murray Crane of Massachusetts, Roosevelt summoned representatives of both sides to a conference at Washington on October 3, 1902.

Roosevelt appealed to the adversaries in the name of patriotism. Mr. George F. Baer, however, supported by his colleagues, burst into round abuse of the President, both for not having sent Federal troops and for having failed to prosecute the miners' union under the Sherman Anti-Trust Act, as Cleveland had done in the railway strike of 1894. Baer referred to the mild and personable Mitchell as a "criminal." The more courteous head of the miners' union, however, expressed willingness to submit the case to an impartial commission appointed by the President, a proposal which the latter considered eminently fair.

The conference ended in a storm, but Roosevelt now used the newspapers with his habitual skill, to make the public understand the cause of the deadlock; and popular anger at the coal barons mounted swiftly.

He wrote to Hanna of his disappointment over the failure of the October 3 conference, not only "because of the great misery ensuing for the mass of our people," but because the obstinacy of the coal operators would serve to "double the burden on us who stand between them and socialistic action." (Always, among the Rooseveltians there was talk of saving the country from socialism.) He concluded with the warning words: "I must now think very seriously what the next move shall be. A coal famine in the winter is an ugly thing." [37]

The situation was actually full of explosive possibilities. Cabot Lodge, beside himself with anxiety, wrote on October 11, 1902, that "The Socialistic feeling is growing apace, and the demand that the government take the mines—one of the greatest disasters that could befall us." [38] Yet the days passed, and Morgan, whose word many felt could end the deadlocked strike, waited silently, as with iron nerves.

[36] Croly, *Hanna*, p. 398.　　[38] Lodge, *Correspondence*, Vol. I, p. 539.
[37] *Ibid.*, pp. 399-400.

Roosevelt, however, armed with immense authority and power, showed a resourcefulness hitherto unsuspected of him. With a purposeful indiscretion he began to utter thoughts out loud concerning the possibility of calling out the army. He informed his Cabinet that he should not even ask their advice, but would "act just as if we were in a state of war"—that is, with emergency powers. He might take over the coal mines, and the army would "dispossess the operators and run the mines as a receiver. . . ." [39] Plans for such action were actually drawn up with General Schofield, the army chief; and with Senator Quay it was also arranged that at a given signal the Governor of Pennsylvania was to ask for Federal troops to halt disorders.

Elihu Root, the old Wall Street attorney in the Cabinet, was worried enough to volunteer his aid to the President. He relates, in a memorandum of the affair:

. . . Roosevelt contemplated sending troops to take possession of the mines. I do not know how far he intended to go. Theodore was a bit of a bluffer occasionally, and at the same time he had the nerve to go on—to take a chance . . . and trust the country would back him up. [40]

On October 9, 1902, Root wrote to Morgan, outlining a plan for a commission of arbitration "appointed by the President or by you," and asking for an early appointment. Two days later he arrived in New York and clambered aboard *The Corsair*, Morgan's very appropriately named yacht which rode at anchor in the bay. His impressions of Theodore's "impulsiveness" and "nerve," traits not hitherto or lately encountered in our political leaders, must have been effectively conveyed to Morgan. With the latter's approval, Root wrote an agreement, which he brought back to Washington.

The coal operators were advised by Morgan to accept a commission of arbitration, whose membership excluded any representative of the miners' union, being composed of several representatives of the mine owners, a philanthropic minister (designated

[39] Roosevelt, *An Autobiography*, p. 475.
[40] Jessup, *op. cit.*, Vol. I, p. 275.

by name), and a university professor versed in sociology. Upon this basis, with only minor changes, the strike conference proceeded to a settlement on October 15, 1902.

There was a last-minute hitch over the composition of the arbitration commission. President John Mitchell, on behalf of the mine workers, insisted that unless a labor man were included the pretense of arbitration was absurd, and his men would not abide by the decision. Frantic long-distance telephoning took place in the early morning hours of October 15 between the White House and the Morgan office, where Mr. Baer sat, as obdurate as ever, declaring that only a "sociologist" and no laboring man would be acceptable among the arbitrators. Suddenly it dawned upon Roosevelt that the mine operators would rather endure civil war and revolution than have anyone described *as a laboring man* upon the board of arbitration. But if he were called something else—"an eminent sociologist"—they would relent. Roosevelt recalls that he was overwhelmed with a sense of mingled relief and amusement when he realized that while the operators would "submit to anarchy rather than have Tweedledum, yet if I would call it Tweedledee they would accept with rapture. . . ." And he adds with scorn: "It gave me an illuminating glimpse into one corner of the mighty brains of those 'captains of industry.'" He thereupon gave the hononary degree of Eminent Sociologist to one E. E. Clark, grand chief of the Order of Railway Conductors, and the commission was complete.

At the other end of the telephone in New York, Robert Bacon and George W. Perkins, the Morgan partners, "eagerly ratified" this face-saving formula, and after some trouble forced the mine owners' spokesman, Baer, to accept it.[41]

The verdict of the arbitration committee was a compromise, which the miners afterward felt heavily favored their employers. Only two of the miners' demands had been partially met: the eight-hour demand was compromised at nine hours; the call for a wage increase of 20 per cent was answered with 10 per cent. The

[41] *T. R. Papers*, Roosevelt to H. C. Lodge, Oct. 17, 1902.

other demands were ignored by the arbitration board. Most important of all, union recognition, the real basis of the strike, the real lever of future collective bargaining, was rejected. Thus the road was left open for renewal of the struggle. The miners were none too happy with the outcome of their drawn combat; several times the vote of their delegates had been necessary to stiffen John Mitchell's attitude and prevent him from yielding to a settlement that would have been a complete victory for the operators. Whatever was won, was won not because of Roosevelt's "sympathy" but because of the determined and disciplined spirit of the mine workers.

However, they had gone promptly back to work, as the arbitration commission began its deliberations; coal moved again, and the whole country heaved a sigh of relief and applauded the President. The lion's share of the victory went to him for having forced a settlement of some kind, with bold hands. He could claim that he had defended the legitimate rights of labor, yet had been just to both sides.

Even the extremely conservative New York *Tribune* applauded the "generous and patriotic act of the President" in setting the mines in operation again, filling the empty coal bins as late autumn approached, and extricating the country from a menacing disaster. Was it "a sweeping victory for the miners" or "a bomb in labor circles"? None knew at the time. And the *Tribune* observed sagely that the "public," at any rate, was the gainer.[42] Moreover, the results of the November elections a few weeks later, strongly favoring the Republican party, attested the astonishing, growing popularity of the new leadership.

[42] The New York *Tribune*, Mar. 22, 1903.

V. TOWARD LEADERSHIP:

"ROOSEVELTIANA"

T HE LUSTY Roosevelt almost from the very outset, as we
have seen, gave every sign of profiting from, fostering,
and extending the renascence of political life that came
to America in the first decade of the twentieth century. By his
capacity and will, by his example, he was to carry on a notable
revival of positive political leadership that was the historic feature of an enlightened, critical era. In a sense, he himself was
carried along by a powerful current; but he was a vigorous oarsman, who enjoyed the race and steered boldly through the dangerous rapids as long as he could.

"I did not usurp power," he wrote in afterthought, "but I did
greatly broaden the use of executive power." To the English historian, George O. Trevelyan, with whom he held a long, friendly,
and rich correspondence, he said also:

I have a definite philosophy about the presidency. I think it should be
a very powerful office, and I think the President should be a very strong
man who uses without hesitation every power that the position yields;
because of this very fact, I believe he should be sharply watched by the
people, held to a strict accountability to them, and that he should not
keep the office too long.

The contrasts offered by this concept of executive leadership
and power as against the usages of the immediate, pre-Rooseveltian
past, are important. Political action ceases to be merely *negative*,
must cease to act only to preserve the gains and privileges won by

the ruling groups after the Civil War—the essential counting-house politics of the "Standpatters." It emerges from the closed office of the powerful desk politician and functions more largely than before in the open forum of public opinion. It operates less with Presidents and Senators and Governors acting as the puppets of more powerful managers behind the scenes. Instead, a more direct responsiveness to the popular will, to the sentiment of the masses, is sought. These changes were, to be sure, "relatively" rather than "absolutely" true. Moreover, the Rooseveltian pattern of leadership and power could not have been achieved if the historical and social currents of the age had not so strongly favored the spirit of change.

The evidences of political revival were to be seen on all sides and in many forms. The very atmosphere of the capital was altered. Around the attractive, many-sided personality of the President, a band of loyal followers and lieutenants gathered who were of a type not seen so frequently here in many moons. For while Roosevelt made the concessions of a *Realpolitiker* to the leaders of machines, he also threw open, more largely than before, a career to talent in the national government. In response to his many calls for educated men, for college men to enter public life, young enthusiasts inspired by a new ideal of public service and reform came to his banner. They occupied chiefly minor offices, since the high Cabinet posts were held by the men who had surrounded McKinley. They stirred things up in the dusty old government bureaus. In the Interior Department, an ancient stronghold of the corrupt, where the program of land and forest conservation began to be pushed earnestly toward 1902, the younger, newer men performed feats of patriotic devotion sometimes at the risk of life and health, sometimes at the cost of serious collisions with the men of the old administrative corps and their allies outside.

Here was one of the best sides of the Roosevelt administration, typified by the activities of Gifford Pinchot, the forester, who was himself a young man of education and fortune, actually appointed to his minor office by McKinley in 1897, but given full play and high authority under Roosevelt. James R. Garfield, son of the President who had been killed by a disappointed office-seeker, was another of the devoted young men of education and good family who attached themselves to Roosevelt. He was, naturally, an ardent civil-service reformer. Appointed at first head of the new Bureau of Corporations, established by a law of 1903, he was soon promoted to the office of Secretary of the Interior. At Capitol Hill, Albert Beveridge, brilliant and literary young Senator from Indiana, often described at the time as "engaging, vital, charming"—terms that could easily be used to characterize many of the Rooseveltians—became a devoted, admiring lieutenant of the President, often entrusted with the introduction and expounding of his characteristic legislative measures.

The circle of younger men who surrounded, advised, and took orders from Roosevelt came to be known as the "Tennis Cabinet," being thus differentiated from the Cabinet officers, who were too old and conservative to play at strenuous games in the President's leisure hours. Of the "Tennis Cabinet" and of the corps of younger men who were appointed to fill many offices under this administration, James Bryce, then serving as Ambassador at Washington, said that he had "never in any country seen a more eager, high-minded and efficient set of public servants, men more useful to their country than the men then doing the work of the American Government. . . ."[1] Some of them, now grown old, recall with tears of emotion the stirring days of their service under the beloved "T. R."[2]

"For that once in our history, we had an American salon," wrote a friend of Roosevelt's, nostalgically.[3] Theodore Roosevelt

[1] Rhodes, *op. cit.*, p. 398.
[2] "T. R. told us that we of the 'Tennis Cabinet' were much closer to him than his official cabinet. So he wrote and said to Jim Garfield and myself. . . ." (Hon. Gifford Pinchot to author, Dec. 8, 1938.) The "brain trust" of President Franklin Roosevelt developed directly out of the "Tennis Cabinet" of a generation ago.
[3] Wister, *op. cit.*, p. 125.

had long cherished a more cultured ideal of social life than his predecessors in politics.

To the Rooseveltian circle of men of society who were influential in politics and men of politics who were at home in good society, there was now added the prestige and authority of the White House center. The musty old mansion of tragic memories and ugly furniture was vigorously redecorated by the new President and his wife, at the start of their reign, so that it shone in all its parts. Brilliant seasons of fine dinners and spirited conversations, unlike anything since the days of Jefferson and Dolly Madison, succeeded each other until the social leadership of Washington seemed to rival that of New York and Newport.

Formality, pomposity and dullness, which had ruled at the state occasions of an uncouth Cleveland or a colorless McKinley, now departed. And save for those professional occasions when bosses and financial magnates must be invited, the *dramatis personae* also were changed. Roosevelt said:

I am simply unable to make myself take the attitude of respect toward the very wealthy men which such an enormous multitude of people evidently really feel. I am delighted to show any courtesy to Pierpont Morgan or Andrew Carnegie or James J. Hill, but as for regarding any one of them, as for instance, I regard Professor Bury, or Peary, the Arctic explorer, or Rhodes, the historian—why, I could not force myself to do it, even if I wanted to, which I don't.

Theodore Roosevelt's many-sided cultural interests were well reflected by the presence in the Roosevelt salon of politicians who were also men of letters and historians, such as John Hay, Henry Cabot Lodge, and Beveridge; or the jurist, Oliver Wendell Holmes, whom he elevated to the Supreme Court bench; the French diplomat, who was a distinguished literary critic, Jules Jusserand; the artists LaFarge, John Sargent and Saint-Gaudens. Then, to mingle with these, he introduced the representatives of pioneering, exploring, and soldierly activities, of "the heroic virtues." He believed that "a high artistic and literary development

is compatible with notable leadership in arms and statecraft." [4]
Cowboys and former desperadoes and big-game hunters and pugi-
lists might make their bow at the White House. But these invitations were issued with an eye to good fun and publicity; and
they should not divert us from the significant point that Roosevelt in his social life exemplified a consistently aristocratic concept of culture and the good life; that he could "wear tails when
the occasion called and be at home in them," [5] that he sought to
gather about him an assembly of the "élite" whose aspirations
were turned beyond the crude objectives of the Gilded Age.

None recognized better than himself, Roosevelt wrote in 1904
to a distinguished European poet, that ". . . we of the West, we
of the eager, restless, wealth-seeking nation," after having reached
"a certain, not very high level of material well-being," must turn
to "the things that really count," the things of the spirit. "Factories and railways are good up to a certain point, but courage and
endurance . . . love of home and country . . . love of beauty in
man's work and in nature, love and emulation of daring and lofty
endeavor, the homely work-a-day virtues and the heroic virtues—
these are better still, and if they are lacking, no piled-up riches,
no roaring, clanging industrialism, no feverish many-sided activities shall avail either the individual or the nation." [6]

These strictures upon wealth-getting and material comfort,
these reflections upon arms and glory and culture, that come and
go in Roosevelt's mind during his crowded years of power, all
seem more or less consciously part of his now crystallized outlook
on life. They give point to his relations with organized labor, his
skirmishes with powerful financiers, his shifting tactics toward
professional politicians, his bold foreign enterprises, and his constant pursuit of an ever-extending power. [7]

[4] Speech of Apr. 23, 1910, at the Sorbonne.
[5] Wister, *op. cit.*, p. 125.
[6] *T. R. Papers*, to Frédéric Mistral, Dec. 15, 1904.
[7] I have remarked that Theodore Roosevelt's values were in part "bureaucratic," in part "aristocratic." When in 1910 he made his remarkable European
tour, as the guest of monarchs and nobles, he wrote to Trevelyan of his own
surprise at the sympathy he had been shown by members of the Austrian Em-

2

The problem of power Roosevelt attacked with an intuitive and yet thoroughgoing art, by which future statesmen were to guide themselves more or less well. He saw that the throne of the President was, in effect, a most perilous seat, surrounded by predatory party bosses who might, at will, cut him off from the "big battalions" of party workers; by the managers of Congress who jealously circumscribed his legislative influence; by the lobbyists and lawyers of the great corporations, who furnished the "sinews of war" for party campaigns.

Methodically he courted the popularity of the crowd; this in itself was something of a departure, since no President in forty years had been personally popular with the masses, with the possible exception of General Grant. The second step was the effort to gain control himself of the party machinery and keep it in his own hands. The third step, following naturally, was that of raising war chests, duplicating the work of men like Mark Hanna.

From the White House, through extremely frequent press interviews as well as many speech-making forays, Roosevelt recommended himself to the "plain people" in many ways. For the first time the gentlemen of the press were given a permanent room in the White House. They responded by picturing the new incumbent as a human being, democratically informal and approachable to hundreds of people who visited him every day. He was shown dictating innumerable messages to Congress and to the nation, as

peror's court at Vienna. These feudal personages were impressed because, while he had been president of a republic, he (in his own words) "at the same time had done the kind of thing in war and sport which it would have gratified their ambitions to do . . . ; and then to my intense amusement, I found that they were in cordial sympathy with me because I had attacked the big financial interests, and because I frankly looked down on mere moneyed men, the people of enormous wealth who had nothing but their wealth behind them, and whose power was simply the power of the 'money touch.'" The Austrian nobles felt that Roosevelt had shown himself "aristocratic" in putting the vulgar men of "mere money bags" in their place. (T. R. to G. O. Trevelyan, Oct. 1, 1911, *T. R. Papers.*)

he strode up and down the White House rooms. He was heard shouting with bluff honesty to one whispering Senator: "We have no secrets here!" And to another, that his colleague who had just left the room was a crook. He appeared pre-eminent as a father and husband, a horseman, a wood-chopper, and above all as a hunter. On vacations he hunted the grizzly bear in full view of the national press. Thus he appeared as fearless before physical danger as he was unflinching in his pursuit of even-handed justice. In cartoon or popular song, the dynamic "T. R." appealed as effectively to the mass psychology of the huge middle class as modern dictators have done with the radio broadcast and pageantry. Truly he was the Great White Chief of all the American tribe.

The program that he began to call "my policies" or the "Square Deal" aimed to bring about a synthesis or combination of groups and classes, while preventing them from combining against him. He actually never made a frontal attack upon the whole system of privilege and secret control underlying the political government. Meanwhile his simultaneous onslaughts upon both "anarchists," or "unruly labor leaders," and the "criminal rich" appealed to the great middle class, as if bringing relief to the vague sense of insecurity that often haunted it.

It was Roosevelt's lifelong belief, based, as he told James Ford Rhodes, on his studies of history, that the downfall of the Grecian, Roman, and Italian republics was caused by the fact that when the rich got the power they exploited the poor, and when the poor got the power they plundered the rich. He was to stand midway between the two and prevent excess.[8]

In expounding a middle-road, middle-class program and seeking to make this effective, it was inevitable that Roosevelt should lean strongly upon the moral notes. Lacking the conviction of urgent economic necessity that drove on a Morgan in his trust-building career, feeling nothing of the inevitable class conflict that seemed to inspire a "Big Bill" Haywood, the Red labor leader of the West, he preached with an evangelical fervor the puritan pre-

[8] Rhodes, *op. cit.*, p. 395.

cepts he had long ago learned of duty, morality, honor, and "righteousness."

His more conservative and cynical Cabinet members noticed this trait, and sometimes after an especially fervent sermon twitted him freely. John Hay observed in his diary: "Knox says that the question of what is to become of Roosevelt after 1908 is easily answered. He should be made a bishop." Roosevelt himself said of his public utterances that "he knew there was not much in them except a certain sincerity and kind of commonplace morality which put him *en rapport* with the people. . . ." [9]

The paramount problem in America, Roosevelt felt, was to bring about a kind of "moral awakening," just as other mass leaders, in nations with different historical traditions, devoted themselves by a parallel effort to bring about a military "awakening." He too denied the economic man. Out of his preoccupation with the moral man came the characteristic Rooseveltian demand that the monopolistic corporation should turn itself into the "good" or "reasonable" trust. Because of the same preoccupations, he could ignore for a long time the movement for the eight-hour day and for the elimination of child labor.

The struggle for national unity against both "the turbulent or extreme labor people" and the "malefactors of great wealth" was presented as no affair of pale compromise, but was dramatized with all Roosevelt's natural vehemence of expression. Roosevelt stood as a man committed to righteousness, but he also stood forth as one of those who would be ever ready to "maintain right by force," to whom force was "one of the talents committed to nations by God. . . ." These were the words of his friend, Admiral Mahan. [10]

Roosevelt's readiness for violence of various kinds was seen late in 1903, when a bloodless revolt burst forth mysteriously in Panama, against the government of Colombia. Yankee men-of-war were on hand and the right of way for the Panama Canal overnight passed into the hands of the United States. "I took

[9] Hay, *Diaries*, Vol. V, Jun. 5, 1904; Jun. 21, 1904.
[10] "The Moral Aspects of War," *North American Review*, Oct., 1899.

the Isthmus . . ." Roosevelt would say, indiscreetly, some years later. His propensity to violence was supported by supreme conviction of his own rightness. It was a combination, a "way of getting things done" that impressed the crowds, and showed itself in domestic political battle as well as in the use of our armed forces overseas.

In January, 1903, an act establishing a Bureau of Corporations to engage in fact-finding in the field of the trusts was vigorously urged upon Congress by Roosevelt, but met with resistance from certain politicians who acted at the order of the Standard Oil executive, John D. Archbold. In a dramatic press conference, the President attacked those who blocked his bill. Then after exacting the oath of the reporters that they would keep secret the source of their information, he confided to them, for publication, that "Rockefeller" by telegrams to Congress opposed the Bureau of Corporations law. This proved later to be only approximately true. But in using Rockefeller's name, Roosevelt "demonstrated again his sound grasp of public psychology. . . . Rockefeller personified the evil of the trusts." [11] "Mr. Rockefeller, who had nothing directly to do with the case, declared himself shocked at the President's false revelations." [12]

A few weeks later he dramatized also his chronic clashes with organized labor. On May 18, 1903, a certain William A. Miller, employee in the Government Printing Office, was dismissed by his superior on the ground, as he claimed, that he had been expelled from his labor union. Roosevelt had the case investigated and ordered Miller's reinstatement. He had no objection to unions, he said, but no union rules could be permitted "to override the laws of the United States, which it is my sworn duty to enforce." The men of the American Federation of Labor met and passed resolutions of censure of the President's "open shop" principles. To Samuel Gompers, President of the A. F. of L., who came to protest in person, Roosevelt said, brandishing his fist: he must

[11] Pringle, *op. cit.*, p. 342.
[12] L. W. Busbey, *Uncle Joe Cannon*, p. 216.

govern his actions "by the laws of the land . . . without regard to creed, color, birthplace or social condition. . . ." He would no more recognize the fact that a man "does or does not belong to a union" than he would recognize before the law that he was a Catholic, a Protestant, or a Jew.[13] The trade-union men protested anew in hostile resolutions. But Roosevelt declared publicly that he would adhere to his "open shop" principles, come what may. He thought that "the labor unions and the trust magnates may perhaps unite against me," yet he would win through.[14]

A similar collision occurred May 10, 1905. Roosevelt, speaking in Chicago at a time when a large-scale, spirited strike of the teamsters' union was in progress, was met with a petition of the strikers' committee urging him not to permit Federal interference in their dispute. He replied with the broadest hints that at the first need, he would move with Federal forces for "the preservation of law and order, the suppression of violence by mobs or individuals."

Later that evening, speaking before a business men's club, he repeated these hints, saying that if organizations of laborers as well as capitalists were guilty of wrongdoing, they would be held to strict accountability. "The greatest and most dangerous rock in the course of any republic," he said, "is the rock of class hatred." Addressing directly the Mayor of Chicago, who was among those present, he pledged that the armed forces of the nation would stand behind the city and the state if ever the need arose.[15]

To Cabot Lodge, who complimented him fulsomely after reading a report of the affair in the press, Roosevelt replied that he had "used language so simple" to the strikers "that they could not misunderstand it. . . . So if the rioting in Chicago gets beyond the control of the State and the City, they know well that the regulars will come."[16]

Such incidents went far to pacify the middle class and large

[13] Bishop, *op. cit.*, Vol. I, p. 251.
[14] *Ibid.*
[15] Roosevelt, *Addresses*, Vol. IV, pp. 367-374, 374-376.
[16] Lodge, *Correspondence*, Vol. II, p. 121.

groups among the capitalists made uneasy by Roosevelt's unconventional proceedings under other heads. On the eve of the election of 1904, conservative Republican leaders such as Senator O. H. Platt of Connecticut were able to assure anxious capitalists and large manufacturers that Roosevelt was "sound"; the danger of the enactment of a national eight-hour law, inspired by the Roosevelt administration, was negligible. On November 1, 1904, Secretary of the Navy Metcalf wrote to Senator O. H. Platt: "No manufacturer need fear that the Department has sided, or is siding, with either those who advocate or those who oppose the measure." [17]

Toward the farmers as a class the Roosevelt administration moved with extreme care to avoid offense and disarm the periodic insurgence of the West. Certain favors were granted them, even by Aldrich's group in the Senate, as in the case of the Cuban Reciprocity Bill of 1903, which was adjusted in a manner satisfactory to beet-sugar growers. Anti-railroad agitation was partially appeased by the Elkins Act of 1903, which forbade the granting of rebates to shippers; though this, written by the railroads' friends in the Senate, was soon seen to give but slight relief from the burden of heavy freight charges.

In March, 1903, Governor Albert Cummins, the popular, plainspoken Iowa lawyer, arrived at the White House to urge that Roosevelt advocate the repeal of certain tariff duties "as a means of opposing the trusts." A large faction among the farmers was now reported as eager either for tariff reduction or stern legislation to control trusts and railroads and the burdensome charges they seemed to impose. But here Roosevelt proceeded most cautiously. With a view to gathering popular strength in the West, he made ready for a long speaking tour through the farm belt. Yet before departing, early in April, he submitted his prepared speeches on the tariff and the trusts to Aldrich for advice and

---

[17] Stephenson, *op. cit.*, appendix, p. 460.

approval. "I want to be sure to get what I say on these two subjects along lines upon which all of us can agree."[18]

To Cabot Lodge he reported that the "free trade" agitation in the West troubled his mind. He was not certain of what he could get the party to do in this direction. The year before a Presidential contest would be "a most unwise one in which to enter upon a general upsetting of the tariff. . . ." The tariff, in any case, was "a mere matter of expediency," he thought. In other words, not a moral question.[19]

Roosevelt continued both to fear the temper of the Western agrarians and to lament the possible necessity for appeasing them by tariff reductions. Even a year later John Hay found him still "full of doubt and perplexity" as to tariff revision. Hay noted in his diary:

He is getting very cross with his "fool friends" who urge him to "defy Congress and the people will rally to his support." He said he had sometimes succeeded in fighting the machine, but that was because he himself had chosen the occasion and calculated the chances.[20]

On his "swing" through the West in 1903, Roosevelt therefore confined himself to a castigation of "wicked" trusts and labor extremists. He showed himself to the farmers from the rear platform of his special train as one who, though an Easterner, had lived among them in the West for years, and knew their life, their world. Though wanting the organ voice of a Bryan, Roosevelt touched new heights nowadays as a dynamic speaker, preaching his middle-road sermons with a passion that sometimes seemed to strangle the words in his throat.

This long colorful tour of April and May, 1903, proceeded as far as the Pacific Northwest, and was interrupted by a famous bear-hunt in Colorado, and other picturesque, improvised episodes which Roosevelt now habitually indulged in. The people were intrigued with the Rough Rider and thronged about his train

---

[18] Roosevelt to Aldrich, Mar. 16, 1903; Stephenson, *op. cit.*, p. 219.
[19] Lodge, *Correspondence*, Apr. 22, 1903, Vol. II, p. 6.
[20] Hay, *Diaries*, Vol. V, Dec. 11, 1904.

everywhere to salute him, to his high satisfaction. Yet, momently, doubts assailed him and made him tremble for the future.

The "Hurrahs" were pleasant enough, he told a companion. The people were cheering the President of the United States. But the people forgot quickly; while the corporations and the great party bosses forgot nothing and forgave nothing. What if he should never even be *elected* to the office he now held? "*They* don't want it . . . Hanna and that crowd. . . . They've finished me. . . . I have no machine, no faction, no money. All this [waving his hand to indicate the crowd they had just left] has no significance. You see I cannot hope to be renominated without the support of my own State." The resistance to his nomination, in New York as elsewhere, Roosevelt ascribed to the hidden thrusts of Mark Hanna.[21] Thus it was no accident that, a short time later, on reaching the Pacific Coast, Roosevelt determined suddenly to bring into the open the secret struggle with the national party boss.

3

For two years the astute Mark Hanna had been watching Roosevelt's course, perhaps with inward misgivings, yet making no sign of overt opposition. The two men observed their bargain with each other, though at arm's length. Hanna had been "consulted" frequently; and he had helped the President in settling the coal miners' strike. But when various Republican state conventions at the end of 1902 passed complimentary resolutions recommending Mr. Roosevelt's nomination as the party's candidate for President at the next election, Hanna remained silent. In his very own province of Ohio, where a State Republican convention was to gather in early June, 1903, a plan was on foot to bring up a resolution favoring Roosevelt for 1904. It was directed by the faction led by Senator Joseph B. Foraker, Hanna's old rival, as a means of embarrassing Hanna. The latter, in a newspaper interview, was now forced to oppose the resolution for Roosevelt as be-

[21] McCaleb, *Roosevelt*, pp. 198-200.

ing premature, and unjust to other possible candidates, among whom he declared he was not numbered. Controversy flared up in Ohio, and Hanna telegraphed to Roosevelt at Seattle, on May 25, 1903, in apologetic terms, stating that he had nothing to do with raising the issue of the Roosevelt endorsement. "When you know all the facts," he ended, "I am sure you will approve my course." [22]

Roosevelt, who was busy raising up Western popular support for his aspirations, chose this moment to precipitate a public controversy with Hanna. He replied by telegraph, the same day, and made his dispatch public through the Associated Press.

Your telegram received. I have not asked any man for his support. I have had nothing whatever to do with raising this issue. Inasmuch as it has been raised, of course, those who favor my administration and my nomination will favor endorsing both, and those who do not will oppose.

Roosevelt now openly announced his own candidacy and forced Hanna into a position where he must oppose him in the open or endorse him. In making public his reply he trickily suppressed the fact that it was a reply to a telegram from Hanna, couched in diplomatic and peaceable terms. To his Western audience, which had little sympathy with the Eastern rulers of the Republican party, he appeared to have hurled defiance at Mark Hanna.[23] To Lodge, Roosevelt indicated the little deception he practiced.

At Spokane, the next day, he delivered the hottest speech of the tour; jutting out his jaw and smiting one fist upon the other, he promised the equivalent of "a knockdown and drag-out fight with Hanna and the whole Wall Street crowd. . . ."

Facing the predicament of open party discord, outmaneuvered both by his Ohio rival Foraker and by Roosevelt, Mark Hanna beat a hasty retreat, wiring Roosevelt the next day that he would not oppose endorsement of him by the Ohio party convention.

The initial victory over Hanna, gained by a sudden thrust, and

[22] Croly, *Hanna*, p. 425.
[23] Lodge, *Correspondence*, Vol. II, pp. 18-20.

recorded in the national press, was an important step in breaking down Hanna's dominance of the party organization. Under the circumstances, also, it presented Roosevelt in a most appealing light to the Western citizens as the open adversary of the boss who represented the great "privileged interests." Thus his trip was concluded with triumphal ovations in the cities of the West.

Within little more than a year of taking his unexpected office the new President had shown his mettle as a political strategist with a flair for the attack. Thereafter his efforts to gain a real ascendancy over the party organization were pushed home steadily by discreet wielding of the patronage power. When, late in 1901, he discovered that fifteen officials of the Post Office Department, some of them reputable Republican leaders in their localities, were guilty of corrupt practice, he had them quietly removed. However, the replacements were made with an eye to creating a body of his own supporters.

The naming of the old spoilsman James S. Clarkson, whom Roosevelt had strongly denounced in his Civil Service Commission days under President Harrison, as surveyor for the port of New York, suggested an accommodation of his conscience with earlier ideals. From his post in New York the old spoilsman was reported to be occupied chiefly in "lining up" Southern Republican delegates for the approaching national convention. The dubious appointment (which was later reversed) of a certain W. M. Byrne as United States Attorney for Delaware, also caused some soul-searching among Roosevelt's admirers. The approval of a bill which increased Civil War veterans' pensions by some $5,000,000 per year—though existing pensions had been fairly generous—like the invitation to Dr. Booker T. Washington to the White House for luncheon, so pleasing to colored Republicans, was an instance of rather transparent domestic diplomacy. Thus he built steadily his own faction, his "machine."

While maintaining faithfully his "gentleman's agreement" with Aldrich and Cannon regarding economic legislation, he contended with Hanna in matters of party organization. In the affair of the

Ohio endorsement for his candidacy, he had shown increasing favor to Foraker, Hanna's enemy, who was further armed in the way of Federal appointments. The Roosevelt Papers show also that enormous patronage was dispensed to Senator Quay of Pennsylvania, perhaps even more frequently than to Hanna in earlier days. With Lodge, the dominant New England boss, and his colleague Governor Murray Crane, close business relations were constantly maintained, while in New York, where the aged Tom Platt was finally ousted by his ambitious lieutenants, Roosevelt cemented a practical alliance with the successor boss, Benjamin Odell. By all these dreary expedients Roosevelt gradually thrust himself into the real, rather than the titular, leadership of his party.

"Theodore, do not think anything about a second term," Mark Hanna had said to Roosevelt authoritatively after the death of McKinley. But in 1904, Hanna was sixty-six and in declining health.

Outwardly there was a reconciliation between the two men. Roosevelt paid Hanna the compliment of calling him generous and straightforward. "No one but a really big man—a man above all petty considerations—could have treated me as you have done during the year and a half since President McKinley's death." [24] However, Roosevelt showed determination to take care of his interests himself, in his own way.

In his later years, Hanna was treated more leniently by the national press, which had long pilloried him as an ogre covered with dollar marks. His spirit too had mellowed. By May, 1903, he could say to the Ohio Republican convention: "I believe in organized labor and I believe in organized capital—as an auxiliary." He too criticized capital for its selfish tendency to the "appropriation of the larger share," and in Chautauqua addresses frequently advocated the practice of the Golden Rule. [25]

Whether Hanna himself actually intended to run for President is one of the "problems" for scholars in our recent history. He denied repeatedly and publicly such intentions. He denied them to

[24] *T. R. Papers*, T. R. to Hanna, May 29, 1903.
[25] Croly, *Hanna*, pp. 407-409.

Roosevelt, sometimes in the form of jests. Yet he did not entirely close the door. The financiers of New York and Chicago leaned upon him still. Quietly they pushed preparations to launch his candidacy. They kept him informed of the general suspicion and uneasiness about the Rough Rider in Union League Club circles. Though Hanna too had moments in 1903 and 1904 when he was black with fury at Roosevelt, he bided his time, for his own reasons.

In conservative clubs and counting-houses brilliant intrigues may have been laid to nominate a less "impulsive," less unpredictable candidate for the Republicans in 1904. But Mark Hanna knew that this was now impossible, save at the cost of deadly party strife; even more, at the cost of business confidence. His theory of the public interest, nevertheless, held that the election of Roosevelt by a great popular majority was not desirable. He remained aloof and inscrutable because "he wanted to make the President feel and respect his power." [26]

Reports of constant intrigues by political "sappers and miners" in January, 1904, left the atmosphere of the White House nervously irritable. At a none too secret meeting in the Waldorf-Astoria Hotel, ten railroad presidents offered large subscriptions to the Republican chest "in case Mr. Hanna is the candidate." Their message to him was: "Stop making presidents and become one yourself." [27] News of Hanna's victorious campaign for re-election to the Senate in November, 1903, in spite of the furious onslaughts of Tom L. Johnson, was alarming also; once more he had held Ohio, and named his own Governor and Legislature. But not long after, on his return to Washington in January, 1904, he fell desperately ill.

A fierce unrepentant old man, in an agony of pain, lay dying. He looked back at his own past, so typical of his age: the large wealth he had begotten, the tremendous power he had suddenly seized and wielded so boldly, the far-flung, national, political battles in which he had triumphed. All this power was crumbling

[26] Croly, *Hanna*, p. 443.
[27] *The Nation*, Jan. 21, 1904.

away; while the young leader, medium of the strange new times, magnanimously called to inquire after him and left his card. The gesture touched the inscrutable old magnate's heart, and he responded with a last word of gratitude scrawled in his own hand.

On February 15, 1904, the threat of Mark Hanna's veto power in Republican party affairs passed away. Matt Quay of Pennsylvania had also died, alone and unwept, as the old sinner had wished to die. Boss Tom Platt of New York was retired and in his dotage; in Iowa, Allison was soon to make way for his more progressive colleague Senator Jonathan Dolliver and Albert Cummins; in Wisconsin, Spooner, another famous Republican veteran, passed out of the picture and was replaced by La Follette. Truly the old order was changing in 1904 as Theodore Roosevelt reached forward confidently to grasp the helm of the mighty party organization, President and party boss in one.

4

But who would find money, now that the great Receiver-General of the Republicans was dead?

To make a Rough Riders' legion of office-holders, Grand Army veterans and county or precinct leaders counted for much. But what was needed in order to operate the party Steam Roller in 1904 was money, money above all, and more money. Six months before the party convention Roosevelt, tacking sharply, set forth on his hunt for campaign funds, which he continued through the greater part of 1904 with his superabundant energy.

In February, 1903, Roosevelt promoted his Private Secretary, George B. Cortelyou (who had performed the same confidential function under McKinley), to the office of Secretary of the new Department of Commerce. Cortelyou was the close-mouthed type of political liaison agent; much like President Cleveland's Secretary, Daniel Lamont, he knew his way among the narrow lanes of downtown New York, where the national offices of railroads, insurance companies, and industrial concerns congregated so thickly. To Cortelyou was assigned the problem of raising a war fund.

To strengthen Cortelyou's hand, it was also the President's task to conciliate, as much as possible, the great financial magnates who traditionally supported the Republican party with their donations. Roosevelt's message to Congress in December, 1903, was extremely moderate in tone; it dwelt upon the splendid era of prosperity being enjoyed; it pointed with pride to the "sane and conservative" lines along which legislation was being enacted under his administration; and it gave notice that the malcontents of labor would be held as strictly to account as predatory wealth. On other delicate questions such as tariff and currency, the President was fairly vague. Thus the *Wall Street Journal*, on December 8, 1903, could exclaim that Mr. Roosevelt's policy "neither in intention or fact, is directed against wealth. We admire the courage of the President."

The President had submitted that message, before its completion, to Mr. James Stillman, head of the great National City Bank and a leader of the Rockefeller group, for criticisms and suggestions. At the same season he had made friendly overtures to Henry C. Frick, then a director of the United States Steel Corporation, as well as to J. P. Morgan himself, whom he invited for a consultation at the White House.[28] Yet those great silent men, Stillman, Morgan, and Frick, appeared at first allergic to Rooseveltian charm. The President was filled with anxiety, which he poured out to his close friends, Elihu Root, Hay, Taft, and Lodge. "The criminal rich and the fool rich will do all they can to beat me." The "gentlefolk," he told Owen Wister also, the people he met at the homes of friends or at his clubs, or had known at Harvard, were most bitter in their opposition to him.

From Boston, however, Lodge sent the cheering report that he found friendliness rather than hostility for his friend expressed in State Street, and "even in Wall Street there is a large body of men

[28] *T. R. Papers*, T. R. to J. Stillman, Aug. 29, 1903; T. R. to H. C. Frick, Jun. 9, 1903.

who are with you. . . ." Lodge would continue to do "missionary work" among the Boston bankers, and the President, he hoped, would aid him by continuing as before to show himself firm toward labor-unionists as in the Printing Office case.[29]

The view of Lodge is accurate. High financial quarters were always divided in their attitude toward T. R. rather than consistently hostile. Those who lost money in the market, owing to governmental action against the railroad "merger," were ready to blame him for their losses. Moreover his values, at once bureaucratic, military, and aristocratic, were different from those of most of the giants of Wall Street, who by dint of their "enlightened selfishness" daily contributed to the upbuilding of the nation. Yet there were not a few among the leading capitalists of the nation who felt that Roosevelt as President was much preferable to a Mark Hanna from the point of view of their own real interests; they bore his sermonizing cheerfully, for the sake of the greater real security he brought; they served, if need be, as "whipping boys" for the sake of his superb political acumen and uncanny control of the voting population. Such sophistication, a little rare in America, was long known to the older European capitalist societies, where men of money privately subsidized Radical or Social-Democratic statesmen, while submitting to being pilloried by them in public.

Among those who accepted Roosevelt's assertions that he acted in the long run "conservatively in property's interest," were George W. Perkins, partner of Morgan and Company, director of the U. S. Steel Corporation; and Joseph Medill McCormick, heir to part of the International Harvester Company fortune. Perkins, a most enthusiastic devotee of the Rough Rider, shared Elihu Root's conviction that by his picturesque methods he took the wind out of the sails of Bryan and other radicals, yet left Congress and the nation's purse-strings in safe hands. The vivacious Root would say: "Roosevelt's bark was always worse than his bite." It was Secretary Root, the old corporation lawyer, whom Roosevelt sent to New York to do missionary work among the men of the Union League Club, his old clients and clubmates.

[29] Lodge, *Correspondence*, Vol. II, pp. 19, 24, 57; Wister, *op. cit.*, p. 188.

Here, in a speech of February 3, 1904, replying to those who held that Roosevelt was "unsafe," Root said:

But I say to you that he has been *the greatest conservative force for the protection of property and our institutions*. . . . There is a *better way* to protect property, to *protect capital*, to protect enterprise, than by buying legislatures. There is a better way to deal with labor, and to keep it from rising into the tumult of the unregulated and resistless mob than by starving it or by corrupting its leaders. . . . That way is, that capital shall be fair . . . fair to the consumer, fair to the laborer, fair to the investor; that it shall concede that the laws shall be executed. . . . Never forget that the men who labor cast the votes, set up and pull down governments, and that our government is possible, the continued opportunity for enterprise, for the enjoyment of wealth, for individual liberty, is possible, only so long as the men who labor with their hands believe in American liberty and American laws.[30]

Elihu Root, one of the most intelligent conservatives of his epoch, in these sentences expressed as happily as his chief could have wished the Rooseveltian ideology of "the better way . . . to protect capital." The President testified to this by his many profuse expressions of gratitude to Root. Thus by a form of educational or "missionary" work, the great patrons of the Republican party were induced to come forward and make their donations to the campaign chest.

How powerful was Roosevelt's hold upon the party organization in 1904 was shown by the fact that his handy man, George B. Cortelyou, who had held only a minor post up to recently, was named national chairman of the party, in place of the late Mark Hanna. At the convention in June, Roosevelt's nomination took place without let or hindrance. Even the usual feigned excitement among the delegates was lacking. "The cheering was mechanical," William Allen White observed. The ceremony of nominating Theodore Roosevelt formally was carried off by a New York politician, former Governor Frank S. Black (who privately detested the candidate), with "an electric fountain of rhetorical icicles."

---

[30] Root, *Miscellaneous Addresses*, p. 222; italics mine.

The galleries cheered heartily, at all events, and the politicians on the floor of the arena at Chicago, feeling that they had to do something, "for twenty long minutes . . . turned loose and cheered like mummers." [81]

Then, as if to demonstrate how much the two major parties actually functioned as a unit, the Democrats at their convention in St. Louis set Mr. Bryan in eclipse, and chose the rather colorless conservative, Judge Alton B. Parker of New York, as their leader. August Belmont and Thomas Fortune Ryan, who were believed to be in full control of the party of opposition (chastened by two successive defeats under radical leadership), thus offered a conservative counter-attraction to the more "impulsive" Roosevelt.

Few held doubts concerning the outcome, for the Rough Rider was at the zenith of his popularity.

Nevertheless, Roosevelt remained highly uneasy through much of the 1904 Presidential campaign. The applause of the public and the press he had been schooled to believe was but ephemeral; victories in elections depended upon the efficient working of the canvassing machine, upon the generosity of rich party patrons. The Secretary of War, William Howard Taft, who had been appointed to his office recently, when Root returned to the practice of law, had the impression that Roosevelt was unduly frightened and that certain interests were even using the critical moments of the campaign as occasions in which to wring promises from him. October came, and the President suffered, as John Hay drily remarked, "what we used to call in Ohio an October Scare." Dissensions among the Republicans of New York troubled his soul.[32]

To make matters worse, on October 1, 1904, Mr. Joseph Pulitzer's New York *World* (Democratic) enlivened the campaign by printing on its first page vigorous charges that Mr. Cortelyou, who as a Cabinet Secretary dealt with the corporations, in the post of national chairman drew golden streams of money from them for his campaign fund. How much were the beef trust, the coal trust, the tobacco trust, the oil trust, the railroads, the banks, the

[81] White, *Masks in a Pageant*, p. 313.
[32] Pringle, *Taft*, Vol. I, p. 261; Hay, *Diaries*, Vol. V, Oct. 8, 1904.

insurance companies contributing? What promises, the *World* asked editorially, were being given in return?

Thus it appeared that while the Square Deal President, through his public statements and his stump orators, directed appeals primarily to the masses of "plain people," whom he was to deliver from their wealthy oppressors, in private he made also the most impassioned demands for pecuniary support on the magnates who headed great trusts in railroads or in heavy industry.

Roosevelt also appeared "surprisingly and needlessly alarmed" to George Harvey, who was often the lobbyist for Ryan, Frick, and other great capitalists.[33] He was obsessed with the fear that by sheer trickery and pressure of money his opponents would outdo him, and that donations received for his campaign fund by Cortelyou were inadequate. Taking matters into his own hands, to a great extent, in October he undertook the most strenuous quest for additional funds, to be devoted to the last-hour canvasses in all doubtful areas.

What followed makes a very sad and perplexing chapter in the career of one of the most independent of Presidents: a chapter whose incidents have never yet been fully explained.

As the summer campaign drew to its close, widespread rumors were circulated that chairman Cortelyou was promising freely, to those he approached for donations, a more conservative turn in the Roosevelt administration. Taking note of these rumors, mentioned here and there in the press, the President on August 11, 1904, had written to the party chairman in the following terms:

> I should hate to be beaten in this contest; but I should not merely hate, I should not be able to bear being beaten under circumstances which implied ignominy. To give any color for misrepresentation to the effect that we were now weakening . . . would be ruinous.

And Cortelyou, who was running things in his own way, responded somewhat testily:

---

[33] Harvey, *Frick*, p. 298.

If I did not know you as well as I do I should resent your sending me such a communication. . . . I am conducting this campaign for your re-election on as high a plane as you have conducted the affairs of your great office.[34]

Yet the rumors continued busily as ever; and soon the ubiquitous little journalist and political philosopher Lincoln Steffens (now at the very height of his fame and influence) presented himself one day in September at the White House to make a proposal filled with splendid common sense. He suggested that the President, instead of offering in effect his immense popularity for sale to the great financiers, should ask "the common people who didn't want anything out of the government except general laws and an administration of justice and fair play" to contribute small sums to his campaign fund. Steffens offered to lay down between $1.00 and $5.00, and promised that a million other "little people" like himself would follow suit. The real point was that Roosevelt by such an appeal "would make the millions feel that it was their Government . . . and that you and your administration were beholden to the many, not to the few." [35]

There is no sign that Roosevelt did more than laugh at the notions of his witty friend with the Vandyke beard. The situation was far too serious. To him it seemed that the Republican party organization was in danger throughout the nation. A political party cost money; much money would be needed for watchers and captains to shepherd the tens and hundreds to the polls, especially in the "doubtful" State of New York where the Tammany men offered real dangers. Yet the money was not coming in as it should.

In the first days of October, Roosevelt, overcome by a kind of hysteria, telephoned from the White House to the National Republican headquarters in New York, and asked for chairman Cortelyou or Cornelius Bliss, the treasurer. They were out, and he spoke with Senator Nathan B. Scott, a member of the executive committee. "What is the trouble? . . ." the President asked.

[34] Bishop, *op. cit.*, Vol. I, pp. 324-325.
[35] Steffens, *Letters,* Steffens to T. R., Sept. 21, 1904, Vol. I, pp. 170-171.

"If the election was now, I fear we would be defeated," responded Senator Scott gloomily. The President was expected to win in the country, but his own state, New York, was counted as lost, and Mr. Bliss had no additional funds to give the state committee, which needed some $200,000 more.

"I will send for Mr. Harriman," Roosevelt then said.[36]

Roosevelt now did a fairly unprecedented thing. He made direct appeals for assistance to Edward H. Harriman, then the leading "angel" of the New York Republicans, and to Henry C. Frick, the steel baron, each numbered among the country's ten richest men.

John Hay records in his diary for October 8, 1904: "I lunched at the White House. Frick and Twombly [Hamilton McK. Twombly of the Vanderbilt family and interests] were there." [37] It may have been on the day before that Frick arrived, for he relates that he left New York with a party, in a private train, arriving in Washington as dusk fell, and came after dark to the White House, "entering by the door opposite the Treasury building." According to Frick's account, the occasion was pleasant, though the President appeared highly exercised over the scarcity of funds for the New York State canvass. The men of money promised that they would do their bit. Frick, according to an account by Oswald G. Villard, had the indelible impression that something in the nature of a pledge or promise was given in return. "He got down on his knees before us. We bought the ——— and then he did not stay bought!" [38] It is fairly doubtful, however, that T. R. with his now considerable training at political negotiation gave anything like a precise pledge.

Two days later, October 10, 1904, Roosevelt, who had occasionally kept in touch with Edward H. Harriman, wrote him also that "in view of the trouble over the State ticket in New York," he would like him to come to the White House within a few days for luncheon or dinner. Whereupon Harriman replied promptly, ac-

[36] *Senate Committee on Privileges and Elections*, 1912, testimony, pp. 685-687.
[37] Hay, *Diaries*, Vol. V, Oct. 8, 1904.
[38] Villard, *Fighting Years*, p. 181.

cepting the invitation, stating at the same time that he was busy "correcting the trouble here," and promising that by the time of their interview "conditions will be very much improved." [39]

But if the railroad baron, reputedly worth a hundred millions, gave such assurances, why need a compromising dinner or luncheon be held? And Roosevelt, with a quick change of heart, on October 14, 1904, hastened to write (apparently without justification) that he had heard "in a roundabout way" of Mr. Harriman's embarrassment at visiting the President in the closing weeks of the campaign.

> Now, my dear sir, you and I are practical men. . . . If you think there is any danger of your visit causing me trouble, or if you think there is nothing special I should be informed about, or no matter in which I could give aid, of course, give up the visit for the time being, and then, a few weeks hence, before I write my message [to Congress] I shall get you to come down to discuss certain governmental matters not connected with the campaign.
> With great regard,
> Sincerely yours,
> Theodore Roosevelt. [40]

Mr. Harriman, however, a stubborn sort, evidently decided that helping to make a President was an expensive affair, and was resolved to look this one over in person. After a long-distance telephone conversation with the White House he too came on to Washington, on October 20, 1904. Again the occasion was friendly. Harriman was now politically prominent in New York because, as he testified some time later, he "owned" Governor Odell. His financial ties were with the Rockefeller dynasty, and often clashed with the interests of the House of Morgan. He appeared eager at this time to have Senator Chauncey Depew, who wore the "Morgan collar," kicked upstairs to the office of Ambassador to France, and replaced as Senator by ex-Governor Frank S. Black, who

[39] Kennan, *Harriman*, Vol. I, p. 183.
[40] *Ibid.*, Vol. I, p. 184.

would wear the "Harriman collar." Large affairs were on foot connected with control of the investment funds of great trust and insurance companies, as the Hughes investigation would show a year later, and a fierce financial struggle was actually being waged in secret for control of these institutions. Harriman left convinced that the President had pledged co-operation in the Senatorial business, as a way of clearing up New York's internal political strife. An understanding or "gentleman's agreement," positively denied afterward by Roosevelt, was attested by numerous witnesses at the hearings of the Senate's Committee on Privileges and Elections, in 1912.

Careful study of the testimony before the Senate Committee in 1912 made by witnesses hostile to Roosevelt shows that, in making a "deal" for Harriman's financial assistance in the campaign, the President hedged his promises with a superior cunning. Governor Benjamin B. Odell testified that his friend Mr. Harriman on his return from Washington gave him an account of the interview with Roosevelt. In regard to the kicking upstairs of Senator Chauncey Depew, which Harriman seemed to require in order to rearrange the New York political organization to his ends, "the President had said to him [Harriman] that *if it were necessary he would do as requested.*" [41] Roosevelt in his famous letter of October 8, 1906, written two years after the event, apparently "for the record," differed on this point, claiming that he told Harriman, "I did not believe it would be possible for me to appoint Mr. Depew Ambassador to France." Harriman, Odell, and company were thus consigned to the "Ananias Club" of immortal liars.

In any case, $250,000 was promptly raised by Harriman ($50,-000 of this was his own money) and turned over, in good time, during the last days of October, to the Republican treasury. [42]

By October 24, 1904, John Hay could comment drily that Mr. Roosevelt's man, Cortelyou, "has all the money he needs—about

---

[41] *Senate Committee on Privileges and Elections,* testimony of Governor Odell, pp. 112-113; italics mine.

[42] *Ibid.,* hearings, pp. 112-113, 611-612, 693.

one half what Hanna had." [43] Roosevelt's obligations to the Male-factors of Great Wealth were ostensibly only half as large as those of President McKinley. But his public professions on this point, contrasted with his secret stern chase for funds, show both moral confusion and a fairly Machiavellian worldliness.

Near the end of the campaign he learned that some officials of the Standard Oil Company, with which he had broken lances publicly, had made a very large donation to Mr. Cortelyou's chest, and he wrote virtuously in a letter that became public October 26, 1904:

I have just been informed that the Standard Oil people have contributed $100,000 to our campaign fund. This may be entirely untrue. But if true I must ask you to direct that the money be returned to them forthwith.

But Roosevelt appreciated how dire the need of money was for the legitimate and necessary expenses of a great national campaign, and proceeded to defend his real actions in the following terms. "It was entirely legitimate to accept contributions no matter how large . . . from individuals and corporations, on the terms on which I happen to know that you have accepted them," that is, that no improper obligations of any kind were involved. The donors, even the big corporations, understood that only a "square deal" for them could be expected. Of course these corporations, having a "tremendous stake in the welfare of this country," were but reasonable and proper in seeking the continuance of the Republican party by legitimate contributions. The Standard Oil, however, owing to its past record, lay in a special category. [44]

However, Mr. Cortelyou did nothing about the matter, and only in 1908 did Mr. Roosevelt learn that the money had never been returned. [45]

---

[43] Hay, *Diaries*, Vol. V, p. 320.

[44] Bishop, *op. cit.*, Vol. I, pp. 329-330.

[45] In effect, Cortelyou, though young at his work compared with Mark Hanna, had not done badly. From evidence brought out before the Armstrong Committee of the New York Legislature (Hughes' investigation of the insurance companies), the Clapp Committee in 1912, and the Barnes-Roosevelt suit for libel

While he was dictating the above letter—according to a reminiscence of Taft, divulged in a mood of anger—Secretary of State Knox came into the room and said to him: " 'Why, Mr. President, the money has been spent. They cannot pay it back—they haven't got it.' 'Well,' said the President, 'the letter will look well on the record, anyhow,' and so he let it go." [46]

Wall Street is a huge whispering gallery, and secrets spread rapidly there. On October 22, 1904, Daniel S. Lamont, the old Democratic wire-puller of Cleveland's administration, now a New York bank president, told the Democratic candidate, Judge Parker, of a secret conference at which Edward Harriman, James Stillman, Henry C. Frick, and George W. Perkins had decided that Roosevelt's election was a matter of necessity. They were convinced, as the New York *Sun* had said, that "the impulsive candidate of the party of conservatism" was preferable to the "conservative, temporizing candidate" of the party regarded as "permanently impulsive." [47]

A week before the election, on October 31, 1904, Parker issued his sensational public charge that Roosevelt had "extorted" money from or "blackmailed" the monopolistic corporations with promises of political immunity. The reports of Cortelyou's collections, as given in newspaper rumors, were cited as evidence. Five days later,

in 1915, a representative list may be compiled of the principal donations, as follows:

J. P. Morgan & Company	$150,000
N. Y. Life, Equitable, and Mutual insurance companies (combined)	148,000
George J. Gould (railroads)	100,000
H. H. Rogers and John D. Archbold (oil)	125,000
H. C. Frick (steel)	100,000
C. S. Mellen (railroads)	50,000
James H. Hyde (insurance)	25,000
James Speyer (banking)	25,000
James Stillman (banking)	10,000
Cuba Mail Steamship Company	10,000
William Nelson Cromwell	5,000
General Electric Company	3,000

[46] Pringle, *Taft*, Vol. II, p. 830; W. H. Taft to Helen H. Taft, Aug. 22, 1912.
[47] *Clapp Committee*, Vol. I, pp. 899-900; New York *Sun*, Aug. 11, 1904.

the President issued a thunderous denial in his most indignant phrases, which echoed throughout the land. That corporate donations had been accepted he did not contradict, but held this legitimate, as it had always hitherto been. Judge Parker's accusations were "monstrous" and by their falsity brought infamy upon himself. The vague, ungrounded assertion that there had been "blackmail" was atrociously false. ". . . If elected I shall go into the Presidency unhampered by any pledge, promise or understanding of any kind, save my promise, made openly to the American people, that so far as in my power lies I shall see to it that every man has a square deal, no less and no more." [48]

The election returns of November 8, 1904, overwhelmed, stunned even Theodore Roosevelt, as he said. He had won the largest majority and the largest vote in the electoral college that any candidate for President had ever received.

5

I have likened Theodore Roosevelt to an oarsman steering boldly past dangerous rocks and rapids. The current he rode was of course that of public opinion. In 1904 it ran more swiftly, stronger than ever in the direction of popular reform.

The political revival noted in the administration, with its more critical, sensitive, historically conscious leaders, came undoubtedly in response to the increasing pressure of a more enlightened public opinion. Toward 1904, after seven years of plenty, the financial boom stimulated by the policies of the Standpatters approached its end. Disturbed by uneven economic pressures, reflected by a rising cost of living which outstripped a rising wage level, and a period of more stringent business conditions—financial commentators often spoke of the period as one of "profitless prosperity"—the spirit of criticism, even of disillusionment, was intensified, and strongly favored the trust-busting activities of the Rooseveltian years.

[48] The New York *World*, Nov. 5, 1904.

To the American middle class, even more than to the working class, the new industrial trust became the great bugaboo. Almost everywhere men spoke of the coming end of business competition, perhaps of individual freedom itself, and of the approaching enslavement of the free American citizen. American society was developing into a hierarchy of classes, with the industrial barons at the top, wrote W. J. Ghent at this time in his prophetic work, *Our Benevolent Feudalism.* "The era of competition " he said, "whether free or unfree, is dead, and the means of its resurrection are unknown to political science."

This haunting question had already been raised repeatedly since the 1890's in our popular press, typified by Pulitzer's *World* and Hearst's New York *Journal,* though in hasty, transient form, mingled with sensational, invidious accounts of the debauches of the rich. But in the autumn of 1902, S. S. McClure, the clever publisher of low-priced popular magazines, while on the scent of "startling facts" with which to dazzle his readers, began to publish in *McClure's* Lincoln Steffens' series of articles on *The Shame of the Cities,* and Ida Tarbell's studies in *The History of the Standard Oil Company.* Here were authoritative reports that had been years in preparing, and now provided for a great mass audience a darker, more realistic picture of what our republic had come to be in the fullness of age.

Miss Tarbell, whose oil-digging father had once been "liquidated" by the Rockefeller clan in Pennsylvania, wrote with admirable restraint and clarity a history of the rise of a band of business dynasts who, so to speak, seized the country by the throat. The struggles, the intrigues of the oil barons, constantly defying the law upon shrewd legal advice wherever it restrained them, made history no less picturesque and conspiratorial than that of the Italian princes in the days of Machiavelli. In 1903 and 1904 the whole country talked of the Standard Oil "Octopus," of the mysterious John D. Rockefeller, who had long held himself deliberately in the shade, and whose possible wealth was only now dimly conjectured.

Meanwhile the vivacious Lincoln Steffens, then editor of *Mc-*

Clure's, had set off upon a great tour of the country on the trail of corrupt political rings that festered in our great cities. His series of "exposures," beginning in October (before Miss Tarbell's series) and continuing month by month, were carefully documented and lucidly, even brilliantly, written. They told almost for the first time a coherent but fearsome story of the alliance between professional political machines and business groups. Steffens' *The Shame of the Cities* had an enormous public success. Soon the leading publishers, such as Hearst and Collier, began to devote low-priced weekly and monthly magazines to a literature of informal social criticism, the literature of "exposure," to which T. R. one day would apply the striking name of "muckraking."

Steffens brought to his work a happy combination of qualities, human sympathy and "scientific curiosity." He did not wish to hunt down evil men; it was the process of evil itself that absorbed him. Political corruption, he would say in afterthought, "is a process. It is not a temporary evil, not an accidental wickedness, not a passing symptom of the youth of a people. It is a natural process by which a democracy is made gradually over into a plutocracy." [49]

Without drawing the conclusions at which he arrived long afterward, Steffens' inquiries nevertheless revealed an organic unity working throughout the field of local government. Everywhere, in St. Louis as in Philadelphia or Pittsburgh, there was the tribal chieftain who ruled over the local party organization, a William Flinn in Pittsburgh, a Butler in St. Louis. And behind the Flinns and the Butlers stood the dominant patron of the machine: a rich brewer in St. Louis, or a certain powerful, very secretive banker in Pittsburgh.

But if there were "villains," there were the heroes of Good Government, too. Like an American Diogenes, Steffens searched for honest men, and found and celebrated Tom L. Johnson, the Single Tax mayor of Cleveland. He pictured Johnson as a converted "robber baron" (converted by a reading of Henry George) who had once been a public-utility magnate, a lobbyist, a buyer of

---

[49] Steffens, *Autobiography,* p. 413.

franchises and privilege. Then he described how Johnson brought his wealth, his shrewd knowledge of men and the world, his original turn of thought, his picturesque circus tactics, to fighting the universal enemy: Privilege. ". . . Privilege causes the evil in the world, not wickedness; and not men," he would say. Once the temptations of Privilege were removed from the purview of business men—so that they no longer contested with each other for political advantage—then Democracy (which appeared to be a synonym for Christianity) became possible again. All would play fair together under just arbiters of the laws. Steffens himself shared fervently the belief of Johnson's disciples, such as Brand Whitlock and Frederic C. Howe, that fundamental municipal reform would teach men to do "the clean, decent thing." [50]

The city reformers felt that they worked at the "grass roots" of the industrial society. Many of them like Johnson and Folk of St. Louis were led to wage the holy war of the Single Taxers against "unearned increment" in ground rent. A score of embattled local reformers from Philadelphia to San Francisco staked everything upon activating the passive majority of honest citizens against the rings that defrauded them, and winning a more "direct democracy" by the expedient of the primary and the referendum. The movement of municipal reform, which Mark Hanna contended with in Ohio after 1897, spread more and more broadly during the 1900's, and assumed moral and religious overtones. Brand Whitlock, the radical young mayor of Toledo, declared at this time that he fought chiefly against "the cant and hypocrisy and iniquity of our system." Theodore Roosevelt, in his sermons upon righteousness, reflected the moods of the reformers of his age, who, as a Cleveland minister said, were but "trying to make Christianity possible."

Was democracy a failure? Steffens asked every month in his magazine articles that reached close to a million readers. "Will the people rule? . . . Is democracy possible?"

[50] Whitlock, *Letters*, Vol. I, pp. 171-172.

The public mind, more chastened and self-critical than in the booming, swashbuckling days of '98, now fixed upon these questions. It was haunted nowadays by a picture of the giant corporation extending its tentacles to crush out the small proprietor, the farmer, the laborer. This nightmare picture was soon brought home in all its horrifying details by a series of scandals in high financial quarters, resulting from battles and competitions among the money lords, that came to the surface toward 1904. The scandals of governmental and business misconduct were to bring certain celebrated inquisitions: those of the insurance companies by a New York legislative committee, with Charles Evans Hughes as its examining attorney; those of the powerful New Haven Railroad, led to trial before public opinion by the "people's attorney," Louis D. Brandeis. Thus, every day the evidence of legislative investigations and courts, summed up in the daily press, would be unfolding a monumental tale of financial and political skulduggery, broadly supporting the charges made already by the "muckraking" journalists. The public mind, filled with misgivings and mistrust, observed with a kind of terror the encroachments of the industrial trusts, and listened to incredible rumors of an all-powerful "Money Trust." This mood of dread and insecurity, especially in the middle class, underlay the trust-busting activities of the Rooseveltian era.

Senator Albert Beveridge, the ardent advocate of Hamiltonian ideals, early in 1902 prepared an important address to be given before a state convention in Indiana in which he defended both the new imperialism and the new order of trusts. The trusts, he said, were led by public-spirited men who reduced the costs of production by large-scale management, and who were too intelligent to penalize the public through needlessly higher charges. Scarcely had the speech been put in type when the beef trust (which Charles Edward Russell in Chicago was already investigating) greedily raised the price of meat. Beveridge was indignant, and wrote to George W. Perkins, his fellow-Hoosier, and one of his original backers:

. . . The beef trust in unjustly and arbitrarily raising prices is causing . . . indignation throughout the country. It gives demagogues an
unjust opportunity to answer my arguments. Cannot you bring these
foolish persons to terms? I am aware that you have your hands full,
but it seems to me that . . . you can do nothing better than to see
these people and give them a little sense.[51]

But Perkins, though a member of the House of Morgan now,
and a lyrical advocate of the trusts, could do nothing; and his
friend Beveridge found the incident deeply instructive. Soon the
former panegyrist of big business determined to make a sharp turn
to the left. "It was good form to be a liberal," as Frederic C.
Howe recalls of those years. "Conservative lawyers, bankers, and
men of affairs lent their names to radical movements. . . . The
younger generation was to achieve the things that had been denied
my own." And Beveridge, like so many other politicians, felt himself caught by the new currents. He planned in 1904 a Child
Labor Bill, for which he would fight in the Senate. In May, 1903,
Dr. Harvey W. Wiley, chief chemist of the Department of
Agriculture, made public his "poison squad" experiments upon
many publicly sold foods. And Beveridge soon after prepared to
enter the struggle for a pure-foods law, to the dismay of the Chicago beef barons whom he had formerly defended. For Beveridge,
in his change of heart, had discovered that after all ours was "a
government of the people," and that it should not be pre-empted
or controlled by the possessors of wealth. He too now believed
that political democracy must endeavor to impose an even-handed
justice, fair play, between the opposing economic groups.

Capital is all right in its place. It has a mission, and a mighty and
beneficent mission it is. I do not object to capital. I defend it—only let
it attend to its own business. And public life and special legislation for
its own benefit are not its business.[52]

[51] Bowers, *Beveridge*, pp. 177-178; Apr. 8, 1902.
[52] Beveridge, "The Rich Man in Politics," *Saturday Evening Post*, Jun. 16,
1906.

Meanwhile the deep unrest that he had been noticing among the people pointed to the road that the future statesmen must travel.

I have been carefully studying the present unrest and interviewing numbers of people about it. I am coming to the conclusion that it is not a passing whim, but a great natural movement such as occurs in this country, as our early history shows, once about every forty years. It is not like the Granger episode or the Debs episode. The former . . . affected only the farmers; the latter only the workingmen. The present unrest, however, is quite as vigorous among the intellectuals, college men, university people, etc., as it is among the common people.[53]

The great currents of public opinion Roosevelt studied closely all his life. His hold upon the voters actually resided in the freedom with which he, unlike the Standpatters of the Hanna and Aldrich type, appeared to respond to public opinion. His propounding of the Square Deal in 1904, his air of independence, the unmistakable promise of bold-handed reform, all made for his unprecedented strength among the voters, a strength which he himself grossly underestimated.

The election returns of November 8, 1904, with their character of a political Tidal Wave had stunned even Roosevelt, as he admitted. It was now plain that he had overreached himself in pursuing secretly the masters of corporations for donations to his campaign chest; he had given hostages to the rich, reactionary Republicans, while stirring the emotions of the masses even better than he knew. This paradox provided deep perplexities for the future.

The plain people were jubilant at the outcome of the election of 1904. But so were certain of the masters of capital who felt that credit was owing to them for a share in the victory. Henry C. Frick of the U. S. Steel Corporation telegraphed the President on election night:

The endorsement of yourself and your policies by your fellow citizens is magnificent and truly deserved. Cordial congratulations!

[53] Bowers, *Beveridge*, pp. 223-224.

VI. PRINCIPALLY
WORLD-WANDERING

THE OLD Senators who still ruled Congress seemed surprisingly unhappy over the sweeping Republican party
triumph of 1904.

"What is to be done now with our victory is a pretty serious
question," wrote the canny Orville Platt of Connecticut to Aldrich.[1]
It was a question that Theodore Roosevelt, too, asked himself
continually.

Originally a political "accident," he had won more real power
than any of the dreary Republican worthies who had preceded him
in his office since Lincoln. He was not only the chief magistrate,
but the unchallenged leader of his party organization, seated in the
driving seat of the Steam Roller. The opportunity for positive
leadership lay open for him, with the Presidential power less restricted by indirect controls than ever before, as a similar opportunity fell one day to a later Roosevelt after re-election in 1936.

Moreover he could say, in this great hour, that his re-election,
which vindicated his principles, was owing

not to the politicians primarily, although I have done my best to get on
with them; not to the financiers, although I have staunchly upheld the
rights of property; but above all to Abraham Lincoln's "plain people";
to the folk who worked hard on farm, in shop, or on the railroads, or
who owned little stores, little businesses which they managed themselves.
I would literally, not figuratively, rather cut off my right hand than

[1] Stephenson, op. cit., p. 250.

forfeit by any improper act of mine the trust and regard of these people.[2]

No one could utter braver sentiments than T. R., nor with firmer conviction, at a given moment. His second inauguration, celebrated by a crowd of 500,000 persons who streamed into the capital, witnessed his liberation from pledges to the dead man he had succeeded. "I am glad to be President in my own right," he said to John Hay.[3]

There is evidence that he weighed the trend of the recent elections, and the popular emotions that accompanied it, in serious spirit. One perhaps important symptom was the sharp rise of the tiny Socialist party, led by Eugene Debs, from 100,000 votes in 1900 to 400,000 votes in 1904. Roosevelt duly noted this when he remarked privately in February, 1905, that the growth of the Socialist party was "far more ominous than any Populist or similar movement in the past."[4] William Jennings Bryan, who also watched the popular pulse most carefully, told friends that he now feared the coming of socialism. The new party's rapid growth might lead soon to the capture of one of the older parties, as the Populists had managed to do in 1896. It was proof also "that the Democratic party has been too conservative to satisfy the reform element of the country."[5]

In serious vein, Roosevelt also pondered over the labor problem, though only a minority of American workers were Socialists, while the great majority pinned their hopes upon the economic action of the federated craft unions led by Samuel Gompers. In a long letter, written two days after the election to his Attorney General, Philander C. Knox (retiring now to enter the Senate), Roosevelt explored the possibilities of a Square Deal to labor. Hitherto, with Knox's aid, he had grappled chiefly with the great problems of the day that were connected with organized capital. To Knox, the

[2] Bishop, *op. cit.*, T. R. to Wister, Nov. 19, 1904, Vol. I, p. 345.

[3] Hay, *Diaries*, Vol. V, Nov. 8, 1904.

[4] Pringle, *Roosevelt*, p. 368.

[5] E. E. Robinson, *American Political Parties*, p. 289.

conservative attorney for Carnegie, Roosevelt gave credit handsomely for having given shape to policies which were only "half-formulated" in his own mind. But once in the Senate, there would be occasion for Knox to give as deep thought to the problem of labor as he had given to that of capital.

More and more the labor movement of this country will become a factor of vital importance. . . . If the attitude of the New York *Sun* toward labor, as toward the trusts, becomes the attitude of the Republican party, we shall some day go down before a radical and extreme democracy with a crash which would be disastrous to the nation. We must not only do justice *but we must show the wage-worker that we are doing justice*. We must make it evident that while there is not any weakness in our attitude, while we unflinchingly demand good conduct from them, yet we are equally resolute in the effort to secure them all just and proper consideration.

Here we see in this confidential, artless letter how Roosevelt still never falters in his desire to play the Great Mediator. His hope of upholding the democratic doctrine of "equality before the law" in the conflicts of capital and labor corresponded significantly with the English and European political reform movements of this time, which conceived of social legislation as concessions to be made in time, as a form of "ransom" paid in order to safeguard society and its prosperity. The concessions might be costly; yet, as a Joseph Chamberlain intimated, their costs could be paid out of future profits, and would be outweighed by the gains in security from tragic upheavals.

Roosevelt argued:

It would be a dreadful calamity if we saw this country divided into two parties, one containing the bulk of the property owners and conservative people, the other the bulk of the wage-workers and less prosperous people, generally; each party insisting upon, demanding much that was wrong, and each party sullen and angered by real and fancied grievances.

And what was the answer, what were the measures which, taken in time, would prevent such a fearful outcome? Roosevelt like the corporation lawyers Knox and Root wished to preserve the existing balance of property relations. Further than this he had no definite measures in mind, no time-table, no program. He seemed to offer only a standard, a kind of "moral" imperative, which his conservative colleagues often accepted, but as often wavered from, as it suited their material interests: ". . . Here in this republic, it is peculiarly incumbent upon the man with whom things have prospered to be in a certain sense the keeper of his brother with whom life has gone hard." For "the surest way to provoke an explosion of wrong and injustice is to be short-sighted, narrow-minded, greedy and ignorant. . . ." [6]

Yet vague as was the plan, and wavering the leader, it is true, as Herbert Croly later reflected, that Roosevelt groped in sound directions. His "new Nationalism" or "new Hamiltonianism," while strongly centralizing the government authority, made this augmented authority appear to be more responsive to the popular will; it served not as a bulwark against the rising tide of democracy, but as an effective instrument of the common national welfare. Even in compromise and failure, Rooseveltian leadership gave signs of what could be done; pointed to the "promise of American life."

"In internal affairs, I cannot say that I entered the Presidency with any deliberately planned and far-reaching scheme of social betterment," Roosevelt recollected in writing his autobiography. The more was the pity. What is remarkable at this stage is that, with a record-breaking victory to his credit, and holding an unchallenged position of leadership, Roosevelt confined himself so severely in his actual domestic policies.

While he wondered what to do with his victory, strong influence was brought to bear upon him to see to it that any reform or trust control activities should work, as he put it, "without paralyzing the energies of the business community." [7] From the West came two spokesmen of progressive measures, Governors Cummins

[6] T. R. Papers, T. R. to P. C. Knox, Nov. 10, 1904.
[7] T. R. Papers, T. R. to Sir George Trevelyan, Mar. 9, 1905.

and La Follette, with whom he held a long conference. La Follette advocated strong measures to control railroads and fix the rates they charged; Cummins urged a reduction of the tariff rates that would help, as he thought, to curb the trusts and lower the cost of living. Cummins, on leaving, expressed himself as satisfied with the interview, and counted upon Roosevelt's adherence to tariff reform. He recalled in later years that the President had shown him a passage in his forthcoming Message to Congress indicating as much.[8]

However, something very powerful moved Roosevelt at this juncture, and at almost the last hour before making public his message he veered and changed his mind. Senator Aldrich came to see him; Senator O. H. Platt likewise; and Speaker "Joe" Cannon also came to his desk. To Roosevelt's proposal to do something about tariff reform in the early future, Aldrich coolly answered: "Possibly." Senator Platt may well have reminded the President of the wisdom of holding to the "gentleman's agreement" of 1902 to avoid forbidden subjects. Cannon was even more forthright, according to his own later account. A struggle over the tariff would probably end in failure, and would moreover prevent enactment of the railroad bill Roosevelt had set his heart upon. By telegram, the sentences in the Message of December, 1904, referring to tariff reform, already given out to the press, were "killed."[9]

The Message to Congress of December, 1904, which was to announce a Roosevelt who had "come into his own," and which had been awaited with burning curiosity, proved to be a most moderate document. In a spirit of humanity it recommended laws fostering workmen's compensation and restricting child labor. It was silent upon the tariff issue. Its proposals for the extension of government control over the railroads were the most important ones. Responding to bitter criticisms of existing freight rates, Roosevelt urged

[8] Stephenson, *op. cit.*, p. 235, citing memorandum of A. B. Cummins.
[9] *Ibid.*, p. 462, memorandum of L. W. Busbey; cf. also L. W. Busbey, *Cannon*, pp. 208-209.

that Congress must accord a genuine power to the Interstate Commerce Commission—when complaints were brought—"to decide, subject to judicial review, what shall be a reasonable rate. . . ."

The terms of the Message were conciliatory. Great corporations, the President said, were "necessary," and for their "great and singular mental powers" the masters of corporations were entitled to large rewards. However, they must give due regard to the public interest.

Instant relief was felt now by the anxious railroad lobbyists and "railroad Senators" in Washington. Soon it became plain that, although an administration railroad bill was to be introduced in Congress, nothing would be done during the "Lame Duck" session, and that Roosevelt would not care to call a special session of the new, more liberal Congress, which would normally convene at the end of 1905. It was evident also that Roosevelt had as yet won no agreement of definite support for his bill from Aldrich and Cannon, who controlled Congress still with an unshaken grip. These men waited, and worked to gain time.

It was less well known that the great railroad master Edward H. Harriman, accompanied by his lawyer, quietly visited Washington several times in the winter of 1904-1905, and also in December, 1905, at the time of the new session of Congress. It is evident that in keeping with the friendly alliance between Harriman and Roosevelt, during the late campaign, Harriman was being "consulted" by those who advised the President in framing the proposed law. Yet Harriman disapproved of everything in the way of railroad legislation. He was not an easy man to please, and strain arose between the two aggressive men, more than a year before their public quarrel, almost immediately after the election to which Harriman had given such signal help.

The difficult course of Roosevelt's negotiations with both the railroad magnates and the Standpat leaders in Congress is reflected in certain letters to his Boswell, Joseph B. Bishop, and to Lodge. After a snarl of debate, the railroad reform bill, which had passed the House, died in the committee rooms of the Senate. It was evident that Roosevelt did not press the issue strongly and was easily resigned to waiting for another year, when perhaps the force of public opinion would come to his aid more strongly.

My chief fear is lest the big financiers who, outside of their own narrowly limited profession, are as foolish as they are selfish, will force the moderates to join with the radicals in radical action, under penalty of not obtaining any at all. *I much prefer moderate action:* but the ultra-conservatives may make it necessary to accept what is radical.[10]

In a similar vein he wrote to his old political mentor Lodge, saying that the railroads were opposing his reform bill vigorously and hoped to beat it. ". . . I think they are very short-sighted not to understand that *to beat it means to increase the danger of the movement for government ownership of railroads.*" [11]

These are scarcely the tones of one who, by a tremendous personal victory, had made himself the master of his party. Roosevelt's ventures in legislative leadership (actually very few) show instead that he accepted strict limitations of his power in this field; that he dreaded the wearisome, perplexing task of driving a definite program of legislation through Congress; that he feared the machinelike control of the Senate and the autocratic rule of Speaker Cannon, in the House, would be immune to direct attacks. This machinelike control, especially in the lower House, remained unchallenged by both Roosevelt and Taft, until the insurrection led by Congressman Norris of Nebraska in 1910 suddenly overthrew it.

It was true that the President sought to rally public opinion to his side by making certain fighting speeches, such as that at Philadelphia, January 30, 1905. Here, waving his Big Stick a little, he declared that our free people would not tolerate longer the vast power of corporate wealth, unless "the still higher power" of controlling this wealth in the interests of the whole people were lodged "somewhere in the Government." He asked for "justice" in the way of submitting the railroads to more rigorous supervision by the Interstate Commerce Commission, and gave warning

---

[10] Bishop, *op. cit.*, Vol. I, p. 428, Mar. 23, 1905; italics mine.
[11] *T. R. Papers*, T. R. to Lodge, May 24, 1905; italics mine.

once more that, without such measures, our republic might founder like republics of olden times amid the destructive contests of the Haves and the Have-Nots, the Poor and Rich.

Yet it was all too plain that his mind was distracted by the pernickety controversies that arose over the terms and details of a new empowering act for the Interstate Commerce Commission. Complex economic or financial problems always ended by boring him, for his mind, as his friends knew, was wanting in the spirit of orderly logic necessary to a law-making program. His heart, his emotions, were turned elsewhere in 1905—during this time of painful domestic controversy, financial scandal, and popular unrest—to more distant fields, abroad, where a role of glory, infinitely simpler and more attractive to his nature, beckoned him.

2

"The crowded year supreme" of Roosevelt's official life was unquestionably 1905, according to his authorized biographer. This was the year of the Portsmouth peace conference, bringing to an end the sanguinary Russo-Japanese war. It was the year also when the Morocco crisis brought western Europe to the verge of general war, a crisis in which the President exerted himself to play an important, perhaps a decisive, part in helping to stave off the debacle. Appearing now in the role of a brilliant principal in international *Machtpolitik*, lord of armies and navies, imperial ruler of colonies spreading from the Caribbean to the China Sea, and of their fifteen millions of natives, the Square Deal President inspired Henry Adams to call him "Tsar Rooseveltoff."

For by 1905 the United States formed no longer the "great republic of the West," living its busy life remote from the quarrels and intrigues of Europe's dynastic families; it was a "world power" in a world that had grown perceptibly smaller and whose navies had grown larger and swifter. Operating as the head of a world power was a business that fascinated the "small boy" whom Sir Cecil Spring Rice saw always in this President. As lord of the Army and Navy, and master of the country's foreign relations, his power in this sphere was well-nigh absolute and could even be exercised secretly, up to the point where treaties must be ratified by the Senate. Moreover, in the world outside our borders, the law of force, the law of the jungle, still ruled after all; and the Rough Rider, who preached that one must "speak softly and carry a Big Stick," was well fitted by his aggressive temperament to live in it. For his imperial contemporaries themselves, the Emperors William and Nicholas, or a Chamberlain and a Delcassé often exhibited a temperament no more mature than his. Even their intellectual spokesmen, who preached the ethics of racial superiority (The White Man's Burden) and the "struggle for life," in defending the imperial interests of the day, reflected a philosophy that was at once *"chaste, brutale, héroique et enfantine."* [12]

In the Far East, the interests of the United States as a "world power" now for the first time virtually collided with a whole constellation of the Great Powers. Inevitably the new American foreign policy had marked its enemies and sought to align itself with friends. The American penetration of the Pacific, the seizure of the Philippine Islands, was tolerated and encouraged, as we have seen, by the suddenly benevolent British Empire. More than one British financier-diplomat, like Lord Beresford, expressed the hope that the United States would work in more intimate relations with England in the Far East henceforth, and forestall the swift partition of China, especially by Russia and Germany.

"McKinleyism," with its trust in combinations abroad as well as at home, was responsive to British approaches. In John Hay's Open Door notes of 1899 and 1900 the policy of combination was clearly fostered. The great powers were circularized by the American Secretary of State for an agreement to guarantee to each other's citizens equality of commercial rights in the treaty ports already occupied. Their replies, in truth, were various and hedged with qualifications. But Hay, rather audaciously, declared the Open Door doctrine to be in operation. The declaration of the Open

[12] According to the historian Halévy, cited by Vagts, *Deutschland und die Vereinigte Staaten,* Vol. II, p. 1209.

Door policy gave to American activity in the Far East a humanitarian and righteous appearance, by appearing to protect China's integrity, and thus softened the blows of anti-imperialists at home. In the second place it pleased the American oil, textile, steel, and banking interests who were now entering the Chinese market more vigorously. The "growing necessity for protecting the new markets which American manufacturers and exporters had secured in the Orient, against the counteracting influence of other Powers . . . threatening the partial exclusion of American products," was met by Secretary Hay's skillful Open Door notes. The agreements he gained represented "a *coup d'état* for American foreign trade," according to one spokesman of financial interests.[13] Finally the Open Door agreements were seen to be helpful for the present to British interests in China, serving to stabilize things at a balance favorable to her, and were initiated by Hay, it is believed, as a discreet *quid pro quo* for British retirement from the Caribbean.[14]

John Hay, when he was named Secretary of State, was set down in secret German reports as a confirmed Anglophile. When attacked publicly on this ground by American politicians, he "writhed under the charge but did nothing except to deny it." [15] But even Richard Olney, who had written such ringing, war-like messages to John Bull in 1895, in his old age repented, and in 1900 declared publicly that America "must expand," that of necessity we must have a "friend" and that England alone could help or harm us.[16] Henry Adams, commenting on Olney's change of heart, remarked: "We drift inevitably back to the British. Economical and social interests are too strong. Our administration, whether Olney or Hay run it, must be British; Bayard or Frelinghuysen, or Fish or Seward—it is all the same." [17] Nor was it different when Theodore Roosevelt throned in the White House.

John Hay "believed in the British Empire." In England, "his

---

[13] *Bankers Magazine*, editorial, Jan., 1902.
[14] Dennett, *op. cit.*, pp. 291, 295-296.
[15] *Ibid.*, p. 388.
[16] R. Olney, "Growth of Our Foreign Policy," *Atlantic Monthly*, Mar., 1900.
[17] Adams, *Letters*, Vol. II, p. 270.

friends were always among the ruling classes: Curzon, Chamberlain, Balfour, Harcourt, the bankers, the landed gentry. . . ." It was a cardinal principle of his statecraft—as he declared one day, January 2, 1900, to the German Ambassador—that the "continued existence of the British Empire, even though somewhat humbled," would be of greater advantage to the world than its downfall.[18]

During the Spanish-American War, on May 7, 1898, Spring Rice, reflecting the benevolent British demeanor, had written Hay: "Therefore, as I say again, let us try while we can to secure what we can for God's language." [19] Hay answered that this was precisely in line with his own ideas. It was definitely in line with Roosevelt's ideas also. But Roosevelt was naturally a far more skillful political artist in furthering "friendship" with England, while standing for an unyielding "Americanism" before the home voters.

The British-American sharing of the White Man's Burden evolved rapidly in Rooseveltian days. While American armies, ranging from 60,000 to 100,000 men, formidable even for those days, were deeply engaged in "civilizing" the Filipinos, expansion operations in the Caribbean area were carried forward simultaneously. The late war and Pacific expansion had made the completion of a canal across the Isthmus of Panama a military as well as a commercial imperative. When, early in 1902, the bankrupt Panama Canal Company, launched by the ill-starred de Lesseps, expressed its willingness to sell its uncompleted property and rights to the United States for $40,000,000, Roosevelt moved rapidly to accept the bargain. With the authority of Congress, the earlier project, by which the American government was to build a canal across Nicaragua, was abandoned for that of Panama. The digging of this canal would complete a mighty link in the imperial chain spreading from the Atlantic seaboard to the China coast; and Roosevelt was extremely eager to have the great canal, planned more than fifty years ago, built by the end of his second

[18] Dennis, *American Diplomacy, 1896-1906*, p. 125.
[19] Gwynn, *op. cit.*, Vol. I, pp. 247-248.

term. But first the old Clayton-Bulwer Treaty of 1850, by which Britain and America were to share in the building of such a canal and hold it unfortified, must be altered, in accordance with the new demands of "Americanism" in the Caribbean.

Long-standing disputes between America and Britain had a way of being cleared up with miraculous speed, in these days when Germany's rising industrial and naval power was so keenly feared in Downing Street. The second Hay-Pauncefote Treaty, ratified in February, 1902, yielded to virtually all the American demands that the new canal was to be policed by American forces, and entirely built and owned by the American government. Following up the completion of this agreement (chiefly prepared under Mc-Kinley), Roosevelt undertook by aggressive diplomacy to settle the old Alaska boundary dispute between Canada and the United States. Once more the British seemed ready to yield in changing the line in southern Alaska in accordance with American claims; and evidently perceiving this, Roosevelt did not neglect to hasten them on by drawing out the Big Stick in 1903, flourishing it toward Canada, and speaking out loud about the possible mobilization of American troops at the frontier. The final judgment of the Arbitration Commission, which terminated the affair, represented a cheap foreign triumph for Roosevelt, since the chief of the British delegation, Lord Alverstone, appeared to have been instructed in advance to yield to all the American claims.

Roosevelt's combative manner successfully concealed his real or secret acceptance of the "inevitable" Anglo-American partnership. His innate tendencies were almost as anti-German as John Hay's; and like many high officers in the American navy he singled out the rising German power as "the enemy," while England was held to be the friend of the future. While Britain yielded up control of the Caribbean despite her West Indian possessions, and recognized the new status at Panama, the Germans might not abide by the Monroe Doctrine unless they were encouraged to do so by show of force. The talk of German expansion in South America, even of a possible German naval war against the United States, reached the President. Possibly he knew of Admiral Dewey's strange prediction in 1899 that "the first war of the United States would be with Germany." During the blockade of Venezuela by British, Italian, and German naval forces in December, 1902, owing to non-payment of certain claims, public opinion in America as reflected in the press was permitted to be roused to a pitch of anger at Germany particularly. The German men-of-war, independently of their allies, were said to have bombarded a Venezuelan port in most ruthless fashion. That winter, Roosevelt mobilized the American fleet under Dewey in the Caribbean, as a silent naval demonstration against Germany—though he also hinted at almost the same time that he might invade Canada, because of the pending Alaska boundary dispute. In April, 1903, he confided to Hay his fears that Germany would tend to disregard the Monroe Doctrine. "Both the Dutch and the Danish West Indies in America will be a constant temptation to Germany, unless or until we take them. The way to deliver Germany from temptation is to keep on with the upbuilding of our navy." [20]

That season a very large increase in the naval appropriation, enthusiastically urged by the President, was granted by Congress.

Probably nothing impressed "Tsar Rooseveltoff's" fellow monarchs more deeply than the swift, forthright manner in which he rubbed out large obstacles barring the acquisition of the Panama Canal Zone by the American government. Democracies with their bicameral parliaments are slow to take action in complex business matters. In this case, additional difficulties were provided by the Republic of Colombia, sovereign in the province of Panama, which rightly or wrongly desired in addition to cash and lease rentals a share of the large money payment, namely, $40,000,000, going to those who had taken over the affairs of the defunct Panama Company. To push forward the canal, Colombian opposition must be removed. However, the American proposals, framed in the Hay-Herran convention of January, 1903, after waiting all winter and summer, finally failed of ratification by the Colombian Senate,

[20] *T. R. Papers*, T. R. to Hay, Apr. 22, 1903.

August 12, 1903. The impatience of the Rough Rider now passed all bounds, and veiled threats of force passed from our State Department to the stubborn adversaries at Bogota. By September, plans for a "popular" revolution in Panama were well advanced, and were heard of in Washington as well as in Colombia. At first the eminent New York lawyer William Nelson Cromwell, of Sullivan and Cromwell, attorney for the new group of financiers active for the Panama Company, appeared to be the soul of native revolution. Then the adventurous French soldier of fortune, Captain Philippe Bunau-Varilla, held his place openly in October.

Bunau-Varilla interviewed President Roosevelt at the White House, October 9, 1903. A recently published memorandum of Elihu Root, giving the essence of the conference, throws the clearest light upon that which followed.

Bunau Varilla . . . said that he merely stated what he thought Roosevelt's idea was about the Colombians and by talking about them and what they did, he got from Roosevelt such violent expressions of opinion unfriendly to the Colombians that when he left he told his people in Panama to go ahead, that Roosevelt would never take sides against them with the Colombians. Roosevelt did not say . . . what he wanted to do or intended to do. . . .[21]

Next Bunau-Varilla saw Secretary Hay, and learned from him that the American government was ready for all events; that naval forces in the Pacific had their orders. Hay asked him if he had read a certain novel by Richard Harding Davis entitled *Captain Macklin*, regarding an American soldier of fortune who participated in a revolution in a South American state. The conspirator received the impression from Hay that in case of revolution American warships would be on hand *to prevent* passage of Colombian troops across the Isthmus, rather than to aid them, as previous existing treaties required. According to Henry Pringle's sardonic account of the comic-opera revolution, a new constitution was made ready in a Wall Street corporation lawyer's office; a new

[21] Jessup, *Root*, Vol. I, pp. 403-404.

flag was woven in a room of the Waldorf-Astoria Hotel. The act of "secession" which took place November 3, 1903, on schedule and sans bloodletting, under the watchful guns of American warships, had been openly desired by Roosevelt and Hay, and proved preferable to some other form of violent intervention, which the courageous Roosevelt was also prepared to take.[22] Ten days later, with indecent haste, Secretary Hay signed a treaty with the "minister plenipotentiary" of the new sovereign nation of Panama, handing over to the latter the money originally due to Colombia.

"I took the Isthmus, started the Canal, and then left Congress . . . to debate me," Roosevelt admitted proudly, but indiscreetly, in 1911. The blocked roads of civilization had been forced open quickly. The American public, to whom the news came suddenly, appeared more pleased and amused than shocked. The Roosevelt administration had added new laurels to its world-wide reputation for "doing things." Meanwhile, a large part of the $40,000,000 purchase payment for the New Panama Canal Company, as later investigations showed, undoubtedly passed into the hands of American financiers who had strong political connections, although the actual disposal of the sums has remained to this day a sealed mystery.

3

After the Spanish-American War and Roosevelt's whirlwind, Rough-Rider campaign for the Governorship of New York, Count Speck von Sternburg, Secretary of the German legation at Washington, who had known the Colonel intimately since the early '90's, began to send home colorful reports of the rising statesman for the benefit of the German Foreign Office. Roosevelt was pictured as one of their own kind, inspiring the American upper-class youth with martial spirit; and Sternburg even went so far as to label him "the future military dictator" of the States. These reports came to the eye of the Emperor himself, who wrote upon

[22] Pringle, *Roosevelt*, pp. 316-317, 322-323.

the margin of one of them the ironical comment: "The future military dictator! Europe watch out!??" [23]

When the dynamic Colonel mounted one day to the White House, at his quietly communicated wish, Sternburg, whom he warmly liked, was raised in diplomatic rank and sent back to Washington as German Ambassador. It was a move to overcome the very marked ill-feeling toward Germany manifested in the American press and in high naval circles after the battle of Manila, in May, 1898—when unfriendly gestures were made at each other by the American and the German naval forces.

Roosevelt's extending activities in the Latin American sphere in 1904 completed the grip that the "Colossus of the North" had taken upon the world of the little Latin brother. Following the blockading and bombardment of Venezuela by England, Germany, and Italy, mediation by the American government, brought about in peaceable spirit, had terminated the affair for the time being. But to prevent such complications in the future, Roosevelt wrote to Elihu Root a letter—which the latter read at a public meeting in New York, May 20, 1904—that served to amplify the Monroe Doctrine by the addition of the so-called Roosevelt Corollary. Here and in his Message to Congress of December 6, 1904, Roosevelt declared that though the United States wished no territories in Central and South America, it was desired that the countries neighboring the vital Canal Zone should be "stable, orderly and prosperous." If nations to the south acted "with decency in industrial and political matters," kept order, and paid their obligations, no interference by the Yankee Colossus need be expected. But if duties to civilization and business accounts were forgotten, then the American government would wield a police club. As Roosevelt explained in a subsequent letter to Root, ". . . If we intend to say 'Hands off' to the powers of Europe, then sooner or later we must keep order ourselves." [24]

Despite considerable criticism, it was this new policy that the

[23] Vagts, op. cit., Vol. II, p. 1887.
[24] Jessup, op. cit., Vol. I, p. 470, letter of Jun. 7, 1904.

President pursued in forcing an arrangement upon the government of Santo Domingo (following a dispute with foreign creditors) whereby the American minister, with the aid of American naval forces, would collect customs receipts and allot a regular part of them—to extinguishing foreign debts. The American Senate, irritated at not being consulted, entered upon rancorous debate and refused by a close margin to ratify this significant protocol. But the President, at the height of his power following the election victory of November, 1904, ordered American agents to take charge of Dominican customs notwithstanding; which was done for more than two years, while warships preserved "order" in the island. It was a very high-handed, precedent-making step and, associated with American armed intervention in Cuba during the insurrection of 1906, this time under the "Platt Amendment," it enhanced the reputation for brutal aggression, under virtuous professions, which the government of the Yankees gained among the smaller Latin American nations.

That neurotic and unstable character, the German Kaiser William II, was now willing to believe the reports of his agents concerning the American "dictator's" potential prowess in the *Machtpolitik* of the world. Through the Ambassador at Washington, who stood on the familiar footing of "Specky" to the Presidential family, the most intimate friendly communications were sent from Potsdam in 1904. And from Washington came the friendliest responses in return, indicating that the President felt the Kaiser to be a man of kindred ideals. "The only man I understand and who understands me is the Kaiser," ran one message of October 26, 1904. And William's marginal comment was: "*Sehr schmeichelhaft*" (very flattering).[25] Indeed, he learned from his Foreign Minister, von Bülow, that "The President is a great admirer of your Majesty, and would like to rule the world hand in hand with your Majesty, regarding himself as something in the nature of an American counterpart of your Majesty." [26]

[25] Vagts, *op. cit.*, Vol. II, p. 1186.
[26] Dennis, *Adventures*, p. 390.

The Kaiser feared that *"Teddy ist echt dillettantisch,"* and (as the British Foreign Office observed in a similar case) that the American people, or their elected representatives, might not always follow where he led. But the clue that Roosevelt, like himself, was a man of enormous vanity—"glorieux," a French diplomat called him after the Panama affair—and was eager to "horn into" world power politics was not lost upon him. Thenceforth, from the start of the Russo-Japanese War, so deeply connected with imperialistic tensions in Europe, flattering and confidential messages flowed constantly to Mr. Roosevelt chiefly through the medium of Count von Sternburg. This "playing with kings," which Henry Adams now heard about, was an extraordinary form of intercourse that American Presidents in the past had carefully eschewed. But these were imperial times, even in Washington, D.C.

There was a season when Theodore Roosevelt felt strongly the attraction of the German monarch who with one hand enacted sweeping social reform calculated to appease the restive proletariat, while with the other he commanded the mightiest of land armies. Spring Rice was convinced that his friend "Teddy" envied the Kaiser his uniforms and his prancing cavalry regiments.[27] It also is apparent that, after a glance at the turmoil of world power politics, Roosevelt planned to use as far as possible those balance-of-power stratagems that he had employed against boss Platt in New York and used now in playing rival capitalists, such as Morgan and Harriman, or conservative and radical forces in national politics, against each other.

Thus an extraordinary transatlantic friendship was now cultivated between Theodore Roosevelt and William of Hohenzollern. It sometimes roused the suspicion of the British Foreign Office, although its course was far from even, and the gorgeous friend in Potsdam was often left prey to the darkest misgivings concerning the man in Washington.

Meanwhile, through his other personal friend, Cecil Spring

[27] Gwynn, *op. cit.*, Vol. I, pp. 208-209.

Rice (now familiarly "Springy"), though he was unfortunately stationed at St. Petersburg, equally intimate communications and warnings inspired directly by Downing Street, or sometimes discreetly by Edward VII himself, constantly poured into the White House. Roosevelt flung himself, with a forwardness and zest that no other American chief magistrate had shown, into the "game" of world politics, as if it were an end or a joy in itself, fascinated by its dark and double intrigues, its high and intangible privileges, or dangerous shiftings of chance, that made it all so much more fun than framing and passing a tariff bill.

Shifting his attention from the Caribbean to the Far East, which had been John Hay's special province up to the time of his long illness, in the latter part of 1904, Roosevelt took a strong hand in Pacific affairs. There the final phases of the world-wide contest for colonies and markets were being enacted with breathless speed. The dominant course of world power politics, ever since the end of the nineteenth century, was fixed by England's desperate efforts to gather a coalition of allies against the day when Germany would attempt to destroy her Empire. Germany, the *arriviste* state of Europe, had experienced belatedly an amazing increase of industrial output—her steel-producing capacity increased, between 1881 and 1911, from a figure that was 48 per cent of England's to one that was 220 per cent. In turn, Germany, growing swiftly in population, commerce, and naval force (which the vainglorious William II did nothing to conceal), was possessed with justifiable fear of "encirclement" by her rivals. By 1904 this dominant polar antagonism, around which other rivalries were aligned, and which could be studied in Africa or Polynesia, expressed itself in concealed form in war between Russia and Japan.

Less than two years after the declaration of the Open Door doctrine for China, the "co-operative" policy was a dead letter. England, which had given but lip-service to the Open Door agreements, signed her first Anglo-Japanese Treaty of Alliance early in 1902. Japan now turned to British support and abandoned efforts to conciliate Russia, with whom she clashed constantly in

North China and Manchuria, and war between the two nations was now possible. England could remain unconcerned, since her growing interests in South China and the Yangtze Valley and her immense Indian possessions were rendered all the safer from possible Russian pressure. Meanwhile the German Emperor, pursuing his own designs, pressed his cousin Nicholas to fall upon Japan, seize Korea with its warm-water ports, and make sure of Manchuria as well. The German purpose, it has been judged, was to "mire" Russia in far-off Manchuria, so as to relieve Germany's eastern frontier in Europe from the danger of Russia's vast armies. Beyond this, there were obscure negotiations on foot, pointing to an eventual sharing of North China loot between Russia and Germany, in return for a promise of German support for Russian acquisition of Manchuria—in violation of the Open Door agreements. The vast but obscure schemes of the German rulers also envisaged binding Russia to their projected *Drang nach Osten,* the Berlin-Baghdad drive, though eventually Russian diplomacy saw no good for itself in this adventure. Meanwhile the German rulers, without cost to themselves, riding upon the backs of the Russians, plainly hoped to snatch increased territory in Shantung, north of China's Great Wall, to add to their fortified base at Kiau-Chau, and thus make it more defensible. The expected war began on February 8, 1904, with England, the secret ally of Japan, remaining passive, yet by the threat of her navy giving France (Russia's ally and financial backer), as well as Germany, reason for neutrality.

Britain intended to remain strong in the Orient, not by doctrines but by an alliance with the Japanese regarding mutual aid and "spheres of influence." Japan was a rising power. The weakening of Russia would make her more manageable after the war, and lead to her eventual attachment to the British system of alliances. English officials who watched over the future of India and the Near East were delighted at Russia's embroilment in Manchuria. Meanwhile in April, 1904, during the early stages of the war, the English concluded a second, important treaty, the Entente Cordiale with France, settling all matters of the control of Egypt and Morocco between them. The Kaiser's confused, poorly sustained diplomacy had been outdone at every step by the wily British maneuvers; when the British alliance with Russia was signed three years later—despite William's manly wooing of "Nicky" at Björköe—the encirclement of the too aggressive, heavily armed Germany was a reality.

4

Into this web of international pressures, intrigues, secret treaties, and fomented conflicts, the restless Roosevelt now trod. The American interests lay for the moment in safeguarding our possessions in the Philippines, lately pacified by Governor-General William H. Taft; but the paramount object was to maintain the Open Door for foreign trade in China, whatever the fortunes of the Russo-Japanese War. Hitherto American policy in the Far East, as McKinley and Hay had conceived it, had been identical. But the diplomatic struggle for free and impartial trade rights, among the concessions and spheres of influence of the various powers, was to be a long, losing fight. When Roosevelt sought to uphold the balance of power and made peace moves, ostensibly "for the sake of humanity," Britain moved not to persuade the Japanese.

As soon as hostilities started, the Kaiser appealed to the President, his American "admirer," through Ambassador Sternburg, to urge the belligerents to observe the neutrality of China "outside the sphere of military operations." This excluded, of course, Manchuria and North China, which the Kaiser evidently hoped would fall partly to the larger adversary, Russia, and partly to himself. Roosevelt agreed to circularize the powers with a note to this general effect, after altering the declaration in an important sense, to urge the observance of neutrality *in the whole of China's "administrative entity."* Thus it was from Washington rather than from Berlin that the circular note, boldly reasserting the Open Door policy, was issued on February 10, 1904.[28] The Kaiser thus acted

[28] Dennett, *op. cit.*, pp. 407-408.

as if piously supporting the Open Door doctrine together with his admirer, Roosevelt. This stratagem had little effect on the powers lined up for this war, who responded but indifferently. The Kaiser in this affair behaved with much duplicity toward his American friend, by secretly assuring Russia that he would recognize her conquest of Manchuria. The British government treated the Roosevelt declaration with suspicion, as if words about the territorial integrity of China mattered little against the realities of war and invasion, and of genuine British interests and combinations elsewhere in the world.[29] Russia, suspecting an American neutrality that was actually benevolent toward Japan, paid no heed to Roosevelt's enunciations from Washington upon Chinese territorial integrity. Roosevelt could not understand the Kaiser's underlying motives, but in collaborating with him to a limited extent he at times aroused the suspicions and fears of the British, who hinted that he was being led around by the nose, and insisted that the Kaiser plotted a great coalition against them.

The Rough Rider, in these moments, leaves us with the impression of one moving innocently between the lines of two enemy camps, filled with hidden gunpowder, while assuring the two implacable enemies that there is really nothing to quarrel about. He plainly did not grasp the character of the treacherous ground mined with secret alliances over which he walked, and trusted by informal diplomatic approaches to foster reconciliation, and to win German and British support for his own Pacific balance of power. More than once he assured Spring Rice, and the British Ambassador at Washington, Durand, that reports of the Kaiser's scheming against Britain were misguided. Meanwhile British coolness to his own pursuit of peace and balance in the Far East deeply disappointed him. In the opinion of most students of this period in world politics, Roosevelt failed completely to perceive the deep animosities between the two strongest European powers, as he ignored the real character of their commitments. In the end, more or less wittingly, "inevitably" he drifted into one of the two camps and thus rendered the other all the more desperate.

[29] Griswold, *Far Eastern Policy*, pp. 98-99, 102.

Meanwhile the war had gone hard for Russia, and her dubious friend, the Kaiser, also found no further gains to be derived from it. In January, 1905, before the battle of Mukden, and again in April the American President pressed his good offices for a mediated peace upon the Russian Czar and the Japanese government without effect. For many months, in voluminous diplomatic correspondence and informal approaches through his personal lines of communication, von Sternburg, Spring Rice, and Ambassador Jusserand, he strove to force the two warring nations into a conference, while at the same time he labored to bring England, France, and Germany to the support of his efforts. He believed, as he relates in his autobiography, "that a further continuance of the struggle would be a very bad thing for Japan, and even worse for Russia." At first Roosevelt had been almost as warm a friend of Japan's as England, fearing the Russians more strongly, and expressing in private a willingness to come to the aid of the Japanese, in force if need be. But the sweeping character of the Japanese victories ended by alarming him. At this rate all Asia, and the Philippines included, would be at the mercy of the new conquerors, and unexpected dangers were suggested. Meanwhile, though the usually ferocious Kaiser appeared favorable to Roosevelt's peacemaking, the English were silent, and held off, clearly refusing to second his efforts. Roosevelt, standing between the two alignments, could make nothing of the mutual suspicions and terrors felt on each side, even after the sensational visit of the Kaiser to Tangier in Morocco, March 31, 1905, which suddenly shifted the real theater of world struggle to northern Africa and the Mediterranean Sea. Roosevelt's ignorance was partly due to the lack of an active espionage organization at that time.

In his far-flung interventions and his world wanderings the American leader was like a willing soldier who does not see the whole of the battle front, nor the general configuration of the struggle. He did not know, for instance, until very late, that the English were silent because they were preparing to renew their secret alliance of 1902 with Japan in much stronger form, protecting their main Asiatic possessions more definitely than before—

this at a time, March-April, 1905, when the Japanese waited anxiously for the second Russian fleet steaming around the world to meet them.

But it was time for the war to end. The drain upon Japanese human and material resources was heavy; while the Russians accumulated a tremendous debt to French bankers and investors. Roosevelt, then, did not "stop" the Russo-Japanese war, as we now know. The closing of the purse strings at French and Anglo-American financial sources—for American bankers such as Kuhn, Loeb and Company also gave liberal aid to the Japanese—served as much as the sweeping naval victory of Togo, on May 27, 1905, to halt the war.

In April the French government had already hinted that Russia was ready to make terms. The Japanese, of their own accord, desired that the American President (rather than France) should act as mediator; and the first formal overtures for peace were made by them to Washington, May 31, 1905, immediately after their great naval victory. A week later, pressed by William II, the lethargic ruler of all the Russias indicated to the waiting American ambassador at St. Petersburg that if Mr. Roosevelt desired to act "on his own initiative" in treating with Japan, Russia would agree to a peace conference. The formal invitations to the belligerents then went forward; and Roosevelt busied himself with the essential preliminary work for the conference, which was set for August 10, 1905, at Portsmouth, New Hampshire.

It was to be an affair of novelty and pageantry, the arbitration of a great and terrible war between mighty empires, by the American President. World interest centered upon Oyster Bay, where the President received the envoys with simple ceremony upon the Presidential yacht; then shifted to the little New England city of Portsmouth. A visitor found Roosevelt weary but happy; he had been working tirelessly to carry through the affair, and feared obstacles and treachery at every turn.[30]

At the conference, the Japanese pretended to be firm in their

---

[30] Bishop, *op. cit.*, Vol. I, p 405.

demand for a huge money indemnity, as well as the various territories and spheres of influence they had marked out for themselves or conquered. The Russians, on the other hand, proved to be as hard to bargain with as ever, especially where money was concerned. Roosevelt, though he had favored Japan earlier as the ostensibly weaker adversary, was now keenly aware of the "yellow peril" to the Philippines, and unwilling to see Russia driven out of the Pacific. Therefore his main efforts were directed on the one hand to inducing the Japanese emissaries to give up the notion of indemnities—Russia was bankrupt, and it would have been necessary to capture Moscow to wring money from her. On the other hand, he strove to persuade the Russian government to yield as far as possible to Japan's territorial demands, for the fortress of Port Arthur, a protectorate in Korea, and cession of the southern half of Sakhalin Island. In the end nearly all of the Japanese real, minimum demands were accorded—after long and close negotiation, Russia contenting herself with the boon of having escaped an indemnity. In a sense, Roosevelt's intervention worked well for Japan, who he knew could not continue the war effectively.

Japan was left as virtually the dominant sea power in the Pacific, restrained after 1905 only by her economic exhaustion and her alliance with Britain. Probably her government had not actually counted upon wresting money from Russia; yet the failure to do this was attributed to President Roosevelt's interference. Mob rioting broke out in Tokyo, and Roosevelt—instead of the British government, to whom the peace was extremely important—became the scapegoat, "drawing the resentment of the Japanese people onto his own unpracticed shoulders." [31]

The war had been ended not a whit sooner than the British desired it to end, after their new secret treaty with Japan was initialed. But they wished it ended, within limits, for soon they would also have important treaty business on foot with the wretched Russians. Therefore the happiest solution for them diplomatically was for neutral America rather than themselves

[31] Griswold, *op. cit.*, pp. 121-122.

to stay the hands of their military allies from further conquest.[32]

Moreover Roosevelt, who congratulated himself upon having re-established a balance of power in the Pacific, had actually confirmed a status favoring the Anglo-Japanese domination, while German aspirations in China were thoroughly checked, her concessions in Shantung becoming untenable. The Russian Bear, most of all, had had his claws clipped in the Orient, and threatened less forcibly the British domain in India as well as China. Thereafter, rumors in the chancelleries of Europe told of how the English terrified the Czar with pictures of another Japanese attack upon his possessions (an attack which in 1905 had led to a bloody internal revolution), and which the English alone could restrain. Thus Russia soon became more eager to join the Anglo-French Entente in the West.

Universal applause for the peace-making President accompanied the signing of the historic Portsmouth Peace Treaty on September 5, 1905. Roosevelt in his toast to the Russian and Japanese emissaries at the opening of the conference had said that he prayed for a "just and lasting peace" not only for the two powers here represented, but for "all civilized mankind." [33] It was with this end in view, ostensibly, that he participated and intruded himself so vigorously into the affairs of the whole world. In studying the pattern of bold Rooseveltian interventions in the incessant struggles of the world's imperial rivals, we must ask ourselves constantly how much the real interests of the American republic were aided, and how much this international activism in Washington

[32] Roosevelt was scarcely neutral in the negotiations. For on July 29, 1905, preceding the peace conference, Secretary of War Taft on a tour of inspection to the Philippines was instructed to call at Tokyo as the President's special plenipotentiary. He bore a "memorandum," in effect a secret treaty, by which the United States was to recognize Japan's acquisition of Korea, while Japan agreed not to attack our Pacific possessions, the Philippines, etc. Yet the status of Korea, as a part of China's "integrity," was to be settled at the approaching Portsmouth conference. The Taft-Katsura "memorandum," and the later Root-Takahira "gentleman's agreement," remained in force, putting the United States in an informal alliance with Japan and Britain in the Far East.

[33] The New York *Tribune*, Aug. 6, 1905.

actually changed the order of things or furthered the humane end of world peace.

No sooner were measures taken to quench the flames in one part of the world, than they roared up in another place. Even while the Russo-Japanese War drew to its close, and Roosevelt's mediating efforts were bearing fruit, the world crisis over Morocco, with its menace of a general war of all the great powers in Europe, burst forth in the early spring of 1905. The mercurial President's attention now swung to the focal point in the Mediterranean, where once more he would endeavor to play his characteristic, leading part.

Once having begun, he must continue. After the Portsmouth Conference, Roosevelt said:

> In foreign affairs, we must make up our minds that, whether we wish it or not, we are a great people and must play a great part in the world. It is not open to us to choose whether we will play that great part or not. We have to play it. All we can decide is whether we shall play it well or ill.[34]

5

On March 31, 1905, the anxious motives of the German Emperor in seeking new friends, even as far afield as North America, became painfully clear. On that day he had disembarked at Tangier, Morocco, from a German cruiser, and, addressing the Sultan of Morocco in a deliberately "aggressive" speech (while trembling nervously at his own audacity), declared his hope and wish that Morocco would remain independent and free to the trade of all nations. The inwardly tormented, outwardly bellicose William II acted in accordance with the deliberate plan of his Foreign Minister, von Bülow, who convinced him that the hour had come to smoke out the secret terms of the Anglo-French Entente of 1904, relative to the partition of northern Africa, by an open challenge in that area and a demand for the Open Door. The German government in the discussions that followed William II's

---

[34] *Presidential Speeches*, Richmond, Va., Oct. 18, 1905, Vol. IV, p. 461.

visitation demanded that the status of neutral rights in Morocco be clarified, and that a conference to determine this question as well as that of "neutralization" of the Moroccan government be held. This the French, who were on the ground, refused; the English supported them, and secret mobilization began. Thus, as we have seen, the stage setting of the world-wide imperialist drama was shifted from the frozen prairies of Manchuria to the tropical, palm-fringed shores of Morocco.

William II and von Bülow, whose courting of Roosevelt had both titillated and mystified the man, now called upon him earnestly to defend with them the sacred and enlightened principle of the Open Door, the "co-operative" policy, in northern Africa as well as in China. The United States was asked to join Germany in requesting the other interested powers to agree to an international conference regarding the future status of Morocco, a conference in which the United States was to participate as an equal member, by virtue of previous though somewhat obsolete conventions with former Sultans. The Germans revealed the utmost anxiety to escape from the isolation which threatened them in the hostile world arena.[35]

The Emperor urged upon the President the gravity of the situation, telling him in memoranda transmitted through Sternburg that the Moroccan question was not an isolated one, but might lead either to war or to a new grouping of the world powers. "If England is successful in causing the refusal of France to join in a conference to settle the Morocco question, Germany will have to choose between war with France or between an understanding with France with regard to Morocco. . . . Everything he [William II] thinks depends on the attitude *you* may

[35] A. Vagts, *op. cit.*, Vol. II, pp. 1835-1843.

Dr. Vagts, after long study of German archives touching this period, attributes the idea of calling for American participation to the purpose of showing "peaceful" intentions on the part of Germany. Should war have come—and only the resignation of the French minister, Delcassé, averted it—then American participation in the preliminary discussions would have been a gauge of Germany's good faith in seeking peaceful solutions.

consider fit to take toward a conference of the treaty powers to settle the Morocco question." [36]

Thus "everything depended upon" Theodore Roosevelt, the Emperor of Germany assured him! General war, for which secret preparations were under way—or peace. The Kaiser through his Ambassador communicated charges of the plotting of England and France to gain an absolute ascendancy over Germany, and urged the President not to permit such an outcome, which would vitally affect the balance of power in the East, perhaps to the ultimate injury of American interests there. America must therefore help to bring about the conference over Morocco. Yet at this very time William himself returned to the wooing of Czar Nicholas, to whom he proposed a military alliance against England at a conference on board his yacht July 24, 1905.

Faced with the possibility of working for the balance of power in the Western World, to the advantage of Germany, Roosevelt turned less than impulsive, and hesitated prudently. With a very moderate enthusiasm, while admitting that the United States took only slight interest in Morocco, he made diplomatic overtures to both the French and the British governments for holding an international conference. In London, Lord Lansdowne appeared cool to any suggestion of a conference, and determined to fight in behalf of France if Germany attacked. Roosevelt, still unaware of the shaping of secret military alliances in Europe, and the secret agreements between France, England, Italy, and Spain to divide Morocco and Tripoli, decided at length to press for the international conference that might lessen the European tension, and also further peace in the Far East.

He approached the French, then, in serious vein. To Jules Jusserand, with whom Roosevelt was also upon very intimate, informal terms, he remarked that it might be advisable to make "concessions . . . that one can honorably make to avoid a conflict. . . . You must grant some satisfaction to the immeasurable

[36] Bishop, *op. cit.*, T. R. to Whitlaw Reid, Apr. 28, 1906, Vol. I, p. 471.

vanity of William. And it would be wise to help him save his face, if by doing so one could avoid war." [37]

Roosevelt then offered to employ his "initiative" in bringing about the conference, in a spirit friendly to France. Although United States interest in Morocco was slight, vigorous support would be lent France, if such a conference were held, in order to see to it that "unjust attacks by Germany upon French interests" would not succeed. [38]

In short, although the President in the Far Eastern war had favored Japan against Russia, in the Western crisis he favored France against Germany, saying, "France was right," and promising that he would not serve as a "decoy duck" for the Kaiser. Most important of all, he told the French ambassador in advance just what he would say to the German ambassador in regard to a conference whose conditions and limits were to be fixed by the French and the English! [39] Moreover, the United States would not "accept the invitation to the conference unless France was willing." Upon these safe terms, France agreed on June 23, 1905, to let the President intervene for the maintenance of peace.

Roosevelt might flatter the Kaiser and remain his "admirer," desirous of going "hand in hand" with him; but in a pinch, to the intense disappointment of the German Foreign Office, he drifted toward the French, and more or less knowingly, the Anglo-French orbit.

He did continue to reason, like Admirals Mahan and Dewey, that while England could be forced to act as our friend, Germany, if she disposed of her European rivals, was to be feared as an ultimate enemy. Was not the configuration of the "Atlantic System" that John Hay saw accepted also by Roosevelt, in spite of his outward obeisances to William II? By this concept, America was

[37] *Documents Diplomatiques Français*, 2" Série, Tome VII, Paris, 1937. Jusserand to M. Rouvier, Jun. 18, 1905.

[38] Bishop, *op. cit.*, Vol. I, p. 478.

[39] *Documents Diplomatiques*, 2" Série, Tome VII. Jusserand to Rouvier, Jun. 25, 1905.

bound to be vitally affected by a shift in the western European balance. As Henry Adams stated it: "We have got to support France against Germany, and fortify an Atlantic system beyond attack; for if Germany breaks down England or France, she becomes the center of a military world, and we are lost." These were prophetic words, stating a formula which, right or wrong, was to be followed by American statesmen of either party in all the great crises of the twentieth century.[40]

Recently published documents, issued by the French government in 1937, reveal more strongly than ever how decidedly Roosevelt swung to the support of France in the Moroccan crisis.

On June 6, 1905, secret negotiations between France and Germany had led to the resignation of the bellicose Premier Delcassé, as partial appeasement for Germany. Yet nothing further was yielded in Morocco. The conference was to be one whose program, by the terms of the Anglo-French Entente, was fixed inalterably in advance. For the Kaiser to accept such a limited conference, under such narrow conditions, meant to take the appearance of things in place of the substance of them. He was to satisfy himself with the resignation of the hated Delcassé and the mere acceptance of a conference by his adversaries, while silently a great diplomatic triumph was scored for the Anglo-French Entente, which both excluded Germany from northern Africa and fashioned an iron ring of "encirclement" around her.[41]

At a time when tension between Germany and France made direct negotiation difficult, Roosevelt played the important part of pressing the Kaiser (through Sternburg) to swallow the bitter pill as really good candy. The French Diplomatic Documents, now reaching to 1906, show that in framing these letters to the head of the German government, the President showed them to Ambassador Jusserand in advance of delivery. "The letter to Baron von Sternburg . . . the President let me modify . . . while he dictated, and adopted without hesitation divers suggestions which

[40] Adams, *Letters*, Paris, Aug. 27, 1905, Vol. II, p. 461.
[41] Vagts, *op. cit.*, Vol. II, pp. 1858, 1860-1864.

I permitted myself to make." [42] In these messages Roosevelt warned Germany of the consequences of war.

Without mentioning the certain loss of your colonies and your fleet which England will bring about, suppose that you triumph over France, the addition to your State of a new French Province would only increase the number of your enemies within your frontiers: it would be like a poison to you. [43]

Jusserand remarks in his secret reports to Paris that Mr. Roosevelt favored the cause of France more and more in public statements at this time. Roosevelt and Jusserand agreed also concerning the formula for the conference: there was to be officially "no program" and no discussion of points where either power was "engaged by honor, by previous engagements"—in short, a huge loophole permitting the program to be fixed in advance. Jusserand remarks:

In all this the President has certainly sought as best he could and with the sincerest friendship, the most practical means in his judgment for avoiding the calamity of war. He has in any case despite the advances and solicitation of William II, refused to do or say anything that might range him on the side of the Germans in this quarrel. On the contrary, it is our cause that he has wished to defend, while observing, nevertheless, all the forms rendered necessary by the character of the German sovereign, and without which his words would have no effect.

Jusserand even paid tribute to Roosevelt's political courage in ignoring a numerous German voting population in America. [44] "Germany was to have her conference; France, Morocco." To Germany a momentary, illusory prestige from the affair; to France, empire over rich territories she had seized, and to Britain security for the imperial "life-line" running via Egypt and the Suez Canal to the Orient. Such is the consensus of German historians. [45]

[42] Documents Diplomatiques, IIe série, tome VII, pp. 126, 134, 157. Jusserand to Rouvier, Jun. 23, 24, 26, 1905.

[43] Ibid., p. 157.

[44] Ibid., pp. 180-181.

[45] Vagts, op. cit., Vol. II, 1864.

Roosevelt declared that he feared a war that was to be a calamity for all of civilization, "what would literally be a world-conflagration." Hence he busied himself in sending to the Kaiser pleas couched in the most fulsome terms of flattery, that he preserve the peace of the world and earn the gratitude of untold generations, by accepting the empty conference offered him. The willingness of France to confer, he pretended, was a magnificent "triumph" for the Kaiser's diplomacy. Let him not cloud his high and honorable fame by raising difficulties over mere "minor details." [46] These minor details, as Roosevelt himself soon admitted privately, gave the "kernel of the nut" to France, and but the shell to Germany.

Henry Cabot Lodge, the chairman of the Senate Foreign Relations Committee, declared that the "local dispute in Morocco is a matter of indifference to us, but it is of very great importance to give France all the help we can." [47] Both Lodge and Roosevelt now expressed fear of the "young, aggressive military power, Germany." In designating Henry White to head the American delegation, Roosevelt wrote him:

I want to keep on good terms with Germany and if possible to prevent a rupture between Germany and France. But my sympathies have at bottom been with France and I suppose will continue so. Still I shall try to hold an even keel. [48]

Elihu Root, now Secretary of State after Hay's death in July, 1905, instructed White that the American delegation must be careful to avoid injuring the Anglo-French Entente, "or be made a means of breaking that up. . . ." White was to "help France get what she ought to have," but also to make it as difficult as possible for anyone to pick a quarrel. [49]

At the Algeciras Conference, sitting from mid-January to April, 1906, the American delegation labored to throw the moral influ-

---

[46] Bishop, *op. cit.*, Vol. I, pp. 481, 484-488.
[47] Lodge, *Correspondence*, Aug. 14, 1905, Vol. II, p. 172.
[48] *T. R. Papers*, Aug. 23, 1905.
[49] Nov. 28, 1905; Nevins, *White*, p. 267.

ence and diplomatic weight of the United States into the balance for peace—though on conditions unfavorable to Germany. According to the amusing account of Harold Nicolson, whose father Sir Arthur, hero of *The Portrait of a Diplomatist*, was the British representative at the conference, the Americans worked with the British and French delegations almost better than they knew to force German surrender on all important points.

At one stage of the affair, March 21, 1906, the Kaiser balked at accepting the Franco-British formula for predominantly French police and military rule of the Moroccan ports (a disguised, or "creeping," annexation). Roosevelt once again put pressure upon the Germans, threatening before Sternburg to publish the entire correspondence with the Kaiser (some of it of very embarrassing nature) if a break-up of the conference were forced by German resistance. On the other hand, if the Emperor would yield, Mr. Roosevelt would issue public statements crediting him for the success of the conference and preservation of peace, and would also undertake to receive at the White House a delegation of German war veterans with special honors, as an occasion for public manifestation of United States friendship for Germany and her monarch. Roosevelt contended that the Emperor had promised to accept a solution which he, Roosevelt, held to be "fair." Reports of increasing anti-German feeling in America, again, helped the Emperor to yield on this point. The public encomia for the Emperor by the President and the public reception of German veterans at the White House were then duly demanded and given.[50]

A year after the Algeciras Conference, the British were able to complete their military alliance with Russia. Thus "encirclement" was complete, and the Central Powers lived thenceforth in an atmosphere of military nightmare up to August, 1914. Years of active Rooseveltian intervention in world power politics, as the head of a world power, changed in no way the developing alignment of the great powers that brought nearer the catastrophe of the first imperialist world war. In the Pacific, the Taft-Katsura "memorandum" preserved a friendly alliance between the United

[50] Bishop, *op. cit.*, Vol. I, pp. 500-502.

States and Japan and paralleled and supported the Anglo-Japanese alliance. In the European area, the Square Deal President, despite his fleeting wishes for friendly relations with the German Emperor, ended by supporting firmly the French, and therefore the English, "line" in the Morocco crisis, thus bringing the United States solidly into the Anglo-French axis. For the first time in our history, America was directly involved in the family quarrels of the great European Powers. From the conquest of the Caribbean, the Panama Canal venture, the penetration of the Pacific and China, to the American-European policy indicated at Algeciras in 1906—when our "frontier" first approached the Rhine River—there was a procession of fateful steps leading to an ever deeper involvement of American policy in the power politics of two hemispheres.

VII. THE POLITICS OF REFORM

WHILE Theodore Roosevelt, figuratively speaking, wandered over the world, an imperial monarch with silk hat and Big Stick, the political weather along the home front in America grew unsettled and stormy. Nor was he, who kept always such a sharp eye to the weather, unaware of the unfavorable signs of popular unrest. Returning from his rather glamorous forays among emperors and their plenipotentiaries, he might recall that large tasks of domestic reform and lawmaking, more prosaic and arduous than foreign conquests or diplomatic enterprises, were still left undone. This was largely owing to the obstinacy of the conservative and "greedy" rich, he would recall, and of their Standpat representatives in politics.

I don't at all like the social conditions at the present [he wrote to Secretary Taft]. The dull purblind folly of the very rich men, their greed and arrogance, and the way in which they have unduly prospered by the help of the ablest lawyers . . . these facts and the corruption of business and politics have tended to produce a very unhealthy condition of excitement and irritation in the popular mind, which shows itself in part in the enormous increase in the socialistic propaganda.

Nothing effective, because nothing at once honest and intellectual is being done to combat the great amount of evil which, mixed with a little good, a little truth, is contained in these outpourings. . . . Some of these socialists, some of them [are] lurid sentimentalists; but they are all building up a revolutionary feeling, which will probably take the form of a political campaign. Then we may have to do too late, or almost too late, what had to be done in the silver campaign [of 1896] when in one summer we had to convince a good many people that what they had been laboriously taught several years ago was untrue. . . .[1]

[1] *T. R. Papers*, T. R. to Taft, Mar. 15, 1906.

Here as in his letter to Knox of the year before Roosevelt expresses candidly his fear of the coming of deep class divisions into our politics, with the struggle of the Have-Nots against the Haves imperiling the existing order of things. Once more, it is his conviction, constantly expressed, that he could manage the masses of the people if the "arrogant rich" did not obstruct his program of moderate concessions. At the moment the fate of the long-postponed railroad reform bill urged by the administration hung in the balance in the Senate. As before, the coterie of elder statesmen, headed by Nelson Aldrich of Rhode Island, persisted in opposition tenaciously and skillfully. Would they delay, obstruct, until it was too late?

Albert Beveridge, who, sensing the tide of opinion, fought nowadays in Congress as a champion of social justice, wrote to Roosevelt that it was too late for the slogan of "Let well enough alone!" He concluded:

The truth about it is that nearly all the older politicians are like a bunch of belated travellers who have come to catch a train and stand on the platform waiting for it, when as a matter of fact the train has passed on a long while ago.[2]

The mind of the great middle class continued to be obsessed by the fear of the trusts. Miss Tarbell's *History of the Standard Oil Company* appeared in 1904 in book form and was read by an army of readers. Thus a work of contemporary history contributed to the long series of public prosecutions undertaken against the chieftains of Standard Oil, now to be climaxed by the action of the Department of Justice under Roosevelt.

In February, 1905, *Everybody's Magazine,* following the course of *McClure's,* began publication of a series of articles by Charles Edward Russell which were a study of the methods of the Chicago meat-packing companies—"The Greatest Trust in the World." Each month that year half a million readers learned with horror that the methods of the great beef trust did not halt at poisoning its customers. The feeling of nausea aroused by

[2] Aug. 2, 1906; Bowers, *op. cit.*, p. 238.

the scandals concerning the Chicago packers was enhanced the following year when Upton Sinclair's *The Jungle* appeared. A Federal investigation followed these disclosures, and a stormy demand for a national pure-food law was heard in the land. But even while alarm and anger at the infamies of the trusts penetrated to the pit of the American stomach, Thomas W. Lawson, in his studies of "Frenzied Finance," which appeared in *Everybody's*, disabused not only the "lambs" of Wall and State Streets but the thrifty who entrusted their money in savings accounts and insurance policies to great and respectable institutions.

In December, 1904, Lawson, a spectacular market-plunger, who had fallen on lean days and turned "informer" against his erstwhile confederates, announced somewhat casually that he was going to "cause a life insurance blaze" that would be long remembered. Earlier he had told how rulers of the Standard Oil ("The System"), by controlling a great bank, such as the National City Bank of New York, were able to manipulate the money and security markets at will. Lawson described how the manipulation of the recently formed Amalgamated Copper Company stock had brought to investors a loss of one hundred millions of dollars. Bank deposits belonging to the public, he contended, were diverted to assure control by "insiders" of the $153,000,000 copper trust. But now, he charged, the assets of the four largest insurance companies, totaling three billions of dollars, formed a reservoir of speculative capital for masters of the stock market. The huge New York Life Insurance Company, he said, lay under the control of the Standard Oil; and the policyholders' life savings were at the mercy of the Standard Oil crowd in speculative and piratical adventures.[3]

The public sensation caused by Lawson's general charges against the formerly sacrosanct insurance companies—and met by them only with evasive denials or embarrassed silence—led the publisher of the powerful New York *World* to enter the case. Soon specific exposures followed Lawson's allusions; President John

[3] Filler, *Crusaders for American Liberalism,* pp. 190-193.

McCall of the New York Life Insurance Company resigned, for reasons that remained obscure; in the equally large Equitable Life Assurance Society, dissension burst forth among the executives at the same time. After September, 1905, the investigations of a New York legislative committee into insurance company affairs engrossed the public. Its legal counsel, who examined a long line of political, social, and financial celebrities, was Charles Evans Hughes, described then as "young, thin, pallid, insistent, with merciless, cold gray eyes and a mouth suggesting a steel trap." [4]

The pitiless Mr. Hughes drew a detailed picture of corruption in high places. For many years the great insurance companies, subject to state laws, had exerted themselves to influence state and national governments by regular secret distributions of money to politicians under the head of "legal expenses" or "supply department." George W. Perkins, Morgan's partner and vice-president of the Equitable, usually handled the lobbying and corruption funds. But more important than the tales of the "House of Mirth," set up in Albany for the entertainment of local statesmen, was the picture of interlocking controls by which insurance funds were kept on deposit with chosen banks or trust companies, which were, in turn, subsidiaries of the insurance companies. A second important use of insurance reserves was to invest them in new securities financed by bankers who were also directors of the insurance companies. Thus members of the firm of J. P. Morgan and Company, or Kuhn, Loeb and Company, sitting as directors of the New York Life, or Equitable, would approve readily of the purchase of securities originated and sold by themselves as investment bankers.

The contest of the Morgan and the Rockefeller-Harriman groups for control of the Equitable Life Assurance Society, inheritance of the frivolous young James H. Hyde, now became comprehensible to intelligent Americans. For the prize at stake was nothing less than control of billions in institutional reserves.

[4] The New York *World*, Oct. 11, 1905.

Thus little by little the real contours of the new system of monopoly capitalism, which conquered ever larger areas of American life, became known to thoughtful Americans through the writings of critical journalists and the cross examinations of great lawyers, such as Hughes and Brandeis, who prosecuted the "robber barons" before the bar of public opinion. Among the comfortable but democratic middle classes, uneasiness over the progress of the monopolists grew until it became the central political problem of the age.

Among the working classes, discontent and opposition took stronger form after 1900. An active minority, perhaps a fourth of organized labor, followed Eugene Debs, the inspiring leader of the 1894 general railway strike, in building a new party devoted to the principles of Marxian socialism. Debs delivered in 1904 six to ten speeches every day and carried the message of socialism into every state and territory with such burning zeal that he became a national figure. Yet the majority of the trade-unionists continued to hold by Samuel Gompers' "pure and simple" trade unionism. This meant the solid building of the federated trade unions as a national system, the unending fight for more favorable hours and wages, and for immediate, rather than ultimate, political advantages.

Though the main body of trade-unionists avoided the party of socialism and voted Republican or Democratic, to "reward friends and punish enemies," the mood even of conservative labor grew exasperated in 1906. For many years, ever since 1898, Gompers and P. J. McGuire of the A. F. of L. had lobbied patiently before Congress in an effort to win an amendment to the Sherman Anti-Trust Act that would eliminate its application to labor combinations. In 1906, labor circles reeled under the blow of the famous Danbury Hatters' decision of the Supreme Court, imposing punitive money damages against all the members of a union that had engaged in a strike and boycott.

Gompers now toiled in earnest to exert the force of labor in elections. The American Federation of Labor sent speakers into various districts to oppose the election of Congressmen who had shown a strong anti-labor spirit.[5]

In the Rocky Mountain region, where mining was one of the principal industries, a more militant labor movement had grown up since the late '90's in the shape of the Western Federation of Miners. Here in this rude world but recently carved out by pioneers the industrial conflict often took the form of pitched gun battles between strikers and civil or military authorities. In February, 1906, former Governor Steunenberg of Idaho (who had once called for Federal troops to put down a strike) was assassinated. The alleged confession of a suspect implicated the heads of the Western Federation of Miners—Haywood, Moyer, and Pettibone—as supposed accomplices; and because these men resided at the time in Colorado, an Idaho sheriff took the bold step of kidnapping all three of them and bringing them to face justice in Idaho, scene of the assassination.[6]

The trial of Haywood, Moyer, and Pettibone became a *cause célèbre* of 1906. Throughout the country funds were raised, petitions circulated, and even the American Federation of Labor made the case its own. The writ of injunction in labor cases was bad enough; but now the kidnapping of labor leaders, shorn of those civil rights that all criminals had to defend themselves in an extradition process, aroused immense indignation. To their defense came the colorful Chicago lawyer and radical philosopher, Clarence Darrow, who had defended Debs in 1894; the prosecuting attorney in the long-drawn-out trial was William E. Borah of Idaho. "Big Bill" Haywood and his colleagues were finally acquitted, on the ground of insufficient evidence; but out of the passions roused by this struggle came greater strength for the new Industrial Workers of the World, fathered by Haywood, Eugene Debs, and Daniel De Leon. The I.W.W., planned as an industrial union and dedicated to the "class struggle," proposed to continue the fight by violent as well as peaceful means, "until the workers of the world organize as a class, take possession of the earth and

[5] Gompers, *Seventy Years*, Vol. II, pp. 239-240.
[6] Sullivan, *op. cit.*, Vol. III, pp. 481 ff.

the machinery of production, and abolish the wage system." [7]

To a Theodore Roosevelt, sensitive to the public pulse and also respectful toward violence, the rise of militant "syndicalist" leaders like Haywood, the sudden growth of the Socialist party under Debs, the coming of intellectuals like Darrow to their camp, were signs of a falling political barometer forecasting social storms. Against such eventualities, of which he had so often given gloomy warnings, he must prepare to act, to throw all his powerful influence and force into the balance.

2

But while the labor movement now directed a constant pressure on the political government to yield anti-injunction laws, trust-act amendments, and the eight-hour day, the farm regions too showed signs of a growing disaffection which endangered the ruling party's historic alliance between business and agriculture. Rural discontent was of course chronic, since the protective tariff had long favored manufacturing as against farming. Its recurrence between 1901 and 1904, after several years of good farm prices, followed by a period of sharply rising living costs, was scarcely surprising. The Roosevelt victory in the 1904 elections had brought to Congress a group of agrarian leaders who called themselves Progressive Republicans and voiced the traditional demands of the farm belt. Of these leaders the most prominent was Robert M. La Follette, twice Governor of Wisconsin, and now elected to the United States Senate.

The press of the whole country watched the march of Wisconsin's "Little Giant" upon Washington with mixed curiosity and fear. He had delayed his departure for the East, in the autumn of 1905, and had gone to Chicago with his advisers to complete the last details of the new railroad tax law for Wisconsin, born of many years of struggle. En route to Washington, where he arrived in mid-January of 1906, he was much inter-

[7] Brissenden, *The I.W.W.*, Appendix II, citing preamble to constitution of 1908.

viewed and gave out vigorous public statements on the issues of the day.

The Senator, who was born in a log cabin in Primrose, Wisconsin, child of desperately poor settlers, was a man of wholly different stamp from those who ruled the councils of the brilliant Roosevelt administration. There was grimness and anger in him; he had taken his stand long ago as the champion of the "little American"; thus the contest for office had been made longer and harder, but he arrived at last in the national capital with his hands singularly free. Nor did he need to give thought to the diplomacy of machines and bosses. It was this thoroughgoing, unswerving independence that made political observers rate La Follette, in a day when more than one picturesque crowd leader held the stage—such as Bryan, Pitchfork Ben Tillman, or Tom Johnson—as by all odds the most "dangerous" of the radicals.

La Follette was a Mid-Western Solon. The "Wisconsin Idea" which he championed was a product of the intensely democratic Middle West farmers, who had in earlier times demanded principally liberty from the state. Now the sons of the frontiersmen had turned with the later Populists to erect governmental safeguards to preserve their liberties from abuse by the corporate monopolies of modern times. In pursuing this general plan for Wisconsin, La Follette "consulted" not railroad lawyers nor lumber barons, but professors at the University of Wisconsin, such as Ely, Commons, and Van Hise. A special office for a statistical research director to aid the State Legislature was created, and this contributed largely to the effective writing of laws. Soon, in contrast with the wavering course of a Theodore Roosevelt whether at Albany or at Washington, La Follette had succeeded in pushing through a large body of new statutes, bringing sweeping reforms of child labor and working conditions for women, corporation practice, taxation of railroads and public utilities, primary elections, labor disputes, workmen's compensation. For other states, Wisconsin became a sort of experimental social laboratory where new legislation was carefully tested and perfected in the light of knowledge gained from similar experience in all parts of the world. By developing and applying, for example, the device of the administrative commission of "experts" to regulate and judge of technical questions, which the popular mandate could not accurately decide, La Follette made a very high contribution to our political knowledge. These were the methods pursued later with notable success by men like Alfred Smith (in his liberal heyday) and other followers. What would the Little Giant do? Would he rend asunder the Republican party, as Bryan had rent the Democratic party ten years before? Would he capture its national leadership? Would he continue in his triumphal progress, overriding all opposition single-handed until he reached the Presidency itself?

The Old Guard in the Senate were prepared to waste few courtesies on La Follette. With a touch of wry humor they appointed him to the Committee to Investigate the Condition of the Potomac River Front, a committee which had never yet held a meeting, as La Follette relates, nor had a bill referred to it. Their precautions were justified. From the date of La Follette's arrival, there began the first strong movement of "insurgence" in Congress since the Free Silver uprisings of the early 1890's.

From the start, La Follette declared himself a devoted supporter of President Roosevelt's policies. Debate was proceeding, carried over from the previous session, upon the long-deferred railroad reform bill; and despite the unwritten law that new Senators must make themselves scarce for at least their first year, La Follette, in protest at the bowdlerizing of the administration bill, began on April 19, 1906, his famous first three-day set speech, an open call to revolt against the Aldrich dictatorship. This speech was held, as the correspondent of the Sioux City (Iowa) *Journal* reported, to be "a deliberate insult to the Senate," as well as a defiance of party discipline. In retaliation the Senators showed the new member extreme discourtesy, and one by one they left the chamber, until only three remained to watch him, one of them the aged Allison of Iowa. Walking up and down, "shaking his pompadour in a fine frenzy," and pointing his finger at old Allison, La Follette made his famous prophecy of doom:

Mr. President, I pause in my remarks to say this. I cannot be wholly indifferent to the fact that Senators by their absence at this time indicate their want of interest in what I have to say upon this subject. The public is interested. Unless this important subject is rightly settled, seats now temporarily vacant may be permanently vacated by those who have the right to occupy them at this time.[8]

Several years later, La Follette reverted to his prediction of 1906, pointing out that twenty-four Senators who had refused to lend him their ears, a huge proportion of those who stood for the next election, were now retired to private life.

Theodore Roosevelt's sharp veerings, his lapses into reform, so to speak, can be understood only in relation to the growing pressure brought upon him by the radicals. Left to his own devices, he tended to wait, to hesitate, to temporize, like so many other professed reformers who were ready to believe that the mere occupation of office by themselves meant the winning of the battle. But the arrival of a La Follette, fresh from his provincial successes, to a leading place in national politics was a portent and a reminder.

Now Bryan, the "peerless leader" of the opposition party after 1904, began to urge radical policies for the Democrats. His influential weekly newspaper, *The Commoner*, kept up a constant fire of criticism upon Mr. Roosevelt, pointing out week after week the compromising features of his tactics. According to the indefatigable adversary, Roosevelt was dangerously "Hamiltonian" and believed that "the well-born were born to rule"—a very accurate judgment of the President's convictions. Great opportunities lay before the powerful President, said Bryan, but his own instincts led him to protect the "plutocracy," whatever he might say in his set speeches year after year. Bryan challenged him on a series of issues. What was President Roosevelt doing (1) to advance the Eight-Hour Day, even to the extent of enforcing it in the District of Columbia on government contracts? (2) What was he doing to bring about a constitutional amendment permitting "more democ-

---

[8] *The Commoner*, May 25, 1906; La Follette, *Autobiography*, p. 414.

racy" through the Direct Election of Senators? (3) What of more vigorous prosecution of monopolies? Why were horse-thieves who broke the law given criminal punishment, while trust magnates who broke the law went unpunished? (4) Why was nothing done about the infamous court injunction used in labor disputes? (5) Why was there still no strict regulation of the railroads, after all these years? Why did President Roosevelt still oppose giving to the Interstate Commerce Commission the real power to initiate and fix railroad rates? What truth was there after all in the legend of the "iron man in the White House"? Bryan's organ asked.[9]

Thus after years of good fortune and comparatively smooth sailing Theodore Roosevelt faced an increasingly troubled and critical public opinion at home after 1904. Though he stood at the zenith of his power and glory, thanks chiefly to foreign exploits, his hesitations were noticed, his compromises were measured by would-be rivals for popular leadership.

The danger of party cleavage was always perfectly real to him. In the northwestern tier of states, hitherto staunchly Republican, he felt the constant clamor for downward revision of the tariff and increased trust prosecution. The clamor for more effective railroad regulation, led by La Follette and others, threatened to become a veritable "prairie fire." Yet for nearly two years, up to 1906, the clique of Aldrich and Cannon that still ruled Congress had warily forestalled legislative action.

The essence of Roosevelt's diplomacy, as Professor C. E. Merriam has pointed out, lay in pursuing tactics of combination, and in avoiding the "permanent consolidation of any one group against him. . . ." His "on the one hand" and "on the other hand" policy enabled him to hold the middle class, and alternately to attract and repel the labor group and the business group. "Broadly speaking . . . he was always detaching part of a group, commercial, labor or otherwise, and preventing solid opposition against him."[10] It was in very fear of a rupture within his party and of a

[9] *The Commoner*, Nov. 18, 1904; Dec. 9, 1904; Apr. 13, Apr. 20, 1906.
[10] Merriam, *Four American Party Leaders*, p. 34.

combination of militant sectional and class movements, including Bryan, La Follette, and even Debs, that the Square Deal President now turned resolutely to the unpleasant business of writing large reforms into the statutes. For more than four years he had preached the Ten Commandments, yet no signal legislative achievements were credited to his name.

3

In the late summer and autumn of 1905, at the very climax of his foreign diplomatic adventures, the President in a series of speeches indicated that he was turning to renew his delayed "drive" for domestic reform. On August 11, 1905, at Chautauqua, New York, he spoke of the beef packers as violators of the trust laws, and hinted that their very efforts to evade or resist the law would soon bring sterner laws for their supervision. A few weeks later, in another public address, he promised that he would again seek the passage of an act reinforcing the supervision of the railroads by the Interstate Commerce Commission. He declared that he was opposed to the government ownership of anything that might "be left in private hands," but it would be impossible to go on without "controlling" the railroads. Recently, some public scandal had been caused by the report that a great railway, the Santa Fe, had continued granting rebates to certain large shippers such as the Standard Oil in spite of the Elkins Act of 1903, which expressly forbade such practices. Roosevelt now urged that the I.C.C. must have the power to examine the books of the railroads. He hoped to see all the necessary power granted to the government, but, he qualified, "I would far rather see some of it granted . . . than see a pretence of granting all in some shape that really amounts to nothing." [11]

Roosevelt's speeches that summer and autumn bespoke preparations for an approaching conflict. He talked less often nowadays of the capitalists who "in making fortunes for themselves have

[11] Roosevelt, *Speeches*, Vol. IV, pp. 450-476.

done good to all of us." The recent literature of exposure, sensational articles on the beef trust, the Hughes investigation of the insurance companies, had hardened public opinion and permitted stronger measures of attack. In December, 1905, Attorney General W. H. Moody ordered trust prosecutions by the Federal authorities in many fields. The huge Standard Oil and American Tobacco companies were already under investigation; in addition eight indictments were found by Federal grand juries in December against the Armour, Swift, Cudahy, and Morris packing companies of Chicago, and against certain railroads, notably the Chicago and Alton, accused of granting special rebates on freight charges to the stockyard companies.[12]

Thus the tumultuous Rooseveltian battle for domestic reform was under way as the new "progressive" Congress arrived to hear the President's annual message of December 9, 1905, demanding a varied program of legislation, including a pure-food law, a new enabling act for further measures of forest and soil conservation, a law requiring publicity for party election expenses, and, most important of all, a law that would compel the railroads to grant "just and reasonable" rates. Once more, however, nothing was said about tariff revision.

It was the reading of Upton Sinclair's novel *The Jungle*, early in 1906, that led this literary President to take up the fight for a pure-food law. Finley Peter Dunne ("Mr. Dooley") firmly believed that Mr. Roosevelt was moved to his very bowels by the famous passage in Sinclair's work which describes, with a Zolaësque realism, how a careless workman falls into a vat and is turned into sausage.

"Annyhow, Tiddy was toying with a light breakfast an' idly turnin' over th' pages iv th' new book with both hands. Suddenly he rose from th' table, an' cryin': 'I'm pizened,' began throwin' sausages out iv th' window. Th' ninth wan shtruck Sinitor Biv'ridge on th' head an' made him a blond. . . ."

[12] The New York *Times*, Dec. 14, 15, 16, 1905.

While controversy raged over the truth of Sinclair's tragic and powerful novel of the stockyards inferno, the President dispatched special agents to the scene, and soon had from them a sober report that was if anything more revolting still. A Pure Foods Bill, often advocated by the enthusiastic Dr. Harvey W. Wiley, chief chemist of the Department of Agriculture, was now rapidly pushed through Congress. A companion measure, the Meat Inspection Bill, covering specifically control of the great meat-packing plants, was written by Albert Beveridge, with Roosevelt's strong approval, and introduced in Congress as a "rider" for an appropriation bill.

But the packers and the cattlemen rallied and descended upon Washington with one of the most tenacious lobbies ever seen there. Once more the struggle for "constitutional liberty" (for packing houses) raged in Congress. In the lower House, the teeth of the Beveridge bill were drawn one by one; and only torrential speeches in the Senate and new exposures (through publication of the government's report) were enough to save part of the bill. Beveridge suspected that the President yielded too easily to the opposition, and the two men clashed angrily. In truth, the law was so rewritten that inspection of meats was to be at government expense, rather than that of the accused packers. Amid the popular hue and cry, with Beveridge appealing to the Senate not to "surrender to the next biggest monopoly in the United States, after the Standard Oil," even Aldrich yielded his assent, and a creditable measure was passed at length—a minor victory for the Rooseveltians.[13]

Much closer to the heart of the Rooseveltian politics lay the movement for the conservation of America's natural resources. In the "great barbecue" that followed Lincoln's Homestead Act of 1862, the distribution of the national domain in the West had proceeded in an incredibly rapid and wasteful fashion. The approaching impoverishment of our forests and of our soil—then a nearly incredible notion—was first heard of in the 1890's. Professor Frederick J. Turner, in his famous historical essay, *The Significance of*

[13] Bowers, *op. cit.*, p. 230.

the Frontier in American History, now pointed to the end of the great frontier movements that had been recurring, in wave after wave, since the sixteenth century.

Thanks to a small group of public-spirited citizens an act of 1891 passed by Congress provided for the withdrawal from sale of certain public lands suitable for forest reserves. Thus a far-reaching principle was established that turned away from unbridled individualism and fixed responsibility for the country's natural resources, in some measure, upon the national government. Roosevelt while Governor of New York was one of those who began to support projects for setting up state forest reserves. But in 1902 the movement was given further impetus when a law devised by Senator Newlands of Nevada, providing for the reclamation and conservation of water-power resources, was placed on the statutes.[14]

The heart and soul of the conservation movement was Gifford Pinchot, Theodore Roosevelt's friend and a member of the "Tennis Cabinet." This handsome, wealthy young man had made forestry his life work, having spent years studying the forest reserves of France, Germany, and Switzerland. Returning to America, where he served as head of the government's Forest Service after 1897, Pinchot began to preach conservation everywhere, not merely for the sake of forests, but as a program for a "new patriotism . . . of national service." It meant not merely growing big trees and digging irrigation ditches, but the husbanding of vast resources for the welfare of the people as a whole. It set up the ideal of national husbandry in an age that seemed to be up in arms against land-grabbers or exploiters of political privilege profiting by the unearned increment of land speculation. With a collective

[14] In the years 1862 to 1926, under the Homestead Act and amendments, the government issued 1,391,128 patents for approximately 226,159,053 acres of land, which passed to private ownership. In addition 137,000,000 acres were granted to railroads or to states for railroad building. Of the private lands "commuted" or granted title after six months, by payments of $1.25 to $2.50 per acre, a huge share was taken by large corporations through their agents. A land-office agent estimated for the government that inspection showed that of "commuted" homesteads not one in a hundred was ever occupied as a home. (Hibbard, *History of Public Land Policy,* pp. 387, 389.)

plan that looked toward the future, it opposed the waste and confusion of individual and local land usage. The cause of national
conservation, in short, was peculiarly appealing to the Rooseveltians. Roosevelt and his friends, who recoiled at the notion of
socializing the railroads, could take up the fight for conservation
as a cause embracing all their convictions of "moral righteousness"
in government. Planned conservation, as the ardent, mystical
Pinchot contended, would not merely save our public resources
from the control of the monopolists, but guarantee "an equal opportunity for every American citizen to get the fair share of the
benefit" from these resources. It would both create and distribute
wealth; it would carry democracy into new ground, making of our
country a "Nation of Homes," a society of small landholders,
"bringing the Kingdom of God on Earth." [15]

With the aid of Gifford Pinchot and Secretary of Interior Garfield, Roosevelt explored the provisions of the old Act of 1891;
he found that he could withdraw large quantities of government
lands from distribution, and after 1902 he aggressively pushed the
withdrawal of forest reserves until he could claim that by 1909 he
had increased their area from 43 to 194 million acres. Private corporations, railroads, utilities, and mining companies, which used
government lands, were restricted or regulated under a plan of
"stewardship" for the public. Soon public undertakings that
equaled the vast cost of the Panama Canal were under way for
the development of inland waterways, the irrigation of deserts,
and the preservation of power sites.

The program of conservation was popular among the majority
of the citizens, and La Follette, who sometimes spoke harshly of
Theodore Roosevelt, called it the most constructive and permanent
achievement of his period in office. Yet the removal of large lands
from private use did not go unopposed. Claim hunters and their
political allies, especially in Western states having rich mineral or
timber land, were aggrieved and began to resist Roosevelt's measures actively. Nevertheless, thanks to the enthusiasm he engen-

[15] Pinchot, *The Fight for Conservation*, pp. 26, 115.

dered for conservation, an important act was passed in June, 1906, enlarging the Forest Service and extending its authority.

In the following year the Roosevelt administration pressed its fight for conservation to new victories. A stubborn group of opposition Congressmen who desired to curb the President's occasionally high-handed actions in this field managed, with the help of skillful lobbyists, to have Congress pass a bill prohibiting further withdrawals of public lands in the six northwestern states, unless authorized by Congress. To veto this bill—presented as a "rider" to a routine Department of Agriculture appropriation bill—would have been awkward. Therefore Roosevelt had Garfield and Pinchot map out every acre of the public domain that had a bush on it and could serve for potential timberland. These lands, sixteen million acres in all, he removed from the reach of land-grabbers, by an eleventh-hour executive decree, in accordance with the law of 1891. Then, this done, he humorously signed the new bill which revoked his power to take such action. The opponents of the Forest Service, he recalled afterward, "turned handsprings in their wrath; and dire were their threats. . . ." [16]

4

By strenuous fighting for conservation, for pure-food and meat-inspection laws, and by frequent indictments of trusts, Roosevelt appeared to wage the struggle for reform with increasing vigor. His main objective, however, was still the passage of stronger laws regulating the railroads. To the press he stated frankly that the hour was late, that the people must have relief from the burdensome rates of the railroads. Yet in this contest he feared the outcome. The railroads, he felt, were "crazy" in their hostility. In the winter of 1906, while the railroad bill was being debated, Mr. Harriman and his lawyer, Sidney Webster, came several times to Washington and expressed the strongest objection, not only to the railroad bill but to investigations of the Harriman lines being made

[16] Roosevelt, *An Autobiography*, pp. 404-405.

by the Interstate Commerce Commission. It was plain that Harriman, who had raised $250,000 for the campaign of 1904, was becoming alienated, although in endeavoring to learn what he desired the President could get nothing but "general allegations or sweeping accusations" from him.[17]

In a public address on October 19, 1905, Roosevelt had already hinted that he would willingly accept *only a part* of the power he sought in order to regulate the railroads; it was a hint of compromise. His Message to Congress of December 9, 1905, whose main feature was the appeal for railroad control, also reiterated his prudent position of the year before: "My proposal is not to give the Interstate Commerce Commission power to initiate or originate rates generally, but to regulate a rate already fixed or originated by the roads, upon complaint and after investigation." The new rates to be established were to be, of course, "subject to review by the courts." Full publicity for the accounts of the railroad was another condition he favored.

The remarkable thing was that twenty years after the Interstate Commerce Act had become law, the Commission it established had almost no power to interfere with the activities of railroads. One of the members had even resigned lately, making public protests at the impotence of this regulatory body. Even its limited power had been stripped away—chiefly on the Constitutional ground of "due process"—by the remorseless reasoning of the Supreme Court, the court which Senator Aldrich was said to trust in as he trusted in Providence. The Commission could not of its own authority fix rates for the railroads, for such action might result in "confiscation." On the other hand, if a fair valuation of the railroad properties could once be established, as La Follette urged, then "reasonable" rates permitting fair profits might be fixed. But the very mention of government appraisal of the railroad properties and fixing of their rates aroused terror of a red Socialist revolution in Senatorial breasts.

In January the act enlarging the powers of the Interstate Com-

[17] *T. R. Papers*, T. R. to Sidney Webster, Jan. 31, 1907.

merce Commission, in line with the President's moderate views, was introduced in Congress by Representative Hepburn of Iowa. After brief debate, the bill was quickly passed by the Lower House —Speaker Cannon evidently offering no resistance—and committed to the charge of a committee of the Senate for consideration. Here, the leader of the "Railway Senators," the multi-millionaire Elkins of West Virginia, was chairman; beside him stood Nelson Aldrich, the "dictator," with divers faithful Republican followers. Tillman, on behalf of the Democratic minority in the Senate's Committee on Interstate Commerce, it was expected, would be able to accomplish nothing, and the bill would either be strangled by amendments or altogether killed.

The Old Guard was willing to grant power to the government commission, ostensibly to fix rates, upon complaints brought before it; provided, first, that complaint could be made difficult, costly, and infrequent. That is, a grain shipper with a grievance would be obliged to retain a lawyer and send him to Washington to defend his petition. In the second place, rate cases were to be reviewed after considerable delays, and judged before Federal courts, involving further costly legal process and (probably) very conservative judgment. This was what was meant by allowing for "broad court review" of railroad rate cases. Now the trouble with Hepburn's bill, as sent from the Lower House, was that it provided for no special intervention by the Federal courts, save those normally offered under the Constitution. Aldrich therefore prepared to amend the Hepburn Bill; it was rumored also that rather humorous, dilatory tactics were planned in the shape of a long series of "joke" amendments. Suddenly, to the astonishment of the Senate leader, one of the "regular" Republican members, Jonathan Dolliver of Iowa, rebelled, and with two other Republicans joined the Democratic minority to report the bill favorably.

Dolliver, the genial, studious giant with a pleasing gift for Lincolnesque oratory, long a popular and useful ornament in the conservative organization, had for several years, since 1903, shown signs of wishing to break from the leash. Like Governor Cummins of Iowa, who was soon to enter the Senate in place of the ancient

Allison, Dolliver was sensitive to the strong current of discontent running again through the Granger states. Allison, who had reared him as his protégé since the '80's, and raised him to the party's Inner Circle, had often stayed Dolliver's hand when he thought to revolt, saying: "Don't do it now. Wait until I'm gone. I know it is wrong. . . . I have only a little while left, and I haven't got the strength to break away. But wait until I am gone. . . ." [18] Yet Dolliver now took a leading hand in the railroad bill, and prepared to issue a report in defiance of the Standpat dicta, saying nothing of "broad court review" and leaving the disposition of railway rate cases as the Lower House had voted it.

On the 15th of February, 1906, Aldrich had an interview with the President—possibly a stormy one—of which neither divulged anything to the public. Aldrich fought for delay, and even turned for aid to certain friends on the Democratic side of the Senate. Meanwhile Dolliver worked in close collaboration with Roosevelt to advance the new bill.

When the Senate's Committee on Interstate Commerce reported out the bill, it was seen that the Republican majority had split its vote. The Eastern faction, among them Aldrich, Foraker, Elkins, and Kean, opposed the Hepburn Bill; the Western Republicans, Dolliver and Clapp, joined with the Democratic minority under Tillman to bring about favorable recommendation. This development, undoubtedly forced by the crafty Aldrich, gave him the occasion for his astonishing maneuver by which "Pitchfork Ben" Tillman, the Southern radical Democrat, was designated to report the bill out of committee without the official indorsement of the Republican party. Thus if the bill came to grief or created evil consequences it would not be a Republican affair. Moreover Dolliver, who had hoped to sponsor the bill, was out-flanked, while the President would be placed in an awkward position. For not long ago Mr. Roosevelt had had a resounding personal quarrel with the irascible Southerner Tillman and had barred him from the White House.

[18] La Follette, *Autobiography*, pp. 432-433.

Yet Tillman accepted his mission in good faith. As in the stirring campaign of '96, beside Bryan and Altgeld, he girded himself for a general onslaught upon entrenched corporate wealth and privilege, eager to garner what credit he could for the Democratic party. The President, meanwhile, after enjoying Aldrich's strange pleasantry, made conciliatory statements to the press, declaring that he "did not care a rap" for personal difference, and, in the interests of railroad reform, would co-operate unstintedly with the Democratic leader, "Pitchfork Ben."

For sixty days, during the months of March and April, the Senate chamber rang with a great "Constitutional debate" over railroad control. One by one the conservative Republican orators arose and attacked a measure which ostensibly had the support of their own administration. Foraker of Ohio, the grey-haired hero of the Civil War, condemned the Hepburn Bill as "Democratic" in its inspiration. This old politician, not yet known as the "hireling" of the Standard Oil Company that he was, was heard with respect when he pleaded passionately for liberty to railroad owners. The policy of centralized control that was embodied in the Hepburn Bill, he argued, would "feed on itself . . . and spread like a conflagration until in some form or other it comprehended and applied to every other kind of business, for such were the teachings and plans of Socialism." [19]

Senator Philander Knox of Pennsylvania, formerly Attorney General in Roosevelt's Cabinet, pointed out that the bill placed some ten billions of railroad property under the arbitrary control of government agencies, "beyond the protecting clauses of the Constitution." He urged the inclusion of an amendment providing for "broad judicial review" of all railroad rate cases (which would be, in effect, an invitation to endless court suits). Otherwise, sacred rights, "painfully won from the tyrannies of the past, rights adhering to the rich as well as to the poor, would be forfeited. . . . The courts," cried Knox, in a ringing peroration, "are the guardians of our rights and liberties." [20] Thus the theme of

[19] *Congressional Record*, May 18, 1906.

the opposition was the danger of a tyranny of the poor over the rich!

While Aldrich and his Senatorial lawyers fought to defeat the Hepburn Bill by ingenious constitutional arguments, or sniped at it with a series of amendments, a crowd of Democratic and Republican "Granger" Senators, led by Tillman and Dolliver, defended the bill in torrents of words. They fought for "narrow court review," limiting the injunctive power of the Federal courts to suspend the government's action in railroad-shipper disputes; else, they contended, the floodgates of litigation would be opened. The issue was, simply put: should the Interstate Commerce Commission be given veritable power over the railways, or illusory powers that would be haltered in the courts?

The President for a time pursued the fight with uncommon force and resourcefulness, though Aldrich held the votes of forty Senators in his hand. As Mark Sullivan has recalled it, Roosevelt arranged with his admirers among the newspaper correspondents that a series of vigorous articles on the railroads and on Senators sympathetic to them should appear during the debate over the railroad control bill. In January, 1906, there appeared in the *World's Work* a powerful attack upon Senators Aldrich, Hale, Spooner, Elkins, Penrose, Foraker, Depew, and Kean, as "representatives of corporate business everywhere. . . ." In *McClure's Magazine* for March, 1906, Ray Stannard Baker published a careful, documented study of the evil tendencies of the railroads and their abuse of political privilege.[21] Rumors were circulated in the press, evidently inspired, that the President even hoped to send a few railroad presidents to jail, believing that it would have a wholesome effect on the situation.

News of sensational charges against the Standard Oil and the American Sugar Refining companies, developing from current investigations, was hinted at, as if held over the heads of the opposition. Also, in a series of public addresses during the early spring

[20] *Ibid.*, Mar. 28, 1906.
[21] Sullivan, *op. cit.*, Vol. III, p. 242.

of 1906, Roosevelt made what then seemed radical proposals—proposals for an inheritance tax that would gradually level wealth, and for Federal laws regulating insurance companies within the District of Columbia. These were the days when Roosevelt thundered most heavily against the "malefactors of great wealth." Yet, whatever the popular effect of these broadsides, votes were still lacking in the Senate to encompass the passage of the Hepburn Bill, which he had made the spearhead of his program of economic reform.

In the early stages of the Senate deadlock, Roosevelt made great efforts to gather together a Senate majority. Through an intermediary he communicated privately with Senator Tillman, the Democratic floor leader, and made an "arrangement" for collaboration between the Democrats and himself. Tillman reported that he could count upon the aid of from twenty-six to twenty-eight of the Democratic contingent of thirty-three Senators. In addition, Dolliver promised the support of between twenty and twenty-two Western Republicans, making a majority of from forty-six to fifty votes out of ninety. The delicate negotiations for a coalition with the Democrats—a rather bold undertaking for a Republican President—were completed at a conference on April 14, 1906, in Attorney General Moody's office, both Tillman and Dolliver being present. Roosevelt, as Tillman declared, promised to "stand by" the coalition and contribute executive pressure in support of the bill, whose terms, providing for "narrow court review," were agreed upon.[22]

Roosevelt's public struggles with Aldrich often partook of the character of mock warfare. He respected and bowed before Aldrich's power. "My experience . . . has made me feel respect and regard for Aldrich," he told Taft in 1903, "as one of that group of Senators, including Allison, Hanna, Spooner, Platt of Connecticut, Lodge, and one or two others, who . . . are the

[22] Tillman's account, *Congressional Record*, May 12, 1906; Stephenson, *op. cit.*, pp. 307-308.

most powerful factors in Congress." Though he disagreed with them radically on many questions they were "the leaders, and their great intelligence and power, and their desire . . . to do what is best for the government, makes them not only essential to work with but desirable to work with." [23]

To work instead with the Democrats, in order to pass a bill which Aldrich opposed, meant not only a break in the party harmony, but final departure from the President's tacit "gentleman's agreement" with the Standpatters. It was a decision before which Theodore Roosevelt hesitated deeply. Fortunately, conciliators were there to devise a compromise between the "narrow" and "broad" court review positions, difficult as that seemed. And then the magic of Aldrich accomplished the rest: subjection of the dynamic President, in his first large battle to lead Congress.

Aldrich's magic consisted at this time simply in his subterranean connection with friendly "Railway Senators" among the Democrats. The veteran Joseph Bailey of Texas, a florid, old-fashioned orator, with large black hat, sedate black suit, and string necktie, was at that time the real leader of the Democrats in the Senate. Though he publicly appeared to be sponsoring the "narrow" review clauses of the Hepburn Bill, as well as other popular measures urged by the Democracy, public scandal not long afterward stamped him as a partner in certain dubious oil enterprises that eventually came under the control of the Rockefeller clan. Legend also has pointed to him as the secret lieutenant of Aldrich on the Democratic side, who brought about, when needed, the sudden switch of two or three vitally necessary Democratic votes to the conservative side. For example, one of the amendments that Bailey proposed, an "anti-injunction" clause, had the air of being so radical that the Supreme Court would certainly nullify the whole railroad act.[24]

Tillman himself, according to his memorandum of the proceedings, "suspected the Texan [Bailey] . . . of holding secret con-

[23] *T. R. Papers*, Roosevelt to Taft, Mar. 13, 1903.
[24] S. H. Acheson, *Joe Bailey, The Last Democrat*, p. 201.

ferences with Aldrich," and, as he reported to Roosevelt, kept a close watch on his colleague, lest he "sell out." [25]

Just when victory over the Standpatters seemed assured—though with the dangerous help of a coalition of Democrats and Western Republicans of the La Follette type—the game passed from the President's hands. For at the Democratic caucus, on April 18, 1906, when noses were counted, to everyone's surprise it was found that several recruits were missing. This was all that Aldrich needed.

For Roosevelt the deadlock had been wearying, and the adventure of working with the Democrats, who would seek credit for railroad reform, politically hazardous. He pressed the distraught Tillman to produce the missing Democratic votes; but though Tillman pleaded for time, they were not found in the last two weeks of April. After having held the threat of a coalition with the Democrats over Aldrich's head, Roosevelt was now ready to abandon the comedy of intrigue, and to "trade" or compromise. He wished, as both Lincoln Steffens and La Follette complained, simply to "get something through"; he would content himself in the end with "half a loaf," when half a loaf was worse than none.

On May 4 Nelson Aldrich called at the White House. Reports of this secret interview held that the "dictator" of the Senate was suave and gracious in victory. Roosevelt, judging from his letter to Lodge, acknowledged his defeat in "sporting" fashion, and vowed that Aldrich, who represented only "ten per cent of the people," would be vanquished the next time. Meanwhile an election was approaching, and they must think of the fortunes of their party.[26]

A compromise amendment, made ready by the practiced Senator Allison, was now quickly produced. It had the language of strong railroad reform, but it offered the legal realities of *broadest court review* and restraint in favor of the railroads, in the shape of occult clauses permitting "interlocutory injunctions" and other court in-

[25] Roosevelt to Allison, the New York *Tribune*, May 16, 1906.
[26] Lodge, *Correspondence*, Vol. II, p. 370.

terventions which would limit government control. On the morning of May 4, 1906, it was understood in Washington that the harassed President had yielded suddenly and given his approval to the "Allison amendment," abandoning the Tillman-Dolliver reform coalition. When the Republican compromise terms were made known a week later, they were universally described as a "gold brick."

The vociferous Tillman and his fellow Democrats were outraged by the bad faith, and even "betrayal," they had suffered at the hands of the President. Roosevelt, they cried, had ended by yielding to Aldrich. He was "so constituted," as Senator Rayner of Maryland remarked, "that he cannot look at a trap without fooling with the spring." [27] The Hepburn Act emerged, however, as a simon-pure Republican party measure, supported by the Old Guard. The embittered Tillman then disburdened himself of a remarkable "confession" on May 12, 1906, before the Senate, relating how the President had sought him out and agreed to use his services as leader of the opposition party, then cast him aside in order to effect a compromise with his own party leaders. Roosevelt issued angry denials from the White House; charges and counter-charges filled the air with confusion as the memorable session of Congress drew to its close in June.

Roosevelt had been on the verge of forcing through Congress a measure that would have substantially increased the power of the Interstate Commerce Commission over railroad rates. It would have meant a bitter conflict within his own party, the possibility of overthrowing the old leaders and creating a new political alignment upon progressive and conservative beliefs. Instead he had recoiled, accepted a half-measure that brought no relief from the abuses that agitated a large part of the public. In defending himself, he argued that the bill he signed was the "same thing" that he had asked for; yet few believed him.[28]

[27] The New York *World*, May 12, 1906.

[28] The Hepburn Act extended the authority of the Interstate Commerce Commission over pipe lines, express companies, sleeping-car companies, and railway terminals; it was given the power not to fix rates, but to nullify rates found

As if to conceal his embarrassment, on May 4, 1906, the day when his compromise with Aldrich was announced, Roosevelt delivered his fiercest broadside against the industrial trusts in a message to Congress which laid bare the secret practices of the Standard Oil and sugar-refining trusts and the coal-carrying combination. He promised that his Attorney General would institute prosecutions against all these wrongdoers at an early date.[29] But one of the newspaper men present continued to question the President concerning the Hepburn Act amendments, and his explanations appeared labored. Finally, the reporter who had admired him exclaimed bluntly: "But Mr. President, what we want to know is why you surrendered." To this Roosevelt made no direct reply.[30]

5

By the summer of 1906, Theodore Roosevelt's crusade against the monopolistic trusts seemed to have reached its climax. He was now the very head and front of the anti-monopolistic movement that gripped the plain people of America, and made repeated vows that he would continue the fight until the industrial trusts, which had been as "subjects without a sovereign," were liable to Federal jurisdiction.

In March, 1904, the Supreme Court's decision in the Northern Securities case, reversing its previous opinions of 1895, had dissolved a great railway holding company, and cleared the path for further vigorous prosecution of the trusts. To the President, who sought to serve as an "honest broker" between the rival interests of the republic, this was a notable vindication of the course he had chosen. His aides, James R. Garfield, Herbert Knox Smith, Attorney General W. H. Moody, and later Charles Joseph Bonaparte,

---

unreasonable, on complaints of shippers. "Far from satisfying agrarian demands, the Hepburn Act only stimulated the progressive surge which was soon to induce a political earthquake. . . ." (C. A. and M. R. Beard, *The Rise of American Civilization*, Vol. II, p. 568.)

[29] The New York *World*, May 5, 1912.

[30] Stephenson, *op. cit.*, pp. 314-315, citing memorandum of Richard Hooker.

who succeeded Moody in 1906, worked at his order with a large force to gather information and evidence concerning the monopolized industries. The facts, when they were assembled, astonished Roosevelt himself, though he had occasionally glimpsed at close hand something of high financial chicanery when he served as Governor of New York.

Apparently the snowballing movement toward the consolidation of business had gone on pell-mell, with little regard for honor or truth, or the principles of the Decalogue which Roosevelt so earnestly preached. By 1904 (when a temporary halt in the trust movement followed the Northern Securities decision), there were some 318 greater or lesser industrial trusts, which consolidated 5,300 separate manufacturing plants and were capitalized at over seven billions of dollars, five-sixths of them organized since 1898, and nearly half of them under the favoring New Jersey corporation law which tolerated holding companies. The greatest of all holding companies, the United States Steel Corporation, under a New Jersey charter, controlled 170 subsidiary concerns.

In the case of the other great holding company, the Standard Oil Company of New Jersey, both a "holding" and an operating company, Roosevelt aides brought reports of extraordinary malpractice: there was evidence of over 1,900 violations of the Elkins (rebate) Act of 1903. The Standard Oil had continued, as before, the beneficiary of secret freight rates which gave it a crushing advantage over its competitors; sometimes it paid as little as one-fourth the shipping charges exacted by railroads of "outsiders"; often it forced the railroads to add a surtax increasing the freight costs of its competitors in the oil trade, who, by 1904, were virtually extinct. The sugar trust was found guilty of systematic cheating in payments of customs duties by the use of short-weight scales, in addition to its other unlawful acts in restraint of trade; the American Tobacco Company was little better; while the misdeeds of the combination controlling the Chicago packing industry ran the gamut from poisoning its customers to secret rebates and price extortion.

Roosevelt, learning all this, boiled with honest indignation, which was now shared by all except the great financiers themselves and the Marxian socialists, who believed that the trusts prepared the way for the future society of collective, socialized industry. In a series of fierce verbal onslaughts he promised "without fear or favor" to prosecute the wealthy malefactors, whom he now branded publicly, side by side with Red revolutionists, as "undesirable citizens." In effect, his record by 1909 was impressive when compared with that of his predecessors; forty-six suits for violation of the Anti-trust or Interstate Commerce Act were begun, and over half of these cases were relatively successful in bringing indictments and fines. The most famous of these suits were against the Standard Oil Company of New Jersey and the American Tobacco Company.

What was the real object of the crusade against the trusts? Charles Joseph Bonaparte, who was Attorney General from 1906 to 1909, in a speech in October, 1906, said that it was to restore "fair play" in American business. This wealthy civil-service reformer and distinguished lawyer, who had been a contemporary of Roosevelt's at Harvard, by an amusing metaphor likened the conflicts in the business world to those of pigs in a huge pig pen. The fatter the pigs became, the more money for their owners, and the better for the American people, provided there was a fair field and no favor. But, he added:

Our big, strong, greedy, over-prosperous trusts . . . crowd their smaller and weaker fellows from the feeding-trough, so that they don't get their fair share of our national prosperity. The problem is how to fence off the great beasts so as to give the little ones a show.

Thus President Roosevelt and the Republican party, he declared, were simply trying "to keep each trust in its pen." [31]

The contradictions of such a policy, which sought "fair play and no favors," which differentiated between the "bad trusts" and the "good trusts" (which presumably did not crowd hard against the other pigs), are characteristic of Rooseveltian policy. A quite mod-

[31] Bishop, *Bonaparte*, pp. 128-130.

erate, limited objective was pursued, in contrast with the violence of language used.

"Trust busting" continued in an atmosphere of loud and intemperate controversy, which the press followed with sensational news stories. Week by week, in 1906 and 1907, large corporations fell under indictment, while conservative spokesmen, university presidents, professors of economics, and financiers complained that the Reign of Terror was "tearing down" things and undermining public confidence. It was true that a subsidiary of the Standard Oil of New Jersey on August 13, 1907, was condemned by Federal Judge K. M. Landis to pay a fine of $29,000,000; the American Tobacco Company, organized by the late W. C. Whitney and Thomas Fortune Ryan, was also forced soon after to dissolve into several of its constituent parts. Some of the tobacco company's property was even seized forcibly by Federal officers.

TOBACCO TRUST GOODS SEIZED BY GOVERNMENT

CUSTOMS COLLECTOR TAKES POSSESSION OF 8,750,000 CIGARETTES IN
TRANSIT UNDER SHERMAN ACT—DRASTIC SECTION
OF LAW USED FOR FIRST TIME.[32]

Thus ran newspaper headlines in 1907. Yet the amount of goods involved, worth $7,252.50, was a mere bagatelle for a concern worth a hundred million dollars. The assessment against the Standard Oil was subject to appeal before the Supreme Court, and after litigation for four more years was canceled, and nothing was lost. Finally, the companies that suffered from dissolution decrees, reappearing eventually as separate entities, worked together as a "community of interests," and maintained secret price agreements as harmoniously as ever.

None of the wealthy evildoers was ever put in jail. After from thirty to forty years of "trust busting," beginning with Theodore Roosevelt, the whole effort to prevent monopoly and restraint of trade was judged by a contemporary historian to have failed ut-

[32] The New York *World*, Oct. 22, 1907.

terly.[33] Mr. Louis D. Brandeis, who in his earlier career as a law-yer fought some rousing legal battles with monopolistic corpora-tions and was often in touch with Roosevelt's Department of Jus-tice, felt that this President was "not objective in his thinking" upon the trust question. Brandeis also had visions of setting Amer-ican business free. Roosevelt, in self-explanation, declared that he worked for "the moral regeneration of business"; he directed sim-ply a "movement for honesty." After a time, when the going be-came more difficult, when business conditions were unsettled or de-pressed, he halted his efforts; as if enough honesty had been gen-erated to last for some little while.

Meanwhile, certain episodes of the trust-busting crusade lent drama to the epoch. The Standard Oil clan, on the whole, re-mained sullenly silent under assaults upon their moral character. But this was not true of Edward Harriman, the railroad master, whose vast combinations were often financed by the more specula-tive members of the Standard Oil family.

Harriman was filled with a deep sense of grievance. Theodore Roosevelt, he believed, was under a certain "moral obligation" to him; yet his efforts in personal conferences during two years had won him no favor. In the autumn of 1906 rumors were heard that the government would move to separate his two transcontinental lines, the Union Pacific and the Southern Pacific, and heavy sell-ing in the stock market undoubtedly placed Harriman under some financial strain.

The government attacks upon his property, he felt convinced, were acts of the basest ingratitude for his earlier services; also they seemed to be acts of vengeance, following his stern refusal in the summer of 1906 to donate any money to the Republicans' election chest, when a request was carried to him by an emissary of Roosevelt's. In the second place, he believed that they were in-spired by his powerful rivals in the financial world. According to the memorandum of one of Harriman's attorneys, Maxwell Evarts, who attempted to intercede in the quarrel, Roosevelt burst

[33] Faulkner, *American Economic History*, p. 542.

out on one occasion: "Well, you don't know what Morgan and some of these other people say about Harriman." [34]

Evidently the Morgan partners, who came far more frequently to the White House than was generally realized, carried dark tales about the great financial rival, Harriman, to the trust-buster. And there was not a little to be said about the "reorganization" of the Union Pacific, or the notorious looting of the small bankrupted Chicago & Alton by the Harriman band in 1904. Harriman could never be dissuaded from the belief, expressed in his official biography, that Theodore Roosevelt played favorites in his trust-busting games, a practice that might yield immense profits to Harriman's adversaries.

At this moment of strain, an employee stole several of Harriman's letters and sold them first to Mr. Hearst, and then to Mr. Pulitzer's New York *World*, which on April 2, 1907, published one letter addressed to Sidney Webster, corporation counsel. In this Harriman, writing in December, 1905, spoke of his disillusionment with his political friend Roosevelt, of the promises that had been made to him, the sums of money Harriman had raised in return for these promises, and the subsequent bad faith shown. He had helped Roosevelt "at his own request," and had merely been used to "further his own [Roosevelt's] interests." Harriman vowed that he had been gulled and would never trust politicians again.

In retort, the President handed to the press a letter of his own of a somewhat earlier date, October 8, 1906, to Vice-President James Sherman. (Often he had letters ready—and not fortuitously—in these emergencies.) Here, replying to reports concerning Harriman's dark mutterings against himself, the President presented his own relations with this man as having involved no promises, no obligations, and no requests whatsoever for money donations. (!) It was one of T. R.'s famous "letters for the record." [35] But it closed with the startling words that labeled Harri-

---

[34] Kennan, *Harriman*, Vol. II, p. 224.
[35] The New York *World*, Apr. 2, Apr. 3, 1907.

man "as undesirable a citizen as Debs, or Moyer or Haywood. The wealthy corruptionist, and the demagogue who excites . . . class against class, and appeals to the basest passions of the human soul, are fundamentally alike and are equally enemies of the Republic." Strong words, that deeply wounded the mighty Harriman, pilloried with socialists and syndicalists, raising a memorable storm that enlivened the trust-busting battles.

The clash with Harriman, the powerful legal onslaughts upon the Standard Oil family of corporations, are extremely noteworthy because at this very time the relations between the White House and J. P. Morgan and Company, by contrast, were so uncommonly sweet. After the Northern Securities affair in 1902, there was almost no trouble with the House of Morgan, and the great banker evidently avoided challenging the great politico in his own province. Instead, Morgan's underlings, Perkins and Gary, more prepossessing, more ingratiating than the bluff old man, plied the President with flattery. Elbert Gary, the president of the United States Steel Corporation, wrote to Theodore Roosevelt frequently, saying that he shared his views upon "righteousness," that Roosevelt's investigation of the steel trust had "done good rather than harm," that Gary himself had benefited by following Roosevelt's example and heeding his appeals.[36] Accounts of the steel trust's "profit-sharing" system, applied to a few well-paid workers, were sent to the White House, while nothing was said of the twelve-hour day and the number of spies employed to eliminate union organizers. Thus the biggest of all trusts went unmolested. The gigantic International Harvester Company, organized by Morgan and George W. Perkins, also was granted immunity as a "good" trust. Nor were serious difficulties provided for the Morgan-Vanderbilt coal-carrying railroads, or for the fabulous New Haven railroad monopoly, which by 1906 had swallowed up almost all the surface and marine transportation in the six New England states.

[36] *T. R. Papers*, Roosevelt to Paul Morton, Jan. 24, 1907.

Possibly Roosevelt felt that by attacking one sector at a time, and also avoiding a general frontal advance—by directing his fire now upon one flank and now another—he made victory more certain. In any case, at the time of the government attacks upon the Rockefellers and upon the Harriman lines in the winter of 1907, there was a good deal of uneasiness in financial circles and railway stocks fell sharply in Wall Street. Rumors that the Interstate Commerce Commission planned a series of large "raids" against other railroads brought cries of protest and finally, on March 11, 1907, a visit by a delegation of New York magnates, headed by Mr. Morgan himself. To them Roosevelt said that

. . . No raid was contemplated by the Commission; that nothing would be done in a spirit of resentment, or that would have a tendency to add to, or even continue, the existence of the prevailing public mistrust.[37]

A little later Charles S. Mellen, president of the New Haven, who so proudly wore the "Morgan collar," dashed into the White House to inquire of Roosevelt himself if, under the provisions of the Sherman law, his road would be allowed to keep its Long Island Sound steamers. Roosevelt assured him that "so far as I and my Administration are concerned, if you do not sell, you will have no trouble about those steamship lines." Yet the simultaneous ownership of both railways and competing steamships was a glaring instance of non-competition, of restraint of trade, of monopoly. Again, a few weeks later, Mellen returned to ask Roosevelt if the Interstate Commerce Commission would object to the New Haven's buying the Boston & Maine—a measure which Louis D. Brandeis contested on behalf of independent stockholders. The President said: "I would buy it, if I were you." [38]

In the spring of 1908, following the exposure of scandalous and fraudulent transactions by the management of the New Haven railroad, there were reports that a government suit would be launched. One day the news of this was released, but an hour later

---

[37] *Commercial and Financial Chronicle*, Mar. 16, 1907.
[38] Statement of C. S. Mellen in The New York *Times*, Nov. 11, 1915.

orders came by telephone from the White House to all press associations to kill the news. It was rumored that Morgan's man, Mellen, had again appealed successfully to the White House at the eleventh hour.[39]

These waverings cast a strange light on Theodore Roosevelt as an example of the "honest broker" in politics, a magistrate judging impartially between the rival pressure groups within the state. Gradually the energy of the trust-busting crusade diminished, despite strong talk by Roosevelt of "criminal prosecution of trust magnates." Attorney General Bonaparte cautioned him to go slow in 1907, a year of depression. "I have been on the lookout for several months for a good case, but the chance of getting conviction, and a sentence of imprisonment after the conviction, seems to me to be very poor," Bonaparte wrote in August, 1907.[40]

Despite "trust busting," the United States remained essentially what it had been, "the paradise of capitalists." The great corporations contributed almost nothing in taxes in return for the enormous police and judicial protection they enjoyed. There was no Federal income tax, nor inheritance tax; there was virtually no compensation for workmen killed while at labor; the labor of women and children was subject to almost no restrictions, and efforts to restrict it locally were halted by the Federal courts on Constitutional grounds. The very Sherman Anti-Trust Law itself was used to restrain labor organization. In the commodities and securities markets the most piratical adventures by the speculative leaders of the day were carried off, everywhere with impunity, to the loss of the investing public. Even in 1904 great monopolies, such as the Amalgamated Copper Company, were able to corner the world copper market and double the price of this metal. In that year also a general stock-market panic was traced to the hand of the Rockefeller group, operating through the huge National City Bank. Theodore Roosevelt had moved public opinion powerfully, to be sure, when he left office after seven years.

[39] Lief, *op. cit.*, pp. 146-147.
[40] Bishop, *Bonaparte*, pp. 139-140.

His effectiveness, however, was largely limited to the sphere of "morals."

He clung to his middle-ground position out of deep convictions, and lashed out to the right and the left of him. After using his invectives against the oil trust, he turned to denounce the labor leaders, Haywood, Moyer, and Pettibone, as "undesirable citizens." Thus, as Eugene Debs passionately protested, the chief magistrate publicly condemned men who were then still held innocent under the law, and for whose defense thousands of poorer citizens throughout the country raised funds from their modest earnings.

He veered repeatedly from condemnation of the "criminal rich" to admonitions also to those who, following his example, attacked the rich and the powerful with excessive zeal or, perhaps, with baser motives than his own. Reading the series of articles by David Graham Phillips entitled "The Treason of the Senate," he became very exercised, and on March 17, 1906, at the Gridiron Club dinner in Washington, he lashed out at those who wrote the literature of exposure with an immortal epithet: "Muckrakers." He had taken as his text the passage from Bunyan's *Pilgrim's Progress*, treating of the "man with the muckrake, the man who could look no way but downward with the muckrake in his hands . . . who continued to rake to himself the filth of the floor." The "Muckrake" speech, subsequently repeated at a public ceremony, April 14, 1906, perplexed and disheartened Roosevelt's liberal friends. While denouncing "bad" capitalists, he had also accused the "Muckrakers" of seeking "to make financial or political profit out of the destruction of character," of creating a "morbid and vicious public sentiment." The purpose of the speech, as Roosevelt admitted to his friend Lodge, was to strike at "agitators, at corrupt or sinister or foolish visionaries . . . at preachers of social unrest and discontent. . . ." [41] It balanced the record.

[41] Lodge, *Correspondence*, Vol. II, p. 247.

VIII. THE POLITICS OF DEPRESSION

THE POLITICAL government in the years before the first World War seemed to gather to itself more centralized power than anyone would have dreamed of in recent times. This power now seemed fixed securely in the hands of the man who was at once chief executive of the government and boss of his party. It was commonly remarked among students of political affairs in those days that the President now "overshadowed" all other authorities. Besides his military and police power, he had the right to investigate the management or examine the books of any corporation in the country; he could more or less control railroads valued at fifteen billions of dollars; he sought in addition the power to regulate life-insurance companies with billions of dollars in assets; and it was said that he bent his energies to have laws enacted licensing all corporations engaged in interstate commerce. He could enjoy "smashing" a financial titan like Edward H. Harriman. To a conservative dean of the Yale Law School, all this spelled "the menace of growing centralization."[1] To an intellectual like Herbert Croly, the Rooseveltian tendency meant the redemption of our politics, provided energy and unity of command in a government that had been hitherto divided in all its parts, and made for "the promise of American life." However, the weaknesses in this system, concealed behind its front of deceptive strength, were seldom grasped by those who exclaimed with the editor of the liberal New York *World*, "Where will it all end? Despotism? Caesarism . . . ?" Perhaps the great corporations,

[1] The New York *World*, Oct. 13, 1905.

under pressure, would be driven to the extremity of "launching a revolution" in order "to take possession of the national government." Yet such desperate measures were entirely needless.

' "We still continue to enjoy a literally unprecedented prosperity," Theodore Roosevelt announced with pride in his Message to Congress of December 3, 1906. Fortune had thus far smiled upon his work.

That very winter and in the following spring symptoms of the declining phase of the business cycle were at hand. Financial stress was reported in European centers. Would such adverse developments disturb American industrial activities? Many "experts" thought not, holding that our fabulous supplies of gold, our immense bank reserves, our increasingly strong position as a creditor nation, would henceforth eliminate such panics and depressions as those of 1873 and 1893.[2]

Nevertheless money grew dear—that is, interest rates mounted —toward the end of 1906; grain and stock markets suffered sinking spells, and large railroads were hard pressed to obtain loans for their construction needs that spring of 1907.

By the early autumn of 1907, the credit strain was intense; a half dozen large New York banks were reported to be in difficulties, while thousands of depositors, who struggled to withdraw their savings, stood in long, funereal lines day and night. Farmers could obtain no loans to move their crops; factories were shutting down; hundreds of thousands of laborers were made idle and hungry. The deluge had come; and the "overshadowing," "Czar-like" President could only look on, bewildered.

In spite of moral exhortations of the Square Dealer and his followers, the raging financial panic of October, 1907, revealed many weak spots in our economic system. The immediate or external cause of trouble now appeared to be extravagant "financiering" rather than "overconstruction," as in the 1870's and 1890's. Taking advantage of a legal loophole in the revised New York

[2] Noyes, *American Finance*, p. 364.

State general trust-company law, numerous financiers had toward 1900 launched new trust companies, accepting demand deposits from the public and doing a general banking business. In addition the fashionable new trust companies were almost as free of control as the "investment trusts" and holding companies of a generation later, those of the 1920's; the size of cash reserves, unlike that of banks, was subject to their own discretion; they could buy and sell stocks; they could, as in the case of one trust company, use their own stock as collateral in order to buy other trust companies, until a "chain" of trust companies formed a pyramid that was based on the shaky foundations of very speculative shipping, oil, and copper securities, accumulated for the enrichment of the inner circle of directors. Should any of the stones at the base of the pyramid be dislodged, then the whole structure of overlying banks and trust companies would come falling down.

This was precisely what happened in the week of October 14, 1907, with the group of interlocking trust companies controlled by the shipbuilder C. W. Morse and his partner, the audacious copper baron, F. Augustus Heinze. The stock of the United Copper Company, an independent concern, crashed suddenly from $50 to $10 a share, and with it fell various oil and shipping stocks. At once several large trust companies and banks were in trouble, including the Knickerbocker Trust, the Trust Company of America, the Mercantile National, and others affiliated with the Heinze-Morse enterprises. More than a year before, mysterious warnings of exactly such developments had been given by Jacob Schiff, the head of Kuhn, Loeb and Company, who advocated the establishment of a central bank of reserve.[3]

Now it was discovered how much the Rough Rider, in his collisions with great financial leaders, had "undermined" confidence. In a speech at Chicago, October 22, 1907, which was widely noticed, Roosevelt's former friend and adviser, President Nicholas Murray Butler of Columbia University, exclaimed: *"Do not wreck the credit system."* Roosevelt's reforming activities, especially his

[3] The New York *Times,* Jan. 5, 1906.

recent threat to use the criminal law against monopolists, Butler said, would end by destroying the economic basis "upon which our prosperity and our happiness rests." To such appeals the President answered that he acted but to "turn on the light." In a speech at Nashville, he took notice of the charges that "the policies for which I stand" were responsible for the financial troubles of the moment, and replied that he doubted if this were true. Yet even were the charges true, "it will not alter in the slightest degree my determination that for the remaining sixteen months these policies shall be persevered in unswervingly." [4]

The onward sweep of the crisis would reveal whether the government and its law stood "above" the corporations and their magnates, as Roosevelt boasted. On the very day that Roosevelt spoke at Nashville, October 22, 1907, a large trust company in New York, the Knickerbocker, closed its doors.

In October, J. Pierpont Morgan, the "personal dictator" of the American financial world, had gone to Richmond, Virginia, to attend the General Convention of the Protestant Episcopal Church. As a prominent layman of this church he was busy with all the ceremony and beautiful psalm-singing of a clerical convention when news, more or less surprising, of the tragic bank panic reached him by telegraph on October 19, 1907.

To his friend Bishop William Laurence he confided that he was going back to New York on Saturday, the 19th. "They are in trouble in New York. They do not know what to do, and I don't know what to do, but I am going back."

The Bishop, who happened to return with him in his private car, remembered him as "in the best of spirits" without suggestion of care or anxiety and singing lustily away at breakfast.[5] Morgan sang while banks crashed; their white-faced officers had turned to him for aid. Was it pure religious faith that made him so cheery in these dark hours?

Since 1893 Morgan, by his personal force and will and by his

[4] The New York *World*, Oct. 23, 1907.
[5] Laurence, *Memories of a Happy Life*, pp. 251-252.

strategic relationships with the largest railroad, industrial, and banking concerns, had managed to assert his leadership. In October, 1907, all eyes turned to him as the dictator of the financial world. What passed then for a central banking system consisted of the great New York Clearing House banks, who could decide whether or not the checks of the other metropolitan banks should be accepted for exchange. The bulk of the Clearing House members, as the Pujo Committee investigation would soon show, consisted of institutions directed by Morgan, by his ally George F. Baker, head of the First National Bank, and by James Stillman, head of the huge Rockefeller-owned National City Bank.

As soon as Morgan arrived in New York on Sunday evening, October 20, the city's leading bankers gathered in his home. There, in the famous library with its rare examples of medieval art, its miniatures and Shakespeare folios, the men of money sat in nightlong conference with the Morgan partners, Perkins, Davison, and Steele, who carefully thumbed through their assets and liabilities. There the decision upon the clearing of checks was made. Morgan himself sat in a small adjacent alcove, playing a game of solitaire and smoking his big black cigar. One by one the proposals and estimates would be brought to him on pieces of notepaper. Some he would comment upon in his brief, stolid way; some he would accept; others he would silently tear up. The presence of Stillman, of Baker, of Schiff beside him suggested the mobilization of most of the nation's liquid wealth under Morgan's leadership.

Early in the morning Morgan came, "in his coupe drawn by the familiar gray cob," to 23 Wall Street, the low corner building with large, Roman-arched windows. He passed "through a line of trust company presidents and financiers" reaching from the swinging door outside to the glass-enclosed private office inside. Among those who gathered in the musty old counting house were Edward Harriman, Thomas Fortune Ryan, Elbert H. Gary, Henry C. Frick, and August Belmont, former rivals and enemies who had now closed their ranks. The very head of the national government, frightened by events he could scarcely comprehend, now sent his Secretary of the Treasury, George B. Cortelyou, hurrying to the corner of Wall and Broad Streets with $35,000,000 of the Treasury's surplus funds to throw into the breach.

It was the master of banking who now appeared to hold power of life and death over the nation, a power reflected in the newspapers of the day:

Above the tumult of hysteria and fear one voice sounded strong, clear and reassuring. . . . One face grim and determined shone through the clouds of doubt and foreboding.

It was the voice and the face of J. Pierpont Morgan, called to the throne of finance again; made master of more millions than ever a human being controlled before; with the wealthiest of corporations as his vassals, with financiers of international repute as his aides, and the great U. S. Treasury as his almoner.

Across the street to the frenzied stock exchange word went forth: *"Mr. Morgan requests that you do not sell the market."* It was a threat. To the bankers and financiers who waited to learn of their fate, there was but one command: "You must put yourself unreservedly in the hands of Mr. Morgan." The only questions asked were: "What are you worth? What have you got? How have you been doing business?" [6]

Then the cash and gold marshaled by the banking consortium—the Rockefeller banks contributing nearly as much as the national Treasury—were deposited with those institutions which it had been decided to support. A large part of the government deposits, as Secretary Cortelyou admitted afterward to a Congressional committee, was handed over as call loans to hard-pressed stockbrokers.

The panic and depression were real enough; it had been long brewing. The form it took and the methods of defense used reflected the paramount importance of finance capital in the modern business system. Singular incidents that occurred during the tumult and confusion revealed at the same time how the dominant group of finance capitalists condemned and destroyed rival operators

[6] The New York *World*, Oct. 24, 1907.

whom they had silently marked out as their prey; how by a tacit agreement the Morgan and Rockefeller "crowds" moved swiftly to eliminate menacing opponents, to seize long-coveted prizes in the shape of valuable industrial property, and place these forever among the mass of their own possessions.

Thus it was common rumor in Wall Street that F. Augustus Heinze, the Montana copper baron, had long been a thorn in the side of the Rockefeller copper trust, known then as the "Amalgamated" and controlling the Anaconda mines. Heinze, the independent, owned newspapers and banks as well as oil companies. He paid more liberal wages to miners, signed agreements with the union, and yet in the copper market competed successfully in price with the "Amalgamated." Since 1904, H. H. Rogers, then active head of the Standard Oil combination, had tried to ruin or buy out Heinze. "Rogers . . . told Rockefeller what a dangerous man Heinze was, and they probably both agreed to fight him forever." [7] There was the strange fact that at the height of the panic on October 23, 1907, a New York newspaper published alarming reflections upon the management of a large bank, the Heinze-controlled Knickerbocker Trust Company; and at noon that day the bank closed its doors.[8] The blocks of securities held as collateral for Heinze and Morse were then taken up by new hands, at panic prices. Other banks were saved—except the Knickerbocker Trust—on condition that Heinze, Morse, and their allies resign as directors and officers.[9] Thereafter the independent producers who threatened the monopolies, whether in copper or in shipbuilding, disappeared from the scene.

Like the Rockefeller band, the Morgan group also imposed its terms of surrender. To those who appealed to him, Morgan is credited with having said: "Why should I get into this? I've done enough. I won't take all this on, unless—" and then a gesture signifying "unless I get what I want out of it." [10] Thus it was said

[7] C. W. Barron, *More They Told Barron*, p. 53.

[8] *Commercial and Financial Chronicle*, Oct. 27, 1907, p. 1060.

[9] Noyes, *op. cit.*, p. 371.

[10] Corey, *The House of Morgan*, p. 345.

that when the Trust Company of America, which suffered a tremendous run, losing $34,000,000 of deposits within a few days, was saved by Morgan's bringing up funds of the New Haven railroad, a valuable railway franchise lying in the vaults of this bank as collateral passed into the hands of Morgan's road.[11]

But there were even greater prizes that fell as wreckage of the financial storm to the masters of banking who gathered at Mr. Morgan's home.

On the week-end of November 2, 1907, Elbert H. Gary, president of the United States Steel Corporation, was seen by watching newspaper reporters to enter Morgan's brownstone mansion on Madison Avenue. Henry C. Frick and George W. Perkins, directors of the steel trust, were also reported to have joined him. What the conferees discussed in their nocturnal meetings, it soon appeared, must have been the tremendous bargain which had been temptingly offered in the shape of the Tennessee Coal and Iron Company. This large, independent property, located in a strategic part of the South and believed to possess enormous iron ore deposits, was valued lately at from $150 to $160 a share (of $100 par value), but controlling stock, it was learned, had been assigned to Moore & Schley, a large concern of stockbrokers who were now in serious straits. Mr. Gary earlier had been offered control of the company for $100,000,000, or at $150 a share, but insisted that the price was double what he was willing to have the United States Steel Corporation pay for it. Now, in the midst of the panic, his terms were met, and a bargain was struck by which the steel trust gave its own 4 per cent bonds, worth $40,000,000, for Tennessee Coal and Iron's stock, worth at the time 160, or actually $80,000,000.[12]

The only problem about this "deal" in the minds of the gentlemen congregated at Madison Avenue, New York, was the incalculable one: the President at Washington. Would the United

[11] Barron, *op. cit.*, p. 171.
[12] *Commercial and Financial Chronicle*, Oct. 27, Nov. 3, 1907.

States Steel Corporation, by adding the new property, be liable to prosecution under the Sherman Anti-Trust Act?

On Sunday night, November 4, Mr. Gary telephoned to the White House, spoke to the President's Private Secretary, William Loeb, and succeeded in making an appointment with the President for himself and Henry Frick the very morning following. Taking a special train at once, the two financiers roared through the night to Washington, arriving there early in the morning, and insisted upon calling the President from his breakfast—before the stock exchange opened in New York.[13]

Gary then told the President that a large concern, presumed by Roosevelt to be a "big trust company," would have to go into receivership unless a quantity of shares in Tennessee Coal and Iron were taken from its hands. Gary, in his most pious manner, intimated strongly that the steel trust had no keen desire to purchase the property in question, but would do so only as an altruistic measure. With the President's approval, they would even pay a price "somewhat in excess of its true value," in order to relieve the situation.

Their own company, they argued, controlled slightly more than 50 per cent of the nation's steel trade, and with the new property would still control less than 60 per cent. They insisted upon learning of the government's attitude before the market opened that day.

"I answered," Roosevelt noted after they had left, "that, while of course, I could not advise them to take the action proposed, I felt it no public duty of mine to interpose any objections." Later, in testifying before the Stanley Committee, he explained, "It was necessary for me to decide on the instant, before the Stock Exchange opened, for the situation in New York was such that any hour might be vital."[14] The name of the business concern which was scheduled for failure he had not been told, and he preferred not to ask for it.

---

[13] Tarbell, *Gary*, pp. 201-204.

[14] House of Representatives, *Investigation of United States Steel Corporation* ("Stanley Committee"), pp. 1371, 1375.

At five minutes before ten, Mr. George W. Perkins, waiting at a telephone in the office of Morgan and Company, heard the voice of Gary giving "the glad tidings" from Washington. Instantly word was flashed to the stock exchange and a buying demonstration swept the market upward.[15]

For the Morgan-dominated steel trust, which in its early years often threatened to go into receivership owing to its burden of "watered" stock, the purchase of Tennessee Coal and Iron with its vast reserves of ore proved to be a masterly stroke. Gary admitted a few years later that he would not sell the new property for ten times its cost.

2

The boast of Roosevelt was that the door of the White House would swing open as readily to the labor leader as to the financial magnate. Yet no labor leader was known to have left his door with something equivalent to the government's blessing for executing a plundering raid upon a billion dollars' worth of property. Only lately Mr. Gompers, appearing on behalf of the American Federation of Labor, had presented "Labor's Bill of Grievances," and had been dismissed with evasive replies.

If at times a glimmer of the truth dawned upon Roosevelt, he would admit his own abysmal ignorance of economic problems, which were, after all, the fundamental problems of his time. ". . . When it comes to finance, or compound differentials," he remarked once to Professor J. Lawrence Laughlin, "I am all up in the air." [16] "Judge" Elbert Gary, like all other Morgan men, felt that he owed much to this President, and at the end of his term the steel magnate wrote gratefully:

Notwithstanding that I hear from some of my acquaintances . . . that the present agitation, investigations, prosecutions have a tendency to depress business and slacken prosperity, it is my opinion that sooner or later, probably sooner, the results will be beneficial. . . . I do not

[15] *Ibid.*, pp. 940-941, 1605-1606.
[16] Pringle, *Roosevelt*, p. 432.

hesitate to say that your influence as President of this great republic has been of benefit to me personally and I feel equally certain that it is beginning to have good effect on others who have been reluctant to see their faults.[17]

Under the stress of a great financial storm, which he knew not how to navigate, he turned more and more to the counsel of the men who commanded the big dreadnaughts of the money market. Sometimes he suspected dimly that perhaps the "malefactors of great wealth" were scheming "to bring about as much financial stress as possible" in order to effect a reversal of his declared policies, or to replace his type of government with a reactionary one. This thought occurs in a speech of August 29, 1907, shortly before the decline in financial markets assumed panic proportions.[18] He wrote to one prominent banker, Higginson, that in spite of the pleas that he make reassuring gestures toward the business interests, he could not drop his action against the railroads and monopolies, for such a course would be indefensible "the moment the . . . flurry in Wall Street is over." "I cannot grant an illegal immunity," he concluded, in almost apologetic tones.[19]

But the "flurry" became a long, fierce downpour; and Roosevelt's mood and spirit changed noticeably under stress. In 1907, generally, his attitude was defensive. Soon he was quietly granting indulgences and immunities on every side. The great magnates who came to him asked always for a "breathing spell"; they asked only that the Federal government "keep its hands off them." [20]

He had always worshiped naked power; and now he appeared to bow before the reality of overwhelming economic power. The funds of the Treasury were deposited, for the emergency, where the imperious Morgan directed. Prosecution against the New Haven railroad, as we have seen, was postponed. George W. Perkins, Morgan's lieutenant, who had designed the structure of the

[17] McCaleb, *Roosevelt*, p. 240.
[18] Roosevelt, *Speeches*, Vol. VI, p. 1351.
[19] *T. R. Papers*, T. R. to H. L. Higginson, Aug. 12, 1907.
[20] *Ibid.*, T. R. to H. L. Higginson.

International Harvester Company, a virtual monopoly in the manufacture of farm machines, came to him on August 22, 1907, when this company was known to be under investigation, and urged that it be spared. It was a "reasonable" corporation; it exercised no undue restraint of trade; it gave work to thousands of men, and incomes to thousands of small investors. And Roosevelt quietly dispatched a message to Bonaparte, his Attorney General: "Please do not file this suit until I hear from you." [21]

Herbert Knox Smith, the Commissioner of Corporations, who investigated the International Harvester Company for the President, now reported that it was not an "obvious" monopoly. Justice must therefore be done to a "good" trust whose only wish was to obey the law. Perkins had told Smith that his company, like the other Morgan combinations, was endeavoring to "uphold the policies of the administration and to adopt the methods of modern publicity. . . ." There were no "moral grounds for attack" on the International Harvester Company, Smith concluded; and if one were made on "purely technical" grounds, then Perkins and his associates threatened to fight. Smith concluded:

> While the administration has never hesitated to grapple with any financial interest, no matter how great, when it is believed that a substantial wrong is being committed, nevertheless it is a very practical question whether it is well to throw away now the great influence of the so-called Morgan interests, which up to this time have supported the advanced policy of the administration.[22]

Here in the intimate language of one of Theodore Roosevelt's "Tennis Cabinet" the cat is let out of the bag. We perceive that the Roosevelt administration up to this time (August, 1907) had enjoyed support from "the great influence of the so-called Morgan interests" and *as a practical matter feared to throw this support away*. The decision was made to spare the Harvester Company. This decision and the grounds for it, when examined in 1908 by a Senate Committee, Roosevelt always refused to explain. The

[21] *T. R. Papers*, T. R. to Bonaparte, Aug. 22, 1907.
[22] U. S. Senate, 62nd Congress, 2nd Session, *Senate Documents*, p. 694.

Committee tried to reach the records in the custody of Herbert Knox Smith and the Bureau of Corporations. But Roosevelt ordered Smith to deliver the papers to him, to be held until he stepped out of office. They could only be got, he said, by impeachment. ". . . If they were made public, no end of trouble would ensue." [23] The affair of the International Harvester, like that of the Tennessee Coal and Iron two months after, strongly reveals the narrow limits within which the power of the Honest Broker was exercised.

While Roosevelt stood forth as the fearless adversary of "plutocrats" like Morgan (whom he appeared to assail in public), in private an effective alliance was made—not with Morgan, but with his more prepossessing, more ingratiating lieutenants Gary and Perkins.

The Standard Oil men on the other hand, ever since Miss Tarbell's historical study had appeared, were obvious political targets and easy to pillory. Financial scandal also pursued Harriman. But the character of Morgan and Company for reputable dealing stood high, and few of the "Muckrakers" attacked this group—save for the large scale of their operations—until after the crash of the New Haven railroad. While the Rockefeller men remained silent under attacks, and came not to Washington to ask either for mercy or indulgences, the Morgan lieutenants (several of whose friends were in the Cabinet itself) came often to "consult" the President and appeared to defer to him and to court his approval earnestly by good works.

In November, 1907, rumors of the President's strange services to the leaders of Wall Street circulated actively, and certain of his admirers, such as William Allen White, wrote asking what truth there was in these reports. He replied stoutly: ". . . I shall not 'surrender' to the bankers, or to any one else, and there will be no 'secret, midnight conferences' with any big financiers, or any one else." [24]

[23] McCaleb, op. cit., p. 249.
[24] T. R. Papers, T. R. to T. E. Watson, Nov. 12, 1907; to W. A. White, Nov. 26, 1907.

3

"It is difficult for me to understand why there should be this belief in Wall Street that I am a wild-eyed revolutionist," Roosevelt wrote pathetically to Jacob Schiff. Some day, the men of wealth and substance would realize, he prophesied, that they had been utterly mistaken in their opposition to him, "even from the standpoint of their own interests; and that nothing better for them could be devised than the laws I have striven . . . to have enacted." [25]

As a consequence of the panic and depression of 1907, Roosevelt's attitude toward the great industrial combinations which he had thought to break up, or at least control with a firm hand, began to change noticeably. He began to fear that he might have gone a little too far. As he said to the English historian Trevelyan, he had seen his problem as that of instituting reforms without paralyzing business initiative. He still refused to admit that his "policies" had brought on panic; panic developed from business corruption, "trickery and dishonesty in high places. . . ." But on further reflection he began to believe that "very possibly the assaults and exposures which I made, and . . . which were . . . imitated in the several States, have brought on the panic a year or two sooner than would otherwise have been the case." [26]

To William Allen White he wrote that he felt his reign was ending "under a more or less dark cloud of obloquy," though through no fault of his own.[27]

Yet by sending out word that he would "do everything I can to the very verge of my power to restore confidence," he seemed for the moment to justify the reproaches which the magnates heaped upon him. He even went to the length of issuing certain public statements calculated to instill firmness and hope in the stock markets.

[25] *Ibid.*, T. R. to J. H. Schiff, Mar. 28, 1907.
[26] *Ibid.*, T. R. to Hamlin Garland, Nov. 23, 1907.
[27] *Ibid.*, T. R. to W. A. White, Nov. 26, 1907.

In 1908 the Supreme Court handed down a number of decisions which showed that its members looked not only at election returns but sometimes even at the barometer of the stock ticker. The cancellation of the $29,000,000 fine against the Standard Oil in July, 1908, suggested that moderation in trust busting was now desired. The way was also prepared for the famous "rule of reason," by which the mere size of a corporation was to be judged no offense in itself. Although the President resumed the suit against the Standard Oil at once, there was actually a partial truce in the war against the trusts for nearly three years after 1907; then, under another President, when circumstances warranted, the fate of the trusts would become a political football again.

Roosevelt's friend and patron, George W. Perkins, nowadays passed for a philosopher of big business. He spoke at Chamber of Commerce meetings and published pamphlets and articles urging that corporations should be permitted to grow as big as they wished; they should be subject to "regulation" instead of "repression" or "strangulation." A commission made up of men who were "master minds," who knew intimately the interests of business, should replace the mere politicians and sit in judgment of business problems.[28] Perkins' solution sounded much like that of the protectionist Republican manufacturers who insisted that the tariff should be revised only by its "friends." Yet by the beginning of 1908 Theodore Roosevelt's views had shifted until they resembled closely those Perkins constantly preached.

He now dwelt upon the *inadequacies* of the Sherman Anti-Trust Act and the Interstate Commerce Act. In a message to Congress he said:

It is profoundly immoral to put or keep upon the statutes a law, nominally in the interests of public morality, that really puts a premium on public immorality, by undertaking to forbid honest men from doing what must be done under modern business conditions.

[28] G. W. Perkins, *Wanted, a Constructive National Policy*, Aug. 7, 1910 (pamphlet).

And again he declared:

It is a public evil to have on the statute books a law incapable of full enforcement; because both judges and juries realize that its full enforcement would destroy the business of the country.[29]

Senator La Follette thought these criticisms of the trust laws were a sort of "executive sanction to violate the law."

It is true that the President's behavior suggested that he was carrying out a retreat from reform. Actually this maneuver was concealed, as was so often done by "social-democratic" politicians in Europe, by turning more boldly radical than before in speech. For under the stress of business depression and unemployment and declining farm prices, the mood of the public was, if anything, more critical, more edged with discontent than in the more prosperous years before 1907. Thus Theodore Roosevelt, in a season of popular agitation, and with election approaching, publicly advocated a series of boldly progressive measures. He recommended that Congress pass a direct income tax and inheritance tax; that the government institute a program of workmen's compensation for its employees, partly as an example to be followed by private business. He proposed even that the abuse of the injunction in labor disputes should be curbed; and finally, adopting La Follette's ideas, he declared that the problem of railroad rates could be met only by granting the government power to make a valuation of railroad property and fix rates according to "a fair rate of return." [30]

All this sounded alarmingly radical, until one recalled that the much-compromised and -amended Hepburn Act, moderate as were its provisions, had barely won passage through Congress under its present iron control. Moreover, in these very proposals that sounded so drastic there were also passages, as Roosevelt himself pointed out, that advised important changes in the anti-trust

[29] McCaleb, *op. cit.*, p. 240.
[30] *Presidential Messages*, Message to Congress, Jan. 31, 1908, Vol. VII, pp. 1597 ff.

laws, "in order to make legal proper combinations." [31] Finally, by 1908 the President had lost all control over Congress; and in the Lame Duck session, following the election of November, a loud quarrel broke out between the White House and Capitol Hill. Ordinary appropriations desired by Roosevelt were delayed or refused passage; Roosevelt might still give lip service to progressive, reform proposals as he did in his final messages, yet Congress paid no attention to words that were uttered as if "for the record," and which he himself knew would be wholly ignored. Actually he had abandoned nearly all actions against the trusts and the railroads, writing to a friend in a chastened mood: "As a matter of fact I have let up in every case where I have had any possible excuse for so doing." [32]

To avoid ending his long service as President under a "dark cloud" was an important consideration with such a man as Theodore Roosevelt. It was a coincidence that during the autumn of 1907, while the gloom of depression fixed itself upon America, new strain appeared in the relations of America and Japan; and to these problems the President turned his attention with renewed zeal.

Strong anti-Japanese agitation had broken out in California, and a violent movement to eliminate all Japanese immigration was revived in stronger force than ever. The "memorandum" of an agreement between Taft and Katsura, in 1905, had failed to work. Against the discriminatory and punitive measures of California, the Japanese government protested firmly and with great dignity. Japanese subjects must be treated upon a footing of perfect equality with Europeans; upon this ground the Japanese never yielded. Thus Roosevelt, who strongly deplored the local persecution of the Japanese in California, despite fair and conciliating words, saw relations between the two countries drift from bad to worse. In America the demagogic newspapers of Hearst, both in San Fran-

[31] *T. R. Papers*, T. R. to H. L. Higginson, Feb. 19, 1908.
[32] McCaleb, *op. cit.*, p. 256.

cisco and New York, whipped up a storm of fear over the "Yellow Peril." Throughout the world there was much secret diplomatic gossip of an approaching conflict; and yet, as Roosevelt now recognized, the Philippine Islands were virtually indefensible for our navy—our "Achilles heel" in the Pacific.

Roosevelt said afterward of the Japanese: "I had . . . become uncomfortably conscious of a very, very slight undertone of veiled truculence in their communication . . . and I finally made up my mind that they thought I was afraid of them." He heard also that "the Japanese war party firmly believed that they could beat us" and that other foreign experts also thought so. It was time then for a "showdown." [33]

Suddenly it became known that tremendous preparations had been going on in American navy yards; and soon the news of Roosevelt's decision to send the American battle fleet on a voyage around the world competed in popular interest with accounts of the financial panic. The fleet was to proceed via Cape Horn and the Pacific Ocean, the tour to include a "friendly" visit to Japan, in response to an equally "friendly" invitation. Such a voyage by so large a fleet, requiring such great supplies and organizational labor, had never been attempted before; many doubted that it would succeed. Others strongly believed that the Japanese navy under the formidable Admiral Togo would attack and defeat our ships in the Pacific.

On December 16, 1907, amid enormous popular excitement, the great battle fleet, numbering sixteen battleships with attendant supply and auxiliary vessels and 12,000 officers and men, saluted the President of the United States on the yacht *Mayflower* and steamed out of Hampton Roads. It was to be gone for nearly fifteen months, practicing and maneuvering upon its way around the world, and advertising our navy as one of the most efficient sea forces and the second most powerful, after Great Britain's. Roosevelt recollected:

[33] Bishop, *Roosevelt*, Vol. II, p. 249.

In my own judgment the most important service that I rendered to peace was the voyage of the battle fleet around the world. I had become convinced that for many reasons it was essential that we should make it clearly understood . . . that the Pacific was as much our home waters as the Atlantic. . . . I determined on the move without consulting the Cabinet, precisely as I took Panama without consulting the Cabinet.[34]

Thus, in a troubled hour, without informing the representatives of the people—who sought for a time to withhold funds for the expedition—Roosevelt turned boldly to what was little less than a warlike gesture. He gave his personal orders to the officers of the fleet to keep the peace; but "they were to take exactly the same precautions against sudden attack of any kind as if we were at war with all the nations of the earth. . . ."

Japan might have regarded the move as a provocation, as many authorities predicted. But Roosevelt thought, as he told Tirpitz in 1910, that "we had gained three months" for preparation so that "if they did make war it would be proof positive that I had followed exactly the right course."[35] He noted with satisfaction that all trouble with the Japanese government and press "stopped like magic" as soon as they found that our fleet had actually sailed and was in good trim.

At first, apprehension had mingled with excitement over the possibility of a war. Then, as the great fleet sailed smoothly around the coast of South America, to San Francisco, Japan, the Philippines, and, via European waters, toward home, pride in the navy swept over the country. It was a moment of high triumph for Mahan's sea-power doctrine, since not a few German and British authorities had doubted if so large a fleet could be sailed round the world. The United States was now silently accepted as a great naval power in the Pacific. These mighty floating engines of war advertised a mobile fighting force that could throw its weight wherever it chose. The Japanese had chosen to show a peaceful demeanor, and received the fleet when it arrived with a three-day

[34] Roosevelt, *An Autobiography*, pp. 548-549.
[35] Bishop, *Roosevelt*, Vol. II, p. 250.

celebration of "amity," in October, 1908. Almost a year earlier, at the mere mention of the project, Japanese diplomats had taken the initiative to bring about the Root-Takahira "gentlemen's agreement" restricting Japanese immigration to the United States. Possibly the British ally, in ways as yet unrevealed, exercised a restraining influence. "A real identity of British and American interests in the Far East, based on the common immigration policy [of excluding the Japanese] of the United States and Great Britain's Pacific Dominions, was beginning to emerge." [36]

Roosevelt's campaign to win popular interest in appropriations for a big navy was also furthered. As an English commentator predicted in October, 1907, in the London *Spectator:*

> Next time Mr. Roosevelt or his representatives appeal to the country for new battleships they will do so to people whose minds have been influenced one way or the other. The naval programme will not have stood still. We are sure that . . . this is the aim which Mr. Roosevelt has in mind. He has a policy which projects itself far into the future. [37]

Once more, in the field of foreign and military action, Roosevelt, escaping from the vexing obstacles which beset his course at home, acted with the free hand of an autocrat.

On February 22, 1909—his term soon to expire—he stood again at Hampton Roads, addressing the returned fleet from the flagship, with tears in his voice. This was his hour of highest glory. He spoke of how he and all Americans had "thrilled with pride" as the hulls of the mighty warships lifted above the horizon. "You have steamed through all the great oceans; you have touched the coast of every continent. . . . We are proud of all the ships and all the men. . . ." [38]

4

As all things mortal must come to an end, so the brilliant Theodorian reign approached its term in 1908, and the President who

[36] Griswold, *op. cit.*, p. 128.
[37] Cited in Roosevelt, *An Autobiography*, p. 550.
[38] *Ibid.*, pp. 557-559.

had had the longest uninterrupted term since Ulysses Grant's busied himself with the problem of a succession.

By "playing a great part in the world," as befitted a "great people," Theodore Roosevelt maintained his remarkable popularity to the very end; his foreign forays had a way of following hard upon domestic troubles and reverses that might have dimmed his glory. It must be recalled that the dubious affair of the Tennessee Coal and Iron Company was little spoken of until very late in 1908; the act of submission to Morgan's men, as in the International Harvester case, was not definitely suspected until 1912. To the nation, especially to its large middle class, he remained the "trust buster" at home and the wielder of the Big Stick abroad. Moreover, his uncommon passion for publicity had made the attractive, independent, and forthright sides of his personality part of the everyday knowledge of millions of Americans, who for several years were both diverted and stimulated by him and who truly loved him. But besides holding the affection of the masses as no other recent politician save perhaps the "magnetic" James G. Blaine had held it, Roosevelt's mastery over the Republican party organization was complete.

Little doubt exists that a "third-term movement" of considerable force could easily have been engendered. Politicians in the lower ranks of his party would have welcomed his renomination. A hundred or more of the convention delegates were Federal officials appointed by Roosevelt, and the whole mass of Southern delegates, representing the Republican "rotten borough," would have been compliant enough. As late as May 29, 1908, Roosevelt said: "There has never been a moment when I could not have had the Republican nomination with practical unanimity by simply raising one finger." [39]

Yet, following his triumphant re-election in November, 1904, he had given an unequivocal pledge to the people that he would not be a candidate again for the office of President. The taboo of a third term had ruled Americans ever since Washington's time.

[39] *T. R. Papers*, T. R. to Rev. Lyman F. Abbott, May 29, 1908.

In recent memory, only Ulysses Grant had tested its force in a nominating convention; what the people as a whole felt upon the matter was still unknown. To this taboo Roosevelt himself bowed, saying in a letter to Sir George O. Trevelyan, ". . . The strong man may readily subvert free institutions if he and the people at large grow to accept his continued possession of a vast power as being necessary. . . ." Yet at the same time he expressed the poignant regret that, having acquired and demonstrated his large public power, he must nevertheless "at a fixed date of the calendar abandon certain struggles . . . of vital concern to the national welfare." Alas, he was but forty-nine years of age as he wrote these lines! [40]

Though he must practice a Roman self-denial, the possibility of effecting a succession that would foster *continuity* of Rooseveltian policy and influence obsessed him. For, like Andrew Jackson, he was in a position to name, to "make," the President who succeeded him.

Of his Cabinet members, Elihu Root, who had become Secretary of State after Hay's death in 1905, was the ablest and most distinguished personality, whose long services seemed to make him worthy of elevation. Despite their different careers and background, the two men were in tolerably close agreement in supporting moderate reforms that would work conservatively in property's interests. Elihu Root thought there was really no difference between his own principles and "what Theodore thinks he believes," even though Theodore undoubtedly had given him some bad moments.[41]

Roosevelt, who was deeply fond of Root, and once said that he would willingly "walk on his hands and knees . . . to see Root made President," thought for a long time of setting the old corporation lawyer in his office. There he would have served the people as their advocate as loyally and skillfully as he had formerly served Wall Street. Yet this scheme was eventually aban-

---

[40] *Ibid.*, T. R. to G. O. Trevelyan, June 19, 1908.
[41] Jessup, *op. cit.*, Vol. II, p. 182.

doned, for the West would only see Root in his professional corporate connections, and the heat of a campaign might illuminate
these connections unpleasantly.[42]

New York's brilliant and independent reform Governor,
Charles E. Hughes, was also of Presidential stuff, but was passed
over quickly by the king-maker, who sought instead a man more
amenable to his own influence. It was the Secretary of War, his
good friend Taft, then apparently the most deferent and devoted
member of his Cabinet, to whom he finally turned to hand the
crown.

William Howard Taft, at fifty, had had one of the most distinguished and fortunate careers among the Rooseveltians. Originally
he had been a protégé of McKinley; but it was under the Square
Deal regime that he had figured prominently before the public,
as Governor General of the Philippines, as Secretary of War, and
lately as Roosevelt's active lieutenant. Taft's strong Ohio connections, his eagerness to accept minor public office, had aided his first
steps in politics. He too had gone to a great Eastern university,
Yale; he had been something of a local reformer in youth; and at
the same time, while serving as a judge of an Ohio court during
the industrial warfare of the 1880's, had shown a strong anti-
labor bias (much like Theodore Roosevelt's), which had com-
mended him to both Presidents Harrison and McKinley. He came
of a wealthy family, politically influential—his father, Alphonso
Taft, had been an Ambassador and a member of Grant's Cabinet;
he possessed education and administrative ability; he was handsome, immensely fat, and of an amiable, smiling disposition. He
appealed, even as early as 1903, to conservative groups in the
Republican party, who had singled him out as one of their own.
". . . The trust people and probably some of the machine politicians," he loyally warned Roosevelt at the time, were engineer-
ing a movement to have him, Taft, nominated in place of his
chief.[43]

[42] Davis, *Released for Publication*, p. 54.
[43] Stephenson, *op. cit.*, p. 221, Taft to T. R., Apr. 27, 1903.

Actually Taft had an overwhelming inclination to jurisprudence. His heart's desire was to reach the bench of the Supreme Court. Yet brothers and wife, and all sorts of powerful influences, persuaded him to refuse the robe of the Justice, repeatedly offered him by Roosevelt, so that he might remain available for the Presidency in 1908. Nevertheless it was as a judge, reflecting over evidence, alone, independent, that he was happiest. For all his stout, cheerful, robust exterior, he did not make friends and confidants easily. In all his life, marked with a tolerable if not brilliant juridical and administrative success, he had scarcely ever run for an elective office or learned to be happy jostling about among the lower orders of politicians, giving and taking pleasantries, patronage, and political favors. What Roosevelt did not foresee was how difficult it was going to be for a man who had no talents for the arts of political intrigue—which he himself ate, drank, and breathed—to acquire them in short order.

In those days Taft posed as a militant Square Dealer. When the decision to give full administration support to Taft's candidacy was finally made, early in 1908, Taft indicated to everyone that he stood unswervingly for "Roosevelt policies." If defeated "because I am close to Roosevelt, then . . . I ought to be defeated on that account," he wrote to one of those who prepared his campaign. He declared that he enjoyed being in Roosevelt's Cabinet. "My strength is largely as his friend." [44] Thus it was Taft, more than anyone else, who promised *continuity*.

Indeed, he sometimes expressed even more clearly, more logically than his chief, the great underlying principles of Rooseveltian policy: defense of the existing social-economic system; defense, above all, of property rights against more radical movements or even a possible revolution of socialism.

I agree heartily and earnestly in the policies which have come to be known as the Roosevelt policies [Taft wrote in a private letter of 1907]. These policies, stated succinctly, are that the guaranties of the Constitution shall be in favor of life, liberty and property and shall be

[44] Pringle, *Taft*, Vol. I, p. 329.

sacredly maintained; *that the guaranty with respect to the right of property would be undermined by a movement toward socialism;* that this movement has gained force by the use of accumulated wealth and power in illegal ways . . . to center financial control in a few hands. . . .[45]

And Roosevelt, he concluded, had finally roused the people to the necessity of enforcing the law against rich and poor alike; he had begun to curb those violators of the statutes who by their excesses would have precipitated a revolution not only against the rich but against all property-holders.

Roosevelt himself was convinced that there was little to choose between himself and Taft as "friends of conservatism and order" who would fight the evils and excesses of monopoly.

He would have felt more unhappy about leaving the Presidency, he wrote privately to Trevelyan in a letter of June 19, 1908, were it not that ". . . in Taft there was ready to hand a man whose theory of public and private duty is my own, and whose practice of this theory is what I hope my own is. . . ."

But between the spirit and the letter, between the theory and the practice of a doctrine, there is often a world of difference. Roosevelt had defended property, law, and order, while using the terms of the radical Bryan; thus he was enabled, as he boasted, to keep the adherence of the "one-suspender men"; the rural West remained hopefully attached to the Republican party.

In his letter to Trevelyan which reviewed the significant episodes of his two terms, Roosevelt related how, time and again, simple farmers from the hinterland appeared at the White House, all clean and sober for the occasion, and asked to see him, saying that they wanted only "to shake that honest hand." Roosevelt never failed to appear before them. These horny-handed old fellows touched his heart; to have won their enduring affection was one of his principal political achievements—something that a Taft would know little of.

In short, while Roosevelt collaborated in Congress with those

[45] Pringle, *Taft*, Vol. I, p. 339.

"broad-minded," "patriotic" statesmen, Aldrich, Cannon, and their group, he also conducted a great crusade for "righteousness" that both entertained and heartened the masses. Taft sometimes thought that his friend could literally run with the hares and hunt with the hounds. Could he himself, less imaginative, more methodical, with a mind that moved in straight lines, with limited knowledge of the dark, double ways of politicians and Congressmen, do as much, according to the same tactics?

In mid-January, 1908, Roosevelt indicated plainly that Taft was his political heir. Both were in agreement upon the continuity of policy, and even, in some measure, upon the continuance of most of the officials who made up the Roosevelt administration and gave it its spirit of devoted public service. Both men also agreed apparently that the new administration, if Taft were elected, would limit itself rather to "retrenchment," to the "consolidation of gains" made previously, while experimental legislation was to be avoided if possible. To this extent the Roosevelt policies were to be modified. In general, all circumstances of the transfer of power revealed how much Theodore Roosevelt desired to continue as a force in American politics, perhaps even as the Strong Man of the new government.

From the beginning of 1908, Roosevelt threw into motion all the machinery of publicity he commanded, as well as that of the party organization, in behalf of the Taft candidacy. The hunt for convention delegates was pushed rapidly; Private Secretary William Loeb and Assistant Postmaster General Frank Hitchcock, in preparation for the convention, helped canvass for Taft adherents under Roosevelt's orders.

In addition, Taft men were appointed to strategic Federal posts, which would give them occasion and leisure to aid in the party canvass. Within two months, by March 20, 1908, some 552 delegates out of a possible 980, a clear majority, were claimed for the "Crown Prince"—having been rounded up swiftly by methods of which Taft was not too closely informed. The bulk of expense for the pre-convention campaign was met by Charles P. Taft, the wealthy half-brother of the candidate. Henry Cabot Lodge was designated as "temporary chairman" to conduct the actual convention; and with his help plans to avoid a "stampede" for the Rough Rider were carefully completed. (The Taft family were highly suspicious on this point up to the final hour, according to certain witnesses.) The party platform was "dictated" by Theodore Roosevelt; the successful nominee's formal speech of acceptance was to be written under the eye of the incumbent President.[46] The party's Committee on Credentials, as under Mark Hanna's rule, could pass usually upon delegates approved by the party leader, in disputed cases, and reject opponents. Thus the various Favorite Son movements were easily checked by the Steam Roller machinery, now driven by Theodore Roosevelt. That summer the nomination of Taft was brought about smoothly before a routine convention whose cheers were given mainly for the retiring President.

The platform adopted by the Republican party was liberal in tone. It favored at last a moderate reform of the extremely high protective tariff in force ever since 1897. On this score Taft himself had been outspoken in his public statements. Certain radical demands, such as that of La Follette, for a plank urging the direct election of Senators and more complete government control of railroad rates, were resisted. A spirited effort made by the labor leader Samuel Gompers to win support for an anti-injunction plank was rebuffed. Taft, whom the Democrats would call "the father of the injunction," owing to his record as a Federal judge, said that he would never act to weaken the power of the courts to defend property. Moreover, the National Association of Manufacturers, which took an active part in the Republican convention this year, fiercely opposed the very mention of the labor issue. A compromise plank, wrought in the most cautious phrases, was actually worked out; and when Gompers indignantly objected to it, he was told to "go to Denver"—the site of the Democratic party convention.[47]

---

[46] Stoddard, *As I Knew Them*, pp. 341-344.
[47] Gompers, *Seventy Years*, Vol. II, p. 262.

5

Late in 1906, William Jennings Bryan, the orator of American protest, had returned from a most remarkable world tour, filled with new visions and hopes for new departures. Before an enthusiastic multitude that gathered in Madison Square Garden, New York, to welcome him and to hear him, he sounded ringing calls to battle.

Plutocracy is abhorrent to a republic; it is more despotic than monarchy, more heartless than aristocracy, more selfish than bureaucracy. . . . It is already sapping the strength of the nation, vulgarizing social life and making a mockery of morals. The time is ripe for the overthrow of this giant wrong. In the name of the counting-rooms which it has defiled . . . in the name of the home which it has despoiled; in the name of religion which it has disgraced; in the name of the people whom it has oppressed, let us make our appeal to the awakened conscience of the nation.

Then seizing the bull by the horns, so to speak, with his eye upon the approaching national contest, he announced his decision to make the nationalization of the railroads the Burning Issue of the day: "I have . . . reached the conclusion that railroads partake so much of the nature of a monopoly that they must ultimately become public property . . . and be managed in the interests of the whole community." [48]

Bryan, who had seen his own proposals, adapted originally from the old Populist platforms, taken over by Roosevelt, now served notice that he intended to drive the opposition party forward again toward more radical and more popular policies. Though the Democratic party convention of 1908 was to be cautious, avoiding commitment to government ownership of the railroads, it turned once more to radical policies and leadership.

Bryan sensed the maneuvers of retreat planned by the ruling party. The choice of Taft as Republican standard-bearer, which

[48] Werner, *Bryan*, pp. 152-153.

was so promptly approved in Wall Street circles, gave Bryan the opportunity to seize Democratic party leadership from the hands of the Eastern and Southern conservatives who had met disastrous defeat in 1904. Thomas Fortune Ryan had financed the party in late years, and controlled it through his Tammany Hall and Virginia political friends; he was now pushed into the background. Long before the national convention opened at Denver, twenty-one states had pledged their delegates to the Nebraskan as the party's overwhelming choice for the nomination. Under Bryan's guidance the old party responded, ostensibly, to "the increasing signs of an awakening throughout the country." Its admirable platform contained a series of outspoken resolutions, urging downward revision of the tariff, prohibition of "interlocking directorates" among large corporations, a direct income tax, the direct election of Senators, the elimination of the injunction in labor disputes. The *leitmotif* of the platform was expressed by the phrase: "*Shall the people rule?*" [49]

Once more the "substantial men" ceased their active support of the Democratic party after Bryan's nomination. Woodrow Wilson, president of Princeton University, who had political ambitions, at this time wrote to a friend of his desire that "we could do something, at once dignified and effective, to knock Mr. Bryan once and for all into a cocked hat." Conservative Eastern elements typified by George Harvey, publisher of *Harper's Weekly*, and a confidential aide of T. F. Ryan, had publicly proposed the name of Dr. Wilson himself in place of Bryan; yet little attention was paid at the time to his maneuver. Instead, the mass of organized labor, led by Gompers of the A. F. of L., joined the Western farmers in giving enthusiastic support to Bryan's canvass.

Taft, supported by a unified, disciplined party organization—in contrast with the discordant Democrats—wore the mantle of Theodore Roosevelt that summer. In his speeches, he warned the country that Bryan and his followers were "irresponsible" by nature. Bryan would punish the rich. He was opposed to the accumulation

[49] Robinson, *op. cit.*, pp. 295-296.

of wealth under a strong government. But under the Republican administration, the Roosevelt policies would be continued in a practical spirit, and both the rich and the poor would be held equal before the law. Thus Taft seemed to embody those qualities of "calm thought and moderation and sober judgment" that prominent personages such as Nicholas Murray Butler had found wanting, after the panic of 1907, in the "intemperate" Roosevelt. Taft was "sound." Yet at the same time his public speeches held fair words promising continuance of the Rooseveltian reform activities. He summed up the last four years as "a great struggle between the national administration and certain powerful combinations in the financial world. . . ." He would continue the struggle, for, if the old abuses remained unchecked, if "the tyranny and oppression of an oligarchy of wealth cannot be avoided, *then socialism will triumph*, and the institution of private property will perish." [50] Taft also pledged himself to aid in bringing forth a "reasonable" revision of the protective tariff in force, especially in the schedules for those industrial products such as steel rails and raw materials which no longer needed protection.

Such was Taft's tone in public, especially during the campaigning in Western cities. It was remarked, not long afterward, that Taft had the air of leading a continued reform movement in the West, and at the same time of promising a "restoration" in the East. For, in private, Taft often sounded as if he held notions quite different from his friend Theodore's of how the country must be saved from socialism.

Though the new leader was not a strong or brilliant campaigner, he gained, thanks to the help of the President, the expected electoral victory over Bryan. He held the ground that Roosevelt had conquered, and even extended it in the electoral college returns. It was significant, however, that Bryan increased the Democratic vote by a million over that of 1904. The Socialist party, though it gained only moderately this year, aroused and educated the whole country by its spirited campaign conducted far and wide by

[50] Duffy, *Taft*, p. 204; italics mine.

Eugene Debs from his "Red Special" train. The extreme radical vote, however, was made fragmentary by the intrusion of William Randolph Hearst who, that year, contending with both party organizations, launched his "Independence" party as a venture of his own.

The divergence between the two friends, Taft and Roosevelt, in temperament, in tactics, in the immediate influences they each reflected, really showed themselves during the election campaign. In the month following the election, December, 1908, occurred the first of their differences that foreshadowed the lamentable and historic quarrel between the two statesmen.

Roosevelt knew that under Taft the program of saving the reluctant capitalists from their own excesses would be pursued in a far more prudent spirit. "You see, *you have often preached caution to me . . .*" was a characteristic phrase Roosevelt used in a letter he wrote to Taft a year before the election.[51] Yet in practical diplomacy the proverbially impetuous Theodore could administer many lessons to the habitually tactless Taft. Taft must not be seen playing golf, then a rich man's sport; he must stop at hotels, instead of the homes of rich Republicans; he must shake hands with the people, and allow himself to be handled as public property. These were practices which Taft had not followed of his own accord in ruling over millions of little brown brothers in the Philippines.

Roosevelt told Ray Stannard Baker in August, 1908, shortly after Taft's nomination, that his protégé was a "cool-headed lawyer," such as the country now needed. He concluded:

Well, I'm through now. I've done my work. . . . People are going to discuss economic questions more and more: the tariff, currency, banks. They are hard questions, and I am not deeply interested in them; my problems are moral problems, and my teaching has been plain morality.[52]

[51] *T. R. Papers*, T. R. to Taft, Sept. 19, 1907; italics mine.
[52] R. S. Baker in *The American Magazine*, Sept., 1908.

In the same vein he told another journalist, in the last days of his administration, that the time had probably come to cease the "crusading" that he had felt himself forced to do to save the country from "intolerable conditions imperiling everything." Henceforth all attention would be given to "what you call the business problems of government," which had no appeal to Roosevelt. Taft, however, would know how to "round out and shape up the policies of the last four years." He had a legal mind. "He's a constructive fellow, I am not. . . . The ground is cleared for constructive work. . . ." [53]

Taft himself, in formally accepting the nomination, had tried to differentiate his purposes from his predecessor's:

> The chief function of the next administration in my judgment is distinct from and a progressive development of that which has been performed by President Roosevelt. *The chief function of the next administration is to complete and perfect the machinery by which these standards may be maintained,* by which the lawbreakers may be promptly restrained and punished, *but which shall operate with sufficient accuracy* and dispatch *to interfere with legitimate business as little as possible.* [54]

Here at any rate was a hint of Taft's natural, human prompting to be President in his own right. If he had not sought to be this, his whole solid, respectable, determined family would have pushed him to it. To write the speech of acceptance cited above, the candidate had made a journey to Oyster Bay and submitted his work to the approval of the overshadowing party chief. But then he had journeyed to his native Cincinnati and closeted himself in the bosom of his family, who persuaded him to accept certain changes and amendments.

The family, especially Charles P. Taft (the half-brother) and brothers Henry and Horace, were all strong characters. Not the least of these was his wife, whose dislike and suspicion of the Roosevelts was often noticed. Mrs. Taft, who had been triumphantly right in advising her husband not to enter the Supreme

[53] Stoddard, *op. cit.,* pp. 352-353.
[54] The New York *Times,* Jul. 29, 1908; italics mine.

Court, urged him to separate himself as much as possible from the "Roosevelt policies." She said: "Let the Corporations rest for a while." [55]

Charles P. Taft, for example, would never have passed for a good Rooseveltian. He was a successful corporation attorney, had seen a good deal of the inside of political life—once as Congressman for a single term from Ohio, but chiefly from behind the scenes. For many years he had contributed a generous annuity to fill out his distinguished younger brother's income from public service, and for the sake of his brother's elevation to the Presidency he had donated large sums, representing a small fortune. But the election being over, brother Charles also discovered political ambitions in himself; he announced that he would stand for the Senate in Ohio, after the retirement of Foraker. Presumably he hoped to go to the Senate, "as the Mark Hanna" of his brother's administration. But a public outcry at Charles Taft's schemings, at his attempt to pass over those Ohio party veterans who were next in succession for the Senate, caused the whole plan to be hastily abandoned. [56]

Another glimpse we have of this curious, rich brother, is on the occasion when he is closeted with Mr. J. P. Morgan at the latter's home, and he sends an urgent message to brother "Will," just then passing through New York, to join him promptly at Morgan's for a conference. However, the new President felt obliged to rebuke his brother, pointing out the impropriety of such a visit, and asking that Charles Taft and Morgan come instead to see him in Washington. [57]

Yet the President-elect in his first letter to Roosevelt after the election tactlessly attributed his success as much to his brother's money as to Roosevelt's political support: "You and my brother Charley made that possible which in all probability would not have occurred otherwise." [58]

However, a passage in another letter of this time from Taft to

[55] Pringle, *Taft*, Vol. I, pp. 329-330.   [57] A. Butt, *Letters*, Vol. II, p. 443.
[56] Stoddard, *op. cit.*, p. 349.   [58] Sullivan, *op. cit.*, Vol. IV, p. 315.

Colonel Roosevelt was phrased in the terms of that extreme deference which, I suspect, led Roosevelt to name Taft his Crown Prince:

I can never forget that the power I now exercise was voluntarily transferred from you to me, and that I am under obligation to you to see that your judgment in selecting me as your successor and bringing about the succession shall be vindicated according to the standards which you and I . . . have always formulated.

This letter was made public by Roosevelt during the rupture of 1912.[59]

It is clear that the brother heartily disliked Roosevelt, and hoped that Will would not think too long of his obligations to the other man, or preside under his shadow. The influence of Charles P. Taft, like that of the first lady, "Nellie" Taft, was thrown squarely against the idea of "continuity." One perceives this source of discord at an early date in the new regime, according to the gossiping journal of Major Archie Butt, who was the personal military aide of both Presidents. Speaking of his brother to Archie Butt early in 1909, Taft said, laughing:

What troubles Charlie is, he is afraid Roosevelt will get the credit of making me President and not himself. . . . I am always amused at Charlie's determined position that Roosevelt had nothing to do with my nomination and election. . . .[60]

More important still for Roosevelt's hope of continuity of policy was the retention of certain Cabinet officers and minor officials by the new administration. Taft, in a pleasant humor after his big victory, had voluntarily promised as much in the case of James Garfield, Secretary of the Interior, and certain others; and Roosevelt had conveyed the good news to those Cabinet members who wished to stay in the service. Then, belatedly, Taft realized that he might want to select new men, who would be beholden entirely

[59] The New York *Times*, Apr. 27, 1912.
[60] Butt, *Letters*, Vol. I, p. 104.

to him rather than to "T. R.," men who would be fitted for the different tasks he had in view. Therefore James R. Garfield, the head of the "Tennis Cabinet," and enthusiastic conservationist, was asked finally to give way, and was replaced by a lawyer and politician, who for a time had been his assistant: Richard *Achilles* Ballinger, former Mayor of Seattle. Taft was determined to dismiss Roosevelt's friend Garfield "because I *knew* him," he said later.[61] The selection of Ballinger, who soon proved to be a vigorous opponent of Rooseveltian policies and sought to reverse them, was a key case; he was to be the "Achilles heel" of the new administration.

In the awkward interim period, Taft wrote most apologetically to Roosevelt of his regret at changing the Cabinet personnel, "with a view to a somewhat different state of reforms, which you have instituted, and which I must carry on." But this scarcely relieved the strain, which had begun immediately after the election, when Roosevelt found that he already counted for very little in national affairs.[62]

The final exchange of letters between the outgoing and incoming executives consisted in mere amenities, labored and cold, despite Taft's attempts at epistolary endearments. At the very end Roosevelt spoke with irritation of his protégé, saying to Mark Sullivan: "*He's weak. . . .*" News that Taft, before assuming office, had made gestures of submission to the rulers of Congress, Senator Nelson Aldrich and Speaker Cannon, in order to further his legislative program, ran about Washington. Roosevelt had worked with these men, had advised Taft to do so; but he had

[61] Pringle, *Taft*, Vol. I, p. 386.
[62] Taft to Roosevelt, Feb. 1, 1909, McCaleb, *op. cit.*, p. 271; also Gifford Pinchot to author.
Political action is a continuous, eternally unfinished process. There existed unfinished business in the State Department, a "gentlemen's agreement" with Japan in which Taft as Secretary of War had had a hand; the Big Navy program was also an important part of Rooseveltian policy; the work in progress in the Department of the Interior and the Forest Service (which Gifford Pinchot continued to head) involved reclamation, setting up land reserves, eternal warfare against land-grabbers—all this depending greatly on the continuance of the personnel and *esprit de corps* created under Roosevelt.

been accustomed to holding them at arm's length, or even to appearing as their opponent in public. Taft, it was now said, was using utterly different tactics, calculated to bring about a kind of Restoration Period. At the Gridiron Club dinner, held in Washington early in April, 1909, at the very outset of the new regime, the players burlesqued a "Restoration." Aldrich and his colleagues in the Senate, as well as Joe Cannon, were shown as having the run of the White House, and were told by its incumbent: ". . . Fix up the tariff to suit yourself and the boys." It was an extraordinarily accurate forecast.[63]

Theodore Roosevelt could scarcely conceal his depression as his term of official rule drew to its end. Part of this was because he so thoroughly enjoyed the burdens of his great office. Part was undoubtedly due to disappointment in his hope of a large, continuing, indirect power, through transfer of the Presidency to his once deferent and humble lieutenant Taft. The evening before the inaugural ceremonies, March 3, 1909, the Tafts were, in accordance with custom, White House guests. In a letter four years later Taft still vividly recalled the dinner gathering that evening as "that funeral." [64]

The real end of the seven years' reign actually came at the large luncheon which Roosevelt tendered to the "Tennis Cabinet" on March 1, 1909. Here were present his favorite Cabinet members such as Garfield, and the intimate friends among the minor officials such as Gifford Pinchot, who would have laid down his life for him. Roosevelt toasted his "generals" for the last time, thanking them for their able, loyal service, and saying magnanimously that the credit which had come to him, as the chief, belonged truly to them. His words were simple, but they were very moving; and the thirty-odd guests who had long loved him, and who had never suffered from boredom in his service, could scarcely abide the thought of his exile. Many of them, conquered by emotion, broke down and wept unashamed.[65]

---

[63] Dunn, *Gridiron Nights*, pp. 216-217.
[64] Pringle, *Taft*, Vol. I, p. 393.
[65] Roosevelt, *Presidential Addresses*, Vol. VIII, pp. 2177-2179.

BOOK TWO

IX. AN ATTEMPTED "RESTORATION"

THE FOUR years of the Taft administration, designed to be a period of "calm" and "confidence," were filled with the turmoil of controversy. These were years of political drama, both sensational and inwardly significant. The "inwardness" of the political drama—like that of the preceding eighty years of American political history—can best be charted in terms of centripetal and centrifugal movements. The bureaucratic tradition and the needs of the deep-rooted party system work to pull things together; the economic and sectional forces in society work with outward-driving thrusts, to break up the partisan lines, to clash among themselves, then to coalesce into a new balance.

So, under the outwardly amiable Mr. Taft's reign, movements of tremendous energy, the stronger for having long been pent up, worked again, driving the liberal middle class, the farmers and organized labor in a crusade for "social justice"; and, gathering an unheard-of force, threatened to destroy the former equilibrium of the old party system.

For a long time the leaders who dominated the ruling party more firmly than ever, the so-called Old Guard—now that the Great Hunter devoted himself to pursuing lions and water buffaloes in Africa—ignored the signs of gathering stormy weather as much as the Chief Magistrate himself ignored them. They went forward with plans for their "Restoration"; they returned to high-handed methods of forcing the bonds of party discipline upon dissenters, or attaining the practical ends in view by tactics already too crude and old-fashioned for existing public opinion. By such measures they aroused and shocked great numbers of citizens who were nowadays more jealous of their rights, more discontented, more aware of the painful contrasts between the "promise of American life" (which a Theodore Roosevelt often seemed to hold out to them), between the "American dream," and the ugly realities of the time. Against such stresses and discontents, the strenuous, acrobatic "Teddy" had held the ruling party together and bedazzled the voters. Even a powerful (Democratic) opponent, Joseph Pulitzer, conceded that Roosevelt had worked wonderfully to overcome "discontent and socialism among the masses. . . ." If Roosevelt had committed a hundred times more mistakes, or had been a hundred times "more impulsive, changeable, unpresidential in dignity . . . inaccurate, loud and vociferating," Pulitzer thought, he must be given eternal credit for his service to the nation in turning "the great machinery of the government and the force and majesty of the law" toward prosecuting the "great offenders." [1]

The change from Roosevelt to Taft, as Elihu Root drily said, was like changing from one of the new automobiles to a horse-cab.

William Howard Taft, in equipment of education and training, was superior to most of the mediocre types selected for the Presidency by politicians. Yet it cannot be said that he was a man of real intelligence or large character; the considerable mass of his intimate letters and papers and the details of his private life, published lately, do not add to his stature. He appears Pickwickian rather than tragic. In his heart he had wished not to be President but to be a Supreme Court Justice. He had been pushed into the office in spite of himself, as he was to be pushed into other misadventures. Thus he approached his difficult role, in which so few Americans have distinguished themselves, with not a little fear and trembling. The sum of his errors or blunders would overcloud the sum of his creditable achievements while in office. For he was not a bold fellow, and lacked the imagination and flashing intui-

[1] Seitz, *op. cit.*, letter of Aug. 7, 1907, p. 320.

tions of strategy that his friend Theodore possessed. He was well-meaning and strove to please more than one faction in order to have harmony; yet he won few friends because of small, narrow traits of character easily exposed by the stress of public life, and contrasting strangely with his vast, loose, genial physical bulk. He shrank from strenuous political combat, longing for peace and order; yet opened himself to heavy attacks from various sides, and lived through a long nightmare of political war.

From the start of his administration Taft proceeded as if "the time for rhapsodies and glittering generalities" had passed—these were his own words. He proposed to continue on the road of "even-handed" justice to the poor or rich without fear or favor. But the Ship of State must be held to its course more steadily than before by the large, fat man at the helm. Government was to be conducted with more Constitutional purity, with more thorough legality than under the "impulsive," wayward, sometimes high-handed T. R. And who could best assist him in steering such a course? The people best fitted, he argued, to administer the government "without injury to the business interests" were "those lawyers who understand corporate wealth. . . ." The distinguished corporation lawyers whom he installed in his Cabinet, from Philander Knox, as Secretary of State, to George W. Wickersham, as Attorney General—he reasoned, a little too logically—by knowing corporate evils well would be best able to put the trusts in their place. They would gain a better hearing before Congress than the "more radical members" of his party. Taft expected to be criticized for the composition of his Cabinet. But even before assuming office he was reconciled to being "charged with reactionary tendencies." [2]

Taft little thought that he was already sowing dissension in his own administration. Under Roosevelt one of the intangible gains was the improvement that had been brought about in certain branches of the public service by the introduction of vigorous, educated, and genuinely patriotic young men. In the Departments of

[2] Pringle, *Taft*, Vol. I, p. 182, letter of Feb. 23, 1909.

the Interior and Agriculture—the former long malodorous for its grafters and claim thieves—Roosevelt's favorites, Garfield and Pinchot, had been leading a veritable crusade against waste, grabbing, and speculation in national lands. Their enthusiasm had spread to the young men in the ranks, lower officials and agents, some of whom, as in the Forest Service, endured willingly hardships and adventures in which life and limb were endangered for the great public cause. It is out of such devotion and *esprit de corps* that the administration of a good society is developed. And here, though perhaps guilty of oversights or at times of overzealousness, Roosevelt and his followers had made solid beginnings.

The appointment of Richard A. Ballinger, the lawyer-politician from Seattle, to replace Garfield as Secretary of the Interior, suggested the reversal by Mr. Taft of the conservation policies that had brought such credit to the preceding administration. Ballinger had for several years been Commissioner of Public Lands, working under Garfield; then had resigned early in 1908 to return to the practice of law and increase his earnings. His connections with Western politicians and land claimants who were interested in lands that the government had withdrawn was found afterward to have been close and friendly. What purpose lay behind the appointment of a Ballinger? To the Pickwickian Taft, the problem shaped itself as one of being more strictly legal or "Constitutional" in dealings with the public lands. He had the impression that Secretary Garfield had been overzealous, while he termed Gifford Pinchot a "fanatic." Ballinger would be more careful. Under him there would be a change of emphasis—but also dissension, from the very start, between his faction and the Pinchot faction of ardent conservationists.

For the legislative program being prepared under the new administration, a change of emphasis was also the rule. A revised tariff act and a new central banking and monetary act, demanded for years by great financial interests, were the most important measures planned. Immediately after his election Taft held a number of conferences with Senator Nelson Aldrich, the boss of the Senate, and Speaker "Joe" Cannon, the boss of the House of Representatives. These were the wise, strong leaders, with whom Roosevelt, it must be said, urged Taft to collaborate. But whereas Roosevelt would certainly have engaged in horse-trading with these Standpatters, reports soon indicated that the President-elect had yielded them a free hand in framing the new protective tariff. A special session of Congress was to be called for the tariff legislation; and the new act, Cannon predicted as early as November, 1908, would be drawn up largely in accordance with the wishes of the "intimate friends of the protective tariff"; that is, the protected manufacturers.

There were times when Taft felt deep misgivings about his "wicked partners"—as he sometimes called Cannon and Aldrich in private speech. The powerful Speaker, a cynical and profane old man, given (alas) to whiskey and poker, he found especially distasteful. There had been some talk of the new President's helping the Progressive wing of the Republican party to elect another Speaker who might impress the public as less cheerfully cynical than "Joe" Cannon. But as reports of Taft's secret conferences with Cannon and Aldrich spread, the Progressives knew that this was not to be; the President would give them no aid or comfort.

Before taking office, Taft wrote to his brother Horace that he had made an "investigation" to learn whether Speaker Cannon could be beaten, and found him "so strongly entrenched . . . that it was impossible. . . . I therefore gave up any hope of doing so or any effort to do so." [3] The search was not exhaustive, apparently; and the spirit shown here is like the courage of the Sabines rather than the Romans.

Two weeks after his inauguration, Taft wrote a long letter to Theodore Roosevelt bidding him *bon voyage*, and describing also, in somewhat gloomy terms, the series of compromises or "arrangements" made with the Standpatters which he clearly foresaw would bring down upon him the anger of the reform wing. But

[3] Duffy, *Taft*, p. 237.

the die had been cast; the party caucus, led by Cannon, had spoken and marked out the party "line." And Taft wrote:

I have no doubt that when you return *you will find me very much under suspicion by our friends in the West.* I think I am already so because I was not disposed to countenance an insurrection of thirty men against 180 outside the caucus. . . . I knew that unless I sat steady in the boat, and did what I could to help Cannon and the great majority of the Republicans to stand solid, I should make a capital error in the beginning of my administration in alienating the good will of those without whom I can do nothing to carry through the legislation to which the party and I are pledged.

Taft is already "on the defensive." Cannon and Aldrich, he argues, had promised "to stand by the party platform and to follow my lead. They did so, I believe, for you, in the first Congress of your administration." Actually the initiative, the party leadership, which Roosevelt had held, passed to Aldrich, Cannon, and their associates in Congress. And Taft implies this when he expresses the fear that he may not be able to manage Congress as well as had his predecessor. He lacked, as he felt, Roosevelt's prestige and popular support as well as

. . . the faculty for educating the public . . . through talks with correspondents, and *so I fear that a large part of the public will feel as if I had fallen away from your ideals;* but you know me better and will understand that *I am still working away on the same old plan* and hope to realize in some measure the results that we both hold valuable and worth striving for.

There are moments of pathos in this long letter when Taft appears to wrestle for the shrinking friendship of his great benefactor and friend. He explains his not having consulted Roosevelt more, on the ground that he had refrained from imposing upon the outgoing President's "well-earned quiet." (But when did Theodore Roosevelt ever ask for rest or quiet?) He insists that he is still following the lights of his patron, "the same old plan"— of exorcizing that Old Devil, socialism—but Roosevelt would not have done that with the open public assistance of the "wicked partners," Cannon and Aldrich. Finally the letter is the confession of a soldier weary before the battle has been joined, and seeing the future as through a glass darkly.[4]

The plans for a "Restoration" were, nevertheless, pushed forward rapidly. Opponents were brushed aside or chastised; the state of public opinion was ignored.

Nelson Aldrich, the real leader of the ruling party, thankful that the erratic, unstable Roosevelt was abroad, busied himself with vast, Hamiltonian plans for establishing a central bank of reserve—the embryonic Federal Reserve System—made possible by the recent passage of the Aldrich-Vreeland Act of May 30, 1908. He had traveled to the great financial centers of Europe, studying the foreign banking systems with Davison, of Morgan and Company, and George Reynolds, of the First National Bank of Chicago, by his side. Returning, he conferred with Paul M. Warburg, member of Kuhn, Loeb and Company, who had also labored long in the vineyard for a new banking act, but expressed fear that the political obstacles were too great to be overcome.

". . . You say that we cannot have a central bank, but I say we can," exclaimed Aldrich with his determined mien and piercing eyes.[5] It was with the same ruthless, determined spirit that he approached the task of enacting new tariff schedules under the law which was to bear his name. Aldrich had had the determining voice in the framing of financial and tax laws for thirty years. He saw no great obstacles before him now; least of all in the White House, whose incumbent now responded readily to his least call. Aldrich, though erect and proud as ever, was seventy; he was older than he realized. He had forgotten nothing and learned nothing.

2

Since 1906, William Jennings Bryan's farm paper, *The Commoner*, then widely read throughout the interior, had been speak-

[4] Duffy, *op. cit.*, letter of Mar. 21, 1909, pp. 226-227; italics mine.
[5] Stephenson, *op. cit.*, p. 340.

ing hopefully of a possible alliance between the independent or "Progressive" Republicans, as they now came to be called, and the Democratic opposition. Such an alliance would seize the balance of power from the conservative leaders. It was broached actively in the spring of 1907, when there was much talk of a union between La Follette and Bryan.[6] In the more recently founded farm paper, *La Follette's Weekly*, doctrines but little different from those of the Bryan Democrats were voiced, and nearly all the new Senators from the West, such as the brilliant William E. Borah of Idaho, seemed to take their tone and inspiration from the Little Giant of Wisconsin. They gave warning that the plain people, the farmers and the producers, were too largely ignored in Washington. They reiterated interminably the views to be read in *La Follette's Weekly* that

The Middle West, that great agricultural Mecca [sic] between the Rockies and Alleghenies, between Canada and the Gulf, is the battleground upon which the American farmer, the American laborer, the American capitalist, must fight his political, his moral, his social battles. It is the crucible of God—the "melting pot"—where the best of all the races of the world have congregated and amalgamated to produce America's working citizens, who love their country and are not ashamed of honest labor. . . . It is the bread basket of the world. It is here the American farmer must fight for a "square deal." [7]

The clamor for "more direct democracy" often heard from the West, the demands for stronger control of the railroads and trusts, for the curbing of speculation in grains, for tariff reform (in the interest of the agriculturists), for direct primaries, direct election of Senators, reform of the rules of Congress, even popular control of the judiciary through the "recall of judges"—the cry for all that would equalize the political unbalance now rose stronger than ever, a crescendo of protest.

After 1906 the filibustering tactics of La Follette in the Senate

[6] *The Commoner*, May 24, 1907.
[7] *La Follette's Weekly*, Jul. 17, 1909.

meant something more than the behavior of a Lone Wolf in politics. If the imperious Aldrich had read *The Commoner* or *La Follette's Weekly* he would have seen that La Follette worked systematically to bring about a new grouping of the opposition, one that would burst through the old superstitious limits of the parties. A beginning of this was to be seen in the struggle over the abortive Hepburn Act in 1906. Theodore Roosevelt had flirted for a time with a Democratic-Insurgent-Republican combination, based upon economic—that is, anti-railroad—lines, but then abandoned it.

The same combination was headed in the summer of 1908 by La Follette in the contest over the Aldrich-Vreeland Act, which broadened the monetary basis of the national banks and provided for a Monetary Commission, headed by Aldrich, to draw up a plan for a central bank of reserve. Here again was the specter of that United States Bank which the common people, and especially the farming class, had fought since the days of Alexander Hamilton and Andrew Jackson. Once more, as La Follette argued, it was to be a central bank cast in a form desired by the great financiers and with all its vast centralized economic powers placed in their hands.

La Follette used sensational methods in an attempt to alarm the country; in a final effort to prevent passage of the monetary act he filibustered for three days. He ranged over all subjects interminably, harping especially upon his favorite reform measures. He treated his listeners to an unvarying flood of irony; he railed at the machinelike control of the Senate's Philistines by the "little handful of men" that dominated its important committees. He was literally Peter the Hermit "alone in the Senate," thoroughly hated by most of the members of its comfortable little club, yet building himself an ever greater following in the *Hinterland* beyond the Mississippi River. When La Follette weakened, members of the Democratic minority willingly took his place. It was while one of them, the blind Senator Gore of Oklahoma, paused in his flight of words—thinking his allies were present to take up the burden—that the clerk of the Senate, by previous arrangement, instantly called Aldrich's name, and the filibuster was broken. The Aldrich-Vreeland Act was then swiftly passed.[8]

La Follette's example of systematic defiance of the Congressional and party "hierarchy" was considered a most dangerous provocation by the Old Guard. Manifestation of a similar insurgent spirit in other Republicans now brought fearful parliamentary reprisals in the House of Representatives. The thirty "young insurgents" from the West (of whom Taft had spoken in his letter of farewell to Roosevelt) had joined with the Democrats in a fight to depose Speaker Cannon at the start of the special session in 1909. One by one, Cannon demoted the "insubordinates," such as George K. Norris of Nebraska and Victor Murdock of Kansas, from the committee chairmanships and privileges they had earned by years of service.

In the Senate, Jonathan Dolliver, the Iowa veteran, in addition to La Follette, was also marked for demotion. He had combined with the Democrats in 1906 in an effort to bring about a more drastic railroad act; he had been guilty of other sins of insubordination. The unforgiving Aldrich excluded Dolliver from membership in the powerful Finance Committee of the Senate, a committee to which he should have gone by seniority as well as personal distinction. Dolliver had hoped, by attaining the important committee post, to lead in the framing of a historic tariff-reform act which might bear his name, thus paving the way to higher things. The failure of appointment was a most bitter blow. La Follette had often appealed in vain to this lovable giant, whose heart was known to be on the progressive side, to join him in opposition, to stand "at the head of a movement here in the Senate and the country, for the public interests." Dolliver could now believe what his colleague La Follette said of the "tyranny" of the financial East over the West. For he learned that when appeals were made to Aldrich on Dolliver's behalf, Aldrich had said firmly and coldly

[8] *Congressional Record*, Vol. 42, Part 8, 60th Congress, 1st Session, May 29, 30, 1908.

that it would be impossible for them to work together in preparing a new tariff.[9]

Meeting Dolliver in the corridor of the Senate, one day after the committee appointments were announced, La Follette said to him:

"Jonathan, are you pretty nearly ready to have that conference with me?"

He answered: "Yes, I am coming over to see you."

"Well," I said, "come now."

And he went with me to my committee room. We spent several hours together.

From that day, Dolliver is said to have resolved that he was going to be "independent." He had saved his money and put it into a farm.

"I am going to judgment in the next twenty years," he said, "and I am going so that I can look my Maker in the face. . . . I can take my books, my wife and children, and, if I am dismissed from the service for following my convictions, I will go out to my farm and stay there until the call comes." [10]

3

The Payne-Aldrich Tariff Act of 1909 differed little from earlier Republican legislation in its field. Nor did it differ in the bitter debates, the rumors of corruption, the criminations and recriminations, it aroused. What chiefly distinguished the contest that began shortly after the special session of Congress opened was the fact that Democrats and Republicans as such were no longer clearly divided upon the line of protection. Even the Southern Congressmen now sought protection for Louisiana sugar or Alabama iron or tobacco. Opposition formed chiefly among the "Insurgent" Republican Congressmen hailing from the Granger states such as Wisconsin, Minnesota, Nebraska, Iowa, and Kansas. Nor did these men demand Free Trade—in a world of competing com-

---

[9] Stephenson, *op. cit.*, p. 345, citing memorandum of Senator Albert Cummins.
[10] La Follette, *op. cit.*, pp. 432-434.

mercial empires which erected Chinese walls of customs duties about themselves. On the contrary, a number of them sought increases of duties that would specifically aid agricultural and forest products such as hides and lumber. But mainly they fought against the Payne-Aldrich tariff as a means of fighting the tariff-favored trusts, which, a large minority of the Western Republicans believed, were responsible for the high cost of manufactured consumer goods. The tariff contest of 1909 was waged on economic rather than on partisan lines. It was accompanied by the strongest revolt within the Republican party since the Free Silver struggles of the 1890's.

The elaborate, technical business of writing a national revenue law was as usual little understood by most of the public, which looked on with mixed, confused sentiments. It was a situation made to order for Aldrich, who had been framing tariff laws for thirty years by his own system of compromise, horse-trading and "sudden thrusts." The only doubtful factor, this time, was that the Republican party platform in 1908 had declared itself for genuine and "unequivocal" revision of the tariff, and the President in various campaign addresses (though not in his inaugural) had been more outspoken still in urging necessary downward revisions of rates. The problem was therefore how to give the appearance of supporting the President's moderate demands, or how to sacrifice him a little while saving his face.

The bill introduced before the Lower House by Chairman Sereno Payne of the Ways and Means Committee on April 10, 1909—after some cursory hearings of "experts" and lobbyists—promised very slight reductions in the schedules, causing not a little disappointment. But soon it was improved by the addition of an amendment, providing for a direct income tax, a clause which it was now hoped the Supreme Court would not nullify as in 1895. But Aldrich's bill, presented in the Senate in the guise of a series of amendments and made ready with remarkable speed by April 12, 1909, administered a shock in that it embodied *increases* rather than the promised reductions. The Senate's "dictator" presented his bill with only a brief oral statement, asking immediate consideration of its 300 pages and hundreds of increases over the rates in the House bill.

Even before the bills were introduced, a large Wall Street investment house, Hayden, Stone and Company, had sent out a telegraphic market letter to its clients informing them that "we are reasonably sure . . . there cannot be any radical reduction." [11]

Ten days later, the attack of the dissident Republicans led by La Follette and Dolliver burst forth with a vehemence that none had awaited. Where was the downward revision promised to the people? they asked. Their first onslaught made a "profound impression" upon a public opinion already deeply agitated by great financial scandals and depression. [12]

But Aldrich asked coolly in return: "Where did we ever make the statement that we would revise the tariff *downward?*" Soon the Standpatters were to avow openly that all the talk of lowering the tariff rates was but a "concession, a sop thrown by those lacking in confidence to the voters." [13]

The "Payne Bill" had shown a desire to appease the consuming public, placing iron ore, hides, and wood pulp on the free list, and a forty per cent reduction in duties on shoes. It was when this bill with its amendments returned from the Senate's Finance Committee that, as in Lewis Carroll's tale, the Cheshire Cat gradually disappeared until only the grin was left. But Aldrich had promised President Taft that the tariff act would be in accord with his pledges, so that he would have no occasion to veto it. What would the President now do? the press asked. [14]

The new President was even more undecided than he appeared, as his letters now show. Taft wanted, Lodge said, only "a tariff that will strike the country favorably." [15] But his own view of what

[11] *Collier's Weekly*, Apr. 3, 1909.
[12] The New York *Times*, Apr. 23, 1909.
[13] *Congressional Record*, Jun. 8, 1909, p. 2950; Apr. 22, 1909, p. 1499.
[14] The New York *Tribune*, Apr. 13, 1909; *Literary Digest*, Apr. 17, Apr. 24, 1909.
[15] Lodge, *Correspondence*, Vol. II, p. 334.

this would be was not firmly asserted; he seemed unready to exert Presidential force to impose it, and inclined rather to let Congress (and its managers) lead the way. Thus he seemed to lean now to one side, now to the other. La Follette and Beveridge, who communicated with the President, felt sometimes that he encouraged them to "insurge" and raise the pressure from their side against the Standpatters. "Saw Taft—he is with us," Beveridge wrote his wife on one day.[16] But Aldrich proceeded confidently without fear of lightning bolts from the White House. Indeed the crafty old horse-trader was prepared to make certain seeming concessions to Taft, in items lowered from extremely high rates and no longer important to the great lay Republicans of big industry; free hides, a lower rate on lumber and upon leather gloves, and reduced tariffs for the Philippines were gifts which, in June, filled the President's heart with joy.[17] Yet in the case of the all-important wool and cotton schedules, which Aldrich insisted upon as representing his own requirements, Taft showed himself complaisant or indifferent. Thus Dolliver, with a flash of wit, was led to remark in the Senate one day that Mr. Taft was "an amiable man entirely surrounded by men who knew perfectly what they wanted."

But it was worse. Privately, to friends, to his brothers, to members of his Cabinet, to Elihu Root, Taft actually complained that Speaker Cannon was not playing square with him, that he mistrusted Aldrich's motives in keeping certain rates too high; that the attitude of the Standpatters was "most unfortunate." [18] These were his private thoughts, for at heart he felt himself something of a "low tariff man." But, in action, he invited Aldrich and his coterie to White House good-will dinners, fed them of his meat and good wine, and then bowed to their councils.

In the last week in May, as the tariff debate prolonged itself, Jonathan Dolliver heard that the President had turned against the Insurgents, saying that "he would not have anything to do with

[16] Bowers, *op. cit.*, Jun. 12, 1909, p. 349.
[17] Butt, *op. cit.*, Vol. I, p. 162.
[18] Jessup, *op. cit.*, Vol. II, p. 220; Pringle, *Taft*, Vol. I, pp. 429, 430.

such an irresponsible set of fellows." Beveridge on the floor of the Senate, May 25, 1909, cited passages from the President's speeches of 1908, promising moderate but definite reductions of the tariff rates, so that they would bear less heavily upon the masses of the people. He called upon the Republicans to support the President's original declarations and keep the party faith. The next day when Beveridge visited the White House, he found, as he said, "the coldest atmosphere I ever encountered in politics." [19]

Taft now came to think Beveridge, ardent supporter of Rooseveltian policies, an insufferable egotist and poseur, who bored him to death. He hated to meet the "fanatic" La Follette even at a public ceremony; and thought it equally a waste of time to see those "blatant demagogues," Dolliver and Cummins,[20] men who talked incessantly, wearyingly, shrilly, and endangered the future of the party itself.

Legends of the overweening vanity of the Insurgent leaders, La Follette, Beveridge, Dolliver, and Cummins, have been perpetuated by certain historians. ". . . Of the sum of the egos of all 96 Senators, the 10 Insurgents had more than half," according to Mark Sullivan. Yet in the tariff battle of 1909 this group of Senators, who had only hitherto fired occasional, sniping shots at the Old Guard, made a demonstration of organized minority resistance, of devoted teamwork, that was spectacular and rare in our parliamentary history.

From the rostrum of the Senate Chamber they educated the people. A "prairie fire" was growing in the West, as one keen observer related at the time. Men talked everywhere of the need for new leadership, and a "new national party." Such a development was "nearer than the Republican party of 1855." [21] It was the sense of this historic opportunity that fused the bloc of Insurgent Senators, including La Follette, Beveridge, Dolliver,

[19] Bowers, *op. cit.*, p. 343.
[20] Pringle, *Taft*, Vol. I, pp. 430-431.
[21] Mark Sullivan in *Collier's Weekly*, Dec. 11, 1909. In those days Mr. Sullivan was an ardent Progressive.

Cummins, Bristow of Kansas, Moses Clapp of Minnesota, Knute Nelson, and Norris Brown, into a determined, well-drilled team, whose members each mastered the parts they must play. Soon, as they knew, they were to be proscribed, "outlawed," and must depend solely on the voters of their own states for continuance in public life. They were convinced that they had nothing more to look for in the Aldrich-Cannon leadership and must either rebuild their party from within or form a new alignment.

"It is incumbent upon the reformer who seeks to establish a new order to come equipped with complete mastery of all the information upon which the established order is based," La Follette wrote not long afterward. La Follette brought to the group the Wisconsin tactics of mastering facts, of using exact knowledge as a weapon against the adversary. The work of organized opposition was thereupon divided among the Insurgent Senators: thus Dolliver prepared to speak on the cotton rates, La Follette on the wool and other textiles, Cummins on the metals, while Beveridge acted as floor leader. They engaged experts to furnish them with information in each field, and from the early days of May to the torrid ones of June, gathered together every night at La Follette's or Beveridge's apartment—with a case of beer to quench the large Mr. Clapp's thirst—and prepared their speeches and mapped out the strategy of debate in consultation.[22] Every evening they planned questions which they would ask of each other on the morrow, on the floor of the Senate, in order to bring out plainly all points to the most innocent listeners. That spring the American people, hearing of the concerted attacks, day by day, learned something of what tariff legislation meant.

Dolliver, for instance, whose speeches were probably the most interesting and wittiest of the period, delivered an all-day speech on the cotton-textile schedules, which he proved to be higher than the Dingley rates of 1897, tremendously favorable to Massachusetts mill owners, whose lobbyists had demanded the new rates. Aldrich, greatly put out of countenance, warned Dolliver that he

<hr>

22 La Follette, *op. cit.*, pp. 441, 442, 445.

was assaulting "the very citadel of protection." But Dolliver answered with the defiant challenge that henceforth he would take
his orders from his constituency and not from Mr. Aldrich. He
perorated:

I want to see an end to the scandal that has accompanied the framing of every tariff bill. . . .
So far as I am concerned I am through with it. I intend to fight it.
I intend to fight without fear—I do not care what may be my political
fate. I have had a burdensome and toilsome experience in public life
now these twenty-five years. . . . I do not propose that the remaining
years of my life, whether they be in public affairs or in private business,
shall be given up to a dull consent to . . . all these conspiracies, which
. . . use the lawmaking power of the United States to multiply their
own profits and to fill the marketplace with witnesses of their avarice
and of their greed.[23]

The Insurgents made serious charges of secret alterations of the
tax rates, such as the reduction of the cigarette tax in committee
at the demand of the tobacco trust. Beveridge told of how the
same trick had been worked before; and how it was being worked
now. And his accomplice La Follette would rise and ask him with
malice: "Does the Senator think that remarkable legislation . . .
was an oversight?"[24]
Aldrich grew angry, embarrassed, silent. At times he demanded
discipline. The tariff would be passed, he hinted, as written by the
majority; the majority were on his side. He threatened Beveridge
and the others, styling them "free traders" and no Republicans.
Yet day by day the testimony of Aldrich's "experts" seemed over-
weighed by the Insurgents' marshaling of facts. At last it was apparent that they actually meant to vote against the bill. Aldrich
was astonished; he had thought they talked but for the record. In
answer to his menaces, Cummins of Iowa replied: "There will
come a time presently when the clamor of millions who want re-

[23] *Congressional Record*, May 3, May 5, 1909; Tarbell, *The Tariff*, p. 357.
[24] *Congressional Record*, May 14, 1909.

lief will sound like the roar of a thousand Niagaras from one ocean to another." [25]

Aldrich scorned to consider such warnings; he pressed on to votes. Danger existed, because the House version of the tariff bill included an amendment providing for an income tax of 2 per cent upon incomes of over $5,000, the Democrats joining with the Insurgents to support this clause. Aldrich, who fought the income tax for twenty years, was finally forced to the unpleasant expedient of accepting as a compromise measure the proposal of a corporation excise tax of 2 per cent, in return for which the Insurgent-Democratic combination abandoned the personal income tax. Then, as a separate measure, both Houses passed a resolution for a Federal income-tax amendment to the Constitution to be submitted to the states.

The Payne-Aldrich revenue bill, when it was finally passed, contained good mixed with evil. Its increases were moderate; there were provisions for sliding rates, and for a tariff commission to be appointed by the President. But the nation, deeply aroused by the long, sensational debate in Washington, remembered chiefly the ruthless tactics used in forcing passage. They saw that the protective tariff rates were made higher when it was pledged that they should be made less burdensome. The ten Insurgent Senators who, burning their bridges, voted opposition to the very end, were known thereafter as martyrs to Aldrich's "Star Chamber" proceedings. ". . . A promise to a people is sacred!" Beveridge had exclaimed, when the final roll call was taken.

While the President cheerfully signed the bill, the citizens were already protesting that they would be forced to pay more for their woolen clothing. Even conservative newspapers such as the New York *Sun* (on August 2, 1909) made gloomy predictions of an approaching civil war within the Republican party which would continue "until the leadership of one faction or the other is driven from power." At the other side of the country, the farm paper of La Follette drew its own conclusions, saying:

[25] *Literary Digest,* May 15, 1909.

The lesson has been a costly one to the people, but it has been well-learned. . . . The tariff-favored trusts won out. . . . But their victory will unquestionably be short-lived. Soon the people who must buy food and clothing and other necessaries of life will send other representatives to Washington.[26]

It was the evident truth that underlay such dire predictions as those above, the reports from field agents of a "prairie fire," that sent the indolent Mr. Taft upon a speaking tour of the Middle West late that summer. He had decided to "get out and see the people and jolly them." [27] From Minnesota the party wheelhorse, Representative Tawney, who had much to do with the recent tariff act, had called for help in a local election campaign. Taft planned to make his speech at Tawney's native town of Winona, in the heart of the radical agrarian region, a defense of the Payne-Aldrich bill. Unfortunately he delayed writing his speech until the last hours, when it was prepared with great haste.

Neither the Republican party nor himself, ran Taft's speech of September 17, 1909, had promised that tariff rates would all be revised downward. (This resembled unpleasantly Aldrich's equivocations.) Then, after a long, labored defense, he concluded: "I would say without hesitation that this is the best tariff bill that the Republican party has ever passed, and therefore the best tariff bill that has been passed at all. . . ." [28]

Only afterward, when he took account of the outburst of ridicule this speech evoked in the press, did Taft realize that he had made a political mistake. In this same speech he also made disparaging allusions to the Insurgent Senators, challenging them either to "stay in line and work for party solidarity," or leave the party openly, as their individual consciences dictated. The "Progressive" Senators accepted this as an attempt to "read out of the party" those who opposed the Payne-Aldrich bill.[29]

[26] *La Follette's Weekly*, Aug. 14, 1909.
[27] Pringle, *Taft*, Vol. I, p. 457.
[28] The New York *World*, Sept. 18, 1909.
[29] *La Follette's Weekly*, Sept. 25, 1909.

The Mid-Western countryside rang with the protests of the Insurgents, recorded in numerous newspaper interviews:

TAFT HAS SURROUNDED HIMSELF WITH CORPORATION ATTORNEYS

TAFT HAS MADE STUDIED EFFORT TO REPUDIATE THINGS
PREDECESSOR STOOD FOR

The Insurgent leaders were now more determined than ever to overthrow the Old Guard and recapture the Republican party for Lincoln's plain people. It was nothing less than this that La Follette and his colleagues patiently planned: once a half dozen large Western states were seized, the rebuilding of the party from within could be completed rapidly, as in Wisconsin. That summer and fall the Insurgent leaders, returning to their constituents, told their tale of outrage and betrayal and won strong local approval. Some of them as in the case of Beveridge were soon to face re-election campaigns, and they arranged to stump for each other.

Jonathan Dolliver, ill and worn out from the long summer debates, nevertheless addressed a cheering letter to Beveridge in September. Formerly the very paragon of regularity and tolerance in Congress and party, Dolliver wrote as one who had come to see the light of revolution late in life.

If we had a direct line from the skies we could not have done a better job for ourselves than we did when we stood on our convictions against all comers including the Big Chief [Aldrich]. The penalty of doing right exists only in the imaginations of grafters and time-servers. If you never see the inside of the Senate Chamber again, the last three months of your labors will make your life notable and famous when biographies are written. . . .

We don't need money to fight them. *We will go in with the common weapons of justice and common sense and make a new era in national life. . . .*[30]

When the "man mountain" of Iowa, Dolliver, believed that the central party organization could be defeated with "the weapons

---

[30] Sept. 14, 1909; Bowers, *op. cit.*, p. 371; italics mine.

of justice and common sense," surely the times were out of joint. The plans for a "Restoration" had grievously miscarried. It was scarcely a year since the Rough Rider had gone abroad, and the party he had held unified was torn by internal strife. Soon a wave of scandal would engulf it.

As the party elections of 1910 approached, Elihu Root, now Senator for New York, had forebodings of disaster, and went about "like old Noah," warning his political associates "that this is no ordinary shower but a flood," and that they had "better hurry up and get into the Ark." Yet few of his friends believed him.[31]

[31] Jessup, *op. cit.*, Vol. II, p. 154.

X. THE BALLINGER CASE:

AN AMERICAN AFFAIRE DREYFUS

THE CONSERVATION of America's immense natural resources for the benefit of the people made the chief glory of Theodore Roosevelt's years in power. Not only were great forests of magnificent timberland saved from destruction, but millions of acres of coal, of mineral land, and above all of water-power sites were held from pre-emption by claimants who would eventually have turned them over to the hands of monopolistic groups.

The soul of the conservation movement in the early years of the present century was undoubtedly Gifford Pinchot. His eyes, as Owen Wister recalled, seemed to look always "as if they gazed upon a Cause," and his face was "one of marked and particular beauty, in which enthusiasm and asceticism" were blended.[1] There were those who, like President Taft, could be ironical at the expense of this "fanatic," this "transcendentalist." But that his idealism was constructive and invaluable could scarcely be denied.

In their zeal the conservationists undoubtedly exceeded a Pickwickian interpretation of the law. Garfield as Secretary of the Interior and Pinchot as an under-officer of the Department of Agriculture used their authority to compel those who developed power sites or established electric power lines across government lands to charge only moderate rates for their services. These tactics were extremely irritating to the forerunners of the Electric Bond and

[1] Wister, *op. cit.*, p. 114.

Share Company and other utility monopolies.[2] When Taft became President, he immediately put a stop to this practice, upon legal grounds. In any case he thought Pinchot "a good deal of a radical and a good deal of a crank. . . ."[3] But Gifford Pinchot, though a minor government official, enjoyed the influence of a full Cabinet officer; he had been a favorite at Roosevelt's court, and to dismiss him would have meant an open repudiation of Rooseveltian principles.

However, Taft's naming of Richard A. Ballinger as Secretary of the Interior—despite his awareness that Pinchot and Ballinger worked with poor accord—was an indication that limits were to be marked out for the conservation movement. Henceforth everything would be done "within the law" and according to the "limited powers" granted by the Constitution, even though land-grabbers and public utilities benefited thereby.

No one offered greater contrast to Gifford Pinchot, surely, than Secretary Ballinger. His face and manner was that of a hardheaded "old school" lawyer and politician who had grown up with the West. Taft appointed him, probably, at the urging of Western party leaders, remarking at the time that the appointment "would satisfy the West coast."[4] In the Far West conservation policies were said to be less popular than elsewhere. The Western politicians demanded continued liberal distribution of public lands in their vicinity to "pioneers" who would settle and develop them. In reality the latter-day pioneers were often but claim agents leagued with the politicians, to whom the Department of the Interior had been a source of spoils for a century. Eventually the claims would turn up in the hands of some large syndicate that could furnish the capital or build the railroads necessary for the exploitation of the copper, coal, or timber lands.

Under the Roosevelt administration, for several years, Ballinger as General Land Commissioner had exhibited only restrained en-

[2] Stahl, *The Ballinger-Pinchot Controversy*, pp. 77-78.
[3] Pringle, *Taft*, Vol. I, p. 480.
[4] *Ibid.*, Vol. I, p. 478.

thusiasm for the current conservation policies. In one case, in 1907, he had shown himself ready to approve certain claims for coal lands in southern Alaska, known as the "Cunningham Claims," which special agents of the Interior Department had considered as being of fraudulent title. There were reports that most of these claims to Alaskan coal lands were being taken for the Guggenheims, who were then developing copper mines in Alaska, or were to wind up in the hands of a "Morgan-Guggenheim syndicate" eventually. One special agent of the Interior Department who had become suspicious of the Cunningham Claims opposed Ballinger's action so vigorously that Secretary Garfield was induced to delay approval of them until further government investigations were completed.

In March, 1908, Mr. Ballinger resigned from the service and resumed the private practice of law in Seattle. It happened oddly enough that among the private cases he defended was that of the self-same Cunningham group which still petitioned the government for title to some 5,280 acres of coal land. Later, Ballinger explained that he took this case largely as a friendly service, accepting only the small fee of $250, which barely paid his expenses for a trip East. The fact that while employed in the government service he had obtained information of possible value to his clients presented no ethical problems to his mind. The Cunningham affair, however, continued in suspension; and there matters rested until 1909, when by a most curious coincidence Ballinger, returning to the Interior Department as its chief, took it under consideration once more.

From the start Secretary Ballinger showed that he believed in a form of conservation that encouraged private exploitation of government lands in the Western states and territories. Within thirty days after taking office he, with Taft's approval, restored to entry a great part of the land that his predecessor, under Roosevelt, had withdrawn "illegally" in a sort of last-hour coup.

It is apparent from the Taft Papers that Gifford Pinchot came at once to Taft and protested vehemently at Ballinger's reopening of large water-power sites to entry. Pinchot contended that Taft by supporting Ballinger's orders was going back on the principles of the Roosevelt administration which he had vowed to continue. And Pinchot would not endure such a change silently, but, he hinted, would resign from the service he loved and defend the cause of conservation before the public.[5] There were three conferences in April, 1909; and though Taft did not enjoy the visitations of the "fanatic," he retreated, and ordered Ballinger, who acted under protest, to restore the water-power lands in question to the forest reserve.[6]

Under the surface a constant struggle was now waged between the two adversaries, Pinchot and Ballinger, and their respective cohorts; and Taft, aware of the dangerously growing dissension within his government, was alarmed and wearied by it. He wondered how to end it without running the political danger of banishing Pinchot, who had already threatened to resign. Large principles and even vast natural wealth were at stake; yet the President did not treat the matter in this light. Then, at the end of the summer, the internal struggle suddenly rose to a climax.

In August, 1909, Pinchot, through Forest Service officials, got wind of the contested Cunningham Claims and learned that Ballinger was endeavoring to have them validated, although more than one subordinate who had investigated the claims reported that they were fraudulent. Louis R. Glavis, the young chief of the Field Division of the Interior Department who had been in charge of this case, had come to the conclusion that certain of the Alaskan coal lands, including forest reserves under the jurisdiction of the Interior Department, were to be disposed of to claimants who evidently represented the Morgan-Guggenheim "Alaska Syndicate."

Glavis had been in the service about four years, and had the reputation of being a very able, intelligent, and faithful official. He was only twenty-five years old and it was not surprising if he

[5] Gifford Pinchot to author, Dec. 18, 1939.
[6] Stahl, *op. cit.*, pp. 85 ff.

took to heart the many moral exhortations of Theodore Roosevelt that one should fight to the uttermost for the welfare of the nation against the forces of money and greed. In 1907 he had already crossed swords with Ballinger, when the latter was his superior as General Land Commissioner, and by a direct appeal to Secretary Garfield he had prevented the disposal of the Cunningham Claims. But now Ballinger, in full command of the department, pressed Glavis to have the Cunningham affair concluded in short order, or have the claim approved. Glavis was distraught at this command, since his investigations required traveling over wild territories and seeking the depositions of persons who sometimes lived thousands of miles apart. He telegraphed to Washington, pleading for more time. On May 17, 1909, he went to Washington himself and saw Secretary Ballinger, submitting his partially completed report. Ballinger and his legal aides thereupon overruled Glavis's judgment on the fraudulency of the Cunningham Claims. But Glavis, who later exhibited a remarkable memory and mental capacity, felt that he knew the law and that a great deal was at stake. He relates:

Without consulting with my superiors, I went to Attorney General Wickersham and stated the matter to him. I understand that he asked Mr. Ballinger to refer the matter to him. . . . Ten days later the Attorney General . . . upheld my contentions and saved the Alaska Coal cases.[7]

That is to say, Glavis was given further time for investigation. But soon the Interior Department superiors pressed him again to hasten the affair. It was now mid-July and Glavis, who had returned to the West, saw Ballinger, then visiting Seattle, and made a last, vain appeal for more time to prepare for a final hearing.

By now the whole affair was overshadowed by mutual suspicion and hostility. Glavis knew that his own position was precarious, that his cause was seen with little favor and would eventually be overruled. But more than his own career, the Alaska coal cases

---

[7] *Collier's Weekly*, Nov. 13, 1909.

involved "the future coal supply of the United States." The hidden interests who, thanks to their railway dominance in Alaska, would soon take over the coal fields, would in his opinion secure "a monopoly similar to that of the Pennsylvania coal fields today." [8] As a last resort, Glavis appealed for aid to a friend, A. C. Shaw, who was an assistant to Gifford Pinchot in the Forest Service. He saw Pinchot on August 5, 1909, at Spokane, and held a long talk with him, and Pinchot thought the story was serious enough to warrant sending the young official with a letter of introduction to President Taft himself.

The stout Chief Magistrate was vacationing at Beverly, Massachusetts, after the steaming days of the tariff warfare, when, on August 18, 1909, Glavis came to him with his complaints and charges, over the head of his superior officer. Glavis charged that entries for over 5,000 acres of valuable coal and timber land had been made for the indirect benefit of the Morgan-Guggenheim syndicate; like Gifford Pinchot, earlier, he accused Secretary Ballinger of being faithless to the conservation program inaugurated under Roosevelt and officially espoused by President Taft. Later, on September 5, 1909, Glavis returned and delivered into the hands of the President a large dossier, several hundred pages of technical reports, and testimony taken in the field.

It was plain that Taft was in no humor to enjoy the highhanded, even insubordinate performance of the minor official Glavis—though it was done in the name of public duty. Besides, Glavis came straight from Pinchot, who stood behind him, and who was believed to be responsible for recent press criticism of the administration's handling of conservation problems. Taft was busy preparing for his speaking tour in defense of the unpopular Payne-Aldrich tariff; he was busy and yet needed rest—and golf,

---

[8] L. R. Glavis to A. C. Shaw; testimony of Jan. 26, 1910; 61st Congress, *Investigation of Interior Department*, Vol. 34. Conflicting views have been expressed upon the value of the Alaska coal lands. Mineral resources are usually of uncertain value, until promotional capital, machinery and transportation are applied to exploiting them. At the time, 1909, there was much talk of railway building in southern Alaska by larger railroad interests.

which made him happy. During that week of September 6, 1909, the President was visited by Attorney General Wickersham and by Secretary Ballinger, who came with his legal counsel, Lawler. It is evident that the whole unpleasant matter, including the Glavis documents, was taken up with these men. Normally a ruling in the case should have come from the Attorney General. But Mr. Wickersham, as it transpired, was extremely busy with many more important affairs all that week; and so it came to pass that Mr. Ballinger, the accused, with the aid of Mr. Lawler, his counsel, judged the Glavis charges and presented his summary report to the President.

It was of course a judgment that completely exonerated himself and set down Glavis as a neurotic young man, filled with delusions of grandeur and obsessed by mere "shreds of suspicion." Taft now moved with unusual promptness, since the dangerous Pinchot was in the background of the case; he disposed of the whole business (as he hoped) with a vigorous public letter addressed to Secretary Ballinger, exonerating him and requesting him to dismiss the offensive Glavis. Afterward, he would claim that he spent several days and sat up until three o'clock one morning going over the evidence in the case.[9] In reality he asked Oscar Lawler, the attorney assigned to the Interior Department, to draft a report "as if he were President," exonerating Ballinger, which Lawler did. This was duly signed by Taft, with perhaps a few slight changes introduced by him.

The letter of September 13, 1909, to Secretary Ballinger, Mark Sullivan wrote at the time in *Collier's Weekly*, appeared as "a ponderous, sweeping letter of exculpation and endorsement intended . . . to refute all present charges against Ballinger and make future ones impossible." Taft told Ballinger that he had "examined the whole matter most carefully" and reached the conclusion that Mr. Glavis's case was without substantial evidence. For having attempted to file "a disingenuous statement unjustly

[9] Taft to Senator Knute Nelson, May 15, 1910, the New York *Times*, May 16, 1910.

impeaching the integrity of his superior officers," Taft authorized Mr. Ballinger to dismiss the said Glavis from the service, as the Secretary had intended.

The President, as he departed on his Western tour to quench Western prairie fires by this forceful public statement, doubtless intended to teach a lesson not only to Glavis but to Pinchot and his fellow agitators. Newspaper talk of Alaskan land-grabbing had started in the latter part of August, and La Follette already thundered accusations against Ballinger for helping the "water-power grab." The source of the public rumors lay within the government itself: the Forest Service, conducted by Pinchot.

2

But while Taft was falling into grievous blunders in his Minnesota speech, another prairie fire was kindled in the East by his letter to Ballinger. It was the heyday of social reformers, who spoke through many organs. One of the largest and most powerful of the muckraking magazines was *Collier's Weekly*, whose owner was a close friend of Gifford Pinchot, and whose editor was the able Norman Hapgood. In a vigorous, well-informed editorial, Hapgood attacked the Taft administration that week, arguing that the Roosevelt conservation policy was being abandoned, that frauds were being committed again in the oft-pillaged Interior Department, and that the well-meaning Mr. Taft was being led around by the nose. Taft's letter exonerating Ballinger, it was hinted, was not even written by the President; and the President perhaps knew nothing about it.[10]

To Pinchot the punishment of Glavis was a blow at himself and all his works. To defend conservation and "bring the Kingdom of God on earth," he must now help to right the wrong done to Glavis. To the Insurgent bloc of Congressmen the "Ballinger-Pinchot case" seemed a heaven-sent opportunity for renewing their drive against the administration; and they rushed into the

[10] *Collier's Weekly*, Sept. 25, 1909.

fray with a single accord. Soon the great muckraking magazines, which now flourished more widely than ever despite Roosevelt's prohibition, took up the issue; and month by month, in *Hampton's*, *McClure's*, or *Collier's*, attacks upon the Department of the Interior were published. One article pictured Mr. Ballinger as a frank and crude opponent of conservation; it cited his own words in an interview and accused him bluntly of acting in collusion with the Morgan and Guggenheim interests.[11] But the greatest sensation was caused by publication in *Collier's Weekly* on November 13, 1909, of the long, detailed, carefully prepared article by Louis Glavis himself, telling the story of his investigations and preferring charges against Secretary Ballinger. (Though Glavis had been offered $3,000 to tell his story, he had refused payment of any kind, wishing only to clear his name.) The article was prefixed by a sensational headline devised by the editors:

ARE THE GUGGENHEIMS IN CHARGE OF THE DEPARTMENT OF INTERIOR?

The storm now broke in its full force. Demands were made everywhere for a public investigation of the Interior Department by a Congressional committee. On the other hand, Payne Whitney, a scion of New York society, heard talk at the Union League Club of a million-dollar libel suit against *Collier's Weekly* and brought advance news of this to Editor Norman Hapgood and to Pinchot, who had engendered the whole controversy.[12]

One day in December, therefore, Louis D. Brandeis received an urgent telegram from Norman Hapgood, who knew him, asking him to come at once to the offices of the New York firm of Winthrop and Stimson. There Brandeis found a conclave of legal talent, including Henry L. Stimson and George Wharton Pepper, who was engaged by Gifford Pinchot. In addition, James R. Garfield, Norman Hapgood, and Louis R. Glavis were present, the last-named explaining the case to the lawyers. At this meeting

[11] J. L. Mathews in *Hampton's Magazine*, Jan. 1910.
[12] Hapgood, N., *The Changing Years*, pp. 185-186.

Brandeis was strongly impressed with Glavis's sincerity and sense of honor.[13] The Boston reformer and lawyer consented to enter the case. It was understood that a Congressional investigation impended; and plans were laid by the lawyers to represent Glavis and Pinchot at the forthcoming hearings, and thus defend also the owners of *Collier's Weekly*. It was the latter who had retained Brandeis as the strongest lawyer they could get.

Above all things, Taft had dreaded a contest with Gifford Pinchot. At the very time of his dismissal of Glavis and exculpation of Ballinger, on September 13, 1909, he had written: "My dear Gifford . . . I urge that you do not make Glavis's cause your own." The President begged him to take no hasty action.[14]

Yet the logic of events drove Pinchot and the other devoted followers of Theodore Roosevelt into the growing opposition movement against Taft and his Old Guard allies. But yesterday the achievements Pinchot had long dreamed of, in the field of land conservation, had seemed very near. But now it was plain that long-cherished plans and policies of conservation were to be compromised, if not abandoned. This was the meaning of Glavis's dismissal. Pinchot therefore entered the struggle with all his heart. On December 31, 1909, he wrote a long letter to Theodore Roosevelt, then still in Africa, giving his own account of the evil things that had happened since his hero had gone to hunt lions and kings.[15] He also turned to the Insurgents in Congress, who from the opening of the session in December had been fighting for a resolution for an inquiry into the Department of the Interior. To Senator Dolliver, who had led the Progressive opposition to the Payne-Aldrich tariff, Pinchot addressed a long letter on January 6, 1910, that was intended to be read publicly from the floor of the Senate. In this the fiery Chief Forester explained how he had come to mistrust the policy of the President's Cabinet

[13] Lief, *op. cit.*, p. 157.
[14] Pringle, *Taft*, Vol. I, p. 491.
[15] In the early spring of 1910, Pinchot made a journey to Italy, to meet Roosevelt and present "at his [Roosevelt's] request" his account of the controversy. (Gifford Pinchot to author.)

advisers; how he had permitted his two aides, Shaw and Oliver of the Forest Service—though it was clearly an improper and insubordinate step—to help Glavis prepare his case against Secretary Ballinger. Like Glavis, "the most vigorous defender of the people's interests," they had acted out of a high sense of duty, risking their official position rather than the public property. But they had taken this step only after appeals through official channels to the President had failed. The President, Pinchot contended, suffered under "a mistaken impression of the facts." [16] The real question, he said, was "between government by men for human welfare and government by money for profit, between the men who stand for Roosevelt's policies and the men who stand against them."

This indignant letter, exploding like a bombshell in the Senate, gave notice that the break between the Roosevelt followers and the administration had come. It brought from the President the dismissal that Pinchot had courted.

Somewhat tardily, the President realized how the rebellion was growing; how the radical West was breaking away from his party and his attempts at leadership, and how the mantle of Roosevelt, which he had so proudly assumed in 1908, was being torn from him by the friends and political heirs of Roosevelt. He saw a "cabal" against him, rather than an inevitable combination of diverse groups and forces. Assailed on one side because of the unpopular tariff bill, the administration was now assailed on another side for its alleged betrayal of the conservation program. Quietly measures of defense were taken which would strengthen the government for its test.

Pinchot, after his deliberate act of insubordination, made a farewell speech on January 8, 1910, before the assembled officials and clerks of his bureau, to whom he had been as a romantic hero. It was a parting challenge, greeted with rousing and rebellious cheers:

[16] *Senate Documents*, Sixty-first Congress, Third Session, No. 719, pp. 1283-1285.

This fight must go on. It is larger than any man's personal presence or personal failure. . . . Stand by the work! Hold fast to the standard we have set together. Never allow yourself to forget that you are serving a much greater master than the . . . Administration.[17]

3

President Taft had been reconciled, from the beginning, to working with the veteran Speaker "Joe" Cannon, because it was "impossible" to dislodge him. However, the Insurgent bloc in the House had other ideas about Cannon. Led by the mild-man-nered little George W. Norris of Nebraska, they had been plot-ting their stroke of state for nearly four years since March, 1906, and to this end had held frequent conversations with the Demo-crats, who shared with them a deepening sense of wrong. Not only were the Outs and Insurgents shorn of committee privileges, but with increasing arrogance during the "Restoration Period" Cannon had injured them politically by ignoring or postponing indefinitely consideration of bills introduced for the benefit of their districts and states.[18]

When the resolution for an inquiry into the Department of the Interior was introduced before the House in January, follow-ing Pinchot's letter to Dolliver, Cannon as usual was ready to ap-point the House members of the joint committee from his own list of complaisant Standpatters. Possibly, as the Insurgents charged at the time, even the very terms and provisions of the resolution were to be written and the personnel of the committee packed as Ballinger directed. But by the ruse of waiting for an hour when the chairman of the Rules Committee had gone out to lunch, Rep-resentative Norris succeeded in having the House elect its own choice of members. The majority were "sound" Republicans; but the presence of an alert opposition minority, including one strong Insurgent from Kansas, E. H. Madison, and two able Democrats, made a passive "whitewashing" of the affair impossible.

17 Stahl, op. cit., p. 128.
18 The Commoner, Mar. 9, 1906.

Cannon had long managed the House in the spirit of partisan chairmanship perfected by "Czar" Thomas B. Reed in 1890; his despotism depended upon control of the Ways and Means, Rules, and Judiciary Committees. To call up a bill, the legislator must needs go hat in hand to the Speaker's private chambers, negotiate with him, and seek his good will by promising services in return. Then, perhaps, he might be recognized on the floor at some stated time, weeks or months later. Otherwise measures never came to a vote; they died a silent death in the "morgue" of the Judiciary Committee, garroted by the trusted appointees of Speaker Cannon.[19] This despotism had grown less and less benevolent with passing time, and more and more cynical; until on March 16, 1910, ignoring the signs of growing rebellion, and wishing to punish the insurrectos anew, the old Speaker pushed his autocracy to new extremes. Now he sought to abolish the custom of "Calendar Wednesday," a day on which members had a little more than their usual prerogative to be called upon and to speak for their own measures.

On a roll call, so aroused were the less hardened members of his own party that the Speaker was beaten by a sizable vote. The patient Norris had made a study of the rules and precedents in which Cannon had skillfully entrenched himself and for a long time had held himself prepared for just such an emergency as the roll call produced. Suddenly Norris brought forth a resolution that he had carried in his pocket for many months, moving that the Committee on Rules be elected by the House instead of being appointed by the Speaker, as heretofore. There followed a tremendously long and excited debate, lasting for nearly thirty continuous hours and reported by the press in the terms of a great military battle. The control of the Rules Committee was the foundation of the Speaker's autocratic power; and Cannon by every possible resource, all through the day and the night, fought to retain it.

Against the cry of the Standpatters for party discipline, emotional appeals rang out, as that from the respectable Gardner of

[19] Mark Sullivan in *Collier's Weekly*, Mar. 13, 1909, Apr. 3, 1909.

Massachusetts, son-in-law of Henry Cabot Lodge, who demanded the end of "arbitrary rules" and restoration of the "principle of representative government." Norris exclaimed passionately:

I would rather go down to my political grave with a clear conscience than ride in the chariot of victory, a Congressional stool pigeon, the slave, the servant, and the vassal of . . . the owner of a *legislative menagerie*.

Efforts were made, as often before, to rally the sheeplike Tammany Democrats to the rescue of the beleaguered speaker, but Norris denounced them, crying: "Hold up your manacled, wounded, bleeding, shackled hands and let the country see your parliamentary slavery!"

The mood of disaffection among the regulars had gone too far. In the end the Western Republicans with the aid of the Democrats prevailed, and by successive votes forced Cannon to crushing defeat.

In his last extremity, Cannon reverted to the vernacular and exclaimed wearily, "Well, boys, I am a little shot up." Then, as if challenging fate, he himself moved to declare the chair of the Speaker vacant. At this dramatic turn, equal almost to an impeachment, even the Democratic floor leader, Champ Clark of Missouri, burst into tears. The Insurgents and Norris himself, however, shrank from this final step and sustained Cannon in the chair to the end of the session. But the appointive powers of the Speaker were thenceforth severely curtailed, and new, liberal rules were adopted. It was the most humiliating defeat ever suffered by a Speaker of Congress.[20]

Thus, within a year of Roosevelt's departure, an Insurgent-Democratic coalition ruled the House of Representatives. The majority party was divided, its parliamentary machine smashed. Meanwhile the broadening political struggle for "more democracy" that had suddenly liberalized the procedure of Congress it-

[20] Sullivan, *Our Times*, Vol. IV, pp. 380 ff.; *Collier's Weekly*, Mar. 26, Apr. 3, 1910; Neuberger, *Norris*, pp. 39 ff.

self swept on toward new triumphs. More than the political fortunes of Mr. Taft was involved. The schemes for legislation on
currency and a central bank of reserve had been maturing quietly
in Aldrich's committee chamber. The uprising in Congress and the
electoral defeat assured by its demoralizing effect now doomed the
plans upon which Aldrich had set so much store. The central bank
plan was to wait for years, and was to be shaped by alien hands in
a manner wholly different from the purpose of its original authors.

The Insurgent leaders and the opposition party now had a free
hand to direct the attention of the country to the hearings of the
"Ballinger-Pinchot case" before a committee of Congress. The
turmoil in Congress in 1909 and 1910 had aroused the public to
the highest pitch of excitement; and it now followed with rapt
interest the extraordinary inquiry into a branch of the executive
power which, under the masterly strokes of the "people's attorney," mounted to an utterly unforeseen climax in the month
of May.

4

The Ballinger-Pinchot hearings began January 26, 1910, and
continued, with some recesses, for nearly four months. In inquiring into the charges made against Mr. Ballinger and his conduct
of the Interior Department, the Committee of Congress named
Pinchot and Glavis among the important witnesses to be heard.
After a time, out of the distinguished counsel available, Brandeis
was chosen as the principal attorney for the conservationists. With
his rare powers of concentration and analysis, he mastered in a
comparatively short time the evidence and the law touching the
case. Soon Brandeis in his firm, quiet, businesslike way dominated
the proceedings; and the affair to all practical purposes became a
struggle between Brandeis and the administration and all its defenders, whom he prosecuted day by day before the bar of public opinion.

Louis D. Brandeis, a native of Louisville, Kentucky, and descendant of German Jews, had settled in Boston, and there for
more than a quarter of a century had developed an extremely suc-

cessful legal practice. Often he had served as counsel for large corporations, railroads, and trusts. Then toward 1896 a growing fear of the evils which the trusts wrought possessed him. Thereafter he began to devote a regular part of his time to free service in behalf of various popular reforms, free-trade, and anti-monopoly movements. In court and Congressional hearings he appeared as the advocate of the public and the consumers, winning the unofficial title of "people's attorney."

Toward 1905, in fighting the monopolistic expansion of the Morgan-owned New Haven railroad, he opposed no less an adversary than J. P. Morgan and Company, with extraordinary success. Deeply informed of the methods of the big financiers, thorough in his mastery of facts, he stood forth as the most dangerous foeman who had appeared to challenge the "robber barons" of his time. A certain political-economic philosophy, which may here be simply defined as an applied latter-day Jeffersonism, now crystallized in his mind and was to be presented soon in a series of brilliant polemical pamphlets which shaped the progressive thought of this era. To Brandeis' view the problem of democratic distribution of land and resources was now of central importance, and drew him powerfully to the defense of Pinchot and Glavis.

Brandeis, then in his early fifties, was in the prime of life, and in the courtroom had the reputation of a formidable, hard-hitting antagonist. He was very tall and slender, carried himself with a slight stoop, and had a strongly marked face and deep-set piercing eyes that were not easy for an opposing witness to meet. His habitually gentle voice and manner could change with unexpected swiftness when he was ready to strike one of his terrible, paralyzing blows. Against his unhurried resourcefulness of mind, the administration defenders—the committee chairman Senator Knute Nelson and the committee majority, typified by such stalwarts as Senators Root and George Sutherland—found themselves at a sore disadvantage.

Glavis, in his straightforward, clear, extremely well-organized testimony of late January and February, gave a picture of an administration profoundly hostile to the conservation policies set forth by Roosevelt and supported by Congress previously. The points set forth in his *Collier's* article, regarding Ballinger's pressure upon him to approve the Cunningham Claims; Ballinger's professional relations—in the interim when he had resigned from the government service—with the Cunningham claimants; his connection with Cunningham's partner Charles J. Smith, Washington political boss; and charges that the claims were in all likelihood to pass, by option, to the Alaska Syndicate controlled by the Morgan and Guggenheim interests—all this was brought forth. No evidence of corruption or illegal conduct by Ballinger was indicated; only incompetence, dubious ethical behavior, and faithlessness to the declared conservation policies of the government.

Brandeis stressed both the human and the political aspects of the case. Glavis, who had been flung out in disgrace, was defended as a fearless and patriotic public servant; Pinchot too was made a symbol of public-spirited doctrines and constructive social visions which the administration had betrayed. To Brandeis, a Ballinger represented privilege, the power of the Morgans, while Glavis was the "little fellow," the independent in public service. Once more, as in the contest with the New Haven railroad monopoly, Brandeis found himself contending with the overshadowing bankers, here reaching out in secret for the natural wealth left to the public domain.

As in preceding "public" cases, Brandeis directed his main appeal to the force of public opinion. What good was there, he asked, in conservation, if it meant that our natural resources were to be preserved for the rich, while the great multitude of citizens were left "dependent upon certain large capitalists, dependent upon the very limited number of the rich"? [21]

Besides using the committee hearings as a sounding-board for the progressive principles that he and his clients embraced, Brandeis' object was to establish clearly the competence and honesty of Glavis, particularly, and the incompetence and faithlessness of the administration. (Thus the threatened libel suit against *Col-*

[21] Lief, *op. cit.*, pp. 174-175.

lier's Weekly would doubtless be discouraged.) Besides exposing the character of Ballinger and his aides, the lawyer tried to illuminate also the circumstances under which Glavis had been judged and dismissed. A request was made, therefore, to have the report, on the basis of which Taft and Attorney General Wickersham had recommended exonerating Ballinger and ejecting Glavis, submitted as evidence before the committee. After some delays Taft submitted Wickersham's report, a huge dossier containing nearly all related evidence and documents in the case, amounting to some 500,000 words. This bulky report, giving the grounds upon which Glavis had been dismissed in September, was evidently intended as a sixteen-inch gun that would silence all questions.

Examining the documents which included (a part of) Glavis's charges and the replies of Ballinger and three other Department of Interior officials who had been charged with improper conduct, Brandeis began to scent something wrong. It was like a detective story in which the criminal, after completing a "perfect crime," leaves exposed the simplest, the most obvious evidence of his wrongdoing. The vast "Wickersham report" was dated *September 11, 1909*, two days before Taft's letter to Ballinger dismissing Glavis, and less than a week after Glavis had brought (September 5, 1909) his accumulated, written evidence to Taft. It dawned upon Brandeis that the report had been deliberately *antedated*. This was a wholly unexpected development which startled the lawyer, filled him with indignation at the hypocrisy of the administration, and shook his very faith in the government.

The indignant lawyer one night took Norman Hapgood, the editor of *Collier's*, out for a walk and imparted his exciting discovery. Neither Taft nor Wickersham could possibly have made himself acquainted with the facts of the case between September 6, 1909, the day of Ballinger's visit to explain things to Taft at Beverly, and September 11, the date of the report. Glavis, Brandeis reasoned, had simply been dismissed at Ballinger's request, while Ballinger had probably prepared his own exoneration, to be rubber-stamped by Taft.

It was the date affixed to the Wickersham report that had

aroused his suspicions, and the great length of the report had confirmed them. It was filled with the discussion of technical points, and Brandeis himself had taken a full week merely to read it. How long should it have taken to prepare and write it? Some time in November, when attacks multiplied and when a Congressional inquiry was feared, Taft's men had decided to compose their elaborate report of the affair. Then *they had dated it prior* to the time of Glavis's punishment. (For up to now, there existed only the brief memorandum letter of September 13, which Taft had asked Ballinger's legal assistant to write for him.) They had done this "in order to make the public think that in supporting Ballinger, the Attorney General and the President, instead of a political white-wash, had given to the case an attention which at that time they actually had not given to it." [22] By a routine check-up Brandeis informed himself of the daily program of appointments and the movements of Taft and Wickersham in the week of September 6, 1909. Thus he was assured that there had been no time for either one to study the merits of the case at all. Finally, *certain points raised by Glavis, not yet included in the report he had handed Taft, but expressed only in the* Collier's Weekly *article of November 13, 1909, were answered in the "Wickersham report" dated September 11, 1909!*

There were now damning enough traces of the combined dishonesty and stupidity of the administration, but they were circumstantial. Brandeis desired to force from them the admission of their own turpitude. He began now to hint that something was missing in the documents furnished to the committee of Congress conducting the investigation. Day by day he asked patiently, insistently, for reports or memoranda that, he claimed, were being withheld; and each day he was refused.

Then one night in February a young man named Kerby, stenographer in the office of the Secretary of the Interior, and formerly private secretary to James R. Garfield, came to the Pinchot home in Washington with an astonishing piece of news. His conscience

[22] Hapgood, *Changing Years*, pp. 388-389.

had been troubling him, because he had read in the newspapers of a presumed missing memorandum in the Ballinger case; and he himself had in his possession the stenographic notes of the very memorandum, since it had been originally dictated to him. Brandeis was called in, and the confession was repeated, under pledge of secrecy, since the young man feared for his job. The opponents of the Taft administration now had all the knowledge they needed, although there was some uncertainty as to how the information could best be used. Brandeis showed scruples in refusing to call Kerby as a witness against his superiors.

Thereafter Brandeis redoubled his demands for all papers or memoranda that had passed from Ballinger and his aide, Oscar Lawler, to Attorney General Wickersham and the President. An assistant to Ballinger, Finney, who was examined, was asked point-blank:

Brandeis: Is it not a fact that this summary of the Attorney-General which purports to have been made September 11, 1909, bearing the date September 11, 1909, was, as a matter of fact, not completed for more than two months after that time?

Finney: I do not know when it was written, Mr. Brandeis.

The conspirators grew uneasy under the lawyer's pointed questioning. Ballinger, giving testimony, was at once defiant and nervous, and made a poor impression. Yet Brandeis was able, during the cross examination of Secretary Ballinger late in April, to trap the adversary in further false denials.

Brandeis: What did Lawler take with him when he went to Beverly the latter part of the week? [23]

Ballinger: A grip with some clothes in it. I do not know what else he took.

Was there not a memorandum? Was not Ballinger at this very moment withholding this memorandum? "Your question implies an insult! . . ." Ballinger exploded. On the witness stand, Ballinger took the line of denying everything, gave the lie to his

[23] Of Sept. 6-13, 1909.

foes, and called their charges "imaginative" or "maliciously false." [24]

At the committee hearings Brandeis now told the country confidently that President Taft was too busy to have written the letter of September 13, 1909, exculpating Ballinger, without outside help, and that the Wickersham report on which his letter was supposedly based had been antedated. In Congress the Insurgents rose and expressed concern at a government that concealed its actions and suppressed evidence thereof. At first the White House issued formal denials that any material evidence or papers were suppressed. It was left to Attorney General Wickersham to make the damaging admission that his long, bulky report to the President was not completed on the day it was dated, September 11, 1909, but some time afterward.

Finally,[25] on May 14, 1910, the confusion and uncertainty surrounding the whole affair were dispelled when Kerby, the stenographer—probably induced by the offer of a job from a large newspaper chain, that of E. W. Scripps, which desired the news—gave public testimony before the committee. He told how Assistant Attorney General Lawler, with Ballinger's aid, had written the letter exculpating Ballinger, which Taft had simply signed. The original memorandum for the letter had been burned; but Kerby had kept his stenographic notes and had them photographed.

The capital was in turmoil. It was felt, with not a little sense of shame, that the President and Attorney General Wickersham had acted hastily, without a real effort at inquiry, when Glavis

[24] The New York *Times*, Apr. 30, 1910.

[25] A long account of the Ballinger affair is given from the point of view of a defender of President Taft by Henry F. Pringle in *The Life and Times of William Howard Taft*, New York, 1939. It is based largely on the Taft Papers and information furnished by Mr. Wickersham. Yet Mr. Pringle, the authorized biographer, finds serious "errors" and "indiscretions" in the conduct of both the President and his Attorney General. My own account is based on a partial reading of the Hearings and Testimony before the Joint Committee of Congress Investigating the Department of the Interior, as well as published studies of the case, such as Miss Stahl's monograph; also upon conversations with Mr. Gifford Pinchot and Justice Louis D. Brandeis, retired. However, opinions and judgments offered here are my own.

came with his accusations. Ballinger and his aide had dictated Ballinger's own exoneration, and the whole affair was concealed and defended afterward, many assumed, either because real wrong-doing was at the bottom of it or because the Taft people were determined to undo the whole conservation program. In reality the members of the Taft administration had committed no un-lawful deed; but out of timidity and a sense of the weakness of their position, in the face of expected attacks, had been led into a series of subterfuges—especially, the "antedating" of the long Wickersham report—as a means of bolstering their case.

In Presidential circles consternation reigned as the scandal of the Ballinger exoneration gripped the country. On one day the White House declared that the allegations of the stenographer, Kerby, were "absolutely without foundation." But on the next, May 15, 1910, President Taft in a letter to Chairman Nelson of the Joint Committee of Investigation admitted the truth of Kerby's testimony. He admitted that he had told Lawler to write the letter exculpating Ballinger and firing Glavis. He admitted also that the subsequent report of Attorney General Wickersham had been "antedated." But this, Taft now alleged, was because he had heard much "oral" testimony in the week of September 6, 1909, and he and Wickersham had decided to set back the date of the completed report as of the time of the oral evidence heard when they were considering Glavis's charges. The "explanations" which Taft and Wickersham presented were considered disin-genuous, even by conservative newspapers, and did little to lessen the shock and disgust widely felt.[26] The country believed that Taft and Wickersham had engaged in rather clumsy-handed (even needless) dissimulations, and had been caught in the act by the unfeeling Mr. Brandeis.

Ballinger and his aides were not shown to be venal; they were only trying on legalistic grounds to "give away for nothing" cer-tain resources, the lands which, according to the government's de-clared policy, were to be reserved for the benefit of the people.

[26] The New York *Times*, May 15, 18, 1910.

Ballinger and his aides, as the Brandeis brief summed it up, not only would have discredited Pinchot and Garfield, but would have sacrificed the honest Glavis, thus perpetuating

in this country an act of injustice as great as that done Alfred Dreyfus in the Republic of France, and for very similar reasons. The reason here is that men in exalted station must be protected at all hazards, and if they cannot be protected by truth then suppression and lies must be resorted to.

With the sudden, absurd, unawaited outcome of the case, the ruinous libel suit against the magazine which had attacked the administration was dropped. The committee of Congress, made up chiefly of "regulars," which would normally have delayed its recommendations for a year or two, was pressed by its large Insurgent-Democratic minority to make a prompt report. The Standpat majority eventually gave its blessings to the Taft administration and to Ballinger. But the dissenters issued—at the height of an election campaign—a powerful minority report sharply criticizing the President and advising the censure and removal of Ballinger. Though Taft staunchly defended his Secretary of the Interior as the victim of a lying conspiracy, the latter resigned, pleading ill-health, some six months later. In any case the Cunningham and other claims which Glavis had styled as fraudulent were withdrawn by Walter Fisher, the admirable Secretary of the Interior who succeeded Ballinger.

The "Ballinger-Pinchot" case, coming upon the heels of the tariff controversy and the uprising against Speaker Cannon, was a culminating political disaster for the "Restoration" government. As the party that "betrayed conservation" the Republicans were slaughtered, electorally speaking, in the balloting of November, 1910. A strong Democratic majority occupied the Lower House, while enough Insurgents from a half dozen Western states that had broken away from party orthodoxy sat in the Senate to keep the Upper Chamber also hostile to the administration.

Theodore Roosevelt had returned in the late spring of 1910 to find the country aflame with political discontent and controversy.

The great sectional division of the 1890's which he had closed was opened again. The ex-President generally held himself at a distance from his successor in the White House. Though in the campaign of 1910 he endeavored to help his party and the President by some moderate stumping efforts, the results were disappointing. Beveridge, La Follette, and other Insurgents who made pilgrimages to Oyster Bay, left saying that Colonel Roosevelt, as he now preferred to be called, was "more progressive" than ever.[27]

For the ruling party, the prospects were exceedingly dark. Nelson Aldrich, the chief of the Standpatters, weary of it all, announced that he would not stand again for the Senate at the end of 1910. The opposition party, long out of power, saw large opportunities beckoning in 1912. Meanwhile, it was significant that shortly after the elections, in December, 1910, Senator La Follette with the aid of Louis D. Brandeis and others who had fought in the battle for conservation began to organize the dissident wing of the Republican party as the National Progressive Republican League.

[27] Bowers, *op. cit.*, pp. 312-313.

XI. "DOCTOR WILSON"

O NE FINE afternoon in September, 1910, two large, handsome Irishmen proceeded to the charming town of
Princeton, New Jersey, and knocked at the door of the
president of the University. They observed the beauty of the trees
that sheltered the old house; their eyes also took in the terraced
garden below, now in its late summer glory, that the wife of the
scholar had long tended. Ushered into the library of the master,
they viewed with not a little feeling of awe the rows upon rows
of books that lined the room to the ceiling.

One of the men was ex-Senator "Jim" Smith, for twenty years
New Jersey's Democratic boss, and the other was his son-in-law
and first lieutenant, "Jim" Nugent, the boss of Newark. Both were
simple, rough-hewn men of politics; but they were men of feeling
too, and while they waited shared together a sense of foreboding.

Smith finally said to his companion: "Can you imagine anyone
being damn fool enough to give this up for the heartaches of
politics?" [1]

The mission of the two political bosses was to confer with
"Doctor" Woodrow Wilson, as they called him, upon his forthcoming campaign for the Governorship of New Jersey. A short
distance in time beyond the November elections (whose favorable
outcome was firmly counted upon) lay the work of preparation for
the Democratic Presidential nomination, which was the real objective of the Doctor and his supporters. The man who a few minutes
later stood before them was even stranger to them than the place

[1] Kerney, *Political Education of Woodrow Wilson*, p. 62.

and the bold, far-flung plans. He was well on in middle age, bespectacled, gray-haired, and with a cool gray eye. His medium-sized figure was spare and firm; his face bony, deep-lined, with its wide mouth and sharp jaw, no thing of beauty or sweetness. It was a face which to Smith and Nugent seemed a mask of grim-mouthed, inscrutable expression, compounded of the asceticism of the preacher and the super-salesmanship of the college president. A type, in short, wholly unfamiliar to politicians.

Such was Dr. Woodrow Wilson at fifty-three, after a long and apparently distinguished academic career, as he prepared to leave the seemingly peaceful sanctuary of Princeton to launch himself upon the sea of troubles that was American local and national politics. What was worse, he knew pathetically little at first hand of practical politics; he knew what he had read in books, in his fine library. He was a self-confessed amateur, an innocent; and the two shrewd, successful men of affairs, who had eaten and drunk of practical politics since their childhood in the grimy north Jersey towns, scarcely knew where to begin with him.

How Woodrow Wilson came to be "discovered" late in life, how the Presidential crown was offered him, and how he wrestled for it, is an absorbing tale, not without picturesque contrasts and rich in lessons. Born in Staunton, Virginia, the son of a Presbyterian minister, he was of Scotch-Irish stock. Although the Wilsons and the Woodrows had not lived long in the South (his mother, Jessie Woodrow, migrated with her parents as a child of nine from Scotland), they were as proud as most Southerners. The boy grew up during the painful epoch of Reconstruction, and was one of those educated, but poor, Southerners who moved northward in search of opportunity. Yet if he was poorer than his classmates at Princeton, the minister's son was a fellow of strong ambitions and almost pretentiously intellectual tastes. After preparing for the bar, he had found his beginnings at this profession in Atlanta, Georgia, fruitless, and turned away from it with distaste to teaching. Slowly he advanced himself as a fellow at Johns Hopkins, then as a professor of government and history at several Northern colleges, finally at Princeton.

As a scholar, in his chosen field of political science, he had shown a certain promise when in 1885, scarcely thirty, he published his *Congressional Government*. It was a treatise essentially upon the divided authorities of our system of political "checks and balances," a piece of special pleading for the British system of concerted parliamentary leadership. At the height of the Gilded Age, and its crude taste, the young Wilson's studies had led him to admire English literature and political thought; Edmund Burke and the late Walter Bagehot, fastidious Tory apologists, were his chosen mentors. It is important to note that as early as 1885 he had preached unified executive leadership, rather than "divided" and "limited" government, with its cumbersome competitions of the three branches of the service, executive, judiciary, and legislative. In the 1880's and 1890's, Wilson believed, effective "leadership" would have overcome much of the turbulent party strife that weakened our government system; it would have placed emphasis upon programs and policies and removed it from patronage and spoils.

It was in this spirit that Wilson wrote voluminously on law, history, and politics in various magazines and learned journals; in the *North American Review*, the *Atlantic Monthly*. Indeed, he hoped for a long time to win distinction as a writer on public affairs, to have a career in literature. But when he searched his soul, as in those vivid early letters to his fiancée, he showed an honest awareness of his own limitations as a writer; his work was of secondary order. He felt himself temperamentally indisposed to the methodical labor of the secluded scholar, and realized in moments of self-knowledge that his real aspirations were for a role in public and administrative life.

Confined for long years to the study and the classroom, Wilson was a man who longed for a life of action, of struggle, and this to be passed before the eyes of the world. It was really because of his gifts as a lecturer that he rose steadily through the academic ranks. As a graceful phrase-maker and orator at university clubs and dinners of business men who donated funds to universities, he grew more eminent still. In those days he echoed habitually, in a manner pleasing to his listeners, the conventional sentiments they entertained upon public and educational questions.

With the retirement of Princeton's president in 1902, the professor of political science was chosen in his place, reaching a safe and honorable berth at middle age, as one of America's eminent men. But Dr. Wilson was to be denied a life of peace. Within two years he was embroiled in a kind of long drawn-out "village feud" at Princeton, over the administration and expansion of the graduate school. The factions of Graduate Dean West and Wilson fought unremittingly in a seven years' war; and their ill will assumed new forms when Wilson in a sudden, liberal move attempted to eliminate the expensive and fashionable eating clubs long favored by the students' fraternities. Those who had opposed Wilson's efforts to control the graduate school now opposed also his effort to "democratize" Princeton undergraduate social life. The trustees were divided into hostile factions; the university's rich patrons began to cut their endowments—a fatal blow. For years Wilson was the center of an internal storm of university politics, which it became increasingly difficult to hide from the public. In the end, the opposition became overwhelming; though Wilson was a tenacious fighter, the moneyed men among the trustees whom he had always courted, that is, a majority of them, led by the aged and stubborn Grover Cleveland, had turned thumbs down upon him. He was already in the position of a man who would soon be looking for a job, when one of his admirers, the irrepressible Colonel George B. McL. Harvey, hove upon the scene and offered him the chance for the job of President of the United States.

It was the hand of Harvey that was behind the mission of the New Jersey bosses, Smith and Nugent. Harvey, who was an honorary Colonel of the New Jersey militia, was one of the men of substance who had fallen under the spell of Wilson's public, or oratorical, personality. There was in Dr. Wilson at his best moments an evangelical earnestness, inherited perhaps from his Scotch Presbyterian ancestors, that rang forth powerfully in vigorous and happily turned (though often vague) speech. Now

Wilson's public speeches at club gatherings and banquets during the decade before 1910 had been consistently devoted to preaching political conservatism.

Turning against the popular Mr. Roosevelt, and calling to account Mr. Bryan, the entrenched leader of his own party, the president of Princeton would often strike out in defense of the leaders of great corporations who were nowadays so much maligned. For example, an occasion when he spoke on "The Authors and Signers of the Declaration of Independence," at Jamestown in 1907, was used by him to extol, in the name of Jefferson and the founding fathers, the principles of individual liberty which reformist politicians seemed at times to violate. At the time of the financial panic of 1907, Wilson attributed the disaster to the "hostile" legislation, the experiments in government control, especially of railroads, that had been introduced by the trust-busting President.

It was folly, he said, to regulate or punish corporations as such:

When we fine them, we merely take that much money out of their business—that is, out of the business of the country—and put it into the public treasury where there is generally a surplus and where it is likely to lie idle. When we dissolve them, we check and hamper legitimate undertakings and embarrass the business of the country much more than we should embarrass it were we to arrest locomotives and impound electric cars, the necessary vehicles of our intercourse. And all the while we know perfectly well that the iniquities we levy the fines for were conceived and executed by particular individuals who go unpunished. . . .[2]

Therefore, Wilson urged, *individuals* guilty of wrongdoing should be found out and punished, not *corporations*. His conservative hearers, who knew full well how much difficulty the government experienced in winning effective convictions under existing laws, were doubtless satisfied with such proposals that Wilson may have offered in all sincerity at the time. He could be equally fervent in attacking socialism; and his vigorous attacks upon labor unions which aspired to the closed shop—to his mind a

[2] *North American Review*, Sept., 1907.

cardinal sin against our constitutional liberties—were no less appreciated.

Even in his last days at Princeton, Wilson seemed chiefly concerned lest it should become impossible to dissociate the Democratic party, the party to which he had been traditionally attached, from its recent "errors and heresies": Bryanism, money inflation, government ownership of railroads, direct election of Senators. To one who proposed to him the formation of a new party of conservatives, he argued that he did not despair, for his part, of seeing the Democratic party drawn back to the "conservative principles which it once represented." [3]

Colonel Harvey, who had been enjoying Wilson's talk ever since 1902, when he had witnessed his inauguration as president of Princeton, was a most curious character who had all his life worshiped "the god in the machine" and longed to be that himself. As a young newspaper reporter for the New York *World* in the 1890's, he had had the good fortune to win the favor of those two precious "robber barons," W. C. Whitney and Thomas Fortune Ryan, for whom he acted as a confidential agent. Living across the river in New Jersey, he served as liaison officer between the New Jersey politicians and the New York financiers in a series of diplomatic negotiations that concerned the franchises of future traction and public-utility companies. It was Harvey, for instance, who had first brought together Whitney and Ryan, the angels of the Democratic party, and Senator "Jim" Smith, leader of the New Jersey Democrats. After ten years of this kind of work, while still a comparatively young man, George Harvey had himself amassed a sizable fortune and was financially independent for life. Through the friendly interest of J. P. Morgan, to whom also he had sometimes been of service, he was made the head of the old publishing concern of Harper and Brothers, then undergoing reorganization; in his own right he later bought and edited the famous old *North American Review;* he was also the publisher

[3] Baker, *Wilson,* Vol. III, p. 185.

of the somewhat declining *Harper's Weekly*.[4] Now, from his high post in the publishing world, Colonel Harvey was able to indulge his active interest in public affairs: he gave select dinner parties, brought men of note together, attended and spoke at public functions himself as often as possible, and strove in every possible way to become an "influence" in his own right.

In those days of financial scandal, trust busting, and muckraking, the vigor and intelligence of the exponents of radical reform provided sore problems for conservative publicists such as Harvey. It is in this light that Harvey's pleasure in Dr. Wilson may be best understood. Harvey was utterly convinced that in the eloquent Princeton scholar he had found, so to speak, an inspirational conservative of rare power. And the conservative interests now realized that they needed effective ideologues; this was in itself a sign of the higher political culture of the times. There was no mere crude talk of the Full Dinner Pail when the head of Princeton spoke. "That man could win the people," Harvey remarked. He followed and cultivated him, obsessed by the notion that Dr. Wilson might be a distinguished Presidential possibility, that he might lead the nation out of the wilderness of radical reform, while Harvey would be his Warwick, nay, his Mark Hanna. Taking the plunge, on February 3, 1906, at a dinner arranged in honor of Wilson at the Lotos Club in New York, Harvey made his surprising speech offering Wilson as the Democratic candidate for the Presidency of the United States in 1908. It was a moment when the Democratic party, after its 1904 fiasco, showed every sign of returning to the control of the Bryanites. Harvey's personal nomination of Woodrow Wilson "of Virginia and New Jersey" as a contrast to the political idols of the day, Roosevelt and Bryan, was intended to catch the public eye, which it did. The people present at the banquet, the sort who gave their money to party chests, were accustomed to investing in a professional politician. But Harvey proposed that our public life now needed a leader of education, a man of culture and personal distinction,

---

[4] Johnson, *Harvey*, pp. 71-72.

who, though he clung to old traditions, promised to elevate the tone and methods of our politics.

No one would think for a moment of criticizing the general reformation of the human race by Executive decree, but it is becoming increasingly evident that that great work will soon be accomplished. When that time shall have been reached, the country will need at least *a short breathing spell* for what the physicians term perfect rest. That day, now not far distant, will call for a man combining the activities of the present with the sobering influences of the past.[5]

After the Lotos Club demonstration, to which Wilson responded with modesty and reserve, Harvey continued to pursue his hobby of giving publicity to Wilson as a Presidential possibility. Favorable mention of him and articles upon his achievements appeared in the magazines that Harvey controlled, or in friendly newspapers such as the *World*. So much quiet interest was aroused in high circles that one day in March, 1907, Wilson was actually induced to come to New York for "inspection" by a group of newspaper publishers, corporation lawyers, and financiers.

It was at a private dining room of Delmonico's restaurant that the inspection was held; the notables present who catechized Dr. Wilson including Thomas Fortune Ryan; F. L. Stetson, counsel for J. P. Morgan; and Laffan, editor of the New York *Sun*, which also was said to be closely related to the House of Morgan at that time.

"Mr. Wilson talked freely and alluringly to conservative sentiment as if he were conscious of the inspection he was undergoing."[6] This same group had catechized Judge Alton Parker before he was accepted for the Presidential nomination in 1904. Wilson actually prepared and sent his political credo to be studied by Laffan, the editor of the New York *Sun*, and his friends; in the credo he "expressed vigorously his opposition to the tendency of the times to regulate business by governmental commissions."[7]

[5] *Ibid.*, pp. 111-112.
[6] E. P. Mitchell, *Memoirs of an Editor*, pp. 387-388.
[7] Baker, *op. cit.*, Vol. III, p. 35.

Yet, for the moment, nothing came of these pourparlers. Wilson continued to commend himself to the conservative classes by sallies at the Rooseveltians, sometimes in pointed and witty remarks.

"We have heat enough; what we want is light," he said in one public address early in 1909. ". . . Anybody can cry a nation awake to the necessities of reform, but who shall frame the reform but a man who is cool . . . ?" [8] Conservative intellectuals who had been close to the Wall Street group of Whitney and Ryan, which had dominated the Eastern Democracy in Cleveland's time, continued to think well of Wilson as a latter-day Jeffersonian who might halt the centralizing tendency in government where it affected corporate enterprise. Walter H. Page, the head of Doubleday, Page, and Company, himself a Southerner and an old acquaintance of Wilson's, embodied these views fully when he wrote in a letter at the time that Wilson was

. . . a rightminded man of a safe and conservative political faith. He would not have the government own the railroads; he would not stir up discontent . . . he does not speak the language either of Utopia or riot. . . . If the Democratic party should come to its senses again and assert its old doctrines and take on its old dignity, and seek real leadership (and pray Heaven it may!), leaving its Bryans and its Hearsts alone, this suggestion of President Wilson is logical, sound, dignified and decent.[9]

But, alas, he was "not a politician." Boss Smith of New Jersey thought of him at first as a "Presbyterian priest." When Harvey engineered a scheme by which Wilson was to be offered the Democratic nomination for the United States Senate—purely honorary, since the Democrats were then a small minority in the New Jersey Legislature—the affair, even as a publicity enterprise, proved to be an abortion.

But early in 1910, when the Ballinger-Pinchot case raged in Washington and the signs of Republican defeat were on every

[8] *Public Papers*, Chicago, Feb. 12, 1909, Vol. II, p. 100.
[9] Hendrick, *Walter H. Page*, Vol. III, pp. 12-13.

hand, the inner-circle Democrats busied themselves with plans for 1912. Terror of Bryan's resurgence gripped the Easterners; while some of them began to labor on behalf of the veterans, Congressmen Champ Clark of Missouri and Oscar Underwood of Alabama, Harvey redoubled his efforts to advance Wilson as a candidate for the party nomination. From January, 1910, he pursued Boss Smith with his scheme. Finally, at another private conference at Delmonico's between Smith and Harvey, the New Jersey boss was brought to see a great light. His own position in the chess game of New Jersey politics was weak at the moment; the Democratic organization in New Jersey was under heavy attack and badly needed a victory. To be sure, the choice of a college president was a most unpleasant innovation. But would he not be suitable for these strange times? Known to be honest and distinguished, Dr. Wilson as candidate for the governorship would deflect the arrows of reformers, and perhaps prevent a liberal uprising threatening in the Democratic organization itself. The Republicans, it was known, planned to run a candidate who would be both liberal and popular. Perhaps Wilson would produce the needed victory? His high Wall Street connections, furthermore, assured an abundance of campaign funds. The old boss, with some misgivings, accepted Wilson as candidate for Governor. He agreed to "go the whole hog"; and to put the best face upon the matter he would even publicly withdraw from the race for the Senatorship, lest it be said that Dr. Wilson was being used as a respectable "front" to cover his scheme to return to the United States Senate.

Then, as Harvey himself related, he went to Wilson and told him that he would handle the matter of the gubernatorial nomination so that it "shall be tendered to you on a silver platter, without you turning a hand to obtain it, and without any requirement or suggestion of any pledge whatsoever. . . ."[10] Would Wilson, then, accept? Wilson, strongly tempted to escape from the truly unstable ground he held at Princeton, yet fearing also the pitfalls of public life, promised his "very serious consideration." That is,

[10] W. O. Inglis in *Collier's Weekly*, Oct. 7, 1916.

he gave a cautious, qualified approval to Harvey's effort, as before.

In the spring of 1910, Wilson was deeply embroiled in his conflict with the Princeton trustees. In April he made speeches in New York and at Pittsburgh before gatherings of Princeton alumni, in which he defended his plan to eliminate the exclusive eating clubs in his college. At the same time he continued to offer himself as a possible new leader in public life, as a more satisfactory alternative than the current political prophets. In a speech at Chicago before the Princeton Club, at this time, he said in a characteristic passage:

When will leaders arise? When will men stop their questionings and recognize a leader when he rises? When will they gather to his standard and say, "We no longer question; we believe you; lead on, for we are behind you."

America needs men of that sort. Will you encourage them? Will you make your universities such places as can produce them?

Then, in a sentence that is very significant, when we take into account the political fears rampant among the class typified by Princeton alumni, he added:

. . . *You are your own saviours, and when you have come to the determination to save yourselves you will know your leader the moment you meet him, for you will know if he is of your sort and of your purpose.*[11]

In these words Wilson breathes his more or less conscious, more or less secret, political aspirations. The inducements he offers are expressed in cryptic terms; but they are there.

Meanwhile Harvey continued to play a lively little Mephistopheles in tortoise-shell glasses who knew how to tempt the hesitant Dr. Wilson. Rumors were circulated of Wilson's candidacy; and a claque organized by Harvey and Smith in April of 1910 saluted Wilson, on one public occasion, as "our next governor." At a number of later conferences between Smith and friends of Wilson, Wilson was prodded into giving his definite

---

[11] Speech, Chicago, May 12, 1910; italics mine.

consent, and the grounds for an agreement were marked out. In return for the organization support he promised Jim Smith that he would not set about "fighting and breaking down the Democratic organization and replacing it with one of [his] own." These were conditions similar to those the young Theodore Roosevelt had made with boss Platt in New York. Wilson, however, stipulated clearly that the existing Democratic organization machine was to give thorough support of "such policies as would re-establish the reputation of the State and the credit of the Democratic party. . . ." [12] The Big Fellow was now satisfied with this minimal agreement, and ready to work for Wilson's nomination. Time was short; there were other "deserving Democrats," who must be steam-rollered out of the way; and Wilson, who still hesitated before the final plunge, was not surely collared until June 26, 1910, when he was literally hustled off to a dinner and conference at Harvey's country house. Jim Smith and "Marse" Henry Watterson, the Kentucky editor and politician, were present with Harvey when Wilson gave his consent. At a second gathering, soon afterward, in the early days of July, Wilson met a number of New Jersey Democratic leaders, among them Richard V. Lindabury, counsel for the United States Steel Corporation, which as a local concern was an interested party. It was then that Wilson accepted his destiny, and also made his terms, which according to Mr. Lindabury involved no political pledges or obligations.[13]

Smith and his lieutenants now went to work in earnest to win the needed delegates and also to "get the liquor interests behind the Doctor . . . ," as Boss Smith nicely phrased it. What they did, the Doctor was wholly ignorant of, since he believed, as he wrote at the time to one of the Princeton trustees, that other candidates stood ready to withdraw gladly in his favor, and that he was to receive the gubernatorial nomination "by acclamation." [14]

[12] Baker, *op. cit.*, Vol. III, pp. 49-53.
[13] Kerney, *op. cit.*, p. 46.
[14] Baker, *op. cit.*, Vol. III, p. 63; Vol. III, p. 57.

Jim Smith came near to nervous prostration as a result of his struggle to hold the votes of the delegates to the party convention in line. There were three other sons of New Jersey who had long been held deserving of the Governor's office, and who were sworn definitely to the most liberal reforms. It was most difficult to persuade the "boys" that an unusually brazen fraud was not being perpetrated upon them in the shape of the college professor, a hated outsider, who according to dark rumors was being foisted upon them as the "Wall Street candidate." At the Trenton convention one of the local statesmen brought the gathering into a state of frenzy by describing, in a fierce harangue, the corrupt methods used by Smith and Nugent to dragoon a majority of the delegates into the Wilson column. An anti-machine wing, headed by certain young Democrats, aired the record of Dr. Wilson as an enemy of union labor. Up to the last hour, Jim Smith and Harvey feared the loss of forty or fifty votes, which would have been fatal. Yet, despite scenes of brawling uproar that marked this as one of the roughest and dirtiest conventions in years, Smith as so often before succeeded in quelling his opponents by main force. By arrangement, the Doctor was waiting outside of the convention hall, and word was sent to him now that he might come and make his acceptance speech in person.

Now came one of the surprises of the affair. He stepped before the convention, clad in golf costume, looking jaunty and fresh. The party delegates were tired and angry at themselves; they were a crowd of plain "political workers" from the counties, and some of them looked at the Doctor with real distaste. As one onlooker said, his face had the appearance of a man who had "taken a battering from life and . . . given it something of a battering in return." But soon, hitting his stride, Wilson rose splendidly to the occasion and thrilled the convention by the "punch" of his speech.[15]

He thanked the delegates very simply for having conferred upon him the honor of the nomination, and added in most forth-

[15] Kerney, *op. cit.*, p. 55.

right language and with all possible solemnity that he owed his nomination to them, "the representatives of the people," and not to any leader or combination of leaders. The weary conspirators Harvey and Smith could hardly keep their faces straight; and the applause at the beginning was feeble, half-hearted, as if the delegates were incredulous. Was Wilson ignorant, or audacious?

He spoke with a note of independence that seemed needlessly brusque, in a voice that rang musically through the large Trenton House. "I did not seek this nomination," he cried. It had come to him unsolicited; he would enter upon his duties as Governor, if elected, "with absolutely no pledges of any kind" to prevent him from serving all the people. There was to be no mere playing of politics, and no demagogy, cried the "schoolmaster in politics." "The time when you can . . . fool the people has gone by; now it is a case of put up or shut up. . . ." Now cheers from the progressive wing that had opposed his nomination began to resound; Wilson went on to sketch the "renaissance of public spirit, a reawakening of sober public opinion, a revival of the power of the people. . . . We shall serve justice and candor and all the things that make for right," he wound up in a glowing peroration.[16]

The Doctor in short gave a surprising and bold performance that touched the best impulses of the party men. If he were going to be a mere "stool-pigeon for the Interests," as some had charged, then this was the wrong way to begin the business. The Jersey men began to suspect that by some chance a leader had been found who had a backbone under his coat. They applauded him; they followed him.

"His words ring true" was an impression often conveyed in the newspapers that reported the nomination proceedings.[17]

From the very outset Wilson showed resolution and initiative. He knew that he had been called by interests that kept themselves in the background. He may not have known definitely why he was called, or what ulterior purposes he was expected to serve. But he

[16] Tumulty, *Wilson*, p. 21.
[17] Newark *Evening News*, Sept. 17, 1910.

made it clear that they must take him as he was, for better or worse. He was bound to no secret pledges to anyone; his hands were free. Jumping into his new role, bolder, more extroverted than he had ever before been in his academic offices, Wilson soon showed a force of character, a tenacity in negotiation, that troubled the devoted schemer Harvey and the crafty Jim Smith.

He was an innocent in politics. Yet, as he himself said on several occasions, university politics, with its own devious wire-pulling, with its terrible conspiracies and jealousies, was a hard school; by comparison, the Machiavellis of practical politics seemed easy to read. On the other hand the dialectics of Wilson, in conference or negotiation, were hard for the practical politicians to cope with.

On the occasion of that September day when Smith and Nugent called at Princeton, the agenda for the moment included consideration of the claims of local party leaders representing Wilson's home county of Mercer. Wilson had always kept aloof from local politics; he had scarcely ever voted in a local election, and up to 1910 barely read New Jersey newspapers, since those of New York City were easily available. But now, as related by James Kerney, publisher of the Trenton *Times*, the bosses coached Wilson in the diplomacy required for treating with the local leaders and district captains, informing him of their individual hopes and grievances. With an aptitude for affairs natural to him, Wilson quickly grasped what was required.

When the Mercer County leaders had in turn been formally presented by Nugent and had taken seats in the library, Wilson proceeded to discuss local political affairs as if they were the one thing in all the world in which he had been taking interest. He called the various leaders by name and . . . made them feel very much at home.[18]

2

Dr. Wilson's "political education" proceeded at tremendous speed and was concentrated within a very brief space of time: less

[18] Kerney, *op. cit.*, pp. 63-64.

than a year after his nomination for the Governorship of New Jersey, he was launched in the race for the Presidential nomination. Within this time his ideas underwent a very rapid change, and this in itself has given rise to much speculation.

What were Wilson's beliefs? What was his faith? In his writings one searches in vain for marks of intellectual originality. He was accustomed to trace his political doctrines to the influence of Jefferson; but his admiration for the British system of parliamentary leadership, his emphasis upon leadership in government rather than upon limitations of it, belie his Jeffersonism. He was to show no inhibitions whatsoever in adapting himself to the most centralized and "Hamiltonian" tactics.

The real mystery of Wilson, as John Chamberlain has said in his *Farewell to Reform*, is when, and where, and why, he became a Democrat. Frederic C. Howe, who studied under him at Johns Hopkins in the 'nineties, thought he believed essentially in "government by *noblesse oblige*." He thought little of economics, and gave his students glimpses of a glorious ruling caste, upholding the tradition of the Magna Charta, while its power politics were concealed from view.[19] He admired the way of life of the upperclass English leaders, the Arthur Balfours or the Gladstones—and Gladstone too had undergone a famous "conversion" to liberalism. A Calvinist at heart, Wilson believed—as Walter Lippmann remarked—that the world could be set right by the force of human conscience.

In short, there is an evangelical strain in the Wilson who "made political office his pulpit," and there is his heritage of Virginia traditions—absorbed at the law school of the University of Virginia. But it is the tradition of the great Virginians who, while preaching democracy, created more effectively than Hamilton a regime of talent and wealth. Yet signs of some definite, logical body of principles—such as we perceive in Lincoln—are wanting in Wilson. He was to show no abiding loyalty to a conservative's faith, no lasting affinity for the Cobdenism he had sometimes

[19] Chamberlain, *Farewell to Reform*, pp. 283-284.

espoused. Ideas, truths, faiths, systems were not ends for him, but materials for an *ideology*. In the last analysis he triumphed as a dialectician in practical politics. His mind absorbed ideas rapidly from others and threw them into action; his quickness of thought strongly impressed men of more original mental powers, such as Louis D. Brandeis. Whatever successes he had enjoyed, he owed to his mental equipment—rather than to family connections or wealth—and he was proudly conscious of his own intelligence, and inclined to be a little intolerant or impatient of others' stupidity.

He had few or in fact no permanent friendships; yet he had great power over men, to whom he knew how to communicate, by his eloquence of language, something of the cold fire in him, his unlimited ambitions, his intense resolution. He seemed to "love man at a distance," as it was said of Rousseau; and his hopes seem to have been largely self-centered. It might have served as a warning that his main troubles at Princeton were traceable to his habitual quest of augmented power, as in the case of the struggle for control of the graduate school—though in this his efforts may have been justifiable. In the end he had been defeated by the heavy battalions of money on the other side.

But upon emerging from Princeton's neo-Gothic walls, hurled suddenly into the unfamiliar arena of partisan politics, Dr. Wilson found that the components of power were different from those of the schoolman's world. Parties and their organizations had existed long, until they had become traditional. Power, as he saw full well, lay first of all in the hands of those who led the machines that gathered in the voters or the nominating delegates, and controlled the offices of the government. Thus Wilson's first task had been to satisfy boss Smith in some manner. Wilson had written formerly of men such as Smith: "They are the political bosses and managers whom the people obey and affect to despise. It is unjust to despise them." But once in office, extremely conscious of the power—especially the patronage power—he wielded, Wilson would grow far less manageable.[20]

[20] Smith in a fairly illiterate and furious letter, which he wrote after his rupture with Wilson, told Senator Bailey of Texas, August 30, 1911, that Wilson

Beyond the boss and his henchmen there lay another power, that of the moneyed interests that subsidized party organizations. Through Harvey, Wilson had indirect access to these people. Also, the rich Princeton trustees who had supported him, Cleveland Dodge, the copper magnate, and the younger Cyrus McCormick, T. D. Jones, and others, came forward to sponsor his political career.

Yet the party bureaucracy and the moneyed patrons were not the whole story (least of all to Wilson), and especially now in a time when popular discontent ran so strong. As a third component of power, public opinion even in darkest New Jersey, the "mother of trusts," had to be studied and mastered. To this task Dr. Wilson gave himself with an unusually open mind; its problems struck him at once as very different from those he had seen as a scholar.

On certain issues he had been even more conservative than the Wall Street wire-puller, Harvey. A few weeks before the nominating convention at Trenton, when the two men discussed the party platform, Harvey showed Wilson a draft of a resolution in favor of the direct or popular election of Senators. "I don't believe in that," said Wilson. "Neither do I," said Harvey, "and I'll strike it out if possible; but I'm very much afraid the convention will insist upon leaving it in." [21] There were times when even the Harveys and Smiths seemed to yield to the popular will.

As he moved slowly into the hurly-burly of a state campaign,

". . . Is one of the most convincing talkers that you ever listened to, and as our mutual friend Mayor MacLellan informed me two days after the election, is the 'king of liars,' as he termed him. That makes a powerful combination. . . . He has beyond question destructed the Democratic party of this State. . . .

"You will no doubt wonder why I ever nominated him, and then financed him. . . . He convinced me that he would be the most loyal man to me and the organization in the State, that I ever had anything to do with in politics, and that he would do nothing but build us up, and that if he was elected governor, he believed he could be nominated for the presidency."

Smith and his colleagues had seen to it in former years that "backward" New Jersey had very little of the merit system. The Governor had 500 offices to fill, and thus could easily have a large following of his own. (S. Acheson, *"Joe" Bailey*, pp. 303-304.)

[21] Johnson, *Harvey*, p. 151.

Wilson felt the force of public opinion agitated, aroused, on many issues such as that of the direct election of Senators. He felt this force in the breath of the crowds he addressed. The old terms and slogans he had used yesterday before the banquets of Princeton alumni fitted poorly. It needed then some mental sleight of hand, no little dialectical skill—which Wilson always possessed—to turn himself overnight from the man who was reported ready to save the Democrats from Bryan, government ownership, and other Populist notions, to one who would proclaim himself a progressive, who was willing and ready to lead the masses toward the promised land of the New Freedom.

Among the retinue provided the candidate by Smith and Nugent were a few progressive, or anti-machine, Democrats, such as the Trenton publisher James Kerney, the ardently liberal journalist William St. John, and Joseph Tumulty, the youthful Jersey City lawyer and assemblyman. These men warned the ignorant Wilson of the intense discontent rampant among the people, a discontent which he, unwittingly, had been chosen to face. Compared with New York, then under the enlightened Hughes, New Jersey and her citizens seemed left in outer darkness under the shadow of the railroads (especially the Pennsylvania) and the power company, which apparently controlled both parties. Though the public was long weary of Republican rule these last seventeen years, the Democratic leaders by recent maneuvers had aroused even greater disgust, and boss Smith especially had been singled out for his sorry record. One of the greatest grievances was the passenger rate for commutation fares, which the Pennsylvania Railroad had lately increased by 20 per cent while the politicians of both parties remained silent. Wilson was warned that he would be received by the people as a kind of respectable "decoy duck" for the old race-track and gambling crowd in politics. Meanwhile, his opponent, Vivian M. Lewis,[22] owing to an overnight conversion in the Republican party, proved to be an uncommonly independent candi-

---

[22] Kerney, *op. cit.*, p. 70.

date, who made the most forthright pledges of popular relief. Tumulty, the charming young Irishman who soon afterward became Wilson's private secretary, told Wilson frankly that his speeches lacked definiteness, that he was evading the long pent-up issues of the day, such as the regulation of public utilities and the passage of an employers' liability act. Both parties for years had been delaying the enactment of such measures into law, measures that most large states now boasted. Wilson "listened with keen attention," and evidently thought hard. Soon the candidate "struck his gait and astonished me," relates Tumulty, "and all New Jersey with the vigour, frankness and lucidity of his speeches. . . . No campaign in years in New Jersey had roused such universal interest." [23]

By all accounts, Wilson dropped many of his favorite rhetorical devices and employed a plainer, more vivid speaking style suited to the rough and tumble of a state campaign. The results were remarkable. The local audiences could not recall when they had heard more interesting and pertinent political talk. Wilson promised plainly that the Democratic party would be "reorganized"; he insisted that New Jersey was upon "the threshold of a new era." He sang now the praises of the common people, to whom he had given so little attention before.

When I look back at the processes of history, when I look back at the genesis of America, I see this written over every page, that the nations are renewed from the bottom, not from the top; that the genius which springs up from the ranks of unknown men is the genius which renews the youth and the energy of the people. . . .

Then at times he would close with one of his old-time perorations, which were passable imitations of the manner of Daniel Webster:

. . . As the tasks multiply, and the days come when all will seem confusion and dismay, we may lift up our eyes to the hills out of these dark valleys where the crags of special privilege overshadow and darken

[23] Tumulty, *Wilson*, pp. 29-31.

our path, to where the sun gleams through the great passage in the broken cliffs, the sun of God, the sun meant to regenerate men, the sun meant to liberate them from their passion and despair and to lift us to those uplands which are the promised land of every man who desires liberty and achievement.[24]

An unexpected crisis arose during the late stages of the campaign. In reply to charges that he was an impractical schoolmaster, Wilson had issued a challenge to any Republican representative to meet him in public debate upon the affairs of New Jersey. He expressed his disapproval of the methods used by both of the old party machines which formed, as he said, "an illegitimate and abominable partnership between business and politics." At one point he exclaimed bluntly that he did not want anyone to vote for him who believed that he would "listen to a political boss." Smith, sitting on the platform near by and hearing such statements, was seen to smile complacently and was heard to remark that it was "wonderful campaign stuff."[25]

Early in October an answer to Wilson's challenge arrived from the Republican side. George L. Record, a lawyer residing in Montclair, sent word that he was eager to debate with Dr. Wilson in order to learn definitely whether or not he meant to be the tool of the Democratic bosses. Wilson was warned that Mr. Record, a member of the Legislature, might prove a most dangerous adversary; he was a radical reformer, brilliant and most widely informed on current public issues; in short, he was scarcely a proper or "regular" Republican spokesman.

There was a delay in hostilities. Record's challenge was widely spoken of as creating a predicament for the Doctor; and Wilson, who heartily disliked being charged with want of fighting spirit, communed with himself for a week. At length he wrote Record suggesting an exchange of public letters discussing all issues in full and explicit detail, to be published in the New Jersey newspapers.

On October 17, 1910, about three weeks before Election Day,

[24] Tumulty, *Wilson*, p. 33.
[25] Kerney, *op. cit.*, p. 71.

Record's questions came, arranged as nineteen "points," each of them calculated to pin down the candidate upon the most delicate problems. Wilson's advisers were frightened by the "red-hot" issues aroused, such as those of workmen's compensation, public-utility control, and school reform. But Wilson, ignoring his advisers, prepared his own replies, which were published together with Record's questions. Wilson's decision was not to run away from Record. Boldly he cast off the ideas of financial, political, and labor affairs that he had formerly absorbed from the trustees of Princeton. He became uninhibited in late middle age, discovering to himself and to others the qualities of pride and audacity that few men had glimpsed in those cold pince-nez. As he had been wont formerly to appeal energetically to the rich corporation magnates for his "Greater Princeton" campaigns, so now he appealed to the masses of people as a resolute reformer and liberal. It was at this time that he came to the resolution, as he told one of his strong supporters, Oswald Garrison Villard, the publisher of the New York *Evening Post,* that the country needed "a modified Rooseveltism." The "new" emancipated Woodrow Wilson was written large in the public epistolary debate with George Record:

Record: Do you admit that the boss system exists as I have described it? If so, how do you propose to abolish it?

Wilson: Of course I admit it. Its existence is notorious . . . I hate it as thoroughly as I understand it. You are quite right in saying that the system is bi-partisan; that it constitutes the most dangerous condition in the public life of our State and Nation today; and that it has virtually, for the time being, destroyed representative government and in its place set up a government of privilege. I would propose to abolish it by the reforms suggested in the Democratic platform, by the election to office of men who will refuse to submit to it, and who will lend all their energies to break it up by pitiless publicity. . . .

Record: Will you join me in denouncing the Democratic "overlords" as parties to a political boss system?

Wilson: Certainly I will join you or anyone else in denouncing and fighting any and every one, of either party, who attempts such outrages against the government and public morality.

Record had sought to "corner" Wilson by referring to the latter's condemnation of the old Republican bosses, Senators Kean, Murphy, and Baird. Wherein did these men "differ from such Democratic leaders as Smith, Nugent and Davis" who supported Wilson's campaign?

Wilson's bold answer was that the Republican bosses were now in control of the state and must be put out; whereas the Democratic bosses *"are not and cannot be* [in control] *if the present Democrat ticket is elected."* [26] Wilson would serve as "the chosen leader of [his] party and the direct representative of the whole people. . . ." Then he rushed on to say:

You wish to know what my relations would be with the Democrats whose power and influence you fear, should I be elected Governor. . . . If elected I shall not, either in the matter of appointments to office or assent to legislation, or in shaping any part of the policy of my administration, submit to the dictation of any person or persons, special interest or organization. I will always welcome advice and suggestions from any citizen whether boss, leader, organization man, or plain citizen . . . but all suggestions and all advice will be considered on their merits, and no additional weight will be given to any man's advice because of his exercising, or supposing that he exercises, some sort of political influence or control. *I should deem myself forever disgraced should I in even the slightest degree co-operate in any such system or any such transactions as you describe in your characterization of the "boss" system.* I regard myself as pledged to the regeneration of the Democratic party which I have forecast above.

The New Jersey newspapers everywhere remarked how fully and fairly the Democratic candidate had answered Record. ". . . Woodrow Wilson," it was said, "does not appear to have shuffled, evaded or ignored a single issue." [27] Jim Smith may have felt a chill of apprehension and promised himself that Dr. Wilson would "hear plenty" after Election Day. But Record whistled with surprise; he expressed satisfaction with the answers given him, and indicated that he would probably now vote for Wilson.

[26] Italics mine.
[27] Newark *Evening News,* Oct. 25, 1910.

Not long afterward, the brilliant young lawyer who was a friend of Lincoln Steffens, Judge Ben Lindsey, Brand Whitlock, and other reformers became a valuable member of Wilson's Kitchen Cabinet at Trenton.

The effect of the debate, conducted upon so high a plane, upon the New Jersey citizens was electric. They felt Wilson's words could not be unsaid. Even in small towns, the people came out in great crowds to see and cheer him during the last two weeks of the campaign. They gave enthusiastic testimonials of their faith in his leadership, in his independence, which did not fail to move his heart. His speeches of his "new phase" assumed a style of simplicity, clarity, and earnestness that his earlier papers had too often lacked; they were easily the most distinguished expressions of their kind. Even the hardened politicians were astonished at the completeness with which the new leader conquered the old Republican stronghold of New Jersey, carrying over to his cause all the "doubtful" voters and the Progressive Republicans. In 1908 a majority of 80,000 had been given to Taft as Presidential candidate; but in 1910 a Democratic majority of nearly 50,000 was won by Wilson and a Democratic Legislature swept into office. Woodrow Wilson's spectacular victory made him nationally famous overnight. The glowing words in which he called the people to join his enterprise of "regeneration" and reform were cited far and wide; they gave to the New Jersey contest a prophetic significance similar to that which attached to the great Lincoln-Douglas debates in Illinois a half century earlier. Wilson too spoke of the "House of Democracy divided against itself." In his final speech he had said:

We have begun a fight that, it may be, will take many a generation to complete, the fight against privilege; but you know that men are not put into this world to go the path of ease. . . . All through the centuries there has been this slow, painful struggle forward, forward. . . . America has undertaken to lead the way; America has undertaken to be the haven of hope, the opportunity for all men.

3

In tune with the political "revolution" that was sweeping the country, New Jersey in 1910 had adopted for the first time the system of Preferential Primaries to indicate the popular choice for the United States Senator. Instead of having the Legislature name the Senator, as before, in "Room 100" of the Trenton House, its majority party was to abide by the primary vote. Long before it was grasped that Wilson would carry in his wake a majority of the local legislative elections, the nomination for the Senate, without serious resistance on the part of Smith's faction, had gone to a certain James Martine, of Plainfield, who was something of a Bryan follower. But in the late stages of the election campaign rumor held that Jim Smith had reconsidered the Senate primary business, did not regard it as binding, and would seek to return to Washington after all.

Wilson had chosen to ignore the rumors before Election Day. But soon afterward the Big Fellow made his candidacy for the Senate public; the experiment of the Preferential Primary was said to have no serious weight; and Mr. Martine was labeled as "unfit," "inexperienced," and "a silly old man." At once there was a raging controversy, Martine's friends and the younger, progressive element in the Democratic party throwing themselves into the fray with fierce protests at the betrayal of the popular mandate.

The Governor-elect waited silently. The prudent, the "constitutional" course would be to remain neutral, and leave the issue to the Legislature, his conservative advisers at Princeton told him. After Harvey, Wilson was most indebted to Jim Smith for his nomination. He was a "fine fellow," as everyone knew, and longed to return to the Senate, which he had left under a cloud engendered by his former close relations with the exceedingly corrupt sugar trust. If Wilson led the fight against him, it would split the party and endanger the whole ambitious law-making program he had in view.

But the liberals, Kerney, St. John, and Tumulty, besieged Wilson to lead the people in this fight. He had promised that he would act as Governor in the interests of all the people. Many politicians had said that before. But now was the time to see to it that a beginning was made with the popular election of Senators. Here, in fine, was "a clear issue of good faith and observance of party pledges," St. John told him. St. John, who believed that Woodrow Wilson was a great leader in the making and "the most promising figure the genuine progressives ever had," never desisted in his pleas.[28] They were rivaled by those of Tumulty, whom Wilson in his perplexity suddenly visited at his Jersey City law office on November 25, 1910. Tumulty argued that the people were "yearning for leadership" which Wilson had promised to give them. They would turn to another if he faltered at the very beginning. The affair was being widely discussed not only in New Jersey but beyond her borders, in New York and Philadelphia. If Dr. Wilson could make a bold stroke, it would be the first step to the higher calling he sought.

The Governor-elect, however, asked only in a cool, noncommittal voice, and with his usual granite expression, whether Tumulty thought "we could win the fight in case he should decide to enter it." The reply was that the machine was perhaps not more solid than papier-mâché; a hard blow might cause it to fall apart.[29]

In the three weeks that followed the election, Wilson was undecided, though he told George Harvey, his backer, of his belief that the election mandate condemned Smith and his methods. Looking beyond the state boundaries, Wilson perceived the radical tide, and noted that Theodore Roosevelt, now "returned from Elba," also swam upon it. The example and the menace of Roosevelt were ever in back of his mind. Two months before, Roosevelt in his speech at Osawatomie, Kansas, had alarmed the whole country by his announced conversion to a whole series of radical doctrines. Wilson concluded his letter to Harvey with the warning

[28] Kerney, *op. cit.*, p. 80.
[29] Tumulty, *op. cit.*, pp. 54-55.

that if the independent voters who had supported him were disillusioned, they would "surely turn again in desperation to Mr. Roosevelt. . . ."[30]

In December, Wilson's mind was made up. He called upon Smith and in the most courteous terms urged him to withdraw from the Senatorial race. He received only a firm refusal; Smith hoped that the Governor would make only a perfunctory opposition "for the record." Wilson sounded out certain of the powerful city bosses, but found they would not play with him. He then moved energetically, by holding several large conferences, to rally influential members of the Legislature, local leaders, and newspaper editors to his side. He felt his position growing perilous.

On December 9, 1910, he struck hard at the adversary in a manner that Theodore Roosevelt himself could not have bettered, releasing to the press his manifesto in support of Martine and condemnation of Smith's candidacy. Not only New Jersey but the nation heard of "Woodrow Wilson's Challenge to the Bosses." Once more he had written a clear and splendid public paper, stating his position simply and well, and bringing a fresh spirit into New Jersey's sickly political affairs by his whole-hearted action.

The question of who should be chosen to occupy the seat in the Senate was "both a question of political faith and . . . genuine representation . . ." he declared.

I had hoped that it would not be necessary for me to speak; but it is. I realize the delicacy of taking any part in the discussion of the matter. . . . Legally speaking it is not my duty even to give advice with regard to the choice. But there are other duties besides legal duties. The recent campaign has put me in an unusual position. I offered, if elected, to be the political spokesman and adviser of the people. I even asked those who did not care to make their choice of Governor upon that understanding not to vote for me. . . . I cannot escape the responsibility involved.[31]

[30] Wilson to G. Harvey, Nov. 15, 1910; Baker, *op. cit.*, Vol. III, p. 112.
[31] Newark *Evening News*, Dec. 9, 1910.

The vote cast by the people in the primaries must be heeded by the Legislature; Mr. Martine must be chosen Senator. Once more Wilson exceeded the narrow frame of partisan political struggle and made his appeal in the name of eternal principles of justice and democracy. The response showed that the people of New Jersey, long boss-ridden by a whole chain of Tammany Halls, were not too case-hardened to heed him. Pressing the fight, Wilson called several large public meetings in the machine strongholds of Jersey City and Newark. The "amateur politician" talked to great cheering crowds with a vigor and candor that made the "regular" leaders who were pledged to Smith's cause tremble for their future.

Do not allow yourself to be dismayed. You see where the machine is entrenched, and it looks like a real fortress. It looks as if real men were inside, as if they had real guns. Go and touch it. It is a house of cards. Those are imitation generals. Those are playthings that look like guns. Go and put your shoulder against the thing and it collapses.[32]

It was plain that old Jim Smith's cause was lost. He made dramatic charges of heartless ingratitude against this erstwhile protégé. But his frightened followers, fearing the Governor's appointive power, began to give way, one by one. They sent word that they would gladly consider terms for a compromise; but these were refused.

As the Legislature gathered in the capital in the third week of January, Smith, whose whole political life was at stake, made a brave show of confidence, and marched upon Trenton with all his retinue of followers, including a brass band which paraded before the Trenton House to serenade the boss. But shortly after the Legislature convened, the Smith following collapsed utterly, and Martine was quickly elected.[33]

Ex-Senator James Smith, Jr., Democratic boss of New Jersey, was thus the first of Woodrow Wilson's political friends to be thrown relentlessly to the sharks.

[32] *Ibid.*, Jan. 5, 1910.
[33] *Ibid.*, Jan. 22, 23, 1910.

Wilson commented upon his victory in a graphic letter to a friend:

I pitied Smith at the last. It was so plain that he had few real friends,—that he held men by fear and power and the benefits he could bestow, not by love or loyalty or genuine devotion. The minute it was seen that he was defeated his adherents began to desert him like rats leaving a sinking ship. He left Trenton . . . attended, I am told, only by his sons, and looking old and broken. He wept, they say. . . . Such is the end of political power—particularly when selfishly obtained and heartlessly used. It is a pitiless game, in which it would seem, one takes one's life in one's hands,—and for me it has only begun! [34]

Wilson's spectacular victory over the machine not only caught the eye of intelligent citizens throughout the country, but made certain that his legislative program would not be obstructed. He had come, as he realized, in the "fullness of time," when the situation was ripe for change. He had been able to accomplish what Theodore Roosevelt had longed to do with the Platt machine in New York, but dared not, a decade earlier. At once Wilson moved swiftly to seize the helm of the party organization, to fill, himself, the place of the deposed party chieftain.

4

Woodrow Wilson was like a man who all his life carefully avoided vice, but discovering it by chance, in the ripeness of age, pronounced it not too bad, and, in truth, began to enjoy it heartily. He had disapproved of demagogues, and he was far from being one; but he represented himself as "the Governor of all the people," and the masses whom he now flattered in his speeches made his public meetings look like a succession of folk festivals. Other principles and methods than those he once was accustomed to extol before his students he now began to esteem more highly on closer contact. His opinion of the radical agrarian La Follette

[34] Wilson to Mrs. Mary A. Hulbert, Jan. 29, 1911; Baker, *op. cit.*, Vol. III, p. 127.

and his "Wisconsin Idea" changed rapidly, and he began to adopt some of La Follette's measures. Nor did he attack Mr. Bryan in public any longer. Reform, which he had held to be not far removed from vice, lost its terrors; experiments formerly decried as dangerous were now called "new tools of democracy" that permitted the popular will to function through leadership.

He became hospitable to all sorts of new ideas and methods. One day William S. U'Ren, the single taxer and inventor of the so-called "Oregon Plan," dropped into Trenton from the West and held long converse with him. U'Ren, a self-educated son of the frontier, without holding office had become since the early 1890's a most powerful political figure in Oregon, chiefly through his powers of persuasion and organization. He had devised the type of preferential primary which New Jersey, without waiting for a Constitutional amendment, had taken up as a method of bringing about the direct election of Senators; he had generated other measures such as the initiative and referendum as steps toward more "direct" democracy, and they had worked. Wilson's fight against boss Smith had kindled U'Ren's interest in him; and U'Ren in turn made a profound impression upon Wilson, who adopted for his legislative program laws similar to those which U'Ren had brought to Oregon.

Direct popular government under leadership immediately responsible to the people's referendum appealed to Wilson as a great advance over the cumbersome indirection of our political apparatus. To end the tyranny of machines, as it was then hoped, a thoroughgoing direct primary and election bill was made ready for the Legislature.

After U'Ren, the breezy, homespun philosopher, was gone—one met such men so seldom at Princeton!—Dr. Wilson assumed the habit of sitting in his office at the State House with his door open, accessible to all men and women, journalists, labor leaders, social workers and politicians, as if no secrets existed in the Governor's affairs. As late as August 13, 1912, Oswald Villard noted in his diary: "I found [Wilson] in the State House democratically wandering about and talking to the people in the outer office who were waiting to see him. There are no fuss and feathers where he is." [35] He would also go touring the state to the various county seats to report upon his "stewardship" and answer any questions that might be put to him by the citizens face to face, on the spot.

In an intimate letter of this time, he wrote that he felt himself deeply moved at the thought of his "new responsibilities as the representative and champion of the common people." He felt "a sort of solemnity in it all. . . ." [36]

For help in framing his program of reform laws, Wilson on good advice called in George L. Record, with whom he had lately been engaged in debate. Record was something of a "people's attorney" in New Jersey; for years he had fought alone against the bosses of both parties; citing chapter and verse, he could expose, outwit, or confound his opponents with ease. When Record came to Princeton, after the election, Wilson found him a man of idealism and refinement, with a face uncommonly handsome and sensitive. The two men found that party differences could easily be ignored between them—Record was nominally a Republican. At Record's frank counsel that he "cut adrift from the party machine," and seek men he could trust, Wilson gathered a Kitchen Cabinet of his own younger followers, with Record included as the Progressive Republican member. It was Record largely who undertook the tremendous labor of preparing and writing the new reform laws whose passage that year made history in New Jersey.

On January 16, 1911, the day before his inauguration, Wilson took the unusual step of calling a private meeting of prominent New Jersey leaders and legislators at a hotel in New York. Record, according to the editor Kerney, "took command" with Wilson's approval and presented the essentials of a direct primary and

---

[35] O. G. Villard, *Fighting Years*, pp. 218-219.
[36] Wilson to Mrs. Mary A. Hulbert, Jan. 22, 1911; Baker, *op. cit.*, Vol. III, p. 135.

election law, a corrupt-practices act, a public-utility regulation bill, and an employers' liability act.[37]

Wilson also addressed the gathering and imparted to them his hope of enacting promptly reforms pledged to the voters, as well as his views upon primary and election reforms (much colored by U'Ren's influence). Agreement upon a specific program was achieved; and soon, when reports of the "secret" meeting in New York spread, a storm of attack burst upon the liberals. Principal opposition centered upon the election bill, by which, as the Smith-Nugent men said, Wilson the "dictator" would wreck the organization that nominated him.

At a Democratic caucus held early in March to discuss possible amendments which would have softened the election bill, Wilson broke all precedent by making a personal appearance among the members and debating with them for three hours. He spoke with the fire of an old Scotch covenanter, as in a holy cause. The Representatives were won over. But "Jim" Nugent, lieutenant to Smith and chairman of the state Democratic party, held a bloc of a dozen Senators in opposition. Calling Nugent into his private office, the Governor attempted to reason with him. Hard words followed, Nugent insinuating bitterly that the Governor was using his patronage power to destroy the Old Guard. Very sensitive on this point, Wilson showed the Newark boss the door. Thereafter Nugent habitually toasted his Governor as a "liar" and an "ingrate."

In the end it was by the pressure of public opinion, which Wilson knew how to arouse, a judicious use of the patronage whip, and the support of three independent Republicans brought over by Record, that the Old Guard in Trenton were overcome. The drastic election-reform bill, along with its companion measures for utility regulation, employers' liability, and school improvements, were steadily carried through the Legislature, some by narrow margins, and all were made law by April, 1911, when the session adjourned.

[37] Kerney, *op. cit.*, pp. 100-103.

The Governor could hardly forbear to crow a little in private correspondence with a devoted friend:

I wrote the platform, I had the measures formulated to my mind, I kept the pressure of opinion constantly on the legislature, and the program was carried out to its last detail. This, with the senatorial business, seems to the minds of the people looking on, little less than a miracle, in the light of what has been hitherto the history of reform in this state. As a matter of fact . . . I came to the office in the fullness of time, when opinion was ripe on all these matters, when both parties were committed to these reforms, and by merely standing fast . . . and keeping up all sorts of (legitimate) pressure *all the time,* kept the mighty forces from being diverted or blocked at any point.[38]

After so much "noisome and crooked government by compromise and sordid bargaining behind closed doors . . . it was exhilarating to have another Executive administering public affairs in the broad light of day," Oswald Villard wrote.

Overnight, by a political miracle, New Jersey had been placed in the forefront of the progressive states, and Dr. Wilson, the scholar in politics, was saluted as a *successful* reformer. The great press outside now celebrated Dr. Wilson's courage, administrative ability, and gift for public affairs. His victories over the professionals were acclaimed by liberals, intellectuals, Mugwumps, and reformers of all sorts, who held the New Jersey Governor as a new tribune of the people. In these terms, a strong group of influential journalists, including Oswald Garrison Villard in the New York *Evening Post* and *Nation,* Walter H. Page and William Bayard Hale in *World's Work,* and Harvey in *Harper's Weekly,* sang his praises day by day and spread the Wilson cult. Even Bryan's *Commoner* sent supporting broadsides, which to Wilson's conservative backers were as evil omens. Harvey, the President Maker, with Walter H. Page, Cleveland Dodge, and other men of substance, now worked to raise a war chest for the Wilson Presidential boom. There were already widespread fears of a radical combination led

[38] Apr. 23, 1911, to M. H.; Baker, *op. cit.,* Vol. III, pp. 169-170.

by La Follette or Roosevelt or Bryan, or all three, which might break across party lines. Immediately after the adjournment of the New Jersey legislative session, in the early spring of 1911, it was arranged that Dr. Wilson should go forth upon a long speaking tour of the interior that would introduce him to the people of the West.

XII. COLONEL HOUSE'S VISION

THE TIDAL WAVE of November, 1910, was a good index of the degree in which discontent and anxiety had seized upon the country. A massive Democratic majority now held Congress and conducted an aggressive opposition to the Republican administration which was intended to insure its complete defeat in 1912. Even in Massachusetts a reformer-Democrat, Eugene Foss, was elected Governor, while in New Hampshire, another reformer, Robert P. Bass, overcame the Old Guard in the contest for the Governorship.

In the West the Insurgent Republicans, whom Taft had thought of reading out of the party, were everywhere vindicated—save for Beveridge, defeated in Indiana, who now retired to write his *John Marshall*. George Norris of Nebraska, now entering the Senate, ably replaced Beveridge. Despite the sudden, untimely death of the great-hearted Jonathan Dolliver, in the very prime of life, the Insurgents returned stronger than before, to wield the balance of power in the Senate. In a score of Western and Middle-Western states, men in revolt against the methods of the Republican regular organization named the candidates and wrote the platforms. Wisconsin had been a battlefield, with La Follette standing for re-election; though a supreme effort was made to eliminate him from public life, the leader of Insurgency won an overwhelming popular indorsement.

Immediately after the election, La Follette hurried to Washington and helped to launch the new National Republican Progressive League. Its most prominent office-holding members came from the land west of the Mississippi, and from Wisconsin, Indiana, and Michigan. In its statement of principles the following were advocated: the direct election of United States Senators; direct primaries; direct election of delegates to party conventions; the "initiative, referendum and recall"; a corrupt practices act. It was a program for political democracy, primarily. Senator Jonathan Bourne of Oregon was elected its president, and the brilliant young reformer Frederic C. Howe became its secretary. Louis D. Brandeis, who was one of the founders, declared at the time of the Progressive League's inception: "We are confronted in the twentieth century, as we were in the nineteenth century, with an irreconcilable conflict. Our democracy cannot endure half free and half slave. . . ." [1] The League promised that it would bring about the reformation of the Republican party by a nation-wide campaign of education and publicity. Many suspected that its real intention was to transform the Republican party sufficiently to permit the nomination, in 1912, of Wisconsin's Little Giant in place of Taft.

One of the first steps toward a more extended political democracy was achieved at once by the Sixty-Second Congress when, in April, 1911, it passed a resolution for the popular election of United States Senators, initiating thereby the amendment to the Constitution. Soon the Congress was plunged into debate over President Taft's proposed measure of tariff reciprocity with Canada. Yet no less engrossing during the year that followed were the series of investigations initiated by a radical Congress, dealing with interstate commerce, trusts, railroads, and election frauds. Perhaps the most important of these investigations was that begun by the Senate's Committee on Interstate Commerce, which devoted itself to the new industrial monsters of the age, the trusts.

That spring, on May 14, 1911, a very important decision was handed down by the Supreme Court, dissolving the Standard Oil Company of New Jersey into twenty-nine component parts, but enunciating at the same time the so-called "rule of reason" with

[1] Lief, *op. cit.*, p. 205.

regard to restraint of trade by large corporations. By this rule it was assumed that the Court might determine where undue or "unreasonable" restraint of trade took place, according to its judgment. Partial relief was now felt by the owners of large corporations, yet the working of the law remained as obscure and uncertain to them as before. But from the opposing camp a strong outcry of protest greeted the decision and echoed the dissenting opinion of Associate Justice Harlan, who contended that the Court had opened a breach in the Anti-Trust Act, a breach that would soon be wide enough to allow all the monopolies in the land to pass through unmolested.

To the liberals and progressives who had been leading the anti-monopoly movement it seemed that the inner defenses of the Sherman Act had suddenly fallen. The terms of the Supreme Court decision, though they did not satisfy Perkins and other champions of the trusts, gave no assurance that conditions of fair competition would be restored. Various bills were now introduced in Congress which attempted to redefine the Anti-Trust Act, the most notable of these being the one offered by La Follette and written with the aid of Brandeis.

That summer of 1911, before the Senate committee investigating trusts, George W. Perkins was among the financial magnates who testified in favor of the "good" trusts. He ventilated his favorite theories, which proposed a course of admitting the necessity and inevitability of the great trusts, giving a certain publicity to their affairs, and having them regulated in a sane and friendly spirit.

Brandeis, who also played a leading part at the hearings, expressed now probably the most coherent opinion that existed at the time upon a question which seemed to involve the very fate of the republic. He said that the great trusts were "neither inevitable nor desirable." They were more "inefficient" than small-scale business; they blighted and numbed invention and human enterprise with the "curse of bigness." The remedy was not to accept and institute monopoly, until it grew stronger perhaps than all the force of government, and then attempt to "regulate" it; but to regulate unbridled competition at the wage level, where the strong crushed the weak.

The theory of the "curse of bigness" brought a timely note of criticism in days when mere size rather than quality dazzled too many Americans. Many years later, in the 1930's, such views would be repeated in a new form by a school of economists who studied the rigidities and retarding factors of "monopolistic competition" during a great business depression. But at the earlier period Brandeis, like Veblen, argued that the promoters of the great trusts were less concerned with efficiency, as they claimed, than with the rapid gains to be won through floating enormously over-capitalized combinations. The motives of the investment bankers consisted in disposing of "watered stock" promptly, what Veblen would call "planned mismanagement." The case of the New Haven and other railroad and industrial "empires" which had collapsed lately, or were doomed to failure, were cited at length. Meanwhile solemn warning was given that the multiplication of trusts concentrated all of America's wealth finally in the hands of bankers, in a colossal "money trust."

A disturbing picture of a changing America, a land in which equality of opportunity and individual liberty—which Brandeis sincerely believed in—were being rapidly overwhelmed, was afforded by the testimony of the "people's lawyer." Moreover the great monopolies in steel, oil, and other industries, by coercion, espionage, or violence, relentlessly stamped out labor unions, making no provisions for the growth of democracy in industry. Even while the discussion raged, the story of the terrible bombing outrage which had recently been perpetrated at Los Angeles by the MacNamara brothers spread over the country in the daily reports of a famous labor trail. Thus Brandeis warned the public that the ruthlessness of the trusts, and their anti-labor tactics, prepared the way for a revolution of violence. The trusts, he said, "pointed the way to the Socialists." [2] The concentration of wealth

[2] Senate Committee on Interstate Commerce, 62nd Congress, 2nd Session, *Senate Documents*, 98, Vol. I, p. 1258.

in a few hands made it easier for the expropriators themselves to be expropriated. To avoid this, Brandeis proposed that the monopolies should be dissolved, that the conduct of the great corporations should be controlled according to specific, stipulated competitive conditions of trade, and that the trade unions should be encouraged as "a strong bulwark against the great wave of socialism." He concluded with a parable:

> Just as Emperor Nero is said to have remarked in regard to his people that he wished that the Christians had but one neck that he might cut it off by a single blow of his sword, so they [the Socialists] say here: "Let these men gather these things together; they will soon have them all under one head, and by a single act we will take over the whole industry." So Socialists say in regard to Morgan—Morgan pre-eminently the great organizer and great combiner. They say, "He is our best friend, because he is paving the way for us, and we will have only a slight amount of legislation after Mr. Morgan is through with his work." [3]

At this very time, news of financial "extremism" came from New York, where in July, 1911, the gigantic National City Bank announced the formation of the National City Company as its investment "affiliate." The new company was to be capitalized at $10,000,000 and was so organized that it might "make investments and transact other business which . . . may not be within the express corporate powers of a national bank." It could speculate in stocks or buy other banks. [4]

The fears of a money trust were now seen to be more than fancies. Soon afterward Congress designated a committee that was to be known as the "Pujo Committee," with Samuel Untermyer as its legal counsel, to pursue the trail of the Wall Street money trust.

Even in darkest Africa, Colonel Roosevelt heard the reverberations of the political storms in America. When he returned in

---

[3] A. T. Mason, *Brandeis and the Modern State*, p. 99.
[4] Sullivan, *op. cit.*, Vol. IV, p. 579.

May, 1910, after a circuslike round of receptions tendered him by the crowned heads of Europe, the opposing Republican factions besought him for his aid and approval. From Pinchot and his friends he heard the tale of the betrayal of the conservation program; from the regular Republicans came requests that he help his party by stumping in the Congressional elections. He behaved with reserve and decorum for a time. He did not at first approve of the rebellious mood of some of his former adherents such as Pinchot, for he wrote, some months after his return:

> Gifford is going in with some of the extremists in Congress with the expectation of trying to form a third party if Taft is nominated. He has become completely identified with the ultra-extremists, and I can only work with him to a very limited extent.[5]

But Roosevelt, too, had been doing some tall thinking, and, an inveterate pulse-taker, had noticed all the signs of fever among the citizens.

In the trunks that went to Africa there had been placed by chance a copy of Herbert Croly's *The Promise of American Life*, published early in 1909. Thus there occurred a wedding of minds. The Colonel was greatly struck by Croly's penetrating and suggestive study of our political government "as it really was," its weaknesses, its problems and its potentialities. Croly's book, as Walter Lippmann said, "made articulate for Roosevelt his aspiration to combine the social and political reforms initiated by Bryan and La Follette with a Hamiltonian affection for a strong national government." [6] While still abroad, the Rough Rider wrote to the learned political philosopher in New York of the intellectual affinity he felt; and upon his return invited Croly to Oyster Bay for lunch and held a whole long afternoon's talk with him.[7]

The Promise of American Life, though written in a rather abstract style, was the most thoughtful work of its kind since Bryce's *American Commonwealth*, of twenty years before. Croly prophe-

[5] *T. R. Papers*, T. R. to Bacon, Jan. 2, 1911.
[6] *The New Republic*, Jul. 16, 1930.
[7] Mrs. H. Croly to author.

sied an era of sweeping change for the country, and examined the nature of our political traditions, our party system, and the relations between professional politics and big business, in the light of their availability for the age of drastic change which he foresaw. In 1909 Herbert Croly still hoped that the existing party apparatus— detached from its ties with corrupt, corporate wealth—might still be converted to the use of a "new national democracy," more centralized, more authoritative, more energetic and responsive to the popular will.

Believing as he did that many of the abuses we suffered from were traceable to our too sacred Constitution, Croly could not approve either the traditional Democrats who still claimed to be followers of Jefferson, or even the Bryanites, with their lip-service to states' rights and "strict construction." True reform would require a centralizing or Hamiltonian tendency in the government authority, a vigorous "New Nationalism" that would overleap the boundaries set by courts and state lines. Thus Croly came to hold up Theodore Roosevelt as his model, "a Hamiltonian with a difference," who would not make the Federal organization a bulwark against the rising tide of democracy, but would instead give to the Hamiltonian tradition and method a "democratic meaning and purpose." [8]

In nearly all respects Herbert Croly and Louis D. Brandeis were antithetical as political thinkers. Concerning the great trusts and the abuses they had brought, Croly, after much thought, believed that we should "recognize the existing corporate economic organization" and attempt to harness it to the general welfare, rather than call it bad names or seek to mutilate or destroy its parts. How to harness the predatory corporation magnates to the nation's welfare was a matter that was still left vague. Croly put hope in the leveling or redistributing agency of direct taxation, and the regulative power of a devoted, high-minded corps of government commissioners and administrators. Such a policy, he hinted, might well lead to the repeal of the Sherman Anti-Trust

[8] Croly, *The Promise of American Life*, pp. 172-175.

Act and a grand merger of monopolistic business organization with political organization. (It would be, in effect, a frank recognition of that which already existed in indirect, loose form.) Croly, in his early period, before he launched *The New Republic* in 1914, thus combined certain ideas of state capitalism with premonitions of the "corporative" guild state. To Roosevelt, who had originally embraced Hamiltonian ideas of rule by talent and wealth, the "Promise of American Life" according to Croly was alluring, and he borrowed from it whole-heartedly for his program of the "New Nationalism."

Brandeis, on the other hand, applying Jeffersonian doctrine in modern form and with brilliant insight to the Age of Big Business, would have perpetuated a society of individuals; "little men" in constant competition with each other, though in peaceful and civilized manner, under restraints of political and social police. Invention, improvement, progress, he held, came through "struggle," and a steady process of education. Democracy depended upon the spread of intelligence, rather than upon government commissions. His program of trust-breaking, "regulated competition," and social laws to encourage collective bargaining and security as he expounded it in public or in magazine polemics, suggested return to the past but made enormous appeal to the mind of his age, and ended by exercising powerful influence upon the mind of Woodrow Wilson, in particular. While Roosevelt popularized Croly's theories under the slogan the "New Nationalism," Brandeis' ideas emerged in the lucid prose of Wilson's campaign speeches of 1912, under the slogan of the "New Freedom."

Theodore Roosevelt could not be long removed from public life. Soon after his return he became a contributing editor of *The Outlook*, a respectable and influential family paper, and wrote weekly of the issues of the day. In the autumn of 1910, he took an active part in the politics of New York, endeavoring to help the liberal Henry L. Stimson in a gubernatorial contest that failed. Here, as in his occasional speech-making journeys to Western centers,

Roosevelt evidently applied pressure against the conservative leaders of his party. Though there was no outward clash with the Taft administration, he suggested plainly his separation from it by the increasing political radicalism of his speech. Invited to speak at Denver, Colorado, on August 28, 1910, before the State Legislature, he gave plain hints of his dissatisfaction with our Federal courts and their power to review and nullify legislation. The courts, he held, in many ways dominated our whole government—something that was true of almost no other land.

Roosevelt's conservative friend Elihu Root expressed to the President the alarm he felt at hearing the Denver speech, and Taft responded that Roosevelt doubtless had the design of appealing to "the bitter sentiments" now rising "throughout the West . . . and especially in the Insurgent ranks." [9]

But two days later, August 30, at Osawatomie, Kansas, the scene of John Brown's early activities, Roosevelt was even more outspoken in sounding the ideas of the obscure prophet Herbert Croly. After denouncing "swollen fortunes" and the "special interests" who purchased political influence or legal talent to protect them in a sort of legislative neutral ground from the jurisdiction of state and Federal governments alike, he continued:

. . . I ask that we work in a spirit of broad and far-reaching nationalism when we work for what concerns the people as a whole. . . . The betterment which we seek must be accomplished, I believe, mainly through the national government. The American people are right in demanding the New Nationalism without which we cannot hope to deal with new problems. The New Nationalism puts the national need before sectional or personal advantage . . . regards the executive power as the steward of the public welfare. It demands of the judiciary that it shall be interested primarily in human welfare rather than in property. . . .

Roosevelt prophesied that far more governmental interference in business would be seen in the future; and men of all sorts would be compelled to adjust themselves to "new conceptions of the relations of property to human welfare." By these, he asserted, prop-

[9] Jessup, *op. cit.*, Vol. II, pp. 163-164.

erty would be "subject to the general right of the community to regulate its use to whatever degree the public welfare may require it."

Here were bold words. Roosevelt not only asked for the Square Deal and fair play, but suggested that he was willing to see the rules of the game changed, in the name of equality and justice. Here too, in the speech at John Brown's home town, was a passage that borrowed Lincoln's words in praise of labor: property, which man's labor had made, must be "the servant and not the master of the commonwealth." The people "must effectively control the mighty forces which they have themselves called into being."

Roosevelt was now steering into the full current of his time.

2

Dr. Wilson, rolling through the Far West on his long speaking tour, often wondered to himself at the strange fate which had cast him late in life upon a sea of political troubles. The original impetus had come from the inspired George Harvey, who was sometimes called "Morgan's errand boy." Wilson knew that his financial sponsors, Harvey, Dodge, Page, and more lately William F. McCombs, the young lawyer who had once been his pupil at Princeton, all looked to him as a "Grover Cleveland Democrat," who might make head against Bryan's influence. It was hoped also that he might be useful in offsetting any radical leadership, such as La Follette's or Roosevelt's, which might possibly now capture the Republican party.

Yet Wilson, the conservative Democrat, had found himself fighting for his life in New Jersey, against the state boss and his machine from the very start; driven to carrying out a program of long-needed reforms. Thus he had grown strong and found his own legs, while the sponsoring group in downtown New York looked on silently at the upheavals in New Jersey.

Arriving in the West, he had fallen into a land "aflame with the political . . . movements that had descended directly from

Bryanism. . . ." [10] His own convictions had been changing rapidly. The crowds in Kansas City, Denver, San Francisco, and Portland who cheered his liberal messages affected him strongly. En route, a curious incident made a lasting impression upon his mind.

At the small water town of Wymore, Nebraska, the train had stopped to change locomotives. When the Governor descended to take the air upon the platform, a railroad worker in overalls, wiping his hands, came up and introduced himself as Mayor of Wymore. The local worthy, as it developed, had been lately elected upon the Socialist ticket. But why was there so much Socialism in Wymore? "It wasn't Socialism that elected me," the Mayor replied. "Only about 20 per cent Socialism, and 80 per cent protest."

"*That typifies a national condition,*" Wilson observed to his companions as the journey continued. "*There is a tremendous undercurrent of protest, which is bound to find expression. Taft will be renominated by the Republicans; unless the Democrats nominate someone whom the people can accept as expressing this protest there will be a radical third party formed and the result of the election may be little short of a revolution.*" [11]

At almost the same period, though he had not come to an open rupture with Taft, Theodore Roosevelt was seized with forebodings similar to those of Wilson. His later, post-Presidential letters show him convinced that the country was faced with tremendously grave *ideological* problems which his erstwhile protégé could not possibly deal with. It was not that he was actually more liberal than Taft in his purpose; his misgivings arose because he felt that Taft could no longer be counted upon to save the country from revolution.

Confidentially, Roosevelt wrote to Elihu Root that he was "bitterly disappointed with Taft, and consider[ed] much of his course inexplicable." While wishing for his own part to be both "sane and progressive," he felt that Taft had "put himself in commission in the hands of Aldrich, Cannon, Ballinger and Wickersham." He

[10] Kerney, *Wilson*, p. 135.
[11] Baker, *op. cit.*, Vol. III, p. 225, after McKee Barclay notes; italics mine.

had begun to eliminate progressives from any share in the party direction or policy "within forty-eight hours of his election, nearly two years ago." Taft appeared to be steering the Republican party toward an imminent disaster.

The choice between the "wild irresponsible folly of the Ultra-Insurgents" and the "sordid" Standpatters presented Roosevelt with "a situation which is very unpleasant," and Taft and his friends were to blame.[12] How to avoid such a dangerous choice was to be his deepest preoccupation. He was to express this thought constantly in his letters and in public speeches for the next two years. If only men would take warning in time from the dread fate of France in 1789-1793, when the folly of splitting into "two camps of unreasonable conservatism and unreasonable radicalism" had brought the old regime to its debacle. Would America too, in a time of discontent and danger, ignore the moderate counsels of her Turgots?[13]

Thus the more lately arrived "amateur in politics" and the veteran leader, Roosevelt, foresaw with the same mind a tremendous political crisis for 1912. As Wilson could feel the sectional-class bitterness rising in the West, so the "sounding-board" in Roosevelt sensed always the monitory reverberations of distant tumbrels. Both men were friends of the existing system, friends of capitalism, patronized and supported by men high in the councils of Wall Street, and not by I.W.W.'s or even the respectable trade unions; the strategy of both the Doctor and the Colonel now turned upon drawing the protest vote to themselves, and thus preventing the formation of a "radical third party," the break-up of the traditional party system, and results "little short of a revolution." Both men, then, accepted for themselves the historic task of modern capitalist statesmen to save society from a revolutionary break-up. (Roosevelt of course prepared himself for his mission secretly up to January, 1912.) Was it surprising that both gave the appearance of running after strange gods for the while, espousing radical

[12] *T. R. Papers*, T. R. to E. Root, Oct. 21, 1910.
[13] Speech of Mar. 29, 1912, Carnegie Hall, N. Y.

heresies, offering more and more generous concessions (ransom) to the people? Their sponsors might fret and complain; but the political captains could cry that there was now no choice; thanks to the follies of the Tafts and Aldriches and Cannons, and the interests standing behind them, the hour had become desperate. Accept reform from us—Rooseveltian or Wilsonian—they seemed to say, or else take something much worse in the end, from a La Follette, a Bryan, perhaps even a Debs!

3

By prior arrangement the strategy of Wilson's boomers during his Western tour in 1911 was to "sell" him to the press as a "sound" liberal. Wilsonism, it was said in the inspired comments reproduced by the newspapers, was "popular leadership with a safety valve," or a "balance wheel." It was "statesmanship without demagogy. . . ." [14]

In his important opening address at Kansas City, May 6, 1911, before an audience of solid business men, Wilson spoke at first with a becoming moderation. A new political era was dawning. But there was no need for fear. It was not to be "a process of revolution, but a process of restoration. . . ." The movement going on was "one of reform . . . rather than that of a revolution. . . ." The American people were "naturally a conservative people," unwilling to overturn the foundations of their life, revering rights of property and contract. But there must be "change" although sober change. Then he himself skillfully injected a thrill of fear into his bourgeois audience when he said meaningfully:

The man with power, but without conscience, could, with an eloquent tongue, if he cared for nothing but his own power, put this whole country into a flame, because this whole country believes that something is wrong, and is eager to follow those who profess to be able to lead it away from its difficulties.

[14] *Oregon Journal*, May 18, 1911; Baker, *op. cit.*, Vol. III, p. 224.

Wilson would take no such course, it was intimated. He, like all good Americans, felt not "the slightest jealousy of the legitimate accumulation of wealth. . . ." But everyone knew that some of the men who "control the wealth and have built up the industry of the country" sought to control all politics by the iniquitous system of Invisible Government. Our democracy was in danger. What was the solution? A way to "restore and invigorate" representative government had been proposed already. It was the way of the initiative, referendum, and recall, the force of popular plebiscites intervening in courts and legislatures.[15]

Pausing at Lincoln, Nebraska, the capital of the "Bryan Empire," Woodrow Wilson took pains to pay homage to the Great Commoner, who was at the moment on a speaking tour of the East, but whose family and retinue gave the New Jersey reformer a ceremonious reception. And in Wisconsin he paid tribute also to La Follette in moving words:

I have sometimes thought of Senator La Follette, climbing the mountain of privilege . . . taunted, laughed at, called back, going steadfastly on and not allowing himself to be deflected for a single moment, for fear he also should hearken and lose all his power to serve the great interests to which he had devoted himself. I love these lonely figures climbing this ugly mountain of privilege . . . I am sorry for my own part that I did not come in when they were fewer.[16]

Although Wilson actually directed his speeches to the "unselfish public spirit" of the property-owning class mainly, though he endeavored to conciliate and combine all sorts of clashing groups—capitalists and laborers, farmers and townspeople, Gentiles and Jews—he ended by alarming his own conservative patrons. William F. McCombs, who headed the small Wilson bureau in New York, now "wired him . . . to slow up." The less said about the initiative, referendum, and recall, the better for campaign collections in the East.[17] Yet Wilson's tactics were highly effective in

[15] Speech of May 6, 1911, Kansas City, Mo.
[16] Kerney, *op. cit.*, p. 142.
[17] *Ibid.*, pp. 136, 138.

the political sense. Factions opposing the moribund Democratic machine in important states like Pennsylvania sprang to life and rallied to his cause. In Texas, where Senator "Joe" Bailey was now in disgrace, owing to the recent publication of the stolen Standard Oil letters, the majority of the party with its large delegation swung quickly to Wilson's banner.

To the President Maker, Colonel Harvey, the strange proceedings of his own Pygmalion now brought many heart-burnings. Harvey had been silent, giving neither praise nor blame to Wilson's reform activities in New Jersey; but his Western barnstorming showed a positive tendency to "Bryanize," as the conservative press of New York remarked. Later there appeared rumors that Harvey's old master, T. F. Ryan, feared lest Wilson could not be managed; also that J. Pierpont Morgan had been offended by something Wilson said at a public banquet which seemed a hostile allusion to himself.[18]

What was to be done about their converted college president who went about the land awakening the people in the tones of Bryan and La Follette? In the inner circle, a warm discussion sprang up over the question whether Wilson spoke mere rhetoric or actually meant something as bad as Bryan's or Roosevelt's "line." That other honorary colonel, Henry Watterson, who often engaged in these deep counsels of strategy, assured his troubled friend Harvey that a man of Wilson's stamp must be accepted as a Lesser Evil. The trouble with Wall Street was that it lacked "gumption" and political acumen. Its *riffraff of rich noodles who think that money will do it all,* that political movements could be managed according to the laws of the counting-house, were not to be trusted for their own good!

Those Wall Street chaps never do know what is good for them. As to Wilson, it is a case of going further to fare worse. They had better take an intelligent Radical, abreast with the times, who knows how and when to discriminate, and is both upright and his own man, than get a

18 Johnson, *op. cit.*, pp. 181, 187; House, *Intimate Papers*, Vol. I, p. 51; House to Bryan, Dec. 6, 1911.

promissory note for some nondescript, to be repudiated as soon as he is able to feel his oats.[19]

Thus cajoled, Colonel Harvey overcame his misgivings and continued to work for the Wilson cause. Even when rebuffed by a coldness of manner, which could be terrible with Wilson, he continued bravely as ever.

In the local elections of November, 1911, in New Jersey, "Jim" Smith revived his shattered force sufficiently to defeat the Wilson Democrats and help to return a Republican Legislature. The reformist Governor could no longer have his measures passed at will. Yet, despite this hard blow Harvey, after November, 1911, endeavored to capitalize the vengefulness of the boss as giving all the greater credit and glory to his candidate. His local defeats represented a "moral victory." At the top of its editorial page, *Harper's Weekly* now ran the standing head:

FOR PRESIDENT, WOODROW WILSON

But Woodrow Wilson now more and more patently set a distance between himself and the vivacious colonel in tortoise-shell glasses. On two occasions in the late autumn of 1911, he seemed to avoid a meeting with him deliberately. A soft, unfamiliar voice among his counselors whispered to him, late in November, 1911, that he must endeavor to detach himself from Harvey more positively, if he would escape the odium of being "Wall Street's candidate" and win the powerful help of Western Democrats. The younger men in Wilson's entourage had also made the same observations; and he had been thinking hard about it for some months. The journey about the country had opened his eyes to the sentiment of the masses beyond the Appalachian Mountains and the Mississippi; he must win them, and win their leader Bryan, or his cause was hopeless. The time had come, as he sometimes said, "to close his mind and act," cost what it might.

The decision to take a new "line" is well reflected in a letter of this moment, December 6, 1911, written by Colonel Edward

[19] Johnson, *op. cit.*, pp. 179, 181, 182.

House of Texas, still another honorary colonel who now suddenly interested himself in Governor Wilson's career. It was an adroit letter to Mr. Bryan, whom House knew very well, concerning the political situation of the New Jersey Governor. He spoke of a special strain that had arisen between Wilson and his backer Harvey. Only the day before, House had taken lunch with Colonel Harvey and endeavored to learn the man's "real attitude" toward Wilson.

He told me that everybody south of Canal Street was in a frenzy against Governor Wilson, and said they were bringing all sorts of pressure upon him to oppose him. . . .

He said that Morgan was particularly virulent in his opposition to Governor Wilson. I asked him what this was based on, and he said upon some remark Governor Wilson had made in Morgan's presence concerning the methods of bankers, and which Morgan took as a personal reference.

He told me that he believed any amount of money that was needed to defeat Governor Wilson could be readily obtained. He said he would be surprised if they did not put $250,000 in New Jersey alone in order to defeat delegates favorable to his nomination.

We are going to devise some plan by which we can use this Wall Street opposition to [Governor Wilson's] advantage. If the country knows of their determination to defeat him, I am sure it will do the rest. . . .

If you can make any suggestions regarding the best way to meet the Wall Street attack, I would greatly appreciate it.[20]

The die had been cast; Wall Street must efface itself. The campaign to win over Mr. Bryan to the Wilson banner had been begun in a most skillful manner.

On December 7, 1911, Governor Wilson somewhat reluctantly came to New York for a meeting with Harvey, long avoided. Colonel Watterson was present, and the conference took place at Watterson's rooms in the Manhattan Club.

At the end of the discussion, Harvey asked Wilson if there was

[20] House, *op. cit.*, Vol. I, p. 50.

"anything left of that cheap talk during the gubernatorial campaign about my advocating you on behalf of 'the interests'?"

Wilson replied coolly that there was; that at luncheon, the other day, the young men of his "literary bureau" had volunteered the information that Harvey's public support of himself "was having a serious effect in the West."

Harvey: Is there anything I can do, except, of course, to stop advocating your nomination?
Wilson: I think not. At least I can't think of anything.
Harvey: Then I will simply sing low.
(*Pause. Impressive silence from Woodrow Wilson.*) [21]

Watterson, the third party present, found Wilson's coldness of manner infuriating, and left in a rage to tell all the world at Louisville and Washington of Wilson's base ingratitude and the rupture. Some unbending impulse made Wilson sacrifice personal and political friendships mercilessly, when the hour came, like some modern dictator who orders the assassination of outworn retainers. It was only a few days after the meeting with Harvey, when the latter ostentatiously took down Wilson's name from the *Harper's* masthead, that Private Secretary Tumulty reminded the Governor that he might have wounded the other man. Then only, on December 21, 1911, did Wilson send a letter of lame apology, reproaching himself for having a "single-track" mind, and forgetting the marks of gratitude he owed. But it was too late.[22]

In January, 1912, news of the rupture between Wilson and Harvey had leaked out enough to cause a raging controversy. It was noticeable that Wall Street circles gave renewed consideration to the reputed difficulties of Wilson's ungrateful, quarrelsome character. Could he be trusted? On top of this, gossip of a terrible letter which ex-President Grover Cleveland, a resident and trustee at Princeton, had written to a friend concerning Wilson's "habitual untruthfulness," was suddenly spread. Then, as a final blow, there

[21] Memorandum of Harvey; Johnson, *op. cit.*, p. 186.
[22] Tumulty, *op. cit.*, pp. 85-87.

came on January 6, 1912, the sudden publication by Adrian H. Joline, a Princeton trustee and former friend of Wilson's, of a letter Wilson had written five years before, in the days when he had scarcely dreamt of political ambitions, which assailed Bryan and expressed the wish that he might be knocked "once for all, into a cocked hat." This letter had been taken from the shelf and published with the cruel design of ending Wilson's budding courtship of Mr. Bryan.

The early days and weeks of 1912 marked the lowest ebb of Wilson's political fortunes thus far. An admiring and devoted "literary bureau" directed his boom as vigorously as before. A faction of wealthy capitalists, certainly a minority in their class, still donated funds for his nomination campaign at regular intervals. However, the professional politicians in his party, the heads of great city machines, were but slightly interested in him. He had won cheers in the West; but the cheers gave no certain promise of pledged delegations. Week by week came reports of state delegations captured for the amiable veteran of Congress, Speaker Champ Clark of Missouri; other states turned to Favorite Sons such as Harmon and Underwood. Wilson, from advance indications, would stand but a poor second to Clark; even his home state delegation promised to be divided at the convention, a minority led by the embittered Nugent opposing his candidacy.

4

During the summer of 1911, Woodrow Wilson was made aware of a powerful, unknown friend who, from far-off Texas, worked quietly to further his Presidential plans. As early as March, 1911, Harvey had spoken to him of this "exceptionally able man, well-to-do financially and . . . sound politically." [23] Others such as Representative Burleson of Texas also spoke highly of him as one whom he should know: one who, with a skilled, firm hand, seemed to shape political events in the great state of Texas so that its sup-

[23] Baker, *op. cit.*, Vol. III, p. 298.

port was promised to Wilson's candidacy long in advance of other states, and its progressive leaders called to him to come and speak to them, and to lead them. This he did in October, 1911, at the State Fair in Texas, with valuable effect. Yet the mysterious Colonel House, with whom he corresponded twice that autumn, was still unseen. Wilson's curiosity was piqued until late in November, when his strange benefactor came to New York.

On November 25, 1911, Woodrow Wilson went to New York and proceeded alone to the Hotel Gotham. A small, slight man, bald, keen-eyed, well-groomed, with a gentle voice and sympathetic manner, received him. The two men talked for an hour. Each was delighted with the other.

House conveyed to Wilson his own abiding fears of an oncoming political crisis, a possible revolution. Wilson, who shared these fears, outlined those "certain things" which he fervently wanted to do in time, and do intelligently and well. House expressed fullest accord, and promised to devote all his time, and part of his fortune, to this end.

The first hour they spent together, House recalled, laid the basis for their fast friendship. "We found ourselves in such complete sympathy" that each knew what the other was thinking without need for words. There was something almost feminine about Edward House; he seemed to listen to you with so much eagerness, to solicit your confidence; he was so ready to respond, so quick to attune himself to your mood, yet he asked nothing for himself, nothing but to please.

Wilson had so few friends that he deeply needed a *confidant* and an experienced counselor. House relates in his diary:

A few weeks after we met and after we had exchanged confidences which men usually do not exchange except after years of friendship, I asked him if he realized that we had only known one another for so short a time. He replied, "My dear friend, we have known one another always." And I think this is true.[24]

[24] House, *op. cit.*, Vol. I, p. 45.

Edward Mandell House was born in Texas in 1858, the son of a pioneer of Dutch-English descent. His father, who had run away from England, fought in the insurrection against Mexican rule, accumulated large wealth as a merchant, and bequeathed this to his son. Educated in the East, well-traveled, widely read, Edward House with his ample means was able to become a man of leisure. He had the experience of various enterprises to be sure: the management of great cotton plantations, banking, the building of a small railroad. Then in the '90's he had removed to the state capital at Austin, built himself a fine home, and, indulging his interest in politics, had become a sort of Talleyrand of Texas.

In this field, House relates, he "began at the top." Texas was swept toward 1892 by the same Populist-agrarian uprising that in Nebraska produced a Bryan. Here political life was intense and colorful, with a Western as well as a Southern flavor. Among the picturesque leaders who came to the surface here, such as Reagan, Bailey, and Culberson, Governor James S. Hogg was the most honest, courageous, and popular, and to him Edward House attached himself closely—because he found that "the railroads and the entire corporate interests of Texas were combining to defeat him." House was always a progressive, one of his friends, T. W. Gregory, recalled. "He wanted to see advanced ideas placed upon the statute book. . . . Although rated as one of the wealthy men of Texas, he was invariably aligned on the side of the plain people and against most of those with whom he was socially intimate."

Soon House learned to foretell with uncanny accuracy the effect of certain measures or tactics; he was taken into the inner circle of politicians who organized party primaries—in that one-party state —and helped create Governors and Senators. Yet he accepted no office for himself, nor title (save that of colonel of militia). He refused usually to assume the chairmanship of campaign organizations which he directed, preferring to work behind the scenes, and "to put someone else nominally at the head, so that I could do the real work undisturbed. . . ." [25] The delicacy of House's

[25] House, *op. cit.*, Vol. I, pp. 28, 34, 31.

health may have contributed to his secretive habits. Moreover, he had no gifts as a public speaker. He effaced himself not because he was wanting in ambition, as some thought. He said once that his ambition was "so great that it has never seemed to me worth while to strive to satisfy it."

At any rate, House was held in high respect, occupied a desk in the office of several successive Governors, and helped to administer the affairs of Texas as an adviser, political manager, and informal prime minister.

At length, toward 1900, he tired of this role. He desired a place in the national councils of his party, to which his power in Texas entitled him. But Bryan was the leading man of the Democratic party, while the Rough Rider held the stage in Washington. Though House was at one time touched with Henry George's doctrines, he had no taste for Bryan's bimetallism as a panacea. At Austin he came to know Bryan well, Bryan having a ranch near by; but he judged that the Great Commoner thought his ideas "God-given," unalterable. At odds with the dominant Western leadership, Edward House bided his time, traveled, studied, even wrote a novel, while his party bore continued defeats.

But in the spring of 1910 our Talleyrand, now in early middle age, bestirred himself to enter national politics, to make a President. He had seen signs in the skies of great change. Coming East to find a brave and truthful leader, he fixed at first upon whimsical old Mayor Gaynor of New York, the foe of Tammany Hall. But wisdom bade this fine official to shun ambition, and he rejected House's advice that he stand for Governor of New York, in 1910, as a step to the Presidency. House then looked across the Hudson River toward Governor Wilson, and soon became persuaded that the former college professor was the only Eastern leader who might win the country at large by his liberalism. House admired Wilson's "political rhetoric."

Meeting Wilson confirmed his highest hopes, as he wrote home the next day. He had feared Wilson would be vain, but saw no evidence of it. ". . . I would rather play with him than any prospective candidate I have seen." Wilson would be "a man one can advise with some degree of satisfaction. This . . . you could never do with Mr. Bryan." [26]

House's essential plan, as he unfolded it, was to build a bridge running from New Jersey to Nebraska. He had therefore added his pleas to others' that Wilson separate himself from Harvey, "Wall Street's errand boy." Harvey would have resisted the plan of an alliance with Bryan to the bitter end. Wilson's loud rupture with Harvey raised his stock immensely in the West, and was providential, since it brought him at once to Bryan's favorable consideration.

At the small "Wilson Headquarters," House, when in New York, came and went softly every day. McCombs, the nervous young man officially in charge there, thought House a secretive, mousy little fellow filled with grandiose visions. He would say to McCombs, in effect: do thus—"and you and I will control the United States!" [27]

House employed himself with policy making. Noticing that Wilson's stump speeches had not stressed the tariff issue, House called on his friend Professor D. F. Houston, former president of the University of Texas, and a lifelong student of tariff questions, for aid. Houston, who was to be Secretary of Agriculture under Wilson, long remembered the ardent discussions of those campaign days. He observed how House loved the game of power, and enjoyed the sense of power, especially when wielded indirectly. He noticed that House was fairly obsessed with the possibilities of Wilson. "He [House] has a *vision*," Houston wrote of him in a private letter, December 11, 1911. "*I should like to make him Dictator for a while. . . .*" [28]

[26] Nov. 25, 1911, to S. E. Mezes; *ibid.*, Vol. I, p. 46.

[27] McCombs, *Making Woodrow Wilson President*, p. 67.

[28] Houston, *Eight Years with Wilson's Cabinet*, Vol. I, p. 21; House, *op. cit.*, Vol. I, p. 48; italics mine.

5

All those who came close to Colonel House thought that he saw visions. What were they?

Fortunately he has left us fullest evidence of his dreams and ambitions in the shape of the utopian or "tendency" novel *Philip Dru, Administrator,* which he was engaged in writing late in 1911, at the time he met Woodrow Wilson, and published anonymously in the autumn of 1912. "Would that mine enemy would write a book," the proverb runs. To House's book, little noticed at the time of its appearance, we may go to study the hopes, fears, and visions of this singular little man.

Philip Dru is the imaginary story of the coming of a great social revolution to America, set many years in the future, and of the national hero who arises to lead his people to peace, equality, and prosperity. It bears some resemblance to the contemporary work of Howells, of H. G. Wells in *The New Machiavelli,* and Jack London, save that it is by the hand of one untrained to write or organize a work of imagination. By all literary standards it is thin and mediocre stuff. Yet its political commentaries upon the Rooseveltian epoch are keen; and many of the prophecies made were to prove startlingly accurate. *Philip Dru,* in short, embodies the innermost preoccupations, the real social thought, of the reformist leaders of 1912.

Colonel House dedicated his book to the unhappy masses "who have lived and died lacking opportunity, because in the starting, the world-wide social structure was wrongly begun." For his epigraph he quotes a passage from Mazzini, in itself most revealing of the temper of House, his "soulmate" Wilson, and other would-be world saviors of the epoch.

No war of classes, no hostility to existing wealth, no wanton or unjust violation of the rights of property, but a constant disposition to ameliorate the condition of the classes least favored by fortune.[29]

[29] Italics mine.

Colonel House's utopia, we perceive at once, has limits set by a bourgeois, a rentier, with real estate and liquid assets to be spared —though this is no serious reflection upon a man who used his wealth and leisure in so many original ways.

"In the year 1920 . . . ," the anonymous author opens, there were "many indications that the social, financial and industrial troubles that had vexed the United States for so long a time were about to culminate in civil war." Corporate wealth had grown too strong, the masses felt themselves "strangled," even farmers, merchants, and professional men grew "sullen and rebellious"; while all save rich capitalists and their satellites foresaw a "gloomy and hopeless future."

The hero of the romance, Philip Dru, native of Kentucky, graduates from West Point at this time and enters upon an army officer's career. Unlike his colleagues, he is a brooding, Hamletic sort of fellow; he reflects day and night upon the evils of the day, and sees the future darkly. Our civil and military institutions, to his mind, have grown debased. When not employed for petty foreign conquests, the army is used for the intimidation of the people under the guise of the "constitutional protection of property." The omens of the period remind him forcibly of those days in France when the "slumbering, chained giant" arose, struck out blindly, and destroyed a whole society. But out of that revelry of blood, one and a half centuries ago, ruminates Philip Dru, there arose hope of a more splendid day for mankind. The feudal rulers were overthrown. Throughout the Western world "one stratum of society after another demanded and obtained the right to acquire wealth and to share in the government." But then the bolder, more forceful individuals pushed on beyond all bounds. "They who had sprung from the people . . . a short life-span ago were now throttling individual effort and shackling the great movement for equal rights and equal opportunities." It was here, then, in the great republic of the West that the next battle for human liberation was to be fought and won. Then would the spirit of love and brotherhood be born and "the Star of Bethlehem . . . shine again."

Thus ran the reflections of Colonel House's fictive hero, Dru, even when he courted his beautiful fiancée, who was herself the daughter of one of the new "robber barons." Philip Dru's ideas and enterprises epitomize the whole middle class *politique* of the Rooseveltian era. In the last analysis, his motivation is moral and Christian; he seeks a return to a purer Christian ethics, as a way of redemption. "Selfishness" and "greed," he asserts—like Theodore Roosevelt and Bryan—are the root cause of all poverty and evil. And Dru, resigning from the military service, chooses to live in the hideous slums of New York among the poor. For him the solution, the answer to so much selfishness and evil, lay "not in the socialism dreamed of by Karl Marx," but in spreading the practice of unselfishness. In the future men were to work for "spiritual compensations."

Philip Dru now wrote articles and pamphlets decrying the evil conditions he saw on every hand. These effusions were disliked by both the radicals and the conservatives. For—and here again is a point of resemblance with the Rooseveltian social politics—the very moderation of Dru's proposed reforms offended "the ever ready few, who want to remake the world in a day. . . ." A third point of resemblance with the Roosevelts, Beveridges, and Woodrow Wilsons was that Philip Dru believed that he and his girl friend, if they would redeem society, must proselytize among the rich. He tells her:

Do your work gently and with moderation, so that some at least may listen. *If we would convince and convert, we must veil our thoughts and curb our enthusiasm, so that those we would influence will think us reasonable.*

There spoke the real Colonel House, mixture of the prophet and the wire-puller, who, "veiling his thoughts," set forth from Texas to save the country.

Finally, like so many of the young men of wealth and social position in House's time, Philip Dru becomes persuaded that to reach the results he aims at he must "work through politics." For plutocracy in "1920" had banded together in a league of some 10,000 millionaires, using money and intrigue to select its creatures for the Presidency, the Supreme Court, the Congress. Dru, in exploring their secret handiwork in this field, has all the advantages of the author's excellent knowledge of machine politics and skulduggery. "Progressive" Senators are pictured who hail from the agricultural states; refusing moderate measures, they insist upon inserting radical and unsound clauses in proposed reform laws, which result in all being nullified as unconstitutional by a complaisant Supreme Court. But these men are merely the creatures of "*Selwyn*" (a combination of Mark Hanna and Nelson Aldrich), who in his fertile brain conceives and directs all the movements at this political puppet show.

Thenceforth the utopian novel takes flight into fantasy, yet fantasy grounded in the realities of America's recent political history, of which the author shows a full understanding. *Selwyn*, the boss, in his political undertakings collaborates always with *Thor*, described as the mightiest financier of the land—much like the contemporary J. Pierpont (or "Jupiter") Morgan! The two men, at a certain juncture, seek a candidate for President and fix upon *Rockland*, a "progressive" demagogue, and governor of a Middle Western state. The latter accepts their aid and pledges in return adherence to the "unwritten law" of exercising Presidential rule subject to their counsels. An enthusiastic, nation-wide "Rockland sentiment" is manufactured quickly; the conservatives pretend to oppose it and yield so reluctantly that Rockland himself is almost fooled. The election victory is insured by a tremendous organization drive like those of Hanna.

The plotters, *Thor* and *Selwyn*, on the morning of their victory, sit rubbing their hands and counting the vast profits to follow. But a concealed dictaphone records all that they utter; by a leak in the "System" it is stolen and broadcast to the startled people throughout the land. The convulsion of popular anger flames into civil revolution. Philip and Gloria, his Joan of Arc, ride at the head of the armed rebels who move in from the West, cross the Mississippi, and in a single great battle destroy the government army (made up of Easterners). The victorious General Dru now takes over the government and names himself "Administrator of the Republic." With the aid of a council of twelve wise men he decrees a new Constitution incorporating sweeping political reforms which open the way to a new era of peace and riches. These reforms are:

1. Reform of the judiciary.
2. Institution of the partial single tax, largely reducing taxes on "improvements," increasing those on unused land.
3. A Federal income tax.
4. A Federal incorporation act, with labor represented in industry, the eight-hour day, and compulsory profit-sharing.
5. Prohibition of holding companies; regulation of all utilities; nationalization of the telephone company at fair rates.
6. Public relief of unemployment.
7. Loans on easy terms to farmers.
8. Constitutional amendments by simple majority vote.

One reform provision even abolishes the Casket Trust, and makes burial less costly to the poor! Nothing is overlooked in this Single-Taxer's paradise.

But after a period of several years of peace and plenty, the great dictator generously resigns, and with the applause of his countrymen ringing in his ears sails abroad to devote himself to creating lasting peace on earth by organizing a "League of Nations."

In *Philip Dru* we certainly have the epic, although somewhat thin and watery in style, of the age of political enlightenment that came in with Theodore Roosevelt and Woodrow Wilson. To read it is to live again through those days and to hear the very accents of the House-Wilson conversations.

But for the moment, House's visions of "working through politics," making a President, saving the country from revolution, and inaugurating a League of Nations, turned upon such prosaic tasks as winning over state delegates to the coming Democratic convention. Returning to Austin late in December, 1911, he found that the local office-holders and party workers were not sufficiently convinced by the new leader's rhetoric. It was necessary to carry on a state-wide canvass; and House, gathering together "the various pieces of his old political machinery," conducted a contest which, one of his associates said, "was the greatest work of organization that I remember." For three months House's aides labored in every county of the state. Then at last, March 6, 1912, he wrote to Wilson:

> I am pleased to tell you that we now have everything in good shape in Texas and that you may confidently rely upon the delegates from this state.[30]

The large Texas delegation of fifty-eight made a solid nucleus upon which to build the Wilson movement. The influence of House and his Texas political friends had ramifications throughout the South, and was instrumental in having Wilson made "second choice" after Favorite Sons such as Oscar Underwood of Alabama. The veteran Texas politicians would also be of tremendous value in working as a disciplined band at the Baltimore convention to carry out Edward House's far-flung plans for capturing other delegates' votes. These faithful labors were to bring rich rewards one day for House's "Texas crowd."

The second most important task, which House undertook as his own special province, was that of winning over Bryan to their cause. House made it his business to see Bryan in New York during November, and soon after, pursued Bryan as far as his ranch in Texas. He endeavored to "remove obstacles" from Bryan's mind and motes from his eye. He fed him also with his suspicions of Champ Clark (whose aspirations were aided by the "sinister" Hearst). When the unfortunate "cocked hat" letter of Wilson's became public, House redoubled his diplomatic pressure. He even courted Mrs. Bryan, who had much influence over her husband, and wormed himself into her confidence. House guessed that Bryan himself could not win the nomination, and that in choosing among the men available, he would turn at last to the

[30] House, *Intimate Papers*, pp. 57-58.

brave Governor who had "cut loose from the bosses," broken with George Harvey, and turned against Wall Street.

Outwardly Bryan remained neutral between the two leading candidates, Champ Clark and Wilson. But on the eve of the Democratic convention, Mrs. Bryan sent House a confidential message indicating that her husband's feeling was "quite in accord with the talk we had."

6

William Jennings Bryan in his later years played an extraordinary role in our national politics. He failed for sixteen years to win the office he aspired to, and other offices, for instance that of Senator, he spurned. He himself sometimes wondered if he would have enjoyed being President—a point which he still kept secret from the public. But it was as a Voice that he dominated the Democratic party; he alone could expose and smash the designs of his adversaries, as he lectured up and down the land before his immense Chautauqua and church following. His mere presence in Washington caused anxiety among the Congressmen, and his powerful pressure could upon occasions turn the balance for or against important national legislation. Thus the Democratic party, as a professional organization for electoral contests, lived willy-nilly under his domination through long years that had brought only national defeat; and throughout the West and the South few Democratic politicians cared to invoke his displeasure.

In a remarkable letter written in 1904, just after his defeat at the St. Louis convention, Bryan has presented better than anywhere else his own sense of his true mission.

I do not know what my real work in life is and I have often been impressed with our scant knowledge of the future—even of our own lives. I feel that I have been able to do something to raise political ideals and if my life is spared, I hope to do much more. My great concern has for years been, and still is, to throw whatever influence I may have, be it small or great, upon the right side of each question, to the end that human rights may be sacredly defended and public interests advanced.

While I have been a candidate for office, this had been merely incidental and no part of my general plan. I do not want to hold office except as it may assist in realizing the plans that I have laid for the advancement of the interests of the common people. In fact I shall feel relieved if I am permitted to work as a private citizen and can leave the cares and responsibilities of office to others. My life is now an ideal one. With a happy home to which I can retire when weary and from which I can go refreshed; with a sufficient income for my modest needs and with nothing upon my mind and heart but the work in which I am engaged, what more could I ask? If I have been defeated in my political aspirations the defeats weigh like dust in the balance against the blessings that I have received and that I now enjoy. . . .[31]

Through these lines there shines the soul of a truly good man, although one of rigid virtue that could make itself unpleasant to the worldly sort. In these calmer days, following his meteoric youth, the stamp of the inveterate crusader and uplifter contending against the too numerous infidels, the unwearying expounder of the Bible, the orator of the Chautauqua circuit, drew sadder lines upon Mr. Bryan's handsome countenance. But on the other hand it was a riper, more statesmanlike Bryan who emerged in 1912 after so many defeats. In holding his whip over the enthusiastic Democratic multitude that followed him, in exercising his "balance of power," Bryan was now more disinterested than any political figure of his period—none of whom he resembled.

Bryan had first heard of Dr. Wilson as the "awakened scholar," after the New Jersey victory of 1910; news of Wilson's legislative achievements aroused his curiosity. Further, he praised Wilson in *The Commoner;* and he wrote letters to him, catechizing, on various grounds of policy, the man who had in earlier years been proposed as an anti-Bryan leader.

In March, 1911, Bryan, who had never been invited to Princeton (unlike so many other Elder Statesmen), arrived there to lecture. Mrs. Ellen Wilson, the first Mrs. Wilson, who was both intelligent and diplomatic, determinedly arranged a dinner for

---

[31] Bryan to Rev. Dr. W. M. Hindman, of Kenton, Ohio; quoted here with permission of Mr. E. F. Cigrand, Aurora, Ill.

Bryan and saw to it that her husband was there. A few weeks later they spoke together at a public meeting, and Wilson, turning from his earlier convictions as an Eastern hard-money Democrat, now paid marked and gracefully phrased compliments to the Commoner, who had so long "cried America awake." [32] Bryan had shown at best a polite neutrality toward the aspirations of both Champ Clark and Wilson—behind which, many surmised, there lay a hope of wresting the nomination for himself out of a deadlocked convention. But the airing of Wilson's old anti-Bryan letter to the railroad lawyer, Adrian Joline, seemed likely to destroy even this friendly neutrality, a few days before the Jackson Day Dinner took place at Washington.

Wilson's friends rushed to Bryan with their explanations. They found him generous and broad-minded, yet reserved. He had insisted everywhere that he would fight to have a decided progressive nominated by the party in 1912. He hinted therefore to Wilson's emissaries, Dudley Field Malone and Josephus Daniels, that the best thing for Wilson to do was to show his progressivism and independence as clearly as possible.

The foremost Democrats on that night of January 8, 1912, Clark, Wilson, Alton B. Parker, Underwood, and Harmon, all entered the limelight and were passed in review by the leaders or bosses gathered there, Bryan, Hearst, Charles Murphy of New York, Roger Sullivan of Chicago. Almost every ambitious schemer connected with the party was present; the goggle-eyed George Harvey sat directly opposite Woodrow Wilson and closely watched the effect he made.

Wilson had been coached to pay his tribute to Bryan and to do so without appearance of craven apology or truckling. The keynote of the evening was "harmony"; and when Wilson arose toward the end, immediately preceding Bryan's speech, he was equal to the occasion. Ever supple in speech, he managed to be general, vague, yet "progressive." He touched upon his favorite theme nowadays, the uprising against "invisible government" and

[32] Baker, *op. cit.*, Vol. III, p. 211.

the need for "setting the government of this country free and the business of this country free." Then turning to Bryan, he said with conviction:

He kept the fires burning which have heartened and encouraged the democracy of the country. . . . Let us apologize to each other that we ever suspected or antagonized one another; let us join hands once more all around the great circle of community of counsel and of interest which will show us at the last to have been indeed the friends of our country and the friends of mankind. . . .[33]

There was a flattering burst of applause. But to those present the face of Mr. Bryan "was a study."

[33] The New York *World*, Jan. 9, 1912.

XIII. THE MENACE OF LA FOLLETTE

O N THE eve of the Presidential year 1912, signs of a tremendous political crisis were seen in increasing force by all who had eyes to see. Herbert Croly's observation in *The Promise of American Life* that our politics "had suddenly been made much more interesting and significant than at any time since the Civil War" was being fully borne out. To a La Follette or a Bryan it was a moment of thrilling hope for the resumption of the advancing movement. To a President Taft, however, the nation seemed to be falling upon evil days. In September, 1911, he wrote to his brother Charles:

There is so much demagoguery these days and the people seem to like it. . . . Intelligent men have lost their heads and are leaning toward fool, radical views in a way I never thought possible. . . .[1]

Somewhat later, in 1912, Taft in a confidential letter summed up the political crisis as follows: "*The great trouble that we are facing . . . is the division of parties into groups, such as they have in France and Germany, and now in England.*"[2] What Taft meant of course was that he foresaw class conflicts and the coming of class parties in America. Woodrow Wilson in one of his New Jersey speeches, expressing the mood of the times, also alluded to the possible realignment of the parties into groups with opposing interests and faiths, rather than rival office-seeking concerns. The only real parties, he said, would be those of the reactionaries and the liberals.

[1] Pringle, *Taft*, Vol. II, p. 761.
[2] Duffy, *op. cit.*, p. 299; italics mine.

The pressure of groups or classes seeking to burst the bonds of the old professional party institution asunder is the story of 1912. At the bottom of the social scale, radical labor appeared to be in more militant humor than ever before. The early days of the Taft administration had witnessed an explosion of labor-union violence in California, where the sensational MacNamara bombing case lent credence to reports that labor had determined to declare war upon the existing order. Rebuffed by Standpatters, such as Speaker Cannon, who swore that "he wouldn't recognize anyone who spoke for the Eight Hour Day law," Gompers redoubled his efforts to organize the pressure of labor in the political field. Taft had given to labor little more comfort than in the days when he was known as "the injunction judge," and the A. F. of L. was now driven as in 1896 to transferring the votes of its members in a body to the opposing party.[3]

The more vigorous efforts of the A. F. of L. to exert pressure in the political field, to "reward its friends and punish its enemies," even in the separate Congressional districts, were much stimulated by the mounting influence during these days of the National Association of Manufacturers in Republican party councils. The weakness of the A. F. of L.'s political tactics stemmed, however, from the peculiarly deep-rooted character of the party system and its permanent personnel. The trade-unionists applied the pressure of their votes once in two or four years; but seldom (save for 1912) did they produce any fundamental results, for the professional party men worked the year round.

Similar causes of failure were to be seen in the spirited Socialist movement, which reached its zenith between 1908 and 1912. A solid minority of labor, especially in the large cities of the East and the Middle West, regularly supported the Socialist party and its perennial standard bearer, Debs. The Socialists brought their fixed, doctrinaire, Marxian interpretation to bear upon the American capitalist order and proposed constantly their program of nationalization of industrial and natural resource monopolies to

[3] Gompers, *Seventy Years*, Vol. II, p. 239.

be effected by democratic process, at the ballot box. To this end an extremely energetic and ardent educational campaign was conducted from 1904 on. Moreover, a series of celebrated "conversions" to Socialism took place among men and women of wealth and social position, university professors, and leading journalists.

But the recruits soon found that their labors were to be limited chiefly to proselytizing and educational work. Politically speaking, joining the Socialists was like entering a monastery. At election campaigns the Socialists conducted their proselytizing with utmost ardor; then they would relapse into relative inactivity until the next November. No fragments of the existing parties and their habitual office-holders were ever carried over to Socialism, save in certain local or city elections. Socialism, which had won such enormous electoral victories in Europe, with its parliamentary governments, encountered the strong walls of the professional party system in America, manned by its tens of thousands of adept followers who had long depended for their political life upon holding office. Pre-war Socialism failed to exert a direct, active pressure in politics such as the later Marxians, the Communists, by more militant and continuous tactics, brought into play when, though small in number, ill-led, or misguided, and with scanty funds, they labored in the vineyard with the fanatical discipline and constancy of the humblest Tammany heelers. The Socialists, however, did enjoy their largest and most salutary *indirect* influence toward 1912, when their limitations were less well understood.

That year the incredibly bitter and agonizing strike of the woolen workers at Lawrence, Massachusetts, beginning in January, engrossed the nation. William D. ("Big Bill") Haywood, the leader of the Industrial Workers of the World, hitherto chiefly active in the West, directed a large organizing program. Soon he succeeded in entering the Eastern textile field and combining 50,000 strikers as "one big union," owing to the previous apathy of the American Federation of Labor in this sector. A great strike against intolerable conditions followed. That winter the excessive cruelty of the local authorities and police, the stories of famine in Lawrence, helped to arouse public opinion and win the strike. The terrible Lawrence strike provided a graphic, living lesson in Marxism. Socialists and I.W.W.'s had worked together in the cause; and a few months later Haywood, whom Lincoln Steffens described as "crude, rough, violent and true," joined forces with the gentler Eugene Debs, becoming a member of the Executive Committee of the Socialist party. The Socialist party vote in November, swelled by new recruits, reached nearly 900,000, numerically the largest in its history, when we consider that women did not vote and the total population was then about three-fourths that of 1940.

Far more likely to upset the apple cart was the new political organization publicly launched by Republican Senator Robert M. La Follette of Wisconsin and his progressive friends in January, 1911. Ostensibly, the National Progressive Republican League represented an effort, as La Follette told Brandeis, to "get men of our stamp" to work together.[4] In reality, it bore a good deal of resemblance to a Trojan Horse; for its function might well be that of transforming and capturing control of one of the great parties. A machine whose immediate purpose seemed educational was being erected; it had a national office at Washington, and allies at work in the interior organizing meetings, rallies, and lectures. In time it could become also the vehicle for a new national party if the necessity for that arose, calling to its banner the progressive elements among the Democrats and the Republicans alike.

Some of the Progressives, such as Gifford Pinchot, hero of the fight for conservation, even in 1910 were proclaiming that the Special Interests would soon be driven from politics. ". . . The old party ties are slipping off; . . . the progressives in both parties are the true representatives of their parties and the people." [5]

[4] Lief, *op. cit.*, p. 203.
[5] Speech at Detroit, Oct. 26, 1910; Newark *Evening News*, Oct. 27, 1910.

It is evident that La Follette always had kept the possibility of a new party in his eye. He was a tenacious political leader, cautious in his strategy, bold in tactics. In his campaign autobiography of 1912 he argued that it needed something equivalent to a revolution in America in order to launch a new national party. Parties were "born, not made." When he later ignored his own axiom, in 1924, he came to grief. At the time he held that the country was ripe not for revolution but for reform. The prevailing temper of America was middle-class; the majority of its organized workers endeavored to "control the job" rather than to bring about class war; its farmers hoped that land values would rise again, and the cost of living fall; the capitalist mode of production, though guilty of great unevenness and inequalities, was the most fortunate and abundant in all the world, and no other full-grown system stood ready to replace it overnight.

The little American feared and hated monopolies, grumbled at the high cost of living—eggs were now 65 cents a dozen!—and longed to make secure the small property-holder's way of life. It was this American, in the mass, "Jacobin" rather than Socialist, that La Follette chose to represent, and to whom he seemed the providential leader.

It was President's Taft's misfortune that, after having outraged many Eastern liberals by his conduct in the Ballinger case, he also gave mortal offense to the men who stood in Congress as Insurgents and Progressives. That he neither liked nor understood them is all too clear from his private correspondence, in which he alludes to men like La Follette and Norris as "yellow dogs." In January, 1910, Norris of Nebraska, in most judicious and respectful language, warned the President that he was opening himself to the charge that he used his executive power "to influence and control the members of the legislative branch in the exercise of their constitutional function." In shorter words, he was depriving them of patronage. Taft's reply was merely evasive, although not more so than other Presidents' statements in such circumstances. But before 1910 was well under way, his biographer relates, "President Taft had abandoned even the pretence that he did not discriminate against the Insurgents." [6] Thus a whole group of active Western leaders were rendered desperate: Senators Bourne of Oregon, Clapp of Minnesota, and Norris of Nebraska, and Representatives Murdock of Kansas, Charles A. Lindbergh, Sr., of Minnesota, and Lenroot of Wisconsin, were but a few of the able, trained politicians who were driven inevitably to fight by the side of La Follette, as a solid bloc, against the Old Guard.

The well-intentioned, blundering Taft, growing highly alarmed at the trend of opinion in the country, made a series of patently conciliatory moves after November, 1910. Having supported Secretary of the Interior Ballinger through thick and thin, even to the extent of falsifying the date of a report, Taft retreated on this issue, and when Ballinger, to his vast relief, resigned, he replaced him with Walter Fisher of Chicago, an ardent, idealistic conservationist, his polar opposite. After having called the Payne-Aldrich Tariff Act the best ever framed, he devoted himself in 1910 to a plan of reciprocity with Canada which would, in effect, scale down some of its objectionably high rates.

Reciprocity was an ancient idea, formerly espoused by such a staunch Republican as McKinley himself, and applied in the form of a preferential agreement to our trade with Cuba. But in the case of Canada, the plan had often foundered upon the shoals of a jealous American protectionism and Canadian-British suspicions of economic encirclement.

By January 26, 1911, after frequent negotiations quietly conducted with the Canadian authorities and party leaders at home, Taft sent a special message to Congress calling for a reciprocity agreement that provided free trade with Canada in a long list of articles and lowered customs rates upon hundreds of others. It was a statesmanlike message; and behind it, as Taft informed the dying Nelson Aldrich, was the thought that only by such a measure could the "American system" of protection be saved, and

[6] Pringle, *Taft*, Vol. II, pp. 612-613.

the expected vengeance of triumphant Democrats be averted after 1912.[7]

The message was well•received by the country. Eastern financial, railroad, and manufacturing interests were now favorable to a limited tariff reduction in special spheres. But to the disappointment of the President, the Western Republican bloc, whom he had alienated, succeeded in defeating passage of the bill in the Lame Duck session of Congress. The Western politicians now argued that the tariff concessions given to Canada would be helpful chiefly to Eastern manufacturers, who would be provided with free raw materials, but would burden our agriculturists by permitting the competitive import of Canadian cattle, hides, and grain. La Follette in vigorous speeches contended that the proposed reciprocal duties contained many of the evil practices of past tariff legislation, which he outlined in his habitually painstaking and factual manner. The vote in the Senate revealed the terrible weakness of the administration in the whole Western tier of states—California, Oregon and Washington, the Dakotas, Nebraska, Kansas, Iowa, Wisconsin, and Minnesota.[8]

Acting with an energy unusual to his character, Taft called a special session of the new Congress to meet early in April, 1911, a half hour after the old session died. Although farm organizations, such as the powerful National Grange, now warned him that their membership felt the measure would discriminate against them, Taft valiantly fought for reciprocity, making vehement speeches that summer and vowing that he would carry on "even if it should cost his party the farmer vote."[9] This time the predominantly Democratic Congress passed the bill after long and bitter debate, Eastern Republicans and Democrats overcoming the resistance of a large group of Western and Insurgent Senators. But Taft's victory, credited to the Democrats, soon proved to be no more than Pyrrhic. The Hearst newspapers and Democratic Speaker Champ Clark had spoken too often and too openly of

[7] *Ibid.*, Vol. II, p. 590.   [9] Sullivan, *op. cit.*, Vol. IV, p. 398.
[8] Robinson, *op. cit.*, p. 315.

ultimate annexation of Canada by gradual economic means; Taft
himself, with his habitual tactlessness, alarmed the Canadians by
allusions to "the parting of the ways" and the "light and imper-
ceptible" ties that bound Canada to the mother country. The general election in Canada brought the crushing defeat of the Liberal
party, which had espoused reciprocity, and the President saw his
pet scheme rejected peremptorily by the Canadian people. The
President, for all his pains, found his party more sharply divided
on sectional lines than ever before, the Progressive faction having
stood against him to the end, as hard-headed advocates of the
American farmer.

After more than two years very little was left of Taft's original
plan to steer a cautious middle course, consolidate the reform gains
of the Roosevelt administration, and thus outflank that Old Devil
revolution. The politically unlucky Taft administration (which in
its routine conduct of affairs was more honest and effective than
most of its predecessors), had acquired a marked unpopularity and
nothing it attempted seemed to repair the mischief. The Supreme
Court decision in the case of the Standard Oil of New Jersey, dissolving the trust but imposing its "rule of reason," had provoked
a fierce controversy during which many leaders of public opinion,
especially those of the Progressive stripe, declared that the trust
law was rendered more uncertain than ever, that the people were
more exposed to the plunderings of the trusts and were left without remedy. "Are the trusts and combinations stronger than the
government?" Bryan and La Follette asked of their sober Chautauqua audiences, up and down the land, all that year. Criticism
of the Supreme Court itself and its conservative judgments became
more widespread than ever. That summer at the hearings of the
Stanley Committee, Brandeis gave warning that the existence of
the trusts imperiled the continuance of American democracy.
". . . Our sacred constitution," he declared, "protects not only
vested rights, but vested wrongs. . . ." Alluding to such industrial monsters as the United States Steel Corporation, he commented: "We risk our whole system, judicial, political, and industrial, by creating a power which we cannot control. . . ."

President Taft, who believed religiously in the Supreme Court, and who appointed three extremely conservative justices to the bench he had long desired to occupy, fervently upheld the Standard Oil decisions in public statements. There is reason to suppose, however, that he and his chief adviser, Attorney General Wickersham, were more embarrassed than appeared on the surface. It is difficult to avoid the deduction that at this stage they took stock of the situation and either cast about for a new "line" to follow, or took up one that had been held in reserve for such an emergency.

As Mark Sullivan relates, Taft acted

as men in desperation sometimes do when they find the strength of the tide running against them too strong. . . . Left to himself he would have let the tide against him go on to whatever fate might bring him. But some of his advisers suggested that the tide . . . might be reversed, the Progressives placated, and the Democrats disarmed, by a policy of thorough-going prosecution of the trusts.[10]

It was resolved that the Sherman Anti-Trust Law, although it lay under a cloud of judicial doubts, should be enforced to the hilt. Within two days after news came of the final defeat of reciprocity by Canadian voters, on September 21, 1911, a remarkable interview given by Mr. Wickersham appeared in a large New York newspaper. It forecast a renewed onslaught against the trusts: a hundred or more great corporations would be called before the courts; criminal procedure would be instituted against their officers. Among those who were now to be judged was the United States Steel Corporation, which had been wholly immune from prosecution in the first ten years of its life.[11]

Thus the Taft administration veered to the "left" in the autumn of 1911, while a seismic shock of fear swept through Wall Street. Soon there were compiled twenty-two bills in equity and forty-five indictments. Stocks and bonds sank calamitously; Taft's friends in financial circles were in despair, feeling that he performed his

[10] Sullivan, *op. cit.*, Vol. IV, pp. 406-407.
[11] The New York *World*, Sept. 23, 1911.

political tasks with an unfeeling awkwardness, and ill requited their original faith in him. To the antagonism which the labor movement and the Western farmers felt for the ruling administration, there was added now the implacable hostility of an important group of great finance capitalists.

2

"Ohio would be on fire from one end to the other if a real Progressive like La Follette came in," wrote Brand Whitlock, the reform Mayor of Toledo, in the summer of 1911.[12] From Minnesota, Senator Moses Clapp wrote Beveridge at the same time that

. . . Senator La Follette is being pressed to stand as a candidate for the Republican nomination, and I do not see how he is going to be able to resist. From all over the country there is a demand that there shall be a candidate who stands for old-time Republican policies as exemplified by men like Lincoln. . . .[13]

Lincoln Steffens, who was then in California, besieged his friends by letter throughout the country, from San Francisco to Boston, for small contributions to the La Follette movement. In the East, Gifford Pinchot and his brother Amos gave unstintedly of financial and vocal support. Writers and intellectuals such as Ray Stannard Baker and Frederic C. Howe, Francis J. Heney, George Record, and Ben B. Lindsey worked together with liberal millionaires such as Rudolph Spreckels of San Francisco, Charles R. Crane and Medill McCormick of Chicago, Joseph Fels of Philadelphia, and A. E. Filene of Boston, to carry on the La Follette "boom," all through 1911.

The boom had been launched as early as April, when the Insurgent faction in Congress, in a conference at Washington, passed a resolution inviting Senator La Follette to become the Progressive candidate for the Republican nomination. When it became

[12] Whitlock, *Letters*, Vol. I, p. 127.
[13] Jul. 11, 1911; Bowers, *op. cit.*, p. 412.

clear, in 1911, that the unpopularity of the Taft administration spelled certain defeat for the party in the event of the President's renomination, there was a great deal of speculation as to what Colonel Roosevelt would do. What would he do also about the Progressive movement? His personal friends, however, especially Gifford Pinchot, James Garfield, and McCormick, were seen to be busily occupied in supporting Senator La Follette's aspirations.

Theodore Roosevelt suffered from a certain embarrassment because he had designated Mr. Taft as his successor. After promising to retire from active political service, he had in the elections of 1910 consented to help the Republican forces. He had tried to do this especially in New York State, where (in opposition to the New York machine) he had thrust himself into the chairmanship of the party convention, forced the nomination of his friend, Henry L. Stimson, for Governor, and then taking the stump for Stimson, suffered a grievous defeat at the hands of the Tammany men. Since November, 1910, Colonel Roosevelt seemed to feel that his political usefulness was ended, and that not a little of this misfortune flowed from the ineptitude of his former protégé, Mr. Taft. But so far as the Progressive movement was concerned, he refused to lend his name to its league, and maintained merely a friendly neutrality, indicating that he thought the Progressives should not put forward a candidate of their own.

But in May of 1911, after a speaking tour in the West, Roosevelt's spirits seemed to revive and he apparently saw the light. Only now, it must be recorded, did he seem to be convinced that Taft's tactics had been too "reactionary." His motives were much mixed and confused, and we shall revert to them later as they declare themselves. But in the meantime, late in May, 1911, La Follette relates, there came to him Gilson Gardner, a devoted follower of Colonel Roosevelt, who was the Washington correspondent for the Scripps newspaper syndicate, then extremely liberal and independent. Gardner came from Oyster Bay as the

bearer of a most important message. Roosevelt, he said, had entirely changed his mind regarding a Progressive candidate against Taft; he now believed that the Progressives should put forward a candidate, that I should be that candidate, and that I should get into the fight at once. . . . He, Roosevelt, could not openly oppose Taft, whom he had made President . . . could not for the same reason openly advocate my candidacy against Taft; but . . . he would . . . commend my work from time to time in *The Outlook* and help along.[14]

Having Roosevelt's ultimate support, Gardner said (perhaps on his own recognizance) La Follette's nomination for the Presidency was virtually certain.

In May, 1911, Roosevelt passed through Wisconsin on a speaking tour, met La Follette and his lieutenants, and appeared impressed by the strength they had developed and the "scientific" character of the Wisconsin reforms. Truly the country was "going Progressive," he exclaimed.

In his widely read organ, *The Outlook*, Theodore Roosevelt wrote most favorably of the Wisconsin Senator. For once, he wrote, we need not go to foreign lands for examples of social reform. "We can now . . . look for leadership in Wisconsin." There the students at the state university as well as its professors served as aides and experts in "realizing schemes of social betterment." Human rights rather than property rights were the first considerations. And yet there were no signs of dangerous "professional radicalism" (such as T. R. had previously seen in La Follette). Reforms were undertaken with "cool-headed caution and wisdom," concluded Roosevelt, "in the true progressive spirit."[15] He approved the "Wisconsin Idea" and its progenitor both.

La Follette now called together his adherents and besought them for promises of solid, unflinching support. He proposed to make a most active fight for the nomination, one that would involve much labor, time, and money. Thus he would make a "respectable showing," he hoped. ". . . To a few of my most intimate friends I said from the beginning that I would not be

[14] La Follette, *op. cit.*, pp. 512-513.
[15] *The Outlook*, May 27, 1911.

leading a wholly forlorn hope." [16] La Follette then appointed Walter L. Houser, former Wisconsin Secretary of State, as his campaign manager; funds were gathered, approximately $5,000 a month being raised chiefly among the more affluent Progressives, such as the Pinchots (who gave $20,000 in all), McCormick, Spreckels, Crane, and Brandeis (who gave $500).[17]

After July, 1911, the drive was on in earnest. A mass of pamphlet literature was produced and broadcast throughout the country. La Follette meanwhile took the field in a tremendous speaking tour that was designed to disseminate Progressive ideas among all the people. Afterward he recalled that summer as one of the happiest and most eventful of all his life. He moved about in a series of mass ovations. "The people," he thought, "were much in advance of the Progressives in Washington."

By the autumn the La Follette boom seemed to have gathered a powerful momentum. His supporters now counted upon placing from 300 to 350 Progressive delegates at the approaching Republican national convention of 1912, and needed but 200 more to win. This may have been an overestimate; yet reports made for the E. W. Scripps newspapers indicated that the proverbial political "prairie fire" was actually raging through the Middle West and Pacific Coast, as in 1896. Early in October La Follette's lieutenants decided to issue a call for a Progressive convention to be held in Chicago, on October 16, 1911, with representatives from thirty states gathered to give their formal endorsement to La Follette's candidacy.

La Follette in 1911 was in his early fifties; he was by nature a hard worker, and directed his boom with a magnificent, quenchless energy. The project of conquering the regular organization of his party and effecting his own nomination and the adoption of Progressive standards was truly an audacious scheme; yet it was in tune with all of La Follette's earlier, uphill career.

---

[16] La Follette, *op. cit.*, p. 529.
[17] *Clapp Committee Reports*, Vol. II, pp. 541, 1184-1185.

In effect, La Follette's career resembled rather that of certain great Social Democratic leaders in the Europe of his time, such as John Burns in England and Jean Jaurès in France. He labored consistently, uncompromisingly toward a program, a set of principles and standards in politics, in a period when our parties were primarily rival corporate bodies bent upon the gathering of office spoils and only incidentally, or rarely, concerned with enacting programs of principle. Yet unlike a Jaurès or a Bebel, La Follette had no set of dogmas, no distinctive body of theory, which proposed to transplant society from the painful realities of the present to the utopia of the future. Nor did he boast some single cure-all, such as Bryan's monetary inflation or George's Single Tax plan. He believed that men must win an ever-extending democracy by education and experience. It was to be a process of growth that he would lead, at the end of which men would be more fitted than before to face the social problems of the day. To the crying question of the time: "Are the trusts and combinations stronger than the government?" his answer was to erect a flexible but "constructive platform" for reducing the strongholds of monopoly, and encouraging more "direct government," more intense popular rule on every side. The tentative measures to be taken toward this end included direct nominations and elections, income and inheritance taxes, parcel post, government ownership and operation of the express business, physical valuation of the railways and trusts as a basis for control. La Follette's answer to popular protest embraced measures that brought no simple panacea, but fixed an ever closer grip upon the organs of government by the electorate.

La Follette had a sense of history; he knew how to "dramatize facts" in his vigorous, tireless speeches. To thoughtful men, to a Brandeis, his grasp of social problems and his proposals for their solution seemed always more "constructive" and more comprehensive than any other's. He "worked hard." To the masses the evidence of his social conscience was unmistakable. He understood the aspirations of labor far better than those latter-day Hamiltonians, Roosevelt and Taft, and had enacted in Wisconsin the most enlightened social laws in the land. He acted as if *"he really cared."* [18]

To his essentially pragmatic program of gradual reforms, La Follette applied himself with a crusading zeal and fanaticism that was not rivaled by the Socialists of the period. There were many who believed that he had no hope of bringing about his own nomination but desired to make so strong a demonstration that Progressive standards would be forced upon his party in 1912. For there were dangerously, harshly uncompromising traits in this man which were rare in a Presidential candidate, who invariably seeks to please many different factions. He believed that compromises but injured a cause by removing "constancy of purpose." A "clean-cut, uncompromising campaign, *even though a losing one,*" would help later to gain the ends he sought for now.[19] Here was an important point: La Follette was always ready to fight alone; he was willing to "lose." La Follette heard at one time that Roosevelt hesitated to fight Taft for the Republican nomination, holding that even if he could win, the party would be so divided and the Democrats so strong that he would lose the election. This made the Wisconsan laugh: "Why should a man think only of winning an office?" he would say.

Thus the Little Giant of Wisconsin spent himself freely. This effort in a thousand lectures and long tours up and down the country alone should have given the lie plainly to the stupid commentators who recorded his strange "egoism." Certainly he was a proud man; the tilt of his prominent, finely cut jaw, the gleam of his piercing eye, the pose of his stocky, short, wrestler's body, all bespoke pride and militancy and courage. But what held him to his course, despite fearful disappointments, as his friends relate, was his supreme conviction that history and time would bear witness to "the rightness of the principles by which he guided himself."

Donald Richberg, who was a follower of "Teddy" in 1912 and

[18] Hon. L. D. Brandeis to author.
[19] La Follette, *op. cit.*, p. 528.

felt hostile to La Follette at the time, changed his tune drastically when he came to know "Battle Bob" well a few years later. Far from being the obstinate, vindictive and egotistical man he was painted by adversaries, Richberg found him immensely tolerant, especially when compared with the pious Bryan. He had a sudden winning smile that lighted up his whole face, erasing its lines of struggle and anxiety, and was remembered even by his enemies. Richberg, then young, recalls:

> He appealed to me—as I am sure he did to many other young men—to give the utmost of time and energy. He did not offer hopes of quick victories, but the prospect of glorious defeats.

There was so much work to do, he seemed to cry out. If the people only knew how badly they were ruled, how dishonest were the "great men" they were expected reverently to follow, then what big things might be accomplished yet! The struggle would draw itself out for many years. Was it vain? La Follette, even in old age, with the shadows lengthening for him, would say: "It is a bitter, discouraging struggle—many defeats for a few victories—but it brings inner satisfactions that are lasting and repay for all the pain." [20]

He would exclaim: "I am telling you the truth. If only the people know the truth, they will vote the right way. . . ." Or, singling out a person in the audience, he would ask repeatedly—after a long patient exposition of the trust situation, the Supreme Court's "rule of reason," or the Ballinger-Pinchot case—"Now do you understand me? Do you? I will explain again." Or at the end of a Chautauqua meeting in some small town, he would call the young people in the audience to him, and say: "I have done; but I have a few hours before my train leaves, and have lots of time for you. I will answer any questions you care to put."

To many among the confused, uncertain, troubled multitudes who saw him at his best, in his prime, during 1911 and 1912, he was primarily "a forceful man," his voice powerful rather than

[20] Richberg, *Tents of the Mighty*, pp. 132-134.

sweet, his body muscular and nervous from the sole of his feet to the crown of his head with its "shock of hair rebellious to the comb." Forceful in his far-reaching voice, forceful in his dramatic gestures, forceful in the form and resoluteness of his statement. He was in short the "real leader of the Progressives"; he offered no middle-of-the-road line, yet he seemed to challenge all: "Come on, and I'll save you!" Some in the crowds hissed him; but he seemed, like Wendell Phillips of Abolitionist days, not to dislike this.[21]

La Follette had always mistrusted Theodore Roosevelt. He knew the Colonel well, and had studied his record and manner of doing things from close by. La Follette's memoirs pay tribute to T. R.'s usefulness in "awakening" the public conscience to higher ethical standards by appeals expressed both picturesquely and vigorously. But, La Follette concluded, the man's actual ignorance of affairs, his "want of definite conception always invited to compromise, retarding or defeating real progress." Too often T. R. was willing to take "half a loaf" in lieu of none, as he said. But in politics it was often better to demand the full loaf, since the seductive half loaf "dulls the appetite and destroys the keenness of interest in attaining the full loaf." La Follette's epitomization of the Rough Rider ended with a passage that was stamped with his own insight and that, written in 1912, has remained classic:

His most savage assault upon special interests was invariably offset with an equally drastic attack upon those who were seeking to reform abuses . . . demagogues and dangerous persons. In this way he sought to win approval both from the radicals and the conservatives. This cannonading, first in one direction, then in another, filled the air with noise and smoke, which confused and obscured the line of action, but when the battle cloud drifted by and quiet was restored, it was always a matter of surprise that so little had been accomplished.[22]

As the year 1911, year of political crisis, wore on, Roosevelt's relations with the La Follette movement remained as equivocal as

[21] The New York *World*, Jan. 3, 1912; *The Outlook*, Feb. 3, 1912.
[22] La Follette, *op. cit.*, pp. 478-480.

ever. Obscurity has long shrouded the real negotiations between Roosevelt and La Follette emissaries. No letters exist in which Roosevelt pledged direct support of La Follette's candidacy, and probably none will ever be found. It is doubtful, in any case, if he would have committed himself in writing. He was as "cagey" as if he were dealing with a Harriman, or the Japanese ambassador. The tradition among the La Follette adherents has been that T. R. sent encouraging messages through emissaries, or indirectly. Others believe he said to Gardner that he was "not against La Follette," and did not say he was "for" him, in so many words.[23] For he was never above such mildly Machiavellian intrigues, as William Allen White has said. But the La Follette Progressive "boom" rose in a tide through the first nine months of 1911. Suddenly in mid-October the movement began to slow up, with shoals and reefs showing ahead.

At the Progressive "convention" held in Chicago on October 16, 1911, by informally chosen representatives from many states, La Follette was enthusiastically endorsed as its "logical candidate" for the Presidency. The only discordant note was sounded by James R. Garfield, Theodore Roosevelt's former Secretary of the Interior, who proposed that "this endorsement is to be regarded as a recommendation rather than a committal of the movement to any one man." Garfield had just returned from a visit to Oyster Bay.[24]

Why did the friends of Roosevelt among the Progressives and Roosevelt's organ, *The Outlook*, resist, or struggle to delay, the endorsement of La Follette's candidacy?

For La Follette, the great stumbling block continued to be—as 1912 drew near—the equivocal attitude or hidden opposition of Theodore Roosevelt. Men who worked for La Follette wondered out loud whether he would be supplanted in the end. As late as November 26, 1911, Roosevelt in an interview said that he was not a candidate and "discouraged" the idea. But soon afterward

[23] Charles Willis Thompson to author, Dec., 1938.
[24] *The Outlook*, Oct. 28, 1911; La Follette, *op. cit.*, p. 533.

he was rumored to have said that he would not shirk his duty if the call came to him from the people. He was believed to be un-decided in his mind, because he suspected that even if he were nominated the Republicans were fated to lose to the Democrats at the next election—"in which case I shall not only be assailed but derided." [25]

La Follette believed that Theodore Roosevelt always had in back of his mind the hope of returning to power in 1916, but not in 1912. But when in the closing months of 1911 reports of the widespread unpopularity of Taft and the strength of radical and Progressive sentiment all over the country, reports also from pow-erful machine politicians that even Ohio would be lost under Taft, came to him, the possibility of an earlier return to power began to sway his mind. La Follette was convinced all his life that he had been chosen by the conspirators friendly to Roosevelt "to feel out the enemy's strength." In October, Gilson Gardner, returning from Oyster Bay, is said to have told La Follette that "Roosevelt is not only surprised at the development of your candidacy, he is disappointed." [26]

Meanwhile a large Progressive conference in Ohio was sched-uled for January 2, 1912; and well in advance of it, Garfield and Gifford Pinchot prepared to block passage of a resolution endors-ing La Follette's candidacy. In December, 1911, even a Democrat such as Brand Whitlock, the mayor of Toledo, knew that Stand-patters disguised as Progressives were "trying to bring [Roosevelt] out as a candidate *in order to head off La Follette*." [27]

In mid-December, 1911, according to the La Follette side, emis-saries came to the Wisconsin Senator and urged him to make way for the Rough Rider. La Follette indignantly refused. There was a heated conference in Chicago between La Follette and the Rooseveltians in his camp. In the midst of it he was called out-side to verify a story published that day in a Chicago afternoon

[25] Lodge, *Correspondence*, letter of Dec. 13, 1911, Vol. II, p. 417.
[26] La Follette, *op. cit.*, p. 534.
[27] Whitlock, *op. cit.*, Dec. 5, 1911, p. 147; italics mine.

newspaper to the effect that he had already abandoned the race for the nomination. He vehemently denied this; but the constant leak of rumors of this sort filled him with apprehension.

Soon afterward, the appeals of prominent persons to La Follette to retire from the race, and "spontaneous" meetings and resolutions calling upon Roosevelt to save the country, were featured in the press. *"La Follette's Last Hope Gone"* ran one remarkably informed or inspired dispatch from Washington to a Western newspaper, that reported bitter dissension among the Progressives. ". . . The Republicans do not want La Follette and will not have him." [28] These rumors were doing great damage to the La Follette movement, despite firm denials from his lieutenants.

In New York the "Insurgents' Club," headed by Fred Howe, planned a great gathering to be held at Carnegie Hall, January 21, 1912, in honor of La Follette, who was to be principal speaker. Roosevelt also was invited. But he arranged a dinner uptown, and, as long as he could, held a number of the Progressives who were to appear at the La Follette meeting that evening, by regaling them with interminable and merry after-dinner stories. [29] Some of them never got to Carnegie Hall that night, where "Battle Bob," his back to the wall, feeling himself more alone than ever, made one of his most vibrant speeches before a crowd that packed the hall to standing room. The absence of Roosevelt, who was expected to speak for La Follette, was widely noticed in the press. [30]

To most people it looked as if Roosevelt was still possessed by his doubts. That week in January, Lincoln Steffens with his clear insight reported the feverishly fluctuating situation in a letter:

. . . [Francis J.] Heney and La Follette have been here, and we have had long talks. And Heney and I have seen T. R. It looks bad at the moment. *The Colonel is mussing up the whole Progressive movement* with his "To be or not to be." And he won't make a statement.

[28] San Francisco *Examiner*, Jan. 14, 1912.
[29] Fred Howe to author, Dec. 20, 1939.
[30] The New York *Times*, Jan. 22, 1912; San Francisco *Examiner*, Jan. 21, 1912.

He talks to us privately, but not convincingly. . . . La Follette is bully. *He is for the cause, not himself, and wants to act at once, and in the best interests of ultimate results.*[31]

Even at this time, extraordinary rumors were becoming current which should have opened La Follette's eyes to the nature of the opposition; they held, in effect, that a "Wall Street boom for Roosevelt's nomination" was soon to be launched, and that George W. Perkins and Frank A. Munsey, the wealthy publisher, and a large shareholder in the steel trust, were to furnish his financial backing.[32] Other important recruits were Walter Brown, the Ohio boss, and Daniel Hanna, the son of the late Mark, who through his large Ohio newspapers urged Roosevelt to "go in."

Fierce dispute now raged among the Progressive leaders. At one meeting on January 14 at the Pinchot home in Washington, La Follette proposed to send a letter to Theodore Roosevelt that would ask him to declare himself. But Gifford Pinchot and Gardner insisted that there must be no break with Roosevelt. Should this come, they now threatened plainly, they would quit the camp and go over to the Rough Rider in a body. Then on the afternoon of January 29, 1912, there was another stormy gathering at Pinchot's, at which Louis D. Brandeis was also present. The followers of "Teddy"—Gifford Pinchot, the hero-worshiper in particular—presented an ultimatum to La Follette, insisting that he give way. They believed now that their old idol would place himself at their head; that they "could win" with him. The cleverer thing, the more practical politics, the short cut to Progressive goals was by way of Roosevelt's glamorous leadership. La Follette, indignant at their change of front, berated them bitterly, warned them that they pursued a mirage. "I know Roosevelt's strength and I know his weakness," he exclaimed. He refused to give way. The angels with money, Medill McCormick,

---

[31] Steffens, *Letters*, Vol. I, p. 287; Jan. 24, 1912.

[32] San Francisco *Examiner*, Jan. 17, 1912; the New York *Times*, Jan. 22, 1912.

Gifford Pinchot, and Amos Pinchot—the last with some reluctance —now left La Follette's side for good.[33]

"La Follette is in the race to the end" was the announcement that issued from this meeting. Little more was said in public. But several weeks later the suspicions that the Senator had formed, his deep sense of being aggrieved, were intensified when he read Gifford Pinchot's public statement:

> Senator La Follette's candidacy was undertaken for two clear and specific purposes, first, to hold the Progressives together as an effective fighting force, and, second, to prevent the renomination of a reactionary Republican President.

On the very day of the secret rupture in the La Follette camp, while the Rough Rider still remained silent as a Sphinx, news came that Roosevelt-for-President headquarters had been opened up in Chicago by Medill McCormick.[34]

Everything was ready for the stampede to the Roosevelt bandwagon when La Follette, disillusioned, bitter with the thought that the movement he led was sapped and mined from the beginning, made his tragic appearance at the banquet of the Publishers' Association in Philadelphia, February 2. He himself had been ill, his nerves were worn thin, and that night he knew that his youngest daughter was to go under the surgeon's knife. And before him were the distinguished men of the press who, in his conviction, so consistently and malevolently misled and deceived the great public.

His prepared speech was in fact an admirable presentation of the best thought of the Progressives, based in great measure on Mr. Brandeis's theories. La Follette gave his view of the developing crisis of democracy: the nation had passed from a stage of small property-holding and mercantilism through a phase of large, competitive, industrial enterprises, after the Civil War, to a culminating stage of control by great financiers and trust magnates,

---

[33] La Follette, *op. cit.*, pp. 593-595; Fola La Follette to author, Jan. 21, 1940; San Francisco *Examiner*, Jan. 30, 1912.

[34] The New York *Times*, Jan. 30, 1912.

in which competition and individual liberty were being strangled before their eyes. His specific recommendations embraced those measures which would be made famous under the "New Freedom," and in a second wave of reform, under the "New Deal." The government through its agencies must control the great monopolists of banking and transportation; powerful dikes must be set up against the license of the ruthless industrial trusts; the power of the Federal courts to alter legislation by their effectual revisions of the laws of Congress—as in the "rule of reason" decree—must be curbed; the trusts must be prosecuted, but "cutthroat competition" must also be restrained by government controls, by social laws which encouraged the healing growth of labor unions and collective bargaining.

But that night the gentleman from Wisconsin was less interested in his chosen doctrines; ridden by bitter, conflicting emotions, he at length shoved aside his speech and began a tirade against the pundits of the publishing world, his lifelong enemies. What he said, in truth, was prophetic. The spirit of monopoly, of regimentation having conquered our large industries, he contended, was now gaining over the press. The forces of pooled advertising— not yet strong in the heyday of muckraking magazines—would end by dominating the entire newspaper and magazine press, he predicted, and all would then bow down to common taboos, all would voice the same conventional canons of political and social respectability. Beside himself with passion, the Little Giant of Wisconsin lashed out again and again at his well-fed, well-clad, complacent listeners. These influential gentlemen found him graceless and harsh, when they had come expecting an amiable parade of Presidential "possibilities" before their eyes. He had begun late in the evening and his tirade continued for over two hours. By their accounts he repeated himself endlessly, unintelligibly, then at last broke down and slumped to his seat with his head sinking to the table.

A ghastly finish for an evening of conviviality. Did this episode mark the collapse of the strongest heart and best will among the reform leaders? Was it the tragic "farewell to reform" that John Chamberlain has described in a moving passage of his study of this political epoch? The bandwagon was about to start and the music ready to strike up, while the "lost leader" sat alone, abandoned.

The hoary legend that La Follette's physical breakdown forced the influential Progressives of 1912 to turn from him to Roosevelt, on that night of February 2 in Philadelphia, should long ago have been exploded. (No one found anything wrong with La Follette's head, the next day; and the devoted Brandeis continued to stump for him up to the day of the Chicago convention.) It was not the weakness of La Follette that led to his proscription, but rather his alarming strength, the positive, aggressive character of the movement he led, the very capacity he showed for linking together all the dissident factions, among farmers and laborers and the intelligent middle class, into a unified party of concrete principles and program.

La Follette, in 1912, led squarely toward a new party alignment, if the fight to capture the old Republican organization should fail. He said nothing of such plans. That was a bridge he would cross when he came to it. But if the great, inevitable demonstration against Republican conservatism that year had been committed to his hands, it would have resulted not merely in a *temporary* schism, a futile quarrel of personalities, a prating of "righteousness" and the Decalogue—but the formation of a true opposition party. This probability as we shall see was what frightened and hardened the influential citizens who underwrote the Progressive movement that year.

Lincoln Steffens' final word upon the mental confusion, histrionics, and "revivalism" that swept the political arena and caused all sight of truth and fact, of the deeper issues of the day, to be lost, was written in a letter of the time: *"Heroes and Devils still rule our minds!"* [35]

The great parade now began. The men of good will, the Wil-

[35] Steffens, *op. cit.*, Vol. I, p. 308; Sept. 12, 1912.

liam Allen Whites, Pinchots, Garfields, and all their like, were swept along by the mass fervor which the great politico knew well how to use. Shouting and cheering, raising the dust, the marching men swung off in a new direction.

La Follette sat with bowed head. Yet he would revive his strength on the morrow, if only through knowledge of the fear and hatred of him that ruled in high quarters. He would continue. He would continue to be La Follette, prepared by his stoical faith to embrace willingly yet greater "defeats"—as in April, 1917, on the eve of America's entrance into war—if such defeats could point the way to the ultimate victory.

XIV. "ARMAGEDDON"

O<small>N</small> <small>FEBRUARY</small> 10, 1912, there was made public a "spontaneous" petition, signed by the Republican governors of seven states (namely, New Hampshire, Michigan, Missouri, Kansas, Nebraska, West Virginia, and Wyoming), addressed to Theodore Roosevelt, and asking him to become a candidate for the Presidency. It set forth that the Republican rank and file now hungered for the Colonel's leadership; that he alone represented the principles that answered popular demands; and that it was a matter of "plain duty," despite his reputed preference for private life, for him to stand for the nomination and endeavor to save the country from reaction.

Two days later, on February 12, President Taft, who had long been brooding over real or fancied wrongs which his former patron was doing him by his opposition, struck out in a speech at New York against

. . . those who in apparent despair at any ordinary remedy are seeking to pull down . . . the pillars of the temple of freedom and representative government. . . . Such extremists would hurry us into a condition which would find no parallel except in the French Revolution or in that babbling anarchy that once characterized the South American Republics. Such extremists are not progressives; they are political emotionalists or neurotics.[1]

The epithet of "emotionalist" and "neurotic," ostensibly aimed at himself, was believed to have offended Theodore Roosevelt mortally.

[1] The New York *Times*, Feb. 13, 1912.

Now things began to happen. In a prepared speech on February 21, 1912, at Columbus, before the Ohio Constitutional Convention, Roosevelt uttered memorable words which could not easily be unsaid. Once more, but more challengingly than before, he expounded the principles of the New Nationalism. Property rights must be made subject to human rights; government must be set free of the control of money in politics. To this end he advocated, "as weapons in the hands of the people, all . . . devices which will make the representatives of the people more easily and certainly responsive to the people's will." The devices were those of the initiative and the referendum, in which such high hopes were held in 1912. Further than this, Roosevelt went on to express his approval of the plan advocated for some time by La Follette and other Western leaders: the recall of judicial decisions. Thus not only the legislatures, but the courts, hereafter, would to a great extent be subject directly, immediately, to popular will.

Excitement over these bold utterances mounted even higher when it was learned that on the very day of the so-called "Charter of Democracy" speech at Columbus, February 21, 1912, Roosevelt had said to a reporter in response to a question: "My hat is in the ring." Three days later he answered the petition of the seven Governors formally, saying: "I will accept the nomination for President if it is tendered to me. . . ."

Outwardly it appeared that the Colonel had come to a final break with the gentleman he had placed in the White House and with the orthodox leaders of his party. Heeding the popular call, he had resolved, after long inward debate, to lead the fight against reaction in behalf of an aroused public conscience.

Had Theodore Roosevelt become a "radical"? His former political associates did not think so. Cabot Lodge and Elihu Root were deeply shocked at the "new departure" of their old comrade; they held that the new doctrine concerning the power of the courts was not characteristic of him, Root observing: "I have no doubt he thinks he believes what he says, but he doesn't. *He has merely picked up certain popular ideas which were at hand as one might pick up a poker or chair with which to strike.*" [2]

In reality Theodore Roosevelt had a habitual dislike of radicals. Henry Lothrop Stoddard, then the editor of the New York *Evening Mail*, relates that at about this time, in January, 1912, the Colonel spoke to him of his prejudice against the men who formed the "lunatic fringe" of politics, who "want to be revolting all the time." He added: "I cannot be their candidate." [3]

In 1911, La Follette found that Colonel Roosevelt *was firmly opposed* to the "recall of judges." But late in January, 1912, Western politicians had visited the Colonel and told him that this was a Burning Issue in the West, "as dear to the La Follette men as 16 to 1 was to Bryan. . . . Several days of discussion resulted in Roosevelt's concession that the recall of judges might be advocated as a 'last resort.' . . ." [4] Roosevelt thus borrowed La Follette's doctrine; he himself was frightened by the storm that followed his outspoken plea for such a measure in the Columbus speech.

It was not a passion for revolution that drove Colonel Roosevelt back into the political arena. Nor was it an irresistible popular call that furnished the original impetus. An account exists of the secret conferences that took place in late January between Roosevelt and his supporters at the office of *The Outlook* in New York. Howland, an assistant editor of *The Outlook*, felt that Roosevelt's hesitation concerned chiefly the formula and timing of his entrance into the Presidential contest. On January 20, 1912, Howland noted in his diary: "All agree . . . time is here." The wording of the seven Governors' petition was actually prepared by Roosevelt and his friends. On January 22, 1912, Frank Knox of Michigan set forth to gather the signatures of the Governors designated. This was done many days before questions arose as to Senator La Follette's health; the "popular call" was then released in accordance with a prepared plan. [5]

---

[2] Jessup, *op. cit.*, Vol. II, p. 180, letter of Mar. 9, 1912; italics mine.

[3] Stoddard, *op. cit.*, p. 394.

[4] *Ibid.*, p. 395.

[5] H. Howland, *Roosevelt*, pp. 210-211.

Taft, as he told the White House Boswell, Major Archie Butt, could no longer understand his friend Theodore's deep animus against himself. To him the decision of his old mentor to enter the race, disastrous to Taft's fortunes as to party harmony, was born of overweening ambition, vanity, and jealousy. The play of such emotions can never be ignored, to be sure, in a "moral science" such as politics. Theodore's prominently developed bump of egoism was legendary. Yet in his cooler moments, he would recall that he had given his pledge against standing for a third term. He knew that he now flew in the face of a great taboo, which he had respected in 1908. He would provoke discord among the Republicans; it was very doubtful that he would win; and in any case, he would be accused always, like Caesar, of consuming personal ambition. All this he had foreseen and told Joseph B. Bishop, in December, 1911.[6]

The causes of Roosevelt's final public rupture with Taft and with the Old Guard Republicans have constituted a minor historical mystery up to recent days, when the later Roosevelt Papers, those subsequent to 1908, were made available to students. His displeasure with Taft arose not merely because he considered the latter a "good lieutenant" and a "poor leader," who heeded only his conservative relatives and the Standpatters. What goaded the Colonel was the fact that, soon after his return from Africa, he felt himself "neither consulted nor considered," as he wrote Elihu Root in confidence. In the state and Congressional elections of 1910 he was called upon to help the party, and responded freely. Yet, as he said, the very men who begged him to stump and make speeches for the President and the party desired to keep him on the shelf. ". . . In spite of their anxiety to use me at the moment, [they] were exceedingly anxious to limit that use to before elections with the understanding that I should have no say afterward."[7] Roosevelt explained that he would have favored infusing a little judicious progressivism into the conservatism that Taft

[6] Bishop, Roosevelt, Vol. II, pp. 312-313.
[7] T. R. Papers, T. R. to E. Root, Oct. 21, 1910.

followed. Yet platforms and candidates were "arranged deliberately on the theory that the progressives, the men whom I stand with, were not to be given any share in directing the party policy before the nomination and after the election. . . ." To them and to him was left the duty only of supporting the ticket chosen. Surely he had not foreseen that in helping Taft to succeed him, things would turn out so that he, T. R., would have "no share in directing the party policy."

There is the nub of the personal rupture with Taft and his friends. But it is not enough to explain the raid upon La Follette, the rising against the dominant party organization, the "bolt" of June, the braving of almost certain defeat.

Theodore Roosevelt took a pardonable pride in his record as chief magistrate. He had awakened the public conscience as no other leader since the Civil War. What he would be most remembered for, he felt with pride, was his resounding attack upon the "malefactors of great wealth," his deeds as Trust Buster. A shadow had suddenly been cast upon his achievements in this field by the Taft administration's renewal of the anti-trust crusade. Following the defeat of its Canadian reciprocity measure in September, 1911, a vigorous attack had been launched upon the greatest monopolies, among them the United States Steel Corporation. One of the facts cited by the government in evidence of the steel company's unlawful character was its purchase of the Tennessee Coal and Iron property in 1907 with President Roosevelt's approval, an approval which was held to be unwarranted and gained, it was charged, by deception. Since 1907 there had been some unpleasant criticism of Roosevelt in this merger of the steel interests—but now, according to the charge of the Taft administration, he was made out to be either a fool or a knave. Within the week that followed the filing of the steel trust suit, October 26, 1911, Roosevelt published a most vehement and bitter retort to the aspersions against him. The steel men had told him the truth, he asserted. ". . . Nothing . . . is gained," he said, "by breaking up a huge industrial organization *which has not offended otherwise than by its size. . . .*" [8]

Roosevelt's pride was deeply attaint. Major Butt, meeting Roosevelt's sister at lunch in Washington, learned that the Colonel would never forgive the President "for introducing or allowing his name to be introduced into that steel suit. . . ." What was worst of all was that Taft, with his habitual carelessness, had not known or noticed the reflections upon Roosevelt's integrity contained in the government's charge.[9]

If Roosevelt had not been sufficiently convinced that Taft's tactics would lead to a debacle in 1912 by opening wide the breach between Eastern and Western Republicans, then the reflections upon himself in the government's steel trust suit, and the President's pointed tirade against political "neurotics," furnished enough added emotional incentive for him to take up the gauge of battle. But none knew better than the Colonel that political victories are not won simply by emotion. His decision to run was strengthened by the fact that party bosses began to come to him in groups late in 1911, after the steel suit had begun, and urge him to intervene in the nomination contest. Among these were Walter Brown of Ohio, Edward Lee of Indiana, and Frank Knox of Michigan (then), each the chairman of his state Republican organization and members of the Republican National Committee. They spoke of the "hopeless outlook" for the party unless he consented to run. There would be no offices for their henchmen. Brown told him that Wilson and Taft, speaking at Columbus, made scarcely a ripple; whereas if Roosevelt would come there, "there will be such a crowd that the whole traction system . . . will be tied up." [10] These men, together with "Bill" Flinn of Pittsburgh and William Ward of Westchester County, New York, promised that they would carry to his banner great masses of the party delegates.

[8] *The Outlook*, Nov. 16, 1911; italics added.
[9] Butt, *op. cit.*, Vol. II, p. 813.
[10] Stoddard, *op. cit.*, pp. 390-393.

In addition to the professional politicians urging him on, there was a most important group of financial leaders who were highly aroused by Taft and Wickersham's renewal of legal warfare against the trusts, under circumstances that strongly suggested a political "diversion movement." Pleas that Roosevelt stand for the nomination now came as often from south of Fulton Street in Manhattan as from the regions West of the Mississippi. These gentlemen offered not only their votes but their purse.

Since the panic of 1907, Theodore Roosevelt had done a heap of thinking upon the "trust question"; and not a little of this thinking had been influenced by his old friend George W. Perkins. Roosevelt had come around to a "radical" position upon certain current political issues such as those of the "initiative, referendum and recall"—in order to sustain that synthesis of the Haves and Have-Nots that he had always sought to preserve. But at the same time he was persuaded that it was now high time to end the warfare against the trusts, to cease using them as a "football," and let them grow as big as they wanted to grow, so long as they were "good" or "reasonable" trusts. The new Roosevelt of 1912 thus offered, "on the one hand," more direct democracy to the masses (though under his personal guidance), and "on the other hand," governmental tolerance of the great monopolies, though under certain presumed safeguards.

Thus the preaching of Perkins during the last decade was bearing fruit, at length. Perkins had "proved" to Colonel Roosevelt unwearyingly that U. S. Steel and International Harvester practiced the Golden Rule. He had spread wherever possible his doctrine that wise policy would provide for the "regulation" and not the oppression of our grandiose industrial concerns. The intensified trust prosecution set in motion by Taft and Wickersham after October, 1911, aroused Mr. Perkins to fever pitch. It was noticeable that the Morgan companies, long relatively immune (while the Rockefeller concerns were being pilloried), now came under government fire. Perkins now took up the cudgels for the trusts in earnest. In a series of speeches before gatherings of business men and magazine articles that were widely published he lustily belabored the Taft administration.

The Republican party, he argued, had gone back on the letter and especially the spirit of its platform of 1908, when it promised to seek certain amendments to the Sherman Anti-Trust Law that would clarify the trust situation. Now the government was launched upon a course of "repression" rather than "regulation"; and all was in confusion.

If anybody wants to know what is the matter with business; why we are not as prosperous as we should be; why the country is torn asunder politically—let him contemplate what has happened and . . . he will be filled with amazement that such colossal blundering can take place in such an enlightened country as ours is supposed to be.[11]

Smarting under the reflections against himself—for he had taken a large part in the Tennessee Coal and Iron affair and in squelching a suit by Roosevelt against the International Harvester Company—Perkins moved heaven and earth to organize the opposition against Taft and his associates. He declared himself to be an unmitigated "progressive." He preached "righteousness" in business, the enforcement of publicity and uniform systems of accounting, even the establishment of a "business court"—this last device suggesting strongly the contemporary Nazi "Court of Business Honor." At heart Perkins never ceased to long for the kind of government regulation which had been enjoyed under Theodore Roosevelt, when he was wont to telephone his advice to the White House at will.[12] But Perkins and his close business partner, Frank

[11] G. W. Perkins, "Business and Government," *Saturday Evening Post*, Mar. 16, 1912.

[12] Mr. Perkins' idea of government regulation is illustrated by the following memorandum of William Loeb, Dec. 29, 1902: "Mr. Perkins telephoned from New York that he is very much disturbed by a message received from Washington this afternoon that the Attorney-General is to institute proceedings tomorrow against the coal companies. He cannot believe this. If anything of this kind were done, there is danger of serious trouble here in New York, and he hoped the President will give him an opportunity of talking with him about the matter." (*T. R. Papers.*)

A. Munsey, who was a large stockholder of United States Steel, as well as a powerful newspaper publisher, could not for a moment abide the brand of Progressivism offered by a La Follette. The would-be President Makers, Perkins and Munsey, turned instead to the "Hamiltonian" Theodore Roosevelt, who was now in full accord with their plans for business. Roosevelt, the popular idol, they now pursued constantly with their appeals that he help to save the country both from a Taft, whose more rigorous application of the Anti-Trust Act harassed the great financiers, and from a La Follette.

In December and January, Perkins and Munsey exerted themselves to head off the dangerously strong La Follette movement. On January 11, 1912, the Munsey newspapers published an editorial on their first page, signed by Mr. Munsey, discussing the possibility or probability of Roosevelt's candidacy. It prophesied: ". . . If ever the call does come, he [Roosevelt] will buckle on his armour and 'go to it' with all his old-time impetuosity and energy." [13]

The rumors of a "Wall Street boom" for Roosevelt were not wholly without foundation.

More than a fortnight before La Follette's famous *crise de nerfs* at Philadelphia, Perkins and Munsey knew that Theodore would accept the crown. In answer to an entreaty of Munsey's, in a letter that was private and confidential, on January 16, 1912, he had written:

I am not and shall not be a candidate. I shall not seek the nomination, nor would I accept it if it came to me as the result of an intrigue. But I *will not tie my hands to a statement which would make it difficult or impossible* for me to serve the public by undertaking a great task if the people as a whole *seemed definitely to come to the conclusion that I ought to do that task. . . .* [14]

It was at this same time, in mid-January, that the Rooseveltians, hearing of the good omens from Oyster Bay, began to desert the

13 New York *Press*, Jan. 11, 1913.
14 Bishop, *op. cit.*, Vol. II, p. 314; italics mine.

La Follette camp; rumors of dissension leaked out in the press and were denied. La Follette's reported "breakdown" at Philadelphia was but a pretext for the Gifford Pinchots and the Medill McCormicks to return to the standard of the Rough Rider. Those who paid for political parties had, with good reason, lost all hope in the Senator from Wisconsin. He was *constant, uncompromising*—in short, totally unlike typical Presidential candidates, who invariably conceal their hand and endeavor to please various factions before election.

Afterward, when the fighting was over, Roosevelt in a long statement to Amos Pinchot explained his association with such curious Progressives as George W. Perkins, Frank A. Munsey, and H. H. Wilkinson, president of the Crucible Steel Company. These men, Roosevelt stated, had all joined the Progressive cause for the same reason that Wilkinson had given him one day:

. . . Namely, that he had become convinced that something must be done to help the condition of the wage workers, and have justice done so as to better the condition of the small man, and that he was in the Progressive Party because the triumph of the Progressive Party and the adoption of all its principles meant *the elimination of the possibility of his children having to face revolution*.[15]

But La Follette, the Jacobin from Wisconsin, represented to Roosevelt and his friends that which they all desired to spare their children from. Senator William E. Borah has left us an account of how, after the Republican convention in June, Roosevelt sent for him and asked him to "bolt" the Republican party and attend the proposed rump convention which was to nominate him. Borah counseled against holding such a convention and against launching a third party. But Roosevelt exclaimed: "If they don't nominate me they will nominate La Follette." [16]

The grand design was to outflank Western radicalism and preserve the "benevolent" trusts. In effect this was partly what was accomplished in 1912. "The advent of the Roosevelt candidacy de-

---

[15] *Amos Pinchot Papers*, T. R. to Amos Pinchot, Dec. 5, 1912; italics mine.
[16] Johnson, *Borah*, p. 149.

stroyed the unity of the Insurgent movement in Congress as in the nation." [17] The class-economic forces which in America so often assumed a *sectional* form continued afterward their weak but persistent efforts to gain ascendancy over the lines of the old party institution; the Western and other dissident groups were driven to combine with other opposition elements from other sections of the country, when opportunity offered itself, but failed for a long time to stand together as a socially consistent movement.

Meanwhile the Rough Rider, writing his speech of February 21, 1912, in favor of the referendum and the recall of judicial decisions, endeavoring thus to gather for himself La Follette's Progressive following, did not fail to submit this speech in advance to the eyes of Perkins and Munsey.

Munsey's advice at this point is not without a certain interest, since he, principally, shared with Perkins expenses of approximately a million dollars for the Colonel's campaigns that year. The Wall Street speculator, to whom William Allen White later ascribed "the morals of a green-goods grocer," appears not in the least frightened by Roosevelt's denunciations of "money in politics," and his demands that wealth be made the servant and not the master of the people. Munsey asked only that Roosevelt should speak out against "all this ponderous legal warfare" and "this onslaught on business" that Taft now carried on in order to satisfy "a technical statute, which, in its present form, to my mind, never should have existed. . . ." He proposed that Roosevelt introduce mention of "*a constructive policy—business activity, industry, full dinner pails.*" Among the brethren of Wall Street, he indicated, he had been seeking converts to their progressive cause, and had already assured them, whenever they asked him what kind of an administration Mr. Roosevelt would have if he were re-elected, that it would be "the finest constructive administration this country has ever known." [18] Munsey for his part understood or assumed

---

[17] Robinson, *op. cit.*, pp. 318-319.
[18] *T. R. Papers*, Munsey to T. R., Feb. 13, 1912.

that Roosevelt as President would bring "better business, humming activities all along the line." For he saw in him *the statesman, the saviour, if you please, of our industrial and commercial
life.*" [19]

In sum, by helping to overthrow Taft and his regime—too
"standpat" or now too "legalistic" to suit them, the millionaires
who embraced the Progressive cause in 1912, Perkins, Munsey,
McCormick, and Wilkinson, hoped to kill various birds at the
same time. They would eliminate "the possibility of their children
having to face revolution," and yet they also hoped to save the
trusts, restore business activity, increase profits—"constructive regulation of trusts instead of destructive litigation," was the very
phrase James R. Garfield used in this connection.

To the excited marching men and women of 1912 it was hard
to comprehend or analyze the political potpourri that made up the
Rooseveltian "synthesis." La Follette had long known that Roose-
velt's talk, his ideology, was "at right angles" to his real actions.
A Brandeis, with clear sight, asked what it meant to have George
W. Perkins, the apostle of the great trusts, as prime minister to
the "Rooseveltian party." Was it not like serving both God and
Mammon at the same time?

Those who, in Donald R. Richberg's phrase, "thought they
were Progressive" did not halt to consider the contradictions of the
new leadership. A wave of generous enthusiasm swept over the intellectuals of the middle class, at the announcement that T. R.
would run again. They were for T. R. "first, last, all the time . . .
for him right or wrong"; "Roosevelt or Bust" was the slogan that
William Allen White set at the masthead of the *Emporia Gazette*.
The idealistic social worker Jane Addams was swept into the cheering torrent of humanity along with the venal city boss, Bill Flinn.
The scholarly university professor Albert Bushnell Hart joined

[19] *Ibid.*, Munsey to T. R., Feb. 17, 1912; italics mine.

But how faithful would T. R. have been? These words above strangely re-
semble those used by Mr. Fritz Thyssen, the German steel magnate, in introducing
Mr. Adolf Hitler to a gathering of German business men in 1931. Capitalists in
political action are as apt to be deluded by their hopes and their emotions as others.

with the money-greedy Munseys in the rush to the colors of the beloved leader "returned from Elba."

2

National party conventions in America are to the naked eye great folk festivals filled with brass music, parades, beer, and patriotic or eulogistic oratory. Under cover of the tumult and shouting the procedure for nominating a candidate and making resolutions of policy is usually carried off, according to plan, by the wire-pullers. This was as true of the Republican convention of 1912, at Chicago, as of other gatherings, though it was the most dramatic and disastrous convention in the party's history.

Colonel Roosevelt's decision to run again for the Presidency filled the orthodox party leaders with a holy rage. Some of these leaders, such as William Barnes of New York, or Boies Penrose of Pennsylvania, had either disliked or merely tolerated him in the past as an "instable," impulsive adventurer in their field. In seeking a third term against the will of the party's regular leaders he embodied the lust for personal power; to make the sacred Republican party his engine of personal power this Catiline would foment discord and disorder. In the crisis they stood firmly by Mr. Taft, who had generally heeded their counsels and collaborated with them in matters of patronage—this despite the fact that they too were invariably linked with the big capitalists, and the Taft administration had lately been unpleasantly busy "saving" the capitalist system by attacking the trusts. The capitalists themselves were divided, a large minority among them supporting Theodore Roosevelt.

The conservatism of the Old Guard bosses of the Republican party in 1912 was both emotional and *institutional*. Their instinct, probably sound, told them to form themselves together in a desperate hollow square, in order to fight off the attack of the swashbuckling politico whose methods left the party no peace. Once rid of him, they would continue at all events to hold the national party organization in their hands, though the price were temporary loss of public office.

Taft of course sought vindication. He felt that his old chief had become a "megalomaniac," bent upon wreaking a vengeance which Taft never believed he had merited. He abandoned his dignified silence and, during the pre-convention struggle for pledged delegates, though he said it "wrenched his soul," struck back in public speeches at his adversary with invective as personal and emotional as Roosevelt's. It is doubtful that the public, which had been roused to great interest in the question of the trusts and of "invisible government," now understood the welter of charges and denials, the cries of "liar" that were hurled by each camp.

But though the internal party contest appeared to be predominantly one of personalities, one of "Heroes and Devils" solely, as Lincoln Steffens said, even Taft in cooler moments understood the real issues at stake. He foresaw defeat for himself, in any case, in November. But, he observed, in a letter of July, 1912, written shortly after the Chicago convention:

The Republican party needs the discipline of defeat, and the great object that I have in carrying on this campaign is saving the parts of the party which can be saved, and making a solid disciplined force which will be ready to take advantage of the errors of our old-time enemy the Democrats. . . .[20]

It was not that Roosevelt himself now stood for "revolution." But if he should succeed in overthrowing the old Republican organization, the very precedent would most likely lead to that fateful "division of parties into groups" or classes that men like Taft had always feared; it would bring possibly the disintegration of our old bipartisan political institution, and in its place, something unknown.

None realized better than Roosevelt that the reigning President and his followers held the advantage in the pre-convention contest.

[20] Duffy, op. cit., p. 299.

Roosevelt himself had run the Steam Roller, as national party boss, in 1908; the National Committee and the important Credentials Committee, which decided cases of disputed seats in the convention, had formerly done his bidding. But now the tables were turned. The Old Guard held control of the Southern "rotten boroughs" and of the delegates under orders of the largest state machines. Therefore the tactics of the Roosevelt boom were designed to create noise and terror. No pains were to be spared in demonstrating to the country and the party how truly popular the Colonel was, how unmistakably he was the idol of the rank and file, and how disastrous it would be to pass over him.

A "war of Chinese noises" was conducted from the stump and by means of printed "literature" upon a stupendous scale, in order to demonstrate to the Old Guard leaders that "only Roosevelt could win." They scarcely needed to be shown. How much the average American of 1912 enjoyed and was amused by the inimitable Rough Rider, the present writer recollects vividly, since as a small boy of ten or eleven he had the good fortune to attend with his father a Roosevelt rally. From the moment the stocky man in the big black hat came rolling vigorously through the crowded door of the hall, there was a joyous pandemonium; the belligerent gestures of the Colonel evoked delight, the fiercely aggressive passages of his speech brought interruptions of fairly blood-curdling yells which one still hears ringing in the memory after nearly thirty years.

In a prodigiously expensive and energetic stumping campaign, the Colonel attacked one by one the important Republican states. Perkins and Munsey cheerfully provided an initial $50,000 for publicity and organization. Subsequently, it was charged, these two men, aided by those other recent recruits to progressivism, Daniel Hanna, Alexander T. Cochrane (the Carpet King), Medill McCormick, Wilkinson of Crucible Steel, and T. Coleman Dupont, raised approximately a million dollars for the nomination campaign. The lavish scale of the stumping, the manner in which the Colonel's luxurious special train (furnished by Dan Hanna) zigzagged the length and breadth of Ohio, gave some color to these charges.[21]

At any rate, for those who stood inside the fortifications Roosevelt made it an extraordinarily warm contest. The delegates of Taft's own state of Ohio, California, New Jersey, and other regular Republican strongholds fell to him quickly. In the Western states wherever there were preferential primaries he was the overwhelming choice of the voters. For a time, fear spread that the Colonel would win easily; and there was a short break in Wall Street followed by a quick recovery. Gossip in Wall Street then reported that "assurances have been given" that "the most radical of candidates, if nominated and elected, will in office set aside radicalism. . . ."[22]

Yet the Steam Roller slowly ground out its narrow victory, in spite of the magnificent struggles of the Rooseveltians. Advance polls showed that the Taft men at the convention would have a minimum of 550 delegates, a majority, and Roosevelt approximately 100 less than this. It was then that heroic measures were decided upon to halt the action of the administration-controlled Credentials Committee, which sat, in time-honored manner, awarding disputed delegates' seats to the Standpatters. Vociferous charges of "robbery," "fraud," "naked theft," that alarmed the country as never before, were raised against the majority side by the Roosevelt camp; yet the disputed seats went to Taft delegates—although reversals in all these contested cases, it was shown later, would not have been enough to nominate Roosevelt. The Roosevelt faction then centered its fight upon preventing the election of Elihu Root as "temporary" chairman, presiding over the convention procedure—a strategic position. Here, too, it was known ten days before the convention formally opened that they were defeated.[23]

Three days before the party ceremonies opened on June 15, 1912, Roosevelt took a train and departed for Chicago, the scene of the convention: an unprecedented thing for a candidate to do. There

[21] The New York *Times*, May 18, 1912.
[22] *Ibid.*, May 30, 1912, financial section, p. 12.
[23] *Ibid.*, Jun. 7, 1912.

were now clear indications that the Roosevelt men planned to "bolt" and form their own party. The elaborate preparations made for the Colonel's headquarters at Chicago were in themselves signs of extraordinary measures on foot. The night following the Colonel's arrival was one of tumultuous excitement, punctuated by fist fights in the crowds outside his hotel. On the eve of the convention, Roosevelt spoke at a vast rally of his followers in the Chicago Auditorium, giving strong hints that defeat was momently expected; that, as he held, "stolen delegates" would rule the convention's decision on the morrow, but that such a decision must not be held binding. In solemn and religious vein, also, he proclaimed his progressive political faith, and warned his hearers against the leadership of men whose souls were seared, whose eyes were blinded, "men of cold heart and narrow mind, who believe we can find safety in dull timidity and dull inaction." A period of change was upon us, and we could not stand still if we would. Roosevelt cared little what happened to himself; he was "to be used, as in doubtful battle. . . ." Then in his peroration, which became as famous as Bryan's "Cross of Gold" épopée, he cried:

We fight in honorable fashion for the good of mankind; fearless of the future, unheeding of our individual fates, with unflinching hearts and undimmed eyes; we stand at Armageddon, and we battle for the Lord.

Despite the grotesque disorder that gripped the convention, the Republican party managers proceeded to the nomination of Taft. Neither filibustering, parades, threats of bolt, nor the protests of beautiful women wrapped in the American flag, deterred the cool, cynical, good-humored chairman Root from carrying the meeting to its ordained conclusion on the first ballot of June 22. It is interesting to remark that there was on this occasion little conflict over the platform resolutions. The Progressives at the last hour modified their more radical doctrines, and even refused to commit themselves, in response to labor-union requests, in favor of a definite anti-injunction plank. The Standpatters on the other hand adopted the most liberal platform conceivable for them. But toward the candidacy of Roosevelt no compromise was shown.

In silent protest 344 of the 451 Roosevelt delegates abstained from voting. As in the third-term contest for General Grant, in 1880, an unyielding opposition developed; there was no occasion or thought of surrender.

The night before, on June 21, a midnight-to-dawn session was held in Colonel Roosevelt's hotel rooms, while every possible alternative to that of "bolting" was examined. What was to be done, now that the outcome was clear? Where should they go? For three months on end, a nation-wide movement of politicial protest had been organized; a considerable part of La Follette's radical following had been taken over. Yet the Old Guard had stood fast, blocking this powerful current, preferring certain defeat in the election to yielding its control. Where would this protesting mass, many of its members furiously aroused, go? To the Democrats—who were now certain to nominate a liberal candidate? Or would it turn to the "professional radical," La Follette, as Roosevelt feared? The energies of this movement must in some wise be channeled. And where was Roosevelt to go? Was he to disappear as a political force, the victim of "fraud"? He constituted a whole political problem in himself, suffering, in his early fifties, the "living death" of an ex-President. Other motives strong in Perkins and Munsey and other leaders, as well as in the Colonel, sought to insure the defeat of the adversary. To do nothing, then, was inconceivable now, especially for Theodore Roosevelt. To go forward, hazardous and costly though the enterprise might be, with the launching of a new nation-wide third party, was the one solution which met many needs of various sorts.

"Colonel, we will see you through," Perkins and Munsey said when the night had waned. And Munsey, tense with emotion, added: "My fortune, my magazines, my newspapers are with you." [24] Amos Pinchot, who was present, felt that he was witnessing the birth of a great new party of the plain people.

---

[24] Stoddard, *op. cit.*, p. 305.

On the night following the nomination of Taft, June 22, an informal "rump" convention was called and addressed by Roosevelt in most moving terms. The plan to establish a third party, to be known as the Progressive party, was announced. The faithful followers (others, like Borah, returned to "regularity") were asked to go to their several homes, find out the sentiment of the people, and come together again in August in representative convention to name a candidate and a platform. Thus they departed from Chicago, as they were bid, with high resolve and solemn spirit.

3

One very interested witness of the stormy proceedings at Chicago was William Jennings Bryan, in his capacity of press correspondent. The cleavage of the Republican forces into a conservative and radical wing, like the smaller Republican Free Silver "bolt" of 1896, quickened his hopes. The Democrats were now sure to win the Presidential election provided that they declared in favor of progressive policies and nominated a liberal Democrat. More than ever was he resolved, now that great opportunities beckoned, to bend the party to his principles.

Bryan's position of leadership, his powerful influence over the Democratic Western wing, as we have seen, gave him virtually the deciding voice in a Presidential convention. Whatever his deeper motives may have been—at the time many tongues wagged about his secret hope of wresting the nomination again for himself—there was no doubt about his fervent wish to support liberal policies; there was no doubt about his almost religious animus against the "financial East." Word came, while he still watched at Chicago, that the Democratic National Committee, urged by boss Charles Murphy of Tammany Hall, had decided to recommend Judge Alton B. Parker, leader of the anti-Bryan faction, for "temporary" chairman of the convention, an official endorsement that virtually assured him this strategic post. At once, on June 21, Bryan from Chicago sent telegrams to the leading Democratic candidates, Clark, Wilson, Harmon, and Underwood, pointing out that the naming of a "reactionary" chairman to preside over a convention which sought to be "overwhelmingly progressive" was a grievous error, and asking that they join him in opposing the selection of Parker.

From the headquarters of Champ Clark, the leading candidate, there came but an evasive reply that pleaded for party harmony. Only from Woodrow Wilson did there come, by telegram, a fairly forthright, courageous answer which promised support of Bryan's action against Parker and the conservatives. In truth Bryan's message had embarrassed Wilson's aides. Only at the last moment was the campaign manager, William F. McCombs, overruled by the pressure of the Texas and New Jersey liberals, who heeded House's injunction to conciliate Bryan at all costs. In any case Wilson's reply served to stiffen Bryan's faith in the New Jersey Governor. The newspapers judged that Wilson had "played a master stroke," and reported that he was now being advertised to all the delegations arriving at Baltimore as "standing shoulder to shoulder with Mr. Bryan" for a progressive ticket and platform.[25]

As the various delegations marched into Baltimore, with brass bands playing, it was obvious that a marked tide had set in in favor of Speaker Clark of Missouri. This pleasant, personable Democratic veteran could have passed for a conservative or a progressive at will. With his conciliatory nature, resembling McKinley's, he was not unpleasing to Tammany and to the Eastern capitalists, and by his former attachment to Bryan and Free Silver in earlier days he had earned the official support of the party's Western wing. The Nebraska delegation, headed by Bryan, was pledged to Clark. Bryan had not opposed Clark in the Nebraska primary. He had assured Colonel House that either Clark or Wilson would be an acceptable candidate. His only stipulation was that either one must stand as a progressive. But Bryan evidently had reservations concerning both men. Was Wilson genuine in his tardy conversion to liberal principles? And was not Champ Clark a good

[25] Kerney, *Wilson,* p. 224; Tumulty, *op. cit.,* pp. 110-111; the New York *Times,* Jun. 21-23, 1913.

deal of a straddler? Moreover, Bryan was troubled by the impression that Clark drank whiskey, was "addicted to the excessive use of alcohol." [26] One of Bryan's most charming habits was that of serving as a public conscience for Democratic politicians, and hectoring them frequently. Only lately he had noticed Clark's vacillation upon certain bills before Congress, and had felt obliged to address him in a rather tart letter, of May 30, 1912, as follows:

A leader must *lead*; it is not always pleasant to oppose friends, and one who leads takes the chances of defeat, but these are the necessary attendants upon leadership. Wilson is making friends because he *fights*. His fight against Smith was heroic. He fought for the income tax and a primary law. The people like a fighter. . . . The right wins in the end. . . . One can do better to be defeated fighting for the right than to win on the wrong side. I hope you will pardon this intrusion. . . .[27]

Was not Bryan cooling toward Clark, as Colonel House had calculated he would? His eyes opened further when he saw that Clark's men indirectly co-operated with boss Murphy's Tammany delegates to support Parker for the convention chairmanship against Bryan, whose name was submitted in opposition. Bryan threw himself into the struggle from the opening moments of the convention, on June 25, 1912.

For the second time since 1896, Bryan, appearing personally at the convention, by his main strength, with his single voice, like a Danton dominated the vast, unruly gathering of party deputies. Taking the floor, serious and tense, he began a long arraignment of Parker and the conservatives, using every art of platform oratory, now waiting patient and determined, while explosions of anger or approval came alternately from the great crowd; now indulging himself in personal anecdotes and sharp sallies at the enemy: "The Democratic party is true to the people. You cannot frighten it with your Ryans nor buy it with your Belmonts." [28]

Thomas Fortune Ryan, one of the "money kings," was sitting

[26] Kerney, *Wilson*, p. 286.   [28] The New York *World*, Jun. 26, 1912.
[27] Bryan, *Memoirs*, p. 163.

there together with August Belmont. He had slipped into Baltimore in his private railroad car, and taken the unusual step of appearing in person at the party convention as a delegate.

In the first skirmish, Parker was elected chairman over Bryan, by a rather close vote of 579 to 508, a majority of the Clark delegates aiding in this result. Under the Democrats' traditional "two-thirds" rule, however, the Nebraskan still held, as the press termed it, "a menacing sway over his party." [29] He served notice that he would fight, with almost half the delegates under his leadership, to hold to his progressive line. The first collision had only hardened his resolve. The lines were drawn; and as one of his Texas admirers roared: ". . . Bryan is on one side and Wall Street is on the other." [30]

On the night of Wednesday, June 26, after a two days' struggle over the platform resolutions, in which Bryan had imposed his will, the Nebraskan heard reports from his brother Charles W. Bryan that the New York contingent, nominally pledged to Governor Judson Harmon of Ohio, had made a "deal" to switch its support to Clark on the second ballot. It was then that he determined to present an unprecedented resolution of his own device from the floor of the convention, the next morning, before the balloting began. [31]

Turmoil greeted his rising on Thursday, June 27. The resolution, which shocked even his own friends, read in part:

Resolved, That in this crisis in our party's career and in our country's history this convention sends greetings to the people of the United States, and assures them that the party of Jefferson and of Jackson is still the champion of popular government and equality before the law. As proof of our fidelity to the people, we hereby declare ourselves opposed to the nomination of any candidate for President who is the representative of or under obligation to J. Pierpont Morgan, Thomas F. Ryan, August Belmont, or any other member of the privilege-hunting and favor-seeking class.

[29] The New York *Times*, Jun. 26, 1912.
[30] *Proceedings*, Democratic Party Convention, 1912, p. 13.
[31] M. R. Werner, *Bryan*, p. 186.

Be it further resolved, That we demand the withdrawal from the convention of any delegate or delegates constituting or representing the above-named interests.

It was a most fantastic, unheard-of resolution, though perhaps bespeaking, as the Nebraskan said, "the extraordinary conditions" of the time. Those distinguished Democrats, Ryan, Belmont, and Charles Murphy, sat as if stunned, and the hall was silent for a moment. Then pandemonium burst forth, while Bryan stood there quietly, fully believing that blood would be shed and he himself killed. Yet the resolution did its work well. Bryan himself consented to withdraw the second part of his resolution, banning Ryan, Belmont, *et al.,* by name, and left it as a simple denunciation of the "privilege-hunting" class. In this form, few delegates chose to record themselves as opposing it, and the thing was passed by a vote of 883 to 201.[32]

Bryan dramatized the struggle within the convention; he barred the way to the conservatives, who were by now convinced that it would be impossible to unhorse him without such a fratricidal battle (akin to the recent one at Chicago) as would ruin the greatest chance for a Democratic victory in twenty years.

The Wilson delegation at Baltimore, led by William F. McCombs, William G. McAdoo—the famous builder of the Hudson Tubes—Mayor Newton D. Baker of Cleveland, and the group of House's Texas politicians headed by Senator Culberson, made a very spirited fight from the outset, despite some dissension in its ranks. Colonel House had made all his preparations, left clear instructions, and then taken passage for Europe—to escape the wearying heat or the nervous excitement at Baltimore. Against House's advice, McCombs, who was officially the manager of the Wilson forces and had close New York connections, evidently labored to win over the massive New York delegation. Rumors were heard that McCombs promised the Tammany men that Wilson, if elected, would not appoint Bryan to his Cabinet. But from

[32] The New York *Times,* Jun. 27, 1912.

New Jersey, Wilson, upon astute advice, felt obliged to overrule McCombs, and in a public statement repudiated any pledges given in his name. Thus *he refused to say that he would not include Mr. Bryan* in his Cabinet.[33]

The first ballot showed Clark leading with 440½ votes; then came Wilson a strong second, with 324; Harmon, with 148; Underwood, 117½; and the rest scattered among Favorite Sons. The contestants remained relatively unchanged in their position until the tenth ballot, taken on the second day of voting, when Murphy, the New York boss, suddenly swung the big New York delegation from Harmon to Clark. The latter now had 556 votes, an actual majority—though not the two-thirds vote required for the choice of a candidate—against Wilson's 350½ votes.

"This is . . . a loss for Clark," exclaimed Bryan, who now announced that he was casting his vote for Wilson and invited the Nebraska delegates to join him. The Bryan following now brought, in the nick of time, a strong support to Wilson, who soon drew up almost even with Clark. Bryan's threat to "bolt" the Democratic party, if a candidate were named with the aid of the New York faction, threw the convention into greatest excitement.[34]

There were some who now accused Bryan of "treachery" in seeking a deadlock. "From the first he favored Wilson, pretending to be neutral between him and Clark," wrote one active participant privately. ". . . After Clark's success in Nebraska, Bryan conspired to defeat him. . . ."[35] Whatever his motives, he had kept the affair in the open, brought the light to play upon every phase of it, and aroused public opinion throughout the country. It was thanks to Bryan—and in a sense vengeance fitting enough—that the gathering at Baltimore became a "people's convention." The deadlock continued for some time; but the situation had become too dangerous to permit of any shady compromise. The majority of the Democratic press now petitioned for the nomination of the bril-

[33] Tumulty, *op. cit.*, pp. 110-111.
[34] The New York *Times*, Jun. 29, 30, 1912.
[35] *T. R. Papers*, George Fred Williams to Senator R. F. Pettigrew, Jul. 8, 1912.

liant New Jersey Governor as a solution to the problems which Bryan had raised of liberalism versus machine control. On the seventh day of this long convention, and on the forty-third ballot, the powerful Illinois and Indiana bosses, Roger Sullivan and Thomas Taggart, led the "stampede" which brought Wilson's nomination.

Woodrow Wilson, waiting at a summer resort on the New Jersey shore, received the news of victory, it was said, with serious and grave mien.[36] He had come to the end of one road; for the election of a Democratic President was almost a certainty that year. He had originally undergone his "political education" and entered public life under the sponsorship of a "Wall Street agent," Harvey, and of the machine bosses, Smith and Nugent. But he had found himself quickly, as a reformist leader. Then the conservative groups had undoubtedly undergone a change of heart toward him, especially after Republican dissension suggested to them that a more pliant candidate than Wilson might well be named at Baltimore. Events had so shaped themselves that Wilson must stand forth as a progressive, as the "people's candidate." It was the insistent fighting of the radical Democrat Bryan and an aroused public opinion that had made the victory.

4

The Rooseveltian Progressives, on August 5, 1912, met in convention in that same vast Chicago Auditorium, where they had seen themselves undone six weeks earlier. Though obliged to pay their own traveling expenses, two or three times the number of delegates called arrived in Chicago. Here were plain people from the hills jostling with uninhibited, Rooseveltian corporation magnates such as George Perkins and Oscar Straus; intellectuals and college professors such as Amos Pinchot, Charles E. Merriam, and George W. Kirchwey; machine bosses such as "Bill" Flinn, and social workers and near-Socialists such as Ben B. Lindsey, Miss

[36] The New York *Times*, Jul. 3, 1912.

Jane Addams, and Walter Weyl. All were now inspired with the same fervent faith in the Colonel and his program, though yesterday they might not have remained peaceably in the same hall together. "There was room on that platform," wrote one young Bull Moose, Donald Richberg, "for anyone who had seen Peter Pan and believed in fairies." The National Progressive party convention was a church, a "great revival meeting." One of the hardened reporters present wired his newspaper: "I can't make fun of this convention. This is a religion." [37]

They sang "John Brown's Body" and "Onward Christian Soldiers." They joined in a passionately evangelical, hymn-singing celebration of the crusade for "righteousness" that they launched. They stood with Colonel Roosevelt at Armageddon, "put on shining armor and went forth to battle for the Lord."

In truth, historic opportunities lay before the founders of the new party. The Old Guard Republicans, like the old Whigs of Lincoln's day, had refused to obey the voice of the people; they had refused to see the handwriting on the wall. "The old party is gone. . . . We are really founding a new and great party," wrote Albert Beveridge to his wife. His children would be proud of what he had helped to do. [38]

Beveridge, part jingo, part reformer, part poet, had hastened to join Roosevelt's party on being assured that it was to be a vital and permanent organization. His insurgency had led to his defeat for the Senate; his old hope of reaching the White House was all but destroyed. Now he stood, making the "keynote" address. In passages of this torrentially eloquent speech he appears to recognize well the contradictions of the old system, and the tremendous opportunities looming before the new party. Thus he said:

The people vote for one party, and find their hopes turned to ashes on their lips; and then, to punish that party, they vote for the other party. So it is that partisan victories have come to be merely the people's vengeance; *and always the secret powers have played the game.*

[37] Richberg, *op. cit.*, pp. 31-32, 36.
[38] Bowers, *op. cit.*, p. 424.

Here they had come, however, to found a party of definite ideas and interests, rather than one dedicated to patronage and power. The sham warfare of the past would be ended. This much was truly enlightening.

But for the rest the keynote speech given by the former laureate of the Republicans was characteristic of the strangely contradictory rhetorical promises and political bargains embodied in the new movement. Beveridge had begun in a strongly euphuistic style:

We stand for a nobler America. We stand for an undivided Nation. We stand for a broader liberty, a fuller justice. We stand for social brotherhood, as against savage individualism. We stand for an intelligent co-operation instead of a reckless competition. We stand for mutual helpfulness, instead of mutual hatred. We stand for equal rights . . . for rule of the people. . . . We battle for the actual rights of man.

Then came a riot of promises. The Progressive party would abolish the boss system, it would end Invisible Government and make sure the rule of the people. It would also end depressions, profitless business ventures, unemployment, and poverty. "Hunger should never walk in these thinly peopled gardens of plenty." The aged would be granted insurance or pensions. Child labor and degrading labor for women would be eliminated.

Prosperity would be brought about by the Progressives; but it was to be a prosperity distributed among the many. "The Progressive motto is 'Pass Prosperity around.'" And how would this be done? By a national supervision of Big Business, wiping out its evils and directing its power to the service of the people; ending the uncertainty of business men as to their rights and chances and duties. The "misleading" and "destructive" Sherman Anti-Trust Act, which touched not the root of the evil, would be abandoned. Business would no longer be destroyed.

We mean to try to make little business big and all business honest, instead *of striving to make Big Business little,* and yet letting it remain dishonest.

Thus among the musical notes intended to appeal to the masses were also strong calls to the friends of monopolistic industry. But everyone wept or cheered when Beveridge had ended, and sang "The Battle Hymn of the Republic."

Roosevelt's prepared speech on the evening of the following day when he was tendered the Presidential nomination was extremely long. He called it his "Confession of Faith." It reviewed his entire career, passed on to the wickedness practiced at the regular Republican convention, justified his insurgence, and outlined the various measures of reform he now espoused. Like Beveridge, he vigorously attacked the recent Democratic party resolution that promised to reinforce the Sherman Anti-Trust Act. The directors of great monopolies were also to be made happy, in the Rooseveltian millennium, by a government police that would firmly preserve them from wrongdoing while protecting them also from injury to themselves.[39]

In short, the Roosevelt Progressivism, as Mr. Donald R. Richberg has summed it up,

did not question the existing order. It proposed changes in law largely for the purpose of compelling or inducing men to be "good" instead of "bad." . . . Big business would be encouraged if "good" and punished if "bad." The wicked strong people would be controlled, and the good weak people would be protected.[40]

The exaltation of 15,000 enthusiastic followers venting itself in Niagaras of cheers now overcame all misgivings concerning such cracks as showed themselves in the new political edifice. Even the careful New York *Times* on August 5, 1912, noted that the Bull Moose platform was to be "progressive but not alarming." The Bryan Democrats at Baltimore had definitely pledged relief to labor in the form of an anti-injunction law; the Progressives avoided this difficult point with rhetorical generalities.

But behind scenes a raging struggle had gone on all the night

[39] The New York *Times*, Aug. 6, 7, 1912.
[40] Richberg, *op. cit.*, pp. 34-35.

before within the Resolutions Committee which wrote the platform. A long series of legislative proposals, some of them vague, some of them enlightened, ranging in subject from woman suffrage to social and labor welfare, were all drawn up and passed, even George W. Perkins, whom Roosevelt had chosen as chairman of the Executive Committee, giving his approval. But when it came to the concrete issue of the trust question, bitter dissension showed itself. The radical faction, in the majority, favored specifying or cataloguing what were violations of the Sherman Anti-Trust Act. Their thought was phrased as follows:

We favor strengthening the Sherman law by prohibiting agreements to divide territories or limit output; refusing to sell to customers who buy from business rivals; to sell below cost in certain areas while maintaining high prices in other places; using the power of transportation to aid or injure special business concerns; and other unfair trade practices.

But Perkins stoutly opposed all mention of the Sherman law. Amos Pinchot, also a member of the Resolutions Committee, was convinced that Perkins desired "the protection of the trusts." Had he not lately resigned from the banking firm of J. P. Morgan in order to devote himself, as he said, to ending all industrial warfare and promoting a partnership between capital and labor? Some of the Progressives might look at Perkins as an embarrassing or unwelcome stranger in their midst; but he was the money-bags of their party. They could pass their own trust plank (as they apparently did), but Perkins would leave the camp.

Thus pocket-book makes cowards of us all . . .

sang Donald Richberg afterward, paraphrasing Shakespeare in an allusion to wavering political leaders' souls.

That night Perkins ran back and forth between the hotel room in which the Resolutions Committee was wrangling bitterly and the bedroom in which Colonel Roosevelt was supposed to sleep. Although Roosevelt had begun by approving the committee's version of the trust plank, he ended by also giving consent to an amended version of it which Perkins wrote, in which reference to strengthening the Sherman law was eliminated. Afterward, Roosevelt admitted privately that he had allowed Perkins to overrule the Resolutions Committee "in a somewhat irregular manner" owing to the "harrowing" confusion of the moment.[41]

The next day, as Dean W. D. Lewis, Chairman of the Resolutions Committee, read off the party platform, either by mistake or through someone's subterfuge he recited the unamended, "radical" version of the trust plank, as the Committee majority had written it. (Later he said that in his fatigue he had taken into the hall "both planks on the Sherman law . . . and by mistake . . . read the wrong one.") [42]

Perkins in great agitation listened while this was read and adopted by the general convention enthusiastically. Turning excitedly to Amos Pinchot, he exclaimed: "Lewis has made a mistake. That does not belong in the platform. We cut it out last night." Perkins shoved back his chair and proceeded to leave the hall, two or three of his wealthy friends following him. In the crisis, a hurried conference was called, Roosevelt authorizing Oscar King Davis, New York *Times* political correspondent, and secretary of the Progressive National Committee, to hurry to the press associations and newspaper offices and "kill" the offending plank, sending the amended version as approved by Perkins in its place.[43] The newspapers and the party pamphlets all printed the trust resolution in its amended form "protecting the trusts." Amos Pinchot, then a zealous, clear-sighted reformer, felt that he was learning something about politics. He began to have his qualms about the Roosevelt-Perkins "progressivism." Perkins, he observed, had "succeeded in eliminating the trust plank twice." [44]

Thus the newly born party of the plain people continued throughout the season, and afterward, to suffer endless embarrassment thanks to its national chairman and the trust question. There

---

[41] *Amos Pinchot Papers*, T. R. to A. Pinchot, Dec. 5, 1912.
[42] O. K. Davis, *op. cit.*, p. 333.
[43] *Ibid.*, pp. 334-335.
[44] *Amos Pinchot Papers*, A. Pinchot to T. R., Dec. 8, 1912.

were moments when the more earnest members such as William Allen White and the Pinchots would hint to Perkins that despite his managerial experience and resources he might benefit the party by removing his name from the head of its Executive Committee. But the determined Perkins replied, with some justice, that it was scarcely fair to accept the funds he was raising, while concealing his name and removing him from a position in which he could "exert some influence over their expenditure."

While the Progressive orators Roosevelt, Hiram Johnson, and Beveridge toured the country giving speeches calculated to instill morality into our politics and business life, the wily Perkins raised money, managed the national organization that was quickly thrown up, bred dissension within the party, and served as the target for the opposition.

Even Beveridge complained: "Perkins, Munsey and —— are too much in evidence. If we're not careful we'll be labeled a Wall Street promotion."

As the summer passed, both opposing parties directed their fire in good measure upon George W. Perkins rather than Roosevelt, while debate over the perennial trust question occupied the country. From Progressive headquarters there went forth whole crates of pamphlets defending Perkins, entitled: "Is Perkins Honest?" His speeches and articles were reprinted under Progressive auspices. In these, and in pamphlets prepared by others at his order, it was maintained that Perkins was nothing less than a "true Progressive," who had liquidated all his business investments and planned to devote himself thenceforth to the common weal. His goal was ostensibly the establishment of "partnership," profit-sharing, and social justice. This he had already begun to achieve, it was claimed, in the corporations with which he had been connected.

He went to the Morgans, and the Garys, and the Rockefellers and the McCormicks and showed them that any great business was a partnership between directors and working men. . . . His next job would be the solution of industrial problems, the bringing in of a better understanding and a more equitable distribution of the good things produced equally by labor and capital. . . . Mr. Perkins wants the American business man to do the square thing without having it forced on him. He wants him to see that the square deal is not business loss but business gain. . . . It is brotherhood brought down to the pay envelope. . . . Perkins is, therefore, a prophet to the rich. Other men are able to tell the masses what they ought to have. But Perkins, with his proved business ability, his . . . complete knowledge of the situation from the rich man's point of view, is able to tell the captains of industry what *they* ought to *do* in order to be saved. . . .[45]

The citations above also tell better than any of Roosevelt's speeches what the true inward nature of the Bull Moose party was, and what was its mission. They tell us why Perkins, in spite of the "lunatic fringe"—who, Roosevelt himself complained, wanted "a sort of I.W.W. movement"—clung to control of its organization, and held it as his own instrument. They tell us why the liberals, disheartened by the contradictions within their own ranks, eventually abandoned the Progressive party, which collapsed when Perkins and Munsey withdrew their financial support in 1914.

5

The diplomacy of the 1912 Presidential campaign was made fairly simple for Woodrow Wilson, thanks to the intrusion of the Roosevelt "bolters." He had the aid of the aggressive Bull Moose attacks in splitting the Republican opposition in the North, while the Solid South remained safely Democratic. Moreover, the two parties that now stood on the left were virtually alike in their pledges of reform—except for the trust issue. Here the Democratic ideologue had Colonel Roosevelt on the hip.

In the late summer, while the controversy over Mr. Perkins was at its height, a committee of Congress, the "Stanley Committee," was hearing expert evidence upon the trust question. Louis D. Brandeis and John Fitch, the latter an authority on the steel

[45] *Amos Pinchot Papers*, A. Pinchot letter to J. Dixon, May 23, 1914.

trade, appeared and testified that the United States Steel Corporation, of whose benevolence Perkins boasted, actually enforced the longest possible hours, low wages in all its unskilled departments, and resorted to espionage to crush out labor unions. Brandeis pictured "conditions of repression, the like of which you cannot find, I believe, this side of Russia."

Wilson, who had been much interested by Brandeis's bold crusading against the enemies of conservation and against the Morgan railroads, as well as by his keen pamphleteering in the muckraking magazines, now called the "people's lawyer" to his service in the campaign. With the La Follette boom officially ended, Brandeis was glad to furnish concrete advice upon the trusts and methods of restraining them. Thus while Roosevelt drew inspiration for his sermons upon the "New Nationalism" from the writings of Herbert Croly, Wilson drew generously upon Brandeis's teachings in the series of speeches delivered on the subject of the "New Freedom."

Tilting at Roosevelt, Wilson declared that he, for his part, did not want to live under the benevolent despotism and by grace of the trusts. The increased size and power of the monopolies, he held, would, under mere regulation and supervision, result in the trusts' capturing control of the government and supervising and regulating government itself. Like Brandeis he denied that the big monopolies introduced greater efficiency. They grew great by crushing out effective competitors, by buying out efficient independents like Carnegie. But thereafter they "staggered about" like water-logged giants under the artificial burden of their overcapitalization. This was the "curse of bigness." Wilson believed that whenever a trust's share of the market exceeded, say, 40 per cent, it should be broken up; and progress through individual effort should be encouraged. In addition he favored regulating competition by social and labor laws prohibiting a cruel human exploitation. In general, Wilson outlined the specific measures of the future Clayton Anti-Trust Act, which Brandeis furnished him, as he had already done for a similar measure La Follette had vainly introduced in Congress.

Ridicule was heaped by Wilson upon Roosevelt's distinctions between "good" and "bad" trusts. Epitomizing the best liberal thought of the epoch, Wilson exclaimed: "I do not care to live in a country called free even under kind masters." [46]

While offering himself as an enlightened reformer with a successful record in New Jersey, the university scholar kept himself on high ground, spoke in moderate tones, and stood that season, between Taft and Roosevelt, as "the middle-of-the-road candidate, a sort of conservative liberal." [47]

He said, almost soothingly, at a moment of his New England tour:

I believe that the ancient traditions of a people are its ballast. . . . You must knit the new into the old. If I did not believe that to be progressive is to preserve the essentials of our institutions, I for one would not be a progressive. . . .

You have no right to promise Heaven unless you can bring us to it, for, in making promises, you create too much expectation and your failure brings with it only disappointment and sometimes despair. . . . I can only see a little distance up the road. . . . A great industrial system has been built up in this country under the fosterage of the Government. . . . Changes must be brought about first here, then there, and then there again. We must move from step to step with as much prudence as resolution. . . .

And while we do so we must create by absolute fairness and open-mindedness the atmosphere of mutual concession. There are no old scores to be paid off, there are no resentments to be satisfied; *there is no revolution to be attempted.*

In the three-cornered contest, Theodore Roosevelt appeared less effective than in former years, despite his violently vocal radicalism and spectacular personal stumping tour, which included a nearly fatal encounter with an assassin. President Taft, on the other hand, said to himself: "I have no part to play but that of a conservative, and that I am going to play." [48] Under these condi-

[46] Wilson, *The New Freedom,* pp. 162 ff.
[47] Kerney, *Wilson,* p. 241.
[48] Pringle, *Taft,* Vol. II, p. 823.

tions, the outcome of the election was a foregone conclusion, and (calculating population increase) a total of 500,000 less people came to the polls than in 1908. The Democrats, though winning a tremendous electoral majority, were in point of number of votes a minority party, Wilson with 6,294,293 votes running 116,000 behind Bryan's total vote in 1908, and carrying by a real majority only the Southern and "Bryan states." The Republicans, winning only Utah and Vermont, with 3,486,000 votes, suffered their most disastrous defeat, and were a poor third to the Progressives, with 4,117,000 votes and six states in the electoral college.

The old party that Abraham Lincoln had helped to found seemed upon its last legs; while the new Rooseveltian party had made the strongest showing recorded for a third party in America since 1856. Yet it was the Bull Moose who was fated to become an extinct animal, while the Elephant was soon to nurse himself back to health and power.

6

It was as if the fates conspired against the emergence of a new radical-conservative alignment of the political parties in America. Taft and the Standpatters clung tenaciously to their control of the Republican organization, and demonstrated in time its amazing vitality and permanence as an institution. Roosevelt and his monopolistic friends did much to cast discredit upon the new Progressive party; Wilson, who might have led a new liberal party, ended by respecting the traditions of Democratic partisanship, while offering, for the moment, successful competition to Roosevelt's Progressive movement.

"If Governor Wilson had not been nominated at Baltimore," Brand Whitlock wrote at the time to Newton D. Baker, "we should have had a new liberal party and the alignment at last would have been clear." [49]

But who killed the Progressive party? As O. K. Davis, secretary

[49] Baker, *op. cit.*, Vol. III, p. 388.

of the Progressive party's National Committee pointed out, there was too little time, after July, 1912, to set up local or state organizations in sufficient force. A very small number of Progressive Congressmen won election in their districts. Thus there was no national field organization of any size to carry on the work of the party and provide its local branches with "loaves and fishes" in the shape of public offices or partial sinecures. Practically speaking, the Progressives were in the position of the Socialists as political outsiders, even though they had money behind them. A deeper cause of the debacle of third-party hopes was the underlying discord and disillusionment, the clash between varying faiths and cross-purposes.

In the month that followed the 1912 elections the Progressive leaders began to take stock of their situation and thought of the future. The "radical" faction now made a determined effort, as a first measure of improvement, to oust Mr. Perkins from his controlling position. Amos Pinchot was one of those who besought Roosevelt for aid to this end. The Progressive party, he wrote, professed to dedicate itself to "economic justice," yet stood deeply compromised by the character of its executive management. Some rumors of the filching of the Progressive trust plank had already spread about during the late campaign. What would happen if the whole story should come out, as it well might some day? Let us quit the counsels of careful cowardice, the younger Pinchot urged, and henceforth work unremittingly and whole-heartedly "to free the industrial slaves" of the modern world as Abraham Lincoln fought to free the chattel slaves of yesterday.[50]

In a long and somewhat lame reply, Roosevelt argued that the trouble with the Progressive party in the last election was not that it was too compromised, but that it was too "radical" and frightened the moderates. As to the stolen trust plank, Roosevelt said in effect that he agreed with Perkins. The whole argument had been about "tweedledum and tweedledee," though he confessed that Perkins had been somewhat "irregular" in his operations, and that

[50] *Amos Pinchot Papers*, A. Pinchot to T. Roosevelt, Dec. 3, 1912.

the old rascal might need talking to. But Roosevelt stressed the fact that he wished the Progressives to avoid quarreling among themselves, to remain "practical" lest the party "sink into an adjunct to the Debs movement." Had not Lincoln been applauded after he was gone "because he got things *done*"? The way to get things done, he held, was to continue to work with Perkins, Munsey, boss Flinn, Wilkinson, and other men of wealth who were ready almost to give their all so that their children might not face a real revolution.[51]

In truth, Roosevelt's real idea of progressivism was almost identical with that of Perkins and Munsey. Before cheering crowds, the Rough Rider could utter rousing slogans in behalf of justice and the Square Deal. But alone with Perkins, or in his family circle, he could express himself with the most withering contempt for "cranks" or "parlor socialists," or "so-called reformers who came dangerously near the mark of lunacy."[52]

Soon the moneyed exponents of capitalist-labor conciliation began to show diminished fears of an imminent revolution. Within two months of the election, Roosevelt reported that Mr. Munsey had "kicked over the pail"—that is, quit the Progressive party. Some of the other rich patrons such as the Carpet King, Alexander T. Cochrane, were still willing to help provided that the Progressive party would "get to business . . . have a decent practical policy, leave reform alone."(!)[53] Mr. Munsey, using the current Wall Street jargon, even urged that the Progressives should "amalgamate" with the Republicans.

During the Congressional and state elections of 1914 Roosevelt showed an indifference amounting to apathy. As a personal vehicle the new party interested him less and less; and the crisis of world war would provide grounds for ridding himself of its burdens.

Besides, the Colonel was once more by 1915 the jingo par excellence, resigned to conservatism in domestic politics, and asso-

[51] *T. R. Papers,* T. R. to A. Pinchot, N. Y., Dec. 5, 1912.
[52] *Ibid.,* T. R. to Kermit Roosevelt, Jan. 27, 1915.
[53] *Ibid.,* T. R. to C. J. Bonaparte, Jan. 14, 1913; A. T. Cochran to W. Cochran, Nov. 14, 1912.

ciated in his old age with the most reactionary of capitalists. He reflected that the appeal of the Progressive party to men's ideals of righteousness was after all too "advanced" for the masses. With a flash of insight he said that "the fundamental question that interested the average man and the working man" was "the purely economic question of how he could best shape conditions so that he could earn his own living." Toward this end, he himself admitted, the Progressive party had offered the average man too little. Prosperity had returned, and Roosevelt's old indifference to or dislike of the laboring class returned. The working man, he judged, was not "interested in justice." [54]

Here and there a few independent casualties of the political arena, for whom there was no place in the regular Republican set-up, continued as Progressives, without benefit of Roosevelt's support. Albert Beveridge, stumping Indiana for re-election to the Senate in 1914, was one of these, an upright, high-minded, rather confused gentleman in politics to the end. Repudiated by the machine managers, yet failing to reach the people's votes, he poured forth his eloquence at every hamlet and crossroads village of his state, in vain. He was defeated: and turned again to the republic of literature which he graced so well.

[54] *Ibid.*, T. R. to C. J. Bonaparte, Nov. 7, 1914.

XV. "THE NEW FREEDOM":

CLIMAX OF

THE LIBERAL REVOLUTION

B
UT NOW it is come—the real thing; at any rate a man somewhat like us, whose thought and aim and dream are our
thought and aim and dream." Thus wrote Walter H. Page
glowingly of his great expectations as Woodrow Wilson prepared
to take power.[1]

For Wilson was heir to the bloodless, liberal revolution of the
ballot boxes that had arrived in 1912. Burdened with no pledges
or damaging political connections, imbued with high concepts of
leadership, and committed to long-demanded, sweeping reforms,
Wilson would at last put the democratic idea into action.

Those who knew something of Wilson or had glimpsed the cold
fires that blazed in him sensed that historic political events were in
the making. In effect, the first thrust of the Wilson administration
was to provide a year or two of miracles, "the most remarkable
program of national legislation enacted within the same length of
time since the stirring epoch of the Civil War . . . legislation
conceived principally in the interests of 'small folk,' planters,
farmers, and organized labor." [2] For the first time in half a century the tariff was materially reduced; a central banking system
was set up under presumably democratic safeguards; the Anti-
Trust Act was strengthened; a Federal Trade Commission was

[1] Hendrick, *op. cit.*, Vol. I, p. 121.
[2] Beard and Beard, *op. cit.*, Vol. II, p. 607.

established to ensure fair business practices; labor was exempt from the operation of the trust law and further aided by a Seaman's Act, while the eight-hour day for railroad workers was enacted into law; and farmers and small business men were provided with a more elastic currency, through the Federal Reserve System, and with more liberal credit by a Farm Loan Act. Moreover the first of these measures, for tariff, banking and trust reform, were all conceived as part of a systematic program and carried through Congress with unheard-of rapidity. The cumbersome American legislative machinery leaped forward under the whip of an invincible executive leadership. Political power itself seemed dominant over economic groups and privileged interests as it never was even under Theodore Roosevelt. One felt the change electrifying the life of the capital itself.

"I had been familiar with affairs in Washington since the days of the Cleveland administration," relates Mr. Justice Brandeis. "Suddenly it seemed as if we had climbed mountain heights and entered into a purer, more rarefied atmosphere." [3]

During the interval following his election—even during the months before November, when he foresaw the result—Wilson planned and prepared a large legislative program, a whole series of measures, which he proposed to drive through Congress at the very start of his term. (These were tactics which some of the younger men in his entourage remembered to use in a great emergency over twenty years later.) After November 8, 1912, Wilson shut himself off from the world, to which he had been so democratically accessible, even from journalists who sought him. For one thing, he was keenly aware of the tremendous difficulties, the whole troubled future, that faced him. Once a victory had been achieved, he seemed, as House described him, to take little joy in it, but looked forward to the next struggle and feared again the possibility of error and failure. His obsessive fears and anxieties he hid from all eyes, under a public mask of cold, impassive firm-

[3] Mr. Louis D. Brandeis to author.

ness that was seldom removed. Charles W. Eliot thought that Wilson "like most reformers . . . had a fierce and unlovely side." House recorded in his journal Wilson's fear that the burdens of his office would kill him. At times ". . . he spoke of the loneliness of his position in a way that was saddening." [4]

Yet his aloofness, his habits of loneliness, stood him in good stead when he was besieged by the small politicians who came rushing to flatter him. The Democratic party had been out of office for sixteen years, and its various factions, whom he had held together under his banner, conservative and liberal, Northern and Southern, clamored for office. These people he met with icy mien. Even some of those who had labored for his victory by his side, such as McCombs, were affronted by his coldness when they tried to sway his mind toward their own designs, or to learn from him in advance what policies he planned. Thus big business men knew nothing of his intentions, any more than did the party leaders, such as Clark and Underwood, who made journeys to New Jersey. They could say with Franklin K. Lane that "nobody comes home from Trenton knowing anything more than when he went. . . ." [5]

The last legislative measures he carried through in New Jersey, including one drastically changing the famous corporation law that had been so favorable to great trusts, gave conservative business an unpleasant foretaste of what might come. Gloom therefore spread in stock markets, and the late autumn of 1912 was filled with talk of a heavy depression.

At one of the few occasions when he spoke out, at a dinner of the Southern Society in New York, Wilson in an unusually irritated and vehement manner referred to the "sinister predictions as to the trouble we are going to get into down at Washington." It was charged that business would be "disturbed" by the proposed reforms of the incoming Democratic administration. He retorted that business could be disturbed only by business men whose minds were disturbed. Perhaps, he hinted, there were men who

[4] House, op. cit., Vol. I, p. 118.
[5] Lane, Letters, Vol. I, pp. 112-113.

were not unwilling to use their own resources and existing financial machinery to bring about an artificial panic for their own gain. If there was any man who "dares use that machinery for that purpose," the President-elect promised him "a gibbet as high as Haman's." [6]

No one knew then whether the academic thinker wrapped in his clouds of theories might not choose for his Cabinet independents and "radicals" who represented no traditional political weight. Walter H. Page, who had helped much in the late campaign, feared that Bryan and his friends would dominate the Wilson government. Page was a successful publisher, and considered himself a "conservative liberal"; he was also a member of the board of the Rockefeller Foundation at this time and reflected opinion in high quarters such as Wilson had not heeded of late. He observes, on December 31, 1912:

. . . I made up my mind that his real friends owed it to him and to what we all hope for to break over his reserve and to volunteer help. . . . So I began to write memoranda about those subjects of government about which I know something and have opinions and about men who are or who may be related to them.[7]

But even Page, though he bombarded Wilson with his suggestions, had only a slight effect.

In a stubborn silence, in seclusion, save for the presence of one or two confidential advisers, Wilson planned his program, struggled with the problems of selecting a Cabinet, and prepared to put into action the ideas of executive leadership that he had expounded many years ago in his book, *Congressional Government*. He held that our whole machinery of government was too cumbersome, too often at cross purposes amid its checks and balances, which operated—as certain interested groups desired—to hold government weak. Wilson told House, in whom he was never afraid to confide, that he hoped to put into law the real desires of the

[6] Speech of Dec. 17, 1912; the New York *Times*, Dec. 18, 1912.
[7] Hendrick, *op. cit.*, Vol. I, p. 122.

people. With the force of popular opinion behind him, the President must organize and lead Congressional action after a prepared plan.

Colonel House was never more active as adviser and political "adjuster" for Wilson than at this period. The suspicious Wilson was deeply moved when he perceived that his new friend, offered a post in the Cabinet, earnestly refused the title or emoluments of any public office. That was not House's idea of his chief usefulness, which could be achieved best by *indirection*. What House sought was a role such as Wilson had even long ago visioned for himself when he thought of entering politics: that of confidential adviser to the statesman who is plunged in action, serving as eyes and ears to him who is too occupied to "hear all and see all." As in Texas, House felt that he could perform these services best if unhampered by official title or duty.

Soon Wilson, who presented the appearance of a strong, self-willed man, came to depend in an enormous degree upon House's peculiar, soft-treading, self-effacing services. He trusted the man; he was convinced of his disinterestedness. House, moreover, had a nearly feline ability to anticipate his thought, and at the same time knew how to soften Wilson's frequently harsh words and gestures.

This "strange friendship" makes a strange, arresting chapter in the study of power and personality. Great fortune or great power, suddenly experienced, like great adversity provides a stern test of a man's character. A Theodore Roosevelt blooms happily under the sun of power; a Woodrow Wilson becomes increasingly difficult and lonely. Intimate associates who had quarreled with him, such as George Harvey, told of his great intelligence and strength, but also of his "unyielding mind," and of how he was "hard to advise." Others who admired him, such as Brandeis, felt that the inhuman responsibilities he assumed during his entire public life weighed him down. He was not "hard to advise," but he was undoubtedly intolerant of human stupidity when it came too close to him. He did not seek to be autocratic, he did not wish to "wield a big stick," but he wished to "lead through reason" toward "the accomplishment of a common purpose," he said of himself in a private letter.[8]

Yet his inaccessibility, his intellectual loneliness, stares one in the face. To perceive these qualities one need only read the warning letters of House advising those who called on the terrible Doctor in the White House—even a man who was to enter Wilson's Cabinet—"never to go into long-winded arguments," or mention unimportant details, and to refrain, in short, from disputing with him. Lincoln Steffens, a fine judge of character, gave the same cautionary advice to John Reed on his way to the great man for an interview.[9]

Between the lines we read the character of a man who had immense pride in his own will and in the superiority of his own reasoning power (which had carried him so far), who assumed habitually the air of implacable strength, but showed unconscious fear or anger toward those who would oppose him or hold him in error. Here was a man who might go far, but who could also go grandly wrong, yet none could stay him.

How useful, then, House was to this difficult, lonely nature with the bleak Scotch face! House soon became the *alter ego*. To a politician who inquired whether House represented the President's own views accurately in a certain affair, Wilson replied:

Mr. House is my second personality. He is my independent self. His thoughts and mine are one. If I were in his place I would do just as he suggested. . . . If anyone thinks he is reflecting my opinion by whatever action he takes, they are welcome to the conclusion.[10]

In that first winter of power, in 1913, the strange influence of Mr. House was much spoken of, and he was titled in newspaper gossip the "Assistant President." The Democratic office-seekers who stormed the administration, whipped on by a famine of twenty years, came first into the presence of House, who was actually the

[8] To M. A. Hulbert, Sept. 21, 1913; Baker, *op. cit.*, Vol. IV, pp. 182-183.
[9] House, *op. cit.*, Vol. I, p. 142; Steffens, *op. cit.*, Jun. 6, 1914, Vol. I, p. 342.
[10] *Ibid.*, Vol. I, p. 114.

ex-officio prime minister or head of the Cabinet. The burden of calming jealous passions and real or fancied slights fell upon the quiet little man from Texas. Even a great steel magnate, privately seeking an "arrangement" of a government anti-trust suit, would be sent to Mr. House rather than to the harsh Chief Magistrate. The terms of negotiations might be proposed and set by House even before the master opened his mouth to speak.

House: You had better let me tell Frick that you referred me to the Attorney General and suggested that whatever proposal came to you should come through the Attorney General's office.

Wilson (smiling): You may consider it has been said.[11]

The two men's minds worked in a beautiful accord. In his lately published utopian novel, *Philip Dru, Administrator,* House as an author had pictured the imaginary career of a fictive Woodrow Wilson facing the emergency of revolution. Wilson was his "Philip Dru" in the flesh, older, less charming or handsome, but good enough. At any rate, House began to live through the experience of ruling vicariously the affairs of the nation. Indeed there was almost nothing of Wilson's aspirations and program that House had not foreseen in his novel. The action that followed resembled astonishingly the matter of the novel. There were, of course, certain things that could not come to pass, as yet, under the American scheme. In his romance House had pictured a Cabinet chosen of "experts, economists and others," well versed in public affairs. The real Cabinet was to be something wholly different from the ideal. But, for the rest, the novel had proposed as a plan of reform: (1) a tariff law which would be a step toward ending the system of protection; (2) a graduated income-tax law equalizing the burden of taxation; (3) a "new banking law affording a flexible currency, bottomed largely upon commercial assets, the real wealth of the nation," and eliminating the money trust, "the greatest, the most far-reaching . . . the most pernicious trust of all"; (4) the control of industrial life, with monopolies to be curbed, and labor

[11] House, *op. cit.,* Mar. 24, 1913, Vol. I, p. 129.

to be protected by social laws instead of being left as "an inert commodity to be bought and sold by the law of supply and demand."

These were the grand lines of policy which (Philip Dru) Wilson and House pursued together, at the outset. Both Franklin K. Lane and Bryan expressed their amazement at the degree in which the novel seemed to shape the President's thought. "All that book has said should be comes about. . . ." [12]

Was it to be at last government by the pure intelligence of high-minded men? In theory, House's political romance provided the norm, the ideal. But in practice House himself was the first to depart from its idealism. The thought of having a Cabinet that would be a departure from previous Presidential Cabinets in that it would be chosen from experts and "best minds" exerted a strong appeal upon Wilson, who was not without boldness of sorts. House ended by advocating insistently a Cabinet that would partially recognize "political claims" and expediency. The fear that "the Governor" (as he called Wilson) would appoint for his Cabinet only "irregular party men," who would not be on speaking terms with Congress, ended by harassing Colonel House beyond all measure. He went so far as to beseech Mrs. Wilson to help him sway the mind of the President-elect. [13]

In the end, the Wilson Cabinet was a compromise between political expediency and the President-elect's own preference for "experts." The hope of including men like President Charles W. Eliot of Harvard University, or Dean Henry B. Fine of Princeton College, as Secretaries or Ambassadors was laid aside for various reasons. Rumors that former Governor Joseph Folk of Missouri, a militant reformer, would be named to a high office proved groundless. The enlightened, "non-partisan" idea of retaining Taft's admirable Secretary of the Interior, Walter L. Fisher, who had replaced the unfortunate Ballinger with so much distinction, was also regretfully abandoned.

[12] Lane, op. cit., Vol. I, p. 297.
[13] House, op. cit., Vol. I, p. 103, Jan. 14, 1912.

One man Wilson had stubbornly desired to invite into his Cabinet, as either Attorney General or Secretary of Commerce, was Louis D. Brandeis. The brilliant "people's lawyer" strongly impressed Woodrow Wilson as one fitted to be an expert adviser, though in a manner different from that of House. But rumors that he counted upon having Brandeis as a member of his Cabinet brought the pressure of the most powerful financial interests upon Wilson. The friends of the New Haven railroad, of the United Shoe Machinery Company, and of Boston's large banks marshaled their forces and sent Wilson's friend and financial angel, Cleveland Dodge, to plead with him against Brandeis' appointment. House too notes in his diary that he helped to eliminate Brandeis as a candidate for the Attorney General's post, which was finally given to James C. McReynolds of Tennessee.[14]

Wilson, still determined to find a place for Brandeis, in January and February, 1913, considered him for Secretary of Commerce. But at the last a respectable Democratic party hack, Congressman W. C. Redfield of Brooklyn, became the compromise choice.

Other appointments that suggested yielding to circumstances included that of William G. McAdoo as Secretary of the Treasury. McAdoo was a "Wall Street promoter" whose one notable achievement was the successful promotion of the Hudson-Manhattan Tubes, which had many New Jersey "political angles." The selection of William B. Wilson as Secretary of Labor; D. F. Houston, a Western college president (originally from Texas) as Secretary of Agriculture; and the veteran Congressman, Albert S. Burleson —another Texan—as Postmaster General, seemed nondescript or mediocre. Burleson, who was charged with dispensing the party spoils and patronage through the Post Office Department, was a friend of Colonel House; so was T. W. Gregory, also a Texan, who soon succeeded McReynolds as Attorney General, when the latter was elevated to the Supreme Court. Thus the ubiquitous House, who appeared everywhere, had his hand in everything,

[14] Lief, *op. cit.*, pp. 259-260; Baker, *op. cit.*, Vol. IV, p. 450.

held much of the actual machinery of official power while keeping himself hidden behind the Presidential throne.

The highest post of all, that of Secretary of State, went to William J. Bryan, the man who seemed at first glance less expert than anyone else, least of all in foreign diplomacy. Wilson suffered at the thought of having Bryan by his side. Many schemes for "disposing" of him were considered. He was offered the post of Ambassador to Russia, where it was hinted that he might be of service to world peace, a subject that was now of great interest to Bryan. But he sent word to Wilson's adviser that he did not care to be "exiled." House at last convinced Wilson that Bryan was more dangerous outside the administration than in it; and most reluctantly, even coldly, Wilson offered him the post of Secretary of State, which Bryan promptly accepted.[15] With Bryan there came also one of his ardent followers, Josephus Daniels, who was named Secretary of the Navy; he was a lively young newspaper editor from North Carolina and formerly something of a Populist.

It was a strange, inchoate Cabinet. At one end was Franklin K. Lane, Secretary of the Interior, who as a member of the Interstate Commerce Commission had a proved record of ability and character; at the other end was Bryan, the idealistic Chautauqua lecturer, political orator, and party leader. Yet though conservative citizens rubbed their eyes at seeing the "Tiberius Gracchus of the West," with his quaint, undiplomatic notions, ruling over the State Department, he proved to be of immense help in carrying through the Wilson legislative program. He represented strongly, courageously the Western progressive influences in the Democratic party amalgam. In retrospect he seems to have been a great power for good, by force of his character and deep convictions; his two years as Secretary of State are seen now as the most meritorious of his crowded and uneven career.

In his utopian novel Edward House wrote like a lion; in day-to-day politics he behaved more like the fox. Thanks to the influence of House and other "practical" advisers, Wilson frankly

[15] House, *op. cit.*, Vol. I, p. 95.

played organization politics. Under the quasi-revolutionary emblem of the New Freedom under the philosopher-President, the old, narrow Democratic partisanships were continued. One wonders if Wilson fully realized what was happening, what kind of officers were being chosen to fight in his crusade.

On March 5, 1913, immediately after his inauguration, he announced that office-seekers would be barred from the White House. House, McAdoo, and the young Tumulty, who came to Washington as Private Secretary to the President, saw them all in his place. And Postmaster General Burleson dispensed over 56,000 civil offices with a partisan hand, while Bryan "felt content to entrust our affairs abroad to every-day folks" who had been loyal Bryan men since 1896.[16] Dr. Wilson thereafter wrapped himself in his robes of a prophet, ascended his mountain, and fixed his attention upon higher, less mundane things. Behind him, whilst he looked the other way, the old partisanship raged and the old lust for office and privilege fed itself freely under new Democratic priests in the temple, much like those they supplanted.

What did it matter if the Cabinet were filled chiefly with indifferent or mediocre men? The new President hardly ever spoke to his Cabinet Secretaries after a time. (Sometimes he sent House to carry a rebuke or an order.) After some months had gone by, the traditional Friday Cabinet meetings were discontinued. A man might be Secretary of State, but the President conducted our foreign relations with his own hand. Wilson's colleagues in the administration did not speak to their difficult chief unless they were spoken to; they did not offer advice unless it was asked for.

2

Wilson desired above all to impose executive leadership upon Congress and upon the nation. He had an ambitious program of law-giving before him, its grand lines set forth clearly in his campaign speeches and in his brief, beautifully written inaugural ad-

[16] Kerney, *Wilson*, p. 319.

dress of March 4, 1913: tariff reduction, currency and banking reform, laws to strengthen the Anti-Trust Act and to safeguard and extend the rights of organized labor. It would need strenuous, unremitting fighting by the leader for this program, and behind him a convinced, loyal, and well-knit army of political foot-soldiers. Was the old Democratic party, with its Smiths and Nugents, its Murphys and Taggarts, an adequate instrument for his great objectives? Wilson in the past two years had often asserted that the Democratic party must become progressive or disappear; indeed his constant effort in the last campaign had been to lure away from the turbulent Colonel Roosevelt his progressive followers.

In his first interview with Postmaster General Burleson, Wilson who knew well why the man had been appointed, was extremely suspicious of him. To this ruddy-cheeked, side-whiskered Southern conservative he declared bluntly that his administration was intended to be "a progressive administration." He asked to see Burleson's papers bearing upon pending appointments. The wishes of reactionary or Standpat Congressmen, he added, would be given scant consideration; and he desired to supervise Burleson's appointments personally so that only able and forward-looking men were placed in office.

Burleson relates that he felt horrified at what he heard. He decided to make his fight then and there. He argued that if the President pursued such methods, his administration would be a failure. "It means the defeat of the measures of reform that you have next to your heart." The thousand and one little offices upon which Congressmen set such great store meant little to the President. By according them Wilson could escape the dissensions which Grover Cleveland provoked; he could make the Democratic party progressive, as Cleveland made it conservative. The essential thing was to "adopt a policy of harmony and observe the laws of human nature."

Wilson seemed obdurate. He recalled the bitter opposition of the reactionary party leaders in New Jersey. Should he not work to weaken their power in the national party? But Burleson contended that he had 56,000 appointments to fill, and proposed to fill them by consulting with the members of Congress from the various districts and states. Burleson warned the President, out of wisdom gained from thirty years in the House of Representatives, that if the wishes of the Congressmen and Senators in patronage matters were ignored, they would "hate" him and vote against all his measures.

Wilson was silent. Subsequently he made some efforts to deal with numerous selected cases among the masses of post-office appointments. In the end he surrendered and simply asked Burleson, when he arrived with his *dossiers:* "Where do I sign?" [17]

By seniority, the chairman of the Senate Finance Committee, who replaced Aldrich, was F. M. Simmons of North Carolina, a narrow, Negro-baiting Southern Bourbon. Simmons would, in the normal course of events, have in his charge the tariff-reform bill upon which the Democratic President set such great store. But his record was a doubtful one: in Cleveland's second term, when the Wilson-Gorman tariff act was passed, this Democratic Senator had joined with Aldrich's Republicans to increase the tariff duties, especially in cases which favored the home industries of his state. How could Simmons then be safely left as floor leader in charge of a bill reducing the protective tariff duties? Wilson, therefore, seriously considered having Simmons removed, through the pressure of other Senators more friendly to his own principles. But Simmons showed fight. It meant his ruin to be superseded. Even Secretary Josephus Daniels, Simmons's liberal compatriot in the Cabinet, advised that factious strife should be avoided, and attempts be made to collaborate with the reactionary Senator. Moreover Simmons sent pledges that he would be a loyal soldier and would fight valiantly for Wilson's tariff ideas. The President, after long hesitation, finally withdrew his opposition to the man.

Though Wilson may have promised himself and the public that he would work only with the progressives in his party, he formed

[17] Baker, *op. cit.,* Vol. IV, pp. 44-47.

working alliances with the old partisan leaders, Burleson and Simmons, and strove to conciliate his rivals of yesterday, Champ Clark and Underwood. The old Standpatters in his own party, he was assured, though they had been loyal soldiers of reaction, would under his leadership be as loyal fighters for reform. "You may be able to lead them along progressive lines," Josephus Daniels said hopefully.[18]

What better course could he have followed? asks his biographer, Ray Stannard Baker. Time was short; bills must be passed. He who had yesterday declared that there were only two real parties, those of "the reactionaries and the liberals," made one of the most fateful decisions of his entire career, at the beginning of his term, when *he elected to work with his party as it stood.*

Through hard fighting for direct control of the national party organization, he might, like La Follette in Wisconsin, have suffered delays in enacting his great legislative program. But he would have built out of the half-corrupt, secretly reactionary Democratic party a renewed, truly progressive party. More vital than the legislative victories of that season would have been the fundamental change and overhauling of our professional party system, which might have remained a lasting monument to Wilson's glory. But this was not to be. Wilson's secret decision, made in his first days as President, goes far to explain the strange and confusing consequences that followed in later years, and that so easily undid the initial personal victories for liberalism.

Once more the deep-rooted professional, institutional character of our party system survived a veritable revolution of the ballot box. The permanence of new principles of law, of sweeping reforms hung upon the fate of a single political personality. So long as the apocalyptic moods possessed Wilson, the new regime worked with clean hands, immune to a surprising degree to the pressures of special interests, Wilson standing as a just, even-handed, and sometimes terribly aloof magistrate. But in time Woodrow Wilson himself became accustomed to working "through" his party and

[18] *Ibid.*, Vol. IV, p. 102.

found it convenient to accord credit to it for his victories—though Insurgents, such as La Follette, strongly supported him also. His tactics became increasingly partisan, even to the extent of lending his personal intervention one day in certain Congressional elections. When he was gone, the old "crowd," surviving reform and war, would show themselves unregenerate as ever.

A very determined effort was made by Wilson from the start to sever those private wires that always seemed to run from the President's mansion to the financial centers in New York and elsewhere. Louis D. Brandeis warned him that

. . . The conflict between the policies of the administration and the desires of the financiers and of big business is an irreconcilable one. Concessions to the big business interests must in the end prove futile. The administration can, at best, have only their seeming or temporary cooperation. In essentials they must be hostile. . . . It is extremely dangerous to follow their advice, even in a field technically their own.[19]

Besides, the unfortunate experience of Theodore Roosevelt in the Tennessee Coal and Iron affair was enough to cause Wilson to shut the back door of the White House firmly, making himself more unapproachable to Wall Street than any other President theretofore. The younger Morgan, succeeding to the place of his father in 1913, inherited and cherished his father's deep dislike of the apostle of the New Freedom.

Yet the connections between the radical political government and finance were not entirely destroyed. Big business still ruled the American people's everyday economic existence. Whether this were recognized or not some contact must be established; and the "contact man" turned out to be Edward House. His diary tells us that on March 22, 1913, "Mr. Frick came at eleven . . ."; that the New York banker, James Speyer, communicated with him urgently on March 12 regarding the need for stopping "these attacks by Government agencies" on the railroads, unless catastrophe

[19] Memorandum of Jun. 14, 1913; Lief, *op. cit.*, p. 274.

were to follow; that the Boston investment banker, Henry Lee Higginson, sent to House his frequent complaints of business "uncertainty," though like the other conservatives he dared not personally approach Wilson. Further—during the preliminary, secret discussions of the Federal Reserve Act—we find that House, on December 19, 1912, "talked with Paul Warburg . . . regarding currency reform"; and on February 26, 1913, with Frick and Otto Kahn; on March 13, 1913, "Vanderlip and I had an interesting discussion . . ."; on March 27, 1913, "Mr. J. P. Morgan, Jr., and Mr. Denny of his firm came promptly at five." [20] This arrangement of having an "Assistant President" was most curious and had its conveniences.

3

"There has been a change of government" were the first impressive words Wilson uttered in his first inaugural address. In a brief, simple, lucidly written speech that showed no trace of compromise or evasion, he pictured an America grown great through its genius for enterprise yet stopping not "to count the human cost," while evils festered within the fabric of our society and government. The changed government, instead of ignoring these things, would now look at them with "a new vision," and would undertake whole-heartedly the long-needed work of "restoration" and reconstruction. He announced his three-point program of legislation, touching tariff, banking, and social laws, saying: "Society must see to it that it does not crush or weaken or damage its own constituent parts." In solemn, determined tones, he added: "This is not a day of triumph. It is a day of dedication. . . . I summon all honest men, all patriotic, all forward-looking men to my side. God helping me, I will not fail them. . . ."

The first pictures of Dr. Wilson at work were those of a granite-faced, long-nosed, bespectacled, gray-haired man whom the nation would respect but not love. There was no Inaugural Ball as of old on March 4, 1913; there were no jollifications. Wil-

[20] House, *op. cit.*, Vol. I, pp. 129-134, 160-161.

son announced that he would have no time to make appearance at dinners, or travel about the country. Commentators predicted "a regime of plain living" and "higher thinking." [21]

But the Wilson regime was not to be wanting in Rooseveltian boldness and "new departures." Congress was promptly called by President Wilson in special session to enact the promised tariff and currency legislation. When the two houses convened, April 8, 1913, the President appeared at the Capitol in person to read his message on the proposed tariff act, thus suddenly reversing a tradition which, since the time of Thomas Jefferson, emphasized the jealous separation of our government authorities. Wilson, on the contrary, boldly stressed the unity or teamwork which must be brought about between the branches of the government. The President henceforth was to be "a person, not a mere department of the government hailing Congress from some isolated island of jealous power . . . a human being trying to co-operate with other human beings in a common service." Thus he framed in action his ideas of leadership, patterned after his favorite English parliamentary models, and expounded long before in his books. Henceforth he would follow every step of debate or maneuver in Congress; he would move closely in step with the legislators, instead of feigning that he could not shape their opinions or guide them; he would be, by grace of the nation's support, the active leader of his party and the activating agency of the Congress.

Some protests were made at these precedent-breaking proceedings; even in his own party, certain Congressmen of the "Jeffersonian" type spoke of the "autocratic schoolmaster" in Wilson and of "imperious" ways that Colonel Roosevelt himself had not assumed. Yet Wilson's simple dignity of manner disarmed criticism.

The personal descent upon Capitol Hill symbolized a new technique of national political leadership that triumphed over the "divided" character of our government. Occasionally foreshadowed or suggested by Theodore Roosevelt, it was now perfected by

[21] *Review of Reviews*, Apr., 1913.

Wilson. It was a technique of leadership that seemed all but imperative in a period of drastic political reform.

The forthrightness of the President's message on tariff revision was widely remarked as showing the most decided contrast with the timid and equivocal attitude of Mr. Taft and his colleagues four years earlier. He stressed the system of "privileges and exemptions" that had grown up under protection, and against which the nation must now make head. As in his campaign speeches of 1912, so now he grounded his appeal upon classical principles of economic "freedom": business must be set free; the new tariff act must at last "open once more the free channels of prosperity to a great people. . . ."

When the administration bill was introduced in Congress by Representative Underwood of Alabama, even the piously Republican New York *Tribune* praised the bill "as expressing fairly and justly the [Democratic] tariff attitude during the campaign." [22] There were many reformers and free-traders who had cursed the protective tariff all their lives as the crowning evil of our politics; they had seen administrations committed to tariff revision come and go, and nothing done, until they were ready to believe that no President would ever dare to lower the tariff rates. Yet the Underwood-Simmons Bill provided for free wool, free paper and wood pulp, free steel rails, free lumber, free trade with the Philippines, and free sugar (after an interval of three years). Its main feature was its effort to lighten the cost of the "market basket" by moderately lowering the cost of living for the little man, especially with regard to shoes and clothing, while duties upon luxuries, precious stones, furs, and perfumes and fashionable garments were left unchanged. However, the reductions were so moderate or even "nominal" that the protective character of our fiscal system—now so widely imitated by the great European powers—was in no sense violently altered. The Underwood-Simmons Bill was hailed as "the most intelligent" tariff act ever framed.

[22] *Ibid.*, May, 1913.

Late in February, 1913, the Sixteenth Amendment to the Constitution, initiated nearly four years earlier, enabling Congress to levy direct taxes upon incomes, was fully ratified. Thus the Underwood-Simmons Bill was permitted to incorporate a clause providing for an income tax ranging from 1 per cent on earnings of $3,000 (for unmarried men) to 6 per cent on incomes above $500,000 per annum. The income-tax clause, fruit of the first Constitutional amendment since the dramatic days of Reconstruction forty years ago, made the Underwood-Simmons Bill a historic, almost a revolutionary event, the culmination of twenty years of political struggle.

Passage of the tariff law was helped not only by Wilson's eager efforts to hold his party "in line," but by the important liberalization of Congressional rules which Norris's uprising had brought in 1910. As a consequence, the chairmen of the strategic committees were far less autocratic in their powers. In the upper chamber Senator Simmons, chairman of the Finance Committee, was watched sharply by the majority of Democratic liberals and by the Insurgent La Follette, who was now at last a member of this powerful committee. On the floor, Bryan's progressive followers led the fight in both houses.

The heavy Democratic majority in the Lower House brought quick passage of the bill, with few revisions, on May 8, after only two weeks' debate. But in the Senate, where the opposition had a strong minority, the debate was keener; resistance was organized at the bottlenecks of committees and reinforced by a swarm of lobbyists, made up of corporation lawyers, ex-Congressmen, and even detectives and spies, who quickly converged upon Washington. They petitioned and entertained the politicians as of old. Masses of letters and telegrams, simulating a "spontaneous" public protest (in behalf of the woolen and sugar lobbies), were dispatched to those Senators thought to be most wavering.

On May 26, 1913, using tactics invented by Theodore Roosevelt at the height of his power, Wilson struck a powerful blow at the opposition by giving out for publication a statement on "the extraordinary exertions being made by the lobby" endeavoring to obtain changes in the tariff bill and defeat a popular mandate. It was a serious thing, he protested, that the people should be, in effect, voiceless, while "great bodies of astute men seek to create an artificial opinion . . . for their private profit." He summoned a real public opinion to help rid Congress and the government of the "intolerable burden" created by the paid lobbyists.

The President's public warning and appeal aroused a storm in the Senate, Republican opponents moving indignantly for a resolution of investigation into the lobby, a move accepted by the Democrats. That summer a Congressional committee held hearings on lobbying activities. Testimony taken concerning the large sums expended by the great trade associations—$750,000 had been disbursed by the sugar combination alone in a few recent years—as well as revelations of the National Association of Manufacturers' secret activities, increased popular resentment and suspicion, and broke the resistance of certain high-tariff Democrats in Congress.

In addition, Wilson on several occasions drove to Capitol Hill to hold conferences with the Senators in the President's Room of the Senate. A party caucus designed to force disciplined action, which the turbulent Democratic party so often lacked, brought on July 7 a resolution that the proposed tariff bill was a "party measure." On July 11 the bill was formally "reported" to the Senate by Mr. Simmons without important changes or amendments. As foreseen, no insoluble disagreements between the two Houses of Congress arose in joint conference over the terms of the bill; and after brief, routine delays, it was passed and signed by Wilson on October 3.

The pertinacious Wilson, according to press comments of the time, had

jammed through Congress . . . a tremendous and all-embracing piece of legislation . . . by using all the prestige and authority of his party leadership and all the power of his executive office, without tolerating amendment or encouraging debate.[23]

[23] *Review of Reviews*, Jul., 1913.

Tremendous, nation-wide applause greeted this first victory. To many Americans it seemed that a providential leader had arisen and that the first great steps toward social justice were being taken by the philosopher President who guided the republic.

4

As early as June 23, 1913, when the safe passage of the tariff bill was already assured, Wilson had appeared before the united bodies of Congress for a second time with a special message asking their urgent consideration of another large reform measure which, as he said, "should press close on the heels of the tariff changes. . . ." It was a plan for a new central banking and currency law, the Federal Reserve Act.

Shortly before his inauguration, in a speech at Chicago, Wilson had made reference to the facts brought forth by the committee of Congress then investigating the so-called "money trust." "I am not indicting the bankers," he said; "they have been convicted." An "inner circle" composed of a handful of powerful or strategically placed Eastern financiers now held the main reservoir of the country's credit through their banking, insurance, and investment institutions. Business men nowadays could obtain virtually no credit save on the sufferance of this "inner circle" of the money trust. Wilson declared, "We must see to it that the business of the United States is set absolutely free of every feature of monopoly." [24]

The House Committee on Banking and Currency (known to fame as the "Pujo Committee"), with the aggressive lawyer Samuel Untermyer examining witnesses, held hearings upon the workings of the "money trust" from May, 1912, to January, 1913, and soon afterward presented its report and recommendations to Congress. All previous notions of the dangers implicit in the trend of our economic life to monopoly—even in the alarming exposures by the muckrakers—paled into insignificance beside the judicial re-

[24] *The Outlook*, Jan. 25, 1913.

port of the Pujo Committee. It showed that the great monopolies in transportation, public utilities, and heavy industry had been combined directly through banker control and interlocking directorates into a grand "community of interests" having aggregate resources of $22,245,000,000. The members of the firm of J. P. Morgan and Company and the directors of their controlled trust companies, along with the directors of the National City Bank (Rockefeller-dominated) and the First National Bank, held 341 directorships in the 112 principal financial and industrial corporations making up the community of interests. The system extended itself also through subsidiary networks and subsidiary syndicates that controlled the investment of capital. For many years no important financing amounting to as much as $10,000,000 was carried out save through the hands or with the participation of the controlling group and its several satellites: Kuhn, Loeb and Company; Kidder, Peabody; or Lee, Higginson.[25] In effect, by controlling the largest banks and insurance companies, the Morgan-Stillman-Baker group constituted a central banking agency holding the entire credit of the country in its private hands.

Morgan stubbornly denied that a monopoly of currency and credit was possible. But George F. Baker admitted to Untermyer that the existing situation was "not entirely a comfortable one" for the banking and currency system of a great nation.[26] The committee of Congress soberly concluded in its report that the proofs of a concentrated money and credit monopoly were incontestable. (Its extremely intelligent recommendations for the reform of evil banking and investment practices, recommendations which might have mitigated the rigors of the 1929-1933 banking collapse, were to be adopted twenty years later.)

The men who established our great industries [the Pujo Committee summed up] have added to the prosperity of the country during the period of the upbuilding of these industries; but they, none the less, violated the law when they reversed the process under which the country

[25] Pujo Committee, *Report*, Feb. 28, 1913, pp. 86, 160.
[26] *Ibid.*, Feb. 28, 1913, p. 106.

had grown and prospered, by combining to throttle the competition upon which they had thrived. Whilst they were struggling against one another for supremacy they were a valuable asset to the country; since they have pursued the opposite policy they have become a menace.

Monopoly, in short, had reached the stage of its development where it throttled progressively all competition, as forecast by Karl Marx in his *Capital*. But the overwhelming demand of the liberals who had triumphed at the polls was to restore competition rather than to suffer that the trusts should "regulate the government and the citizens of the United States," as Brandeis, La Follette, and Borah believed they meant to do. Nor did they wish to wait, as the Socialists advised, until the big capitalists had "pushed the cart up the hill," and then confiscate the nationally consolidated industries. Wilson, in his message to Congress of June 23, 1913, as before, urged that "American business must be set free." In his public papers the ideology of the New Freedom embodied a renewed quest for liberty by farmers, workers, and small tradesmen; a return to classical, individual competition.

Tariff reform was designed to render the American people free of an oppressive protective system. It was now imperative, Wilson added, that a remodeled banking and currency system should be provided by which our business men "can make use of the freedom of enterprise and of individual initiative which we are about to bestow upon them." The controls of the Money Trust, as the Pujo Committee had implied, "clogged" the arteries of credit. These controls, Wilson held, must be henceforth public, not private; must be vested in the impartial government itself "so that the banks may be the instruments, not the masters, of business. . . ." With this salvo, the historic Federal Reserve Bill was introduced by Representative Carter Glass of Virginia and Senator Robert L. Owen of Oklahoma, even while the Underwood tariff waited for adoption.

Since 1907 the creation of a new central bank of reserve and issue had been the fondest project of Senator Nelson Aldrich, now retired. The Aldrich-Vreeland Act of 1908, revising our national

banking laws, was but a temporary expedient; meanwhile the proposals of the monetary commission it had set up for a Federal
Reserve System had met the resistance of the Insurgents and the
deep prejudice of the currency radicals, typified by Bryan, who
constantly feared lest the control of the country's gold supply pass
forever into the hands of a clique of Eastern bankers. The patient schemes of the Republican conservatives had been frustrated
by the great political defeat of 1912.

However, the modern need for an "elastic" currency and bank
of reserve went unanswered. Very shortly after his election, Wilson took up this question in earnest, with the aid of Colonel House,
who was a former banker. Conferences were held privately with
Representative Carter Glass, Chairman of the Committee on
Banking and Currency, and with Glass's financial adviser, Professor H. Parker Willis; later, Secretary of the Treasury William
G. McAdoo, Senator Owen (who was making a special study of
the problem), and leading bankers, such as Paul M. Warburg,
Otto Kahn, Frank A. Vanderlip, and the younger J. P. Morgan,
as well as Samuel Untermyer, counsel to the Pujo Committee,
were all brought into the discussion.

Colonel House relates that on March 27, 1913, J. P. Morgan, Jr., and a member of his firm came to him with a central
banking plan "already formulated and printed." He discreetly advised Morgan to have a plain typewritten copy of the plan made
to be shown the President. How embarrassing it would have been
if Bryan had seen that a scheme all complete and printed was being submitted by the Morgans! [27] For the Nebraskan, like his
great forerunner Andrew Jackson, who had led the radical farmers, detested the idea of a central bank that might become an instrument of the "plutocracy." No plan corresponding to Aldrich's
could escape a powerful attack by the Bryan men in Congress.
Indeed Bryan had catechized Woodrow Wilson on this point early
in 1912, before lending him support. Thus House, Glass, and

[27] House, *op. cit.*, Vol. I, p. 161.

their advisers worked as quietly as possible to prepare their bill and to enlist for it the support of the great bankers.

A draft of the bill, as first written by Glass and his aides in April, 1913, was subjected to the criticism of the New York bankers, who through their spokesman, Paul M. Warburg, protested that it did not go far enough toward setting up a strong central bank, and did not make sufficient provisions for having the issue of currency notes controlled by the bankers themselves.[28] One Boston banker, Josiah Quincy, threatened that the bankers might "withdraw their national bank charters and take out state charters."

Late in April, Bryan obtained a copy of Glass's draft, and set off on the warpath. He was utterly convinced that the bill, as drafted by Glass, Warburg, and Willis, left predominant control of the central bank's board to the private bankers rather than to government officers, and actually surrendered control of the issuance of money to the bankers. Bryan insisted that the new Federal Reserve note issues, instead of continuing to be obligations of the national banks (that entered the system), should be "government money." In addition Bryan wished to reinforce the "regional" as against the "central" organization of the system. To his support Bryan drew Senator Robert L. Owen, in charge of the bill being prepared in the Senate, and Samuel Untermyer.

The first plan prepared by Glass and Willis, according to Samuel Untermyer, had set up twenty reserve banks under control of a central directory of forty-three members, only three of whom represented the government, the rest being private bankers.[29] On the other hand, a rough compromise plan, which Glass soon shaped with Wilson's approval, while not meeting the objections of the progressives, came under the fire of the Eastern bankers who protested vigorously that it did not meet their minimum demands and had unsafe features.

Thus there was a spirited tug-of-war behind the scenes in the

[28] Glass, *An Adventure in Constructive Finance*, pp. 53-54; House, *op. cit.*, Vol. I, p. 161.
[29] Untermyer, *The Federal Reserve Act*, p. 11.

spring and summer of 1913. The essential ground of dispute, between the faction led by Bryan and that headed by Carter Glass (whose conservative financial views the President seemed to favor), was that of control of the Federal Reserve System by the representatives of government or of banking. Senator Owen, who was supported by Bryan, in his Senate bill showed a serious divergence from the plan of Glass being prepared in the House.

Going to the White House with Untermyer by his side, Bryan warned the President that if the Glass bill were introduced, "he would use all his influence . . . with the members of Congress to accomplish its defeat." [30] Some weeks later, in the first days of June, the President himself sent for Bryan and endeavored to persuade him to drop his resistance to the Glass bill. Bryan, though courteous in tone, insisted upon his original point of view. His firmness, however, gave hints that he might resign from the Cabinet and fight Wilson within the Democratic party. [31]

They seemed to have come to the parting of the ways, according to Tumulty, who relates that he was asked by Wilson to go to Bryan that very night. The Secretary of State expressed his faith in the President's sincerity, but he asked bluntly: "Who from Wall Street has been discussing this bill with the President?" [32]

During this raging controversy, which was somewhat concealed from the public, Secretary of the Treasury McAdoo came forward with a third plan, a compromise that tried to meet some of the demands of the radical faction. Meanwhile the bankers, through the press, conducted an intense agitation against "government control," and signs of financial panic were reported from New York.

At this crisis Wilson turned to Louis D. Brandeis, and laid the whole problem before him. Brandeis argued in a logical manner for Bryan's main contentions. The role of the private bankers in the governing board of the Federal Reserve System, he held, should be limited to that of an advisory council, and the power to issue currency (against commercial paper) should be vested exclu-

[30] *Ibid.*, p. 11.
[31] Bryan, *op. cit.*, pp. 370-372.
[32] Tumulty, *op. cit.*, p. 179.

sively in government officials appointed by the President. A hue and cry had been raised against the threat of the government's "entering the banking business," and this contributed to panic. Brandeis besought the President not to be frightened into passing an inadequate bill. The imperative thing, he reminded him, was to "curb the money trust. . . ." While the bankers' views should be given the most careful hearing, their advice in their own field might often prove unsound.[33]

Wilson now decided that he must make his terms quickly with the progressives. He summoned McAdoo, Glass, and Owen to a conference at the White House on June 18, 1913, and, reversing himself completely, proposed that the bankers be excluded from direct representation upon the central governing board of the Federal Reserve System. Glass, who "was very definitely committed to banking representation," made stormy protests. (Subsequently, visiting delegations of bankers made even louder protests, without effect.) A second point on which the President now insisted was that the Federal Reserve notes that would be issued were to be "obligations of the United States," and not of the constituent banks that deposited reserves in the System. Glass and his aides objected fiercely; but in a technical sense the difference was negligible, and the President prevailed.[34]

On other points compromises were rapidly worked out, and the support of the redoubtable Bryan was won. Wilson was able to call successfully for the united support of his party in his historic message to Congress of June 23, 1913, when he recommended the Federal Reserve Bill for passage. A long and confusing debate followed, which was sharpened by the last-ditch resistance of bankers like Vanderlip, head of the National City Bank, who continued to predict calamitous consequences. Yet passage of the bill was ultimately won on December 23, 1913, and marked another notable triumph for Dr. Wilson.

The Federal Reserve Act of 1913 was essentially non-partisan

[33] L. D. Brandeis to Wilson, Jun. 14, 1913; Lief, *op. cit.*, pp. 273-274.
[34] Glass, *op. cit.*, pp. 112-115, 124-130.

legislation, long needed. It created a government depositary and central rediscount "bank for bankers" in which most of the nation's banks became subscribing members. In its final form, with its "decentralized" organization of twelve regional reserve banks underlying the Federal Reserve Board—unlike Europe's central banks—it appeared to redistribute New York's financial domination of the money supply, thus yielding to progressive or "Jacksonian" demands. Moreover, the Federal Reserve notes, "government obligations," based on commercial assets as well as government bonds, became the basic money of the country; the gold standard, backed by a gold ratio of 40 per cent, existed only "in theory" and the emission of currency was controlled by a Board of Governors appointed by the President. A broad basis of currency resting on commercial paper, the nation's short-term business credits, broader than Bryan's "Free Silver Coinage," was thus created at last. On the other hand, elasticity, the ability to expand or contract the supply of money as required by modern economic conditions, was introduced.

Did the new system eliminate the Gold Bugs' control of the nation's financial resources? Only the future would tell. Much depended upon the personnel who would direct the reserve banks. It was significant that the big private bankers who had at first shown great apprehension came to the support of the Federal Reserve System afterward. "The bill is a good one," wrote Jacob Schiff to House; "anyhow good enough to start with." [35] The appointment by Wilson of men like Paul Warburg, W. P. G. Harding, and Benjamin Strong to the Board of Governors went far to reassure the bankers, and mitigated greatly the appearance of "government control." Within two years of its inception, more than 33 per cent of our banks had subscribed to stock in the Federal Reserve regional banks; by 1928 nearly 49 billions of banking resources were joined within the System.

Its establishment on the very eve of the World War and world panic of 1914 was undoubtedly a stroke of fortune for American

[35] Seymour, op. cit., Vol. I, p. 174.

business, which had been hampered in its growth by an obsolete banking and currency institution.

5

Woodrow Wilson felt that he must force the pace at the start, that "his first months would be his safest," commented Norman Hapgood, the liberal journalist, at this time. The great policy measures must be driven through; the tariff, currency, and trust pledges redeemed—before "one of those false reactions" came that would make the going more difficult.[36]

In the winter of 1913-1914 Wilson proposed determinedly to carry on his sweeping legislative reforms by enacting laws strengthening the Sherman Anti-Trust Act, setting up a Federal Trade Commission to regulate the trusts, safeguarding the rights of labor unions, and establishing more liberal credits for farmers, with government aid. In financial circles that winter, gloom spread widely at the news of a new Anti-Trust Act with specific provisions framed according to the ideas of La Follette and Brandeis. There was tension and uncertainty at the threat which the austere President seemed to offer. Then suddenly, before the new anti-monopoly laws were announced from the White House, there came the sensational news that the younger Morgan, together with George F. Baker, president of the First National Bank of New York, intended to withdraw from directorships they held in a large number of corporations. In a public interview, at the beginning of the new year, Morgan stated that this step was being taken in deference to "an apparent change in public sentiment in regard to interlocking directorships. . . ."[37]

This public gesture, apparently deliberate and intended to conciliate the government and public opinion, did not fail to bring a thrill of triumph to Woodrow Wilson. He had established an apparent primacy of the national government over the most pow-

[36] *Harper's Weekly*, Jun. 27, 1914.
[37] The New York *Times*, Jan. 3, 1914.

erful financial interests in America. By telegram House exultantly reported to Wilson, then resting from his heavy labors at a vacation resort near New Orleans, that the action of Morgan and Baker was "an indication that big business is preparing to surrender unconditionally." Tumulty corroborated this report, saying that the financial interests now showed as much readiness to "come into agreement with the government and work in harmony with it *as the government is to come into agreement with them.*" [38]

In Wilson's special message of January 20, 1914, asking Congress for new legislation upon trusts and labor unions, there was a tone of triumphant pride, but there was also *magnanimity* toward the Enemy. Was not the final coming of the New Freedom within sight? ". . . At last," he remarked, "the masters of business on the great scale have begun to yield . . . in honorable surrender." But then he added:

What we are proposing to do, therefore, is, happily, not to hamper or interfere with business . . . or in any sense to put it under the ban. The antagonism between business and Government is over. . . . The Government and business men are ready to meet each other half-way in a common effort to square business methods with both public opinion and law.

Woodrow Wilson was naturally a most skillful dialectician, or "ideologue," and he avowed that the reforms he sought were intended to bring "peace" and success to the average American business man. By reducing the "area of debatable ground" surrounding the Sherman Anti-Trust Act, by making it more explicit, the government could be fairer to all sides, including labor. He argued that "the best informed men of the business world" shared his view that only good might come to them from a program that would be comprehensive, but not "radical" and "without revolution of any kind." He then outlined the provisions of the acts which were to be known as the Clayton Anti-Trust Act and the Federal Trade Commission Act: prohibiting "interlocking direc-

[38] Jan. 6, 1914; Baker, *op. cit.*, Vol. IV, p. 369; italics mine.

torates," specifying what were acts in restraint of trade and fair competition, declaring discriminations and "tying" agreements illegal, providing for the publicity of accounts for the government commission, and for penalties (threefold damages) which, however, were not to include criminal penalties. Two clauses of the Clayton Act seemed to fulfill honestly the pledges given by the Democratic party in 1912 to organized labor: by one clause "labor, agricultural and horticultural organizations" were exempted from the operation of the Anti-Trust law; while the second forbade the use of the injunction process in a strike, unless—here was a loophole—*deemed necessary to prevent irreparable injury to property rights.*

In the 1920's the Supreme Court would find a way of drawing the teeth from the Clayton Act's no-injunction provisions—but at the time of its enactment the bill was hailed as a "Magna Carta for American labor." Only the year before, President Taft in one of his last acts had condemned and vetoed a similar bill, passed as a "rider" to an appropriations bill, as "class legislation of the most vicious sort." But for the moment men opened their eyes wide in amazement at the manner in which the inspired Wilson, leading an aroused public opinion in the summer of 1914, drove through Congress social laws they had scarcely hoped to see in their lifetime. These measures were crowned in the two years following by the Federal Farm Loan Act, the La Follette Seamen's Act, and the Adamson Act establishing an eight-hour day on interstate railways. Even a Child Labor Act (though soon declared unconstitutional by the Supreme Court) was passed by 1916, in the last wave of the Wilsonian crusade.

The magnitude of Wilson's achievements during the first, peacetime phase of his administration has been forgotten, owing to the long, dark shadows cast by the war that followed. His almost unequaled legislative achievements sprang, as he himself said, out of the experience of a whole generation which, though often balked or turned aside, marched steadily toward a more extended democracy, toward "social justice."

Wilson's "system," his ideology, revealed itself fully in his first year of power. By the passage of his reform laws he brought, as he contended, a new "constitution of peace" for our society. For the farmer, the laborer, and small business man he provided strengthened government controls over predatory economic groups, which seemed to guarantee the liberties that the little American hungered for. To the big capitalists, who brought heavy complaints of the government's interference with business, he could say (like Theodore Roosevelt) that the policy he pursued "was absolutely necessary to satisfy the conscience of the country . . . that it was a great deal better to do the thing moderately and soberly now than to wait until more radical forces had accumulated and it was necessary to go much further." [39] Like Theodore Roosevelt, he promised, in effect, to save their children from Red revolution. He too was the honest broker, save that, endowed with more intellectual power and purposefulness, more deeply informed, he seemed to work more effectively to "regulate competition" and to put the weak upon an equality with the strong. Thus, conducting government by a "communion of consciences," or as Walter Lippmann has phrased it, by *noblesse oblige*, his efforts seemed to promise unmistakably that new social equilibrium that men had longed for.

His very detachment, his aloofness from commonplace, day-to-day politics, fitted him the better to administer an even-handed justice between the jealous interest-groups in our society. He did not seem to fear labels or Sacred Cows. That a bill calling for a government-owned railway in Alaska was termed socialistic did not deter him from urging its passage. Even so astute an observer as Lincoln Steffens came to believe that Woodrow Wilson embodied the "forward movement" in the country, that he had triumphed over the inertia of his own party and swallowed up the Progressive faction.[40]

Had a lasting method of co-operation between capitalism and

[39] Baker, *op. cit.*, Vol. IV, p. 376.
[40] Steffens, *op. cit.*, Dec. 23, 1913, Vol. I, p. 331.

democracy been discovered? asks his biographer, Ray Stannard Baker. If the World War had not broken out at this juncture "would the nation have accepted the new arrangements and gone forward upon the new basis? . . . Is it possible that a real *modus vivendi* in the relationship of capitalism and democracy might have developed as a counterpoise for the spreading doctrines of communism?" [41]

In reality the masters of big business, as wc now clearly see from accumulated evidence of their private opinion, had in no sense "surrendered," but merely had executed a strategic retreat. With seeming good grace they quit certain interlocking directorships, as required by the new law, and sundered various giant holding companies—though the divided parts of the Standard Oil Company, for example, through a secret community of interests, worked perfectly together. What these people truly thought of the philosopher-President may be judged from the private remarks of Mr. J. P. Morgan, the younger, made after his requests for an interview at the White House were rebuffed. To his friend Henry White he wrote:

The general situation here is perfectly unspeakable. I cannot begin to write about it, but I hope to have the pleasure of seeing you sometime later in the summer . . . and then we can mutually pour forth to each other. A greater lot of perfectly incompetent, apparently thoroughly crooked people has never, as far as I know, run, or attempted to run, any first-class country. The Mexicans are far better off because their various bosses only murder and rape, but our bosses run the country and make life intolerable for a much larger number of people. [42]

Presumably the great financiers took no patriotic pride in the regime of the New Freedom, and bought no stock in it. By all accounts, the years between 1913 and 1915 represented a low ebb for the House of Morgan. Investments languished, markets declined, and large business failures were suffered, such as that of

[41] Baker, *op. cit.*, Vol. IV, pp. 375, 380.
[42] H. *White Papers*, J. P. Morgan to Henry White, Jun. 5, 1914.

the dry-goods house of H. B. Claflin in New York. The growing business depression was attributed to the harsh controlling hand of the government; in the press an immense clamor for a truce, a "breathing spell," was set up, as so often before. The country, it was said, was "tired of reform." Pressure was brought upon the intimate advisers of Wilson. "Something must be done," wrote one banker to Colonel House, "and *done soon* in a big and courageous way to stop these attacks by Government agencies . . . if disaster is to be averted." [43]

In the President's own Cabinet several members, such as Secretary D. F. Houston, showed alarm and urged caution. From London, Walter H. Page, though giving high praise to the President's achievements in 1913, urged House to point out to Wilson that

. . . he was not seeing enough business men, and was not talking to them in "their language." . . . Everything [Wilson] was doing for the country was absolutely right, but he failed to give proper assurances to the business world that he had their welfare at heart. . . . The President should invite some of them to lunch and show them some marked social attention. . . . [44]

The New Freedom still advanced, though more slowly, driven by a Wilson who commanded the prestige of marvelous political victories. And still in the future lay the tremendous struggle with conservative forces over the appointment of Brandeis to the Supreme Court, which Wilson so courageously joined in 1916. But now there began an era of postponements, compromises, and concealed defeats. Wilson had thought of appointing George Record, who had done so much for the reformation of New Jersey, to the new Federal Trade Commission, but was forced to drop the plan, leaving Record waiting empty-handed in Washington for the word that never came. Other plans such as those for government ownership of the telegraph and telephone companies, which Wilson had strongly favored, were postponed; new conservation

[43] James Speyer to House, Mar. 12, 1914; House, *op. cit.*, Vol. I, p. 132.
[44] House, *op. cit.*, Vol. I, p. 127.

projects were abandoned as opposition mounted on all sides. At an impromptu and informal speech before the National Press Club in Washington, on March 20, 1914, Wilson spoke feelingly of how stupendous and difficult the task of "reconstruction and renewal" now seemed to him. He felt himself besieged by appeals to reform everything on the calendar. When he thought of the varieties of salvation men pressed upon him, it made him tremble with a sense of his own inadequacy. He began to doubt himself, and was silent or impassive (he said apologetically) because he was "trying not to make any colossal blunders." He exclaimed impetuously: "God knows there are enough things in this world that need to be corrected."

In his second year forces outside and within him stayed his hand; he lived under an increasing tension for many months before Sarajevo.

Certain historians have perpetuated the misconception that Wilson's magnificent design for a future order, the clear and definite program in which he was engaged, was sharply interrupted when the catastrophe of World War suddenly halted him, in August, 1914, and made him turn to face external dangers. Actually the American movement toward social democracy, though managed under native traditions and partisan institutions, followed in great measure the pattern of earlier social democratic movements in western Europe. These had gradually come to a halt toward 1912, when the epoch of imperialist general war appeared already at hand and inescapable. European finance, it is now known, was fully prepared for war after 1912. The war's repercussions, though at first remote or limited, would be felt upon the American continent, overshadowing the elaborate plans for social equilibrium which a Wilson endeavored to construct upon shifting sands.

Wilson had forced the pace at the start. Now, in the summer of 1914, as remarked by the well-informed Norman Hapgood, editor of a rejuvenated, progressive *Harper's Weekly*, there had been sixteen months of Wilson; the moment had come when "fatigue" overtook the reform movement; it struggled with its own limitations and the renewed opposition of powerful, deeply hostile elements. The first signs of reaction were already perceptible.[45]

Alone and remote from men, Woodrow Wilson one day in September, 1914, confided to his one intimate friend, House, that he felt he would be much happier if he did not have to stand for re-election in 1916. House pointed to the brilliant successes he had gained and his "duty" to continue along the same line. But Wilson, inconsolably, replied that

what frightened him was that it was impossible to make such an effort in the future as he had made in the past, or to accomplish anything like what he had accomplished in a legislative way. He feared the country would expect him to continue as he had up to now, which would be impossible.

House referred to other things he could do, which would be more "delightful" to pursue and "would add even more to his fame. I referred particularly to his foreign policy, which, if properly followed, would bring him world-wide recognition." [46]

But these remarkable proposals evoked little interest on Wilson's part. He spoke at this time as if he wished to keep far away from the great war that had begun. It was to him barbarous and indefensible from any point of view, and arose from "economic causes." [47]

On still another occasion House spoke in his flattering vein of Wilson's success in his domestic reforms, but the President refused to show elation or satisfaction. He had vague, indefinable apprehensions. He said "his Princeton experiences hung over him sometimes like a nightmare; that he had wonderful success there, and all at once conditions changed and the troubles, of which everyone knew, were brought about. He seemed to fear that such a dénouement might occur again. . . ." [48]

[45] *Harper's Weekly*, Jun. 27, 1914.
[46] House, *op. cit.*, Vol. I, pp. 295-296; italics mine.
[47] *Ibid.*, Vol. I, pp. 295-296.
[48] Dec. 22, 1913; *ibid.*, Vol. I, p. 120.

XVI. LEADERSHIP THROUGH WAR

T HE SHOCK of general European war, arriving suddenly on a summer day of 1914, seemed to set a period to the program of reform and "grand reconstruction" that Wilson directed in America. This program, as we have seen, appeared to have reached its climax already, and established its limits, early in the second year of the New Freedom. But now the storm of elemental forces, such as the liberals had seldom included in their rationalistic schemes, swept from war-torn Europe to distant North America. The passion and fear of war reached us; a financial panic gripped the country from August on, causing at first a stoppage of markets and industries.

At its best, Wilsonian liberalism had been slowly extending the influence of political democracy over increasing areas of American life, without of course changing the fundamental relations of property or the real disposition of economic and social power. Its social philosophy, its historical outlook, was still liberal, rationalistic, and optimistic, like that of English leaders toward the close of the nineteenth century. To keep the domestic peace, concessions were granted to the masses of people, a kind of "ransom," as English politicians had phrased it. The costs were to be borne through the continued, habitual increase of wealth and profits under the capitalist system, as in the past. Everything seemed to promise the continuance of this system by the spread of education and the discovery of new inventions and industries. And the masses of people, to whom political democracy was preached every day by the liberal statesmen of the pre-war era, were taught to look for constantly increasing blessings, benefits, and privileges from the same system in the future.

For example, when the organized railroad workers in 1916 threatened a general strike, President Wilson intervened, and won from the railroad owners concessions to labor in higher wages and shorter hours (the Adamson Act), a great part of the increased cost being met by higher freight charges to the general public, which he also approved. But such methods of balancing things off, which liberal statesmanship hoped to continue, had obvious practical limits; in the long run they brought no improvement in the railroad situation.

As he was liberal in domestic policy, so Wilson also endeavored from the very beginning to pursue a "democratic" diplomacy in foreign affairs. American foreign policy for more than a decade had alternately followed (1) the line of expansion through "dollar diplomacy," especially in Latin America and the Far East, or (2) the line of "balance of power," as in the time of the Russo-Japanese war and the Moroccan crisis in 1905 to 1906.

Wilson, having a free hand in foreign affairs save for the Senate's treaty-making power, desired undoubtedly to win distinction for his administration by an enlightened policy. His first moves would show traits that marked his behavior in foreign politics up to the end. These were a penchant for the use of idealistic verbiage in executing perfectly practical purposes; second, a rigidity in procedure which led him into progressively difficult situations whence he could not extricate himself without doing violence in some measure to the humanity and idealism he professed. In the end the entrance of the United States into its grandest and most costly war adventure, lending itself to the most reactionary designs, was to be carried out in the terms of the most exalted ideology ever used by any of our statesmen.

In March, 1913, when Wilson entered office, the infamous four-power loan was being forced upon the Chinese republic. The American financiers who considered entering the banking consortium arranged by Britain, France, Russia, and Japan actually felt that "dollar diplomacy" had paid but little in China; they were willing and ready to retire from the field, unless the government of the United States supported them abroad with its fullest authority.

Wilson abruptly reversed the program in the Far East; the conditions of the proposed loan to China he judged to be shameful in that they mortgaged China's administrative sovereignty by controlling her customs receipts at the treaty ports. In a declaration of March 12, 1913, Wilson proposed that the United States, with regard to the Chinese republic, should "assert and apply the old democratic and moral principles" of friendly co-operation and mutual respect, rather than open or veiled coercion.[1]

Thus Wilson, in his first application of the New Freedom to our foreign affairs, proceeded as if the world were made up of peaceful democracies that observed constitutional law, acted by popular consent, and respected human and property rights. The American bankers were going to retire from the China loan, on practical grounds, in any case. But it happened that Dr. Wilson used the occasion to repudiate "dollar diplomacy" in the noblest phrases. Meanwhile the large American navy still stood guard over the Pacific.

In Mexico confused civil strife persisted for years after the overthrow of the iron-handed Diaz in 1911. Here again, taking high, democratic ground, Wilson refused recognition to the government formed by General Huerta, who was said to have ordered the assassination of his predecessor, Madero. The real problem was whether "order" was to be imposed through the agency of a military gang backed by a great British oil baron, Lord Cowdray, or other opposing Mexican groups. Here Wilson's attitude clashed with the practical purposes of the British Foreign Office. However, in spite of Wilson's high moral position, our troops since 1912 had stood threateningly at the Mexican border; unpleasant incidents succeeded each other rapidly, until they culminated in the "insult to the American flag" and the forcible occupation of Vera Cruz by American naval parties on April 21, 1914, at the order of the President.

[1] Griswold, *op. cit.*, pp. 171-172.

Four American sailors were killed and twenty wounded in the operation. Wilson, hearing the news, "looked preternaturally pale, almost parchmenty. . . ." The death of American sailors and marines seemed to leave him "positively shaken." Something strange happened inside the great liberal when he perceived, for the first time, that commands given in pursuance of high, democratic principles might lead to the death of human beings.[2] He shut his mind; he refused to alter his position. Wilson, Bryan, and House had hoped to strengthen friendly relations with Latin America. But democratic diplomacy was evidently not to be all clean fun. The Mexicans, who had suffered far heavier losses at Vera Cruz, were inflamed with hate and suspicion of the "Colossus of the North," and swung to the support of the bloody Huerta, who may well have provoked the whole episode. Nor did the later expedition of General Pershing in pursuit of Villa improve things. When Wilson, in view of infinitely greater problems raised by the European war, at length turned his face away from unhappy Mexico, good intentions, edged with rigid tactics, had made a fiasco of his efforts to spread democracy and peace to our southern neighbor.

Toward 1912 various plans for promoting world peace and creating a World Court, advanced by philanthropists such as Andrew Carnegie and warmly supported by President Taft, became highly fashionable. William J. Bryan was a sincere pacifist, and from his post of Secretary of State endeavored in 1913 to place our government at the service of humanity and promote a new world order through the exchange of a series of mutual peace and disarmament pacts between the great powers. Colonel House, who was really the *de facto* Secretary of State, and who had similar visions (already outlined in his utopian romance), held many conferences with President Wilson on this subject. With the President's blessing he set forth for Europe to make preliminary inquiries regarding the possibility of effecting "an understanding between France, Germany, England and the United States re-

[2] H. J. Forman memorandum; Baker, *op. cit.*, Vol. IV, p. 330.

garding a reduction of armaments." Before leaving, House on December 2, 1913, had had a talk with Sir William Tyrrell, Grey's secretary, who was then visiting Washington, regarding his plans, and with the English diplomat's approval, he decided to make his trip a succession of secret visits to the rulers of Europe. Most important on his list was the Emperor William II of Germany, to whom he meant to present himself as "the power behind the throne" in America while proposing terms of general disarmament. Even as early as 1913, the honorary Colonel from Texas, by virtue of several vacations abroad, had reckoned himself deeply informed upon European politics. It was in the balmy month of May that Wilson's secret ambassador-at-large arrived in Berlin, saw the Kaiser, then proceeded to London, where he held talk with Foreign Minister Grey.

The first impressions are sometimes the best. From Berlin, House sent confidential word to President Wilson that each of the great groups of military allies lived in terror of the other, that there was little to choose between their motives or modes of justification.

The situation is extraordinary. It is militarism run stark mad. . . . There is some day to be an awful cataclysm. No one in Europe can bring about an understanding. There is too much hatred, too many jealousies. Whenever England consents, France and Russia will close in on Germany and Austria.[3]

It was the last time that the hopeful amateur diplomat looked at both sides in the great conflict, then impending, as equally to blame. He dared to think that by his talks he had made progress in moving the world a little on the path to disarmament. No one had given him the slightest ground for such optimism. He had made "contacts," at any rate, he claimed upon his return. But the most important of these was with Grey, the British Foreign Minister, who evidently fascinated the Texan. Grey had promised to "co-operate."

[3] House, *op. cit.*, May 29, 1914, Vol. I, pp. 242, 249.

It was in the midst of this amateur peace-making (with Secretary of State Bryan fairly ignorant of House's activities) that the earthquake of general European war arrived. The first timid offers of mediation by Washington, on the eve of the war, were quickly thrust aside by both the Entente and the Central Powers.

Wilson in August, 1914, saddened by the death of his first wife, at first looked with only a sick heart and lack-luster eye at the European tragedy. House had found Wilson "almost" enthusiastic upon giving report of his May, 1914, mission. Now the President, though he expressed himself as "unsympathetic with the German attitude" (like so many other Americans high in public life who had inherited British blood and British traditions), said that he "did not wish either side to win"; that the causes of the war were historic and economic; that he did not believe there was the slightest danger to this country from foreign invasion, even if the Germans were successful.[4]

But soon the persistent House, virtually the only adviser whom the inaccessible Wilson permitted to approach him closely, returned to press the attack. In his curiously effeminate manner he had a way of speaking both with a flattery and candor that none other used; he allowed himself to voice the President's most intimate hopes and fears, or his most vertiginous aspirations. The European crisis, as his thought ran now, formed the One Big Question before them. The President still seemed "more interested in domestic affairs" in the early months of the war, and House vowed to himself, as he notes in his diary, September 28, 1914, that he would try to "get him absorbed in the greatest problem of world-wide interest that has ever come, or may ever come, before a President of the United States."[5]

House, by virtue of the *Intimate Papers* he has left us, becomes the Boswell of a powerful American President in a time of world tragedy. We may read thus his own innermost motives and those he described in his chosen master. We perceive how he begins to

---

[4] *Ibid.*, Vol. I, p. 300.
[5] *Ibid.*, Vol. I, p. 296.

enjoy more and more zestfully his strange role as secret emissary or "personal Secretary of State"; how, feeling himself "a power behind the throne," he saw in the international upheavals of 1914 opportunities to extend his own role until, with the President's compliance, he himself might yet play a mighty part upon the world stage. So eager is he to keep this business in his very own hands that he shows himself intensely jealous and suspicious of Bryan, and hostile to the latter's desire to mediate at every possible moment of the conflict. Moreover Bryan would have exerted *equal* pressure upon both groups of combatants, a policy soon abandoned by House, Ambassador Page, and Robert Lansing, counselor to the State Department, who were all ready to correct the "Boy Orator's" presumed ignorance of foreign affairs. Even in August, 1914, House had warned the President to hold back Bryan's first moves toward mediation.[6]

Then, as we have seen, on days when he found the President gloomy concerning the prospects for continuance of the domestic reform movement, House assured him that this was now an indifferent matter. As if uttering his own heart's yearnings he would speak in the early weeks of the war of those "other things" Wilson might do henceforth, those immense opportunities in foreign policy "which if properly followed would bring him world-wide recognition," to cap his glory at home.[7]

Besides, from London, the same glittering opportunities were held before Wilson steadily, with some evident authority.

When the first timid offer of mediation was made on August 4, 1914, Walter Page reported to Wilson from London on August 9, 1914, that at the right moment "you will be called on to compose this huge quarrel." Lord Bryce also wrote to "My dear President" that "a time may come when an offer of mediation from you as the greatest and most respected neutral may be helpful."[8] Wilson undoubtedly recalled how much world glory T. R. had won by his effective mediation in the Russo-Japanese war.

[6] Tansill, *America Goes to War*, p. 433.   [8] Millis, *The Road to War*, p. 79.

[7] House, *op. cit.*, Vol. I, p. 296.

It is difficult to judge at what precise moment in the early stages of the war the chance for the President to play a deciding part in establishing, as House phrased it, "the greatest peace the world has ever seen," began to absorb him fully. But soon a whole complex of pressures thrust him toward this enterprise, which he was then led to believe possible only with the success of the Allies. All the more reason for proceeding slowly and keeping the inept Bryan from "upsetting the apple-cart."

One of the most decisive factors that swayed the judgment of the President (as of his chief adviser), one that has been much overlooked in studies of the "causes" of the war with Germany, was the growing conviction that the program of domestic reform and renovation encountered ever-narrowing limits. The liberals and progressives of 1912, as one keen commentator, Professor Frank Tracy Carlton, wrote at approximately this period, had rallied the farmers, the middle class, and most of the skilled wage-earners to their banner; but they had no "definite plan," their strength was "negative" rather than positive. The growth of monopoly was not actually arrested for long, despite the zeal of Wilson's first Federal Trade Commission—which in any case could give only "cease and desist" orders, subject to court interference. The deep trend toward mechanization of all industry, toward larger units, and toward the destruction of competition by secret agreements, was not checked. In agriculture, the increase in the number of tenant farmers, a very marked tendency of the first decade of the new century, continued strongly until farm prices rose during the war, and was resumed in the 1920's. But to contend with these deep social forces was far from the thought of the Wilsonian liberals.

Their work was already done, so far as the big business group, that had introduced itself into both the Roosevelt and Wilson movements, were concerned. Men like George W. Perkins or Cleveland Dodge, whose interests lay chiefly in having an efficient and contented labor force, had shrewdly joined the movement that promised "social justice." These "far-seeing big business leaders" may even be said to have helped direct the movement. No doubt, as Professor Carlton observes, ". . . they wished to dilute radicalism and to soothe the restless insurgents. . . ." [9] They thoroughly approved of the plan for instituting a certain "benevolent feudalism" through government commissions, much as Prince von Bismarck had backed a similar social policy in Germany about a generation earlier.

But by the end of 1913 these interests had had enough reform, and their friends or spokesmen, such as Walter Page, within the councils of the government, were crying for a "breathing spell." House himself, who had outlined such ambitious reforms in his anonymous novel, by the summer of 1914 told Wilson that the country neither expected nor wanted any more of them.

Compared to the effects of his own limited measures of "social justice," those of the war crisis were volcanic. At first the disastrous down-swing of depression; then, after six months, early in 1915, a strong upswing in trade, a boom in farm produce and war munitions, and expansion of approximately 100 per cent in the "favorable balance" of our export trade. Soon the Allies, while blockading Germany, depended on us as their supply base for munitions, food, cotton, copper, and raw materials of all kinds. Thus, as Lord Grey has said, any political decision of the American government or its President "which in any wise affected the shipment or supply of these commodities was of fateful importance." [10] It was of fateful importance also to President Wilson's ideas that he was now directing a nation fully engaged in war industries, whose gains affected the economic life of millions of American farmers and factory workers as well as capitalists.

In the mirror of his own mind Wilson often likened himself to Mr. Gladstone, who had swung from the Conservative to the Liberal party, in obedience to his own conscience, and helped carry through historic reforms. But as 1915 opens, and especially after

[9] Carlton, *Organized Labor*, pp. 193-196.
[10] Grey, *Twenty-five Years*, Vol. II, p. 107.

1916, it becomes increasingly difficult to recognize the liberal par excellence in Wilson. Ray Stannard Baker, the admiring apologist and official biographer, notes a "swing to the right" from 1915 on. Because of the exigencies and dangers suggested by the war, his former opponents are seen hastening to make peace with him. George Harvey, from whom he had been divorced since 1911, called at the White House for the first time in October, 1915; Henry Watterson also sued for peace and was welcomed, Baker relates.

As a politician Wilson had travelled far in two years. It was now no longer "only progressives on guard," nor yet the sovereign "appeal to the people." . . . He no longer exhibited contempt for the devices of political mechanism. . . . We have seen him smoothing the ruffled plumage of the millionaires and meeting George Harvey with a wry smile. He was to go a long step further—to win the support of the old "bosses" of the Democratic party.[11]

It was in these days that he told Postmaster General Burleson that he felt he could depend more on the old Standpatters of his party than on "some of his own crowd," that is, the progressives. To his private secretary, Tumulty, he avowed: *"My head is with the progressives in the Democratic Party, but my heart, because of the way they stood by me, is with the so-called Old Guard in the Senate.* They stand without hitching."[12]

How explain these shifts? Like Theodore Roosevelt before him he found it convenient to administer the affairs of the government "through his party," and by full use of its practical mechanism. The unquestioning discipline of the professional politicians was now valued more than the often critical attitude of a Claude Kitchin, liberal Representative for North Carolina and floor leader in Congress, or of a Bryan, who raised difficult questions within his own official family. For Wilson, more heavily burdened, had dropped the open democratic manners he used at

[11] Baker, *op. cit.*, Vol. V, pp. 88-89.
[12] Tumulty, *op. cit.*, p. 101; italics mine.

Trenton, and become more aloof, remote, inaccessible than ever before. His coldly impassive expression became even more marked at those conferences with politicians, government officials, or influential citizens for which he had so little liking.

He was infinitely lonely after the death of his first wife, knew little relief from the responsibilities that preyed heavily upon him, and his hair turned wholly white. The gracious and intelligent Ellen Axson Wilson had had a decided vein of idealism and generosity. But Edith Bolling Galt, the handsome, wealthy young widow who took her place late in 1915, stemmed from a wholly different background and scarcely represented a liberal influence in the President's private life. The first Mrs. Wilson, with fine political instincts and great good will, had helped to cement the alliance with Mr. Bryan. But Edith Galt Wilson, when the President confided to her that Bryan threatened to resign his post of Secretary of State owing to differences over policy, urged Wilson to "give Mr. Bryan what he wants"—that is, let him go.[13]

In short, Wilson had come to the end of a certain road. The orator and ideologue in him was now overshadowed by the powerful party leader, who used the conveniences of partisan politics. He had won political fortune by deflecting the wrath of the people by tariff reform, and by laws that promised to benefit farmers and workers. He had brought into existence a long-needed central banking system which, even conservative finance soon admitted, served its purpose exceedingly well in a time of financial stress at the opening of the war. He was then in the position of a man who wields great power, yet feels convinced that his mission has nearly been completed, or has reached its natural limits. For beyond the limits set by the statesmanship of equilibrium, of balanced reforms, and concessions, if one dared to contemplate them, there remained all the work of revolution, the overturning of all property and social relations. At this point the middle-class statesman invariably halts. He had halted there in western Europe, before 1914.

[13] E. Wilson, *My Memoir*, p. 63.

Such a moment is dangerous. A great part of the work appears to be done, yet the leader is convinced that he must continue to lead—to furnish "positive leadership" as Wilson phrased it—if only because he thinks now of his place in history. And for Woodrow Wilson a future of dazzling, historic opportunities, worthy of his large talents, with immense possibilities for "positive leadership," perhaps even, as House whispered to him, for being arbiter of the world's destiny, was opened by the general war.

2

In the press of America controversy over the merits of the warring nations raged higher and higher. The redoubtable Colonel Roosevelt had said in his first public utterances on the war, in August, 1914, that there was little to choose between the two groups of adversaries. (Four years earlier, after his European tour of 1910, he had given a confidential report to President Taft, forecasting the near approach of general war and accurately predicting the German flanking invasion of Belgium as an "inevitable" move.) By October, 1914, writing in *The Outlook*, he veered to strong partisanship for the Allied cause and passionate condemnation of Prussian militarism.

While war news, war propaganda, tales of German "atrocities" in Belgium, and the accelerated industrial boom occupied the public, there smoldered in the President's Cabinet the same divisions, partisanships, fears and hopes.

From London Wilson's ambassador, Walter Page, the old colleague of Johns Hopkins days, began now his long, earnest campaign to win the President to the English and Allied view of the war and of German guilt in precipitating it. Page interlarded his diplomatic correspondence with ecstatic passages, veritable purple patches, upon the beauties of the English countryside, English conversation, and garden parties in the spring when the rhododendrons are in flower. Becoming deliberately "more English than the English," he chose to serve chiefly as the spokesman of British interests before the head of his own government—an extraordinary lapse from his official duty. There were times in the first years of the war when Woodrow Wilson feared to read Walter Page's letters.

Within the Cabinet, Secretary of the Interior Lane, who had relatives fighting in the British army; Secretary of Commerce Houston; and Secretary of War Garrison were staunch partisans of England, the green England to which Wilson himself was bound by blood of kin, and which in imagination he had loved, which he had often toured with delight on vacations from Princeton, and whose poets and orators he knew by heart. The day came —at the time of the *Lusitania* affair—when Bryan, who embodied the sentiments of the West, during a Cabinet conference burst out in indignation at Lane and Houston as "pro-Ally" spokesmen within our government; and Wilson rebuked Mr. Bryan for his outspoken charges.[14]

Essentially, there were three possible lines of action with regard to the European crisis. First, there was General Washington's now historic policy of American isolation, of "no entanglements" with Europe; and Wilson, in his first famous proclamation, two weeks after the opening of the war, took this ground as his point of departure, when he urged that Americans be "impartial in thought as well as in action. . . ." Second, there was the possibility of attempting a more or less even-handed mediation between the combatant powers. This role also Wilson attempted, although, as we shall see, without real vigor and with discouraging results. Third, there was the possibility of ultimately taking a positive part, of intervening on the side of one or the other of the adversaries; and by the orientation of American policy away from isolation, since 1898, such intervention could only tend to favor the Anglo-French group, under the concept of the "Atlantic System."

Consistently John Hay, the champion of "McKinleyism" abroad; Theodore Roosevelt, wielder of the Big Stick; and Elihu Root, the friend of "dollar diplomacy" in successive episodes,

[14] D. F. Houston, *Eight Years*, Vol. I, p. 137.

had shown that they favored a world balance of power dominated by Britain and France, our Atlantic neighbors. Under this arrangement, the United States diplomats felt that we would be safer and would run into no serious points of friction. An unfortified Canada was a "pawn" for British good behavior. But the intrusion of a fourth great power upon this harmonious scene, such as Germany, was thought to offer all sorts of unknown menaces. The United States would have to arm to the teeth to defend her "sphere of influence" in the Americas; the Monroe Doctrine would be challenged sooner or later and would have to be defended with arms. In the decade preceding the World War, Germany's trade penetration of the Pacific, or her activities in South America, always aroused much sharper, bitterer emotions in political-minded Americans—sometimes even a wave of anti-German feeling, as in the Venezuela incident of 1903—than did similar movements by the British. Men as different as Henry Adams, Colonel House, and Charles W. Eliot all were agreed in voicing their fear of aggressive German designs. If the present war were won by Germany it would mean "the unspeakable tyranny of militarism for generations to come," wrote House on August 22, 1914. He told Wilson: "Germany's success will ultimately mean trouble for us. We will have to abandon the path which you are blazing as a standard for future generations, with permanent peace as its goal and a new international ethical code as its guiding star, and build up a military machine of vast proportions." Dr. Eliot went even further in writing Wilson, as the war opened, that the prospect of German success, and the burdens it would bring to us, justified "the abandonment of Washington's advice that this country keep out of European complications." [15]

These sentiments of the foremost American educator Wilson fully shared. Sir Cecil Spring Rice, now the British Ambassador at Washington, felt that Wilson had had, at any rate, an "English education"; he loved English literature. Did not the Lake Poets, especially Wordsworth, bring tears to his eyes? But for all his

---

[15] House, *op. cit.*, Vol. I, pp. 285, 288.

sympathies, did he not owe it to the world, also, to prevent the spread of the conflagration? Did he not owe it to his country to save it from a war in which the million-masses submitted themselves to a kind of mystic blood sacrifice? Wilson's first impulse disposed him to a rigorous neutrality.

The humane desire to preserve our civilization and our peace were, however, very quickly modified under the impact of current realities. The panic of August, 1914, the closing of our chief stock exchange, the withdrawal of European funds here, the initial fall of the dollar followed by its recovery in 1915, and the no less alarming decline of sterling as the balance of money exchanges now swung heavily in favor of America—all these were powerful facts. They spoke of the immense manufacture and shipment of war supplies, which under the circumstances of the rigid British blockade made us, as Lord Grey said, "the main reserve arsenal of the Allies." The British blockade, against which many official protests were to be made in the name of American rights upon the sea, and the counter-blockade of German submarines, brought to the head of the greatest neutral power further harassing problems, reminiscent of the tensions of 1809-1812. Early in 1915 the problem of credits or loans to the belligerents made the course of neutrality uneasier still. Moreover, neither the press nor our leading public figures retained their calm impartiality long. The tireless Roosevelt, aided by General Leonard Wood, seized upon the issue of Preparedness as the political *pièce de résistance* for a Presidential race looming beyond 1915. Soon President Wilson himself, urged by his advisers, must needs take up a little American flag in his hand and by a double step or two place himself at the head of the Preparedness parades being held in our principal cities. Such is the atmosphere in which the political leader lives and makes decisions.

In December, 1914, Wilson and House decided upon their first effort at direct but "unofficial" mediation. House was to proceed to London, Paris, and Berlin as the President's unofficial or "personal" Secretary of State—Mr. Bryan being largely ignored—and attempt to obtain peace offers from both sides. He was actually to explore the possibilities of "a plan for a general convention of all neutral and belligerent nations at which [Wilson] will be called upon to preside and which should be called upon your invitation." [16]

Arriving in London by the *Lusitania* early in February, 1915, House held conferences with Grey and other members of the British war cabinet. In March he was in Berlin, to hear the proposals of the German government. No tangible results of any kind came from this first peace mission. The British would not move, when the tide of battle ran against them, and House indulgently complied with their wishes by not insisting. The German government, on the other hand, would offer no terms save such as recognized their military victories. Moreover, the Germans now perceived that the main supply lines for the Western Front extended across the Atlantic to the United States. To them the American suppliers of shells and bullets that fell upon their soldiers were *no neutrals*. Despite existing conventions concerning neutral rights of trade (clearly favoring the English rulers of the sea), it became their overwhelming preoccupation henceforth to cut the supply lines from America by using for counter-blockade, the destructive submarine weapon.

Analysis of the events of 1915, in the perspective of a quarter of a century, shows how, step by step, the United States in the World War crisis was eliminated as a "neutral power," as one fitted for impartial mediation. The deciding moves took place alternately at the economic level and at the political level.

An economic decision of highest importance was made as early as August, 1914, when the State Department, with the approval of Bryan and Wilson, in response to inquiries declared that Americans had the right to sell and ship materials of war, even though they were declared "contraband" by one or the other of

[16] House, *op. cit.*, Vol. I, p. 375.

the belligerents. The proposal of Senator La Follette that America should impose an embargo upon the export of munitions of war was resisted as a denial of our rights of neutral trade. Coming in wartime, even the pacific Bryan held, such a measure would in itself represent an "unneutral act" and would be an "unjustifiable departure from the principle of strict neutrality. . . ."[17]

Thus the way was open for the rapid development of a huge munitions trade in the United States. It supplied the alarming deficiencies of Britain and France, a large part of whose steel industry was in German hands. By January, 1916, the United States constituted for the enemies of Germany "a base of supplies of such magnitude," as one authority warned our State Department, that the fate of empires literally depended upon control of the output of American factories.[18]

Soon a financial decision of even graver importance faced the government. In the second week of the war, on August 15, 1914, Secretary Bryan, in whom later historians have found the character and common sense of a true statesman, had issued by telegram to J. P. Morgan and Company the opinion that "loans by American bankers to any foreign nation which is at war are inconsistent with the true spirit of neutrality." In Cabinet conferences and elsewhere, Mr. Bryan repeatedly thereafter expressed the view that money and credit formed "the greatest of all contraband of war."[19]

But the two great banking groups of Morgan and Company and the National City Bank were being besieged from abroad with demands for loans to finance the Allied purchases here. Messrs. Vanderlip of the National City Bank and Lamont and Davison of Morgan's cautiously pressed the Wilson administration for further "clarification." Mr. Bryan's statement was, after all, but an

---

[17] Bryan to Bernstorff, Apr. 21, 1915, Tansill, *op. cit.*, p. 56.

Professor Tansill notes that Holland and the Scandinavian countries embargoed materials of war; that Wilson in the Mexican crisis, May 14, 1912, had forbidden the shipment of munitions of war from the United States to either side in the Mexican civil struggle as the "best practice of nations." (*Ibid.*, p. 64.)

[18] C. C. Hyde to Lansing, Jan. 11, 1916; *Senate Reports on the Munitions Industry*, 74th Congress, 2nd Session, 1936, No. 944, Part 5, pp. 115-119.

[19] The New York *Times*, Aug. 16, 1914; Tansill, *op. cit.*, p. 73.

"opinion," not a *legal* ruling; yet if implemented it would bring prostration to the industrial and banking world. By mid-October, 1914, Secretary Bryan, confused by the opposition he met, retreated from the firm position on foreign loans that he had taken in August. It was admitted that the government had no legal right to prohibit trade relations between our citizens and belligerents. Then with the help of Mr. Lansing, assistant to Mr. Bryan, but considered afterward the "mouthpiece" of Big Business, further important and definite modifications were gained in the State Department's ruling on loans to belligerents.

An officer of the National City Bank, in a conference with Mr. Lansing, had discussed the bankers' need for granting short-time credits to the European governments engaged in purchasing supplies here, credits that would not become public issues but that were supposedly necessary in the normal course of trade. The gist of this conference was then also summarized in a letter which was given to Lansing, and which he merely copied and showed to President Wilson that same night, October 23, 1914, as representing his own view of the proper policy regarding the temporary banking credits.

That night Lansing, who occasionally exercised a strong influence over the President, won Wilson's agreement to "look the other way" at the temporary credit accommodations that were being supplied the French and British treasuries. Wilson, who had earlier supported Bryan's position, now executed a strategic retreat from a position based upon "the true spirit of neutrality" to one based upon "strict legality." [20]

Thus, no firm or definite policy of neutrality was formulated at the beginning of the European war by the Wilson administration, nor even by Mr. Bryan, such as the Senate attempted, at least, to formulate in 1936, after the Nye Committee hearings. Two months after hostilities began, Ambassador Jusserand was able to inform officers of the National City Bank that while our

[20] *Hearings, Senate Committee on the Munitions Industry*, Exhibit No. 2047; Beard, C. A., *The Devil Theory of War*, pp. 30 ff.

government authorities were not granting "permissions" for credits to foreign belligerents—permissions "neither asked for, nor wanted" —they were ready to "abstain from objections." [21] The Wilson government, then, made no real quest of neutrality. Here, as Charles A. Beard has pointed out, while false, hair-splitting distinctions between "credits" and "loans" were being established, the cornerstone was laid for the vast structure of American financial aid to the Allies.

Soon the remarkable arrangement was perfected by which J. P. Morgan and Company, our leading private bankers, became the general purchasing agents for the Allied governments, and the machinery of credit now speeded up the war trade. Soon the Federal Reserve Bank itself was being used to bolster the pound sterling, by discounting American guaranteed acceptances of bills on London. Not long after, in the spring of 1915, the great New York banks were lending indirectly huge sums of thirty to forty-five millions upon collateral to the French government, by the medium of French bankers' paper.[22]

In the political and diplomatic as well as the financial field the ground of American neutrality shrank month by month. On February 10, 1915, after warnings by Germany were received in Washington that a war zone subject to submarine blockade was to be established, the first stern note was dispatched to Berlin condemning attacks without warning on unarmed merchant vessels, declaring that damage to American vessels or property would be regarded as "an indefensible violation of neutral rights," and warning Germany that she would be held to "strict accountability" for such damage. The Germans in their dilemma were forced to balance the evil of American displeasure against the danger of slow starvation under naval blockade. Their attitude wavered in accordance with the tide of the war, which now placed more cautious civilian politicians in the saddle, or now military or naval

---

[21] *Hearings, Senate Committee on the Munitions Industry,* Exhibit No. 2048.
[22] Tansill, *op. cit.,* pp. 86-89.

leaders who promised quick subjugation of England by undersea ruthlessness. With a certain show of logic, the German government asked Washington to persuade England to relax her blockade, especially for foodstuffs, which struck at German women and children, as a condition for restrictions upon the submarines. Yet no serious American diplomatic efforts were made in this direction.

Meanwhile, English interference with our shipping, their navy's hateful orders in council, also brought diplomatic protests from Washington, although in a wholly different spirit from those directed to Berlin. The notes, usually written by Lansing, were comprehensive in argument, but as Professor Tansill has remarked, were intended primarily as "noisy" demonstrations. Rarely did the notes to London convey a serious threat of rupture of relations that would permit no peaceful issue. Whenever they did approach this limit, the American ambassador, Page, or the oft-traveling House, was there to advise Sir Edward Grey that only an effect upon the home public had been intended.

In the midst of these wavering negotiations came, on May 7, 1915, with the force of a great bomb explosion, news of the torpedoing of the *Lusitania*, giant British passenger liner, and the loss of 1,100 lives, including 124 Americans. Woodrow Wilson, reading the tragic reports of the affair, strove for the moment to resist the mood of hysteria that was reflected in the American press. He spent, as he told Tumulty, "many sleepless hours thinking about this tragedy." He estimated that the bulk of our citizens, perhaps 80 per cent, were for keeping their heads and preserving peace. In California, for example, it was reported that the *Lusitania* disaster aroused only mild excitement.[23]

That very week Wilson had prepared a speech, to be given in Philadelphia on May 10, 1915, in which he voiced those ideals of peace and humanity that he had always formerly cherished. He spoke these words—and who could truly hold them "cowardly" or "craven," rather than noble?

[23] Tumulty, *op. cit.*, p. 232.

The example of America must be the example not merely of peace because it will not fight, but of peace because peace is the healing and elevating influence of the world and strife is not. There is such a thing as a man being too proud to fight. There is such a thing as a nation being so right that it does not need to convince others by force that it is right.

Removed from its context, the phrase "too proud to fight," so bitterly ridiculed by the bellicose Colonel Roosevelt, served to mitigate the harshness of the note of May 13, 1915, sent at the same time to Berlin, which had the character of an ultimatum. House, then in London, had the impression that a final step toward war was being taken, that the parting of ways had actually come already—despite Wilson's calming utterances at home.

Once more our State Department wrote that we would "hold the Imperial German Government to strict accountability" for losses of life and property suffered by American citizens exercising their right to travel on belligerent merchant vessels. Unrestricted submarine warfare was condemned in the name of reason, justice, and humanity.

At Cabinet meetings, Secretary Bryan argued that the *Lusitania* had carried a large store of munitions; the German embassy had advertised that this ship was subject to torpedoing. Bryan had urged that an official restraint be placed upon the presumed right of Americans to sail on belligerent ships through the war zone. He wrote letters to the President; he showed extreme agitation at Cabinet meetings. But Wilson now followed the counsel of Lansing (who confided to his diary that he could no longer maintain an impartial attitude) and of House for a firm stand.[24] The second *Lusitania* note, of May 31, following a German attempt at "explanation" and complaints of the "hunger blockade," brought to a head the impending resignation of the "Great Commoner," who had enjoyed so little control over his State Department these two years. His chief objections were that our government no longer showed an equal firmness or equally peaceful attitude toward both

[24] Tansill, *op. cit.*, p. 325.

sides in the conflict. The President, he felt, had already chosen sides and drifted toward war. To his lasting glory, racked by deep emotion, Bryan resigned from his office on June 7, 1915—an action that was neither clearly understood nor given its due credit at the time, least of all in Germany.

3

Mr. Bryan had groped toward neutrality, and failed. Dr. Wilson, despite his resolute manner, drifted uncertainly, hoping to be neutral, and yet hoping also to determine the outcome of the war; hoping to "save" civilization, and at the same time desiring "subconsciously" to retain the booming munitions trade and the mounting export trade with neutral nations that were bringing wealth untold to our people.

The remarkable report of the Senate Committee on the Investigation of the Munitions Trade, in 1936, has laid bare virtually all the pertinent evidence and documents touching the steps on the road to our war with Germany in 1917. Various able scholars such as Millis, Grattan, Beard, and lately Tansill have sifted this and other evidence. Senator Gerald K. Nye, chairman of the Senate committee that inquired into the munitions traffic, has pointed the finger of accusation at the arms manufacturers, the "Merchants of Death," and at the bankers who leaped at opportunities to finance the colossal war traffic and a world-wide neutral foreign trade opened to us by the absorption of Britain and Germany in war. Professor Tansill has borne hard upon Lansing, who succeeded Bryan as Secretary of State; others have reproached Edward House or Walter H. Page for their unquestionable partisanship, or Wilson himself. All this however has only a partial truth, so far as the origin of the war is concerned.

The heads of the Morgan and Rockefeller banks were not so much pro-English or pro-war as pro-profits; and in being so they were not remarkably different from the farmers who sold wheat at $2 to $2.50 a bushel. The real causes of the war, if we may speak of "causes," were as Woodrow Wilson himself said in his clairvoyant moments, "historic and economic." American interests were deeply, inextricably caught within the world-wide net of these historic-economic forces.

In the last third of the nineteenth century the great powers had entered the decisive "imperialist" phase of their economic growth. Thereafter, their ruling groups, instead of trying to use the knowledges and techniques gained through applied science to increase production of goods and services at home, raising wages, lowering prices, and elevating the standard of living and rate of consumption of their own people, turned away from problems of internal reform and applied their accumulated capital and savings to winning new foreign markets, to opening new sources of raw materials and channels for investment. Business was organized along nationalistic lines, and proceeded usually where the native flag was carried by the navies or armies; patriotism was linked with commercial or economic conquests and fed by it. Then, as John A. Hobson relates, "under the urge of nationalist sentiment, supported by appeals to self-sufficiency, for purposes of defence," each of the powers strove to conserve its markets for its own producers, jealously excluding rivals.[25] The armament race accompanied the last rush for undeveloped territories, and terminated in the long-foreseen general conflict of 1914 between the two groups of powers led by the British and the expanding, challenging German Empire.

The United States, as a belated or quasi-imperialist power since the late 1890's, was inextricably enmeshed in the world-wide imperialist competitions and struggles. It gravitated constantly toward one of the imperialist groups, and was hostile to the other. Even our military theorists such as Mahan favored the "Atlantic States" policy, holding that the British navy acted as a protective wall for our own dominance of the Western Hemisphere. Its economic and financial ties with the Anglo-French Entente were strongest, and by 1915 were almost exclusive.

The submarine weapon, then, threatened a very large part of

[25] Hobson, *Imperialism*, Introduction, p. xi.

our new-gotten trade and wealth as certainly as German military might threatened England's investments in India. This threat was a culminating, rather than an exclusive, factor in the complex of "causes." We were "neutral" but we were the chief suppliers of one of the parties to the conflict. Our munitions industry was believed to be working at capacity by 1917. The German general staff aimed its submarines precisely at the ships which carried the goods and munitions from whose sale our recent prosperity derived. The decision in 1916 to accelerate this traffic by financing exports upon a vast scale (our "secret war," the Germans called it) was soon followed by the German decision to renew "unrestricted" submarine warfare.[26]

Meanwhile the far-wandering diplomat, Colonel Edward House, stood in London looking at the dazzling mountains in the distance which Grey pointed out to him. It was a vision of a future day when wars were to be outlawed, and a great parliament of man, a "League of Nations," presided over by Colonel House's protégé, Wilson, would be convened to decree eternal peace. Previously Grey, in a letter of September 22, 1915, had asked House if the President would accept the idea of a League of Nations whose members would be bound to act against any aggressor or treaty-violating power. He discussed here also the probability of American involvement in the World War on the side of the Allies. House had implied earlier, as Grey reminded him, that the American people might soon be willing "to go to limits heretofore unthinkable to bring about a just solution," that is, to prevent the final disappearance of Britain and France as powers that counted in the world.[27]

On his previous visit, early in 1915, House had shown that American efforts at mediation would be managed in accordance with British wishes in the matter. Now, on his second visit to London since the war, in January, 1916, he discussed with Grey noth-

[26] Cf. Professor Paul Birdsall, in *Science and Society*, Vol. III, No. 2, pp. 224 ff.
[27] House, *op. cit.*, Vol. II, pp. 88-89.

ing less than the possibilities of an Anglo-American entente. A tremendous change in American foreign policy was planned—for without the knowledge of the American people or Congress, Wilson and House promised, first, to offer mediation only when the Entente desired it, and second, if this were refused, to enter the war on the side of the Allies.

At Paris, House saw the French government leaders, Briand and Jules Cambon, and told them that if France could not win unaided, the American government, at their signal, would intervene "to save them and guarantee a peace based on justice." This was also the substance of the House-Grey agreement, recorded by Sir Edward Grey in a written memorandum of February 22, 1916.

President Wilson, "on hearing from France and England that the moment was opportune," would "propose a conference to put an end to the war. Should the Allies accept this proposal and Germany refuse it, the United States would probably enter the war against Germany.

"Colonel House expressed the opinion that, if such a conference met, it would secure peace on terms not unfavourable to the Allies; and, if it failed to secure peace, the United States would (probably) leave the conference as a belligerent on the side of the Allies, if Germany was unreasonable." [28]

The word "probably" in parentheses was inserted by Wilson when he approved the memorandum on March 8, 1916.

In sharp contrast with these important exchanges at London and Paris, House's second wartime visit to Berlin, after he passed through Paris, brought not even perfunctory results. The Germans, though they had lately shown a more yielding attitude in the *Lusitania* affair, deeply mistrusted both the American government and its secret spokesman.

Wilson perceived now that the Allies might be ready to call him to his role upon the world stage of mediation—with armed intervention as a threat. Recent plans to preserve a stricter neutrality, yielding on certain points to Germany and calling Britain to account more vigorously, were hastily reversed at the telegraphic

---

[28] House, *op. cit.*, Vol. II, pp. 163, 201-202.

advice of House from London. It was at the time of these high-handed and secret covenants in February, 1916, that certain progressive Democrats in Congress, such as Kitchin of North Carolina and Senator Stone of Missouri, heard rumors that the President was hurrying us into war. At several conferences in the White House, especially the "sunrise conference" of the early morning of February 22, 1916, the President by his "strong words" gave the impression that he meant to force Germany to declare war upon us.[29]

Greatly alarmed by the President's belligerent mood, which all Congress heard of, the progressive Democrats led a muffled revolt, introducing on that same day the McLemore Resolution (espoused by floor leader Kitchin) requiring that official warnings be issued to American citizens not to take passage on belligerent vessels and thus threaten the safety of their whole country. This was with difficulty circumvented by Wilson's exertion of the fullest party discipline.

Yet Wilson's haste was needless, because the Allies themselves were not ready to call upon the secret partners in America. Their own Secret Treaties, soon to be exposed to the world by the Bolsheviki one day in 1918, embarrassed them in dealing with such a "political idealist" as Wilson, who spoke of his conception of the future peace as embracing freedom of the seas, no dismemberment of Germany, no war indemnities. It was desired to use the American intervention only in the last resort; but to call in Wilson now would have implied coming to some agreement with him upon the future peace terms. Perhaps the drift of things, economic forces at work, even German stupidity, might bring America into the war—utterly without strings!

If the situation continues as now, and if Congress does not restrict him [Wilson], *everything will go through as planned.* His recent victory in Congress was complete. . . . *It is now squarely up to you to make the next move, and a cable from you at any time will be sufficient.*

[29] David Lawrence in New York *Evening Post,* Feb. 23, 1916, and Mar. 2, 1916; Gilson Gardner in *McNaught's Monthly,* Jun., 1925.

Thus wrote Colonel House to Lord Grey, March 10, 1916, in a dispatch recording the President's "complete approval" of the House-Grey memorandum of February 22, 1916.[30]

"If you think best, I will send a cable every fortnight repeating the offer, so it may be used in the way planned," he added.

House, with Wilson at his elbow, was ready and eager to "mediate" now. All that was needed was a signal from the British Foreign Office. Also, some friendly yielding by the British in the matter of infringement of our rights by her own blockade methods. At this moment, because of renewed submarine ruthlessness, it was thought that a final break with Germany would come any day. House early in April, 1916, dropped in to see Secretary of War Newton Baker, spoke of the imminence of war, and inquired after the disposition of troops which, in case of trouble with the masses of people, "would be available for the protection of New York, Chicago and larger centres. . . ." In case the city proletariat should rise against the foreign war, our humanitarian House advised Secretary Baker "to use a firm hand." It would be "mistaken mercy to temporize with troubles of this sort. . . ."[31]

Following Wilson's stern notes in April, the Germans now seemed to be swinging for the moment toward a relaxation of the submarine attacks. Thus the chance for American intervention on the Allied side might be lost.

But sinister motives stayed the Allies' moves in the game with Washington, and perhaps delayed our entrance into war for a year. Doubtless they feared the President's meddling with the rich stakes they had carved out for themselves and their friends in the Secret Treaties with Russia and Italy. They pressed on at Verdun, and prepared hopefully for the tremendous offensive of the Somme. Sir Edward Grey simply sent his regrets to Colonel House that the British Government could not press their French and Russian allies to such a "peace conference" as had been planned between them.

Wilson and House were definitely snubbed by the Allies in

[30] House, *op. cit.*, Vol. II, p. 220; italics mine.
[31] *Ibid.*, Vol. II, p. 232.

Grey's note of May 12, 1916. There were moments when House saw a little light. In his diary on April 30, 1916, he noted how nauseatingly the French and British spoke of America's lack of "high ideals" in the war crisis, and observed bitterly: "It is the old story. . . . What the Allies want is to dip their hands into our treasure chest." To Wilson, who now showed a high degree of irritation, House spoke sadly of the "utter selfishness" of governments in their dealings. While in Paris and London earlier, he had heard whisperings of secret treaties, of harsh terms and great loot counted upon in the day of victory—but he had delicately turned his ears away from such scandal. He sometimes wondered if the English and British democracies were truly fighting for democracy at all.

A somewhat sharper message, of May 19, 1916, which House wrote and Wilson wholly approved, was designed to push the British government a little. "America has reached the crossroads. . . ." Soon her people would be demanding that "We assert our undeniable rights against the Allies with the same insistence we have used towards the Central Powers. . . ." [32]

At this very moment, on the home front, House and Wilson were planning to conduct the 1916 campaign for re-election under the slogan "He Kept Us Out of War." That summer and autumn the nation rang with the praises of the peace-loving President who spared his people the sufferings of war. Yet the narrow self-interest of British and Allied policy, reflected by Grey and Balfour, and the incredible optimism of the Allied military leaders—who hoped always that Germany would "collapse" under a few more mass assaults—should equally have won credit for the non-belligerent position of America thus far.

4

The strategy of the 1916 campaign for re-election was based by the Democrats upon two points: first, the "successful" neutrality

[32] *Ibid.*, Vol. II, pp. 264, 286.

policy of Wilson; second, the great reform measures (crowned by the Adamson Eight-Hour Act, in August, 1916) inaugurated under Democratic leadership and appealing to liberal and progressive elements. The Republicans, who selected the able Justice Charles E. Hughes as their candidate, suffered from both divided and timid counsels; Roosevelt the firebrand was with difficulty muzzled; the Progressive schism was only partly bridged; and the Republican party was forced willy-nilly to stand upon wholly conservative ground in opposition to the Democrats.

In an election campaign Colonel House, the *de facto* chairman of his party, was in his element, bombarding the enemy's weak points—that is, all "doubtful" states—with his inveterate skill. A complete blueprint of the canvass written by House, and carried out everywhere to the last detail of organization—"organization," rather than "enthusiasm," he held, would win the day—remains to show how uncanny were his calculations of election quantities. The East, deeply concerned with the war and munitions production, was virtually given up for lost. Victory would turn upon Ohio, momentarily "liberal," and the West and Far West, strongly neutral in sentiment.

Though he worked in the field of foreign politics to bring America into the war, so far as the home front was concerned, House as early as May, 1916, urged Wilson to play for the liberal vote, the peace vote.[33]

Woodrow Wilson needed no urging. In eloquent words he reiterated his earlier vows to hold to the ways of peace. Even during his "Preparedness tour" he had exclaimed:

. . . No voice has ever come to any public man more audibly, more unmistakably, than the voice of this great people has come to me, bearing this impressive lesson, "We are counting upon you to keep this country out of war." And I call you to witness, my fellow-countrymen, that I have spent every thought and energy that has been vouchsafed me in order to keep this country out of war.[34]

[33] House, *op. cit.*, Vol. II, p. 355.
[34] Speech at Des Moines, Iowa, Feb. 1, 1916.

At a time when there was much loose talk in the press of expanding Pershing's Mexican expedition into a full military occupation, Wilson strove to breast the jingo tide:

... I have constantly to remind myself that I am not the servant of those who wish to enhance the value of their Mexican investments, but that I am the servant of the rank and file of the people of the United States.[35]

Practiced public orator that he was, Wilson's pacific utterances carried a passionate conviction to troubled minds. In those days of 1916 the two characteristic movements inspired by the tragic events in Europe were for Preparedness, directed by Theodore Roosevelt and Leonard Wood, and for a League to Enforce Peace, launched by the earnest pacifist Professor Theodore Marburg, and supported lately by former President Taft. Appearing before a gathering of this body at Washington on May 27, 1916, Wilson in a magnificent address so clearly and vigorously expressed his desire for world peace, and his view of the conditions required therefor, that it was impossible for the Republicans at their approaching convention in June to offer anything better.

Dark as were the days of war, certain great truths were dawning upon men and even statesmen, he said. The great nations of the world must in some way band themselves together "to see that . . . right prevails as against any sort of selfish aggression. . . ." There must be freedom of the seas, open diplomacy, recognition and safeguarding of the sovereignty of small nations, and the protection of peace from selfish aggressors by a "feasible association of nations formed in order to realize these objects." In this great undertaking, Wilson declared, "the United States is willing to become a partner." As to the present war—"with its causes and objects we are not concerned."

The slogan "He Kept Us Out of War" carried Wilson in 1916 to a second, narrowly won victory over the reunited and long-dominant Republican party. The Republicans argued that all our

[35] Speech at New York, Jun. 30, 1916.

foreign policy recently was wrong, but Wilson, on September 30, 1916, pointed out with deadly logic:

If it is wrong and they are men of conscience they must change it, and if they are going to change it, in what direction are they going to change it? There is only one choice as against peace, and that is war.

Yet even as he stood publicly before the people, a shining apostle of peace and world-wide justice, Woodrow Wilson permitted new turns of the screw that made our abstention from war well-nigh impossible. While on the political level the ground for American mediation had narrowed to a condition of tacit subservience to Britain and France, so at the economic level the area of choice shrank sharply after the summer of 1915. The pound sterling had suddenly slumped until it seemed that the power of the Allies to buy materials of war in America must soon be lost. "Normal" short-term credits for Allied purchases appeared to have been. stretched to the limit. The only measure that would save the situation, as a leading Chicago banker (very close to the Morgan-Baker group) wrote to the vice-governor of the Federal Reserve Board at Washington, was "the flotation of a large British loan in this country. . . ." In cryptic language the banker inquired whether the political government (not mentioned as such, but referred to mysteriously as "parties") would (1) be favorable to or encourage such a loan; (2) take no action with regard to it; (3) discourage it, but not actively or openly; (4) offer such resistance as to make it practically impossible.[36] Mr. H. P. Davison, partner of Morgan and Company, also had a long conference with Secretary of the Treasury McAdoo, now President Wilson's son-in-law, regarding

[36] Senate Committee on the Munitions Industry, *Hearings*, J. B. Forgan to F. A. Delano, Aug. 17, 1915, Exihbit No. 2220.

Benjamin Strong, of the Federal Reserve Board, urged upon Secretary McAdoo that ". . . certain steps should be taken with a view to the country's financial position." (*Hearings*, Part 30, Exhibit No. 3124, B. Strong to W. G. McAdoo, Aug. 2, 1915.) The outlook was "gloomy" according to Strong; England might soon restrict our exports, owing to the fall of her exchange. (*Hearings*, Exhibit No. 3119, B. Strong to F. I. Kent, Jul. 10, 1915.)

the "serious" exchange situation. And Secretary McAdoo turned to his austere father-in-law with the pressing question: How could the great cycle of prosperity which had begun here in April, 1915, be sustained unless it were *financed* by us? [37]

Our prosperity is dependent on our continued and enlarged foreign trade. To preserve that we must do everything we can to assist our customers to buy. . . . To maintain our prosperity we must finance it. Otherwise it may stop, and that would be disastrous.

A term loan of "at least $500,000,000" to Britain was "imperative" to fund all the floating credits in the hands of our bankers, he urged. The new Secretary of State, Lansing, seconded McAdoo's pleas and Colonel House did likewise. Meanwhile Bryan's ban on direct public "loans" to foreign governments, in the shape of bonds, still stood as the declared policy of the political government.

Wilson, before whom Lansing placed the confidential letter from the Chicago banker inquiring as to the attitude of "parties" (that is, President Wilson) toward foreign loans, now confronted a "hard dilemma, fateful for bankers, manufacturers, farmers, industrial workers, American boys who were to die in France, and all the families who were to suffer losses on the battlefields. . . ." [38] On August 26, 1915, very quickly, Wilson made his decision, which was secretly communicated to those "entitled" to know and only "orally." He revoked Bryan's prohibition; yet realizing perhaps the delicacy and weightiness of this order, made it oral only— that is, informal. He wrote to Lansing:

My opinion in this matter is . . . that we should say that "parties would take no action either for or against such a transaction," [this was one of the alternatives in the banker's letter, and in his own words] but that this should be orally conveyed, so far as we are concerned, and not put in writing. [39]

[37] *Ibid.*, Aug. 21, 1915, Exhibit No. 2219.
[38] Beard and Beard, *America in Mid-Passage*, p. 414.
[39] Senate Committee on Munitions Industry, *Hearings*, Wilson to Lansing, Aug. 26, 1916, Exhibit No. 2224.

Secretary McAdoo now moved to liberalize the regulations of the Federal Reserve Banks, two of whose Governors, Warburg and Miller, seemed "pro-German" and stood for restricting the financing of munitions exports. The way was now opened for a vast expansion of our "export trade" and for the Anglo-French loan of $500,000,000, floated in September, 1915, by the Morgan syndicate for a gross commission of about 22 millions, the greatest foreign loan ever known in this country. By election time in 1916, some 1.5 billions in bonds of the Allied powers were circulating among bankers and investors in this country. By April, 1917, the amount had risen to 2.7 billions.[40]

The British Ambassador, Spring Rice, in a letter to Grey, October 7, 1915, pointed with satisfaction to the President's change of heart concerning public loans to belligerents. With Mr. Bryan he had opposed such loans one year ago, ". . . but when it became apparent that a loan was necessary in order to give a credit for American exports to Europe, many secret forces began to act in its favour." In a second letter, reverting to this point, a month later, the Ambassador said: "The brutal facts are that this country has been saved by the war and by our war demand from a great economic crisis. . . . Our orders here are absolutely essential to their commercial prosperity." [41]

In a remarkable passage of a speech before a gathering of business men at Detroit, July 10, 1916, President Wilson had called to the attention of his hearers the significant fact that since 1914 America had "ceased to be a debtor nation and become a creditor nation." The gold of the world was being heaped on our shores, he said, adding:

. . . Our business hereafter is to lend and to help and to promote the great peaceful enterprises of the world. We have got to finance the world in some important degree, and those who finance the world must understand it and rule it with their spirits and their minds. We cannot cabin and confine ourselves any longer. . . .

[40] Tansill, *op. cit.*, pp. 107-108.
[41] Gwynn, *op. cit.*, Vol. II, pp. 281, 300.

Meanwhile, no "great peaceful enterprises" were pointed out, but mostly war enterprises were given financial encouragement upon a vast scale. Soon the creditor would be locked in the death grip of his debtor. A tremendous money inflation had spread throughout our industrial system, which by 1917 was producing coal, iron ore, petroleum, and copper goods at a pace from 50 to 100 per cent higher than in 1913. On the agricultural front, cotton was rising to its peak of 35.9 cents a pound, wheat was at times above $2.50 a bushel, and hides and meat, also produced in unheard-of quantities, were at corresponding levels of value. In the cycle of inflation the expansion of profits and incomes and prices and cost of living rose similarly.

Yet all this booming trade, this flood of industrial activity and prosperity, with its joyous new thousands of millionaires, was linked with the fortunes of the Allies, as Wilson was periodically reminded nowadays. At one turn of the wheel the high structure of our prosperity could be sent crashing to the ground. Would the great debtors ever be able to pay their colossal debts to the full sum? Occasional downward plunges of sterling exchange caused fear—Britain alone was estimated to have upwards of 15 billions in foreign securities throughout the world, most of it invested in her colonies and dominions. She did not yet convey the certificates for this wealth to her chief foreign creditors in the United States. She waited. (Eventually the floating debts of 1917 and far more were transferred to the back of the United States government, and ultimate repayment was postponed, apparently forever, in the 1931 moratorium.) Meanwhile, what would defeat for the Allies mean to the United States? And there were months, after the Russian collapse, when final disaster seemed very near.

On March 5, 1917, Walter H. Page, from London, summarized the whole perilous economic position in a cablegram which remained buried from public view up to January, 1936. The international financial situation, he said, appeared "most alarming to the American financial and industrial outlook." The Allies might soon halt their huge purchasing program.

France and England must have a large enough credit in the United States to prevent the collapse of world trade and of the whole European finance. If we should go to war with Germany the greatest help we could give the Allies would be such a credit. . . . Trade would be continued and enlarged until the war ends, and after the war Europe would continue to buy food and would buy from us also an enormous supply of things to re-equip her peace industries. We should thus reap the profit of an uninterrupted, perhaps an enlarging trade over a number of years. . . . Perhaps our going to war is the only way in which our present prominent trade position can be maintained and a panic averted. The submarine has added the last item to the danger of a financial world crash.[42]

In December, 1916, the Central Powers made their "peace drive," offering terms which the Allies held unworthy of consideration. Wilson's last proposals for mediation, which Secretary Lansing opposed, also fell on barren ground in late December, 1916. Germany, suspecting the American government's "neutrality," with good reason, indicated that some other medium would now be preferred. The last hope of Wilson for essaying his great peace-making role—*save through participation in the war on the side of the Allies,* always held out to him still—was gone. Meanwhile, the announcement on February 1, 1917, of a renewal of unrestricted submarine warfare, with the ruthless Admiral von Tirpitz at the helm again, ended the German "truce" with America. Great Britain's life-line of supplies was threatened, a situation perhaps dooming her to early defeat, certainly offering chances of a gigantic financial disaster for the United States. For America was involved from one end to the other on a vast output of war *matériel,* and a tall financial pyramid of loans and credits was now based on this trade.

In March, 1917, three American merchant vessels passing through the war zone were torpedoed without warning and sunk. The German government had repudiated its pledges to spare unarmed merchant ships, and the time for words had passed. As often

[42] *Foreign Relations of the U. S.,* 1917, Supplements, No. 2, Vol. I, p. 516.

happens at such a crisis, the fated enemy now assumed his worst guise. Revelations concerning stupid German propaganda and conspiratorial activities, the secret "Zimmermann notes," dealing with a plotted rising in Mexico and invasion of Texas and California, and of the Papen-Boy-Ed schemes to destroy munitions plants, agitated the whole country profoundly and helped to the desired end.

In the few, calm moments that were left before the inevitable rupture of relations with Germany, the President could still reflect that *"Every reform we have won will be lost. . . . We have been making a fight on special privilege. We have got new tariff and currency and trust legislation. We don't yet know how they will work. They are not thoroughly set. . . ."* [43]

Then, in the next breath, he remarks that if war comes he means to be "ruthless," to use "force, force, to the uttermost. . . ." For how else could war be pursued? And was not the prize at stake a great one, the very destiny of the civilized world? Though he had detested war, Wilson, "like the maid of Orleans . . . had a habit of hearing voices," voices calling him to a historic role, the settlement of the war and the peace, the making of a League of Nations and the parliament of the world. He isolates himself still further, refuses appeals to form a coalition war Cabinet, and takes personal command of the government.[44]

Even Wilson's language in these days reflects a transformation of his character in the crucible of the world drama. We have the impression that he saw himself constantly as standing before the judgment of all posterity at one of the fateful turns of man's long, violent history. The awful, extraconstitutional power and the responsibility that now fall into his hands stir his considerable literary imagination. "I stand here and have taken the high and solemn oath," he says in his second inaugural address of March 6, 1917, ". . . because the people of the United States have chosen

[43] Baker, *op. cit.*, Vol. V, p. 77; italics mine.
[44] Kerney, *Wilson*, pp. 390-391.

me for this august delegation of power and have . . . named me their leader in affairs."

A few weeks later, April 2, 1917, calling upon Congress for the declaration of war, he speaks again in his peroration as if utterly transported: "There are . . . many months of fiery trial and sacrifice ahead of us. It is a fearful thing to lead this great people into war. . . . But the right is more precious than peace." And to the right, America could well dedicate the lives and fortunes of all her people if need be, "everything that we are and everything that we have," to preserve those conditions and principles "that gave her birth and happiness."

XVII. THE MARTYRDOM

OF DR. WILSON

THE ENTRANCE of the world's richest and potentially strongest nation into the war on the side of the Allies, in the early spring of 1917, was most fortunate for them, coming as it did at the dark hour when the Russian front collapsed. Although Germany prepared all through 1917 for her supreme effort on the Western Front the following spring, the great turning of the tide could already be discerned. The wealth of all broad America, her youthful energy, flung generously and devoutly into the battle, was sufficient, when added to the Allied forces, to close the breaches in their land lines, clear the seas, and bend back the gigantic offensive of Ludendorff in March to July, 1918.

Under the emergency powers of wartime, Dr. Wilson took "personal command" of the government of the United States. He became "the dictator . . . with unlimited control of the country's finances; the dictator of the farms, of all business . . . and dictator as to who of our youth should live or die—greater power by far than had ever been Abraham Lincoln's." [1] From his desk in the White House, where he sat alone, the decrees flew to the Capitol. Notes went one after another to the floor leaders of the House and Senate, asking Congress to pass measures of military action and measures providing for vast money appropriations. His tone in the messages and communications of 1918 grew imperious and urgent. Almost as soon as his communications were received,

[1] Villard, op. cit., p. 326.

Congress, acting with wartime discipline, enacted them into law.

More inaccessible than ever, he sat in his study framing his lofty public declarations and messages, while a Draconian censorship and political police now harshly suppressed all dissent, all criticism, all opposition. He had predicted, in intimate conversations, that if war came it would be pushed pitilessly and our people would "forget there ever was such a thing as tolerance." Pacifists, radicals, and other opponents of the war were imprisoned, mobbed, or even tortured; liberals who spoke in public in those days had agents of the Department of Justice shadowing them, or taking down their words verbatim. Hourly they waited for arrest. "One had a sense of having come to a sudden short stop at the end of an intellectual era," observed Randolph Bourne. Soon the ponderous machinery of suppression and censorship rolled on under its own momentum; yet the Professor-President virtually never interceded to help or save its victims.

Edward House had once observed to Wilson that he thought him too sensitive, too intelligent, and too refined to conduct a war. But Wilson disclosed an unexpected side of his nature when he held himself deaf to all appeals against official injustice during the war. The time comes, he would often say, when one must shut his mind and act.

In one of his occasional moments of intimacy with Private Secretary Tumulty, Wilson himself alluded to the truth in those accusations of "coldness" which were leveled at him. He said: "I am cold in a certain sense. Were I a judge and my own son should be convicted of murder . . . I would do my duty even to the point of sentencing him to death. It would be a hard thing to do, but it would be my solemn duty." [2]

Although he did not find it necessary to call together a coalition cabinet, embracing leaders of both major parties—holding that this would only hamper and embarrass his efforts—the President did summon the leading financiers, industrialists, administrators, and "best" minds to join in directing the hugely expanded action of the

[2] Tumulty, *op. cit.*, p. 475.

war government. These manned the Council of National Defense and its chief subdivisions, the War Industries Board, the National Food Commission and Fuel Commission, the shipping and railroad boards, and the War Labor Board. Centralized control and integration of our industries and economic resources, under a President who had championed liberal doctrines, was carried out to an extent never before known here, though under conditions which in most cases richly favored their private owners. The railroads passed (temporarily) into government hands, in March, 1918. In other vital industries production schedules and consumption were controlled, prices were *fixed*, usually at very high levels, by agreements with the "Dollar-a-Year" men who directed the government's control boards.

The machinery of planning and control assumed a collectivist form, and after a period of preliminary confusion, worked with creditable energy under men like B. M. Baruch, Chairman of the War Industries Board, Herbert Hoover of the Food Commission, Secretary McAdoo and Daniel Willard of the Railroad Administration, Edward Hurley, Charles M. Schwab, and James Farrell of the Shipping Board, and Dwight Morrow and Thomas W. Lamont, who were detailed to help the Treasury in its huge wartime financial operations. Wilson supported his administrative "experts" as he supported the army and navy officers he had placed in command. But neither in the military field nor on the economic front at home did his leadership assume any distinctive form, either by striking errors of judgment or triumphs of personal command. A collective war machine, patterned after those built up in England as well as in Germany, functioned impersonally, sometimes with strange effects. The President would be called in to determine points of policy as they arose; but his main interest lay elsewhere, one might say, beyond the war operations themselves.

It is not part of our plan to review the events of the war, so often chronicled, but rather to weigh its effects upon an epoch of peaceful, enlightened political action in the United States, and upon the fortunes of the man who had become the most eminent model of that enlightenment.

Within a short time after America entered the war, President Wilson became the most famous and most powerful statesman in all the world, one to whose leadership hundreds of millions of human beings everywhere looked with fervent hope. It was the American President rather than the French or English leaders that the masses in the Allied countries trusted to bring their deliverance from present and future wars. For even more remarkable than the effect of American arms and material was the unawaited, inspirational force of Wilson's public utterances on the weary and despairing peoples of Europe. The apotheosis of our Dr. Wilson, the Calvinist minister's son, into a latter-day saint or savior of the world, was one of the more wonderful effects of the last years of a war whose pity and terror turned unbelievers into mystics. "Out of the New World came the Professor-President, as though with warming breezes to thaw out the winter numbness of the Old. A godlike atmosphere surrounded the man in scholar's garb who had lifted himself above the crowned and the chosen of Europe. His arrival inspired wonder and awe. . . ." Thus commented a great European journalist upon the advent of "Saint Woodrow." Wilson's crusading he likens to that of Henry VII, hero of a tumultous age, of whom also it was once said that he would "purge the earth of iniquity, restore to the Roman Empire its holiness, and insure to all mortals the blessings of just and righteous rulership." But Henry VII, after coming to pacify Italy, conquering, winning the Iron Crown, was very soon betrayed; and, returning, was jeered and derided along his way, dying on the road to Germany, at Buonconvento, with few so poor as to do him honor.[3]

On the eve of America's entrance into the war, Wilson had voiced noble doctrines, such as no other war leader dared to utter. In a message to Congress, one of the most momentous speeches

[3] Maximilian Harden, *I Meet My Contemporaries*, pp. 57-58.

ever given there, he had defined the essential terms of peace as including an association of nations that would guarantee the permanence of peace, "a force . . . so much greater than the force of any nation now engaged or any alliance hitherto formed or projected that no nation, no probable combination of nations, could face or withstand it." The present war, then, must be resolved as no mere "struggle for a new balance of power." For who could guarantee that again? To crush the antagonist entirely would be both wrong and vain. There must be instead *"peace without victory."* And, he added, "the paths of the sea must alike in law and in fact be free. . . . The freedom of the seas is the *sine qua non* of peace, equality, co-operation." Wilson spoke for liberty, for the sovereignty of the helpless small nation, for the "consent of the governed." Such were the principles envisaged in his war making, as lofty, noble, and spiritual as that of any knight who in earlier times set forth to win the Holy Grail.

Wilson believed that he spoke out what the people of the United States would wish him to say.

May I not add that I hope and believe that I am in effect speaking for liberals and friends of humanity in every nation and of every programme of liberty? I would fain believe that I am speaking for the silent mass of mankind everywhere who have as yet had no place or opportunity to speak their real hearts out concerning the death and ruin they see to have come already upon the persons and the homes they hold most dear.[4]

These were golden words, rhythmic and pure in style, moving even the hearts of the enemy soldiers when they came fluttering down in white leaflets behind the battle lines. To his colleagues at the head of the Allied governments, Wilson may have provided embarrassing moments, if they thought of the Secret Treaties by which they bound themselves as partners in the common war enterprise. Yet they remained silent on this point, biding their time, grateful for the powerful help given by the American President's exalted ideology.

[4] Jan. 22, 1917, message to Congress.

It was the American statesman, rather than the leaders of Britain, who gave the highest and perhaps final expression of the historic principles of liberalism (developed originally in England during the eighteenth and nineteenth centuries) applied to international politics. In calling for the declaration of war on April 2, 1917, he promised "peace and justice in the life of the world"; the subject populations of the selfish, autocratic powers were to be free and self-governed. Unfolding the same theme in later public papers, he promised that secret diplomacy was to be abolished as well as selfish, secret alliances; territorial boundaries were to be fixed according to the lines of nationality; armaments were to be reduced, economic barriers were to be removed and equality of trade conditions established among the states banded together for peace. It was a dream of world-wide free trade, the Heavenly City of the laissez-faire economy.

As an earnest of his intentions, Wilson could declare that the American government had asked for no share of the spoils of war. "We have no selfish ends to serve. We desire no conquest, no dominion. We seek no indemnities for ourselves. . . . We are but one of the champions of the rights of mankind."

Woodrow Wilson, Princeton University professor who had become an amateur of politics as part of the movement of talent and wealth to improve the tone of our public life and save us from radical extremes, had traveled a long distance in less than seven years. He had striven to set business men and bankers, farmers and laborers, free in America, before 1914. But now, on March 5, 1917, he exclaimed: "We are provincials no longer." He dedicated himself, in effect, to the task of making "the world itself at last free."

While Wilson on the ideological front represented the Allied governments as champions of human values, of "the rights of mankind," more effectively than their own accomplished orators, a sudden counter-offensive that promised the most serious embarrassments for this line of argument was begun by the former allies, the Russians.

After the first, moderate revolution in March, 1917, overthrew the house of Romanoff, Wilson had paid a joyful salute to the free Russian republic. The Russian revolution was "a wonderful and heartening" event. "The great generous Russian people have been added . . . to the forces that are fighting for freedom. . . ." [5]

But soon came the second, "October Revolution," led by the Left Wing Socialist (Bolshevik) party, and Lenin, turning boldly from the course of the preceding Kerensky regime, led his people out of the trenches to peace, land, and bread. What was more, he contended that the general war now raging in Europe was the business of deadly imperialist-capitalist rivals, and called upon the masses of people everywhere to cease fighting each other and to rise against those who, for their own greed and pelf, led them to war. By way of illustration, Lenin in December, 1917, published the text of the Allies' Secret Treaties of 1915, providing for the division among the winners of vast territorial loot after the war. These were published in certain American newspapers and reprinted as a pamphlet late in January, 1918. The world now learned of how it was planned to distribute German territories to France, Austrian territories to Italy, and Turkish provinces to Russia, with England and France receiving the lion's share of the German African colonies, while Japan was to be given Shantung.

Was Woodrow Wilson ignorant of the Secret Treaties of 1915, as he later claimed to have been? There is good reason to believe that he learned something of them during Balfour's visit to America in the summer of 1917. Charles R. Crane, who had headed a first mission to Russia with Lincoln Steffens in his retinue early in 1917, heard talk of the Secret Treaties, and reported on them to House. [6]

At any rate the revelations that came from the Russian archives, showing the Allies to be little nicer in their scruples than the German imperialists, created a sudden dilemma. On January 3, 1918,

[5] Speech of Apr. 2, 1917.
[6] L. Colcord in *The Nation*, May 17, 1919; Steffens, *op. cit.*, Jun. 20, 1917, Vol. I, p. 399.

Edgar Sisson, who accompanied a second American mission for the purpose of helping to rally and finance the battered Russians, cabled to George Creel, American director of public information, urging that the President be asked to "restate the anti-imperialistic war aims and democratic peace requisites of America, thousand words or less, short, almost placard paragraphs, short sentences." [7] Such a manifesto could be used with effect upon both the German and Russians.

The Professor-President now showed his mettle. As a counterblast to Lenin's exposures, which he officially ignored, Wilson before a joint session of Congress on January 8, 1918, stated the war aims and peace terms of the United States in the famous "Fourteen Points" declaration, already embodied in earlier papers and now summarized and formulated in a most effective form.

The effect of this memorable declaration was long remembered even by General Ludendorff. Copies of Wilson's Fourteen Points rained down upon the German armies and behind their lines. "While her army was victorious in the field of battle," Ludendorff relates, "Germany failed in the fight of intellects [ideology] against the enemy peoples."

Even German soldiers began to awake from the stupefaction and frenzy of war, as they read or heard of the pledges of a just peace made by the President of the great republic. They were led to wonder at their hard fate and to dare to hope again. Wilson himself was aware in his cooler moments that by his utterances he at times aroused hope among the people that was almost tragic, hope that "runs out to such depths that *we cannot in the nature of things satisfy it.*" [8]

Beyond the borders of the United States Wilson aroused incredible hope among men of a lasting peace and a just, "free" world order, while he ignored the previous pledges exchanged by

[7] Beard and Beard, *Rise of American Civilization*, Vol. II, p. 651.

[8] Speech to Democratic National Committee (privately), Feb. 28, 1919; Tumulty, *Wilson*, p. 367 (after stenographic notes); italics mine.

the Allied governments with whom he on the other hand had no agreements at all concerning peace terms. To those who studied Wilson's conduct at home with clear sight, the outcome of his foreign crusade need have been no great surprise. He who had set forth to win the New Freedom for Americans, to "set business free," administered a final death blow to the old liberal individualistic, competitive economy by leading the nation into war. During the tremendous industrial expansion the giant corporations dominating each field were assured certain and fabulous profits if they could increase their output capacity. The restraints upon monopolies, which the Justice Department and the new Federal Trade Commission had begun to impose vigorously, were necessarily relaxed. While American doughboys advanced against the German lines in northern France, the masters of heavy industry extended their profits to unheard-of figures. Their own "victories" during the war and immediate post-war period from January 1, 1916, to July 1, 1921, after all Federal income and excess profits taxes were deducted, totaled thirty-eight billions, half of this going to the 1,000 largest corporations. They themselves had been called in to manage the "business side of war," Wilson being convinced that this called for "business experts." The kings and near kings of industry and finance had flocked to the capital to take control of the collective wartime production. "At every point of vital business contact," wrote one onlooker, "some Morgan partner or agent —direct or indirect—was close at hand to inform or guide. . . ." [9]

The wartime "co-operative" planning of our industrial production has been likened to Fascist economic planning in later years. Yet the results then were very different from those of recent Fascist planning, since the great capitalists emerged from the process not to walk the plank but enriched beyond their dreams. The number of millionaires rose more than twofold, to over 15,000, within four years. In the wake of war, social inequalities became more marked than ever; the large industrial units, hugely over-expanded, when peace came were compelled to merge with each

---

[9] Kerney, *Wilson*, p. 394.

other into still greater combinations in very self-defense, fixing more completely and irrevocably than ever the system of monopoly which Wilson had promised to abolish.

Directing huge war finances, government bond issues of twenty-five billions, and financing great foreign loans, domestic capital flotations, and a world-wide foreign trade that trebled the pre-war records by 1920, the bankers also found that under the liberal reformer Wilson they had amassed greater gains than under a long line of conservative Presidents. Indeed the bankers, especially the investment bankers, who controlled the flow of capital to industry, emerged in full command of the industrial system at the end of the war, as Veblen had predicted. More than one of them, like Thomas W. Lamont, had entertained visions of American finance dominating all the world. In April, 1915, this member of the Morgan firm, in a speech before the American Academy of Political and Social Science at Philadelphia, pointed out that "if the war continues long enough" America would buy back all its own securities, becoming one of the principal creditor nations in the world, and a "lender upon a really large scale," not only in Europe but for the private and public enterprises of South America and other parts of the world. The dollar, "if the war continues long enough to encourage us," he said, "would take the place of the pound sterling as the international standard of exchange." [10] Such words, suggesting the real hopes of powerful American financiers who manned the government controls of our wartime economy, cast strong doubt upon the pure disinterestedness of America's intervention in the war.

Yet Dr. Wilson continued to ignore the facts at home, as abroad, as he had a way of doing, while he contemplated the "eternal verities." Some men, especially French and British diplomats, began to doubt his sincerity. Lincoln Steffens, who observed him long and sympathetically, has set him off in a sparkling passage as "a righteous man. . . . He had ideals; they were high and they were sincere, *but they were so high that he did not expect to*

---

[10] Lundberg, *America's Sixty Families*, pp. 139-140.

realize them." So long as he could feel he had done his best for them, he was satisfied. Steffens recalled meeting many earnest reformers of the same type in American towns.[11]

Meanwhile over all the grand, collective outpouring of life and money, the gigantic toiling, desperate enjoying, killing, and wealth-getting, the austere philosopher in the White House, aloof and remote from men as ever, drew his concealing mantle of lofty ideology. "It is not of material interests . . . that we are thinking." And further: "My theme is of those great principles of compassion and of protection which mankind has sought to throw about human lives. . . ." "We have always professed unselfish purpose. . . ." "Our motive will not be revenge or the victorious assertion of the physical might of the nation, but only the vindication of right. . . ."[12]

At last news came of the approaching Armistice. Those who knew Wilson had seen for a long time that he was devoured by the desire to "dictate the peace," the peace that would redeem all the loss of blood and treasure, the eternal peace. The plan of House's old League of Nations, so strongly espoused in the "Fourteen Points" speech, was ready to hand. The talk in circles close to the ruling groups in Washington held that Wilson now desired to cap all his recent glories, in peace and war, with that of becoming "President of the world"!

"Thus the war comes to an end," Wilson said solemnly to Congress, on November 5, 1918, a few days before the Armistice was signed. A month later he stood before the two houses of Congress and announced his precedent-breaking intention to sail for Europe and "join in Paris the representatives of the governments" with which we had been associated in the war. Wilson declared now (what he had decided many months before) that he felt it his "paramount duty" to participate directly and give his personal counsel in the peace conference, although the Allies were agreed

[11] Steffens, *Autobiography*, p. 786.
[12] Speeches of Mar. 4, Apr. 2, 1917.

in principle upon acceptance, he believed, of his January 8, 1918, declarations of war aims (the Fourteen Points).

"I shall be in close touch with you and with affairs on this side of the water, and you will know all that I do," Wilson promised. Might he not hope in return, he concluded as he bade farewell, in view of the delicate tasks before him to have "the encouragement and the strength of your united support"? [13]

Another detail overlooked. Before the November elections of 1918, and just before the Armistice, the President had appealed to the electorate for a vote of indorsement. The result was a decisive defeat in the Congressional elections by which the Republicans came into control of Congress. Yet the President, as he took ship on December 4, 1918, reflected that this reverse for his party would make his task only a little harder; his confidence in his star was unshaken. On his voyage to Paris, he was accompanied by a large retinue of "expert" aides and journalists, but no prominent leader of the opposition party, no member of the Senate which held treaty-ratifying power, was invited to be a member of the American delegation.

The receptions given to President Wilson when he set foot in France were in measure with such a grandiose mission. The "savior" in Paris was greeted by the people in a manner scarcely ever seen before in all history. His proud wife recalls: as they rode through the streets, in procession, "every inch was covered with cheering, shouting humanity. The sidewalks, the buildings, even the stately horse-chestnut trees were peopled with men and boys. . . . Roofs were filled, windows overflowed, until one grew giddy trying to greet the bursts of welcome that came like the surging of untamed waters. Flowers rained upon us until we were nearly buried." [14]

It was with an eye to the possible effects of these crowd ovations and the strength they added to his thesis—against the Allied statesmen at the Peace Conference—that Wilson continued his

[13] Annual message to Congress, Dec. 2, 1918.
[14] Edith Wilson, *op. cit.*, p. 137.

imperial progress before the masses of England and even Italy. Flanked by royalty, riding in historic state carriages, with liveried and wigged coachmen, footmen and outriders, he made his memorable appearance in the cities of England. One observer relates:

In all my journalistic experience I have never attended a meeting so moving and reverential as that in the historic Manchester Free Trade Hall on December 30, at which Mr. Wilson spoke. I am sure that if it had been Christ Himself returning to this earth, His reception could not have been more impressive or awe-inspiring. When that great crowd rose to its feet as Mr. Wilson appeared, there was an atmosphere around me—yes, all through the hall—that defied description. Reverence, profound gratitude, the feeling that there stood the saviour of the world, the creator of a new and better universe—all of these feelings were expressed on every countenance. . . . It would have taken very little more for that audience to have gone down on its knees.[15]

Only twenty years before, American diplomats had turned American foreign policy toward participation in the world balance of power. Seven years later, Theodore Roosevelt had carried this policy still further when he strode upon the stage of world power politics during the Russo-Japanese and Moroccan conferences. But Dr. Wilson, in 1919, seemed to stand virtually alone, the refulgence of his world glory dimming the lights of the other statesmen who came to the peace council which was to dispose of the earth itself.

2

When the last-hour liberal government of Germany sent word to Washington on October 5, 1918, that it was ready to accept the peace terms outlined by President Wilson, they were referred to General Foch, the Allies' supreme military commander, for the terms of an armistice. The extremely harsh armistice terms should have offered an unmistakable clew to that which followed: a repetition of the Congress of Vienna, whose members, released from

[15] Villard, *op. cit.*, p. 381.

the fear of ruin after Waterloo, set for themselves the sole task of restoring and protecting the *status quo ante*.

The rulers of France desired vengeance, reparations, and the permanent crippling of the German nation. The British exacted for their part the destruction of the German navy, the confiscation of her large merchant marine, and the distribution of her colonies. The scheme for the partition of the Central Powers' territory or colonies principally among Britain, France, Italy, Roumania, and Japan had been established in 1915 and was not to be abandoned in 1919. In short, the rulers of the Allied Powers looked to the present, or to the past; as for the future, with its new, promised order of peace and justice, which seemed to concern President Wilson so greatly, that could take care of itself.

They quite evidently prepared themselves against the influence of the President. His visits of state, at which the European masses welcomed him as their Moses, were allowed to continue until the popular excitement over Wilson diminished. The intentionally delayed peace council of thirty-two nations held its formal opening more than a month after Wilson's arrival. Then it was announced quickly that a supreme council in which only the United States, Great Britain, France, Italy, and Japan were represented would transact the business of the conference. Soon Japan retired, and Italy, angered by Wilson's refusal of its maximum territorial demands, also withdrew, and "The Big Three," ignoring Wilson's promises of open covenants, conducted the peacemaking behind closed doors.

At Versailles, Wilson smiled at the earthy Clemenceau and his peasant craft. Was he not the purer, the stronger man? Had not the cheers of the people of England rung for him rather than for Lloyd George? Yet in a room alone with these two shrewd premiers, he was at a disadvantage, he was in a trap. He constituted a minority of one, as the American military contingent was only one among the armed forces that overlooked the conference.

Wilson had begun by deferring to the feelings of the French, who had borne such fearful material losses. From this concession

Lloyd George and Clemenceau pressed him, step by step, to the sanctioning of Austria's partition, the semi-partition of Germany, and the division among the Allies of the colonial loot, none of which America shared. To be sure, there were compromises forced by his resistance; the reapportionment of the map of Europe followed to some extent his concept of racial divisions or "national self-determination," and he pressed successfully for the establishment of outlets to the sea for inland states. Yet each new state set up, each coal field moved across a border, was designed principally to complete forever the military and economic subjugation of the enemy.

In compensation for these drastic defeats, the plan of a League of Nations was also incorporated in the voluminous clauses of the peace settlement. It was both a weak and an inadequate League of Nations, and one that, subject to the dominance of the Allied partners in the war, might prove also a dangerous instrument. Yet Wilson, who was believed to have undergone much mental suffering during the secret sessions of the conference, was finally convinced that, through the League of Nations alone, the means existed to repair any possible errors or wrongs embraced within the peace settlement.

The terms of the peace were "severe," Wilson finally admitted, in a cabled message to Congress on the day when the German representatives were dragooned into signing it. They were severe "only because great wrongs done by Germany are to be righted. . . ." [16]

In the end he became convinced that the Treaty of Versailles actually embodied his Fourteen Points. Questioned upon this very matter by newspaper reporters, as he departed for the United States, he answered earnestly and thoughtfully: "I think that we have made a better peace than I should have expected when I came here to Paris." [17]

[16] Speech of Jun. 28, 1919.
[17] Steffens, *Autobiography*, p. 789.

Certain hard, immovable facts had led to the Carthaginian peace settlement at Versailles and its evil, tragic fallacies, which made hope of an economically free and stable world order vain. Wilson himself in unguarded moments that year admitted freely (quite in the terms of Lenin) the "imperialistic" character of the late war—though he attributed this character only to Germany.

The real reason that the war we have just finished took place was that Germany was afraid her commercial rivals were going to get the better of her, and the reason why some nations went into war against Germany was that they thought Germany would get the commercial advantage of them. The seed of the jealousy, the seed of the deep-seated hatred, was hot, successful commercial and industrial rivalry. . . . This war, in its inception, was a commercial and industrial war.[18]

But that the peace too was one of commercial and industrial jealousy, hatred and vengeance, did not enter into his discourse.

Still denying to himself that the splendid edifice of world peace he had envisaged had crumbled away in the conference rooms of the Quai d'Orsay, Wilson returned to America, doomed to experience personal tragedy as remarkable and imposing as his brief years of world glory.

Beyond the determining economic and historic forces that led to the ill-concealed catastrophe of Versailles, there were in Wilson's character and outlook on life personal qualities and forces that led to his tragic failure—at a moment in history when he possessed still such immense power for good. His personal disaster, his swift, steep fall from the very heights of world rulership, became the symbol of the disaster which overtook his whole political movement, his followers, his generation.

Ray Stannard Baker, in his adulatory ten-volume biography of Wilson, has not neglected to point out how much his character drew from the teachings of his father, the Presbyterian minister, a Calvinist who saw life as a struggle against danger and tempta-

---

[18] Speech of Sept. 5, 1919, at St. Louis.

tion at every hand. Even in youth, at college, Woodrow Wilson had been "withdrawn" and a little "high-minded" in manner.

Men who are lost in sin and saved by the grace of God cannot but think with awe of the difference between themselves and the rest of the world. They are full, at the best, of what may be called humble superiority; at the worst, of fierce prejudices, intolerance, even burning fanaticism.

Such were the influences under which he had grown up as a boy.[19] In the man at the zenith of his power and success the fierce pride and intolerance of an overruling ego blazed under the impassive mask he so often wore, his "bleak, Scotch face," as he himself called it. He trusted few men and despised the self-interest he suspected in each of them. He used them and cast them aside. Assuming always a mask of silent strength, he dreaded most of all being found in error, and easily attributed his failures to his advisers. One by one his friendships were ruptured; at Versailles even House, his *alter ego* of many years, was thrust away forever.

His coldness of manner, as he had admitted in an informal talk, was born of fear and trembling "at my own inadequacy and weakness." He seemed circumspect and cold because he was "so diligently trying not to make any colossal blunders." [20] Yet at Versailles, his lack of human resourcefulness and roundedness in a trial of wits with harder men of equal or superior force of character, and certain of their ground, did not spare him what he most feared: colossal blunders.

Wilson's mask of cold strength concealed then a considerable fund of indecision and weakness, which House sometimes observed from nearby as a disposition to shun unpleasant details, to flee from bad news. Meanwhile, his pride, though it did not prevent him from being at home with and strongly attracting intelligent women, increased with age and success and power. His intense pride is well revealed in his second inaugural address, of March 5, 1917, in which he looks back at his own record of four years.

[19] Baker, *op. cit.*, Vol. I, p. 70.
[20] Speech before National Press Club, Washington, Mar. 20, 1914.

We had sought, he says, "to put our house in order . . . quicken the processes of our national genius and energy and lift our politics. . . ." He adds: "It is a record of singular variety and singular distinction." Here, at the eve of entrance into the dangerous European adventure, there is none of Lincoln's humility and self-restraint.

With such lonely pride, a man could easily become fiercely intolerant of those who disagreed with him. Of the opponents of his peace treaty, he was to say: "Of all the blind and little provincial people, they are the littlest and most contemptible. It is not their character so much that I have a contempt for, though that contempt is thoroughgoing, but their minds. They have not even got good working-imitations of minds." [21] Woe unto those who disagreed with him. For did he not rule "in God's providence"?

Here, at any rate, are a few of the traits which, combined with qualities of courage and high intelligence, made up Wilson's complex, highly charged, and troubled soul. They serve to explain something of the mystery which has always clung to him. They are surely bound up with his strange surrender before difficult, tenacious opponents at Versailles and the subsequent self-deception which he practiced. That he had been hugely gulled, that he had failed, and failing betrayed the millions of suffering men and women who placed so much hope in his leadership, who had knelt in the streets of Old Europe as he passed, was not in his character to admit. A cry of bitter disillusionment had been raised in America at the first rumors and then at publication of the peace terms in May, 1919. But against all those who questioned the merits of the treaty, which he now conceived of as his crowning glory before posterity, Woodrow Wilson set his face like flint.

The Treaty of Versailles, with its covenant of the League of Nations, he assured the country on June 28, 1919, brought to an end "the old intolerable order"; ruthless ambition for power and dominion were now barred; all that remained was for the greatest

[21] Speech to Democratic National Committee, Washington, Feb. 28, 1919; Tumulty, *op. cit.*, pp. 377-378.

of free governments to give its guarantee to a system that promised to consecrate right and justice forever.

3

After the Armistice and the elections of November, 1918, the country was ripe for a tremendous party struggle such as Grover Cleveland had faced in his second term over the issue of depression and Free Silver. The war, conducted upon a scale never known before, touching every phase of our economic life, had produced massive dislocations. The cost of living was high, and wages were high. Three million soldiers must be returned to civil life. A revival of labor organization meanwhile, encouraged by the legislation of Wilson's first term and the scarcity of labor during the war, brought the American Federation of Labor to the largest enrollment of members in its history, and vigorous efforts were made in 1918 and 1919 to extend unionization into heavy industries, such as steel, which had been closed to it previously. The growth of the labor movement in turn produced apprehension among employers, who combined to resist labor with extreme energy.

In the meantime, the oppressive political controls introduced for the war emergencies were continued under Attorney General Mitchell Palmer, and directed chiefly against radicals and labor for a full year or more, contributing to the spreading feeling of unrest which gripped both the upper and the lower layer of society.

The business community, as the war ended, pocketed its profits in a somewhat chastened mood, anxious to liquidate the war and its authoritarian rule by "The All-Highest"—as Wilson was called—anxious to "get out of Europe" as quickly as possible. Extreme disillusionment was felt at the situation there. Europe could never repay its debts to us, and in returning to peace would become a desperate competitor in all the world markets which our merchants had temporarily dominated. The business men, like the masses of people, were weary of wartime discipline and of the aloof autocrat in Washington, whose lofty ideology now seemed clearly to have far outrun its usefulness.

All these various discontents provided of course a sound opportunity which the reviving Republican opposition was determined to capitalize. During the war itself their line of attack upon the administration had occasionally taken the ground that it tended to be too lenient or "liberal" with the enemy. But Wilson's conduct of the peace negotiations, very high-handed and secretive according to American custom and tradition, had given the Republicans still larger openings. The Senate had been bitterly offended. Interrupting the Paris Peace Conference, Wilson late in February made a brief return trip to Washington, dispatched business that waited for his signature, and appeared before the Senate Committee on Foreign Relations to defend or explain his projected League of Nations Covenant and the terms of the treaty in which it was incorporated. The Senators were unmoved; thirty-nine of them (more than one-third their number) signed a "round-robin" declaration which warned him that the peace negotiations should be completed promptly and that a League of Nations Covenant would be rejected. Wilson accepted a few reservations proposed for the Covenant by moderate critics, providing against immigration or tariff control, and for recognition of the Monroe Doctrine. Yet, for the rest, he vowed that he would not change an iota of his plan to combine peace treaty and League and to hold them to the form already shaped, including the much disputed Article X of the League Covenant. This provided that America as a League member would protect the territorial integrity of other members from external aggression.

When Wilson returned to Washington finally, on July 10, 1919, to submit to the Senate the completed, signed peace treaty, with the League Covenant firmly "tied" to it, it was already clear that a two-thirds vote for ratification was lacking. A bitter debate had been raging in Congress ever since May, when the terms of the peace had reached Washington indirectly, through no wish of Wilson's. Yet he warned the Senators at once that he would accept neither amendments nor reservations to the finished construction. "The stage is set," he cried, "the destiny disclosed. It has come about by no plans of our conceiving, but by the hand of God who led us into this war. We cannot turn back. . . . The light streams upon the path ahead and nowhere else."

But the Senators in their "hard-boiled" post-war mood were now cold to the Wilsonian rhetoric. Progressives who assailed the vengeful terms of the "war-makers' peace," and conservatives who objected to the large commitments involved in the League Covenant, coalesced into a solid opposition with surprising speed. La Follette, Borah, and Johnson of California, the radical "isolationists," combined with the Standpatters, Henry Cabot Lodge, Philander Knox, and Boies Penrose, in crying down any "permament alliance with European Powers."

The chance for uniting the conservative and progressive wings of the Republican party upon the issue of the League was quickly grasped by the veteran Henry Cabot Lodge, who led the opposition in the Senate. At first glance it seemed difficult even for an opposing political party to appear to repudiate the settlement of a war in which the whole nation had given of blood and treasure. Therefore Lodge's first maneuver was "to unite the Republicans so far as I could . . . on strong and effective reservations." [22] For Lodge himself was not opposed to some sort of league for the promotion of peace.

But Wilson's fiercely uncompromising spirit, his refusal to accept any effective reservations, played into the hands of his opponents, who determined to arouse the whole people on the issue of "Nationalism versus Internationalism." Soon Lodge, now seventy years of age, who had long felt a jealous hatred of the other scholar in politics, placing himself at the head of the Irreconcilables in the Senate, regaled the country with his bitter tongue. While the Progressives, La Follette and Borah, were sincere in their "isolationist" convictions, Lodge and the Standpat faction, in

[22] Lodge to Beveridge, Aug. 4, 1919; Bowers, *op. cit.*, p. 507.

planning for defeat of the treaty and a Republican victory the following year, had deeper motives.

Through the defeat of Wilson the radicalism potential in Wilson and his following must be utterly crushed, in order to insure return to the old, comfortable order which would soon be called "normalcy." The current struggles waged by union labor were also no small factor in these calculations.

Although Wilson had moved far from his liberal phase of 1910-1914, the conservatives still feared or pretended to fear in him some incalculable and autocratic threat of instituting state socialism here. This at least was the view of Henry Cabot Lodge, who in April, 1919, had said privately:

> . . . The fact is that the Republican party is the only organized force we have to rely upon to defeat the Wilsonian movement toward Socialism and breaking down the constitutional government of the United States. If the Republican party as an organization fails us there is nothing else.[23]

Opinion in the country was confused on the subject of the League Covenant. While radicals and liberals denounced the whole treaty as a work of undisguised vengeance, certain prominent peace-loving Republicans, such as ex-President Taft and George Wickersham, favored the League with certain reservations. Other Eastern conservatives, especially the international financiers, showed sympathy with a plan for preserving the peace of the world by common action with the great powers of Europe. In Senator Lodge's native Boston, a state Republican convention repudiated his counsels by adopting a resolution favoring the League of Nations.

In the Progressive and radical West, however, opposition was overwhelming. The people did not wish to send "our gallant young men to die in obscure fights in the Balkans or Central Europe . . ." as Colonel Roosevelt had said in one of his last utterances before his death in January, 1919. Among great capi-

[23] To G. Harvey; Johnson, op. cit., pp. 270-271.

talists there was a similar unwillingness to tie up American capital, and to link American military and political support with European imponderables.

George Harvey, Wilson's estranged political backer of yesterday, who had lately turned Republican, now took up the fight against the League with passionate enthusiasm, gathering funds, issuing a magazine, and organizing a nation-wide speakers' bureau for the sole purpose of saving our sovereign republic from "the morass of Socialism" and internationalism. With the war ended, Harvey found that great capitalists such as Henry C. Frick and Andrew Mellon, who had formerly favored thrusting our nation into the struggle for world balance, were now eager to stay close to shore under the protection of our own naval police force. Chiefly through the generosity of Frick and Mellon, Harvey raised a fund of approximately $100,000 for an anti-League campaign in the summer of 1919, while the Senate, holding the treaty in the Senate Foreign Relations Committee, delayed its decision. Frick, the old steel magnate, was convinced that the commitment of the United States to the provision of Article X of the League Covenant was from a business man's point of view "a crazy thing to do." [24]

Beyond the defeat of Wilson's treaty and League, Harvey, the President Maker of 1910-1912, scented a great political overturn and the opportunity for more President making under Republican auspices.[25] Woodrow Wilson, too, understood the full scope of the crisis, and, while waiting for the verdict of the Senate, determined to go to the country in a nation-wide speaking tour which would bring the pressure of popular opinion to bear upon the Senate.

[24] Harvey, *H. C. Frick*, pp. 327-328.
[25] Harvey was one of the little group of men who in a "smoke-filled hotel room" of Chicago, the next year, chose Senator Warren G. Harding of Ohio as the Republican candidate for the Presidency.

4

Reconstruction had begun, wasteful, chaotic, violent. In 1919 the new, massive, twentieth-century America came into being, with jazz and cheap motor cars, amid fierce political strife over the League question, booms and panics in financial markets, race riots in Chicago, and dramatic labor uprisings in Pittsburgh and Boston. Postmaster General Burleson still continued censorship over the press and mails; Attorney General Palmer waged his "war on the Reds," raiding meetings, rounding up and arresting "suspected" persons and deporting aliens. It was at this season of stress and change that certain of President Wilson's advisers, reviewing the whole dangerous post-war situation, cast about for new programs of political action. They endeavored to call to the attention of the President, first, the pressing problem of domestic reconstruction, and second, that of launching anew an advancing social movement, which would consolidate the partial gains of pre-war reforms and war-time measures of control, now plainly ready to be lost.

In the spring of 1919 the liberal followers of Wilson, both labor leaders and capitalists, while struggling to regain their footing, developed the plan of calling a National Industrial Conference, representing all sides of economic life, which would attempt to face the problems of peacetime reconstruction and social reform. Once more the excellent George L. Record, who had been Wilson's most valuable political adviser in the New Jersey days, though he had been long thrust aside, was moved by the serious complexion of affairs to come forward with his offers of counsel. In March, 1919, Record came to Washington, consulted Tumulty, and at the latter's suggestion sent to the President, then still in Paris, a long memorandum in which the proposal for a National Industrial Conference was discussed, and a kind of Five-Year program sketched in outline.

Proposing at this time a course utterly different from that which the President pursued, one that would have placed the Philosopher-President once more at the head of the forces of progress, steering the nation toward vigorous social change, Record's little-known letter of March 31, 1919, is a paper of remarkable historical interest. It defines the deepest problems of 1919 with clear insight, prophesies the future dangers that threaten if they are not met, and epitomizes perfectly the Roosevelt-Wilson epoch at its close.

Assuming, as he says, that Wilson was "big and broad enough to welcome frank speech," George Record plunges into a coldly logical analysis of recent events that exposes the insubstantiality of the President's achievements up to that time. Upon the validity of the peace treaty and the League of Nations Covenant he casts the gravest doubts, and goes on to prophesy only evil to come from their adoption. The obscure prophet then begs the leader, standing at the zenith of his world glory and flattered by nearly all men, to abandon those vague, ill-founded international projects and return to "fundamental" things.

"As conditions are now," Record began with almost brutal candor, "your political fortunes are at a low ebb, your prestige impaired, and your party demoralized." What was the reason for this condition? Record continued:

> . . . *Nothing you have done as President, nothing that you are proposing in the League of Nations idea, will give you a place in history as a great man, because at the end of your terms you will have rendered no great and lasting service that will lift you above the average of our Presidents, and you have ignored the great issue which is slowly coming to the front, the question of economic democracy, abolition of privilege, and securing to men the full fruits of their labor or service.*[26]

There was neither "glory" nor real "service," Record pointed out, in standing, nowadays, for the principles of "political democracy." Once it was dangerous to advocate those principles, and our fathers a century and a half earlier had won a just glory therefor. But nowadays to hold to their position was "like advocating the Ten Commandments." American political democracy was now, as before

[26] Italics mine.

Wilson, controlled by a privileged minority. And he pointed to the current Supreme Court decision, declaring unconstitutional the recent Child Labor Act of Congress, thus sanctioning the employment of little children in mills.

Was the nation we looked at now, with its fearful social inequalities, that which "our fathers had fondly hoped for"? For nearly a century, the existence of frontier territories and their boundless resources, enabling us to give land freely to all comers, "covered up the fact that by establishing political democracy we had not rid ourselves of privilege." Industrial conditions in modern America were beginning to approximate those of the old world; the nation's resources had passed into a comparatively few hands; the percentage of our people who owned their farms or homes was actually shrinking rapidly. A dreary poverty festered in the great cities side by side with extreme forms of wealth. Recently, while the cheers of multitudes were ringing in the Presidential ears, "the teachers of New York City . . . shocked the public by revelations of the fearful privations inflicted upon the children of the poor," against whom a great milk trust exploited its monopoly of this necessity of life. There had been too little change! Millions of Americans, Record contended, still worked long hours, winning barely enough to provide food and shelter, while odious monopolists, such as the Food and Meat Trusts ("as reported by your own Trade Commission"), swindled the public. Yet these "powerful criminals" went untouched by the law, while "our courts send to prison for long terms poor, weak socialists, who have been driven to intemperate speech by the contemplation of monstrous injustice. . . ."

The peace treaty and the League Covenant, Record held, would provide no cure for war. Record, who knew Wilson well, pointed his appeal to the man's aspiration for a place in history:

The League of Nations idea will not help your position, either now or in history, because like all your other policies, it does not go to the root of the problem.

Every modern state, he held, was actually governed by the privileged, by those who controlled railroads, lands, mines, banks, and credit. "These men thus obtain enormous and unearned capital, for which there is no use in the country where it is produced, because the poverty of the workers limits the home market. Those who control this surplus capital must seek new countries and new people to exploit, and this clash of selfish interests leads to war." The way to end war was to bring about "the reign of justice, that is, the abolition of privilege in each of the great nations." Record refused to believe that Wilson could set up machinery which would maintain justice in international relations among governments which denied justice to their own people.

It was entirely possible, if not probable, he reasoned, "that such a League, established by the present governments of the Allies, is very likely to be used as an international bulwark of privilege." [27]

Meanwhile the modern world's one great social experiment was that being attempted in varying forms by Russia and—as then believed—by socialist Germany. Wilson could not fight this movement by ignoring it, or denouncing its leaders, or putting them in jail. At home, our republic faced a similar crisis, just as it had faced the issue of slavery between 1830 and 1860: the problem of industrial or economic democracy. "If you fail to attempt to solve this problem, you will stand in history . . . exactly as the leaders of the Whig and Democratic parties stood when they turned their backs upon the rising question of slavery." Wilson, he exhorted, must attempt to meet the menace that threw its long shadow forward, he must cease to occupy his high talents with "second rate tasks," he must now offer a bold program for the "removal of injustice in our industrial and social relations."

[27] At this time Mr. Herbert Bayard Swope, accompanying Wilson to Paris as a newspaper correspondent, wrote home: "A curious, ostrich-like policy is being maintained by most leaders of public opinion on the question of a social uprising, evidence of which is seen on all sides, but which is seemingly to be checked by the mere denial of its existence. [President Wilson] preaches a vast political reform . . . but he is silent upon the bigger social questions, which are, after all, the taproots of world politics." (The New York *World*, Jan. 8, 1919.)

In America, liquidating its war work, with soldiers returning from the battlefields and training camps and men and women being discharged from factories *en masse*, no workable solutions were being proposed. The average politician was bewildered. For this very reason Wilson was faced by greater opportunities than ever before.

"You should become the real leader of the radical forces in America and present to the country a constructive program of fundamental reform, which shall be an alternative to the program presented by the socialists and the Bolsheviki, and then go to the country with it." At once, the intelligent and forward-looking elements would cast off their discouragement and gather about Wilson again.

Record ended by proposing that the President send a message to Congress, and call for a special session, which would enact (among others) the following measures: (1) public ownership of all railroads, public utilities, pipe-lines and natural resources owned by trusts; (2) the opening of all patents to general use and manufacture by anyone on payment to the owner of a royalty fixed by the government; (3) the employment of all land now held out of use for speculation or monopolistic purposes; (4) the limitation of great fortunes by inheritance and income taxes.

The Republicans, Record concluded, had no ideas. "This program would completely turn the flank of the Republican plan of attack, and put them on the defensive." Wilson, by offering a "positive program of relief," would "split wide open the Republican party"; or failing, he would certainly split both parties so that "a new party embodying these ideas would be spontaneously brought into existence . . . which would have a great historic career, and would always be identified with your leadership." True, Wilson might be defeated, but he would go down "with colors flying," and "when the ideas triumph, as they inevitably must, your place in history, and consequently your service, would be recognized as that of a truly great man." [28]

[28] Kerney, *Wilson*, pp. 438-448.

Thus Record, foreseeing that the downfall of a whole era of political enlightenment was bound up with the fortunes of Wilson as a leader, must have sat through the night devotedly writing his appeal. He proposes, for the historic emergency, another way out, an alternative program, a "new deal" one might say. That Wilson —though he acknowledged the letter cordially—would ignore the call was a foregone conclusion. Yet Record's letter still rings with truth twenty years after, for both the leader of the New Freedom and those who came after him.

It was foregone, then, that the reactionaries should, at this turning point in our history, seize the reins of power from the faltering hands. That summer Lincoln Steffens in Paris perceived as never before that Wilson "does not see fundamentals at all; he sees things only politically and morally. . . . *He is the most perfect example of the Culture which has failed.*" [29]

"*Let us kill no more Kaisers, save in our own hearts,*" was Steffens' bitter epigraph for the Wilsonian crusades.

In the summer of 1919, after the President had returned to Washington, numerous other advisers strove to fix his attention upon the dangerous industrial crisis. Great strikes were impending in the steel trade and in the bituminous coal fields. The United States Steel Corporation, which the Supreme Court would soon absolve as a "reasonable" corporation, refused to treat with the union men among its employers. Gompers' appeal to the President, urging him to intercede and call a conference between both parties in the struggle, actually went unanswered during August. Then suddenly on September 10, Wilson (while on tour in San Francisco) issued a call for a National Industrial Conference, to be held on October 6, 1919, at Washington, and urged the American Federation of Labor to postpone all action until after the conference. It was too late. The date for the strike had already been set; sporadic violence had broken out, and blood was being shed in the steel towns. On September 21, 1919, some 275,000 steel

[29] Steffens, *Letters*, Jun. 28, 1919, Vol. I, p. 474. Italics mine.

workers stopped work, beginning one of the largest and bitterest industrial struggles in our history.

The National Industrial Conference, composed of twenty-two prominent employers and labor leaders, duly met to "devise new relations between labor and capital." Soon its members burst into discord and the conference broke up without result. But it is doubtful that Wilson followed with even half an eye the reported proceedings of this unhappy gathering.

The belief has persisted that Wilson was a sick man, even before he departed for Paris.[30] Overborne by constant suffering and fatigue, he thought nothing of the sufferings of those who languished in Federal prisons, the Socialist Debs or the pacifist Roger Baldwin, who had opposed the war. The domestic crisis, the industrial warfare upon the home front, touched him little in his last phase of transported "internationalism." Thus the closing period of his administration, with its unbridled political reaction and suppressions of civil liberties, has overshadowed the brilliant record of his peacetime leadership.

With his last remaining force, he gathered himself to fight in defense of his Peace Treaty and League Covenant, threatened with utter defeat in Congress. He told Tumulty now that he felt himself at the end of his tether. The tremendous, exhausting tour of the country, in which he would "go to the people" once more, was now decided upon as a last resort. "For if the Treaty should be defeated, God only knows what would happen to the world as a result of it," he exclaimed. He was now "an old man, grown grayer and grayer," but grim in his determination, "like an old warrior, to fight to the end." [31]

The Treaty wholly absorbed his mind and body, worn out by long labor, in his days and his white nights. Leaving Washington on September 4, he set off on a great swing around the circle, a journey of 10,000 miles during which he was to deliver from two to three speeches a day.

[30] Confidential source.
[31] Tumulty, *op. cit.*, p. 435.

To him, the thought was intolerable that the United States, after using all her magnificent strength and resources to send two million young men across three thousand miles of ocean into the World War, should abandon the prime object of the struggle. A plan for a stable world order of international law and peace had been devised; and it needed America's enormous power in the world balance to establish the permanence and reality of the League and its Parliament of Man at Geneva. For Wilson this issue now transcended all other questions.

Nevertheless the series of forty public addresses which he gave in the twenty-two days of his final pilgrimage from September 4 to September 26, 1919, were far weaker than his earlier public papers. In tone they had a curious air of unreality; they indulged in moral and political generalities, and suggested a transported or dimmed mind. He did not see the wrongs and fateful errors in the peace settlement; he was blind to the fact that the peace settlement was *imposed*, and not negotiated; he refused to perceive the emotional recoil, weariness, and disillusionment of the people after war.

One of the characteristic phrases that recurs in these speeches was contained in a passage where Wilson exhorts his listeners not to defeat "this great enterprise," and to *"Forget the details and . . . stand with me. . . ."* [32] Borah and Lodge, however, touring the country in the wake of the President, reminded men every day of those very details.

Another theme, often touched in an extremely emotional, highly symptomatic fashion toward the end of the tour, revealed how the President's heart and nerves were ready to give way at the thought of final failure, and at the pursuing thought that the whole mighty war effort might have been in vain. Sometimes he seemed literally *haunted*, when he spoke of the beautiful graveyards he had visited near Paris, where "rank upon rank of departed American soldiers" lay buried. He had seen the sheeted dead. "What of our pledges

[32] Speech of Sept. 15, 1919; italics mine.

to the men that lie dead in France? . . . To see to it that there was never such a war again." [33]

The "last chance for civilization, the salvation of the world," depended upon acceptance by the Senate of the Treaty and the League Covenant. Hence there could be no compromise, no agreement upon reservations—refused both in November, 1919, and in the spring of 1920 at Wilson's order. It was in these days that Wilson showed signs of persecution mania. To Tumulty he spoke frequently of "our enemies who have poisoned the wells of opinion." He had dismissed the faithful Colonel House from his side at Paris; now he drove Lansing from the Cabinet. On the day of his speech at Pueblo, Colorado, September 25, 1919, Wilson felt warning pains and an unwonted weakness, yet he mounted the platform once more. That speech was the most emotional of all, and his wife, his friends, and aides who stood by, moved by his tones, wept freely at its heart-breaking, tragic peroration.

Again and again, my fellow citizens, mothers who lost their sons in France have come to me and, taking my hand, shed tears upon it not only, but they have added, "God bless you, Mr. President!" Why, my fellow citizens, should they pray God to bless me? *I advised the Congress of the United States to create the situation that led to the death of their sons. I ordered their sons overseas. I consented to their sons' being put in the most difficult parts of the battle line, where death was certain, as in the impenetrable difficulties of the forest of Argonne.*

The very manner in which these words were uttered reveal to the psychologist an overpowering, harrowing sense of "guilt." And Wilson spoke again, as if obsessed, of the beautiful hillside cemetery in France, where lay, rank upon rank, the young men he had "ordered" there. Yet all the mothers had "forgiven" him.

Why should they weep upon my hand and call down the blessings of God upon me? . . . They believe, and they rightly believe, that their sons saved the liberty of the world.[34]

[33] Speech at Pueblo, Colorado, Sept. 25, 1919.
[34] Speech of Sept. 25, 1919, at Pueblo, Colorado; italics mine.

In the night hours that followed that speech, on the Presidential train riding through Kansas, Woodrow Wilson fell stricken, one side of his face paralyzed, one side of his body, the left, motionless. His health was shattered, never to be recovered again, and the four years of life that followed were a kind of living death.

Eighteen months remained to the end of his term, and in the preceding half year he had been mostly in Paris, absorbed by the Peace Treaty. Thus for two years, after the Peace Treaty which brought to an end the great war that closed an era of American political enlightenment, our government drifted, rudderless. Men took things in their own hands; "normalcy" returned almost involuntarily even while Wilson lay on his bed of pain. A lasting memory of the painful interval of confusion and disillusionment that came with the debacle of liberal statesmanship was implanted in men's minds, while the high purposes, the promise of the enlightenment, were forgotten.

SOURCES

I am under obligation to various persons who were witnesses or participants in events described in this work: among them, former Governor Gifford Pinchot and Mr. Justice Louis D. Brandeis, for information conveyed to me; to Mr. Amos Pinchot, for permission to use letters from his collection; to Mr. Elihu Root, for permission to study his father's papers; to Fola La Follette, George Middleton, and Miles L. Colean, for advice and information concerning the elder Senator La Follette; to Charles Willis Thompson, for his oral recollections and advice. None of these, however, are in any sense responsible for what I have written.

I am indebted also to the staff of the Manuscript Division of the Library of Congress for courtesies and aid; and to the Library of Columbia University for use of the Brander Matthews papers. Also, for use of the collection and aid of the staff of Roosevelt House.

Passages from James Kerney's *The Political Education of Woodrow Wilson* have been quoted with the kind permission of the Appleton-Century Company; passages from Charles Seymour's *The Intimate Papers of Colonel House*, with the permission of Houghton Mifflin Company; those from R. S. Baker's *Woodrow Wilson*, with permission of Doubleday, Doran.

I am indebted finally to Professor Thomas C. Cochran for having read proofs; and to my wife for both research and editorial assistance.

MANUSCRIPT SOURCES (UNPUBLISHED)

Bryan, William Jennings: Collection in Division of Manuscripts, Library of Congress

Lodge, Henry Cabot: Collection in Library of Congress, and Library of Harvard University

Matthews, Brander: Collection in Library of Columbia University

Pinchot, Amos: Collection privately held

Roosevelt, Theodore: Collection in Library of Congress

Root, Elihu: Collection in Library of Congress

White, Henry: Collection in Library of Congress

HISTORICAL WORKS, BIOGRAPHIES, MEMOIRS, PUBLISHED LETTERS

Acheson, Sam H., *Joe Bailey, The Last Democrat*, New York, 1932

Adams, Henry, *The Education of Henry Adams*, Boston, 1918

—— *Letters*, edited by W. C. Ford, Boston, 1930 and 1938, 2 vols.

Adams, Brooks, *The Law of Civilization and Decay*, New York, 1895

Alexander, De Alva S., *Four Great New Yorkers*, New York, 1923

Baker, Ray Stannard, *Woodrow Wilson, Life and Letters*, New York, 1931-1938, 6 vols.

Barron, C. W., *More They Told Barron*, New York, 1931

Beard, C. A. and M. R., *America in Mid-Passage*, New York, 1939

—— *The Rise of American Civilization*, New York, 1927

Beer, Thomas, *Hanna*, New York, 1929

Bishop, J. B., *Charles Joseph Bonaparte, His Life and Services*, New York, 1922

—— *Theodore Roosevelt and His Time*, New York, 1920, 2 vols.

Bowers, Claude G., *Beveridge and the Progressive Era*, New York, 1932

Brissenden, P. F., *The I.W.W.: A Study of American Syndicalism*, New York, 1920

Bryan, William Jennings, *Memoirs*, Philadelphia, 1925

Busbey, L. White, *Uncle Joe Cannon, The Story of a Pioneer American*, New York, 1927

Butt, Archie, *The Letters of Archie Butt*, edited by Lawrence F. Abbott, New York, 1924

—— *Taft and Roosevelt; The Intimate Letters of Archie Butt*, New York, 1930, 2 vols.

Carlton, F. Tracy, *Organized Labor in American History*, New York, 1920

Chamberlain, John, *Farewell to Reform*, New York, 1932

Chapman, John Jay, *Causes and Consequences*, New York, 1898

Cleveland, Grover, *The Letters of Grover Cleveland*, edited by Allan Nevins, Boston, 1933

Corey, Lewis, *The House of Morgan*, New York, 1930

Cowles, Anna Roosevelt, *Letters from Theodore Roosevelt to Anna R. Cowles, 1870-1918*, New York, 1924

Croly, Herbert, *Marcus Alonzo Hanna*, New York, 1912

—— *The Promise of American Life*, New York, 1909

Davis, Oscar King, *Released for Publication*, New York, 1925

Dennett, Tyler, *John Hay, From Poetry to Politics*, New York, 1933

Dennis, Alfred L. P., *Adventures in American Diplomacy, 1896-1906*, New York, 1928

Depew, Chauncey M., *My Memories of Eighty Years*, New York, 1922

Duffy, Herbert S., *William Howard Taft*, New York, 1930

Dunn, Arthur W., *Gridiron Nights*, New York, 1915

Faulkner, Harold U., *American Economic History* (Fourth Edition), New York, 1937

Filler, Louis, *Crusaders for American Liberalism*, New York, 1940

Ghent, L. J., *Mass and Class*, New York, 1904

Ford, Henry Jones, *Rise and Growth of American Politics*, New York, 1898

Fuess, C. M., *Carl Schurz, Reformer*, New York, 1932

Glass, Carter, *An Adventure in Constructive Finance*, New York, 1927

Godkin, E. L., *Problems of Modern Democracy*, New York, 1896

Gompers, Samuel, *Seventy Years of Life and Labor*, New York, 1925, 2 vols.

Grey, Viscount Edward, *Twenty-five Years; 1892-1916*, New York, 1925

Griswold, A. Whitney, *The Far Eastern Policy of the United States*, New York, 1938

Gwynn, Stephen, *The Letters and Friendships of Sir Cecil Spring Rice*, Boston, 1929, 2 vols.

Hapgood, Norman, *The Changing Years, Reminiscences of Norman Hapgood*, New York, 1930

Harvey, G. B. McL., *Henry Frick, The Man*, New York, 1928

Harden, Maximilian, *I Meet my Contemporaries*, New York, 1925

Hay, John, *Letters and Diaries* (privately printed), 1908

Hendrick, Burton J., *The Life and Letters of Walter H. Page*, New York, 1925, 3 vols.

Hibbard, B. H., *A History of the Public Land Policies*, New York, 1924

Hobson, John A., *Imperialism, A Study*, new edition, London, 1938

House, Edward M. (anonymously), *Philip Dru, Administrator*, New York, 1912

Houston, D. F., *Eight Years with Wilson's Cabinet*, New York, 1926, 2 vols.

Howe, M. A. de Wolfe, *John Jay Chapman and His Letters*, Boston, 1938

—— *The Portrait of an Independent, Moorfield Storey*, Boston, 1932

Howland, Harold, *Theodore Roosevelt and His Times*, New Haven, 1921

Jessup, Philip C., *Elihu Root*, New York, 1938, 2 vols.

Johnson, Willis F., *Colonel George B. M. Harvey, A Passionate Patriot*, Boston, 1929

Johnson, Claudius O., *Borah of Idaho*, New York, 1936

Josephson, Matthew, *The Politicos*, New York, 1938

Kennan, George, *E. H. Harriman*, Boston, 1922, 2 vols.

Kerney, James, *The Political Education of Woodrow Wilson*, New York, 1926

La Follette, Robert M., *Autobiography*, Madison, Wis., 1913

Lane, Franklin K., *The Letters of Franklin K. Lane, Personal and Political*, Boston, 1922, 2 vols.

Laurence, William, *Memories of a Happy Life*, Boston, 1926

Lief, Alfred, *Brandeis: The Personal History of an American Ideal*, New York, 1936

Lloyd, Caro A., *Henry Demarest Lloyd*, New York, 1912, 2 vols.

Lodge, Henry Cabot, *Selections from the Correspondence of Theodore Roosevelt and Henry Cabot Lodge, 1884-1918*, New York, 1925, 2 vols.

—— *Alexander Hamilton*, Boston, 1882

Lundberg, Ferdinand, *America's 60 Families*, New York, 1937

Mason, A. T., *Brandeis and the Modern State*, Washington, D. C., 1936

Mayo, L. S., *America of Yesterday, as Reflected in the Journal of John Davis Long*, Boston, 1923

McCaleb, Walter F., *Theodore Roosevelt*, New York, 1931

Merriam, C. E., *Four American Party Leaders*, New York, 1926

Millis, Walter, *The Martial Spirit*, Boston, 1931

—— *The Road to War*, Boston, 1935

Mitchell, Edward P., *Memoirs of an Editor*, New York, 1924

Neuberger, R. L., and Kahn, S. B., *Integrity, the Life Story of George W. Norris*, New York, 1937

Nevins, Allan, *Henry White, Thirty Years of American Diplomacy*, New York, 1930

Noyes, Alexander D., *Forty Years of American Finance*, New York, 1917

Olcott, Charles S., *Life of William McKinley*, Boston, 1916, 2 vols.

Pinchot, Gifford, *The Fight for Conservation*, New York, 1910

Platt, Thomas C., *Autobiography*, New York, 1910

Pringle, Henry F., *Theodore Roosevelt*, New York, 1931

—— *The Life and Times of William Howard Taft*, New York, 1939, 2 vols.

Puleston, William D., *Mahan; the Life and Work of Captain Alfred T. Mahan*, New Haven, 1939

Pyle, J. G., *The Life of James J. Hill*, New York, 1917, 2 vols.

Richberg, Donald R., *The Tents of the Mighty*, Chicago, 1929

Rhodes, James Ford, *The McKinley and Roosevelt Administrations*, New York, 1927

Robinson, E. E., *The Evolution of Political Parties*, New York, 1924

Roosevelt, Theodore, *An Autobiography*, New York, 1926

—— *Presidential Addresses* (*Review of Reviews* edition), New York, 1910, 8 vols.

—— *Works* (National Edition), New York, 1925, 20 vols.

Root, Elihu, *Miscellaneous Addresses*, Cambridge, Mass., 1917

—— *Military and Colonial Policy of the United States*, Cambridge, Mass., 1916

Seitz, Don C., *Joseph Pulitzer, His Life and Letters*, New York, 1924

Seymour, Charles, *The Intimate Papers of Colonel House*, Boston, 1926, 2 vols.

Stahl, Rose M., *The Ballinger-Pinchot Controversy*, Northampton, Mass., 1926

Steffens, Lincoln, *Autobiography of Lincoln Steffens*, New York, 1931
—— *Letters*, New York, 1938, 2 vols.

Stephenson, N. P., *Nelson W. Aldrich, A Leader in American Politics*, New York, 1930

Stoddard, Henry L., *As I Knew Them, Presidents and Politics from Grant to Coolidge*, New York, 1927

Sullivan, Mark, *Our Times*, New York, 1926-1932, 4 vols.

Tansill, Charles C., *America Goes to War*, Boston, 1938

Tarbell, Ida M., *The Life of Elbert H. Gary, A Story of Steel*, New York, 1925
—— *The Tariff in Our Times*, New York, 1911

Thayer, William Roscoe, *Life and Letters of John Hay*, Boston, 1915, 2 vols.

Tumulty, Joseph P., *Woodrow Wilson as I Knew Him*, New York, 1921

Untermyer, Samuel, *Who is Entitled to the Credit for the Federal Reserve Act* (pamphlet), New York, 1927

Vagts, Alfred, *Deutschland und die Vereinigte Staaten in der Weltpolitik*, London, 1925, 2 vols.

Villard, Oswald G., *Fighting Years, Memoirs of a Liberal Editor*, New York, 1939

Werner, M. R., *Bryan*, New York, 1929

Wilson, Edith, *My Memoir*, New York, 1939

Wilson, Woodrow, *The Messages and Papers* (*Review of Reviews* edition), New York, 1924, 2 vols.

White, William Allen, *Masks in a Pageant*, New York, 1928

Whitlock, Brand, *The Letters and Journal*, New York, 1936, 2 vols.

Wister, Owen, *Roosevelt, The Story of a Friendship*, New York, 1930

INDEX